Lecture Notes in Computer Science   892

Edited by G. Goos, J. Hartmanis and J. van Leeuwen

Advisory Board: W. Brauer   D. Gries   J. Stoer

K. Pingali   U. Banerjee   D. Gelernter
A. Nicolau   D. Padua (Eds.)

Languages and Compilers for Parallel Computing

7th International Workshop
Ithaca, NY, USA, August 8-10, 1994
Proceedings

Springer-Verlag
Berlin Heidelberg New York
London Paris Tokyo
Hong Kong Barcelona
Budapest

Series Editors

Gerhard Goos
Universität Karlsruhe
Vincenz-Priessnitz-Straße 3, D-76128 Karlsruhe, Germany

Juris Hartmanis
Department of Computer Science, Cornell University
4130 Upson Hall, Ithaka, NY 14853, USA

Jan van Leeuwen
Department of Computer Science, Utrecht University
Padualaan 14, 3584 CH Utrecht, The Netherlands

Volume Editors

Keshav Pingali
Department of Computer Science, Cornell University
Ithaca, NY 14853, USA

Utpal Banerjee
Intel Corporation
2200 Mission College Blvd. P.O. Box 58119, RN6-18
Santa Clara, CA 95052, USA

David Gelernter
Department of Computer Science, Yale University
51 Prospect St., New Haven, CT 06520, USA

Alex Nicolau
Department of Information & Computer Science, University of California
444 Computer Science Bldg., Irvine, CA 92717, USA

David Padua
Center for Supercomputing Research and Development
465 Computer and Systems Research Laboratory
1308 West Main St., Urbana, IL 61801, USA

CR Subject Classification (1991): F.1.2, D.1.3, D.3.1, B.2.1, I.3.1

ISBN 3-540-58868-X Springer-Verlag Berlin Heidelberg New York

CIP data applied for

© Springer-Verlag Berlin Heidelberg 1995
Printed in Germany

Typesetting: Camera-ready by author
SPIN: 10479285   45/3140-543210 - Printed on acid-free paper

Foreword

The papers in this volume are revised versions of papers presented at the Seventh Annual Workshop on Languages and Compilers for Parallel Computers which was held in Ithaca, NY August 8th-10th, 1994. This workshop series has traditionally been a forum for the presentation of state-of-the-art research in languages, restructuring compilers and runtime systems by leading groups in the US, Europe and Japan. This year, we received about 45 submissions in response to the call for papers. Because of time constraints, we were unable to accept all papers, and these proceedings contain the 32 papers that were selected for presentation.

Thanks are due to many people for making the workshop a success. The members of the standing program committee — Utpal Banerjee, David Gelernter, Alex Nicolau and David Padua — were a great source of advice and information. Helene Croft put the entire database of names and addresses online, which should make it easier to run this workshop in future years. She was also relentless in tracking down tardy authors, referees, speakers and attendees, which made the workshop run like clockwork! Thanks are due to the referees: Utpal Banerjee, Carrie Brownhill, A. Capitanio, Sudeep Gupta, David Gelernter, Laurie Hendren, J. Hummel, Richard Johnson, Indu Kodukula, David Kolson, Vladimir Kotlyar, Wei Li, Mayan Moudgill, Alex Nicolau, Rishiyur Nikhil, Steve Novack, F. Onion, David Padua, Anne Rogers, Paul Stodghill, Thorsten von Eicken, H. Wang and Richard Zippel. Finally, the Cornell Department of Computer Science, and the Cornell Theory Center gave generous financial grants, which allowed us to reduce the registration fee for participants.

October, 1994

Keshav Pingali
Program Chair

Table of Contents

What Next?

Back to Basics: Program Analysis

Languages for Parallelism: Something Borrow, Something New

And Now, for Something Completely Different

When Your Program Runs (Finally)

How to Communicate Better

Automatic Parallelization Considered Unnecessary

Fine-grain Scheduling under Resource Constraints

Paul Feautrier

Laboratoire PRiSM,
Université de Versailles, 45 Avenue des Etats-Unis,
78035 VERSAILLES FRANCE

Abstract. Many present-day microprocessors have fine grain parallelism, be it in the form of a pipeline, of multiple functional units, or replicated processors. The efficient use of such architectures depends on the capability of the compiler to schedule the execution of the object code in such a way that most of the available hardware is in use while complying with data dependences. In the case of one simple loop, the schedule may be expressed as an affine form in the loop counter. The coefficient of the loop counter in the schedule is the initiation interval, and gives the mean rate at which loop bodies may be executed. The dependence constraints may be converted to linear inequalities in the coefficients of a closed form schedule, and then solved by classical linear programming algorithms. The resource constraints, however, translate to non-linear constraints. These constraints become linear if the initiation interval is known. This leads to a fast searching algorithm, in which the initiation interval is increased until a feasible solution is found.

1 Introduction

Thinking about parallel programs is a notoriously difficult task. One of the most successful techniques for dealing with this problem is *scheduling*, i.e. the construction of a timetable for the operations of the program. Scheduling is a difficult problem. Various special cases have been proved to be NP-hard or NP-complete. Most of the complexity of scheduling can be assigned to the conjunction of two type of constraints:

- dependence constraints, which express the fact that some computations must be executed in a specified order if the meaning of the original program is to be preserved; these constraints are usually expressed as a dependence graph.
- resource constraints, which express the fact that the number of simultaneous operation at any given time is limited by the available resources in the target computer.

While any one of these constraints can be handled easily, it is their simultaneous presence which is at the origin of the difficulty. Fortunately, in many cases of computer science interest, it is possible to handle the resource constraints in an approximate way. It is customary in this context, to distinguish between *coarse grain*, *medium grain*, and *fine grain* scheduling.

In coarse grain scheduling – e.g., job shop scheduling or macrotasking – the tasks and the resources are few. The schedule is represented in tabular form, and there are approximate techniques, like list scheduling, with precise bounds on the approximation.

In medium grain scheduling, there are many tasks – typically as many as there are operations in an execution of the source programm – and many identical resources – the processors in a massively parallel computer. The schedule must be obtained in closed form. One may ignore the resource constraints in computing the schedule [Fea92a, Fea92b], and then fold the schedule on the available processors. One may prove [Fea89] that this solution is *asymptotically efficient*, provided that the source program has enough intrinsic parallelism.

The situation is different for fine grain scheduling. Here the number of tasks is large. The resources are few and discrete. At the most, resources may be partitioned into classes, each class having a small number of identical resources.

Fine grain scheduling started some thirty years ago when the first computers with multiple functional units – like the CDC 6600 – were put on the market. It is now a very important technique, due to the advent of many computers with instruction level parallelism, like pipelined computers, VLIW or superscalar processors.

In fine grain scheduling, it is impossible to ignore the resource constraints. Several techniques have been proposed for solving the problem, at least in an approximate way (see [RF93] for a comprehensive review of the subject). Trace scheduling [Fis84] applies list scheduling to basic blocks; it tries to detect critical paths in the program control graph and to enlarge basic blocs by moving code around test instructions.

Software pipelining [RG81] applies to simple loops and aims at executing several instances of the loop body in a staggered way so as to maximize resource usage and minimize the total execution time. A solution to the software pipelining problem for a given loop is characterized by its *initiation interval*, i.e. the time span between two successive iteration of the loop. It is easy to derive bounds for the initiation interval: an upper bound is given by the sequential execution time of the loop body. A lower bound is deduced from an analysis of resource usage, see section 2.2, and another one can be obtained by constructing an unconstrained schedule.

In many algorithms for software pipelining, one assume the iteration interval is given, and applies list scheduling, taking care that each resource allocation is folded modulo the initiation interval when constructing the reservation table (see e.g. [Lam88]). The interval of admissible initiation intervals is explored by binary search until the optimal value is found.

The algorithm of [GS92] applies only if there is only one resource class. The program is first scheduled as if there were no resource constraints. Analysis of the resulting schedule allows one to delete some dependences, and the resulting dependence graph is cycle free. The final schedule is obtained by applying list scheduling with resource constraints to this graph. The resulting schedule is not optimal, but the authors show that the usual bound on the list scheduling approximation applies.

This paper is an attempt to extend the scheduling techniques of [Fea92a], which are based on linear programming, to fine grain scheduling. The next section is a review of these techniques. The main theme of Section 3 is how to convert the resource constraints into bilinear constraints. This is done in two cases. In the first one, there is one unique resource of each type; in the second case, there may be several copies of a resource. In the conclusion, I discuss the complexity of the algorithm and point to some direction for future work.

2 A Review of Scheduling Techniques

I will consider here the problem of scheduling a single loop:

do $i = 1, \ldots$
    $S_1; \ldots S_n$
end do

where the S_k are scalar or array assignments. I have emphasized the fact that the upper bound of the loop is irrelevant for the present problem. The solution must be in the form of the repetition of a uniform pattern, the loop upper bound controlling only the repetition factor.

A schedule is defined by n functions from the iteration counter, i, to an integral time. I will suppose that an appropriate unit of time has been chosen – e.g., the clock cycle – and that all delays and durations are integral multiple of this unit. Schedules are supposed to be of the form:

$$\theta(S, i) = \lfloor ai + b_S \rfloor, \tag{1}$$

where a and the b_S are rational numbers. a is known as the initiation interval of the schedule. The main objective of software pipelining is its minimization.

There are several reasons for choosing such a form. Firstly, all known methods for computing schedules apply only to affine forms. It is true that a schedule whose values are not integral has no meaning, but it has been shown that the floor of a causal schedule is also causal, and that if the iteration domain is large enough, schedules of the above form are nearly optimal [Qui87].

Before embarking on the solution proper, let us observe that there is some leeway in the selection of b_S in (1). a is necessarily a rational number – if it where not so, the schedule would not be periodic. It is easy to prove the following lemma:

Lemma 1. Let $a = A/D$ be the representation of the initiation interval in lowest terms. Any schedule of the form (1) is equivalent to a schedule of the form:

$$\theta(i) = \left\lfloor \frac{Ai + B_S}{D} \right\rfloor \tag{2}$$

where the B_S are integers.

Recent research on medium-grain scheduling [MQRS90, Fea92a] favors schedules in which each statement has its own initiation interval. In the case of fine grain parallelism, such a schedule generates very complicated code [2], hence our insistence on the same initiation interval for all statements.

All schedules must satisfies the so-called *causality condition*: let us write $(S_k, i) \perp (S_l, j)$ if (S_k, i) and (S_l, j) are in dependence, and $(S_k, i) \prec (S_l, j)$ if (S_k, i) is executed before (S_l, j) in the original program. The schedule must verify:

$$(S_k, i) \perp (S_l, j) \wedge (S_k, i) \prec (S_l, j) \Rightarrow \theta(S_k, i) + \partial(S_k) \leq \theta(S_l, j), \qquad (3)$$

where $\partial(S_k)$ is the duration of S_k.

2.1 Dependences

The choice of the dependence relation in (3) is somewhat arbitrary. Ordinary dependences include both the effect of data flow from operation to operation and the constraints generated by the pattern of memory usage in the object program. Value based dependences are much less constraining and are easily computed by Array Dataflow Analysis [Fea91]. There is a value-based dependence between (S, i) and (R, j) iff (S, i) writes into some memory cell $\mathbf{a}$, if (R, j) reads $\mathbf{a}$, $(S, i) \prec (R, j)$, and there is no write to $\mathbf{a}$ between (S, i) and (R, j). The result of Array Dataflow Analysis may be represented by a Dataflow Graph (DFG), whose vertices are associated to statements and edges to dependences. Each edge e from S to R is decorated with a polyhedron $\mathcal{P}_e$ and a transformation h_e such that if $i \in \mathcal{P}_e$ then there is actually a value-based dependence from $(S, h_e(i))$ to (R, i). One may say that after Array Dataflow Analysis, all values produced by the source code have been given distinct names, and the program has been rewritten using these names. Array Dataflow Analysis may thus be seen as a compile time counterpart of Tomasulo Algorithm.

The shape of the dependence is given by the function h_e. The simplest case is that of *uniform* dependences for which h_e is a translation:

$$h_e(i) = i - d_e$$

where d_e is known as the dependence distance. One may encounter more complicated cases, where h_e is an affine function, or even a sublinear function[3]. The scheduling technique of [Fea92a] works whenever the dependence is affine and is not limited to uniform dependences.

Value based dependences will be used throughout this paper. In this context, the causality condition (3) simplifies to:

$$\forall e \in DFG, \forall i \in \mathcal{P}_e : \theta(R, i) \geq \theta(S, h_e(i)) + \partial(S). \qquad (4)$$

---

[2] The size of the code grows as the least common multiple of the initiation intervals.
[3] A sublinear function contains integer divisions by constants.

This condition expresses the fact that since operation (R, i) uses a value which is computed by $(S, h_e(i))$, it cannot start before this operation has terminated.

The solution method starts by substituting the form (1) into (4). In the case of uniform dependences, one may prove that:

Lemma 2. *The causality condition (4) is equivalent to:*

$$ad_e + b_R - b_S \geq \partial(S). \tag{5}$$

Proof. That (5) implies (4) is proved in [Fea92a] Theorem 6. To prove the reverse implication, choose for i a multiple of D. Notice that if n is an integer, we have the identity $\lfloor n + x \rfloor = n + \lfloor x \rfloor$. (4) simplifies to:

$$\lfloor B_R/D \rfloor \geq \lfloor (B_R - Ad_e)/D \rfloor - \partial(S).$$

Since the left hand side of this inequality is an integer, we have:

$$\lfloor B_R/D \rfloor \geq (B_R - Ad_e)/D - \partial(S).$$

Now, obviously, $x \geq \lfloor x \rfloor$, hence:

$$B_R/D \geq \lfloor B_R/D \rfloor \geq (B_R - Ad_e)/D - \partial(S),$$

Q.E.D.

By the above lemma, each uniform dependence may be translated to a linear constraint on the a and b's coefficients. For more complicated dependences, one has to resort to the Farkas algorithm [Fea92a], but the result is still a set of linear constraints. One then selects a particular solution according to some objective function. Of particular interest for fine grain scheduling are the minimum latency schedules, in which one minimizes first the initiation interval a, and then the b_R.

2.2   Resource constraints

In operation research, a *resource* is an entity which may or may not be used by tasks or operations. To each resource is associated a constraint: namely, that the execution intervals of two operations which use the same resource cannot overlap. One may have resource *classes*. In that case, at any given time, the number of active operations which use a given resource cannot exceed the number of resources in the class. I will suppose here that all operations which are instances of the same instruction use the same resource class. For simplicity, I will assume that each operation uses only one resource. This restriction can be easily lifted in case of need. In fact, in this work resource classes will simply be sets of statements. If ρ is a resource class, $S \in \rho$ means that statement S uses a resource from class ρ.

In the case of unique resources, the non overlap constraint may be translated to simple inequalities on schedules. Suppose that S and T use the same resource. If $\langle S, i \rangle$ is scheduled before $\langle T, j \rangle$, then we must have:

$$\theta(T, j) \geq \theta(S, i) + \partial(S),$$

while in the opposite situation the constraint is:

$$\theta(S, i) \geq \theta(T, j) + \partial(T).$$

Since the two situations are exclusive, we may write the resource constraint as:

$$\forall i, j : \theta(T, j) - \theta(S, i) \geq \partial(S) \vee \theta(S, i) - \theta(T, j) \geq \partial(T). \tag{6}$$

Beside that, two operations which are instance of the same instruction necessarily use the same resource and cannot overlap:

$$\forall i, j : i < j \Rightarrow |\theta(S, i) - \theta(S, j)| \geq \partial(S). \tag{7}$$

This condition gives a very simple bound on a. Suppose a large number N of iterations of the loop body are executed in time t. The total usage of resource ρ will be:

$$t_\rho \approx N \sum_{S \in \rho} \partial(S).$$

Suppose there are P_ρ copies of ρ:

$$t \approx Na \leq N \sum_{S \in \rho} \partial(S)/P_\rho,$$

from which one deduces the lower bound for a:

$$a \geq \max_\rho \sum_{S \in \rho} \partial(S)/P_\rho. \tag{8}$$

If the initiation interval satisfies the above constraint, (7) is automatically satisfied.

In actual processors, resource utilization may be a much more complicated affair than the simplified scheme above. Pipelined resources, for instance, do not appear to be busy for the whole duration of one operation. This is easily taken care of by replacing $\partial(S)$ in (6) by another timing characteristics, the *stalling time* of operation S, noted $\sigma(S)$. The resource constraint is now:

$$\forall i, j : \theta(T, j) - \theta(S, i) \geq \sigma(S) \vee \theta(S, i) - \theta(T, j) \geq \sigma(T). \tag{9}$$

An ordinary functional unit will have $\partial(S) = \sigma(S)$, while a pipelined unit will have $\sigma(S) \ll \partial(S)$.

There may be links between resources, as for instance when one cannot use a functional unit unless there is a free data path to it. That kind of constraint must be handled heuristically.

The problem is more complicated if some resource class has more than one element. A resource is in use at time t if some statement S which uses it has been initiated less than $\sigma(S)$ time units before t. If we identify a resource class with the set of statements which use it, we may write the constraint for resource ρ as:

$$\text{Card } \{(S, i) \mid S \in \rho \wedge t - \sigma(S) < \theta(S, i) \leq t\} \leq P_\rho. \tag{10}$$

3 Two Scheduling Algorithms

Basically, the scheduling method of [Fea92a] works by replacing (4), which represents a potentially infinite system of affine inequalities, by a finite set of constraints on the coefficients a and b_R. The first problem is to find a similar reduction for (9). Due to the non-convexity of (9), the result is non linear. Hence, one cannot directly use linear programming to solve the problem. However, the problem lends itself to a simple and efficient solution by searching the space of possible values for a.

3.1 The singular resource case

For schedules of the form (2), the floor function in the expression of (6) may be ignored:

Theorem 3. *Let $\tau(S, i) = \frac{Ai + B_S}{D}$ and $\theta(S, i) = \lfloor \tau(S, i) \rfloor$. Then the two conditions:*

$$\forall i, j : \theta(T, j) - \theta(S, i) \geq \sigma(S) \vee \theta(S, i) - \theta(T, j) \geq \sigma(T). \qquad (11)$$

and

$$\forall i, j : \tau(T, j) - \tau(S, i) \geq \sigma(S) \vee \tau(S, i) - \tau(T, j) \geq \sigma(T). \qquad (12)$$

are equivalent.

Proof. Suppose first that (12) is true. Let us be given two arbitrary integers i and j. We may suppose, without loss of generality, that $\tau(S, i) - \tau(T, j) > 0$. We have, successively:

$$\lfloor \tau(T, j) \rfloor \leq \tau(T, j),$$
$$\lfloor \tau(T, j) \rfloor + \sigma(T) \leq \tau(T, j) + \sigma(T) \leq \tau(S, i),$$

and, since the left hand side is an integer,

$$\lfloor \tau(T, j) \rfloor + \sigma(T) \leq \lfloor \tau(S, i) \rfloor,$$

Q.E.D.
    Conversely, suppose that (12) is false for some values of i and j. Set $x = i - j$. We have both: $Ax + B_S - B_T \leq \sigma(T)$ and $B_T - B_S - Ax \leq \sigma(S)$. Set $B = B_T - B_S$ for short. We may suppose that $Ax - B > 0$. The other case is handled in a symmetrical fashion. We have, for all j:

$$\tau(S, j + x) - \tau(T, j) = \frac{Ax - B}{D} \leq \sigma(T).$$

Since A and D are relatively prime, a j may be selected in such a way that $\tau(S, j + x)$ is an integer. We then have:

$$\lfloor \tau(S, j + x) \rfloor = \tau(S, j + x) \leq \tau(T, j) + \sigma(T),$$
$$\lfloor \tau(S, j + x) \rfloor \leq \lfloor \tau(T, j) \rfloor + \sigma(T),$$

(11) is also false, Q.E.D.

With the help of this result, the resource constraint above may be written in the form:

$$\forall x \in Z : \frac{Ax - B}{D} \geq \sigma(T) \vee \frac{B - Ax}{D} \geq \sigma(S).$$

Now $\frac{Ax-B}{D}$ is an affine function of x whose zero is $x_0 = B/A$. For all values of $x > x_0$, the second inequality is certainly not verified. Hence, the first one must be true, and a necessary and sufficient condition is that:

$$A(\lfloor B/A \rfloor + 1) - B \geq D\sigma(T).$$

The other case is handled similarly and gives: $B - A\lfloor B/A \rfloor \geq D\sigma(S)$. These conditions may even be simplified by observing that, if they are true, then there exists a unique integer q such that:

$$A(q+1) - B \geq D\sigma(T) \wedge B - Aq \geq D\sigma(S). \tag{13}$$

As a consequence, the resource constraints in the singular case are given by the following rule:

For all statements S and T which use the same resource:

- Create a new integer variable q_{ST},
- Write the two constraints:

$$A(q_{ST} + 1) - B_T + B_S \geq D\sigma(T), \tag{14}$$
$$B_T - B_S - Aq_{ST} \geq D\sigma(S).$$

These constraints are to be added to the dependence constraints and solved for A and the B_S, A being the objective function to be minimized. Now the constraints generated by (14) are clearly non linear. However, they become linear if the value of A is known. Remember that we have one upper bound for $a = A/D$ which is simply the sum of the duration of all statements in the loop body – the *sequential* upper bound – and two lower bounds. One of them, the *resource usage* bound, is given by (8), and the other, the *free* bound, is obtained simply by solving the scheduling problem with no resource constraints. The maximum of these two bounds gives the *parallel* lower bound. The problem is that, since a is a rational number, exploring its possible range of values is not a finite process. As has been observed many times, the schedule (2) has period D. D iterations of the loop body are scheduled in A clock cycles, giving a mean activation interval of A/D. When generating code from such a schedule, the loop body has to be replicated D times, which means that D cannot be too large. In the singular resource case, the resource usage bound is an integer. The free bound may be rational, but the actual value of its denominator is no indication, because simplification may occur depending on the values of the statement durations. A better guess may be obtained by observing that when computing the free schedule, one has to solve a linear programming problem by a process analogous to Gaussian elimination. By the familiar Cramer rule, the denominator of the solution is the determinant of a submatrix of the problem tableau, the basis matrix. The value of this determinant can be easily extracted from the linear programming code, and is a good candidate for the unrolling factor.

We have found in practice that the following heuristic gives satisfactory results :

1. Compute the free bound, the resource usage bound and the parallel lower bound, l, which is their maximum.
2. D is set equal to the determinant of the basis matrix or to 1, depending whether the parallel lower bound is the larger bound or not.
3. Set $A = \lceil Dl \rceil$.
4. Solve the complete scheduling problem for A and D.
5. If the problem has no solution, increase A by 1 and start again at step 4.

Let us consider first a very simple example:

```
program A

      do i = 1,n
1         r1 = a(i)-b(i)
2         c(i) = c(i-2) + r1
      end do
```

Suppose that all operations are executed in unit time. Let $\theta(1, i) = ai + b_1$ and $\theta(2, i) = ai + b_2$ be the prototype schedules. There are two dependences:
- The first one is from $\langle 1, i \rangle$ to $\langle 2, i \rangle$ and gives the constraint: $b_2 - b_1 \geq 1$.
- The second one is from $\langle 2, i - 2 \rangle$ to $\langle 2, i \rangle$ and gives: $2a \geq 1$.

It is easy to see that the minimum latency solution is:

$$\theta(1, i) = i/2, \qquad \theta(2, i) = i/2 + 1.$$

Suppose now that both statements of the example are executed on the same resource. This gives the following additional constraints:

$$a(q + 1) + b_1 - b_2 \geq 1, \qquad b_2 - b_1 - aq \geq 1.$$

Since there are two statements in the loop and only one resource, we must have $a \geq 2$. An attempt to solve the remaining constraints with $A = 2, D = 1$ succeeds and gives:

$$\theta(1, i) = 2i, \qquad \theta(2, i) = 2i + 1.$$

Since A has an upper and a lower bound, it may seem that a binary search for the right value might be a good idea. However, experiment shows that the solution is always near the lower bound. In that case, a simple linear search is sufficient. Let us consider the following example:

```
program B

      do i = 1,n
1        r0 = a(i-2)/2.0
2        r1 = r0+a(i-3)
3        r2 = r0+a(i-4)
4         a(i) = r1*r2
      end do
```

Suppose that the available resources are an adder, a multiplier and a divider, and that addition takes one cycle, multiplication and division taking two cycles. Analysis of resource usage shows that the minimum initiation interval is two cycles. Dependence analysis shows that statement 1 has to be executed first, that 2 and 3 can be executed in parallel, and that 4 is to be executed last. However, since the cycle is closed by a dependence from 4 at iteration i to 1 at iteration $i + 2$, this gives a minimum rate of $5/2$, and this is the parallel lower bound. Hence, we set $D = 2$. The first value of A to be tested is 5, and the integer programming algorithm finds that there is no solution. A is thus increased to 6, and there is a solution. It is easy to see a *posteriori* that this solution is optimal. In fact, since there is only one adder, statements 1 and 2 must be executed sequentially. Hence each iteration of the loop cannot take less than 6 cycles. The resulting initiation interval is $6/2 = 3$, indicating that no unrolling is necessary.

Suppose now that the multiplication time is reduced to 1 cycle. The free bound decreases to 2, but the determinant of the basis matrix is still 2. Hence, we set $D = 2$ and $A = 4$. The first solution is found at the second iteration when $A = 5$, giving an initiation interval of $5/2$ with an unrolling factor of two. The schedule is:

$$\theta(1, i) = 5/2i, \qquad \theta(2, i) = 5/2i + 2,$$
$$\theta(i, 3) = 5/2i + 3, \qquad \theta(4, i) = 5/2i + 4.$$

To solve this problem, three calls to the integer programming algorithm PIP where needed, which took 0.43 seconds on a low end workstation.

3.2 The many resource case

In the many resource case, the resource constraint is given by (10). In the singular case, the scheduler has to guess the value of D and to search for the value of A. The many resource case is evidently more complicated. Hence, I will suppose that the algorithm structure is the same, namely that the problem is to test whether, A and D being given, there is a possible assignment for the B_S which meets all the constraints of the problem.

Here again, the first step is to get rid of the floor function. Suppose t is given, and that we are trying to count how many instances of S are active at time t. The iteration counter of the active instances is a positive integer such that:

$$t - \sigma(S) < \left\lfloor \frac{Ai + B_S}{D} \right\rfloor \leq t. \tag{15}$$

All terms in these inequalities are integers. Hence, they can be rewritten as:

$$t - \sigma(S) + 1 \leq \left\lfloor \frac{Ai + B_S}{D} \right\rfloor < t + 1.$$

Now $t - \sigma(S) + 1 \leq \lfloor \frac{Ai+B_S}{D} \rfloor$ and $t - \sigma(S) + 1 \leq \frac{Ai+B_S}{D}$ are equivalent. In one direction, this is because $\lfloor x \rfloor \leq x$, and in the other, it results from the monotony of the floor function.

For the other inequality, $\frac{Ai+Bs}{D} < t+1$ clearly imply $\lfloor \frac{Ai+Bs}{D} \rfloor < t+1$. In the reverse direction, $\lfloor \frac{Ai+Bs}{D} \rfloor \leq t$ implies $\frac{Ai+Bs}{D} < t+1$ by definition.

As a consequence, the iterations of S which are active at time t are solutions of:

$$Dt - D\sigma(S) + D \leq Ai + Bs < Dt + D.$$

The problem is to count the solutions of these inequalities with i as the unknown as a function of t.

Introducing an "excess" variable x, the constraints may be transformed into an equation:

$$Ai + Bs = Dt + D - 1 - x, \tag{16}$$

provided that x satisfies $0 \leq x < D\sigma(S)$. If $N_S(t, x)$ is the count of solutions of (16) for given t and x, then the number of active iterations at time t is:

$$N_S(t) = \sum_{x=0}^{D\sigma(S)-1} N_S(t, x).$$

The first observation is that equation (16) has at most one solution, which is given by:

$$i = \frac{Dt + D - 1 - x - Bs}{A}.$$

To be a legitimate iteration number, this solution has to be a positive integer. i is obviously positive for large enough t. The effect of ignoring the positivity condition, is to overestimate the resource usage for the *prologue* of the loop nest. It is customary in the field to ignore this factor by considering only very long loops, and this is the best one can do at compile time, since, for most loops, the iteration count is a variable. It may be possible to do better under user guidance: for instance, to inhibit software pipelining when the user knows that the iteration count will be small.

The integrity condition is simply:

$$Dt + D - 1 - x - Bs \equiv 0 \pmod{A}. \tag{17}$$

This has to be evaluated for all values of t. It is clear, however, that the condition depends only on $t \bmod A$. It thus has to be tested for $t \in [0, A-1]$. Another point is that the correspondance from t to $Dt \bmod A$ is bijective, since A and D are relatively prime. As a consequence, one may introduce a new variable $t' = Dt \bmod A, 0 \leq t' \leq A - 1$. The number of solutions of (16) may be written:

$$N_S(t, x) = \delta((t' + D - 1 - x - Bs) \bmod A),$$

where δ is a variant of the Kronecker symbol:

$$\delta(0) = 1, \quad \delta(i) = 0, i \neq 0.$$

The total number of solutions is now:

$$N_S(t) = \sum_{x=0}^{D\sigma(S)-1} \delta((t' + D - 1 - x - B_S) \bmod A).$$

All in all, (10) translates to:

$$\sum_{S\in\rho} \sum_{x=0}^{D\sigma(S)-1} \delta((t' + D - 1 - x - B_S) \bmod A) \leq N_\rho. \tag{18}$$

The next step is to "linearize" the Kronecker symbol. This is possible by rewriting B_S as:

$$B_S = AC_S + \sum_{k=0}^{A-1} ky_{S,k}, \tag{19}$$

where the $y_{S,k}$ are integral variables such that:

$$0 \leq y_{S,k} \leq 1, \sum_{k=0}^{A-1} y_{S,k} = 1 \tag{20}$$

To see that this change of variable is legitimate, suppose that the value of B_S is given. Take first $C_S = B_S \div A$, and $r = B_S \bmod A$. Setting $y_{S,r} = 1$, all others $y_{S,k}$ being 0, gives the required equality (19).

It is now easy to prove by enumerating cases that:

$$\delta((t' + D - 1 - x - B_S) \bmod A) = y_{S,(t'+D-1-x)\bmod A},$$

and that, as a consequence, the resource constraint (18) takes the form:

$$\forall t' \in [0, A-1] : \sum_{S\in\rho} \sum_{x=0}^{D\sigma(S)-1} y_{S,(t'+D-1-x)\bmod A} \leq N_\rho. \tag{21}$$

This is the required linearization. The solution process may be summarized as follows:

1. Select a value for D, in a manner that will be discussed presently.
2. Set $A = \lceil Dl \rceil$, where l is the lower bound for the initiation interval.
3. For each statement S in the loop nest, create $A + 1$ new unknowns C_S and $y_{S,k}, k = 0, A - 1$, write the equality (19) and the constraints (20).
4. For each resource in the system, write the constraint (21).
5. Express the causality constraint in term of the new unknowns, applying the Farkas algorithm if necessary [Fea92a].
6. If the resulting system is feasible, the problem has been solved. If not, add one to A and start again at step 3.

The unrolling factor D has to be choosen, as above, by heuristic arguments. Since the resource lower bound is no longer an integer, there are two denominators to choose from. Possible suggestions are to take the largest one, or their least common multiple, or the denominator of the largest bound.

Consider the following loop, which is taken from [GS92].

```
    program G
    do i = 0,n
1       a(i) = a(i)+d(i-2)
2       b(i) = a(i)/e(i-2)
3       c(i) = a(i)*e(i-2)
4       d(i) = c(i)+b(i-1)
5       e(i) = e(i)+b(i)
    end do
```

The target computer has three identical processors on which each statement takes unit time, with the exception of 2 which takes two cycles. In our notations, for statements 1, 3, 4 and 5 $\partial(S) = \sigma(S) = 1$, while $\partial(2) = \sigma(2) = 2$. As has been observed by Gasperoni et. al., the free schedule is:

$$\theta(1, i) = 3/2i, \qquad \theta(2, i) = 3/2i + 1,$$
$$\theta(3, i) = 3/2i + 1 \qquad \theta(4, i) = 3/2i + 2,$$
$$\theta(5, i) = 3/2i + 2.$$

with an initiation interval of $3/2$. This means, in fact, that two iterations can be initiated every three clock cycles. Since each iteration needs 6 cycles, and there are three processors, full utilization of the resources is obtained for an initiation interval of 2. The proposed algorithm succeeds immediately and find the following schedule:

$$\theta(1, i) = 2i, \qquad \theta(2, i) = 2i + 1,$$
$$\theta(3, i) = 2i + 1 \qquad \theta(4, i) = 2i + 2,$$
$$\theta(5, i) = 2i + 3.$$

Two calls to PIP are needed, taking less than 2 seconds. The present solution is optimal; this is to be compared to the solution obtained by Gasperoni et. al., whose initiation interval is 3.

4   Conclusion and Future Work

In this paper, I have shown how to translate resource constraints into systems of bilinear inequalities. For a given initiation interval, the inequalities become linear. When added to the dependence constraints, they can be tested for feasibility by any integer programming algorithm, in our case, an implementation of the Gomory algorithm. One then has to search for increasing values of the initiation interval until a solution is found.

Extracting the object code from the schedule is a well known problem, which is best explained by an example. Let us consider program G. The first step is to invert the schedule, i.e. to decide who is doing what at any given time. Since the initiation interval is 2, we have to distinguish between even and odd times. Let us suppose that t is even. The solution of $2i = t$ is $i = t/2$. Hence, we know that some processor will be executing iteration $t/2$ of statement 1 at time t. Similarly, $2i + 3 = t$ has no solution, but $2i + 3 = t + 1$ has. Hence, we know that some processor will be executing iteration $\frac{t-2}{2}$ of statement 5 at time t+1. Proceeding in this way, we obtain the following diagram

t	$\langle 1, t/2\rangle$			$\langle 4, \frac{t-2}{2}\rangle$	
$t+1$	$\langle 3, t/2\rangle$	$\langle 2, \frac{t-1}{2}\rangle$	$\langle 5, \frac{t-2}{2}\rangle$	

The construction of the actual code is now strongly dependent on the machine architecture. On a VLIW processor, for instance, the above diagram directly gives the statements to be packed in two successive instruction words. The problem may be more complicated if the hardware has provision for dynamic rearrangement of operations.

The method has been implemented by extending the scheduler of [Fea92b]. All exemples in this paper have been solved on this implementation. There are many possible improvements on this solution, some of which have already been tested. For instance, in the case of mixed problems, with single resources and resource classes, it is possible to combine the two algorithms, using (13) for single resources and (21) for resource classes.

The controlling factors for the complexity of the algorithm are the size of the initiation interval, A, and the number of statements in the loop body. The algorithm is not sensitive to the number of resources in a class. For instance, the following table gives the initiation interval and the solution time in seconds for program G, for 1 to 4 CPU's, at which time the free schedule is obtained:

CPU	Interval	Time
1	6	1.58
2	3	2.0
3	2	1.86
4	3/2	0.71

Obviously, the space and time requirements of the algorithm may become prohibitive for very large exemples. The question now is: is there a better way of solving directly the non-linear constraints (13) or (21) than by a combination of integer programming and search?

Acknowledgment

All exemples in this paper have been run using Zbigniew Chamski's multiple precision implementation of PIP.

References

[DGN92]   Vincent H. Van Dongen, Guang R. Gao, and Qi Ning. A polynomial time method for optimal software pipelining. In Luc Bougé, Michel Cosnard, Yves Robert, and Denis Trystram, editors, *Parallel Processing: CONPAR 92-VAPP V*, pages 613–624, Springer, LNCS 634, June 1992.

[Fea89]   Paul Feautrier. Asymptotically efficent algorithms for parallel architectures. In M. Cosnard and C. Girault, editors, *Decentralized System*, pages 273–284, IFIP WG 10.3, North-Holland, December 1989.

[Fea91]   Paul Feautrier. Dataflow analysis of scalar and array references. *Int. J. of Parallel Programming*, 20(1):23–53, February 1991.

[Fea92a]   Paul Feautrier. Some efficient solutions to the affine scheduling problem, I, one dimensional time. *Int. J. of Parallel Programming*, 21(5):313–348, October 1992.

[Fea92b]   Paul Feautrier. Some efficient solutions to the affine scheduling problem, II, multidimensional time. *Int. J. of Parallel Programming*, 21(6):389–420, December 1992.

[Fis84]   J.A. Fisher. The VLIW machine: a multiprocessor for compiling scientific code. *Computer*, 45–53, July 1984.

[GS92]   Franco Gasperoni and Uwe Schwiegelshohn. Scheduling loops on parallel processors: a simple algorithm with close to optimum performance. In Luc Bougé, Michel Cosnard, Yves Robert, and Denis Trystram, editors, *Parallel Processing: CONPAR 92-VAPP V*, pages 625–636, Springer, LNCS 634, June 1992.

[Lam88]   Monica Lam. Software pipelining: an effective scheduling technique for VLIW machines. In *Proc. of the SIGPLAN '88 Conf. on Programming Language Design and Implementation*, pages 318–328, Atlanta, June 1988.

[MQRS90] Christophe Mauras, Patrice Quinton, Sanjay Rajopadhye, and Yannick Saouter. *Scheduling Affine Parameterized Recurrences by means of Variable Dependent Timing Functions*. Technical Report 1204, INRIA, April 1990.

[Qui87]   Patrice Quinton. The systematic design of systolic arrays. In F. Fogelman, Y. Robert, and M. Tschuente, editors, *Automata networks in Computer Science*, pages 229–260, Manchester University Press, December 1987.

[RF93]   B. Ramakrishna Rau and Joseph A. Fisher. Instruction-level parallel processing: history, overview and perspective. *The Journal of Supercomputing*, 7:9–50, 1993.

[RG81]   B. R. Rau and C. D. Glaeser. Some scheduling techniques and an easily schedulable horizontal architecture for high-performance scientific computing. In *IEEE/ACM 14th Annual Microprogramming Workshop*, October 1981.

Mutation Scheduling: A Unified Approach to Compiling for Fine-Grain Parallelism*

Steven Novack and Alexandru Nicolau

Department of Information and Computer Science
University of California
Irvine, CA 92717

Abstract. Trade-offs between code selection, register allocation, and instruction scheduling are inherently interdependent, especially when compiling for fine-grain parallel architectures. However, the conventional approach to compiling for such machines arbitrarily separates these phases so that decisions made during any one phase place unnecessary constraints on the remaining phases. Mutation Scheduling attempts to solve this problem by combining code selection, register allocation, and instruction scheduling into a unified framework in which trade-offs between the functional, register, and memory bandwidth resources of the target architecture are made "on the fly" in response to changing resource constraints and availability.

1 Introduction

In this paper we present Mutation Scheduling (MS), a unified, compiler-based approach for exploiting the functional, register, and memory bandwidth characteristics of arbitrary single-threaded fine-grain parallel architectures, such as VLIW, super-scalar, and super-pipelined. MS is a "value-oriented" approach to instruction scheduling that allows the computation of any given value to change dynamically during scheduling to conform to varying resource constraints and availability.

Generating code for single-threaded fine-grain parallel architectures consists of three phases: code selection, register allocation, and instruction scheduling. Code selection refers to deciding which sequence of machine operations will be used to compute each value needed by the program. Register allocation determines when these values will reside in the registers and when they will be transferred between memory and the register file. Instruction scheduling refers to mapping the selected operations to the appropriate functional units of the architecture so that the order of execution minimizes execution time while preserving the semantics of the original program. Conventional compilers perform these phases separately so that decisions made during code selection and register allocation can unnecessarily constrain the ability of the scheduling phase to utilize available machine resources. This problem exists even for conventional pipelined architectures, but becomes more critical for fine-grain parallel machines. For example, consider a super-scalar architecture consisting of three functional units, an adder, a shifter and a multiplier. If we want to generate the value "$Y \leftarrow X * 2$", three possible single operation code selections are immediately obvious: "(add Y X X)", "(mul Y X 2)", and "(lshift Y X 1)". The code selection phase would generally associate a cost, such as the sum of operation latencies, with each possible code sequence, and choose the one with the smallest cost. Of these three single-operation sequences, "(lshift Y X 1)" would generally be selected as the quickest (e.g. by a reduction in strength optimization pass), thus forcing the instruction scheduling phase to assign the operation to the shifter unit. However, when scheduling "(lshift Y X 1)" it might be the case that the shift unit is already committed to computing other operations (*at that point in the schedule*),

---
* This work was supported in part by NSF grant CCR8704367 and ONR grant N0001486K0215.

while one or both of the other two units remains simultaneously idle. In this context, even though the shift operation has the lowest code selection cost, one of the other operations may have been more appropriate. Similarly, if registers are allocated prior to scheduling, spurious dependencies, such as write-after-write and write-after-read, are created that can prevent operations from being scheduled in parallel.[2]

Mutation Scheduling integrates code selection and register allocation into the instruction scheduling phase in an attempt to "adapt" a given program to best fit the physical characteristics of the target architecture. MS works by associating each value, VAL, defined in the program with a set, called MUTATIONS(VAL), of functionally equivalent expressions, each of which computes VAL using some different resources of the target architecture. At any given time during parallelization, exactly one of the expressions in MUTATIONS(VAL) will be used in the program graph to compute VAL. When scheduling the expression, EXPR, that currently generates VAL, if the resources for EXPR are unavailable, then another expression, or *mutation*, of VAL that better fits the resources may be substituted for it from MUTATIONS(VAL). When this happens, we say that VAL has been *mutated*.

MUTATIONS sets are also used for integrating register allocation into the scheduling process by allowing the MUTATIONS sets to change dynamically during scheduling to contain new expressions that may become available for a value. When a value, VAL, has already been computed and resides in a register, a reference to that register will become one of the expressions in MUTATIONS(VAL). If VAL is spilled to its "home" location in memory, then the expression "(load VAL home(VAL))" is also added to MUTATIONS(VAL). If at some point during scheduling, VAL is needed by some other expression, an evaluation function is applied to choose from MUTATIONS(VAL) the "best" way of accessing, or if necessary re-computing, VAL. If a register reference for VAL is still in MUTATIONS(VAL), then that register can simply be used. Otherwise, VAL must be "regenerated" by scheduling some expression from MUTATIONS(VAL). To allow for register spilling we will always insist that the two operation expression "(STORE home(VAL) VAL), (LOAD VAL home(VAL))"[3] be a member of MUTATIONS(VAL). In addition, if VAL has already been spilled to memory then MUTATIONS(VAL) will also contain the single operation expression "(load VAL home(VAL))". Finally, MUTATIONS(VAL) may also contain other expressions that are capable of re-computing VAL from data already stored in the register file. Note that these expressions may be as simple as semantically equivalent operations derived from a simple understanding of the target architecture or as complex as some of the esoteric operation sequences generated by a "superoptimizer"[12]. The actual expression chosen from MUTATIONS(VAL) to regenerate VAL depends on the relative merits of accessing memory versus re-computing the value, which in turn depends on the functional, register, and memory bandwidth availability *at that time* in the scheduling process.

2 Related Work

In recent years, a number of techniques have been developed that, to one extent or another, redefine the boundaries between the conventional separation of code selection, register allocation, and instruction scheduling concerns. For example, instruction scheduling and register allocation are integrated in [9, 14, 3, 17, 13, 19, 2]. Techniques like [14, 17, 13, 19] start with an initial register allocation and then during scheduling allocate unused registers using dynamic renaming[5] to remove false dependencies.[4]

---

[2] Although, some compilers[14, 17, 13, 19] do partially mitigate the effect of early register allocation by removing spurious dependencies using dynamic register renaming[5]. Others [22] perform a potentially very expensive post-scheduling register re-allocation.

[3] If this expression is selected as a new mutation for VAL, then it will be instantiated in its entirety, but nevertheless the STORE and LOAD will be scheduled separately so that the final locations of the STORE and LOAD will not generally be in adjacent instructions.

[4] Some of these techniques also try to eliminate spill code that becomes unnecessary as a result of scheduling.

Unlike these techniques, which do not release allocated registers for use in other computations (e.g. by introducing spill code), the techniques presented in [9, 3, 2] do full register allocation and instruction scheduling "on the fly", including register spilling when appropriate.

The *re-materialization* technique presented in [4] is a register allocation technique that, unlike the above methods, partially integrates the code selection pertaining to re-generating needed values. In this technique, a conventional register allocation phase is performed, but when a live value needs to be removed from the register file, the operation that originally computed the value may be used to re-compute it in place of using spill code so long as doing so is worthwhile by some heuristics measure and semantics preserving. Some traditional compiler optimizations, like Strength Reduction and Common Subexpression Elimination (CSE)[1] exhibit similar trade-offs between code selection and register allocation, but traditional compilers eliminate the *trade-off* (e.g. by performing the transformation prior to or after register allocation).

Finally, Incremental Tree-Height Reduction (ITHR) partially integrates code selection into instruction scheduling. THR[11] is a well-known technique for changing the structure of expressions by exploiting the associative and distributive properties of most arithmetic and logical operators. *Incremental* THR[16] was used to change (on the fly) dependencies encountered during instruction-level scheduling when doing so would increase the degree of parallelism.

Each of the abovementioned techniques has successfully out-performed techniques that rely on the conventional separation of concerns when compiling for fine-grain parallel architectures, and collectively, these successes provide much of the motivation for Mutation Scheduling (MS). MS differs most notably from the previous techniques in that it unifies all three aspects, code selection, register allocation, and instruction scheduling, into a single framework in which trade-offs among all three can be made, but MS does share some similarities with each technique:

- Like the techniques used in [9, 3, 2] MS attempts to do full register allocation in conjunction with instruction scheduling, but unlike these techniques, MS follows the same paradigm as used in [14, 17, 13, 19], of starting with an initial register allocation and then modifying it during scheduling in response to changing resource availability.
- Like re-materialization, MS allows code other than a spill/reload sequence to re-generate a value previously removed from the register file, but MS allows the use of any functionally equivalent computation, the choice of which (including spill code) depends on the relative merits of each with respect to current resource availability at the current point during scheduling.
- Like the incremental THR technique, MS allows the code used to compute expressions to change during scheduling in response to changing resource dependencies, but does so with greater generality as any functionally equivalent expression may be substituted,[5] not just those derivable using THR.

Of course, like the previous techniques, MS does by necessity depend on heuristic guidance since the problems it deals with are each NP-hard. However, MS has the advantage of allowing a single uniform heuristic to provide trade-offs among code selection, register allocation, and instruction scheduling within a unified framework. Within this framework, the heuristic aspects are encapsulated away from the actual code transformations so all three problems can easily be tuned by adjusting the heuristics, and without modifying the code transformation algorithms themselves.

---

[5] Including those derivable using CSE, re-materialization, and strength-reduction, as well as more complex sequences such as those that may be derived by a programmer with expert knowledge of the target architecture or a super-optimizer[12].

3 Value-oriented TiPS

MS schedules operations using a system of parallelizing program transformations called Trailblazing Percolation Scheduling (TiPS)[19]. TiPS is a hierarchical extension of Percolation Scheduling (PS)[15] that preserves the completeness of PS while enabling non-incremental transformations on a type of hierarchical control flow graph called the Hierarchical Task Graph (HTG)[8]. To facilitate the "value-oriented" view used by MS, we augment the HTG structure with a slightly modified version of the Static Single Assignment (SSA) form of [6]. In the pure SSA form of a program, each use is reached by exactly one definition. When definitions from multiple control paths are needed by a use, a special ϕ-function is inserted at the confluence of the control paths that merges the multiple values into a single definition. In SSA form, each variable name corresponds to a value that is defined once and used at least once. At any given time during execution, the value defined by a ϕ-function is just the ϕ-function's use which is reached along the current control path. The unique name for each definition in SSA form makes it natural to view each variable as a "value" produced and consumed, in the dataflow sense, by its definition and uses. For this reason, SSA variables are usually referred to as "values" in this paper.

For simplicity of exposition, we assume that LOAD's and STORE's of elements of arrays and structures are represented using the Access, Update, and HiddenUpdate operations defined in [6] which, in terms of *dataflow*, treat each element LOAD/STORE as a scalar read/write of the entire array or structure. The actual method used in our compiler is very similar to this, but allows for less conservative handling of ambiguous references and incremental updates of SSA form. While the issues involved in handling ambiguous references are somewhat interesting in the context of SSA form, they are not especially relevant to MS itself and will not be discussed further in this paper.

The parallelizing transformations provided by SSA enhanced TiPS are essentially the same as those of normal TiPS. The only significant difference is in maintaining the SSA form as scheduling progresses. In order to expose more parallelism during scheduling, we often allow operations below the join-point of a conditional to "move" into the conditional by duplicating them into its "true" and "false" branches. If such an operation, OP, depends on a ϕ-function at the join-point of a conditional, then OP is control dependent on the conditional and may use and define different values depending on which branch is taken through the conditional. If OP is copied to OP' along one branch, say B, of the conditional, then each use in OP' that depends on the ϕ-function will be replaced by the ϕ-function's use that is reached through B.   Similarly, if OP defines the variable X then the copy of OP on each branch will define a new variable, say X' and X'' respectively, and the ϕ-function $X \leftarrow \phi(X', X'')$ will replace OP at the join-point. Note that if OP does not depend on any ϕ-function at the join-point, then OP would not be control dependent on the conditional and identical copies of OP could be duplicated onto each control path, without requiring a new ϕ-function — this is a slight structural relaxation of true SSA form which requires a unique destination name for each *textual* occurrence of an operation, but is fundamentally consistent with the intended meaning of SSA form since each *value* is still given a unique name. Note that this relaxation also allows multiple textual occurrences of the same value to occur when "re-generating" values that have been released from the register file.

4 Mutation Scheduling

This section describes Mutation Scheduling. MUTATIONS sets are defined in Section 4.1. Techniques for finding and constructing multiple functionally equivalent "mutations" for values are discussed in Section 4.2. Section 4.3 describes the MUTATE transformation that provides the mechanism for using the MUTATIONS sets for integrating both code selection and register allocation into the scheduling process as detailed in Section 4.4.

4.1 Mutation Sets

Conceptually, we view each MUTATIONS set as a set of arbitrarily long expressions, each of which computes the same value. However, since the intermediate values defined within any expression may themselves have multiple expressions (i.e. mutations), we represent expressions as follows. Given an expressions, E, that computes VAL, the *tree form* of E consists of *leaf* nodes and *interior* nodes. Each leaf corresponds to either a constant or a value produced for E by some other expression. Each interior node corresponds to an operation in E that uses the values defined by its "children" in the tree and defines a value for use by its "parent" in the tree. Edges in the tree join each operand used by an operation (i.e. interior node) to its definition: either a leaf or the destination operand of some other operation. The root of the tree corresponds to the operation that defines VAL. This tree form expression for VAL is represented in our system using MUTATIONS sets by storing the operation, OP, associated with the root of the tree in MUTATIONS(VAL) and creating new MUTATIONS sets for each (sub)expression rooted at a non-leaf child associated with a use in OP. We assume that each expression is already in SSA form with respect to the program (even though the expression itself may not be present in the program) so any new MUTATIONS sets created will be for new values.

Note that in the set theoretic sense, MUTATIONS(VAL) only contains *operations*; however, in the remainder of this paper, we will say an *expression, E, is in* MUTA-TIONS(VAL) if E can be re-constructed from the MUTATIONS sets by reversing the above process, starting with an operation from MUTATIONS(VAL) as the root of the tree for E. This representation of expressions is similar to value numbering[1] except that instead of representing multiple identical subexpressions as a single subexpression, referenced multiple times within a directed acyclic graph, we represent multiple identical equivalence classes of expressions (i.e. MUTATIONS sets) as a single equivalence class referenced multiple times by its value name.

4.2 Finding Expressions

Any technique may be used for generating the initial set of expressions stored in the MUTATIONS sets as long as the abovementioned guidelines are followed. One simple, but useful technique is to initialize the MUTATIONS set for each value, VAL, defined by the operation, OP, to MUTATIONS(VAL) = {OP}, and then take the transitive closure of each MUTATIONS set with respect to a (constructive) functional equivalence relation, $\cong$, defined as follows. Given expressions A and B in tree form, A $\cong$ B if and only if all of the following are true:

1. The leaves of A and B reference the same set of variables (i.e. A and B have the same "inputs").
2. The operations associated with the roots of A and B define the same variable (i.e. they have the same "outputs").
3. For all valid assignments to the leaf variables of A and B, the values produced by A and B are identical, and this equivalence can be determined by the compiler (thus $\cong$ is a "constructive" relation).

Note that this definition says nothing about the internal structure of either expression which may be arbitrarily complex or simple. For instance, THR can often yield a large number of functionally equivalent expressions,[6] each of which may have different numbers and kinds of operations in addition to a different structure.

The rules used in step 3 to determine functional equivalence will, by necessity, be incomplete due to the undecidability of the "program equivalence" problem; however,

---

[6] Although, due to the finite precision of computer arithmetic, the actual values produced at run time may differ somewhat for some THR-equivalent expressions. Whether or not these differences are significant is application dependent.

for any given target architecture, simple but important classes of functional equivalence can usually be determined. For instance, the following three types of functional equivalence generally lend themselves to constructive characterization for most architectures and application domains:

Synonyms When restricted to specific functions, many operations have "synonymous" meanings. For instance, "X ← Y", can be performed on most architectures, in a number of ways: (ASSIGN X Y), (ADD X Y 0), (MUL X Y 1), (OR X Y 0), etc. Each of which may require different resources, and may or may not have different latencies depending on the particular architecture.

Composition/decomposition Many architectures offer specialized "compound" operations that perform the same function as multiple sequences of other operations. It is often possible to change the resource requirements and latency of a given computation by "composing" such a sequence of operations into an equivalent compound operation, or by "decomposing" a compound operation into a sequence of operations. For instance, most processors designed for use on Digital Signal Processing applications offer a single Multiply And Accumulate (MAC) operation that performs the computation "A ← B + C * D", which could also be "decomposed" into the two operation sequence "t ← C * D, A ← B + t". Executing the MAC operation takes less time than the decomposed pair of operations; however, the MAC operation typically requires MULTIPLY and ADD functional units to be used "back to back", which may not be possible at a particular point in the program if some other operation has already been scheduled onto one of those units. In this case, if the MULTIPLY and ADD units were separately available then the decomposed sequence of operations might produce the same result sooner.

In addition, some architectures, such as the Intel i860, provide a more general mechanism that allows fairly arbitrary "compositions" of operations executed on some functional units by allowing an operand address to specify that the output of one functional unit be fed directly into the input of the same or another unit, thus bypassing register access stages of the execution pipe. This type of explicit register-file bypassing feature is complicated by the fact that the result from a functional unit is usually only available for bypassing during a specific "hot-spot" cycle in which the recipient must access the value. Fortunately, Mutation Scheduling provides a trivial mechanism for performing "hot-spot" scheduling since it is possible to keep both the hot-spot and register-to-register mutations of an expression for a given value within the MUTATIONS set of the value. Then, at any point during scheduling, the mutation of the value that best utilizes the available resources can be selected.

Tree Height Reduction and Constant Folding Tree Height Reduction (THR) is a well-known technique for changing the structure of an expression in tree form by exploiting the associative and distributive properties of most arithmetic and logical operations [11]. By "flattening out" tall thin expression trees into shorter, wider ones, THR increases the degree of parallelism in the expression, and thereby changes its resource requirements.

Similarly, when the expression contains constant terms, it is often possible to group the constant terms together into the same operation using THR. This then allows the operations involving only constant terms to be performed statically at compile time and replaced by the new resulting constant. This process is typically referred to as Constant Folding. Of course, neither THR nor Constant Folding should be performed if it would result in numerical instability for a given application.

When the above types of functional equivalence combine as mutations during scheduling they may also have the cumulative effect of performing other conventional optimizations. For instance, constant folding, composition/decomposition, and synonym mutations sometimes combine to yield an incremental form of strength reduction.

Other types of functional equivalence might also be employed, including some of the more esoteric "tricks" that might be provided by an experienced assembly language programmer or a super-optimizer[12]. However, even the above "simple" types of functional equivalences are sufficient to yield a large number of functionally equivalent expressions. For instance, even an expression as simple (and common) as the address computation for the array reference, $M[i][j]$, exhibits all three forms of functional equivalence. If C_1 is the row size of M and C_2 is the element size of M, then the address of $M[i][j]$ is ADDR $\leftarrow (i * C_1 + j) * C_2$, which, after Synonym, Composition/Decomposition, and THR closure, is represented using MUTATIONS sets as:

$$\text{MUTATIONS}(\text{ADDR}) = \{(\text{MUL ADDR } t_1 \ c_2), (\text{LSHIFT ADDR } t_1 \ \log C_2),$$
$$(\text{ADD ADDR } t_3 \ t_4)\} \tag{1}$$
$$\text{MUTATIONS}(t_1) = \{(\text{ADD } t_1 \ t_2 \ j), (\text{MAD } t_1 \ j \ i \ C_1)\} \tag{2}$$
$$\text{MUTATIONS}(t_2) = \{(\text{MUL } t_2 \ i \ C_1)\} \tag{3}$$
$$\text{MUTATIONS}(t_3) = \{(\text{MUL } t_3 \ i \ C1 * C2)\} \tag{4}$$
$$\text{MUTATIONS}(t_4) = \{(\text{MUL } t_4 \ j \ C_2), (\text{LSHIFT } t_4 \ j \ \log C_2)\} \tag{5}$$

The above assumes that C_2 is a power of two, which is typical for arrays containing scalar values. Note that the MAD operation (MAD $A \ B \ C \ D$) has the meaning $A \leftarrow B + C * D$. Ignoring resource constraints, the expression "(MAD $t_1 \ j \ i \ C_1$), (LSHIFT ADDR $t_1 \ \log C_2$)" would generally be selected during the initial code selection as the best expression for ADDR; however, at any given point during scheduling, the computation that would actually produce ADDR sooner may very well be one of the other mutations if the resources required for one or both of these operations are unavailable. An example of how this can happen is found in Section 4.3.

4.3   The Mutate Transformation

The core transformation of MS is the MUTATE routine shown in Figure 1. MUTATE is responsible for selecting and scheduling the "best" computation of "VAL", if any, that can be scheduled on the path of instructions described by the Path-Template, P. A Path-Template is a list of 3-tuples of the form (NODE, OPS, RESOURCE-CONSTRAINTS). Each such tuple contains an instruction, NODE, a set of operations, OPS, that would need to be added to NODE in order to compute VAL, and a list of resource constraints, RESOURCE-CONSTRAINTS, that would be satisfied if all of the operations in OPS were added to node. For a given node, N, functional resource constraints specify how many new operations may be scheduled for each functional unit at N, and register constraints generally specify how many new *register-values* may become live at N. A *register-value* is a value defined by an operation that writes to a register, as opposed to a *memory-value* which is defined by an operation (e.g. STORE) that writes to memory. We say that the value VAL is *allocated* a register at N if, and only if, VAL is a live register-value at N. When the target architecture has hot-spots, we treat each hot-spot as a register resource (e.g. latch register) that exists for only one cycle after it is defined (as opposed to normal register resources which always exist). This prevents MUTATE from scheduling the definition of the hot-spot more than one cycle prior to the use of the hot-spot value. Scheduling the definition earlier than this would cause the register holding the hot-spot value to cease to exist at its use, thereby causing the number of live hot-spot values to exceed the number of available hot-spot registers at the use of the hot-spot which is not allowed by the MUTATE transformation.

The first tuple on the Path-Template list corresponds to the node, N, in which the actual definition of VAL is intended to take place. Any subsequent tuples represent a

function MUTATE(VAL, P)
— try shorter mutations first
for i ← 1 ... |P|
  if REALIZABLE-MUTATION(VAL, $(P_1, \ldots, P_i)$) **then**
    REALIZE-MUTATION(VAL, $(P_1, \ldots, P_i)$)
    return true
return false
end function

procedure REALIZE-MUTATION(VAL, P)
for i ← |P| ... 1
  if |Preds(Node(P_i))| > 1 **then**
    ISOLATE(Node(P_i))
  Insert(OPS(P_i), Node(P_i))
  REMOVE-REDUNDANCIES(NODE(P_i))
  UPDATE-LIVE-INFO(NODE(P_i))
end procedure

function REALIZABLE-MUTATION(VAL, P)
if VAL **in** LIVE(NODE(P_1)) **then**
  return true
while OP ← CHOOSE-OP(MUTATIONS(VAL))
  if OPS(P_1) ∪ { OP} satisfies RESOURCE-CONSTRAINTS(P_1)
  and (Reads(OP) ⊆ LIVE(NODE(P_1)) **or**
      |P| > 1 **and** (∀U ∈ Reads(OP), REALIZABLE-MUTATION(U, $(P_2, \ldots, P_{|P|})$))))
  then
    OPS(P_1) = OPS(P_1) ∪ { OP }
    return true
— VAL is not realizable, so forget any subexpressions
for i ← 2 ... |P|
  OPS(P_i) = ∅
return false
end function

Fig. 1. The MUTATE Transformation

path leading to N along which intermediate values needed for computing VAL may be "realized". We say a value VAL is *realizable with respect to the Path-Template*, P, if VAL is already live at Node(P_1), or some operation OP from MUTATIONS(VAL) can be scheduled at Node(P_1) such that the resource constraints, RESOURCE-CONSTRAINTS(P_1), are satisfied and each of the values read by OP are realizable with respect to the rest of the Path-Template after P_1, i.e. $(P_2, \ldots, P_{|P|})$. The REALIZABLE-MUTATION routine shown in Figure 1 is a constructive version of this condition. When called from MUTATE, the OPS sets of each tuple in the Path-Template are empty. As REALIZABLE-MUTATION searches for a realizable mutation, the OPS sets are filled in with the operations that would be needed to compute, or *realize*, VAL. If REALIZABLE-MUTATION succeeds, then REALIZE-MUTATION inserts the operations contained in the OPS set of each tuple on P into the corresponding NODE, removes any redundancies[7] thus created, and updates the live information at the nodes affected. Any affected nodes on more than one control path are duplicated so as to isolate the effect of the new expression to the path specified in P.

Notice that MUTATE always prefers shorter expressions over longer ones, but the maximum length of expressions, the resources they consume, and the order in which mutations are tried all represent heuristics that are completely separate from the MUTATE transformation itself, thus making MUTATE a general transformation that could be used with most, if not all, approaches to instruction scheduling. The specific scheduling approach, in conjunction with the desired application domain and cost vs. performance trade-offs would dictate the actual choices for the MUTATE heuristics.

---

[7] If the target architecture supports conditional write-back as in [7], then it is possible that two operations from the same instruction produce the same value such that the write-back of one operation is predicated on some condition, and the write-back of the other on the negation of the condition. In this case, both operations can be replaced by a single operation whose write-back is not predicated on either the condition or its negation.

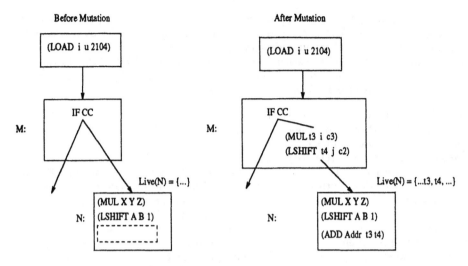

$$\text{MUTATE}(\text{ADDR}, (< N, \emptyset, \text{``1 add unit and 2 registers available''} >,$$
$$< M, \emptyset, \text{``1 add, 1 mul and 1 shift unit available''} >))$$

Fig. 2. MUTATE example

Figure 2 shows an application of the MUTATE transformation to realize a mutation of the value, ADDR, whose MUTATIONS set was defined earlier. Recall that the best mutation for ADDR in the absence of resource constraints was "(MAD t_1 j i C_1), (LSHIFT ADDR t_1 log C_2)". However, REALIZABLE-MUTATION can not return this mutation since the shift unit is already assigned an operation at N. The expression rooted at "(MUL ADDR t_1 c_2)" might also be considered, but this expression is also not realizable at N since the multiply unit is also busy. This leaves the final operation in MUTATIONS(ADDR), "(ADD ADDR t_3 t_4)". This operation does satisfy RESOURCE-CONSTRAINTS(N) but is not yet ready to execute at N since its uses, t_3 and t_4, are not live at N. In this case, since the Path-Template also includes a 3-tuple for M, REALIZABLE-MUTATION will recursively try to realize t_3 and t_4 at M. The value t_3 is realizable at M since a functional unit is available at M for "(MUL t_3 i $C1*C2$)" and a register is available to hold t_3 on entry to N. For t_4, there are two candidate mutations, "(MUL t_4 j C_2)" and "(LSHIFT t_4 j log C_2)". Since the multiply unit has already been (virtually) assigned to the computation of t_3, the first operation is not realizable at M. The shift operation is realizable at M, since the shift unit is available at M and an available register remains at N to hold t_4. The right side of Figure 2 shows the mutation of ADDR that was realized at N by MUTATE.

4.4 Scheduling

This section details how the MUTATE transformation is integrated into an existing Global Resource-constrained Percolation (GRiP)[18] scheduler to yield a Mutation Scheduling system. GRiP scheduling requires that satisfiable resource constraints be an invariant between code motion transformations.[8] Using GRiP, operations are progressively scheduled earlier using PS or TiPS transformations, in ranked order, until blocked by resource constraints (i.e. resource dependencies), true data dependencies, or false data dependencies when no free registers are available for performing dynamic renaming. In Mutation Scheduling, whenever one of these dependencies is encountered

---

[8] As opposed to techniques such as [21] that ignore resource-constraints during scheduling and [10, 2] that satisfy only resource estimates.

during scheduling, MUTATE is used in an attempt to remove the dependence. If an operation that defines VAL is prevented from being scheduled earlier by a true data dependence or functional resource dependence, then we try to find a new mutation of VAL that can be scheduled earlier. If code motion is blocked by a lack of available registers, then MUTATE may be used to free one or more registers by re-generating the values stored in these registers at some later time.

```
procedure MOVE-VAL(VAL, OP, FROM, TO)
if VAL not in LIVE(NODE(TO)) then
   if Writes(TO) ∩ Reads(OP) ≠ ∅
   or not Enough-Resources(OP, TO) then
      t ← GET-CONT-PATH(TO)              procedure DECREASE-REG-PRESSURE(FROM)
      if not MUTATE(VAL, t) then         while VAL ← CHOOSE-REG-VAL(LIVE(FROM))
         return                             t ← GET-REGEN-PATH(FROM)
   else                                     if VAL not in Reads(FROM)
      Insert-op(OP, TO)                      and MUTATE(VAL, t) then
if |Preds(FROM)| > 1 then                       return
   ISOLATE(FROM)                         end procedure
DELETE-OP(OP)
UPDATE-LIVE-INFO(FROM)
if TOO-MANY-LIVE-REGS(LIVE(FROM)) then
   DECREASE-REG-PRESSURE(FROM)
end procedure
```

Fig. 3. The MOVE-VAL transformation

The MOVE-VAL routine shown in Figure 3 is an incremental transformation[9] responsible for trying to schedule the definition of the value VAL, which is currently defined by the operation OP in the instruction FROM, one instruction earlier at TO.[10] Because of the "relaxed" SSA form, which allows multiple definitions of the same variable as long as the value defined by each is the same, it is possible that some other definition of VAL already reaches TO (i.e. VAL ∈ LIVE(TO)). This can happen if a definition of VAL has already been scheduled separately along some other control path through TO, or if VAL was previously defined along some control path leading to FROM, but had to be kicked out of the register file by generating code (including the definition of VAL in FROM) to re-generate VAL. In either case, the presence of VAL in LIVE(TO) when a definition of VAL also exists in FROM indicates that the conditions that originally required that the (re)definition of VAL currently scheduled at FROM have changed so that OP can simply be deleted, thus causing any definition of VAL that reaches TO to also reach the uses that were reached by OP. This facility for "extending" the live range of previous definitions of the same value provides a trivial but useful mechanism for both performing the PS UNIFY transformation, [11] and for "undoing" bad register allocation decisions by eliminating any regeneration code that becomes unnecessary due to changing register pressure during scheduling.

If VAL is not live at TO, then MOVE-VAL begins by testing for either a functional resource or data dependence on TO. If neither dependence exists then the current definition of VAL can simply be scheduled at TO. If a dependence does exist, then MU-TATE tries to realize a mutation of VAL at TO. The GET-CONT-PATH function returns

---

[9] For the sake of notational convenience, we will describe MS in the context of modifying the incremental PS transformation, MOVE-OP rather than its non-incremental counter-part (TRAILBLAZE) used in TiPS (the MS specific issues are identical for both).

[10] Note that VAL must be a register-value or a memory-value — hot-spot values are scheduled solely as a byproduct of the MUTATE transformation.

[11] UNIFY merges multiple definitions that have reached the same point after being scheduled separately along different control paths.

a Path-Template for a path of nodes ending in To along which the computation of VAL may take place.[12] The resource constraints specified within the Path-Template must never exceed the maximum resources available along the specified path of instructions, but may be much less depending on the relative importance of the value being mutated and the resources that would be freed (from the current mutation of the value) if a new mutation were to be scheduled earlier.

If MUTATE fails to realize VAL at To, then VAL is not currently "movable" and is suspended until the condition that blocked its movement changes. If a definition of VAL is successfully scheduled at To (possibly by MUTATE), then the effect of the movement must be "isolated" to the current path along which VAL is being scheduled. If FROM has multiple predecessors then ISOLATE inserts a copy of FROM on all other paths before DELETE-OP (which is called anyway) deletes OP from the copy of FROM that now has no predecessors other than To. DELETE-OP will also recursively delete any definitions that were only used by OP. If OP was the only operation in FROM then FROM no longer exists and we are done. Otherwise, live information is updated to reflect the fact that VAL has become, and other values have possibly ceased to be, live at FROM. If it turns out that the number of live register-values now exceeds the actual number of registers, as might happen, for instance, if VAL is a register-value and no other register-values ceased to be live, then DECREASE-REG-PRESSURE is called to restore the satisfiability of register constraints.

DECREASE-REG-PRESSURE applies some selection criteria (e.g. "furthest next use") to choose register-values from LIVE(FROM) in increasing order of importance. The first such register-value, say X, that is both unused in, and realizable at, FROM will be scheduled at FROM to kill X and thereby "release" the register allocated to X (i.e. X will no longer be live at the entry to FROM). As long as the selection criteria ensures that all register-values are candidates for selection, then DECREASE-REG-PRESSURE will always succeed in restoring correct register utilization since VAL, which must be realizable at FROM, may be selected as the register-value to release. In any case, we delete any previous definition of X that is killed by the new definition of X just scheduled at FROM. Repeated calls to DECREASE-REG-PRESSURE (when the register file is saturated) have the cumulative effect of deferring the definitions of values to the latest point at which they would be useful.

5 Results

Mutation Scheduling "adapts" code to the resources of the target architecture by making trade-offs, on the fly, between functional, register, and memory bandwidth resources in response to changing constraints and availability during scheduling. In this section, we present results from experiments for a few different target architectures that highlight three important aspects of these trade-offs. In the first, we focus on register versus functional resource and memory bandwidth trade-offs; in the second, we focus on parallelism versus register and functional resource trade-offs, and in the third, we focus on trade-offs among heterogeneous and specialized functional units.

Each experiment compares the speedup[13] obtained using a "Mutating" GRiP compiler (as outlined in section 4) for a set of benchmarks against those obtained using a non-mutating GRiP compiler. The presence or absence of Mutation Scheduling transformations is the only difference between the two compilers — each uses the same list scheduling heuristics to rank the order of operation importance and both pipeline loops using the "Resource-Directed Loop Pipelining (RDLP)" technique described in

---

[12] Recall that the length of this path represents the *maximum* length of the expression — the actual mutation is often just one operation. Note that a maximum path length of two is sufficient to exploit most Synonym, Composition/Decomposition, and THR mutations.

[13] i.e. the ratio of sequential to parallel cycles observed during simulation.

bench	RF Size	Speed-up MS	No MS
LL1	10	4.94	2.49
LL2	20	5.32	3.39
LL3	6	3.98	3.98
LL4	9	5.30	3.59
LL5	6	5.47	2.75
LL6	14	6.19	2.08
LL7	15	5.04	2.38
LL8	37	5.46	3.10
LL9	14	5.20	2.64
LL10	5	3.27	2.98
LL11	6	8.81	2.99
LL12	6	4.48	2.99
LL13	13	4.54	2.29
LL14	20	3.94	2.47
Avg	13	5.14	2.87

Table 1. Trading functional units and memory bandwidth for registers

bench	Speed-up MS	No MS
LL1	15.78	14.35
LL2	11.48	11.39
LL3	14.01	7.89
LL4	14.16	10.05
LL5	5.47	5.47
LL6	10.99	10.14
LL7	14.76	14.76
LL8	11.50	11.50
LL9	14.31	14.12
LL10	10.61	14.91
LL11	16.08	8.81
LL12	17.55	8.90
LL13	14.31	14.31
LL14	5.20	5.20
Avg	12.59	10.84

Table 2. Trading resources for parallelism

bench	Speed-up MS	No MS
LL1	11.92	10.70
LL2	8.99	8.93
LL3	7.19	5.76
LL4	5.06	4.22
LL5	6.69	4.61
LL6	6.61	4.98
LL7	10.06	9.97
LL8	9.01	5.92
LL9	4.33	2.85
LL10	2.84	2.53
LL11	5.54	5.04
LL12	7.95	9.24
LL13	3.46	2.75
LL14	3.74	2.53
Avg	6.67	5.72

Table 3. Trade-offs among heterogeneous and specialized functional units

[20]. RDLP works by unrolling and shifting[14] loops during scheduling to expose more operations to parallelize until resources are fully utilized and/or cost vs. performance constraints are satisfied.

For all three experiments, the same exact Mutating and Non-mutating compilers were used on the same set of benchmarks, so the experiments differ only in the characteristics of the target architectures specified for each. For the first two experiments (Sections 5.1 and 5.2) we assume idealized VLIW architectures with homogeneous, unicycle functional units. These simple architectures provide a useful framework for illustrating the ability of Mutation Scheduling to make general trade-offs between resources and parallelism and explicitly factor out its ability to exploit the unusual and specialized features that exist for many realistic architectures, which will be discussed separately in Section 5.3. In the third experiment we use a realistic but hypothetical VLIW architecture that combines some of the functional unit characteristics of the Motorola 88110 Superscalar with explicit pipeline and datapath control characteristics similar to those found in architectures like the Intel i860. We use this model to highlight the ability of Mutation Scheduling to exploit and make trade-offs among heterogeneous functional units and specialized architectural features.

Each of the experiments was run on the Livermore suite. In addition to factoring out distorting (albeit interesting) characteristics, such as cache performance and i/o, these benchmarks are small and well known so the results can easily be understood and interpreted. Below we present each experiment in detail.

5.1 Registers vs. Functional Units and Memory Bandwidth

In the first experiment we focus on the ability of Mutation Scheduling to decrease register pressure when necessary by exploiting unused functional resources and memory bandwidth to recompute or spill/reload values that are removed from the register file. To highlight this ability we compiled each benchmark for a VLIW with eight homogeneous functional units and a "minimal" number of registers. For each benchmark, we define the "minimal" number of live registers allowed during parallelization (i.e. the assumed register file size of the target architecture) to be equal to the maximum number of (virtual) registers live at any point in the initial sequential schedule produced by our GNU C front-end with register allocation disabled. This is the minimum number

---
[14] Loop shifting refers to "unwinding" a loop so that its head becomes a true successor of each of its predecessors, thus exposing new operations from subsequent iterations at the end of the loop for scheduling in parallel with existing operations.

of registers that the target architecture would need to execute the sequential schedule without spilling registers. By allowing each sequential schedule to have as many registers as it needs, we enable the frontend to produce the best schedule that it can with respect to conventional optimizations, such as strength reduction and common sub-expression elimination, and we factor out sequential register allocation constraints on the resulting parallel code. This in turn helps us ensure that speedups represent the ability of each compiler to parallelize good initial schedules rather than to merely remove deficiencies from poor ones.

Table 1 shows the speed-ups obtained when compiling each benchmark using a Mutating version of the GRiP compiler versus a Non-mutating version. Notice that Mutation never does worse than, and in all cases but one, does strictly better than the Non-mutating version. In fact, for 6 of the 14 benchmarks, the Mutation Scheduling version provides between a 2 and 3 fold improvement over the Non-mutating version. In both compilers, renaming to remove false dependencies among register-to-register operations is accomplished by SSA form, so each version is capable of performing the same sort of register re-allocation as is used in [14, 17, 13, 19] by allowing code motion only if the number of live register values after each completed transformation does not exceed the register file size.

The 100-200% improvements often provided by Mutation Scheduling come in part from its ability to *release* registers for use by more critical operations by exploiting available functional and memory bandwidth resources to recompute or spill/reload values when needed, and also comes in part from its ability to select code that decreases register requirements by exploiting opportunities to express computations in terms of values already in the register file, in lieu of introducing new intermediate values.

5.2 Parallelism vs. Register and Functional Resources

Above, we showed how MS can improve performance when the register file is heavily utilized by trading registers for available functional and memory bandwidth resources. In this experiment we show that when the architecture is robust, MS can also improve performance by increasing parallelism at the expense of increased resource consumption. For this experiment we assume a VLIW target architecture with 16 homogeneous functional units and 64 registers.

Table 2 shows the speed-ups obtained when compiling with the Mutating version of GRiP against those obtained using the Non-mutating version. Both compilers produce good speed-ups. In one case, the Non-mutating version out-performs the Mutating version, but in most of the remaining cases, the Mutating version produces significantly superior results — often improving speed-up by as much as 100%. Since the functional units are homogeneous and the register file is large enough, trade-offs between different functional units (as will be discussed in Section 5.3) and between registers and functional units (Section 5.1) do not affect the performance levels of the Mutating compiler. Thus the speed-up differences between the Mutating version of the compiler and the Non-mutating version are caused by the trade-offs between parallelism and resources provided by the Constant Folding and THR mutations defined in Section 4.2.

Sometimes, as for LL10, the mutations performed (e.g. THR) increase resource consumption as well as parallelism. However, since the expressions involved in the mutations are not part of a critical dependence chain, the Non-mutating GRiP compiler is able to achieve the same or greater increases in parallelism just by loop pipelining, without any increases in resource consumption. A more sophisticated mutation heuristic, such as "only choose THR mutations when there is no net increase in resource consumption", would greatly decrease the possibility that MS might degrade performance, without significantly inhibiting the ability of MS to increase parallelism.

5.3 Trade-offs among Heterogeneous and Specialized Functional Units

In this experiment we focus on the ability of Mutation Scheduling to increase parallelism by making trade-offs among heterogeneous functional units and specialized architectural features. The target architecture is a hypothetical VLIW machine combining some of the functional unit characteristics of the Motorola 88110 Superscalar with some explicit instruction issue and and datapath control characteristics found in a few real-world architectures like the i860. For this model we assume 6 types of functional unit: ALU units take 1 cycle to perform integer addition, subtraction, and logical operations; SHIFT units take 1 cycle to perform shift operations; FALU units take 3 cycles to perform floating point addition and subtraction operations; MUL units take 3 cycles to perform integer and floating point multiply operations; DIV units take 3 cycles to perform integer and floating point divide operations; MEM units take 2 cycles to read the cache and 1 cycle to write to the cache (cache misses stall the processor); and finally, BRANCH units take 4 cycles to perform conditional branches. With the exception of the branch unit, which was arbitrarily defined to take 4 cycles, each of these functional unit kinds and latencies are roughly the same as those of the Motorola 88110 Superscalar.

For this experiment we assume that there are two each of ALU, SHIFT, FALU, MUL, and MEM units, and one each of DIV and BRANCH units (i.e. just a little less functionality than a two-wide homogeneous VLIW). We assume a single register file with 64 registers. In terms of control logic we adopt an approach similar in some respects to the i860. Each VLIW instruction specifies exactly one (possibly NOP) operation for each functional unit. Each operation issued to a functional unit can have the optional side-effect of pushing along the execution pipeline of the functional unit.[15] Furthermore we assume that the data paths are set up to allow explicit register file bypassing by allowing each operand of an instruction to address either a register[16] or the output of any functional unit. We assume that register fetch and write-back stages are part of the pipeline for each functional unit, and unless explicitly bypassed as mentioned above, each take one cycle (i.e. without bypassing, the latency from fetch to writeback of any operation is two greater than the execution latency of the functional unit that executes the operation).

Table 3 shows results obtained for this architecture. Both the Mutating and Non-mutating GRiP compilers perform well, but the Mutating version consistently outperforms the Non-mutating version, often by as much as 50%. Note that even though this machine model has essentially the same functional resources as a 2-wide homogeneous VLIW, the Mutating GRiP compiler, and to a lesser extent the Non-mutating GRiP compiler, often produce order of magnitude speed-ups over the sequential case. This is indicative of the ability of each compiler, but especially the Mutating version, to effectively exploit both the spatial and temporal (pipeline) parallelism of the target architecture.

One of the main reasons for the large improvements of Mutation Scheduling over the Non-mutating compiler for this target architecture is the ability of Mutation Scheduling to make better utilization of explicit register file bypassing. One interesting thing to note however is that at times explicit register file bypassing can actually degrade the overall performance of the code, even though locally it always decreases the latency of a computation. To see this consider bypassing the register file for a floating point multiply/add sequence. This decreases the latency of the sequence by two, from 10 total cycles to 8, thus improving the utilization of temporal parallelism. However, loop pipelining could have scheduled the two operations (from different iterations) in parallel spatially, in which case the latency of the sequence would, in some sense, have been only 5 cycles (the total fetch to writeback latency of each operation). The Mutation Scheduling heuristics attempt to handle this trade-off by "unbypassing" operations

---

[15] Even though explicit pipeline control has proven difficult, or at least inconvenient, for many compilers, Mutation Scheduling provides a fairly clean mechanism for scheduling in this environment which allows us to exploit some of the benefits of explicitly controlling the pipeline.

[16] In this context, we treat any immediate fields within the instruction as registers.

when doing so would likely improve performance, but LL12, which is the only benchmark for which the Mutating version did not do strictly better than the Non-mutating
version, is one example where the Mutation heuristics over-zealously exploited the bypassing feature and thus constrained the overall performance of the loop. It should be
emphasized that we currently use very simple Mutation heuristics that could easily
be improved upon; however, an unfortunate reality of dealing with NP-hard problems,
such as resource constrained scheduling, is that no matter how good the heuristics get
there will always be some cases for which they perform sub-optimally.

References

1. A. Aho, R. Sethi, and J.D. Ullman. *Compilers: Principles, Techniques and Tools*. Addison-Wesley, Reading, MA, 1986.
2. D. Berson, R. Gupta, and M.L. Soffa. Resource spackling: A framework for integrating register allocation in local and global schedulers. In *Working Conf. on Par. Arch. and Compilation Techniques*, August 1994.
3. D. Bradlee, S. Eggers, and R. Henry. Integrating register allocation and instruction scheduling for riscs. In *ASPLOS*, April 1991.
4. P. Briggs, K. Cooper, and L. Torczon. Rematerialization. In *PLDI*, 1992.
5. R. Cytron and J. Ferrante. What's in a name? In *ICPP*, pages 19–27, August 1987.
6. R. Cytron, J. Ferrente, B. Rosen, M. Wegman, and K. Zadeck. Efficiently computing static single assignment form and the control dependence graph. *TOPLAS*, 13(4):451–490, October 1991.
7. K. Ebcioglu. Some design ideas for a vliw architecture for sequential-natured software. In *IFIP Proceedings*, 1988.
8. M. Girkar and C.D. Polychronopoulos. Automatic extraction of functional parallelism from ordinary programs. *TOPADS*, 3(2):166–178, March 1992.
9. J. R. Goodman and W. Hsu. Code scheduling and register allocation in large basic blocks. In *ICS*, July 1988.
10. R. Gupta and M. L. Soffa. Region scheduling: An approach for detecting and redistributing parallelism. *TOSE*, 16(4), April 1990.
11. D. J. Kuck, Y. Muraoka, and S. C. Chen. On the number of operations simultaneously executable in fortran-like programs and their resulting speedup. *TOC*, December 1972.
12. H. Massalin. Superoptimizer: A look at the smallest program. In *ASPLOS*, 1987.
13. S. Moon and K. Ebcioglu. An efficient resource constrained global scheduling technique for superscalar and vliw processors. In *MICRO*, Portland, OR, December 1992.
14. T. Nakatani and K. Ebcioglu. Using a lookahead window in a compaction-based parallelizing compiler. In *MICRO*, 1990.
15. A. Nicolau. Uniform parallelism exploitation in ordinary programs. In *ICPP*, 1985.
16. A. Nicolau and R. Potasman. Incremental tree height reduction for high level synthesis. In *DAC*, San Francisco, CA, June 1991.
17. A. Nicolau, R. Potasman, and H. Wang. Register allocation, renaming and their impact on parallelism. In *Lang. and Compilers for Par. Comp.*, number 589 in LNCS Series. Springer-Verlag, 1991.
18. S. Novack and A. Nicolau. An efficient global resource constrained technique for exploiting instruction level parallelism. In *ICPP*, St. Charles, IL, August 1992.
19. S. Novack and A. Nicolau. Trailblazing: A hierarchical approach to percolation scheduling. Technical Report TR-92-56, Univ. of Calif. Irvine, 1992. Also appears in the Proceedings of the 1993 International Conference on Parallel Processing, St. Charles, IL., August 1993.
20. S. Novack and A. Nicolau. Resource-directed loop pipelining. Technical report, Univ. of Calif., Irvine, Dept. of Information and Computer Science, 1994.
21. R. Potasman. *Percolation-Based Compiling for Evaluation of Parallelism and Hardware Design Trade-Offs*. PhD thesis, Univ. of Calif. Irvine, 1991.
22. B.R. Rau and C.D. Glaeser. Efficient code generation for horizontal architectures: Compiler techniques and architectural support. In *Symp. on Comp. Arch.*, April 1982.

Compiler Techniques For Fine-Grain Execution On Workstation Clusters Using PAPERS

H. G. Dietz, W. E. Cohen, T. Muhammad, and T. I. Mattox

Parallel Processing Laboratory
School of Electrical Engineering
Purdue University
West Lafayette, IN 47907-1285
hankd@ecn.purdue.edu
(317) 494 3357

Just a few years ago, parallel computers were tightly-coupled SIMD, VLIW, or MIMD machines. Now, they are clusters of workstations connected by communication networks yielding ever-higher bandwidth (e.g., Ethernet, FDDI, HiPPI, ATM). For these clusters, compiler research is centered on techniques for hiding huge synchronization and communication latencies, etc. — in general, trying to make parallel programs based on fine-grain aggregate operations fit an existing network execution model that is optimized for point-to-point block transfers.

In contrast, we suggest that the network execution model can and should be altered to more directly support fine-grain aggregate operations. By augmenting workstation hardware with a simple barrier mechanism (PAPERS: Purdue's Adapter for Parallel Execution and Rapid Synchronization), and appropriate operating system hooks for its direct use from user processes, the user is given a variety of efficient aggregate operations and the compiler is provided with a more static (i.e., more predictable), lower-latency, target execution model. This paper centers on compiler techniques that use this new target model to achieve more efficient parallel execution: first, techniques that statically schedule aggregate operations across processors, second, techniques that implement SIMD and VLIW execution.

This work was supported in part by the Office of Naval Research (ONR) under grant number N00014-91-J-4013 and by the National Science Foundation (NSF) under award number 9015696-CDA.

1. Introduction

Combining the low cost and high performance of modern workstations with the ever increasing bandwidth of the networks that connect them, the differences between a workstation cluster and a traditional supercomputer blur. However, there are fundamental differences that severely limit the range of parallel applications for which a workstation cluster can achieve good performance. These differences are not inherent in the use of workstations as the processing elements of a parallel machine, rather, they relate to assumptions made about the ways in which the workstation network would be used.

If we assume that each workstation is owned and used almost exclusively by one user, and the network is used primarily for file sharing and email, then it is appropriate to organize the system so that:

- Each workstation runs an autonomous operating system that schedules user process activities and moderates interactions with other workstations.

• Networks are designed to transmit relatively large blocks of data formatted as self-contained messages.

The problem is that this loosely coupled, stateless, organization is not a good match for the aggregate operations within most parallel algorithms, and impedes many of the most important compiler optimizations.

Fortunately, it takes very little modification to the hardware and operating system of a workstation cluster to provide an execution model that is more appropriate for executing fine-grain parallel code. Such a set of modifications is PAPERS: Purdue's Adapter for Parallel Execution and Rapid Synchronization [DiM94].

1.1. PAPERS Hardware

Since our goal is to make a workstation cluster more effective as a parallel machine, the PAPERS hardware is implemented as a simple and inexpensive (less than $50 per processor) add-on unit — neither the workstation hardware nor the network hardware is altered. The PAPERS hardware is connected to the standard Centronics-compatible printer port of each workstation.

Although it is accessed using port I/O operations instead of Load instructions, PAPERS implements the full dynamic barrier synchronization mechanism described in [CoD94]. Because the set of processors participating in each barrier synchronization is specified by each processor giving a bit mask indicating which processors it should synchronize with, the hardware is also completely partitionable, and barriers with nonoverlapping masks have no effect on each other. In any case, the barrier logic is easily implemented to be faster than wire propogation delays, which are in turn negligible in comparison to the processor latency in accessing an external port.

As a side effect of each barrier synchronization performed using PAPERS, an unusual type of synchronous communication is effected. Data from each processor participating in the barrier is simultaneously made available to all other processors (a multi-broadcast communication). In the first PAPERS unit, just one bit of data is sent from each processor, and the gathered set of bits can be directly read by each processor such that each bit in the value read is the data bit that was sent by the processor corresponding to that bit position in the barrier mask. Thus, this hardware allows processors within a partition of the full machine to "vote" and have the result of the vote known by all processors that were involved. For example, this is how the machine can determine at runtime which processors should be included in a barrier mask. It also allows generalized testing of the aggregate machine state, for example, checking if any processor voted 1 (i.e., global or).

Surprisingly, the multi-broadcast operation is actually sufficient for fully general aggregate communications, and can be used to implement random point-to-point "routing" such that all communication patterns are conflict-free. The basic concept is that each sending processor makes data available to every other processor, and the receiving processors simply select which data values they want to use. This is not the standard "shared memory" model, nor is it traditional "message passing," but it yields a more efficient implementation than either of these schemes:

- In both shared memory and message passing, the processor sending a datum must transmit both the datum and the destination address; in contrast, PAPERS' multi-broadcast allows the sender to transmit only the datum. Thus, given a fixed bandwidth (i.e., fixed number of wires), the multi-broadcast operation can send more data per unit time than is possible using either of the more conventional alternatives.

- There is no difference between a permutation and a multicast communication; the number of readers for each datum is irrelevant. This is because there is no dynamic routing. In fact, even if dynamic routing were used within the PAPERS unit, any reasonable delay within the box would be negligible in comparison to the propagation delay time for the cables that connect each workstation to the PAPERS box.

- Because each buffer within PAPERS has only one writer, write operations are always non-blocking. Although future versions of PAPERS might have blocking reads, delaying a read slows only one processor, while delaying a write slows all processors that would read that value.

Although the first PAPERS and TTL_PAPERS units send only one bit per processor, all later versions support four-bit wide communications as single operations.

1.2. PAPERS Workstation Interface

In discussing how each workstation is interfaced to the PAPERS unit, the first thing that should be understood is that adding PAPERS to an existing workstation cluster does not interfere with any of the other capabilities of that cluster. For example, PAPERS does not interfere with operation of Ethernet interfaces, etc. The second concept to understand is that common interactions with PAPERS should all be accomplished directly from a user process, without any operating system intervention.

It might surprise the reader, but most versions of UNIX allow user processes to directly access I/O ports. Typically, this is done by a privileged process calling iopl() to obtain permission to access all ports, and then simply accessing the ports by directly executing port I/O instructions. On 386/486/Pentium processors running the Linux operating system [Wie93], it is possible for a privileged process to obtain access to specific I/O ports by calling ioperm(); the hardware maintains an I/O port access map. Ideally, a new operating system call should be implemented so that a non-privileged user process can obtain access to the I/O ports connected to PAPERS if those ports are not in use by another process; in any case, port access permission need be obtained only once per user process. There is no operating system intervention required in accessing PAPERS aggregate functions.

Unfortunately, there are unavoidable overheads associated with direct use of standard Centronics printer ports:

- Most workstations have port hardware that is deliberately slowed to increase reliability of the printer interface. Depending on the port hardware, the port access time ranges from about $0.2\mu s$ to $4.0\mu s$, much slower than the $0.1\mu s$ limit imposed by cable length and PAPERS circuit speed.

- The use of a unidirectional printer port for all PAPERS I/O severely limits the number of bits that can be transferred per port operation. Each printer port is actually three independently addressed ports: an 8-bit data output port, a 4-bit status output port, and a 5-bit status input port. PAPERS is designed so that normal operation requires use of only the 8-bit output and 5-bit input ports, treating one bit from each as a strobe.

Given these constraints, we can approximate execution time by simply counting the number of port operations required to perform each basic PAPERS function.
Table 1 lists each of the basic aggregate functions implemented by PAPERS, the number of port operations needed to perform that operation on the 4-processor PAPERS1
prototype and on a p-processor PAPERS2, and a short description of each function.
For example, if each port access takes about $1.0\mu s$ and we are using PAPERS2 to perform a p_waitvec() across a 16-processor workstation cluster that is already
roughly synchronized, the approximate execution time would be less than $(2 + 16/2) *$
$1.0\mu s$, or $10.0\mu s$.

PAPERS Function (port ops 4-PE, p-PE)	Description
extern inline void p_enqueue(barrier mask); $(0 .. 1, 0 .. p/4)$	Enqueue the bit pattern given by mask as the group of processors that this processor will synchronize with. This grouping remains in effect until explic-itly changed.
extern inline void p_wait(void); $(0 .. 2, 0 .. 2)$	Wait for a barrier across the set of processors speci-fied by the last enqueued mask. Although the inter-face can be interrupt driven, the wait is currently implemented by polling the input port.
extern inline barrier p_waitvec(int flag); $(0 .. 2, 0 .. 2+p/2)$	Wait for a barrier, simultaneously broadcasting one bit (flag) to all processors that participate in the barrier. The resulting value is a bit vector in which bit k is the flag value from processor k; bits from processors not participating in the barrier are forced to be zero.
extern inline int p_all(int flag); $(0 .. 2, 0 .. 2)$	Like p_waitvec(), except this operation returns a value of 1 if all processors in the barrier had non-zero flag values, and returns 0 otherwise. Note that the all operation is performed in the PAPERS2 hardware, so that transmission of the result bit vec-tor is not necessary. The p_any() operation is also supported.
extern unsigned char p_putget8u(unsigned char datum, int source); $(0 .. 4, 0 .. 4+\log_{16}p)$	This function provides generalized aggregate byte communication, sending the value datum and returning the value that was sent by the processor whose number is source.

Table 1: PAPERS Software Interface

Notice that, although we discuss PAPERS in terms of connecting workstations, it is perfectly reasonable to have multiple PAPERS connections (i.e., multiple
printer ports) on each workstation. ISA bus printer port cards can be purchased for
less than $10 each. Thus, for example, a multiprocessor workstation might well have
one PAPERS connection for each processor it contains. This not only yields a more
symmetric structure for the software, but also yields faster synchronization across

processes within the machine than would normally be obtained using standard UNIX inter-process communication facilities. Using a 486DX/50 workstation running Linux, a simple 1-byte handshake between two processes using a pipe takes $225\mu s$ — at least 68 times as long as an arbitrary operation done using the current PAPERS1 hardware.

2. Static Scheduling of Interactions

Given the low-latency synchronization and communication abilities of the PAPERS hardware, a variety of new compiler optimizations for workstation cluster communication are feasible. The first of these uses the PAPERS hardware not for communication, but as a mechanism for semi-statically scheduling the use of other communication facilities. The second class of optimizations uses the PAPERS hardware instead of the traditional network for performing the actual communications. The ability of PAPERS to quickly examine aggregate state can also be used to impose deterministic simplifications that directly eliminate communications by detecting their irrelevance to the computation, and this forms the third class of compiler scheduling optimizations.

2.1. Scheduling Conventional Network Use

In a recent paper by Brewer and Kuszmaul [BrK94], it was observed that performance of the CM-5 data network could be improved by a factor of 2-3x simply by inserting semantically unnecessary barrier synchronizations to help level network traffic. They also observed that an additional 25% gain could be obtained by slowing the rate of message injection to the network to match the rate of message removal. Given a workstation cluster augmented by the PAPERS hardware, we can achieve a similar gain by using PAPERS to schedule use of the conventional network.

The basic problem noted by [BrK94] is that, without barriers, some processors may race ahead of others, thus causing blocking that further worsens the variation in completion times. Although most conventional workstation cluster networks are relatively simple and do not have blocking properties like those of the CM-5's fat tree, similar problems arise.

For example, the next processor to be given access to a shared bus network (e.g., Ethernet) is essentially selected at random by granting the bus to the first processor that makes an uncontested attempt to access the bus. If multiple processors attempt to grab the bus at the same time, all detect the collision and back-off for a random period before trying again. This type of contention can be eliminated by using the PAPERS hardware to schedule bus accesses. The technique is very simple:

(1) Use a single p_waitvec() to determine which processors would like to access the traditional network. A processor sends a flag value of 1 if it wants traditional network access, 0 if not.

(2) In a statically-determined order, each processor that wants access is given its turn to perform a traditional network access. The accesses are separated by p_wait() operations as necessary to enforce the conflict-free scheduling of traditional network accesses.

This scheduling can be further improved by selecting a static order for each communication so that the processors involved in consecutive communications are disjoint. This is the bus-based analog of matching injection and removal rates in the CM-5's network. For example, in the extreme case, if too much data is buffered in a workstation, that workstations network buffer pool can be exhausted, and additional data received will be discarded. This further damages performance because the lost data will have to be re-transmitted, yielding yet more network traffic. In contrast, the PAPERS hardware can even be used to broadcast information about which workstations currently have buffer space available.

It is also useful to note that a simple p_all() can be used to provide lightweight acknowledgements when data is received using the conventional network.

2.2. Low Latency Multi-Broadcast

As suggested earlier, the PAPERS hardware provides a very low latency multi-broadcast communication mechanism that can be used for general purpose communication, but there are several catches:

(1) Although PAPERS provides low latency, virtually zero communication startup and message formatting overhead, and apparently collision-free "routing," the data transmission bandwidth is severely limited by the use of a Centronics-compatible printer port. At most, just 4 data bits can be read per port operation — in contrast, DMA network interfaces can transfer up to 64 data bits per bus cycle (e.g., using PCI).

(2) The low latency is obtained by direct port access from the user program, implying polled I/O and very little potential for overlap of computation with communication. In fact, all communication using the current version of PAPERS is completely synchronous.

(3) The PAPERS mechanism requires that the sender broadcast data and that the receiver know who to read data from. Given that, however, data always arrives in order and transmission is 100% reliable without an acknowledgement. For the same reason, there is typically no need to construct, send, receive, and decode message headers — a processor never needs to send information at runtime if that information was known to all processors at compile time.

Thus, although PAPERS works very well for most aggregate operations, it probably isn't the best way to do some types of communication. It is up to the compiler to optimize the choice of communication method to match the type of communication required.

A simple rule for compiler scheduling can be derived by examining communication block size. Points (1) and (2) above clearly make sending large blocks of data more efficient using a conventional network than using the PAPERS unit. Thus, for any system, the compiler's decision can be distilled into a single formula for predicting the expected communication time for a collection of communication operations. The cost for sending a block using PAPERS1 or PAPERS2 is four port operations per byte. Using 486DX/33 workstations under Linux, receiving each byte takes about 6.6μs... very low latency, but only 150K bytes/second bandwidth per processor, independent of processor count and routing pattern. In contrast, an Intel EtherExpress Ethernet card on the same system achieves about 580K bytes/second bandwidth, but, through the Linux TCP interface, has a latency of more than 5,000μs. Unless the communication is a simple broadcast, bandwidth available also decreases at least linearly as more processors share the same Ethernet. For this particular 4-processor workstation cluster, the point-to-point communication times always favor using PAPERS1; however, if the operation is a broadcast and the block size is at least 1K bytes, the Ethernet is faster. Incidentally, if the Ethernet were replaced by a 100M byte/second HiPPI, the crossover point for broadcast would have been at a block size of at least 750 bytes. Since PAPERS bandwidth per processor is constant (limited by port speed for reasonable numbers of workstations), adding more processors will make PAPERS faster than bus-based networks for even larger blocks.

A more sophisticated compiler analysis would take into account the issues described in (3) above. Most current compiler analysis is based on creating messages that are targeted by the sender, but the PAPERS hardware requires cooperation from both the sender and receiver. In most cases, this means using the same compiler analysis of communication structure to provide different information, but sometimes it invokes a radical transformation of the communication structure. For example, consider a CMF, MPF, Fortran-D, or HPF statement like:

```
A(1:N) = B( I(1:N) )
```

where A, B, and I all have a layout that places the j element on processor j. Using PAPERS, each processor would simply broadcast the value of B(j). Each processor can then locally select the appropriate datum from the multi-broadcast. In contrast, a traditional message-passing implementation would first send a request message to processor I(j), and then send messages containing B(j) to any processors that requested them. Thus, rather than one set of multi-broadcast operations, traditional message-passing uses 2N messages (not counting acknowledgements) — and there can be serializing conflicts on all 2N messages either due to network topology or destination/source conflicts (e.g., suppose every element of I has the same value).

2.3. Scheduling To Remove Needless Communications

Because the PAPERS unit can provide rapid access to a small amount of global state information, it is possible for the compiler to statically detect communication patterns that are likely to involve needless transmission of data, and to then insert PAPERS operations to detect and eliminate these transmissions at runtime. By far the most common reason that a transmission may be redundant is because it is involved in a race. Fundamentally, if there are n data values racing to be stored in the same location, n-1 of these data transmissions will have no effect on the computed result, and can be eliminated.

Such races are commonly used in MPL [MCC91] code to select representative cases for sets of values. Consider:

```
plural int i; plural double a, b;
router[i].a = b;
```

in which each processor attempts to store its value of b into the variable a residing on processor i. A race exists if the value of i is the same for multiple processors.

Reguardless of whether the data communication (i.e., transmission of b values) is done using PAPERS or the conventional network, it is possible to use PAPERS to rapidly detect these races and select the winners, so that only they need to be transmitted. This is done by simply using p_waitvec() for each processor to transmit the destination it wishes to send to. Each processor can then apply a statically determined algorithm to determine if it was the loser of a race, since it knows which other processors had the same target.

The algorithm can be summarized as follows. For each bit in the destination address, use p_waitvec() to transmit the bit. The returned bit vector is inverted if the bit we broadcast was a 0. By anding all the resulting bit vectors together, we create a race bit mask with a 1 in each position corresponding to a processor that is racing with this processor. Each processor can then determine if it was the loser of a race (and hence, should not send data) by examining the race bit mask. For example, if the race bit mask and the bit mask representing all higher-numbered processors yields 0, then this processor is the highest-numbered processor involved in this race, and hence the winner.

Of course, other methods can also be used to determine the winner from the race bit mask. For example, it is particularly effective to ensure that any processor wishing to send to itself is always the winner of any race involving that communication.

3. Execution Models

An essential part of successfully programming a parallel machine is making effective use of available programming models [BeS91]. A cluster of workstations that provides low-latency aggregate operations can support a wide range of programming models. Different programming models, or even individual programs, may obtain better performance with a particular execution model. Even within the same program, different parts of the program may benefit from using different execution models, for example, mixing MIMD and SIMD execution [BeS91] [Wat93].

Obviously, multiple workstations can run multiple programs, and it is natural to use a cluster as a large-grain MIMD (Multiple Instruction streams, Multiple Data streams) system. However, a PAPERS cluster is a good target for the fine- to medium-grain MIMD barrier scheduling work discussed in [Pol88] [Gup89] [DiO92]. It should be noted, however, that executing fully static schedules for MIMD code may require temporarily disabling interrupts — although this is permitted under most versions of UNIX, disabling interrupts for too long may have strange consequences in the UNIX environment.

The two most common fine-grain models are SIMD (Single Instruction stream, Multiple Data streams) and VLIW (Very Long Instruction Word). Both these models assume a single program counter for the entire parallel machine, and both distribute parallel data across the processing elements. The difference is that SIMD implies that all processors execute the same opcode from each instruction, whereas VLIW allows each processor to use a different opcode field within each instruction. Although it is not practical for workstations to share a single core image and program counter, the same effect can be obtained by placing the appropriate opcode sequence in each processor's memory and using aggregate operations to enforce SIMD or VLIW semantics.

However, these execution models seem to imply instruction granularity. In fact, there is no reason to require that an operation or instruction is an atomic parallel function for the hardware; it could instead be an entire subroutine or sequence of machine instructions. In Table 2, we briefly summarize the effective *minimum* grain sizes for a variety of parallel machines in terms of the minimum communication latency (end-to-end time) measured both as an absolute time and as the maximum number of floating point operations that could be executed by the machine in that time period. Although the Thinking Machines CM-5 and Intel Paragon XP/S both claim to support SIMD execution, they clearly do not support instruction granularity — neither does PAPERS. However, PAPERS is fine-grain enough to enable a large class of SIMD and VLIW codes to execute efficiently.

Machine	Minimum Communication Latency (μs)	Float Operations per Com.	Source of Performance Data
486DX/33 Ethernet (TCP)	5,000	20,000	*measured*
Intel Paragon XP/S	240	18,000	[BrG94]
Thinking Machines CM-5	12-65	1,536-8,320	[LiC94][BrG94]
nCUBE/2	32-110	96-330	[BrG94]
486DX/33 PAPERS1	3.3	13.2	*measured*

Table 2: Comparison Of Minimum Hardware Grain Sizes

3.1. Implementation Of SIMD Execution

SIMD is implemented by each workstation having its own copy of the program, augmented by aggregate operations as needed. Conceptually, SIMD execution would require a barrier synchronization after each instruction. Fortunately, omitting this synchronization between most instructions yields no ill effects [HaL91]. The rule is simply that synchronization is needed for communication or selection of a control flow path based on aggregate state (i.e., does any processor want to take this path?). Because, following SIMD semantics, all processors must conceptually follow the same flow path, processors that did not want to take that control flow path can be "disabled" with enable masking.

3.1.1. Enable Mask Simulation

The SIMD execution model is generally expected to provide support for enable masking: the ability to "turn off" selected processing elements for a sequence of operations.

There are a variety of simple and effective ways in which hardware could disable particular processing elements, but the most practical implementation is probably to have all processing elements perform every operation, nulling the effects on the processing elements that should not have been active. For example, some processors have conditional store instructions that would allow "disabled" processing elements to perform computations, but not update variables with the results. With somewhat greater cost, this nulling can even be done using conventional arithmetic; for example, the parallel assignment:

```
c = a + b;
```

Can be made to execute only when enabled is a bit mask containing all 1s (for true, as opposed to 0 for false) by all processing elements simultaneously executing:

```
c = (((a + b) & enabled) | (c & ~enabled));
```

Another possible implementation is to JUMP over code for which the processor is disabled. However, this must be done very carefully to avoid accidentally skipping operations that should be executed (enable mask operations, scalar code, function calls, etc.). Further, using JUMPs can cause pipeline bubbles that seriously degrade performance.

For the purposes of this paper, we will hide the details of how disabling is implemented by enclosing code that should be executed only by enabled processors within a block marked as EVAL_ENABLED. Of course, having the compiler select the cheapest method for implementing each such block is a fundamental optimization.

In addition to nullifying the effects of disabled operations, there is also the issue of tracking enable status as nested constructs change the set of enabled processors. Traditionally, enable status has been tracked using a special hardware stack of one-bit enable flags, however, this is not practical for most workstations. Alternatively, one word could be used to represent each enable flag on the stack, but this wastes memory space and requires a memory operation for each scope entry or exit. The best method for a workstation cluster using PAPERS is a variation on the "activity counter" scheme proposed by Keryell and Paris [KeP93].

This scheme takes advantage of a simple property of the enable stack deriving from use of structured SIMD enable constructs: the enable stack for each processor always contains a sequence of zero or more 1 bits (enable states) followed by zero or more 0 bits (disable states). Thus, if the program uses only structured enable masking, the same information can be recorded by simply counting the number of disable states that would have been pushed in each processor's enable stack. A counter called disabled is used in each processor to track the number of properly nested constructs for which each processor has been disabled. If this counter is zero, the processor is enabled; otherwise, the processor is disabled. Thus, entry or exit of an enable scope is accomplished by a simple update of the disabled counter. For best performance, disabled would normally be allocated to a register.

However, some SIMD languages provide features that allow "unstructured" changes to processor enable status. For example, MPL's all construct [MCC91] enables all processing elements for execution of the following statement — enabling processors that were disabled at entry to the enclosing region of code. In fact, a statement affected by an all can be a compound statement that contains additional structured and unstructured masking. Another example is MPL's proc construct; proc[i].j refers to the value of j on processor i, reguardless of whether processor i was enabled in the enclosing region of code. Fortunately, this situation can be correctly handled by mixing the activity counter and traditional stacking methods. The disabled counter value is pushed onto a stack at entry to an unstructured change of enable status and is restored at exit from that region.

3.1.2. Example SIMD Code

To illustrate how code with SIMD semantics would be implemented on a group of workstations augmented by PAPERS, code for two parallel constructs will be generated: the parallel if-else and the parallel while. The code for both of the examples makes use of the aggregate test function p_any() and supports operations that may enable all the processing elements in the machine, e.g. the all statement in MPL and the everywhere statement in C*.

3.1.2.1. SIMD Parallel if-else

SIMD semantics do not make a parallel if-else construct change the control flow of the program. Rather, the construct changes enable/disable status of processors as all the processors pass through the code for both the "then" and else clauses.

Although both the new C* [TMC90] and MPL [MCC91] use SIMD semantics, the C* language more literally adheres to the principle that control flow cannot be altered by a parallel construct. Even if no processors are enabled, C* semantics suggest that the complete code sequence should be "executed." In contrast, MPL semantics suggest that code for which no processor is enabled should not be "executed." Thus, before each section of conditionally-executed code, MPL inserts instructions that jump over the code if no processors would be enabled for its execution. This difference in semantics is reflected by the fact that the code of Listing 2 implements the MPL semantics as is, and implements the new C* semantics if the bold code is removed.

3.1.2.2. SIMD Parallel while

Because the new C* does not allow control flow to be altered by a parallel construct, there is no parallel while in C*. However, there is a parallel while construct in MPL. This construct is implemented by the code given in Listing 4.

```
if (parallel_expr){
    stat_a;
}else{
    stat_b;
}
```

Listing 1: Parallel `if-else`

```
if (disabled) ++disabled;
EVAL_ENABLED {
    if (!parallel_expr)
        disabled = 1;
}
if (p_all(disabled))
    goto Else;
EVAL_ENABLED {
    stat_a;
}
Else:
if (disabled < 2)
    disabled ^= 1;
if (p_all(disabled))
    goto Exit;
EVAL_ENABLED {
    stat_b;
}
Exit:
if (disabled) --disabled;
```

Listing 2: SIMD parallel `if-else`

```
while(parallel_expr){
    stat;
}
```

Listing 3: Parallel `while`

```
if (disabled) ++disabled;
Loop:
EVAL_ENABLED {
    if (!parallel_expr)
        disabled = 1;
}
if (p_all(disabled))
    goto Exit;
EVAL_ENABLED {
    fIstat;
}
goto Loop;
Exit:
--disabled;
```

Listing 4: SIMD parallel `while`

3.2. Implementation Of VLIW Execution

VLIW, or Very Long Instruction Word, computation is based on use of a single instruction sequence with an instruction format that allows a potentially different opcode for each function unit. Treating each processing element as a function unit, genuine VLIW [Fis84] [CoN88] execution can be obtained without any hardware changes. Each VLIW instruction is striped across the various local (instruction) memories. I.e., the VLIW instruction at address α is encoded by having address α in instruction memory β be the opcode field for function unit β.

According to Brownhill and Nicolau [BrN90], a workstation cluster would be an effective vehicle for VLIW execution only if it provides:

- Fast communication

- Fast (barrier) synchronization

- An effective implementation for multi-way jumps

Of these, we have already discussed how PAPERS provides the first two; however, PAPERS also is essentially the ideal mechanism with which to implement multi-way jumps.

In order to facilitate more aggressive code motions, ideal VLIW machines allow multiple branch-tests to be executed in parallel. Executing multiple branch-tests within single VLIW operation results in a multi-way jump. In the idealized VLIW model, a central control unit collects these test result bits and selects the appropriate jump target. However, as suggested in [BrN90], the same effect can be achieved by having each processor evaluate its branch-test, set the bit that corresponds to that processor in the global result register to reflect the local branch-test result, perform a barrier synchronization, and then perform a multiway branch using the bit vector that was accumulated in the global result register. There was no prototype hardware implementation and there are several minor flaws in the presentation given in [BrN90], but PAPERS can correctly implement this model using a single p_waitvec() operation followed by a multiway branch based on the value returned.

```
A if (B) { C if (D) { a: E } b: F } c: G
```

Listing 5: Example Program Fragment For VLIW Branching

Processor 0	Processor 1	Processor 2	Processor 3
A	t=B	C	t=D
t=p_waitvec(0)	t=p_waitvec(t)	t=p_waitvec(0)	t=p_waitvec(t)
switch (t) {	switch (t) {	switch (t) {	switch (t) {
case 0:goto c;	case 0:goto c;	case 0:goto c;	case 0:goto c;
case 2:goto b;	case 2:goto b;	case 2:goto b;	case 2:goto b;
case 8:goto c;	case 8:goto c;	case 8:goto c;	case 8:goto c;
case 10:goto a;	case 10:goto a;	case 10:goto a;	case 10:goto a;
}	}	}	}

Listing 6: PAPERS VLIW Code For Multiway Branch

Consider the example program fragment in Listing 5. Listing 6 gives the VLIW code sequence showing how this example is VLIW parallelized so that A, B, C, and D will be executed in parallel on a 4-processor workstation cluster using PAPERS. (For brevity, we have omitted the usual repair code implied by this speculative execution.) Further improvement can be made because most C compilers would compile the switch statement's sparse list of case values into code implementing a binary search. Instead, the compiler should create a nearly perfect hash function to perform the switch without any comparison operations. For example, our hash function generator [Die92] suggests that the mapping from Listing 6 can be implemented directly using a 4-element jump table indexed by `(((-t)>>2)&3)`. Using a 4-processor 486DX/33 PAPERS workstation cluster under Linux, the complete VLIW branch code sequence executes in about 4µs.

In addition to the fundamental optimizations using `p_waitvec()` and a hash function generator, there are a variety of special cases that can be readily optimized by the compiler. A very common special case occurs when a single branch instruction is executed within a VLIW instruction. In this case, it is not necessary to use `p_waitvec()`; a single `p_any()` will suffice. Likewise, in this case, it is not necessary to compute a hash function to index a jump table — an ordinary conditional branch instruction can test the value returned by `p_any()`. The usual techniques for eliminating unnecessary barrier synchronizations also can be applied [BrN90].

4. Conclusion

Many parallel programs are based on aggregate operations, for which traditional workstation clusters have proven to be ill-suited. In this paper, we have presented a variety of new opportunities for compilers to optimize parallel program execution using a conventional UNIX workstation cluster augmented by fast hardware for aggregate operations.

Using the low-latency PAPERS hardware to implement aggregate operations, a workstation cluster can function as a fine-grain reconfigurable parallel machine, rather than a loosely-connected set of autonomous computers. Thus, the compiler issues focus on statically scheduling communication and directly implementing optimized fine-grain SIMD and VLIW execution models. The techniques and performance improvements quoted in this paper represent only the most cursory exploration of this new view of workstation clusters.

To encourage others to pursue this new point of view, the PAPERS hardware design is fully public domain and is optimized to be easily and cheaply replicated. Likewise, as the compiler technology discussed in this paper becomes more stable, we plan to distribute it in the form of both optimization phases that can be used in compilers constructed using PCCTS [PaD92] and as complete public domain compilers for a subset of MPL and a small Fortran 77 dialect called Fortran-P.

References

[BeS91] T.B. Berg and H.J. Siegel, "Instruction Execution Trade-Offs for SIMD vs. MIMD vs. Mixed Mode Parallelism," *5th International Parallel Processing Symposium*, April 1991, pp. 301-308.

[BrG94] U. Bruening, W. K. Giloi, and W. Schroeder-Preikschat, "Latency Hiding in Message-Passing Architectures," *8th International Parallel Processing Symposium*, Cancun, Mexico, April, 1994, pp. 704-709.

[BrK94] E. A. Brewer and B. C. Kuszmaul, "How to Get Good Performance from the CM-5 Data Network," *8th International Parallel Processing Symposium*, Cancun, Mexico, April 1994, pp. 858-867.

[BrN90] C.J. Brownhill and A. Nicolau, *Percolation Scheduling for Non-VLIW Machines*, Technical Report 90-02, University of California at Irvine, Irvine, California, January 1990.

[CoD94] W. E. Cohen, H. G. Dietz, and J. B. Sponaugle, "Dynamic Barrier Architecture For Multi-Mode Fine-Grain Parallelism Using Conventional Processors," *Int'l Conf. on Parallel Processing*, August 1994, vol. 1, pp. 93-96.

[CoN88] R. P. Colwell, R. P. Nix, J. J. O'Donnell, D. B. Papworth, and P. K. Rodman, "A VLIW Architecture for a Trace Scheduling Compiler," *IEEE Trans. on Computers*, vol. C-37, no. 8, pp. 967-979, Aug. 1988.

[Die92] H. G. Dietz, *Coding Multiway Branches Using Customized Hash Functions*, Purdue University School of Electrical Engineering Technical Report TR-EE 92-31, July 1992.

[DiM94] H. G. Dietz, T. Muhammad, J. B. Sponaugle, and T. Mattox, *PAPERS: Purdue's Adapter for Parallel Execution and Rapid Synchronization*, Purdue University School of Electrical Engineering Technical Report TR-EE 94-11, March 1994.

[DiO92] H. G. Dietz, M.T. O'Keefe, and A. Zaafrani, "Static Scheduling for Barrier MIMD Architectures," *The Journal of Supercomputing*, vol. 5, pp. 263-289, 1992.

[Fis84] J. A. Fisher, "The VLIW Machine: A Multiprocessor for Compiling Scientific Code," *IEEE Computer*, July 1984, pp. 45-53.

[Gup89] R. Gupta, "The Fuzzy Barrier: A Mechanism for the High Speed Synchronization of Processors," *Third Int. Conf. on Architectural Support for Programming Languages and Operating Systems*, Boston, MA, April 1989, pp. 54-63.

[HaL91] P. J. Hatcher, A. J. Lapadula, R. R. Jones, M. J. Quinn, and R. J. Anderson, "A Production-Quality C* Compiler for Hypercube Multicomputers" *Third ACM SIGPLAN Symposium on Principles and Practices of Parallel Programming*, Williamsburg, Virginia, April 1991, pp. 73-82.

[KeP93] R. Keryell and N. Paris. "Activity Counter: New Optimization for the Dynamic Scheduling of SIMD Control Flow," *Proc. Int'l Conf. Parallel Processing*, pp. II 184-187, August 1993.

[LiC94] L. T. Liu, and D. E. Culler, "Measurements of Active Messages Performance on the CM-5," University of California Berkeley, CS csd-94-807(dir), UCB//CSD-94-807, May 1994. 36 pages.

[MCC91] MasPar Computer Corporation, *MasPar Programming Language (ANSI C compatible MPL) Reference Manual, Software Version 2.2*, Document Number 9302-0001, Sunnyvale, California, November 1991.

[PaD92] T. J. Parr, H. G. Dietz, and W. E. Cohen, "PCCTS Reference Manual (version 1.00)," *ACM SIGPLAN Notices*, Feb. 1992, pp. 88-165.

[Pol88] C. D. Polychronopolous, "Compiler Optimizations for Enhancing Parallelism and Their Impact on Architecture Design," *IEEE Trans. Comput.*, vol. C-37, no. 8, pp. 991-1004, Aug. 1989.

[TMC90] Thinking Machines Corporation, *C* Programming Guide*, Thinking Machines Corporation, Cambridge, Massachusetts, November 1990.

[Wat93] D. W. Watson, *Compile-Time Selection of Parallel Modes in an SIMD/SPMD Heterogeneous Parallel Environment*, Ph.D. Dissertation, Purdue University School of Electrical Engineering, August 1993.

[Wie93] J. Wiegand, "Cooperative development of Linux," *Proceedings of the 1993 IEEE International Professional Communication Conference*, Philadelphia, PA, October 1993, pp. 386-390.

Solving Alignment using Elementary Linear Algebra

David Bau, Induprakas Kodukula, Vladimir Kotlyar,
Keshav Pingali, Paul Stodghill *

Cornell University

Abstract. Data and computation alignment is an important part of
compiling sequential programs to architectures with non-uniform memory access times. In this paper, we show that elementary matrix methods can be used to determine communication-free alignment of code and
data. We also solve the problem of replicating read-only data to eliminate communication. Our matrix-based approach leads to algorithms
which are simpler and faster than existing algorithms for the alignment
problem.

1 Introduction

A key problem in generating code for non-uniform memory access (NUMA) parallel machines is data and computation placement — that is, determining what
work each processor must do, and what data must reside in each local memory.
The goal of placement is to exploit parallelism by spreading the work across the
processors, and to exploit locality by spreading data so that memory accesses
are local whenever possible. The problem of determining a good placement for
a program is usually solved in two phases called *alignment* and *distribution*.
The alignment phase maps data and computations to a set of virtual processors
organized as a Cartesian grid of some dimension (a *template* in HPF Fortran
terminology). The distribution phase folds the virtual processors into the physical processors. The advantage of separating alignment from distribution is that
we can address the collocation problem (determining which iterations and data
should be mapped to the same processor) without worrying about the load balancing problem.

Our focus in this paper is alignment. A complete solution to this problem
can be obtained in three steps.

1. Determine the constraints on data and computation placement.
2. Determine which constraints should be left unsatisfied.
3. Solve the remaining system of constraints to determine data and computation placement.

* This research was supported by an NSF Presidential Young Investigator award CCR-
8958543, NSF grant CCR-9008526, ONR grant N00014-93-1-0103, and a grant from
Hewlett-Packard Corporation.

In the first step, data references in the program are examined to determine a system of equations in which the unknowns are functions representing data and computation placements. Any solution to this system of equations determines a so-called *communication-free* alignment [HS91] — that is, a map of data elements and computations to virtual processors such that all data required by a processor to execute the iterations mapped to it are in its local memory. Very often, the only communication-free alignment for a program is the trivial one in which every iteration and datum is mapped to a single processor. Intuitively, each equation in the system is a constraint on data and computation placement, and it is possible to overconstrain the system so that the trivial solution is the only solution. If so, the second step of alignment determines which constraints must be left unsatisfied to retain parallelism in execution. The cost of leaving a constraint unsatisfied is that it introduces communication; therefore, the constraints left unsatisfied should be those that introduce as little communication as possible. In the last step, the remaining constraints are solved to determine data and computation placement.

The following loop illustrates these points. M is a symbolic constant; the code computes the M-th element of the convolution of two arrays X and Y.

```
     DO 1 i = 1, M
1        Z = Z + X(i) * Y(M - i + 1)
```

Since the loop nest has just one loop, and all arrays are one-dimensional, the virtual processors are assumed to be organized as a one-dimensional grid T. Let us assume that computations are mapped by iteration number — that is, a processor does all or none of the work in executing an iteration of the loop. To avoid communication, the processor that executes iteration i must have Z, $X(i)$ and $Y(M - i + 1)$ in its local memory. These constraints can be expressed formally by defining the following functions.

$\mathbf{C}(i)$: i $\rightarrow$ T – map from loop iterations to virtual processors
$\mathbf{D}_z(i)$: i $\rightarrow$ T – processor that owns Z
$\mathbf{D}_x(i)$: i $\rightarrow$ T – map of array X
$\mathbf{D}_y(i)$: i $\rightarrow$ T – map of array Y

The constraints on these functions are the following.

$$for\ i \in 1..M \begin{cases} \mathbf{C}(i) = \mathbf{D}_z \\ \mathbf{C}(i) = \mathbf{D}_x(i) \\ \mathbf{C}(i) = \mathbf{D}_y(M - i + 1) \end{cases}$$

If we enforce these constraints, we end up with the trivial solution in which all data and computations are mapped to a single processor, since Z can be mapped to just one processor. Alternatively, we can leave the constraint on Z unsatisfied. In that case, we can map the computation so that iteration i is mapped to processor i, and we can map arrays X and Y so that elements $X(i)$ and $Y(M - i + 1)$ are mapped to processor i. This gives a non-trivial solution

48

to the system of constraints; using this, we can compute all the partial products in parallel without moving X or Y array elements[2]. For future reference, we note that the map of loop iterations to virtual processors is a linear function of the iteration number; therefore, this function can be represented by the unit matrix [1], with function application represented by matrix vector product. For example, iteration i is mapped to processor [1] i, which is simply i, as desired. The map of array Y to the virtual processors is not linear but affine; the linear part is represented by the matrix [-1], while the constant part of the map is (M+1).

In this example, the solution to the alignment equations can be determined by inspection, but how does one solve such systems of equations in general? Note that the unknowns are general functions, and that each function may be constrained by several equations (as is the case for C in the example). To make the problem tractable, it is standard to restrict the maps to linear functions of loop indices. This restriction is not particularly onerous in general — in fact, it permits more general maps of computation and data than are allowed in HPF. The unknowns in the equations now become matrices, rather than general functions, but it is still not obvious how such systems of matrix equations can be solved. In Section 2, we introduce our linear algebraic framework that reduces the problem of solving systems of alignment equations to the standard linear algebra problem of determining a basis for the null space of a matrix. The null space problem can be solved through the use of integer-preserving Gaussian elimination of integer matrices, a standard tool in modern parallelizing compilers where it has found use in dependence analysis, loop transformations and code generation [Ban93, LP92]. One weakness of existing approaches to alignment is that they handle only linear functions; general affine functions, like the map of array Y, must be dealt with in *ad hoc* ways. In Section 3, we show that our framework permits affine functions to be handled without difficulty.

In some programs, replication of read-only data is useful for exploiting parallelism. Suppose we change the convolution program so that we convolve the array X with itself (in the program shown above, Y gets replaced with X). In that case, the processor that performs iteration i must own both $X(i)$ and $X(M - i + 1)$. The only linear (or affine) map that permits this is the trivial map that maps everything to a single processor. One way to use M processors is to replicate array X, and map one copy so that processor i owns $X(i)$, and map the other copy so that processor i owns $X(M - i + 1)$. This permits us to run the loop in parallel without moving elements of X during the execution of the loop. Although we could replicate *all* read-only data on *all* processors, it is desirable to conserve space and replicate data only if it helps achieve parallel execution. In Section 4, we show that our framework permits a solution to the replication problem as well.

How does our work relate to previous work on alignment? Our work is closest

---

[2] We are not interested here in the question of whether parallel execution is actually worthwhile for this program — perhaps the sum can be done using a collective communication routine to get some benefit from parallel execution.

in spirit to that of Huang and Sadayappan who were the first to formulate the problem of communication-free alignment in terms of systems of equational constraints [HS91]. However, they did not give a general method for solving these equations. Also, they did not handle replication of data. Recently, Anderson and Lam gave a solution method but their algorithm is quite complex, requiring the determination of cycles in bipartite graphs, computing pseudo-inverses etc. [AL93] — these complications are eliminated by our approach. Complementary to our work is the solution of the (NP-complete) problem of determining the best choice of constraints to leave unsatisfied in overconstrained systems of equations. Heuristics for this problem were first discussed by Li and Chen[LC89] for a limited kind of alignment called axis alignment. More general heuristics for a wide variety of cost-of-communication metrics have been studied by Chatterjee, Gilbert and Schreiber[CGS93, CGST92], Feautrier [Fea92] and Knobe et al [KN90, KLD92]. Incorporating such heuristics into our framework should give a clean and complete approach to alignment.

To summarize, the contributions of this paper are the following.

1. We show that the problem of determining communication-free partitions of computation and data can be reduced to the standard linear algebra problem of determining a basis for the null space of a matrix (Section 2.2).
2. We show that this linear algebra problem can be solved through the use of integer preserving Gaussian elimination (Section 2.3).
3. Existing approaches to alignment handle linear maps, but deal with affine maps in fairly *ad hoc* ways. We show that affine maps can be folded into our framework without difficulty (Section 3).
4. Finally, we show how replication of read-only data is handled by our framework (Section 4).

2   Linear Alignment

To avoid introducing too many ideas at once, we restrict attention to linear subscripts and linear maps in this section. First, we show that the alignment problem can be formulated using systems of equational constraints. Then, we show that the problem of solving these systems of equations can be reduced to the problem of determining a basis for the null space of a matrix. Finally, we show how this standard linear algebra problem can be solved using integer-preserving Gaussian elimination.

2.1   Equational Constraints

The equational constraints for alignment are simply a formalization of an intuitively reasonable statement: 'to avoid communication, the processor that performs an iteration of a loop nest must own the data referenced in that iteration'. We discuss the formulation of these equations in the context of the following example.

```
DO 2 j = 1,100
    DO 2 k = 1,100
2           B(j,k) = A(j,k) + A(k,j)
```

If i is an iteration vector in the iteration space of the loop, the alignment constraints require that the processor that performs iteration i must own $B(\mathbf{F}_1 i)$, $A(\mathbf{F}_1 i)$ and $A(\mathbf{F}_2 i)$, where $\mathbf{F}_1$ and $\mathbf{F}_2$ are the following matrices:

$$\mathbf{F}_1 = \begin{bmatrix} 1 & 0 \\ 0 & 1 \end{bmatrix} \qquad \mathbf{F}_2 = \begin{bmatrix} 0 & 1 \\ 1 & 0 \end{bmatrix}$$

Let $\mathbf{C}$, $\mathbf{D}_A$ and $\mathbf{D}_B$ be $p \times 2$ matrices representing the maps of the computation and arrays A and B to a p-dimensional processor template; p is an unknown which will be determined by our algorithm. Then, the alignment problem can be expressed as follows: find $\mathbf{C}$, $\mathbf{D}_A$ and $\mathbf{D}_B$ such that

$$\forall\, i \in \text{ iteration space of loop}: \begin{cases} \mathbf{C}i = \mathbf{D}_B\mathbf{F}_1 i \\ \mathbf{C}i = \mathbf{D}_A\mathbf{F}_1 i \\ \mathbf{C}i = \mathbf{D}_A\mathbf{F}_2 i \end{cases}$$

To 'cancel' the i on both sides of each equation, we will simplify the problem and require that the equations hold for all 2-dimensional integer vectors, regardless of whether they are in the bounds of the loop or not. In that case, the constraints simply become equations involving matrices, as follows: find $\mathbf{C}$, $\mathbf{D}_A$ and $\mathbf{D}_B$ such that

$$\begin{cases} \mathbf{C} = \mathbf{D}_B\mathbf{F}_1 \\ \mathbf{C} = \mathbf{D}_A\mathbf{F}_1 \\ \mathbf{C} = \mathbf{D}_A\mathbf{F}_2 \end{cases} \tag{1}$$

We will refer to the equation scheme $\mathbf{C} = \mathbf{D}\mathbf{F}$ as the fundamental equation of alignment. One way to solve systems of such equations is to set $\mathbf{C}$ and $\mathbf{D}$ to the zero matrix of some dimension. This is the trivial solution in which all computations and data are mapped to a single processor, processor 0. This solution exploits no parallelism; therefore, we want to determine a non-trivial solution if it exists.

The general principle behind formulation of alignment equations should be clear from this example. Each data reference for which alignment is desired gives rise to an alignment equation. Data references for which subscripts are not linear functions of loop indices are ignored; therefore, such references may give rise to communication at runtime. Although we have discussed only a single loop nest, it is clear that this framework of equational constraints can be used for multiple loop nests as well. The equational constraints from each loop nest are combined to form a single system of simultaneous equations, and the entire system solved to find communication-free maps of computations and data.

2.2 Reduction to Null Space Computation

We solve alignment equations by reduction to the standard linear algebra problem of determining a basis for the null space of a matrix. Consider a single equation.

$$\mathbf{C} = \mathbf{D}\mathbf{F}$$

This equation can be written in block matrix form as follows:

$$[\mathbf{C}\ \mathbf{D}] \begin{bmatrix} \mathbf{I} \\ -\mathbf{F} \end{bmatrix} = 0$$

This equation is of the form $\mathbf{UV} = 0$ where $\mathbf{U}$ is an unknown matrix and $\mathbf{V}$ is a known matrix. To see the connection with null spaces, we take the transpose of this equation and we see that this is the same as the equation $\mathbf{V}^T\mathbf{U}^T = 0$. Therefore, $\mathbf{U}^T$ is a matrix whose columns are in the null space of $\mathbf{V}^T$. To exploit parallelism, we would like the rank of $\mathbf{U}^T$ to be as large as possible. Therefore, we must find a basis for the null space of matrix $\mathbf{V}^T$. Alternatively, a standard result in linear algebra states that such a basis can be obtained from a basis for the orthogonal complement of the range space of the matrix $\mathbf{V}$, written as range($\mathbf{V}$)$^\perp$ [GVL89].

The same reduction works in the case of multiple constraints. Suppose that there are s loops and t arrays. Let the computation maps of the loops be $\mathbf{C}_1, \mathbf{C}_2, \ldots, \mathbf{C}_s$, and the array maps be $\mathbf{D}_1, \mathbf{D}_2, \ldots, \mathbf{D}_t$. We can construct a block row with all the unknowns as follows:

$$\mathbf{U} = \begin{bmatrix} \mathbf{C}_1\ \mathbf{C}_2\ \ldots\ \mathbf{C}_s\ \mathbf{D}_1\ \ldots\ \mathbf{D}_t \end{bmatrix}$$

For each constraint of the form $\mathbf{C}_j = \mathbf{D}_k\mathbf{F}_\ell$, we create a block column:

$$\mathbf{V}_q = \begin{bmatrix} \mathbf{0} \\ \mathbf{I} \\ \mathbf{0} \\ -\mathbf{F}_\ell \\ \mathbf{0} \end{bmatrix}$$

where the zeros are placed so that:

$$\mathbf{U}\mathbf{V}_q = \mathbf{C}_j - \mathbf{D}_k\mathbf{F}_\ell \tag{2}$$

Putting all these block columns into a single matrix $\mathbf{V}$, the problem of finding communication-free alignment reduces once again to a matrix equation of the form

$$\mathbf{UV} = 0 \tag{3}$$

The reader can verify that the system of equations (1) can be converted into the following matrix equation:

$$[\mathbf{C}\ \mathbf{D}_A\ \mathbf{D}_B] \begin{bmatrix} \mathbf{I} & \mathbf{I} & \mathbf{I} \\ \mathbf{0} & -\mathbf{F}_1 & -\mathbf{F}_2 \\ -\mathbf{F}_1 & \mathbf{0} & \mathbf{0} \end{bmatrix} = 0 \tag{4}$$

Input: A set of alignment constraints of the form $\mathbf{C}_j = \mathbf{D}_k\mathbf{F}_\ell$.
Output: Communication-free alignment matrices $\mathbf{C}_j$ and $\mathbf{D}_k$.
  1. Assemble block columns as in (2).
  2. Put all block columns $\mathbf{V}_q$ into one matrix $\mathbf{V}$.
  3. Compute a basis $\mathbf{U}^T$ for the null space of $\mathbf{V}^T$:
     (a) Factorize $\mathbf{V}$ as in (5).
     (b) Set $\mathbf{U}$ as in (6).
  4. Set template dimension to number of rows of $\mathbf{U}$.
  5. Extract the solution matrices $\mathbf{C}_j$ and $\mathbf{D}_k$ from $\mathbf{U}$.

Fig. 1. Algorithm LINEAR-ALIGNMENT.

2.3 Solving the matrix equation

To solve the equation $\mathbf{UV} = 0$, we have to get $\mathbf{V}$ into a 'rank-revealing' form. The idea is to use row and column operations as needed to get the matrix into a form in which its rank can be determined by inspection. There are many ways to accomplish this, and we describe one such way. Suppose $\mathbf{V} \in \mathbb{Z}^{M \times N}$ and $rank(\mathbf{V}) = r$. Then by doing integer preserving Gaussian elimination with full pivoting [Edm67] we can establish the following factorization:

$$\mathbf{HVP} = \begin{bmatrix} \mathbf{R}_{11} & \mathbf{R}_{12} \\ 0 & 0 \end{bmatrix} \qquad (5)$$

where $\mathbf{H}$ is an $M \times M$ invertible matrix representing the row operations, $\mathbf{P}$ is an $N \times N$ unimodular matrix representing the column operations (which are permutations), $\mathbf{R}_{11}$ is an $r \times r$ upper triangular invertible matrix. It is a property of this factorization that the last $N - r$ rows of $\mathbf{H}$ span the null-space of $\mathbf{V}$ and therefore give us the solution:

$$\mathbf{U} = \mathbf{H}(M - (N - r) + 1 : M, 1 : M) \qquad (6)$$

This also means that during the elimination we need to store only $\mathbf{H}$, the composition of row operations. The general algorithm is outlined in Figure 1.

For Equation (4), a solution matrix is:

$$\mathbf{U} = \begin{bmatrix} 1 & 1 & 1 & 1 & 1 & 1 \end{bmatrix}$$

which gives us:

$$\mathbf{C} = \mathbf{D}_A = \mathbf{D}_B = \begin{bmatrix} 1 & 1 \end{bmatrix}$$

Since the number of rows of $\mathbf{U}$ is one, the solution requires a one dimensional template. Iteration (i, j) is mapped to processor $i + j$. Arrays A and B are mapped identically so that the 'anti-diagonals' of these matrices are mapped to the same processor.

2.4 Remarks

Suppose that the matrix of constraints $\mathbf{V}$ has N rows and M columns and has rank r. Then Gaussian elimination with full pivoting requires $O(rMN + r^3)$ *arithmetic* operations. Note that r is at most $\min(M, N)$. A subtle point is that this complexity measure ignores the sizes of matrix entries during the elimination, but it is a well known result that the sizes of numbers involved grow polynomially at the worst[Edm67]. By exploiting the fact that the matrices arising in alignment are sparse and by reordering them so that symbolic constants are used late in the elimination, it may be possible to speed up this algorithm if necessary.

Our framework is robust enough that we can add additional constraints to computation and data maps without difficulty. For example, if a loop in a loop nest carries a dependence, we may not want to spread iterations of that loop across processors. More generally, dependence information can be characterized by a distance vector $\mathbf{z}$, which for our purposes says that iterations $\mathbf{i}$ and $\mathbf{i} + \mathbf{z}$ have to be executed on the same processor. In terms of our alignment model:

$$\mathbf{Ci} + \mathbf{b} = \mathbf{C}(\mathbf{i} + \mathbf{z}) + \mathbf{b} \Leftrightarrow \mathbf{Cz} = 0 \qquad (7)$$

We can now easily incorporate (7) into our matrix system (3) by adding the following block column to $\mathbf{V}$:

$$\mathbf{V}_{dep} = \begin{bmatrix} 0 \\ \mathbf{z} \\ 0 \end{bmatrix}$$

where zeros are placed to that $\mathbf{UV}_{dep} = \mathbf{Cz}$. Adding this column to $\mathbf{V}$ will ensure that any two dependent iterations end up on the same processor.

In some circumstances, it may be necessary to align two data references without aligning them with any computation. This gives rise to equations of the form $\mathbf{D_1F_1} = \mathbf{D_2F_2}$. Such equations can be incorporated into our framework by adding block columns of the form

$$\mathbf{V}_p = \begin{bmatrix} 0 \\ \mathbf{F_1} \\ 0 \\ -\mathbf{F_2} \\ 0 \end{bmatrix} \qquad (8)$$

where the zeros are placed so that $\mathbf{UV}_p = \mathbf{D_1F_1} - \mathbf{D_2F_2}$.

Finally, one practical note. It is possible for Algorithm LINEAR-ALIGNMENT to produce a solution $\mathbf{U}$ which has p rows, even though all $\mathbf{C}_j$ and $\mathbf{D}_k$ produced by Step 5 have rank less than p. In other words, the solution may use only a low dimensional subspace of the entire template. Mapping the solution into a lower dimensional template can be left to the distribution phase of compiling; alternatively, an additional step can be added to Algorithm LINEAR-ALIGNMENT to solve this problem directly in the alignment phase. For lack of space, we do not describe this modification; the interested reader is referred to an associated technical report which can be obtained from the authors.

3   Affine Alignment

In this section, we generalize our framework to affine functions. The intuitive idea
is to 'encode' affine subscripts as linear subscripts by using an extra dimension to
handle the constant term. Then, we apply the machinery in Section 2 to obtain
linear computation and data maps. The extra dimension can removed from these
linear maps to 'decode' them back into affine maps.

We first generalize the data access functions $\mathbf{F}_i$ so that they are affine functions of the loop indices. In the presence of such subscripts, aligning data and
computation requires affine data and computation maps. Therefore, we introduce
the following notation.

$$\text{Computation maps:} \quad C_j(\mathbf{i}) = \mathbf{C}_j \mathbf{i} + \mathbf{c}_j \qquad (9)$$

$$\text{Data maps:} \quad D_k(\mathbf{a}) = \mathbf{D}_k \mathbf{a} + \mathbf{d}_k \qquad (10)$$

$$\text{Data access functions:} \quad F_\ell(\mathbf{i}) = \mathbf{F}_\ell \mathbf{i} + \mathbf{f}_\ell \qquad (11)$$

$\mathbf{C}_j$, $\mathbf{D}_k$ and $\mathbf{F}_\ell$ are matrices representing the linear parts of the affine functions, while $\mathbf{c}_j$, $\mathbf{d}_k$ and $\mathbf{f}_\ell$ represent constants. The alignment constraints from
each reference are now of the form

$$\forall \mathbf{i} \in \mathbf{Z}^n : \mathbf{C}_j \mathbf{i} + \mathbf{c}_j = \mathbf{D}_k (\mathbf{F}_\ell \mathbf{i} + \mathbf{f}_\ell) + \mathbf{d}_k \qquad (12)$$

3.1   Encoding affine constraints as linear constraints

Affine functions can be encoded as linear functions by using the following identity.

$$\mathbf{Tx} + \mathbf{t} = \begin{bmatrix} \mathbf{T} & \mathbf{t} \end{bmatrix} \begin{bmatrix} \mathbf{x} \\ 1 \end{bmatrix} \qquad (13)$$

where $\mathbf{T}$ is a matrix, and $\mathbf{t}$ and $\mathbf{x}$ are vectors. We can put (12) in the form:

$$\begin{bmatrix} \mathbf{C}_j & \mathbf{c}_j \end{bmatrix} \begin{bmatrix} \mathbf{i} \\ 1 \end{bmatrix} = \mathbf{D}_k \begin{bmatrix} \mathbf{F}_\ell & \mathbf{f}_\ell \end{bmatrix} \begin{bmatrix} \mathbf{i} \\ 1 \end{bmatrix} + \mathbf{d}_k$$

$$= \begin{bmatrix} \mathbf{D}_k & \mathbf{d}_k \end{bmatrix} \begin{bmatrix} \mathbf{F}_\ell & \mathbf{f}_\ell \\ \mathbf{0} & 1 \end{bmatrix} \begin{bmatrix} \mathbf{i} \\ 1 \end{bmatrix} \qquad (14)$$

Now we let:

$$\hat{\mathbf{C}}_j = \begin{bmatrix} \mathbf{C}_j & \mathbf{c}_j \end{bmatrix} \quad \hat{\mathbf{D}}_k = \begin{bmatrix} \mathbf{D}_k & \mathbf{d}_k \end{bmatrix} \quad \hat{\mathbf{F}}_\ell = \begin{bmatrix} \mathbf{F}_\ell & \mathbf{f}_\ell \\ \mathbf{0} & 1 \end{bmatrix} \qquad (15)$$

(14) can be written as:

$$\forall \mathbf{i} \in \mathbf{Z}^d : \hat{\mathbf{C}}_j \begin{bmatrix} \mathbf{i} \\ 1 \end{bmatrix} = \hat{\mathbf{D}}_k \hat{\mathbf{F}}_\ell \begin{bmatrix} \mathbf{i} \\ 1 \end{bmatrix} \qquad (16)$$

As before, we would like to 'cancel' the vector $\begin{bmatrix} \mathbf{i} \\ 1 \end{bmatrix}$ from both sides of the
equation. To do this, we need the following result.

Lemma 1. *Let* **T** *be a matrix,* **t** *a vector. Then*

$$\forall \mathbf{x} \, [\mathbf{T} \, \mathbf{t}] \begin{bmatrix} \mathbf{x} \\ 1 \end{bmatrix} = \mathbf{0}$$

if and only if $\mathbf{T} = \mathbf{0}$ *and* $\mathbf{t} = \mathbf{0}$.

Proof: In particular, we can let $\mathbf{x} = \mathbf{0}$. This gives us:

$$[\mathbf{T} \, \mathbf{t}] \begin{bmatrix} \mathbf{0} \\ 1 \end{bmatrix} = \mathbf{t} = \mathbf{0}$$

So $\mathbf{t} = \mathbf{0}$. Now, for any $\mathbf{x}$:

$$[\mathbf{T} \, \mathbf{t}] \begin{bmatrix} \mathbf{x} \\ 1 \end{bmatrix} = [\mathbf{T} \, \mathbf{0}] \begin{bmatrix} \mathbf{x} \\ 1 \end{bmatrix} = \mathbf{T}\mathbf{x} = \mathbf{0}$$

which means that $\mathbf{T} = \mathbf{0}$, as well. □.

Using Lemma 1, we can rewrite (16) as follows:

$$\hat{\mathbf{C}}_j = \hat{\mathbf{D}}_k \hat{\mathbf{F}}_\ell \tag{17}$$

We can now use the techniques in Section 2 to reduce systems of such equations to a single matrix equation as follows:

$$\hat{\mathbf{U}}\hat{\mathbf{V}} = \mathbf{0} \tag{18}$$

In turn, this equation can be solved using the Algorithm LINEAR-ALIGNMENT to determine $\hat{\mathbf{U}}$. To illustrate this process, let us use the convolution example from Section 1.

```
    DO 3 i = 1, M
3        Z = Z + X(i) * Y(M − i + 1)
```

The array access functions are:

$$
\begin{aligned}
\mathbf{F}_X &= [1] & \mathbf{f}_X &= [0] \\
\mathbf{F}_Y &= [-1] & \mathbf{f}_Y &= [M+1] \\
\hat{\mathbf{F}}_X &= \begin{bmatrix} 1 & 0 \\ 0 & 1 \end{bmatrix} & \hat{\mathbf{F}}_Y &= \begin{bmatrix} -1 & M+1 \\ 0 & 1 \end{bmatrix}
\end{aligned}
\tag{19}
$$

Assume that we want to compute the $X(i)Y(M-i+1)$ products in parallel and them sum them up using a collective communication procedure. The reader can verify that the matrix equation to be solved is the following one.

$$\hat{\mathbf{U}}\hat{\mathbf{V}} = \mathbf{0} \tag{20}$$

where:

$$\hat{\mathbf{U}} = [\hat{\mathbf{C}} \, \hat{\mathbf{D}}_X \, \hat{\mathbf{D}}_Y] \qquad \hat{\mathbf{V}} = \begin{bmatrix} \mathbf{I} & \mathbf{I} \\ -\hat{\mathbf{F}}_X & 0 \\ 0 & -\hat{\mathbf{F}}_Y \end{bmatrix}$$

Using the techniques in Section 2.3, it can be verified that a solution to the equation is the following matrix.

$$\hat{\mathbf{U}} = \begin{bmatrix} -1\, 2 + M & -1\, 2 + M & 1\, 1 \\ -1\, 1 + M & -1\, 1 + M & 1\, 0 \end{bmatrix} \tag{21}$$

From this matrix, we can read off the following maps of computation and data.

$$\hat{\mathbf{C}} = \hat{\mathbf{D}}_X = \begin{bmatrix} -1\, 2 + M \\ -1\, 1 + M \end{bmatrix} \qquad \hat{\mathbf{D}}_Y = \begin{bmatrix} 1\, 1 \\ 1\, 0 \end{bmatrix}$$

This says that iteration i of the loop and element $X(i)$ are mapped to the following virtual processor.

$$\begin{bmatrix} -1\, 2 + M \\ -1\, 1 + M \end{bmatrix} \begin{bmatrix} i \\ 1 \end{bmatrix} = \begin{bmatrix} M + 2 - i \\ M + 1 - i \end{bmatrix}$$

As a check, note that $Y(M - i + 1)$ is mapped to the same processor.

$$\begin{bmatrix} 1\, 1 \\ 1\, 0 \end{bmatrix} \begin{bmatrix} M + i - 1 \\ 1 \end{bmatrix} = \begin{bmatrix} M + 2 - i \\ M + 1 - i \end{bmatrix}$$

Therefore, no communication is required to compute the $X(i)Y(M - i + 1)$ products.

Notice that although the space of virtual processors has two dimensions (because of the encoding of constants), the maps of the computation and data use only a one-dimensional subspace of the virtual processor space. To obtain a clean solution, it is desirable to remove the extra dimension introduced by the encoding. One way to remove the extra dimension is to use the general procedure mentioned in Section 2.4. A faster approach is to use the fact that vector

$$\mathbf{w} = [0\, 0 \ldots 0\, 1\, 0 \ldots 0\, 1 \ldots 0\, 0\, 1]^T$$

(with zeros placed appropriately) is always orthogonal to $\hat{\mathbf{V}}^T$. For lack of space, we defer discussion of this to the associated technical report. Algorithm AFFINE-ALIGNMENT is summarized in Figure 2.

4 Replication

As we discussed in Section 1, communication-free alignment may require replication of read-only data. In this section, we show how replication of data is handled in our linear algebra framework. We have not worked out all the details of replication, so we will restrict attention to a single loop nest here. We use the rank-1 update loop as a running example. In this loop, elements of matrix A are updated by the corresponding element of the outer product of the vectors x and y, as shown below.

Input: A set of alignment constraints as in Equation (12).

Output: Communication-free alignment mappings characterized by $\mathbf{C}_j$, $\mathbf{c}_j$, $\mathbf{D}_k$, $\mathbf{d}_k$.

1. Assemble $\hat{\mathbf{F}}_\ell$ matrices as in Equation 14.
2. Assemble block columns $\mathbf{V}_q$ as in Equation (2) using $\hat{\mathbf{F}}_\ell$ instead of $\mathbf{F}_\ell$.
3. Put all block columns $\mathbf{V}_q$ into one matrix $\hat{\mathbf{V}}$.
4. Compute a basis $\hat{\mathbf{U}}^T$ for null-space of $\hat{\mathbf{V}}^T$ as in the Step 3 of LINEAR-ALIGNMENT algorithm.
5. Eliminate redundant row(s) in $\hat{\mathbf{U}}$ if desired.
6. Extract the solution matrices from $\hat{\mathbf{U}}$.

Fig. 2. Algorithm AFFINE-ALIGNMENT.

```
DO 4 i = 1,100
    DO 4 j = 1,100
4        A(i,j) = A(i,j) + x(i) * y(j)
```

Assuming that we have a two dimensional processor template, let element (i,j) of array A be mapped to logical processor (i,j). The value of the element $x(i)$ is needed to compute all elements of A in row i. In other words, x needs to be replicated column-wise. Similarly, all elements of A in the column j need the value of $y(j)$. In other words, y needs to be replicated row-wise. We would like to derive this information automatically.

4.1 Formulation of replication

To handle replication, we associate a pair of matrices $(\mathbf{R}, \mathbf{D})$ with each data reference for which alignment is desired, and the fundamental equational scheme for alignment then becomes $\mathbf{RC} = \mathbf{DF}$. Up to this point, data alignment was specified using a matrix $\mathbf{D}$ which mapped array element $\mathbf{a}$ to logical processor $\mathbf{Da}$. If $\mathbf{D}$ has a non-trivial null-space, then elements of the array belonging to the same coset of the null-space get placed onto the same virtual processor; that is,

$$\mathbf{Da}_1 = \mathbf{Da}_2$$
$$\Leftrightarrow$$
$$\mathbf{a}_1 - \mathbf{a}_2 \in \text{null}(\mathbf{D})$$

When we allow replication, the mapping of array elements to processors can be described as follows. Array element $\mathbf{a}$ is mapped to processor $\mathbf{p}$ if

$$\mathbf{Rp} = \mathbf{Da}$$

The mapping of the array is now a many-to-many relation that can be described in words as follows:

- Array elements that belong to the same coset of null($\mathbf{D}$) are mapped onto the same processors.
- Processors that belong to the same coset of null($\mathbf{R}$) own the same data.

From this, it is easy to see that the fundamental equation of alignment becomes $\mathbf{RC} = \mathbf{DF}$. The replication-free scenario is just a special case when $\mathbf{R}$ is $\mathbf{I}$. Not all arrays in a procedure need to be replicated — for example, if an array is not read-only or it is very large, we can disallow replication of that array. In the rank-1 update example, we choose to replicate vectors x and y, but not matrix A since A is not read-only. For this problem, the system of equations is the following:

$$\mathbf{C} = \mathbf{D}_A$$
$$\mathbf{R}_x\mathbf{C} = \mathbf{D}_x \ (1 \ 0)$$
$$\mathbf{R}_y\mathbf{C} = \mathbf{D}_y \ (0 \ 1)$$

We solve such systems of equations in two steps as follows.

1. Find communication-free alignment of non-replicated data and iterations, as was described in Sections 2 and 3. In this phase, we only take into account constraints involving non-replicated arrays.
2. Find the alignment (possibly with replication) of the rest of the arrays. We use the computation alignment ($\mathbf{C}$) found in the first step to solve the replication equations $\mathbf{RC} = \mathbf{DF}$, as described below.

Let $\mathbf{C}_{basis}$ be the computation alignment found in the first step. It is easy to see that multiplying $\mathbf{C}_{basis}$ and each $\mathbf{D}$ found in this step by a matrix $\mathbf{T}$ gives another solution to the replication-free equations. In the second step, we implicitly determine such a matrix $\mathbf{T}$ so that the remaining equations are satisfied. The replication equations for the second step can be written as follows:

$$\mathbf{RTC}_{basis} = \mathbf{DF} \tag{22}$$

In the case of a *single loop nest*, all $\mathbf{R}$ matrices in equations like (22) are multiplied on the left by the same $\mathbf{T}$ matrix. This means we can omit $\mathbf{T}$ from the equations[3], and solve the system of simplified equations:

$$\mathbf{RC}_{basis} = \mathbf{DF}$$
$$\Leftrightarrow$$
$$[\mathbf{R} \ \mathbf{D}] \begin{bmatrix} \mathbf{C}_{basis} \\ -\mathbf{F} \end{bmatrix} = 0 \tag{23}$$

We now use the procedure described in Section 2 to solve a system of equations of the form of (23). Algorithm SINGLE-LOOP-REPLICATION-ALIGNMENT is summarized in Figure 3.

We are currently working on extending this idea to handle multiple loop nests.

---

[3] This has the effect of transforming the virtual processor space by matrix $\mathbf{T}$

Input: Replication constraints of the form $\mathbf{RC} = \mathbf{DF}$.

Output: Matrices $\mathbf{R}$, $\mathbf{D}$ and $\mathbf{C}_{basis}$ that specify alignment with replication.

1. Find $\mathbf{C}_{basis}$ by solving the alignment system for the non-replicated arrays using the Algorithm AFFINE-ALIGNMENT. If all arrays in the loop nest are allowed to be replicated, then set $\mathbf{C}_{basis} = \mathbf{I}$.
2. Find $(\mathbf{R}, \mathbf{D})$ pairs that specify replication by solving the $\mathbf{RC}_{basis} = \mathbf{DF}$ equations.

Fig. 3. Algorithm SINGLE-LOOP-REPLICATION-ALIGNMENT.

4.2 Example

We illustrate the above discussion using the rank-1 update example. The only replication-free equation is the one due to array A. Solving this equation gives us $\mathbf{D}_A = \mathbf{C}_{basis} = \mathbf{I}$. Now the equation for the second step of Algorithm SINGLE-LOOP-REPLICATION-ALIGNMENT is the following:

$$
\begin{bmatrix} \mathbf{R}_x \ \mathbf{R}_y \ \mathbf{D}_x \ \mathbf{D}_y \end{bmatrix}
\begin{bmatrix}
\mathbf{C}_{basis} & 0 \\
0 & \mathbf{C}_{basis} \\
-\mathbf{F}_x & 0 \\
0 & -\mathbf{F}_y
\end{bmatrix} =
$$

$$
\begin{bmatrix} \mathbf{R}_x \ \mathbf{R}_y \ \mathbf{D}_x \ \mathbf{D}_y \end{bmatrix}
\begin{bmatrix}
1 & 0\,0\,0 \\
0 & 1\,0\,0 \\
0 & 0\,1\,0 \\
0 & 0\,0\,1 \\
-1 & 0\,0\,0 \\
0 & 0\,0\,{-1}
\end{bmatrix} = 0
$$

This gives us a solution with $\mathbf{R}_x = \begin{bmatrix} 0\ 1 \end{bmatrix}$, $\mathbf{R}_y = \begin{bmatrix} 1\ 0 \end{bmatrix}$ and $\mathbf{D}_x = \mathbf{D}_y = 1$. Therefore, X is replicated in the j dimension, and Y is replicated in the i dimension, as desired.

5 Conclusion

We have presented a simple framework for the solution of the communication-free alignment problem. This framework is based on linear algebra, and it permits the development of simple and fast algorithms for a variety of problems that arise in alignment. A final step would be to integrate a good heuristic to determine which constraints should be left unsatisfied when the system of alignment constraints is overconstrained.

References

[AL93]   Jennifer M. Anderson and Monica S. Lam. Global optimizations for parallelism and locality on scalable parallel machines. *ACM SIGPLAN Conference on Programming Language Design and Implementation (PLDI)*, pages 112 – 125, June 1993.

[Ban93]   U. Banerjee. *Loop transformations for restructuring compilers*. Kluwer Publishing, 1993.

[CGS93]   Siddartha Chatterjee, John Gilbert, and Robert Schreiber. The alignment-distribution graph. In U. Banerjee, D. Gelernter, A. Nicolau, and D. Padua, editors, *Languages and Compilers for Parallel Computing. Sixth International Workshop.*, number 768 in LNCS. Springer-Verlag, 1993.

[CGST92] Siddartha Chatterjee, John Gilbert, Robert Schreiber, and Shang-Hua Teng. Optimal evaluation of array expressions on massively parallel machines. Technical Report CSL-92-11, XEROX PARC, December 1992.

[Edm67]   Jack Edmonds. Systems of distinct representatives and linear algebra. *Journal of research of national bureau of standards (Sect. B)*, 71(4):241–245, 1967.

[Fea92]   Paul Feautrier. Toward automatic distribution. Technical Report 92.95, IBP/MASI, December 1992.

[GVL89]   Gene H. Golub and Charles F. Van Loan. *Matrix Computations*. The John Hopkins University Press, second edition, 1989.

[HS91]   C.-H. Huang and P. Sadayappan. Communication-free hyperplane partitioning of nested loops. In U. Banerjee, D. Gelernter, A. Nicolau, and D. Padua, editors, *Languages and Compilers for Parallel Computing. Fourth International Workshop. Santa Clara, CA.*, number 589 in LNCS, pages 186–200. Springer-Verlag, August 1991.

[KLD92]   Kathleen Knobe, Joan D. Lucas, and William J. Dally. Dynamic alignment on distributed memory systems. In *Proceedings of the Third Workshop on Compilers for Parallel Computers*, July 1992.

[KN90]   Kathleen Knobe and Venkataraman Natarajan. Data optimization: minimizing residual interprocessor motion on SIMD machines. In *Proceedings of the 3rd Symposium on the Frontiers of Massively Parallel Computation - Frontiers 90*, pages 416–423, October 1990.

[LC89]   Jingke Li and Marina Chen. Index domain alignment: minimizing cost of cross-referencing between distributed arrays. Technical Report YALEU/DCS/TR-725, Department of Computer Science, Yale University, September 1989.

[LP92]   W. Li and K. Pingali. Access normalization: loop restructuring for NUMA compilers. In *Proceedings of the 5th International Conference on Architectural Support for Programming Languages and Operating Systems*, October 1992.

Detecting and Using Affinity in an Automatic Data Distribution Tool

Eduard Ayguadé, Jordi Garcia, Mercè Gironés,
Jesús Labarta, Jordi Torres and Mateo Valero

Computer Architecture Department, Polytechnic University of Catalunya
cr. Gran Capità s/núm, Mòdul D6, 08071 - Barcelona, Spain

Abstract. This paper describes some aspects of the implementation of our Data Distribution Tool (DDT), which accepts programs written in Fortran77 and obtains alignment and distribution HPF directives for the arrays used in the program. In particular, we describe the phases of the tool which analyze reference patterns in loops, record preferences for alignment and obtain the alignment functions. These functions are static in the sense that they do not change within the scope of the code analyzed (routine or loop). We propose the use of a set of well-known techniques to extend the scope of the reference pattern analysis and we evaluate their effectiveness in a set of programs from the Perfect Club and SPEC benchmarks.

1 Introduction

Data distribution is one of the key points when programming an application for a massive parallel machine, in which each processor has direct access to a local (or close) memory and indirect access to the remote memories of other processors. Optimizing data distribution for these Non-Uniform Memory Architectures (NUMA) is important in order to fully exploit the available parallelism of the architecture.

Several research groups have targeted their research efforts to this topic. For instance the implementation of PARADIGM [1] on top of Parafrase II and the continuation on the PTRAN II compiler [2] at IBM, or the FCS system [3] are examples of tools oriented to obtain distributions for the arrays used in a program. While High Performance Fortran (HPF [4]) assigns the responsibility of specifying the data distribution to the programmer, the above mentioned authors propose to have a tool to automatically perform this task. For instance, the PTRAN II compiler is a prototype compiler for HPF that, in addition, distributes those arrays whose distribution is not specified by the user. The compiler converts the original Fortran program into a Single-Program Multiple-Data program following the owner computes rule where communication among processors is introduced when necessary. This compilation process is also performed by other tools, such as the Vienna Fortran Compilation System VFCS [5] or the Fortran-D compiler [6]. Both tools are source-to-source translators from Vienna Fortran or Fortran-D into a message-passing Fortran, respectively.

In a different context, [3] proposes a fully-automatic source-to-source translator which accepts programs written in a subset of Fortran90 and determine a data distribution scheme for the arrays of the program. They only analyze array-syntax assignment and WHERE statements to determine the distribution functions. The output of the translator is an equivalent Fortran90 program incorporating directives similar to the ones offered by HPF. They also include, where beneficial, dynamic redistributions.

1.1 An Overview of the Data Distribution Process

The main components of the data distribution environment we are using and developing are shown in Figure 1. We assume as input sequential programs written in Fortran77. The data distribution process specifies how all the arrays manipulated by the algorithm are distributed among the memories of the processors. This decision is done so that communication among processors or the amount of remote accesses is reduced as much as possible, and the communication patterns become as uniform as possible. The data distribution algorithm is based on the ideas proposed in [7] and [8]. The tool is named DDT (Data Distribution Tool) and its implementation has been done on top of ParaScope [9].

The output of DDT is an HPF program in which the original program is annotated with a set of directives that specify how arrays are aligned to a set of virtual target arrays and how the dimensions of these target arrays are distributed among processors.

The xHPF compiler from Applied Parallel Research, Inc. [10] is used to compile the program generated by DDT and generate a Single-Program Multiple-Data node program using PVM3 communication primitives [11]. The simulated execution of the instrumented code generated by xHPF is used to compare the performance of different data distribution strategies and to validate our proposals.

As a benchmark platform, we have used all the programs in the Perfect Club [12] except for SPICE, and some of the numerical codes in the SPEC benchmarks [13]. Within each program, we have selected those routines that are the most time consuming (more than 85% of the execution time) and that reference dimensional data structures within the source code. As a result of the process, 144 out of 824 routines have been selected.

2 Implementation

The basic compilation steps of our approach are described next. First of all, a weighted graph called Dimension Alignment Graph (*DAG*) is constructed from the analysis of the array references in the source program and it records preferences for alignment. Then, an array alignment phase follows. In this step, all dimensions of the arrays in the program are related to each other by mapping them to a set of target arrays (inter-dimension alignment) and shifting them with respect to the dimensions of the target arrays (intra-dimension alignment).

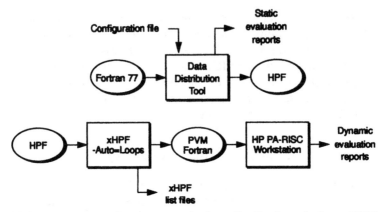

Fig. 1. Main components of our automatic data distribution platform: DDT, xHPF compiler and simulator from APR, Inc.

Communication requirements for those non aligned references are analyzed in order to decide which dimensions of the target arrays are distributed and which ones are internalized. The block-cyclic phase determines for each distributed dimension, whether it should be distributed in a block or cyclic manner. Finally, HPF directives are inserted in the original Fortran77 program, according to the data distribution strategy chosen.

In this paper we analyze in detail the implementation of the two first steps: *i*) reference pattern analysis and *DAG* building, and *ii*) *DAG* partitioning and alignment. A description of the implementation of the other steps can be found elsewhere [14].

2.1 Reference Patterns and Dimension Alignment Graph

The *DAG* is a weighted undirected graph built from the analysis of array reference patterns in loop statements. In this section we review how reference patterns are defined and analyzed for affinity, and how the *DAG* is built from this analysis. We also present and evaluate the use of some basic techniques that increase the amount of reference patterns and, as a consequence, allow us to obtain better alignment and distribution functions.

Reference Pattern Analysis and *DAG* Building The analysis of reference patterns is performed within the scope of nested loops. A reference pattern is defined by

$$A(i_1, ..., i_p, ..., i_m) \leftarrow B(j_1, ..., j_q, ..., j_n),$$

where A is an array that appears in the left-hand side (*lhs*) of an assignment statement located inside a loop, and B is an array in the right-hand side (*rhs*) of the same assignment statement. If the assignment is under the control of conditional statements, then all the arrays in the expressions that evaluate the conditions are considered as if they were in the *rhs* of the assignment statement.

An affinity relation can appear between two dimensions of the data arrays in a reference pattern. In the above generic reference pattern, an affinity relation can appear between any dimension p of array A and any dimension q of array

B (denoted $< A_p, B_q >$). Dimension B_q is said to be affine with dimension A_p if j_q and i_p are linear functions of the same loop control variable.

From the analysis of reference patterns, the DAG is built. Nodes of the DAG represent dimensions of data arrays and edges represent affinity relations between array dimensions obtained examining cross-reference patterns (patterns in which the rhs and lhs arrays are different). Self-reference patterns are not considered in the DAG building step. Nodes in the DAG are grouped in columns; each column contains those nodes representing dimensions from the same data array. An edge $< A_p, B_q >$ in the DAG shows a preference for alignment of dimensions A_p and B_q.

According to [7], edges in the DAG can be weighted in two ways. On one side, each edge is weighted depending on whether it is competing or non-competing with another edge (ε if it is competing and 1 if not). Two edges are said to be competing if they are generated by the same reference pattern and are incident on the same node. A DAG so defined may contain multiple edges between a pair of nodes since there might be multiple reference patterns between two data arrays. Each set of multiple edges can be replaced with a single edge whose weight is the sum of their weights. On the other side, each edge is also weighted with the offset between the two subscripts in the array dimensions involved. In this case, multiple edges are not merged into the same node because each one may store information about a different shift preference. Preferences for stride alignment are not recorded in the DAG in the current version of DDT.

Increasing the amount of affinity relations In this section we propose and evaluate the effectiveness of three techniques that try to increase the amount of affinity relations obtained from the analysis of the sequential program. The aim is to extend the scope of reference pattern analysis by looking for reference patterns between arrays in different statements of the loop body and by considering reference patterns where variables other than loop control variables are used. The techniques we propose are:

- **Expression substitution:** programmers tend to use scalar variables within loops to store temporary results which are later used in other computations within the same loop. The use of these temporary variables hides the existence of affinity relations between arrays used in the computation of the scalar variable and the array that later uses the scalar variable. An example taken from routine RADB4 from the ADM Perfect Club program is shown below:

```
        DO 104 K=1,L1
          DO 103 I=3,IDO,2
            IC = IDP2-I
            ...
            TI2 = CC(I,1,K)-CC(IC,4,K)
            TI3 = CC(I,3,K)-CC(IC,2,K)
            ...
            CH(I,K,1) = TI2+TI3
            ...
    103 CONTINUE
    104 CONTINUE
```

The main idea is to look for the loop statements defining the scalar variables that are used on the *rhs* of the statement being analyzed for affinity. This is equivalent to considering that the programmer would have not used variables $TI2$ and $TI3$ in the example above and instead, he would have written this equivalent version:

```
DO 104 K=1,L1
    DO 103 I=3,IDO,2
    ...
        CH(I,K,1) = CC(I,1,K)-CC(IC,4,K)+CC(I,3,K)-CC(IC,2,K)
    ...
103 CONTINUE
104 CONTINUE
```

In this case, four additional reference patterns are analyzed:

$$CH(I, K, 1) \leftarrow CC(I, 1, K), \; CH(I, K, 1) \leftarrow CC(IC, 4, K),$$
$$CH(I, K, 1) \leftarrow CC(I, 3, K), \; CH(I, K, 1) \leftarrow CC(IC, 2, K)$$

and new affinity relations are found. In this case, they suggest a transposition of the second and third dimensions of arrays CH and CC. Otherwise, this transposition is not detected.

- **Subscript substitution:** the basic idea of this technique is to analyze subscripts which are not linear expressions of loop control variables. For instance, in the same routine shown above, notice that the substitution of the subscript IC in the first dimension of array CC allows us to find that the first dimension of arrays CH and CC are affine. Another example that shows the benefit of this technique, taken form routine GETEU of the DYFESM Perfect Club program is shown below:

```
DO 20 I=1,NNPED
    NODE = ICOND(I,K)
    DO 15 IDOF=1,NDDF
        XE(IDOF,I) = XGLOBL(IDOF,NODE)
15  CONTINUE
20  CONTINUE
```

In this case, due to the substitution of the subscript $NODE$ in the second dimension of array $XGLOBL$, we analyze the reference pattern between arrays XE and $ICOND$. Notice that in this case a preference for transposing arrays XE and $ICOND$ is recorded in the DAG, as indicated by the affinity relation $< XE_2, ICOND_1 >$. This technique has been implemented using just one level of substitution, that is, just looking for the statement where the variable that appear in the subscript is defined. No recursive substitutions are applied.

- **Induction variable detection:** affinity is usually hidden by the use of induction variables in the subscript functions. In this case, it is worthwhile to detect if an induction variable is used and to detect the associated loop control variable. An example from the ADDX routine from the FLO52 Perfect Club program is shown below:

```
DO 30 J=2,J2,2
  JJ = JJ +1
  II = 1
  DO 30 I=2,I2,2
    II = II +1
    DW(I,J,N)     = .5625*WW(II,JJ,N)    +.1875*WW(II-1,JJ,N)
.                  +.1875*WW(II,JJ-1,N)  +.0625*WW(II-1,JJ-1,N)
    DW(I-1,J,N)   = .1875*WW(II,JJ,N)    +.5625*WW(II-1,JJ,N)
.                  +.0625*WW(II,JJ-1,N)  +.1875*WW(II-1,JJ-1,N)
    DW(I,J-1,N)   = .1875*WW(II,JJ,N)    +.0625*WW(II-1,JJ,N)
.                  +.5625*WW(II,JJ-1,N)  +.1875*WW(II-1,JJ-1,N)
    DW(I-1,J-1,N) = .0625*WW(II,JJ,N)    +.1875*WW(II-1,JJ,N)
.                  +.1875*WW(II,JJ-1,N)  +.5625*WW(II-1,JJ-1,N)
30 CONTINUE
```

In this case, detecting that variables II and JJ are induction variables of the loops controlled by variables I and J respectively, allows us to find two new affinity relations $< DW_1, WW_1 >$ and $< DW_2, WW_2 >$.

Next we discuss the usefulness of the techniques proposed. Figure 2 shows the effectiveness of applying expression and subscript substitution. The vertical axis shows the percentage of affinity relations where the use of each technique has been necessary to obtain them. For instance, in the ADM Perfect Club benchmark, 83% and 3% of the affinity relations appear thanks to the use of expression and subscript substitution, respectively. Observe that most of the programs benefit from the use of substitutions. Just one of the programs in the Perfect Club (QCD) does not benefit from the techniques proposed. Observe that the effectiveness of expression substitution is larger than the one of subscript substitution. On the average, 56% of the total number of relations are due to expression substitution, while 18% of them are due to subscript substitution. Notice in Figure 2 that sometimes the two substitutions have to be applied to obtain a new affinity relation (as for instance in the BDNA program, where the sum of the two percentages is greater than 100%).

Figure 3 shows a graphical representation of the percentage of reference patterns where loop control variables (LCV) or induction variables (IV) are used either at the *rhs* or *lhs*. Observe that in most of the cases, loop control variables are used to access data structures in reference patterns $(LCV - LCV$ in Figure 3). However, in some programs the use of induction variables in reference patterns is considerable. For example, in MG3D, OCEAN and FPPPP reference patterns where an IV is used at one side and a different IV' or LCV is used at the other side of the reference pattern are the most frequent. On the average, this technique is useful in 12% of the affinity relations found.

As proposed in [8], reference patterns derived directly from the input program can be optimized before building the DAG with the objective of achieving a more realistic characterization of the code in terms of data movement requirements. One of the most common optimization is to eliminate, when possible, identical patterns within a loop. For instance, for the selected routines in the Perfect Club, 22.8% of the reference patterns can be eliminated from the original set.

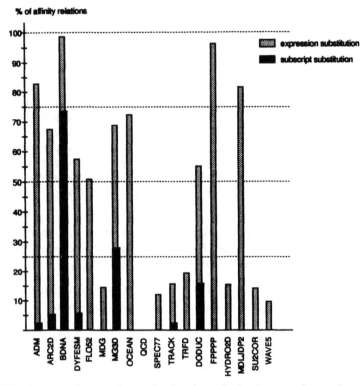

Fig. 2. Effectiveness of expression and subscript substitutions on the number of affinity relations.

This optimization contributes to reduce the complexity of the DAG and thus the computational time of the DAG partitioning step.

2.2 DAG Partitioning and Array Alignment

Two problems are faced when solving the array alignment step. First, the inter-dimension alignment problem tries to decide how array dimensions are aligned into the dimensions of a common target array. This target array has dimensionality equal to the largest dimensionality of all the arrays analyzed. Each dimension of each array is aligned with a dimension of the common array. Second, the intra-dimension alignment problem tries to decide how all the array dimensions aligned into a dimension of the common array are aligned each other. Although this includes offset and stride alignments and reflections, only offset alignments have been implemented in the current version of DDT.

Inter-dimension Alignment Given a DAG G as described above and weighted with the number of affinity relations among nodes, the inter-dimension alignment problem can be stated as follows [7]:

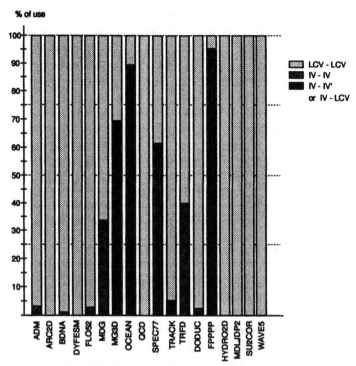

Fig. 3. Effectiveness of induction variable detection on the number of affinity relations.

"Let n be the maximum number of nodes in a column of G. Partition the node
set of G into n disjoint subsets $V_1, ..., V_n$, with the restriction that no two
nodes belonging to the same data array are allowed to be in the same subset."

Nodes in the same subset correspond to dimensions to be aligned. As a consequence, we want to partition the DAG so as to minimize the total weight of
edges that are between nodes in different subsets.

The problem stated above is hard to solve (NP-complete) and an heuristic
algorithm is proposed in [7], which is basically a greedy algorithm. In this algorithm, a single data array is randomly chosen at each step for alignment with
the target array (which is chosen among the data arrays that have maximum
dimensionality). The algorithm applied to a graph G is described below:

> Choose the target column C_T;
> $G_1 \leftarrow G$;
> While G_1 is not empty, do
> $\quad C_x \leftarrow PickUpColumn(G_1)$;
> $\quad G_x \leftarrow FormBipartiteGraph(C_T, C_x, G_1)$;
> $\quad M \leftarrow OptimalAlignment(G_x)$;
> $\quad G_1 \leftarrow ReduceGraph(M, C_T, C_x, G_1)$;

In each iteration of the above loop, an alignment function between the data
array corresponding to column C_x and the data array corresponding to the target
column C_T is generated. The main steps of the heuristic are described below:

- *FormBipartiteGraph*: a graph G_x composed of the nodes in the two columns C_T and C_x is built. An edge is placed between two nodes in the bipartite graph G_x if there is a path between the two original nodes in the DAG. The weight of the edge is the sum of all edges that compose the path. If several paths appear, then the weight is set to the sum of all the edges that compose the paths.
- *OptimalAlignment*: for each bipartite graph G_x, align dimensions of C_x with dimensions of C_T so that the total weight of edges not aligned is minimum.
- *ReduceGraph*: Merges column C_x into C_T, replaces multiple edges between two nodes with a single edge whose weight is the sum of their weights, and deletes all self cycles.

In our implementation, several optimizations in the heuristic have been done in order to obtain better alignments. They are described below:

- In *FormBipartiteGraph*, the weight of an edge between two nodes is set to the min-cut instead of the sum of the weight of all edges that compose the paths. With min-cut, the weight is set to the minimum sum of edge weights in G_1 that we had to eliminate to isolate the two nodes. This represents the cost of not aligning the two nodes. For instance, consider the DAG shown in Figure 4.a (which corresponds to routine TRED2 from the EISPACK library). Figure 4.b shows an step of *FormBipartiteGraph* when a path between T_2 (of C_T) and Z_1 (of C_x in the step) is looked for. In this case, there are two paths: T_2, D_1, Z_1 and T_2, D_1, E_1, Z_1. The bipartite graphs obtained using the original proposal [7] and the min-cut proposal are shown in Figures 4.c and 4.d respectively. *OptimalAlignment* would align $< T_1, B_2 >$ and $< T_2, B_1 >$ in 4.c (with 2 arcs to communicate) and $< T_1, B_1 >$ and $< T_2, B_2 >$ in 4.d (with one arc to communicate). The solution obtained with min-cut is better than the other solution and reflects more the actual communication requirements.
- At each step, *PickUpColumn* chooses a column C_x among all the columns in G_1 as the column that is more critical in the alignment process instead of an arbitrary column. To decide how critical is a column, we inspect direct edges between the target and each column in G_1. For instance consider the same example in Figure 4. Once *OptimalAlignment* and *ReduceGraph* have been done, the graph shown in Figure 5.a is obtained. If we pick up column D, the difference between the two possible alignments ($< T_1, D_1 >$ or $< T_2, D_1 >$) in the number of communications is one. On the contrary, if we pick up column E, the difference is two. So in this case, it is more critical to first solve the alignment of array E rather than array D. Figures 5.b and 5.c show the difference.

The algorithm used to decide the next column is outlined below:

> For each column C_x in G_1, do
> $\quad G_x \leftarrow FormBipartiteDirect(C_T, C_x, G_1);$
> $\quad dif_x = OptimalAlignment(G_x) - WorstAlignment(G_x);$
> Choose column C_x with maximum dif_x

70

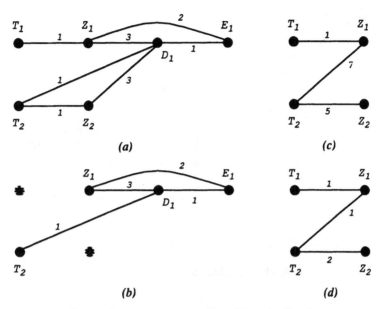

Fig. 4. Min-cut vs. Sum in FormBipartiteGraph.

Function *FormBipartiteDirect* returns the bipartite graph between two columns in a graph that results from direct edges. Functions *OptimalAlignment* and *WorstAlignment* return for a bipartite graph the total weight of non-aligned edges in the optimal and worst possible alignments.

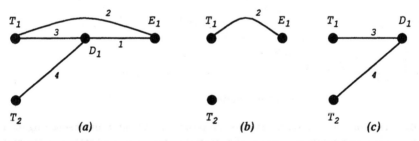

Fig. 5. Heuristic to choose a new column in the graph for alignment: (a) intermediate graph G_1, (b) bipartite graph with domain E and (c) bipartite graph with domain D.

Figure 6 shows the effect of the two previous optimizations. We have considered *DAG* randomly generated with a density of 20% of edges and a variable number of columns with two nodes each. We show the percentage of optimal alignments obtained in each case. Note the difference when the heuristic to choose the new column to be aligned is used. For the non-optimal cases, the min-cut algorithm tends to generate better alignments than the original proposal [7]. Figure 6 also shows the percentage of cases where min-cut resulted in a better alignment than sum and vice versa.

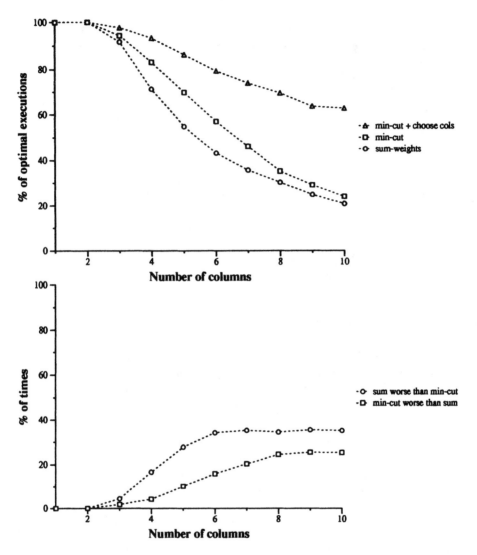

Fig. 6. Effect of the two optimizations proposed to the inter-dimension alignment heuristic: (top) percentage of optimal alignments in each case and (bottom) percentage of times sum is worse than min-cut and vice versa.

The use of min-cut increases the execution time of the algorithm with respect to the sum alternative. However, the use of a heuristic to choose the next column decreases the execution time of the min-cut solution because at each step, the complexity of the remaining graph is lower and the algorithm proceeds faster.

Intra-dimension Alignment The algorithm we propose to find shifts among aligned dimensions is described next. For each dimension of the target array, a directed graph G_2 is created. Nodes in this graph correspond to array dimensions that are aligned with the corresponding dimension of the target array. Edges in

G_2 are the subset of edges in the DAG between the nodes aligned. In this graph, edges are weighted with the offset between the two subscripts in the associated reference pattern. The algorithm implemented is:

> For each dimension of the target array, do
>> Obtain G_2 from G;
>> Mark target node;
>> While not all nodes marked, do
>>> $N \leftarrow PickUpNode(G_2)$;
>>> $S \leftarrow FindShift(G_2, N)$;
>>> $G_2 \leftarrow ApplyRetiming(G_2, N, S)$;
>>> Mark node N.

This algorithm is basically the same that the one proposed by [15] to solve the statement alignment problem in order to reduce synchronization costs in a shared memory execution model. The main steps of the algorithm are described below:

- $PickUpNode$: it returns an unmarked node of G_2 connected with a marked node of G_2. If such a node is not found, then an unmarked node is randomly selected.
- $FindShift$: this function returns the offset S (with respect to the target array) that has to be applied to the node N currently analyzed. This value is obtained from the offset of all the edges between node N and any marked node of G_2. If several edges between node N and the target node appear, the one that is repeated more times is selected. If several edges are candidates, then the one with minimum value is chosen. We have observed that selecting a value different than zero when zero is one of the candidates leads to poor solutions.
- $ApplyRetiming$: the idea of retiming as described in [16] is applied in this function. The offset S obtained in the previous step is subtracted to all incoming arcs into node N, and added to all outgoing arcs from node N.

At the end of the algorithm, each node in G_2 has an associated shift with respect to the target node.

If G_2 is acyclic, a perfect intra-dimension alignment results possible. In this case, all the edges are aligned and no communication is needed. If cycles are present in G_2, then some edges may not be aligned and therefore, communication may be required for them.

3 Some Results

In this section we show the influence of the techniques and optimizations presented in the previous section on the alignment functions for the routines in the benchmark platform used throughout the paper. In particular, Table 1 shows the number of routines selected within each benchmark, and the number of them for

benchmark	number of routines	number of changes
ADM	16	7
ARC2D	10	0
BDNA	1	0
DYFESM	7	1
FLO52	6	0
MDG	6	0
MG3D	14	2
OCEAN	8	0
QCD	7	0
SPEC77	10	0
TRACK	9	0
TRFD	2	1
DODUC	15	3
FPPPP	4	0
HYDRO2D	8	0
MDLJDP2	4	0
SU2COR	8	0
WAVE5	9	0

Table 1. Number of routines in each benchmark where the techniques and optimizations described in Section 2 have modified the alignment function for some of the arrays

which the alignment functions of some of the arrays have been modified because of turning on the techniques and optimizations previously described.

As one can see in Table 1, changes in the alignment functions are obtained in 14 out of the 144 routines evaluated. The key aspect that lead to these low numbers is the following. On the average, routines use 66% one-dimensional arrays, 30% two-dimensional arrays and the rest have higher dimensionality. So only 44% of the arrays used in the routines are candidates to changes in their alignment functions. This high percentage of one-dimensional arrays is due to the fact that some of the applications analyzed assume linear memory models and as a consequence declare one-dimensional data structures to hold higher dimensional ones.

4   Conclusions

In this paper we have presented the implementation of the front-end of our Data Distribution Tool DDT. Our tool tries to automatically determine appropriate array alignment and distribution functions out of the information in sequential programs (reference patterns, parallel and sequential loops, and shapes of the iteration spaces).

DDT has been implemented on top of the ParaScope environment and it is based on the ideas proposed in [7] and [8]. We have described some modifications or extensions that we have made to their proposal in order to improve the quality of the distribution process when dealing with Fortran programs. The extensions that we have proposed can be grouped into:

- Techniques to increase the amount of reference patterns analyzed and affinity relations from their analysis. The aim of the three techniques evaluated (expression substitution, subscript substitution and induction variable detection) is to increase the scope of reference pattern analysis by considering patterns across several statements in the loop bodies and using other than loop control variables in the array subscript functions.
- Optimizations that improve the output of the *DAG* partitioning algorithms, both inter- and intra-dimensional.

We have concluded that these techniques and optimizations are promising and useful to improve the quality of the automatic data distribution process. However, results in the paper do not fully reflect this conclusion because a high percentage of the routines used in our benchmark platform just use one-dimensional data structures, which are less sensitive to the changes proposed than higher dimensional ones.

Although out of the scope of this paper, it is important to notice that the techniques described in Section 2.1 are useful to find new alignment preferences but also to better estimate communication costs. The cost of the new reference patterns obtained when the techniques are applied can modify the distribution functions generated.

Currently we are implementing the phase where dynamic realignment is included. Realignment is considered either between loops in a procedure or between procedures. Due to the high cost of realignment, DDT decides whether it is better to pay the realignment cost penalty and execute a loop or procedure with the appropriate alignment functions rather than execute it with less appropriate alignment functions. Other researchers are considering this topic, either between loops [3] and [17] o within nested loops [18].

5 Acknowledgements

This work has been partially supported by CONVEX Computer Corporation, CONVEX Supercomputers S.A.E, CEPBA (European Center for Parallelism of Barcelona) and by the Ministry of Education of Spain under contract TIC-880/92. We gratefully acknowledge the helpful comments of Miquel Huguet from CONVEX Supercomputer, S.A.E and Robert Metzger from CONVEX Computer Corporation in improving an earlier draft of this paper.

References

1. M. Gupta. *Automatic Data Partitioning on Distributed Memory Multicomputers.* PhD thesis, Center for Reliable and High-Performance Computing, University of Illinois at Urbana-Champaign, 1992.

2. M. Gupta, S. Midkiff, E. Schonberg, P. Sweeney, K.Y. Wang, and K. Burke. PTRAN II - a compiler for High Performance Fortran. In *4th Workshop on Compilers for Parallel Computers*, December 1993.

3. P. Crooks and R.H. Perrot. An automatic data distribution generator for distributed memory MIMD machines. In *4th Workshop on Compilers for Parallel Computers*, December 1993.

4. High Performance Fortran Forum. High Performance Fortran language specification, version 1.0. *Scientific Programming*, 2(1–2), 1993.

5. B. Chapman, T. Fahringer, and H. Zima. Automatic support for data distribution on distributed memory multiprocessor systems. In *6th Workshop on Languages and Compilers for Parallel Computing*, August 1993.

6. S. Hiranandani, K. Kennedy, and C. Tseng. Compiling Fortran-D for MIMD distributed-memory machines. *Communications of the ACM*, 35(8), August 1992.

7. J. Li and M. Chen. Index domain alignment: Minimizing cost of cross-referencing between distributed arrays. In *Frontiers90: 3rd Symposium on the Frontiers of Massively Parallel Computation*, October 1990.

8. J. Li and M. Chen. Compiling communication-efficient programs for massively parallel machines. *IEEE Trans. on Parallel and Distributed Systems*, 2(3), July 1991.

9. K. Kennedy, K. McKinley, and C-W. Tseng. Interactive parallel programming using the ParaScope editor. Technical Report CRPC-TR90096, Center for Research on Parallel Computation, Rice University, October 1990.

10. Applied Parallel Research Inc. xHPF version 1.0, user's guide. December 1993.

11. A. Gueist, A. Beguelin, J. Dongarra, W. Jiang, R. Manchek, and V. Sunderam. PVM3 user's guide and reference manual. Technical Report ORNL/TM-12187, Oak Ridge National Laboratory, May 1993.

12. L. Pointer (editor). PERFormance Evaluation for Cost-effective Transformations report:1. Technical Report 896, CSRD University of Illinois at Urbana-Champaign, July 1989.

13. K. Dixit. The SPEC benchmarks. *Parallel Computing*, (17), 1991.

14. E. Ayguade, J. Labarta, J. Garcia, and M. Girones. Partitioning methods: Implementation report. Technical report, CEPBA European Center for Parallelism of Barcelona, October 1993.

15. J. Peir. *Program Partitioning and Synchronization on Multiprocessor Systems.* PhD thesis, University of Illinois at Urbana-Champaign, 1986.

16. C. Leiserson, F. Rose, and J. Saxe. Optimizing synchronous circuitry by retiming. In *3rd Caltech Conference on VLSI*, March 1983.

17. R. Bixby, K. Kennedy, and U. Kremer. Automatic data layout using 0-1 integer programming. In *International Conference on Parallel Architectures and Compilation Techniques*, August 1994.

18. S. Chatterjee, J.R. Gilbert, and R. Schreiber. Mobile and replicated alignment of arrays in data-parallel programs. In *Supercomputing'93*, November 1993.

Array Distribution in Data-Parallel Programs

Siddhartha Chatterjee [1], John R. Gilbert [2], Robert Schreiber [1] and Thomas J. Sheffler [1]

[1] Research Institute for Advanced Computer Science,
Mail Stop T27A-1, NASA Ames Research Center, Moffett Field, CA 94035-1000
(sc@riacs.edu, schreibr@riacs.edu, sheffler@riacs.edu).
[2] Xerox Palo Alto Research Center, 3333 Coyote Hill Road, Palo Alto, CA 94304-1314
(gilbert@parc.xerox.com).

Abstract. We consider distribution at compile time of the array data in a distributed-memory implementation of a data-parallel program written in a language like Fortran 90. We allow dynamic redistribution of data and define a heuristic algorithmic framework that chooses distribution parameters to minimize an estimate of program completion time. We represent the program as an alignment-distribution graph. We propose a divide-and-conquer algorithm for distribution that initially assigns a common distribution to each node of the graph and successively refines this assignment, taking computation, realignment, and redistribution costs into account. We explain how to estimate the effect of distribution on computation cost and how to choose a candidate set of distributions. We present the results of an implementation of our algorithms on several test problems.

1 Introduction

One of the major decisions in compiling data-parallel programs for distributed-memory parallel computers is the mapping of data and computation to the multiple processors of the machine. A good mapping minimizes program completion time by balancing the opposing needs of parallelism and communication: spreading the data and work over many processors increases available parallelism, but also increases communication time.

Most compilation systems (*e.g.*, Fortran D [11] and High Performance Fortran [10]) divide the data mapping problem into two phases: *alignment*, in which the relative positions of arrays are determined within a Cartesian grid called a *template*, and *distribution*, in which the template is partitioned and mapped to a processor grid. We have dealt with the alignment problem previously [2, 5, 6]. This paper focuses on the distribution problem.

1.1 Distribution

The distribution of a template specifies for each of its dimensions the number of processors p it is spread across and the block size k used in the distribution. Template cell i is located at processor $(i \text{ div } k) \bmod p$. The distribution of a multidimensional template is the tensor product of the distributions of each of its dimensions. The HPF declarations

```
CHPF$ TEMPLATE T(100,200)
CHPF$ PROCESSORS P(4,8)
CHPF$ DISTRIBUTE T(CYCLIC(1),CYCLIC(10)) ONTO P
```

[1] The work of these authors was supported by the NAS Systems Division via Contract NAS 2-13721 between NASA and the Universities Space Research Association (USRA).

specify the distribution of a template to a 4 × 8 processor grid with block sizes 1 and 10 in the two dimensions. The mapping of a data array is determined by the composition of its alignment to the template and the distribution of the template to the processor grid. Note that distributing a template dimension to one processor is equivalent to making that dimension resident in memory.

The distribution problem is to determine template distribution parameters that minimize the completion time of the program. There are two variants of the problem, depending on whether or not we allow redistribution of templates and arrays.

Problem 1 (Static). Given a program and a number of processors, determine a common distribution for all array objects that minimizes the completion time.

Problem 2 (Dynamic). Given a program and a number of processors, determine the distribution at each definition and each use of every array object so that the completion time is minimized.

1.2 Problem formulation

In our system, program data flow is represented as a directed, edge-weighted graph called the Alignment-Distribution Graph (ADG) [4]. It consists of ports, nodes, and edges. Ports represent array objects manipulated by the program, nodes represent program operations, and edges connect definitions of array objects to their uses. See Section 6 for examples. Alignment and distribution are attributes of ports (array objects). Each port has an alignment to a template, and a distribution of the template to a processor grid. With one exception, which is noted in Section 5.3, we treat the ADG in this paper as an *undirected* graph.

Nodes constrain the alignments and distributions of their ports. Alignment constraints have been discussed elsewhere [4]. The distribution constraint at a node is particularly simple: all of its ports must be aligned to the same template, with the same distribution parameters. It is therefore sensible to speak of of "the distribution at a node".

The ADG makes communication explicit. Communication occurs when the alignment or distribution is different at the end points of an edge. ADG edges connect the definition of an object to its uses. *Realignment* occurs along an edge when the alignment of the object at the tail of the edge is different from its alignment at the head. *Redistribution* occurs along an edge when the distribution of the template at the tail is different from the distribution at the head. Alignments are chosen in a previous compilation phase, and are considered fixed here. The interaction of alignments and distributions is quite important in determining good distributions. We cover this topic in Section 5.3.

Let δ be a mapping from ADG nodes to distributions. The computation time T_{comp} of an ADG node u is a function of its computation, the sizes of the array objects it computes, the alignments of its ports, and the distribution $\delta(u)$ at the node. The cost of any realignment that occurs on out-edges of an ADG node can be accounted for at the node, as we show in Section 5.3. Thus, we include a term T_{node}, called a *node cost*, that accounts for computation and realignment, in our model of completion time. All our techniques assume that the dependence of node cost T_{node} on distribution can be made explicit. Section 5.3 discusses techniques for doing this.

The redistribution time T_{redist} of an edge (u, v) depends on the weight w_{uv} of the edge, and the distributions $\delta(u)$ and $\delta(v)$ of nodes u and v. Specifically, we assume that the cost of redistribution along edge (u, v) is the product of three terms: a machine parameter ρ that gives the cost per data item of all-to-all personalized communication; the edge data weight w_{uv} (the total data volume carried by the ADG edge); and the *discrete distance* between the distributions $\delta(u)$ and $\delta(v)$, defined to be 0 if $\delta(u)$ equals $\delta(v)$ and 1 if they differ. (Section 5.1 provides some empirical evidence justifying this model.)

Our model of completion time of the ADG $G = (V, E)$ with alignment map α and distribution map δ is

$$T_{finish}(G, \alpha, \delta) = \sum_{v \in V} T_{node}(v, \alpha, \delta(v)) + \sum_{(u,v) \in E} T_{redist}(w_{uv}, \delta(u), \delta(v)). \quad (1)$$

In the sequel whenever we refer to a "cost" we mean either the node cost T_{node} of an ADG node, or the redistribution time T_{redist} of an edge. To simplify notation, we shall suppress the α in T_{finish} and T_{node} in the sequel, since we assume that α has already been determined, and is not subject to further change.

Given the ADG G and the alignment mapping α, the goal is to determine the distribution mapping δ that minimizes the completion time $T_{finish}(G, \alpha, \delta)$. We shall call a distribution mapping *optimal* if it minimizes T_{finish}, given G and α.

We collect here some definitions and facts from graph theory and linear algebra that we will use in the paper. Let $S \subseteq V$ be a subset of the nodes of the ADG. We denote by $G(S)$ the ADG subgraph induced by S. We assume that the set of candidate distributions D has been determined. (We show in Section 5.2 how to do this.) A distribution mapping of S is a function $\delta : S \mapsto D$. It is *static* if $\delta(s)$ is the same for all elements s of S, otherwise it is *dynamic*. If δ is defined on S, we call the set S static or dynamic depending on whether the restriction of δ to S is static or dynamic.

Let $S \subseteq V$ be given. Define $T_{node}(S, d) = \sum_{v \in S} T_{node}(v, d)$. We denote by $T_{stat}(S)$ the minimum over all $d \in D$ of $T_{node}(S, d)$, and call this the *static cost* of $G(S)$. It is the minimum completion time of $G(S)$, given that all nodes in S are constrained to have the same distribution, since there is no redistribution when S is static. Define a *best static distribution* of the subgraph $G(S)$ as some distribution d that achieves the static cost of $G(S)$.

A partition of S is a set of disjoint subsets of S whose union equals S. We shall primarily deal with partitions of the nodes of an ADG subgraph $G(S)$ consisting of two subsets, S_1 and S_2. For such a two-way partition, define cut$(S_1, S_2) \equiv \{ (u, v) \in E \mid u \in S_1, v \in S_2 \}$, and a redistribution cost cut-cost$(S_1, S_2) \equiv \rho \sum_{(u,v) \in \text{cut}(S_1, S_2)} w_{uv}$.

Let X be any undirected, edge-weighted, n vertex graph with vertices V and edges E. The Laplacian matrix of X is the symmetric $n \times n$ matrix defined by

$$L(X)_{ij} = \begin{cases} -w_{ij}, & i \neq j \text{ and } (i, j) \in E \\ \sum_{k \neq i} w_{ik}, & i = j \\ 0, & \text{otherwise.} \end{cases}$$

If we define the weighted adjacency matrix $A(X)$ in the usual manner and the weighted degree matrix $D(X) = \text{diag}(d_i)$, where d_i is the sum of the weights of edges incident on vertex i, then $L(X) = D(X) - A(X)$. A Laplacian matrix has nonnegative eigenvalues, one of which is always zero. If the graph X is connected, then the eigenvalue zero is simple, and the corresponding eigenvector is the vector $e = (1, \ldots, 1)^T$.

Let x be a real n-vector. We shall make use of p-norms of vectors, defined by

$$\|x\|_p = (\sum_i |x_i|^p)^{1/p},$$

and the ∞-norm, defined by

$$\|x\|_\infty = \max_i |x_i|.$$

Note that the 2-norm is the usual euclidean norm in real n-space, $\mathcal{R}^n$.

1.3 Previous work

Most of the previous work in this area has concentrated on the static version or on simplified dynamic versions of the problem. Wholey [18] uses a hill-climbing procedure to determine the distributions for named variables. (A named variable corresponds, in our formulation, to a subset of the nodes of the ADG. Thus, Wholey considers a restricted version of the dynamic problem.) Gupta [9] uses heuristic methods to determine the distribution parameters. He analyzes communication patterns to determine whether block or cyclic distributions are preferable. He then uses an affinity graph framework to determine block sizes. Finally, he allows at most two array dimensions to be distributed across the processors, and determines the proper aspect ratio by exhaustive enumeration.

Kremer [14] shows that dynamic distribution is NP-complete. Bixby et al. [1] and Kremer et al. [15] present a partial, heuristic solution method. They assume that the user provides a decomposition of the program into phases, which are program fragments that are executed without changing distribution. Dynamic redistribution therefore only occurs between phases. Their system chooses the distribution of each phase. They solve this restricted problem by reducing it to 0-1 integer programming.

The techniques we present here, in contrast, do not require the user to provide any decomposition of the program. We propose, instead, a fast algorithm that first determines node subsets to be given the same distribution and then determines their distributions.

1.4 Organization of the paper

The remainder of the paper is organized as follows. Sections 2 through 4 discuss our algorithm for determining distributions. Section 5 explains details of cost modeling. Section 6 shows experimental results from our implementation of the algorithm. Finally, Section 7 presents conclusions and future work.

2 The distribution algorithm

The dynamic distribution problem is to choose a distribution mapping that minimizes completion time T_{finish} with given ADG and alignment mapping. Our formulation of the distribution problem resembles graph partitioning; but unlike classical graph partitioning problems, there is no intrinsic balance criterion in our problem formulation. Moreover, the tension between T_{node} and T_{redist} makes this problem interesting. Kremer [14] proved that dynamic distribution NP-complete. We therefore seek good heuristics rather than exact algorithms for the problem. This section gives an overview of our algorithm; the next three sections discuss details.

Assume that we have chosen a set $D = \{\delta_1, \ldots, \delta_d\}$ of candidate distributions. (Section 5.2 discusses how we do this.)

Algorithm 1 approximately solves the dynamic distribution problem using the divide-and-conquer paradigm. If it determines that the whole ADG should have a static distribution, then it chooses a best static distribution of G. Otherwise it partitions the ADG into two subgraphs and recursively determines dynamic distributions for each of them. The conquer step which follows chooses the better of two alternatives: either the union of these two dynamic subset distributions, or the best possible static distribution for the whole ADG. Thus, rather than requiring user intervention, Algorithm 1 automatically finds sets of nodes that it constrains to share a common distribution. It then determines distributions for these sets. The key to the algorithm is the partitioner, which must choose a partition that groups strongly related nodes in the same subset.

Algorithm 1 (Top-down partitioning of ADG for distribution analysis.)
Input: S, a set of ADG nodes; D, a set of candidate distributions.
Output: δ, a distribution mapping from S to D; ct, the completion time of set S.

```
 1   sc ← static-cost(G(S))
 2   sd ← best-static-distribution(G(S))
 3   if termination condition is reached then
 4       ct ← sc
 5       δ(v) ← sd for each v in S
 6   else
 7       [S₁, S₂] ← partition(S)
 8       [δ₁, ct₁] ← Algorithm 1(S₁, D)
 9       [δ₂, ct₂] ← Algorithm 1(S₂, D)
10       dynamic-cut ← {(u, v) ∈ E | u ∈ S₁, v ∈ S₂, δ₁(u) ≠ δ₂(v)}
11       dynamic-cut-cost ← ρ Σ₍ᵤ,ᵥ₎∈dynamic-cut wᵤᵥ
12       dc ← ct₁ + ct₂ + dynamic-cut-cost
13       if dc < sc then
14           ct ← dc
15           δ ← δ₁ ∪ δ₂
16       else
17           ct ← sc
18           δ(v) ← sd for each v in S
19       endif
20   endif
21   return [δ, ct]
```

The divide phase calls a partitioning routine on line 7 that returns a partition of the node set S into S_1 and S_2. The conquer phase calls Algorithm 1 recursively on the subsets S_1 and S_2 and determines dc, the completion time achieved using the given partition, with dynamic distribution of each subset (line 12). If this is less than the static cost of $G(S)$, we define the distribution mapping as the (disjoint) union of the mapping returned by the recursive calls. Otherwise, each node of S is mapped to a best static distribution of $G(S)$.

Section 3 discusses partitioning strategies, and Section 4 discusses the termination condition. We show in Section 3 that the costs of our implementations of the function *partition* for an n-vertex subset S are $O(n^3)$. Hence, Algorithm 1 has a worst-case complexity of $O(n^4)$. If the partitions we choose turn out to be well-balanced, however, then its complexity can be as small as $O(n^3)$.

3 Partitioning

A core routine of Algorithm 1 is the partitioner, which takes a subset of ADG nodes S and partitions it into two subsets S_1 and S_2. Algorithm 1 then independently computes candidate distribution mappings for the induced subgraphs. Our key partitioning heurisitic is the following: choose a partition that minimizes $T_{stat}(S1) + T_{stat}(S2)$, the sum of the static costs of S_1 and S_2 and cut-cost(S_1, S_2).

In this section we present two algorithms of polynomial complexity for approximately solving this problem. Both encode the problem as the minimization of a real-valued function of the vertices of the unit n-dimensional cube, and both embed this minimization in an easier continuous problem.

The approximately optimal partitions that these two algorithms provide could be improved further by a subsequent improvement procedure of Kernighan-Lin type, in which nodes are moved from one subset to the other singly, in order to further reduce the cost of the partition. We do not yet know whether such postprocessing is worthwhile.

3.1 The partitioning problem as nonlinear multidimensional optimization

In recasting the partitioning problem in matrix terms, we use techniques seen in spectral graph partitioning methods [16].

Let S be an n-vertex subset of ADG nodes. Assume we are given a partition of S into two disjoint subsets S_1 and S_2. Let x be an n-vector with elements $+1$ and -1 encoding this partition; nodes corresponding to the $+1$ elements of x belong to S_1, while those corresponding to the -1 elements belong to S_2. Let e be the n-vector of all 1's.

As above, $D = \{\delta_1, \ldots, \delta_d\}$ is a given set of candidate distributions. Construct the $d \times n$ node-cost matrix C, such that $C_{ij} = T_{node}(j, \delta_i)$ is the node cost of node j with distribution δ_i.

We now formulate the various costs in terms of matrix expressions. The sum of the weights of the edges crossing the cut is given by $\frac{1}{4}\sum_{(u,v)\in E} w_{uv}(x_u - x_v)^2$, since the term $(x_u - x_v)^2$ contributes zero if x_u and x_v have the same sign and 4 if they have different signs. This may be rewritten using matrix notation:

$$\sum_{(u,v)\in E} w_{uv}(x_u - x_v)^2 = x^T L x.$$

The redistribution cost of edges crossing the cut is therefore $\frac{1}{4}\rho x^T L x$. To get the static costs of S_1 and S_2, we need to extract the nodes belonging to each set. Given that the elements of x are $+1$ and -1, we see that the corresponding elements of the vector $\frac{1}{2}(e + x)$ are 1 and 0, while those of the vector $\frac{1}{2}(e - x)$ are 0 and 1. Element i of the matrix-vector product $\frac{1}{2}C(e + x)$ gives the cost of the $+1$ partition if each node in that partition has distribution δ_i. The static cost of S_1 is therefore $\frac{1}{2}\min_i(C(e + x))_i$, while that of S_2 is $\frac{1}{2}\min_i(C(e - x))_i$. We therefore seek to minimize

$$\frac{1}{4}\rho x^T L x + \frac{1}{2}\min_i(C(e + x))_i + \frac{1}{2}\min_i(C(e - x))_i \qquad (2)$$

over the set of vectors with elements ± 1, not all elements the same. This is the set of vertices of the n-dimensional unit hypercube, without the two elements e and $-e$ whose elements are all of the same sign. We denote this set by H_n.

Rewrite the matrix $C = B - M$, where B is a matrix whose entries are a constant b, larger than $\max_{ij} C_{ij}$; M is the "savings" matrix.

Note that all elements of the products $M(e + x)$ and $M(e - x)$ are nonnegative, as the elements of M are positive and the elements of $(e + x)$ and $(e - x)$ are nonnegative. Hence,

$$\min_i (Cy)_i = \min_i ((B - M)y)_i = b \sum_i y_i - \max_i (My)_i = b \sum_i y_i - \|My\|_\infty.$$

The following constrained minimization problem is therefore equivalent to equation (2):

$$\min_{x \in H_n} \frac{1}{4} \rho x^T L x - \frac{1}{2}\|M(e + x)\|_\infty - \frac{1}{2}\|M(e - x)\|_\infty. \tag{3}$$

Note the two kinds of terms in the cost function. The redistribution term $\frac{1}{4}x^T L x$ is sensitive only to the edges of the ADG. The other two node-cost terms consider only the node characteristics.

The minimization problem (3) is combinatorial, and may be as hard as the original distribution problem! Our heuristic approach is to first change the search space to a convex, closed, bounded region of $\mathcal{R}^n$, and then to replace the objective function by a differentiable approximation. We present two algorithms of this type for approximately solving (3).

3.2   Algorithm NL

The first algorithm (called NL for nonlinear) uses techniques from constrained nonlinear optimization to solve (3). We first change the problem to a continuous version, replacing the ∞-norm by a $2p$-norm for sufficiently large integer p, and minimizing over the surface of the n-dimensional unit $2p$-norm ball rather than over the vertices of the n-dimensional unit hypercube.[3] We return to the discrete domain by taking the sign of the elements of the solution of the continuous problem. We need to exclude the positive and negative orthants, since if all elements of x have the same sign, no partition is produced. A simple constraint, which we use, is to require that x be orthogonal to e. Let $U_p = \{x \in \mathcal{R}^n \mid e^T x = 0, \quad \|x\|_p = 1\}$. The problem thus becomes

$$\min_{x \in U_{2p}} \frac{1}{4} \rho x^T L x - \frac{1}{2}\|M(e + x)\|_{2p} - \frac{1}{2}\|M(e - x)\|_{2p}. \tag{4}$$

Nonlinear optimization problem (4) can be solved by standard iterative methods like successive quadratic programming [7]. While the complexity of each iterative step is independent of p, convergence depends on p. In practice, choosing $p = 2$ appears to be adequate.

The cost of partitioner NL depends on p, on the particular minimization procedure, and on n; the dependence on n is $O(n^3)$ for standard optimization procedures.

---

[3] The definition of the p-norm of a vector involves the absolute values of its components. An even-integer p-norm makes the absolute values unnecessary and is smooth at $x = 0$.

3.3 Algorithm CC

In this section we describe an approximate solution technique that may be significantly less costly than Algorithm NL. The idea in this algorithm (called CC for convex combinations) is to solve approximately the communication-only problem and the node-only problem in the continuous domain and to then search for the minimizer of equation (3) among the convex combinations of the two extremal vectors.

The vector that minimizes the communication term $x^T L x$ among vectors of unit 2-norm is e (since $e^T L e = 0$); among vectors of unit 2-norm orthogonal to e, its minimizer is the eigenvector of L corresponding to the smallest nonzero eigenvalue (called the Fiedler vector). We rescale the Fiedler vector to have unit infinity norm, and call it x_L. (Note that finding a single eigenvector is somewhat cheaper than finding all of them.)

As for the node term, we require a vector x such that $M(e + x)$ and $M(e - x)$ are simultaneously large.[4] Note that M is elementwise positive, so that e maximizes the infinity norm of $M z$ among vectors z with unit infinity norm. We therefore expect that e will be far from orthogonal to the right singular vector x_1 of M corresponding to the largest singular value. (This is the vector z of unit 2-norm that maximizes the 2-norm of $M z$.) By the Perron-Frobenius theorem [17], x_1 must have positive elements. The second right singular vector of M maximizes the norm of $M z$ among unit vectors z orthogonal to x_1. Therefore, if we choose x of infinity norm one in the direction of x_2, then both $x + e$ and $x - e$ will inherit the large component that e has in the direction x_1, making both $M(x + e)$ and $M(x - e)$ large. Call this vector x_M.

We now search along the line between x_L and x_M for the minimizer, i.e., we seek λ in $[0, 1]$ such that the vector $x = \lambda x_L + (1 - \lambda) x_M$ minimizes the objective function in (3). Since both x_L and x_M are only determined up to sign, we replace x_M by $-x_M$ if necessary to make the two vectors agree in sign in at least one element before beginning this line search. (Consider, otherwise, the effect of $x_M = -x_L$.) We explore the search space using golden-section search [8]. Finally, we revert to the discrete domain by taking the sign of the continuous solution.

Our implementation of CC runs in time $O(n^3)$.

4 Termination

The second unspecified element of Algorithm 1 is the termination criterion that determines when to stop dividing. We could recurse all the way down to single nodes, but this is often unnecessary. In this section, we develop certain lemmas regarding structural properties of ADG subgraphs that tell us when we can safely stop the recursion.

First, some definitions. A subgraph $G(S)$ of the ADG G is *optimally static* if some optimal distribution mapping for G assigns the same distribution to all nodes in S. $G(S)$ is *necessarily static* if every optimal distribution mapping for G assigns the same distribution to all nodes in S.

For $v \in V$, let $\delta_{opt}(v)$ be some distribution d that minimizes $T_{node}(v, d)$. We call $\delta_{opt}(v)$ local minimum cost distribution at v. For any $S \subseteq V$, let $\delta_{opt}(S)$ be a best static distribution of $G(S)$, i.e., some value of d that minimizes $\sum_{v \in S} T_{node}(v, d)$.

S is *unanimous* if there is a best static distribution $\delta_{opt}(S)$ that is also a local minimum cost distribution for each node $v \in S$; that is, there is some distribution d such that, for all nodes $v \in S$, $d = \delta_{opt}(v) = \delta_{opt}(S)$.

---

[4] We measure length in the infinity norm; but because of the bound $\|z\|_\infty \leq \|z\|_2 \leq n^{1/2} \|z\|_\infty$ that holds for all $z \in \mathcal{R}^n$, we can switch to the 2-norm $\|z\|_2$ without danger.

Define $\Delta(S)$ as $\min_d \sum_{v \in S} T_{node}(v, d) - \sum_{v \in S} \min_d T_{node}(v, d)$. $\Delta(S)$ gives the difference in node-cost between placing the entire node set at its best static distribution and placing each node at its local minimum cost distribution. Clearly, $\Delta(S) = 0$ if and only if S is unanimous; it is a measure of "dissension" in S. Define $\theta(S)$ as $\min_{v \in S} (\min_{d \neq \delta_{opt}(v)} T_{node}(v, d) - T_{node}(v, \delta_{opt}(v)))$. $\theta(S)$ gives the least possible cost of changing the distribution of a node in S from its local minimum to the distribution of next lowest cost. Let $w(S)$ be the total weight of edges with exactly one endpoint in S, multiplied by the communication parameter ρ. Finally, define mincut(S) to be the smallest possible redistribution cost incurred when S is dynamic, i.e., mincut$(S) =$ min cut-cost(S_1, S_2) where the minimum is taken over all partitions of S into two nonempty subsets.

Now we prove some lemmas regarding the static properties of subgraphs. Our goal is to prove that a subgraph is optimally or necessarily static, because then we know that it is safe to terminate the recursion.

If $\Delta(S)$ is large, then it is hard to satisfy all nodes with a single, static distribution. Also, if $w(S)$ is also large, then the nodes that border S may "pull" its elements toward different distributions. On the other hand, when $G(S)$ has no low-weight edge cutset, it will be expensive to allow it to be dynamic. These competing factors are directly comparable, as we now demonstrate.

Lemma 3 (Min-cut). *If* mincut$(S) \geq w(S) + \Delta(S)$ *for a set* S, *then* S *is optimally static.*

Proof. Omitted in extended abstract. Appears in RIACS technical report [3]

The next lemma establishes sufficient conditions for a subgraph $G(S)$ to be optimally static in the special case where it is unanimous. This strengthens Lemma 3 for this case.

Lemma 4 (Unanimous). *If set* S *is unanimous and* mincut$(S) + \theta(S) \geq w(S)$, *then* S *is optimally static.*

Proof. Omitted in extended abstract. Appears in RIACS technical report [3]

The final lemma shows how an optimally static subgraph may be enlarged while remaining optimally static.

Lemma 5 (Accretion). *Let* S *be optimally static and assume* $v \notin S$. *Define* $w(v, S)$ *to be* ρ *multiplied by the sum of the weights of edges connecting* v *to* S, *and similarly define* $w(v, \bar{S})$ *as* ρ *times the sum of the weights of all other* v-*incident edges. Finally, define* range(v) *as* $(\max_d T_{node}(v, d) - \min_d T_{node}(v, d))$. *If* $w(v, S) \geq w(v, \bar{S}) +$ range(v), *then* $S \cup \{v\}$ *is optimally static.*

Proof. Omitted in extended abstract. Appears in RIACS technical report [3]

Note that the computation involved in verifying the inequalities is dominated by the time taken to find the global minimum cut mincut(S). A naive algorithm for this would run n single-source single-sink minimum cut computations (n being the number of nodes in S) for a total cost of $O(n^3)$ or more. Recently, Karger and Stein [13] developed a probabilistic algorithm for this problem with $\tilde{O}(n^2)$ running time.

5 Modeling

This section fills in certain details concerning the modeling of the distribution problem. The specific issues covered here are use of the discrete metric for redistribution cost, choosing candidate distributions, and building the node-cost matrix C.

5.1 Redistribution cost

Changing distributions typically involves all-to-all personalized communication through the router in a parallel machine. Each processor goes through two steps to complete the process: first, it must examine the data it currently holds, compute the identity of the processor that will hold it in the new distribution, and add it to the message buffer for that processor; then it must send out all the messages to the network. Rather than build a very detailed model of the network incorporating routing algorithms, congestion, and the like, we model such communication using the simple discrete metric. The communication cost is also proportional to the size of the object whose distribution is being changed. Experimental evidence on the CM-5 reveals that this is an adequate model in practice [12]. The program timed was written in CM Fortran. It performs a permutation of the columns of a (BLOCK, BLOCK) mapped square array on a 4×8 processor grid.

5.2 Choosing candidate distributions

The optimization framework described for the distribution problem requires a set of candidate distributions. We now present a heuristic method for generating a reasonable set of distributions based on the characteristics of the array objects present in a program.

A distribution is a partitioning of a t-dimensional template onto the available processors. A distribution may be identified with an ordered pair of t-vectors:

$$((p_1, \ldots, p_t), (k_1, \ldots, k_t)).$$

The first element describes allocation of the processors to the dimensions of the template, and the second gives the block size in each dimension. Thus, template cell $(i_1, \ldots, i_t)$ is located at processor coordinate $((i_1 \text{ div } k_1) \bmod p_1, \ldots, (i_t \text{ div } k_t) \bmod p_t)$.

Generating block sizes requires care. A naive algorithm might simply find the size of the template occupied by the array objects and generate a few block sizes based on that size. However, it is important to recognize and consider the different *feature sizes* of different objects.

We first calculate the extents of all objects in the program. The extent of an array object is the size of the smallest t-dimensional box that encloses it over its iteration space. (Note that the size and position of an object may be functions of loop induction variables.) The extent e of an object is a t-vector.

The collection E of the extents of all objects in the program typically forms a small number of clusters in $\mathcal{R}^t$. We use histogramming to identify these clusters and to select a representative vector for each cluster. Call this set of representative extents R.

The set R is used to generate a set A of processor allocations. Each element of R gives a ratio with which processors are divided among the dimensions of the template. We add to this set an allocation that equally divides the processors if it is not already present. We also add allocations that give only one processor in dimensions for which some extent has a small value.

Block sizes must be chosen based on the extents of objects and also on the manner in which they are used. If an array object varies in size over the course of a program (for example, the active part of the matrix in an LU-decomposition) then a block size of 1 should be examined to achieve load balance over the whole iteration space. Similarly, an array object used in a stencil computation should have a large block size to minimize shift communication.

We extract sets F_1 through F_t of feature sizes from R by projecting individual components. Thus,

$$F_i = \{r_i \,|\, r \in R\}.$$

Additionally, we add a feature size of 1 to F_i if the size of any object varies in dimension i during program execution.

The set D of candidate distributions is constructed from the sets of processor allocations and feature sizes as follows:

$$D = \left\{ ((p_1, \ldots, p_t), (\lceil f_1/p_1 \rceil, \ldots, \lceil f_t/p_t \rceil)) \left| \begin{array}{l} (p_1, \ldots, p_t) \in A \\ \quad f_1 \quad \in F_1 \\ \qquad \vdots \\ \quad f_t \quad \in F_t \end{array} \right. \right\}$$

The resulting set of distributions could potentially be very large. This could render the divide-and-conquer algorithm unusable, because the running times of both our partitioners are sensitive to the number of distributions. In practice, programs typically have only a few feature sizes, and we generate only a few processor allocations. Our feeling is that most programs can be analyzed using a few tens of candidate distributions.

5.3 Building the node-cost matrix C

The model, equation (1), for the completion time of an ADG separates the time into a component depending on the nodes and another component depending on the edges of the ADG.

Nodes perform computation and *intrinsic* communication. Intrinsic communication is communication that is performed as a part of the node computation. An example is the communication of values that happens during the summation of a distributed array. The value of $T_{comp}(v, \alpha, d)$ for an ADG node v with distribution d, and with a given alignment $\alpha(v)$, is determined by finding the largest number of elements held by one processor of the array computed at v under the mapping (of array elements to processors) $d \circ \alpha(v)$, and weighting it by the time per element of the computation done by node v. The only thing that complicates this is that the computation may be performed within a loop nest, and the sizes of the objects being computed can be functions of loop induction variables. So, in general, $T_{comp}(v, \alpha, d)$ is a sum over iterations of the compute time of node v at each iteration.

Edges, on the other hand, perform realignment and redistribution. An individual edge may carry zero or more of these forms of communication. Since alignments are determined in a previous compilation phase, we would like to treat the realignment communication as a known quantity. However, the realignment communication is still a function of distribution. For example, if there is shift communication along an array axis that is memory-resident, the realignment cost is in fact zero. Should an edge carry both realignment and redistribution communication, the realignment communication can be folded into the general redistribution communication at no additional cost.

With this in mind, we use the following approximation in building the matrix C. Here only, we must be aware of the direction of the edges of the ADG, which correspond to the direction of data flow. We find the realignment cost for edge (u, v) assuming distribution d at both head and tail, and add it into the cost $T_{node}(u, d)$ of node u. Thus, in equation (1),

$$T_{node}(G, \alpha, \delta) \equiv \sum_{u \in V} \left(T_{comp}(u, \alpha, \delta(u)) + \sum_{(u,v) \in E} T_{realign}(u, v, \alpha(u), \alpha(v), \delta(u)) \right).$$

$$(5)$$

The cost matrix C is calculated using this definition of T_{node}. It includes the realignment cost of any ADG edge that carries realignment in the node-cost for the node that is the source of the data communicated. The model is approximate; it overestimates communication time when an edge carries both realignment and redistribution communication.

Realignment communication comes in three forms. A change of the array axis to template axis map, or of an alignment stride requires general all-to-all personalized communication; going from a nonreplicated to a replicated alignment (which is how the spread operator of Fortran 90 manifests itself in our system *after* the alignment phase) requires broadcast communication (possibly using a spanning tree algorithm); a change in array offset requires grid communication. We calibrate the communication characteristics of the machine using three parameters ρ, σ, and ν, which give the time per word transferred per processor in the three modes of communication. We use these parameters to scale the maximum processor load in computing realignment time.

6 Experiments

In this section, we compare the performance of partitioning algorithms NL and CC. The test graphs are small, but their characteristics are representative of genuine applications. We implemented both partitioners in MATLAB, and used the number of floating point operations (flops) as measured by MATLAB as a measure of the computation involved in solving a test case.

The first example ADG is shown in Figure 1. It represents the structure seen in multi-disciplinary applications such as the simulation of both the fluid dynamics and the structural mechanics on an airplane wing. In such a simulation, we have two or more data structures that undergo local computation and communication, with occasional transfers of smaller sets of data between them. A schematic of such a code is as follows.

```
REAL A(2000,2000), B(5000,5000)

DO I = 1,N
    A = f(A)
    B(1001:2000, 1) = A(:, 2000)
    B = g(B)
    A(:, 2000) = B(1001:2000, 1)
ENDDO
```

The function f encapsulates the structures computation, and function g encapsulates the fluids computation. We consider two candidate distributions, one being optimal for f and the other being optimal for g. Let the cost vector for the f-node be $10^6[1, 2]^T$ and that for the g-node be $10^6[12, 6]^T$. The two fanout nodes and two section nodes have cost zero (no computation is performed there). The cost of the section-assign (SEC= in

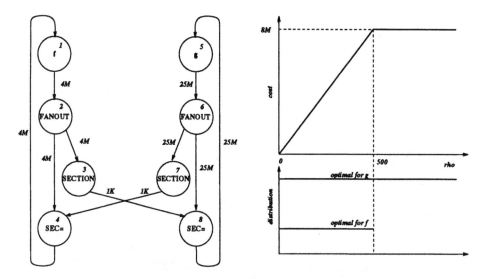

Fig. 1. The ADG for the two-discipline example, and the cost of its optimal partition and the distributions as a function of ρ.

the figure) nodes is negligible compared to the cost of the f- and g-nodes, so we take them to be zero as well. The node-cost matrix of the ADG is

$$C = 10^6 \begin{bmatrix} 1\ 0\ 0\ 0\ 12\ 0\ 0\ 0 \\ 2\ 0\ 0\ 0\ \ 6\ 0\ 0\ 0 \end{bmatrix}.$$

Finally, observe that the size of the left and right sections whose values are interchanged is 1,000.

Applying Lemma 3 to the entire ADG, we see that $w(G) = 0$, $\Delta(G) = 10^6$, and $\text{mincut}(G) = 2000\rho$. If $2000\rho > 10^6$, then the graph is optimally static, with cost 8×10^6. Otherwise, the ADG should be split down the middle, for a cost of $2000\rho + 10^6 + 6 \times 10^6$.

Algorithm 1 with partitioner CC finds this behavior, as shown in Figure 1. Algorithm CC always splits the ADG into two parts down the middle, but the Algorithm 1 checks this against the best static distribution and chooses the best static distribution when $\rho > 500$. Algorithm NL did not always function reliably; the solution depends on its initial starting point, and it often seemed to get stuck in local minima. Algorithm CC required about 7,700 flops, while algorithm NL required between 2.3×10^5 and 2.7×10^6 flops.

The second example is the ADG shown in Figure 2. This example shows the essential features of an alternating-direction implicit (ADI) iteration. We consider three distributions representing row orientation, block orientation, and column orientation. The node-cost matrix of the ADG is

$$C = \begin{bmatrix} 0\ 160\ 160\ 16\ 0\ 640\ 640\ 16 \\ 0\ 320\ 320\ 16\ 0\ 320\ 320\ 16 \\ 0\ 640\ 640\ 16\ 0\ 160\ 160\ 16 \end{bmatrix}.$$

An application of Lemma 3 shows that the ADG should be static at the block orientation if $\rho > 40$ (for a cost of 1,312), and should be dynamic with the first portion of the

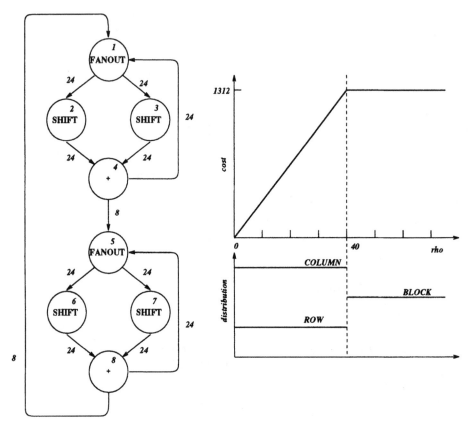

Fig. 2. The ADG for the ADI example, the cost of its optimal partition and the distributions as a function of ρ.

computation being performed in the row orientation and the second portion in the column orientation (for a cost of $672 + 16\rho$).

Again, Algorithm 1 finds the best of the distributions considered, for all ρ between 10 and 70. Partitioner CC was reliable and required about 1.1×10^4 flops, while partitioner NL occasionally failed to find a minimum, and required between 9.8×10^4 and 1.4×10^6 flops.

These examples show that our implementation of partitioner NL is still far from stable. We are investigating the reasons for its aberrant behavior. In any case, partitioner CC requires considerably less computation. The tradeoff between solution time and solution quality is unclear from these small examples; the heuristic used in partitioner CC is quite simple-minded, and it seems possible that partitioner NL may outperform it in solution quality for larger problems.

7 Conclusions

We have formulated the problem of determining data distributions as a partitioning problem on a graph representation of a program, and have presented a divide-and-conquer algorithm to solve the problem. We have developed two different partitioning algorithms for use in this method, and have implemented prototypes of both algorithms. Our tests on some small example programs reveals that these heuristics are reasonable.

We view this work as preliminary. We are currently looking into the effect of weakening the termination criterion on Algorithm 1 in order to limit the number of static subsets explored. This may produce a worthwhile acceleration of Algorithm 1 without worsening the resulting distribution mapping. We are trying to speed up Algorithm CC and are auditioning other hopefuls for the role of the vector x_M in it. We are also experimenting with a procedure that will find optimally static subsets *a priori*, and collapse them before Algorithm 1 is invoked. Finally, we are looking for more difficult and representative problems.

Acknowledgments

Dan Feng suggested the ideas used in Algorithm NL.

References

1. Robert Bixby, Ken Kennedy, and Ulrich Kremer. Automatic data layout using 0-1 integer programming. Technical Report CRPC-TR93349-S, Center for Research on Parallel Computation, Rice University, Houston, TX, November 1993.
2. Siddhartha Chatterjee, John R. Gilbert, and Robert Schreiber. Mobile and replicated alignment of arrays in data-parallel programs. In *Proceedings of Supercomputing'93*, pages 420–429, Portland, OR, November 1993. Also available as RIACS Technical Report 93.08 and Xerox PARC Technical Report CSL-93-7.
3. Siddhartha Chatterjee, John R. Gilbert, Robert Schreiber, and Thomas J. Sheffler. Array distribution in data-parallel programs. Technical Report 94.09, RIACS, 1994.
4. Siddhartha Chatterjee, John R. Gilbert, Robert Schreiber, and Thomas J. Sheffler. Modeling data-parallel programs with the alignment-distribution graph. *Journal of Programming Languages*, 1994. Special issue on compiling and run-time issues for distributed address space machines. To appear.
5. Siddhartha Chatterjee, John R. Gilbert, Robert Schreiber, and Shang-Hua Teng. Optimal evaluation of array expressions on massively parallel machines. In *Proceedings of the Second Workshop on Languages, Compilers, and Runtime Environments for Distributed Memory Multiprocessors*, Boulder, CO, October 1992. Published in SIGPLAN Notices, 28(1), January 1993, pages 68–71. An expanded version is available as RIACS Technical Report TR 92.17 and Xerox PARC Technical Report CSL-92-11.
6. Siddhartha Chatterjee, John R. Gilbert, Robert Schreiber, and Shang-Hua Teng. Automatic array alignment in data-parallel programs. In *Proceedings of the Twentieth Annual ACM SIGACT/SIGPLAN Symposium on Principles of Programming Languages*, pages 16–28, Charleston, SC, January 1993. Also available as RIACS Technical Report 92.18 and Xerox PARC Technical Report CSL-92-13.
7. Roger Fletcher. *Practical Methods of Optimization*. John Wiley & Sons, second edition, 1989.
8. Philip E. Gill, Walter Murray, and Margaret H. Wright. *Practical Optimization*. Academic Press, Orlando, FL, 1981.
9. Manish Gupta. *Automatic Data Partitioning on Distributed Memory Multicomputers*. PhD thesis, University of Illinois at Urbana-Champaign, Urbana, IL, September 1992. Available as technical reports UILU-ENG-92-2237 and CRHC-92-19.
10. High Performance Fortran Forum. High Performance Fortran language specification. *Scientific Programming*, 2(1–2):1–170, 1993.
11. Seema Hiranandani, Ken Kennedy, and Chau-Wen Tseng. Compiling Fortran D for MIMD distributed-memory machines. *Communications of the ACM*, 35(8):66–80, August 1992.

12. Patty Hough and Thomas J. Sheffler. A performance analysis of collective communication on the cm5. Technical report, RIACS, 1994. In Preparation.
13. David Karger and Clifford Stein. On $\tilde{O}(n^2)$ algorithm for minimum cuts. In *Proceedings of the 25th Annual ACM Symposium on Theory of Computing*, pages 757–765, 1993.
14. Ulrich Kremer. NP-completeness of dynamic remapping. Technical Report CRPC-TR93-330-S, Center for Research on Parallel Computation, Rice University, Houston, TX, August 1993. Appears in the *Proceedings of the Fourth Workshop on Compilers for Parallel Computers*, Delft, The Netherlands, December 1993.
15. Ulrich Kremer, John Mellor-Crummey, Ken Kennedy, and Alan Carle. Automatic data layout for distributed-memory machines in the D programming environment. Technical Report CRPC-TR93-298-S, Center for Research on Parallel Computation, Rice University, Houston, TX, February 1993. Appears in *Proceedings of the First International Workshop on Automatic Distributed Memory Parallelization, Automatic Data Distribution and Automatic Parallel Performance Prediction (AP'93)*, Vieweg Verlag, Wiesbaden, Germany.
16. Alex Pothen, Horst D. Simon, and Kang-Pu Liou. Partitioning sparse matrices with eigenvectors of graphs. *SIAM Journal of Matrix Analysis and Applications*, 11(3):430–452, July 1990.
17. Richard S. Varga. *Matrix Iterative Analysis*. Prentice-Hall, Inc., Englewood Cliffs, NJ, 1962.
18. Skef Wholey. *Automatic Data Mapping for Distributed-Memory Parallel Computers*. PhD thesis, School of Computer Science, Carnegie Mellon University, Pittsburgh, PA, May 1991. Available as Technical Report CMU-CS-91-121.

Communication-Free Parallelization via Affine Transformations

Amy W. Lim   Monica S. Lam

Computer Systems Laboratory, Stanford University, Stanford, CA 94305

Email: {aimee,lam}@cs.stanford.edu

Abstract. The paper describes a parallelization algorithm for programs consisting of arbitrary nestings of loops and sequences of loops. The code produced by our algorithm yields all the degrees of communication-free parallelism that can be obtained via loop fission, fusion, interchange, reversal, skewing, scaling, reindexing and statement reordering. The algorithm first assigns the iterations of instructions in the program to processors via affine processor mappings, then generates the correct code by ensuring that the code executed by each processor is a subsequence of the original sequential execution sequence.

1 Introduction

Previous research in vectorizing and parallelizing compilers has shown that parallelization can be improved by a host of high-level loop transformations. These loop transformations include loop fission (or loop distribution), loop fusion, loop interchange, loop reversal, loop skewing, loop scaling, loop reindexing (also known as loop alignment or index set shifting), and statement reordering[1, 2, 6, 7, 8, 9, 10, 16, 17, 18, 19, 20, 21, 22, 23].

A recent focus in parallelizing compiler research has been to devise algorithms that can combine these transformations to achieve specific goals. Loop interchanges, reversals and skewing and combinations thereof have been modeled as unimodular transformations[8, 20, 21]. Algorithms that use unimodular transformations and tiling to improve parallelism and locality on loops whose dependences are represented as distance and direction vectors have been developed. Under this framework, the desired combination of loop transformations is found by finding the suitable unimodular matrix, which can then be used mechanically to generate the desired SPMD (Single Program Multiple Data) code. There are two major limitations in the unimodular loop transformation approach: operations within each iteration are treated as indivisible, and unimodular transformations do not apply to non-perfectly nested loops. Thus unimodular transformations cannot achieve the effects that can be obtained via loop fission, fusion, scaling, or reindexing.

This research was supported in part by DARPA contract DABT63-91-K-0003 and an NSF Young Investigator award.

This paper shows an algorithm that can combine unimodular transformations with loop fusion, fission, scaling and reindexing to optimize programs with an arbitrary nesting of loops and sequences of loops. While it has been shown that these transformations can be modeled as affine transforms[15], researchers are still trying to find algorithms that can exploit this model effectively. In this paper, we show how we can use this affine framework to solve an important problem in parallelization. The following is a synopsis of the key ideas presented in this paper.

Problem formulation: Optimizing for parallelism and communication simultaneously. Experience suggests that minimizing communication is critical to achieving scalable parallel performance. Instead of finding all the parallelism available in a program, we should just find enough parallelism to fully utilize the hardware of a system while incurring minimum communication. This paper solves an important subproblem towards this goal, and that is how to maximize the *degree* of communication-free parallelism. We say that an $O(n^q)$ computation has p degrees of parallelism if it executes in $O(n^{q-p})$ time.

Scope of the algorithm: a comprehensive suite of transformations, and beyond direction and distance vectors. Our algorithm applies to all programs with arbitrary nestings of loops and sequences of loops, whose bounds are large and whose array accesses are affine functions of outer loop indices or loop-invariant variables. Most compilers today represent program dependence information using distance and direction vectors. Our algorithm manipulates the affine access functions directly and are thus more powerful than algorithms based on distance and direction vectors.

An optimization algorithm: Our algorithm finds the maximum degree of parallelism by first assigning the computation to the processors, then generating the SPMD code. We observe that it is possible to tell a particular parallelization is communication-free by simply knowing which iterations are assigned together to the same processor; it is not necessary to know the identity of the processor to which the iterations are assigned. This insight suggests a two-staged algorithm: first determine how the computation is to be partitioned, then determine a particular assignment.

Generating the SPMD code: Given a processor assignment, it is relatively straightforward to generate the correct SPMD code. The code to be executed by each processor is a subsequence of the sequential execution. In contrast, the code generation problem would be very complicated if we had approached the problem by first finding the execution time rather than the processor mappings. More details are discussed in Section 4.

2   Problem statement

We observe that many of the efficient, hand-parallelized computations on large-scale MIMD (Multiple Instruction Multiple Data) machines do not synchronize or communicate in inner loops at all. Instead of trying to first find all the parallelism in a program and reduce the communication later, we ask the question in the opposite direction. Our approach is to first find the maximum amount of parallelism available given that no communication is allowed. Only when the parallelism available is found to be insufficient do we introduce communication and synchronization (in the least frequently parts of the computation) to obtain more parallelism. This paper focuses on a subproblem in this approach, that is, how to maximize the amount of parallelism available in a program that requires no communication. We measure the amount of parallelism by its degree, as defined in Section 1. For example, we are not interested in loop quantization, which increases the amount of parallelism by only a constant factor.

The goal of our algorithm is to find the set of *affine processor mappings* for instructions in the program that maximizes the degree of parallelism in the program. That is, for each instruction S_j, we find an affine mapping $\vec{P}_j(\vec{i}_j) = C_j \vec{i}_j + \vec{c}_j$ which maps each iteration $\vec{i}_j$ of instruction S_j to a (virtual) processor. Suppose we find p degrees of parallelism in a program (with N iterations in each loop). Our algorithm maps the N^p independent threads of computation onto a p-dimensional virtual processor space. These N^p threads can then be distributed across the physical processors in the system. It is easy to derive the data mappings once the computation mappings are determined. Data mappings obtained via this approach are piece-wise affine functions; different regions of the same array may be mapped to processors via different affine mappings.

Affine computation mappings can exploit all the parallelism achievable via a series of loop fission, fusion, interchange, reversal, skewing, reindexing and statement reordering. Nonetheless, affine mappings cannot express all parallelization schemes, therefore algorithms that can only generate affine mappings may not be able to achieve the maximum degree of parallelism possible. For example, we may be able to increase the degree of parallelism by assigning a piece-wise affine processor mapping to each instruction. That is, in code transformation terms, we need to split the index set and schedule different subsets of iterations using a different affine mapping.

Affine mappings also have the limitation that they may lead to a large number of idle processors, processors to which no computation is assigned. This would affect the utilization of hardware and cause poor performance. For example, all the three instructions in the following code have 2 degrees of parallelism.

```
for i₁₁ = 1 to N do
    for i₁₂ = 1 to N do
        x[i₁₁, i₁₂, 1] = x[i₁₁, i₁₂, 1] + ···;      (S₁)
for i₂₁ = 1 to N do
    for i₂₂ = 1 to N do
        x[i₂₁, 1, i₂₂] = x[i₂₁, 1, i₂₂] + ···;      (S₂)
for i₃₁ = 1 to N do
    for i₃₂ = 1 to N do
        x[1, i₃₁, i₃₂] = x[1, i₃₁, i₃₂] + ···;      (S₃)
```

But to exploit all these parallelism using affine mappings, we need to map the iterations of each instruction to a "surface" of a 3-dimensional processor array. The mappings are

$$\vec{P}_1\left(\begin{bmatrix} i_{11} \\ i_{12} \end{bmatrix}\right) = \begin{bmatrix} i_{11} \\ i_{12} \\ 1 \end{bmatrix} \quad \vec{P}_2\left(\begin{bmatrix} i_{21} \\ i_{22} \end{bmatrix}\right) = \begin{bmatrix} i_{21} \\ 1 \\ i_{22} \end{bmatrix} \quad \vec{P}_3\left(\begin{bmatrix} i_{31} \\ i_{32} \end{bmatrix}\right) = \begin{bmatrix} i_{31} \\ i_{32} \\ 1 \end{bmatrix}$$

In this case, a majority of the processors in the processor array would not be assigned any computation. The performance of this parallelization scheme is unacceptable. Fortunately, it is possible to avoid creating any idle processors if we use piece-wise affine mappings.

Ideally, we can find the best piece-wise affine mappings that can find more parallelism than uniform affine mappings, and avoid the creation of idle processors. A straightforward algorithm would be to partition the index set of the iterations into sets with uniform data access relationships. Unfortunately, this technique would be prohibitively expensive. This paper presents an efficient algorithm that can find all the parallelism possible via uniform affine mappings; it introduces piece-wise mappings where necessary to avoid creating idle processors; it is also capable of finding more parallelism than uniform affine processor mappings in some cases.

3 The Algorithm

We first present an outline of the components in the algorithm, highlighting the rationale and explaining how they together solve the problem.

1. The program is first partitioned into slices that do not share any common data, using standard data dependence tests. These different slices can be executed in any order. The following steps apply to each slice.

2. Determine the processor mapping for each instruction in the slice. We observe that it is possible to tell a particular parallelization is communication-free by simply knowing which iterations are assigned together to the same processor; it is not important to know the identity of the processor to which the iterations are assigned. Thus we break this step into the following two substeps.

   (a) Partition the computation into sets of iterations to be executed by a processor. The partition can be described by the nullspace of the linear transformation portion of the affine processor mapping. The goal is to satisfy the constraints that the partitioning is communication-free, while optimizing the degree of parallelism.

   (b) Determine the processor mappings. All the important decisions have been made once the partitioning is determined. This step finds one set of processor mappings that satisfies the partitioning decision above.

3. Generate the SPMD code from the processor mappings. Since no communication is necessary, all the processors execute independently. The SPMD program is correct as long as each processor executes its assignment of operations in the same order as they appear in the original sequential execution.

3.1 Example 1

We now introduce an example that we use to illustrate the steps of the algorithm.

for $i_1 = 1$ to N do
    for $i_2 = 1$ to N do
        $x[i_1, i_2] = x[i_1, i_2] + y[i_1 - 1, i_2];$ (S_1)
        $y[i_1, i_2] = x[i_1, i_2 - 1] * y[i_1, i_2];$ (S_2)

The iteration space for this 2-deep loop nest is shown in Figure 1, assuming
$N = 4$. In Figure 1, the iteration space is divided into rectangular regions where
each region corresponds to one iteration of the loop nest. Within each iteration,
a pair of white and black circles represents an instance of instruction S_1 and
an instance of S_2, respectively. The arrows represent data dependences. It is
easy to see from the figure that the computation can be partitioned into $O(N)$
independent threads. We will show below how our algorithm creates such a
parallel code.

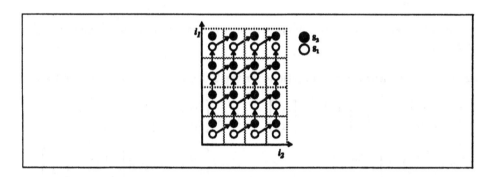

Fig. 1. Iteration space and data dependences for example 1.

3.2 Partition Constraints

No synchronization or data communication is required when the data referenced
by the computation is local to the processor where the computation is executed.
Thus, a communication-free computation partition must satisfy the constraint
expressed in Definition 1.

Definition 1. Let $\vec{F}_{xjr}(\vec{i}_j)$ be the rth array access function for array x in instruction S_j. Let I_j and $\vec{P}_j(\vec{i}_j)$ be the iteration space and processor mapping for
instruction S_j. Then, a computation partition is said to be communication-free
if

$$\forall x \ \forall S_j, S_k \ \forall \vec{i}_j \in I_j \ \forall \vec{i}_k \in I_k \ \forall r, s \ : \ \vec{F}_{xjr}(\vec{i}_j) = \vec{F}_{xks}(\vec{i}_k) \longrightarrow \vec{P}_j(\vec{i}_j) = \vec{P}_k(\vec{i}_k)$$

Definition 2. $R_{jk} : I_j \to 2^{I_k}$ is a *co-reference* function from instruction S_j to S_k if it maps an iteration of S_j onto the set of iterations of S_k that refers to the same data.

$$R_{jk}(\vec{i_j}) = \bigcup_x \bigcup_{r,s} \{\vec{i_k} \in I_k | \vec{F}_{xkr}(\vec{i_k}) = \vec{F}_{xjs}(\vec{i_j})\}$$

A co-reference function is like a data dependence relationship, except that we do not distinguish between read and write operations, and we do not care about the relative execution order of the two instructions. Using the concept of co-reference functions, we can rewrite Definition 1 as Definition 3.

Definition 3. Let R_{jk} be the co-reference function from instruction S_j to S_k. A computation partition is said to be communication-free if

$$\forall S_j, S_k \ \forall \vec{i_j} \in I_j \ \forall \vec{i_k} \in R_{jk}(\vec{i_j}) \ : \ \vec{P_j}(\vec{i_j}) = \vec{P_k}(\vec{i_k})$$

In this paper, we use the notation i_{kb} to denote the bth component of the iteration vector $\vec{i_k}$.

Example 1. The array access functions for the 2-deep loop nest in example 1 are:

$$\vec{F}_{x11}\left(\begin{bmatrix} i_{11} \\ i_{12} \end{bmatrix}\right) = \vec{F}_{x12}\left(\begin{bmatrix} i_{11} \\ i_{12} \end{bmatrix}\right) = \begin{bmatrix} i_{11} \\ i_{12} \end{bmatrix} \qquad \vec{F}_{y11}\left(\begin{bmatrix} i_{11} \\ i_{12} \end{bmatrix}\right) = \begin{bmatrix} i_{11} - 1 \\ i_{12} \end{bmatrix}$$

$$\vec{F}_{x21}\left(\begin{bmatrix} i_{21} \\ i_{22} \end{bmatrix}\right) = \begin{bmatrix} i_{21} \\ i_{22} - 1 \end{bmatrix} \qquad \vec{F}_{y21}\left(\begin{bmatrix} i_{21} \\ i_{22} \end{bmatrix}\right) = \vec{F}_{y22}\left(\begin{bmatrix} i_{21} \\ i_{22} \end{bmatrix}\right) = \begin{bmatrix} i_{21} \\ i_{22} \end{bmatrix}$$

Thus,

$$R_{11}(\vec{i_1}) = \{\vec{i_1} \in I_1 | \vec{F}_{x11}(\vec{i_1}) = \vec{F}_{x11}(\vec{i_1})\} \cup \{\vec{i_1} \in I_1 | \vec{F}_{y11}(\vec{i_1}) = \vec{F}_{y11}(\vec{i_1})\}$$
$$= \{\vec{i_1} \in I_1 | (i'_{11} = i_{11}) \wedge (i'_{12} = i_{12})\}$$
$$R_{12}(\vec{i_1}) = \{\vec{i_2} \in I_2 | \vec{F}_{x21}(\vec{i_2}) = \vec{F}_{x11}(\vec{i_1})\} \cup \{\vec{i_2} \in I_2 | \vec{F}_{y21}(\vec{i_2}) = \vec{F}_{y11}(\vec{i_1})\}$$
$$= \{\vec{i_2} \in I_2 | (i_{21} = i_{11}) \wedge (i_{22} = i_{12} + 1)\}$$
$$\cup \{\vec{i_2} \in I_2 | (i_{21} = i_{11} - 1) \wedge (i_{22} = i_{12})\}$$

Similarly,

$$R_{22}(\vec{i_2}) = \{\vec{i_2} \in I_2 | \vec{F}_{x21}(\vec{i_2}) = \vec{F}_{x21}(\vec{i_2})\} \cup \{\vec{i_2} \in I_2 | \vec{F}_{y21}(\vec{i_2}) = \vec{F}_{y21}(\vec{i_2})\}$$
$$= \{\vec{i_2} \in I_2 | (i'_{21} = i_{21}) \wedge (i'_{22} = i_{22})\}$$
$$R_{21}(\vec{i_2}) = \{\vec{i_1} \in I_1 | \vec{F}_{x11}(\vec{i_1}) = \vec{F}_{x21}(\vec{i_2})\} \cup \{\vec{i_1} \in I_1 | \vec{F}_{y11}(\vec{i_1}) = \vec{F}_{y21}(\vec{i_2})\}$$
$$= \{\vec{i_1} \in I_1 | (i_{11} = i_{21}) \wedge (i_{12} = i_{22} - 1)\}$$
$$\cup \{\vec{i_1} \in I_1 | (i_{11} = i_{21} + 1) \wedge (i_{12} = i_{22})\}$$

A co-reference function maps an iteration of the source instruction to a set of iterations of the target instruction. As illustrated in the example above, the set of target iterations is expressed as a union of subsets of the target iteration space, each of which is described by a set of simple equations. Each of these equations can be of one of two forms. It either expresses a relationship between the source loop indices and the target loop indices, such as $i_{11} = i_{21}$, or it restricts the source or target loop indices to a constant value, such as $i_{11} = 1$. For our simple example, we only have equations relating the two sets of loop indices, and the co-reference functions convey no more information than the distance vectors.

3.3 Objective Function and Affine Mappings

We optimize the maximum degree of parallelism in a program by first finding the maximum degree of parallelism for each instruction, then finding a consistent set of mappings that exploit the degree of parallelism found for each instruction. If we assign an affine mapping $\vec{P}_k(\vec{i}_k) = C_k \vec{i}_k + \vec{c}_k$ to instruction S_k, maximizing the degree of parallelism for this instruction means maximizing the degree of parallelism in $\vec{P}_k$. This is the same as maximizing the rank of the matrix C_k or minimizing the dimensionality of the nullspace of C_k.

Given that our goal is to minimize the dimensionality of the nullspace of P_k, we want to compute the minimal nullspace under affine mappings. Recall that for a communication-free partition, the processor mappings $\vec{P}_k$ must satisfy the constraints in Definition 3. If according to Definition 3, iterations $\vec{i}'_k$ and $\vec{i}_k$ must be mapped to the same processor, i.e. $\vec{P}_k(\vec{i}'_k) = \vec{P}_k(\vec{i}_k)$, then $\vec{i}'_k - \vec{i}_k$ must be in the nullspace of $\vec{P}_k$. Given that $\vec{P}_k$ is an affine mapping, if $\vec{d}_1, \vec{d}_2$ are in the nullspace of $\vec{P}_k$, then any linear combination of $\vec{d}_1$ and $\vec{d}_2$ must also be in the nullspace of $\vec{P}_k$.

Definition 4. The *minimal localized iteration space* of instruction S_k, denoted by L_k, is a minimal set of independent column vectors spanning the space of all $\vec{i}'_k - \vec{i}_k$, where $\vec{i}'_k$ and $\vec{i}_k$ are constrained to be mapped to the same processor by Definition 3.

Before we describe how to find the minimal localized iteration spaces, we introduce another term:

Definition 5. Let G be a *co-reference graph* whose nodes are the dynamic iterations of all the instructions, and the edges connect nodes sharing co-reference relationships. A *simple co-reference cycle* is a cycle in G that begins and ends at iterations of the same instruction, and all the intermediate iterations in the cycle come from all different instructions. The *indirect self co-reference function* of instruction S_k, denoted by R_k^+, maps an iteration $\vec{i}_k$ of S_k to all the iterations of S_k reachable from $\vec{i}_k$ through a simple co-reference cycle in G.

The minimal localized iteration space L_k is the minimum set of column vectors satisfying the following conditions:

1. **Single Instruction:** Map all iterations of the same instruction that reference the same data (directly or indirectly) to the same processor.

$$\forall S_k \ \ \forall \vec{i}_k \in I_k \ \ \forall \vec{i'}_k \in R_k^+(\vec{i}_k) \ : \ \vec{i'}_k - \vec{i}_k \in span(L_k)$$

2. **Multiple Instructions:** If iterations $\vec{i}_j$ and $\vec{i'}_j$ of instruction S_j are mapped to the same processor, all iterations accessing the same data as those accessed by $\vec{i}_j$ and $\vec{i'}_j$ must be mapped to the same processor.

$$\forall S_k \ \ \forall S_j \neq S_k \ \ \forall \vec{i}_j, \vec{i'}_j \in I_j \ \ \forall \vec{i}_k \in R_{jk}(\vec{i}_j) \ \ \forall \vec{i'}_k \in R_{jk}(\vec{i'}_j) \ :$$
$$\vec{i'}_j - \vec{i}_j \in span(L_j) \ \longrightarrow \ \vec{i'}_k - \vec{i}_k \in span(L_k)$$

A straightforward algorithm to compute the minimal localized iteration space would first find R_k^+, for all values of k. Then, initialize each L_k using condition 1, and iterate using condition 2 until all the L_k terms converge. However, it is expensive to compute the R_k^+ terms. Fortunately, we can optimize the algorithm by observing that our ultimate goal is to find L_k, and it is not necessary to compute R_k^+. Space constraints make it impossible to include the full details of the optimized algorithm in this paper. Briefly, our algorithm initializes the L_k values using only the co-reference functions R_{kk}, and uses an iterative step to combine the effects of the indirect self co-reference functions and the affine mapping constraints on the L_k terms at the same time.

We follow the straightforward iterative algorithm to find L_1 and L_2 in our example. We first compute R_1^+ and R_2^+. In this example, we have

$$R_1^+(\vec{i}_1) = \{\vec{i'}_1 \in I_1 | (i'_{11} = i_{11} + 1) \wedge (i'_{12} = i_{12} + 1)\}$$
$$\cup \ \{\vec{i'}_1 \in I_1 | (i'_{11} = i_{11} - 1) \wedge (i'_{12} = i_{12} - 1)\}$$
$$R_2^+(\vec{i}_2) = \{\vec{i'}_2 \in I_2 | (i'_{21} = i_{21} + 1) \wedge (i'_{22} = i_{22} + 1)\}$$
$$\cup \ \{\vec{i'}_2 \in I_2 | (i'_{21} = i_{21} - 1) \wedge (i'_{22} = i_{22} - 1)\}$$

Then the algorithm uses R_1^+ to initialize L_1 and R_2^+ to initialize L_2 according to condition 1. L_1 is initialized to $\{(1,1)\}$ so that all $R_1^+(\vec{i}_1) - \vec{i}_1$ are in the space spanned by L_1. Similarly, L_2 is initialized to $\{(1,1)\}$.

Next, the algorithm iterates using condition 2. We first considering R_{21}. Intuitively, this step finds iterations of instruction S_1 that must be co-located because they use the same data accessed by instance(s) of S_2 which have been mapped to the same processor. From condition 2, we have

$$\forall \vec{i}_2 \in I_2 \ \ \forall \vec{i}_1 \in \left\{ \vec{i}_1 \in I_1 \left| \begin{array}{l} i_{11} = i_{21} \\ i_{12} = i_{22} - 1 \end{array} \right. \right\} \cup \left\{ \vec{i}_1 \in I_1 \left| \begin{array}{l} i_{11} = i_{21} + 1 \\ i_{12} = i_{22} \end{array} \right. \right\}$$

$$\forall \vec{i'}_2 \in I_2 \ \ \forall \vec{i'}_1 \in \left\{ \vec{i'}_1 \in I_1 \left| \begin{array}{l} i'_{11} = i'_{21} \\ i'_{12} = i'_{22} - 1 \end{array} \right. \right\} \cup \left\{ \vec{i'}_1 \in I_1 \left| \begin{array}{l} i'_{11} = i'_{21} + 1 \\ i'_{12} = i'_{22} \end{array} \right. \right\}$$

$$\vec{i'}_2 - \vec{i}_2 \in span(\{(1,1)\}) \ \longrightarrow \ \vec{i'}_1 - \vec{i}_1 \in span(L_1)$$

Since this condition can be satisfied with the initial $L_1 = \{(1,1)\}$. There is no need to increase L_1.

Next, the algorithm considers L_2 using R_{12}. We have

$$\forall \vec{i_1} \in I_1 \; \forall \vec{i_2} \in \left\{ \vec{i_2} \in I_2 \left| \begin{matrix} i_{21} = i_{11} \\ i_{22} = i_{12} + 1 \end{matrix} \right. \right\} \cup \left\{ \vec{i_2} \in I_2 \left| \begin{matrix} i_{21} = i_{11} - 1 \\ i_{22} = i_{12} \end{matrix} \right. \right\}$$

$$\forall \vec{i'_1} \in I_1 \; \forall \vec{i'_2} \in \left\{ \vec{i_2} \in I_2 \left| \begin{matrix} i'_{21} = i'_{11} \\ i'_{22} = i'_{12} + 1 \end{matrix} \right. \right\} \cup \left\{ \vec{i_2} \in I_2 \left| \begin{matrix} i'_{21} = i'_{11} - 1 \\ i'_{22} = i'_{12} \end{matrix} \right. \right\}$$

$$\vec{i'_1} - \vec{i_1} \in span(\{(1,1)\}) \longrightarrow \vec{i'_2} - \vec{i_2} \in span(L_2)$$

Again, the above condition can be satisfied with the initial $L_2 = \{(1,1)\}$. Thus, no addition is necessary for L_2. Upon applying the iterative step, we discover that the initial $L_1 = L_2 = \{(1,1)\}$ remains unchanged and is thus the desired solution. The maximum degree of parallelism m_k for instruction S_k can then be computed from the minimal localized iteration space L_k using

$$m_k = \dim(I_k) - \dim(L_k).$$

Thus, $m_1 = \dim(I_1) - \dim(L_1) = 1$ and $m_2 = \dim(I_2) - \dim(L_2) = 1$.

3.4 Finding the Processor Mappings

If we limit processor mappings to uniform affine mappings, the virtual processor array may need to have more dimensions than the maximum degree of parallelism found in order to exploit all the parallelism. By introducing piece-wise affine transforms where necessary, the dimensionality of the virtual processor array, m_p, is simply the maximum of the maximum degrees of parallelism found among all the instructions. That is,

$$m_p = \max_{S_k} m_k$$

Our algorithm finds affine or piece-wise affine processor mappings such that the following constraints are satisfied.

C1. For each instruction S_k, nullspace of $\vec{P}_k = L_k$
C2. For each pair of instructions S_j and S_k

$$\forall \vec{i_j} \in I_j \; \forall \vec{i_k} \in R_{jk}(\vec{i_j}) : \vec{P}_j(\vec{i_j}) = \vec{P}_k(\vec{i_k})$$

Our algorithm starts by arbitrarily choosing an instruction S among the set of instructions with the largest degree of parallelism, and finding an affine mapping for S such that constraint C1 is satisfied. This decision is then propagated, using C2, to (partially) constrain the affine mappings of all other instructions that share data accesses with S. It is possible that the new constraints on the mapping of an instruction cannot be satisfied by a uniform affine function. However, it can be shown that it is always possible to split the index set of an instruction and find piece-wise affine mapping functions that satisfy all the constraints. The algorithm then repeats this process until all the affine mappings are found.

Note that when calculating any mapping $\vec{P}(\vec{i}) = C\vec{i} + \vec{c}$, non-integer entries in C or $\vec{c}$ can result. Since the mappings are relative, we can always eliminate the rational entry by multiplying all the mappings by the denominator of the rational number.

To continue with example 1, we first compute the number of dimensions m_p in the virtual processor array. We have $m_p = \max(m_1, m_2) = 1$. We then choose a mapping for an instruction S_k with $m_k = m_p$, the largest degree of parallelism. Suppose we choose S_1. The algorithm then finds an affine mapping $\vec{P}_1$ such that constraint C1 is satisfied, i.e. the first row of $\vec{P}_1$ must span the orthogonal space of $span(L_1) = span(\{(1, 1)\})$. Suppose the algorithm sets $\vec{P}_1(\vec{i}_1) = \begin{bmatrix} 1 & -1 \end{bmatrix} \vec{i}_1$.

Next, we propagate the decision of $\vec{P}_1$ to the other instruction (S_2) that share data accesses with S_1. From constraints C1 and C2,

$$\vec{P}_2(\begin{bmatrix} 1 \\ 1 \end{bmatrix}) = \vec{0} \wedge \vec{P}_2(\begin{bmatrix} 1 \\ -1 \end{bmatrix}) \neq \vec{0} \tag{C_1}$$

$$\vec{P}_2(\begin{bmatrix} i_{21} \\ i_{22} \end{bmatrix}) = \vec{P}_1(\begin{bmatrix} i_{21} \\ i_{22} - 1 \end{bmatrix}) = \vec{P}_1(\begin{bmatrix} i_{21} + 1 \\ i_{22} \end{bmatrix}) \tag{C_2}$$

Let $\vec{P}_2(\vec{i}_2) = \begin{bmatrix} a_1 & a_2 \end{bmatrix} \vec{i}_2 + c_1$. We expand the set of constraints to

$$(a_1 + a_2 = 0) \wedge (a_1 - a_2 \neq 0) \tag{C_1}$$

$$a_1 i_{21} + a_2 i_{22} + c_1 = i_{21} - i_{22} + 1 = i_{21} - i_{22} + 1 \tag{C_2}$$

The only solution that satisfies the above constraints for all i_{21} and i_{22} is $a_1 = 1$, $a_2 = -1$ and $c_1 = 1$. Thus, we find an affine mapping $\vec{P}_2(\vec{i}_2) = \begin{bmatrix} 1 & -1 \end{bmatrix} \vec{i}_2 + 1$. Since there is no more unspecified processor mapping, our algorithm terminates.

3.5 Generating Code

Once we have the processor mapping for each instruction, we need to generate the SPMD code. As the computations on different processors are completely disjoint, the code would be correct as long as the code executed by each processor is a subsequence of the original sequential execution. In other words, we can generate the SPMD code by guarding each instruction with the predicate that checks whether the processor should execute the instruction. The SPMD code for our example is

```
for i₁ = 1 to N do
    for i₂ = 1 to N do
        if (p = i₁ − i₂) then
            x[i₁, i₂] = x[i₁, i₂] + y[i₁ − 1, i₂];                    (S₁)
        if (p = i₁ − i₂ + 1) then
            y[i₁, i₂] = x[i₁, i₂ − 1] * y[i₁, i₂];                   (S₂)
```

It is easy to see that the code above is correct, but also that code generated in this manner is extremely inefficient. Instead, we use the following algorithm which can eliminate all the dynamic tests from the innermost loops:

1. Find tight loop bounds for each instruction in the program. This step is based on Ancourt and Irigoin's polyhedron-scanning code generation technique[4]. Let the loop index variables surrounding an instruction be $i_1, \ldots, i_n$, and let B be the set of linear inequalities describing the loop bounds of instruction S_j. We create a new set of inequalities $B' = B \cup \{\vec{p} = P_j(\vec{i})\}$, where P_j is the affine processor mapping for instruction S_j. In the case where we have piece-wise mappings, we apply index set splitting and generate a B' for each subset of instances. We generate the loop bounds of the instances to be executed by a particular processor $\vec{p}$ from B' by projecting the loop indices away in the reverse order of the original loop indices.

2. Merge all the subsequences for each instruction[3]. Let $\vec{i}[1:n]$ denote the first n elements of the iteration vector $\vec{i}$. Suppose instructions S_j and S_k share n common loops. The merged code must execute instance $\vec{i}_j$ of statement S_j before instance $\vec{i}_k$ of statement S_k if $\vec{i}_j[1:n]$ is lexicographically less than $\vec{i}_k[1:n]$, or $\vec{i}_j[1:n] = \vec{i}_k[1:n]$ and statement S_j appears lexically before S_k.

We illustrate the code generation algorithm using our example. Step 1 finds tight loop bounds for each of the two instructions separately. The two loop nests that need to be merged by step 2 are:

$$
\text{MERGE} \left\{
\begin{array}{l}
\text{if } (1 - N \leq p \leq N - 1) \text{ then} \\
\quad \text{for } i_1 = \max(1, 1 + p) \text{ to } \min(N, N + p) \\
\quad i_2 = i_1 - p \\
\quad x[i_1, i_2] = x[i_1, i_2] + y[i_1 - 1, i_2]; \quad (S_1) \\
\\
\text{if } (2 - N \leq p \leq N) \text{ then} \\
\quad \text{for } i_1 = \max(1, p) \text{ to } \min(N, N + p - 1) \\
\quad i_2 = i_1 - p + 1 \\
\quad y[i_1, i_2] = x[i_1, i_2 - 1] * y[i_1, i_2]; \quad (S_2)
\end{array}
\right\}
$$

The second step merges the two subsequences together. It starts with the outermost index p as follows:

$$
\begin{array}{l}
\text{if } (p = 1 - N) \text{ then} \\
\quad x[1, N] = x[1, N] + y[0, N]; \\
\text{if } (2 - N \leq p \leq N - 1) \text{ then}
\end{array}
$$

$$
\text{MERGE} \left\{
\begin{array}{l}
\text{for } i_1 = \max(1, 1 + p) \text{ to } \min(N, N + p) \\
i_2 = i_1 - p \\
x[i_1, i_2] = x[i_1, i_2] + y[i_1 - 1, i_2]; \quad (S_1) \\
\\
\text{for } i_1 = \max(1, p) \text{ to } \min(N, N + p - 1) \\
i_2 = i_1 - p + 1 \\
y[i_1, i_2] = x[i_1, i_2 - 1] * y[i_1, i_2]; \quad (S_2)
\end{array}
\right.
$$

$$
\begin{array}{l}
\text{if } (p = N) \text{ then} \\
\quad y[N, 1] = x[N, 0] * y[N, 1];
\end{array}
$$

The range of p is partitioned into intervals so that the same set of statements is executed by all the possible values of p within an interval. We recursively reapply the algorithm to the indices at the inner levels. The final code for our example is:

```
if (p = 1 - N) then
    x[1, N] = x[1, N] + y[0, N];
if (2 - N ≤ p ≤ N - 1) then
    if (1 ≤ p ≤ N - 1) then
        y[p, 1] = x[p, 0] * y[p, 1];
    for i₁ = max(1, 1 + p) to min(N, N - 1 + p)
        x[i₁, i₁ - p] = x[i₁, i₁ - p] + y[i₁ - 1, i₁ - p];
        y[i₁, i₁ - p + 1] = x[i₁, i₁ - p] * y[i₁, i₁ - p + 1];
    if (2 - N ≤ p ≤ 0) then
        x[N + p, N] = x[N + p, N] + y[N + p - 1, N];
if (p = N) then
    y[N, 1] = x[N, 0] * y[N, 1];
```

4 Related Work

There has been a lot of work on code optimizations for parallel machines. In the following, we restrict our discussion to compiler techniques that are also based on linear and affine transforms.

A significant body of research that uses affine mappings was performed in the context of systolic arrays. In this work, the original loop indices are mapped via an affine function onto the processor-time domain. The virtual processor space is mapped onto hardware directly; dependences in the program are mapped onto communication on the typically neighboring connections in a systolic array.

More recently, Feautrier uses an affine model to schedule instructions for maximum parallelism[11, 12]. His approach is to schedule the instructions to maximize parallelism first, then minimize communication[13]. In the scheduling step, he finds for each instruction an affine mapping to the time domain. Feautrier refers to $O(n^q)$ computations that have $O(n^{q-1})$ degrees of parallelism as computations that execute in linear time. Feautrier has algorithms to find the optimal piece-wise affine scheduling functions for those computations that can complete in linear time. For computations that cannot complete in linear time, he models time as a multi-dimensional space, and has heuristics to schedule the instructions. However, we note that general hierarchical loop structures cannot be faithfully modeled as such; they need to be modeled by a hierarchical time space. Finally, the problem of how to generate code for such schedules has not been resolved.

In contrast, our approach focuses first on minimizing communication and the processor assignment. We only find the affine processor mappings for the instructions and never explicitly represent their time mappings. As no communication is allowed in the problem addressed by this paper, we only need to specify the relative ordering of the instructions executed on each processor. Correctness is guaranteed by making sure that the instructions executed on each processor are a subsequence of the original sequential execution. The SPMD code for each processor inherits the original hierarchical loop structure of the original program.

Huang and Sadayappan also studied the problem of finding a communication-free partitioning[14]. Instead of finding the maximum degree of parallelism in a program, their algorithm only finds one dimension of parallelism. Their program domain is restricted to a sequence of perfectly nested loops, and the instructions within a loop body are scheduled together as indivisible units. Their algorithm thus cannot achieve effects obtainable via loop fusion, fission and reindexing, and it cannot find the same kind of parallelism our algorithm can.

Unimodular loop transforms map a sequential loop nest to another legal sequential loop nest. Parallelizers based on unimodular loop transforms attempt to transform the code such that the outermost possible loops are parallelizable[8, 20, 21]. If the outermost loop is parallelizable, the algorithm has found a communication-free partition for the loop nest. The code in this form can easily be translated into the desired SPMD code because each processor simply executes the code nested within the parallel loop. In other words, the processor mapping is implicitly given by the indices of the parallelized loop. Thus, in a sense, unimodular transforms map the original loop indices to a processor-time domain.

Some of the ideas in this paper are derived from Anderson and Lam's algorithm that minimizes communication across multiple loops[5]. In particular, we use the same approach of first finding the nullspace in processor mappings before determining the rest of the mappings. There are several major differences between the two algorithms. Anderson and Lam ignore neighborhood (or displacement) communication, whereas we do not. Anderson and Lam's algorithm first transforms the individual loop nests using unimodular transforms and loop fission, then finds the data mapping. Our algorithm integrates all the transforms together and is thus more powerful. Our algorithm does not treat loop body as an indivisible unit and it does not use the distance and direction vector abstraction to find parallelism. While Anderson and Lam's algorithm maps data to processors also via an affine mapping, the set of data mappings permitted by our algorithm is larger as the mappings can be piece-wise affine. Finally, Anderson and Lam's algorithm is more complete in that it can introduce communication into the computation when necessary and desirable. We plan to combine some of the ideas used with our algorithm in the future.

5   Conclusion

The first contribution of this paper is in the formulation of the compiler optimization problem. We recommend that compilers should maximize parallelism and minimize communication simultaneously. Thus, instead of asking how much parallelism is in the program, we ask how much parallelism can be exploited for a given amount of communication and synchronization. This paper proposes an algorithm to solve a subproblem in this approach: how to find a communication-free parallelization scheme.

The second contribution of this paper is to show an algorithm that can combine unimodular transformations with loop fusion, fission, scaling, reindexing and statement reordering to optimize programs with arbitrary nestings of loops and sequences of loops. While the relationship between these code transformations and affine transformations has recently been established, developing algorithms in this framework has been met with several difficulties. The three difficult issues in finding an affine time schedule for instructions in the program are: how to determine the dimensionality of time, how we model time in an arbitrarily nested program, and how to generate the SPMD code.

Our algorithm to find a communication-free parallelization has an answer to each of these issues. First, we have developed an algorithm that finds all the degrees of parallelism for each instruction that is achievable via an affine processor mapping. The dimensionality of time for an $O(n^q)$ computation with p degrees of parallelism is simply $(q - p)$. We show a constructive algorithm that parallelizes the whole program in such a way that all the degrees of parallelism found for each instruction are exploited. Second, our algorithm does not explicitly represent the time mapping of each instruction. We recognize that the time domain is fundamentally irregular, so we focus on finding the processor mappings. Third, the code generated is a subsequence of the original program. Efficient code can be produced in a straightforward manner from a processor assignment.

The combination of these ideas together creates a parallelization algorithm that is capable of performing rather complex code transformations. It is interesting to observe that even though the compiler's internal representation of the parallelization scheme is rather simple, the generated code is substantially different from the source. Such code transformations cannot be achieved via ad hoc approaches.

References

1. J. R. Allen, D. Callahan, and K. Kennedy. Automatic decomposition of scientific programs for parallel execution. In *Proceedings, 14th Annual ACM Symposium on Principles of Programming Languages*, Munich, Germany, January 1987.
2. J. R. Allen and K. Kennedy. Automatic translation of Fortran programs to vector form. *ACM Transactions on Programming Languages and Systems*, 9(4):491–542, October 1987.
3. S. P. Amarasinghe and M. S. Lam. Communication optimization and code generation for distributed memory machines. In *Proceedings of the SIGPLAN '93 Conference on Programming Language Design and Implementation*, June 1993.
4. C. Ancourt and F. Irigoin. Scanning polyhedra with DO loops. In *Proceedings of the Third ACM/SIGPLAN Symposium on Principles and Practice of Parallel Programming*, pages 39–50, April 1991.
5. J. M. Anderson and M. S. Lam. Global optimizations for parallelism and locality on scalable parallel machines. In *Proceedings of the SIGPLAN '93 Conference on Programming Language Design and Implementation*, June 1993.
6. E. Ayguadé and J. Torres. Partitioning the statement per iteration space using non-singular matrices. In *Proceedings of the 1993 ACM International Conference on Supercomputing*, July 1993.

7. U. Banerjee. *Speedup of Ordinary Programs*. PhD thesis, University of Illinois at Urbana-Champaign, October 1979.

8. U. Banerjee. Unimodular transformations of double loops. In *Proceedings of the Third Workshop on Programming Languages and Compilers for Parallel Computing*, pages 192–219, August 1990.

9. U. Banerjee. *Loop Transformations for Restructuring Compilers*. Kluwer Academic, 1993.

10. S. Carr and K. Kennedy. Compiler blockability of numerical algorithms. In *Proceedings Supercomputing '92*, pages 114–125, November 1992.

11. P. Feautrier. Some efficient solution to the affine scheduling problem, part II, multidimensional time. *Int. J. of Parallel Programming*, 21(6), December 1992.

12. P. Feautrier. Some efficient solutions to the affine scheduling problem, part I, one dimensional time. *Int. J. of Parallel Programming*, 21(5):313–348, October 1992.

13. P. Feautrier. Towards automatic distribution. Technical Report 92.95, Institut Blaise Pascal/Laboratoire MASI, December 1992.

14. C. H. Huang and P. Sadayappan. Communication-free hyperplane partitioning of nested loops. *Journal of Parallel and Distributed Computing*, 19:90–102, 1993.

15. W. Kelly and W. Pugh. A framework for unifying reordering transformations. Technical Report CS-TR-2995.1, University of Maryland, April 1993.

16. K. Kennedy and K. S. McKinley. Optimizing for parallelism and data locality. In *Proceedings of the 1992 ACM International Conference on Supercomputing*, pages 323–334, July 1992.

17. K. Kennedy and K. S. McKinley. Maximizing loop parallelism and improving data locality via loop fusion and distribution. In *Proceedings of the Sixth Workshop on Programming Languages and Compilers for Parallel Computing*, August 1993.

18. V. Sarkar and R. Thekkath. A general framework for iteration-reordering loop transformations. In *Proceedings of the SIGPLAN '92 Conference on Programming Language Design and Implementation*, pages 175–187, June 1992.

19. J. Torres, E. Ayguadé, J. Labarta, and M. Valero. Align and distribute-based linear loop transformations. In *Proceedings of the Sixth Workshop on Programming Languages and Compilers for Parallel Computing*, August 1993.

20. M. E. Wolf. *Improving Locality and Parallelism in Nested Loops*. PhD thesis, Stanford University, August 1992. Published as CSL-TR-92-538.

21. M. E. Wolf and M. S. Lam. A loop transformation theory and an algorithm to maximize parallelism. *Transactions on Parallel and Distributed Systems*, 2(4):452–470, October 1991.

22. M. J. Wolfe. *Optimizing Supercompilers for Supercomputers*. MIT Press, Cambridge, MA, 1989.

23. M. J. Wolfe. Massive parallelism through program restructuring. In *Symposium on Frontiers on Massively Parallel Computation*, pages 407–415, October 1990.

Finding Legal Reordering Transformations using Mappings

Wayne Kelly

William Pugh

wak@cs.umd.edu, (301)-405-2726   pugh@cs.umd.edu, (301)-405-2705

Dept. of Computer Science
Univ. of Maryland, College Park, MD 20742

Abstract. *We present a unified framework for applying iteration re-ordering transformations. This framework is able to represent traditional transformations such as loop interchange, loop skewing and loop distri-bution as well as compositions of these transformations. Using a uni-fied framework rather than a sequence of adhoc transformations makes it easier to analyze and predict the effects of these transformations. Our framework is based on the idea that all reordering transformations can be represented as a mapping from the original iteration space to a new iter-ation space. An optimizing compiler would use our framework by finding a mapping that both corresponds to a legal transformation and produces efficient code. We present the mapping selection problem as a search problem by decomposing it into a sequence of smaller choices. We then characterize the set of all legal mappings by defining a search tree.*

1 Introduction

Traditionally, optimizing compilers attempt to parallelize programs and improve their performance, by applying transformations, such as loop interchange, loop skewing and loop distribution [Wol89]. Each of these transformations has its own special legality checks and transformation rules. This makes it difficult to find sequences of transformations that obtain some desired goal.

To overcome these problems, many researchers have proposed frameworks that unify some of these reordering transformations [Ban90, WL91, LMQ91, LP92, Fea92a, ST92, DR92]. We have developed a framework that handles more reordering transformations than most existing transformation frameworks. Our framework is based on the idea that a transformation can be represented as a mapping from the original iteration space to a new iteration space. Our frame-work is more expressive than most because we allow a separate mapping to be associated with each statement and do not require that the mappings be uni-modular.

Like all other frameworks, our framework needs to be able to perform the following three tasks:

- Determine which mappings correspond to legal transformations.
- Determine which of these legal mappings will produce efficient code.

```
      do 30 i = 1, n
10       s(i) = 0
      do 20 j = 1, i-1
20       s(i) = s(i) + a(j,i)*b(j)
30    b(i) = b(i) - s(i)
```

$$T_{10} : \{ [\, i \,] \quad \rightarrow [0, i, \quad 0, 0] \}$$
$$T_{20} : \{ [\, i, j \,] \rightarrow [1, j, \quad 0, i] \}$$
$$T_{30} : \{ [\, i \,] \quad \rightarrow [1, i - 1, 1, 0] \}$$

$$I_{10} : \{ [\, i \,] \quad | \, 1 \leq i \leq n \}$$
$$I_{20} : \{ [\, i, j \,] \| \, 1 \leq i \leq n \wedge 1 \leq j \leq i - 1 \}$$
$$I_{30} : \{ [\, i \,] \quad | \, 1 \leq i \leq n \}$$

```
         parallel do 10 i = 1, n
10          s(i) = 0
         do 30 t = 1, n-1
            parallel do 20 i = t+1, n
20             s(i) = s(i) + a(t,i)*b(t)
30          b(t+1) = b(t+1) - s(t+1)
```

Fig. 1. Original program, iteration space, sample mapping and transformed program

– Generate the transformed source code from a given mapping.

We will present the combination of the first two of these tasks as a search problem. The first task corresponds to defining the search tree and the second task corresponds to selecting a path within that tree. This paper will deal almost entirely with the first task, i.e. defining the search tree. Interested readers are referred to our previous work [KP93a, KPR94] for more information on the second and third tasks.

Section 2 explains how mappings can be used to represent reordering transformations; Section 3 describes tuple relations and how they are used to represent both mappings and data dependences. In Section 4 we state the legality test for a complete mapping. In Section 5, we present the process of finding legal mappings in terms of defining a search tree with further details in Sections 6 and 7. In Section 8, we discuss related work, and finally in Section 9, we state our conclusions.

2 Mappings

We allow a potentially different mapping to be used for each *atomic statement*. An *atomic statement* is a code segment that is being transformed as a unit, and might be a single statement, a basic block, an if-then-else statement or even an entire loop nest.

Each atomic statement s_p has associated with it an iteration space I_p, which is a subspace of Z^{m_p} (where m_p is the number of loops nested around s_p). A statement's iteration space is the set of iterations for which that statement will be executed. Figure 1 shows a program and its associated iteration space.

We represent reordering transformations as 1-1 mappings from the original iteration spaces (the I_p's), to a new iteration space I'. We restrict the mappings to be those that can be described by affine constraints. We use the following notation for each mapping:

$$T_p : [i_p^1, \ldots, i_p^{m_p}] \rightarrow [f_p^1, \ldots, f_p^n]$$

- $i_p^1, \ldots, i_p^{m_p}$ are the index variables of the loops nested around statement s_p.
- The f_p^j's (called *mapping components*) are affine functions of the index variables and symbolic constants.

This mapping represents the fact that iteration $[i_p^1, \ldots, i_p^m]$ in I_p is mapped to iteration $[f_p^1, \ldots, f_p^n]$ in I'. For example, the mapping in Figure 1 maps iteration $[5, 7]$ in the original iteration space of statement 20 to iteration $[1, 7, 0, 5]$ in the new iteration space.

Given a section of code and a mapping, we need to be able to produce a new section of code that results from applying the transformation represented by that mapping. Since we are only considering reordering transformations, the transformed code will contain the same atomic statements as the original code, but will contain different loop structures. The new loop structures must execute all iterations in the new iteration space and no others. The transformed code also has the important property that all of the iterations are executed in lexicographical order based on their coordinates in the new iteration space. Note that this property specifies a total order on all iterations (even between iterations belonging to different statements), since all iterations in the original iteration spaces are mapped to a common iteration space.

Figure 1 shows the code that is produced by applying the given mapping to the program in Figure 1. Since the do 10 i ... and the do 20 i ... loops carry no dependencies, they can be run in parallel. The mapping does not specify which loops are made parallel, although given the mapping and dependences, it is easy to determine which loops could be made parallel. The algorithm we use to generate the transformed code is relatively complicated and is not described in this paper, but details can be found in [KPR94].

We have demonstrated [KP93b] how mappings can be used to represent all transformations than can be obtained by applying any sequence of the following traditional transformations:

- loop interchange
- loop skewing
- loop reversal
- loop alignment
- loop fusion
- loop distribution
- statement reordering
- loop scaling

Figure 2 gives some interesting examples of mappings. In this paper we do not give details of how to select these particular mappings.

3 Tuple Relations and Sets

Most of the previous work on program transformations uses data dependence directions and differences to summarize dependences between array references. For our purposes, these abstractions are too crude. We describe dependences exactly using integer tuple relations. We also use integer tuple relations to represent mappings.

Code adapted from CHOSOL in Perfect club (SD)	Code adapted from OLDA in Perfect club (TI)
Original code	**Original code**
| ```
        do 3  i=2,n
1        sum(i) = 0.
         do 2  j=1,i-1
2          sum(i) = sum(i) + a(j,i)*b(j)
3        b(i) = b(i) - sum(i)
``` | ```
        do 2  p = 1, n
          do 2  q = 1, p
            do 2  i = 1, orb
1             xrsiq(i,q)=xrsiq(i,q) + f1(p,q,i)
2             xrsiq(i,p)=xrsiq(i,p) + f2(p,q,i)
``` |
Dependences	**Dependences**
$d_{12} : \{[i] \rightarrow [i, l] \mid 1 \leq l < i \leq n\}$ $d_{22} : \{[i, l] \rightarrow [i, l'] \mid 1 \leq l < l' < i \leq n\}$ $d_{23} : \{[i, l] \rightarrow [i] \mid 1 \leq l < i \leq n\}$ $d_{32} : \{[i] \rightarrow [i', i] \mid 2 \leq i < i' \leq n\}$	$d_{11} : \{[p, q, i] \rightarrow [p', q, i] \mid 1 \leq q \leq p < p' \leq n\}$ $d_{12} : \{[p, p, i] \rightarrow [p, p, i] \mid 1 \leq p \leq n\}$ $d_{22} : \{[p, q', i] \rightarrow [p, q', i] \mid 1 \leq q < q' \leq p \leq n\}$ $d_{21} : \{[p, q, i] \rightarrow [p', p, i] \mid 1 \leq q \leq p \leq p' \leq n\}$
Mapping (for parallelism)	**Mapping (for parallelism)**
$T_1 : \{[i] \rightarrow [0, i, \quad 0, 0]\}$ $T_2 : \{[i, j] \rightarrow [1, j, \quad 0, i]\}$ $T_3 : \{[i] \rightarrow [1, i-1, 1, 0]\}$	$T_1 : \{[p, q, i] \rightarrow [i, q, p, 0]\}$ $T_2 : \{[p, q, i] \rightarrow [i, p, q, 1]\}$
Transformed code	**Transformed code**
| ```
      parallel do 1  i = 2,n
1        sum(i) = 0.
         do 3  t2 = 1, n-1
           parallel do 2  i = t2+1,n
2            sum(i) = sum(i) + a(t2,i)*b(t2)
3          b(t2+1) = b(t2+1) - sum(t2+1)
``` | ```
       parallel do 12  i = 1,orb
         parallel do 12  t2 = 1,n
           do 21  t3 = 1,t2-1
21           xrsiq(i,t2)=xrsiq(i,t2) + f2(t2,t3,i)
11           xrsiq(i,t2)=xrsiq(i,t2) + f1(t2,t2,i)
22           xrsiq(i,t2)=xrsiq(i,t2) + f2(t2,t2,i)
           do 12  t3 = t2+1,n
12           xrsiq(i,t2)=xrsiq(i,t2) + f1(t3,t2,i)
``` |
| **Transformations required normally** | **Transformations required normally** |
| • loop distribution
• imperfectly nested triangular loop interchange | • index set splitting
• loop distribution
• triangular loop interchange
• loop fusion |

Fig. 2. Example Codes, Mappings, and Resulting Transformations

3.1 Integer Tuple Relations and Sets

An integer k-tuple is simply a point in Z^k. A *tuple relation* is a mapping from tuples to tuples. The relations may involve free variables such as n in the following example: $\{[i] \rightarrow [i+1] \mid 1 \leq i < n\}$. These free variables correspond to symbolic constants or parameters in the source program. We use Sym to represent the set of all symbolic constants.

Tuple relations and sets are represented using the Omega Package [Pug92, PW94] which is a collection of routines for manipulating affine constraints over integer variables. We introduce variables corresponding to each of the input positions and output positions. Relationships between these variables and those corresponding to symbolic constants are represented as a disjunction of convex regions.

3.2 The Gist Operation

We make use of the gist operation, originally developed in [PW94]. Intuitively, (gist p given q) is defined as the new information contained in p, given that we already know q. More formally, if $p \wedge q$ is satisfiable then (gist p given q) is a minimal set of constraints such that $((\text{gist } p \text{ given } q) \wedge q) = (p \wedge q))$; otherwise it is **False**.

4 Verifying the Legality of Mappings

Not all mappings correspond to legal transformations, so we need a way to distinguish between legal and illegal mappings. A mapping is legal if the transformation it describes preserves the semantics of the original code. This is true if the new ordering of the iterations respects all of the dependences in the original code. So we have the legality requirement:

$$\forall i, j, p, q, Sym \quad i \rightarrow j \in d_{pq} \Rightarrow T_p(i) \prec T_q(j) \tag{1}$$

where $\prec$ means lexicographically precedes. To be well formed, the mapping must also be 1-1.

5 Defining the Search Tree of Legal Mappings

So far we have shown how to represent reordering transformations as mappings and how to verify the legality of a given mapping. To make use of such a framework, optimizing compilers would need to be able to find legal mappings that would produce efficient transformed code. In this section we show how this can be modeled as a search problem. More precisely, for a given section of code, we will define a search tree whose leaves correspond to all legal mappings for that section of code. A complete search tree could never actually be constructed by a compiler as such search trees are all infinitely large. However, a well defined search tree, lets us use any search algorithm to find a good legal mapping. Some examples of possible search algorithms include:

- Using a heuristic to choose which branch to follow at each fork.
- An interactive tool where a human user can select some or all of the branches to follow at each fork.
- Defining a function from the nodes to the integers which satisfies the monotone property [Nil80]. This would allow us to use admissible search algorithms such as the A^* algorithm [Nil80]. In a previous paper [KP93a], we described an approach along these lines.

Depending on the search algorithm used, parts of the search tree may actually be constructed, or may only exist implicitly. We will not discuss search algorithms further in this paper, but will instead concentrate on defining the search tree.

5.1 Divide and Conquer

In order to define a search tree, we must first decompose the mapping selection problem into a sequence of choices. There are many different ways in which this problem can be decomposed. The decomposition that we have chosen has the desirable property that all partial legal sequences of choices can be extended into a complete mapping.

5.2 Coarse Grained Decomposition

At the highest level, we decompose the mapping selection problem into the smaller problems of choosing each of the mapping components. The order in which these choices are made is very important. We require that the mapping components for levels $1, \ldots, k$ be chosen before the mapping components for level $k+1$. Level k is defined as the set of mapping components $\{ f_p^k \mid p \in \text{Stmts} \}$. To understand why we require that choices be made in this order, we need to consider the following property of the lexicographically precedes operator. Given any tuples $(x_1, \ldots, x_k)$ and $(y_1, \ldots, y_k)$, it is always possible to find x_{k+1} and y_{k+1} such that $(x_1, \ldots, x_k, x_{k+1}) \preceq (y_1, \ldots, y_k, y_{k+1})$ iff $(x_1, \ldots, x_k) \preceq (y_1, \ldots, y_k)$. So, given any partially specified mapping (where only the first k levels of the mapping has been chosen), we know that it can always be extended into a legal complete mapping iff

$$\forall i, j, p, q, Sym \quad i \rightarrow j \in d_{pq} \ \Rightarrow T_p^k(i) \preceq T_q^k(j) \tag{2}$$

where T_p^k is the mapping consisting of only the first k levels of statement s_p.

If Equation 2 has been maintained while selecting mapping components for levels $1, \ldots, k$, then to maintain it at level $k+1$ we simply need to ensure that:

$$\forall i, j, p, q, Sym \quad i \rightarrow j \in d_{pq}^{k+1} \ \Rightarrow T_p^{k+1}(i) \preceq T_q^{k+1}(j)$$

where $d_{pq}^{k+1} = \{i \rightarrow j | i \rightarrow j \in d_{pq} \wedge T_p^k(i) = T_q^k(j)\}$ is the set of dependences that have not already been guaranteed to be respected by mapping components chosen at levels $1, \ldots, k$.

5.3 Fine Grained Decomposition

We distinguish two parts of a mapping component: the *variable part* and the *constant part*. The variable part is the largest subexpression of the mapping component that is a linear function of the index variables. The rest of the expression is called the constant part. For example in the mapping $[i, j] \rightarrow [2i + j + n + 1, 0, j]$ the first mapping component has variable part $2i + j$ and constant part $n + 1$.

We further decompose the problem of selecting all mapping components at a given level into the problem of first selecting all of the variable parts for that level, followed by selecting all of the constant parts for that level. We decompose in this way because we can partially analyze the legality of variable parts in isolation. As will be seen in Section 6, we can sometimes determine that a particular variable part can not be used for a particular statement, even if we do not know which variable parts will be used for the other statements and do not know which constant parts will be used.

6 Characterizing Legal Variable Parts

This section deals with the problem of selecting all of the variable parts at a given level k. For each statement s_p we will define a set V_p such that if variable part $v \notin V_p$ then v can not be used as a variable part for statement s_p at level k. This gives us a necessary for a variable part to be legal. We would like to also give a sufficient condition but we can't do so without considering constant parts. We will therefore wait till Section 7 to give a sufficient condition.

6.1 Direct Self Dependences

To be legal, a variable part must respect the direct self dependences of the statement it is going to be used for. It is possible to determine whether self dependences will be satisfied without knowing what constant part will be used because the constant parts cancel out in the case of self dependences.

6.2 Transitive Self Dependences

It is also necessary for variable parts to respect transitive self dependences, as is demonstrated by the example in Figure 3.

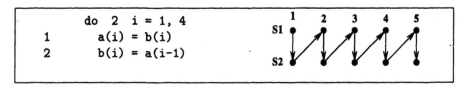

Fig. 3. Example where considering only direct self dependences is insufficient

In this example, variable part $-i$ is legal for both statements with respect to direct self dependences (there aren't any), but is not legal with respect to transitive self dependences.

To compute all transitive dependences[1] we can use an adapted form of the Floyd-Warshall algorithm for transitive closure. The algorithm is modified because we need to characterize each edge, not simply determine its existence. The algorithm is shown in Figure 4. In an iteration of the k loop, we update all dependences to incorporate all transitive dependences through statements $1..k$.

The key expression in the algorithm is $d_{kj} \circ (d_{kk})^* \circ d_{ik}$. We include the $(d_{kk})^*$ term (the transitive closure of relation d_{kk}) because we want to infer transitive dependences of the following form:

If there is a dependence from iteration i_1 of statement s_p to iteration i_2 of statement s_q and a chain of direct self dependences from iteration i_2 to iteration i_3 and finally a dependence from iteration i_3 to iteration i_4 of statement s_p then there is a transitive self dependence from iteration i_1 to iteration i_2 (see Figure 5).

---

[1] We only actually want the transitive self dependences, but it is easier just to compute all transitive dependences.

```
for k := 1 to n do
    for i := 1 to n do
        for j := 1 to n do
            d_{ij} = d_{ij} ∪ d_{kj} ∘ (d_{kk})* ∘ d_{ik}
```

$$d_{ij} = d_{ij} \cup d_{kj} \circ (d_{kk})^* \circ d_{ik}$$

Fig. 4. Modified Floyd-Warshall algorithm

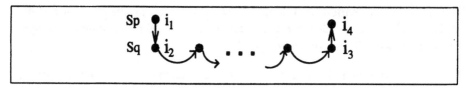

Fig. 5. Transitive Closure Example

There are three problems with computing transitive closure:

1. We would like to be able to say that if $v \in V_p$ then we can use variable part v for statement s_p provided that we carefully choose variable parts for the other statements. However, if we determine inclusion in V_p based solely on transitive self dependences then we cannot make this claim, as the example in Figure 6 demonstrates. Since there are no self dependences for statement

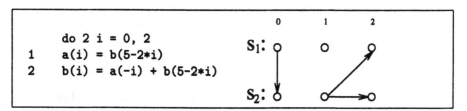

Fig. 6. Example program and associated dependence graph

1 (even including transitive dependences), any variable part appears legal for statement 1. However, if $-i$ is used as the variable part of the mapping for statement 1, there is no possible affine mapping for statement 2 that would respect the dependences.

2. This algorithm is guaranteed to compute the exact transitive closure of a statement graph, assuming that we can compute $(d_{kk})^*$ exactly for each relation d_{kk}. Unfortunately, the exact transitive closure of an affine integer tuple relation may not be affine. In fact, we can encode multiplication using transitive closure: $\{[x,y] \to [x+1, y+z]\}^*$ is equivalent to $\{[x,y] \to [x',y+z(x'-x)] \mid x \le x'\}$. Adding multiplication to our other supported operations would allow us to pose undecidable questions.

3. The number of disjunctions used to represent each dependence relation often grows quite large during execution, making the algorithm infeasible for large problems.

Each of these problems can be attributed to the presence of the $(d_{kk})^*$ term. We set out to solve the first of these problems by trying to find something stronger than $(d_{kk})^*$. To understand why it is legal to use something stronger than $(d_{kk})^*$ we need to consider the following alternative definition of transitive closure:

Definition 6.1 (Transitive Closure) *The transitive closure R^* of a self dependence relation R is the maximum relation R' such that any mapping component that respects R will also respects R'.*

From this definition it is clear that we are not making use of the important knowledge that the mapping components under consideration must be affine. This observation leads naturally to the following definition:

Definition 6.2 (Affine Closure) *The affine closure $R^{\odot}$ of a self dependence relation R is the maximum relation R' such that any affine mapping component that respects R will also respects R'.*

Using $(d_{kk})^{\odot}$ rather than $(d_{kk})^*$ partially solves the first problem since it produces a stronger set of ordering constraints. Unfortunately, we still can not make the claim that we wanted to make, because we make use of the information that the mappings are affine within each statement, but not between statements.

A surprising but extremely important consequence of using $(d_{kk})^{\odot}$ rather than $(d_{kk})^*$ is that it completely solves the second and third problems.

6.3 Affine Closure

This section explains how to compute $R^{\odot}$ for an arbitrary self dependence relation R. The algorithm is given in Figure 7 and is explained below.

Algorithm to compute Affine Closure of R

1. $\Delta = \{j - i \mid \exists Sym \text{ s.t. } i \to j \in R\}$
2. Compute $F(\Delta)$ from Δ
3. Compute Δ^c from $F(\Delta)$
4. $\Delta^{\odot} = (\Delta^c)^*$
5. $R^{\odot} = \{x \to x + d \mid d \in \Delta^{\odot}\}$

Fig. 7. Affine Closure Algorithm

Step 1. Consider two iterations i and j of a statement such that there is a self dependence from i to j. We say that that statement has a *self dependence difference* of $j - i$. We use Δ to refer to the set of all self dependence differences of a particular statement. Dependence differences would generally be considered a weaker abstraction than dependence relations because they do not indicate exactly which iterations are involved in the dependence. If $d \in \Delta$ then it simply means that $\exists i, j$ s.t. $j - i = d \land i \to j \in R$; it does not necessarily mean that $\forall i, j, \; j - i = d \Rightarrow i \to j \in R$. However, since we are dealing only with self dependences and we have assumed that the mapping components must be affine, the imprecision becomes irrelevant. This is due to the following property of affine functions:

Property 6.1 *If f is an affine function and i and j are two points such that $f(i) \leq f(j)$, then for any other two points i' and j' such that $i' - j' = i - j$, $f(i') \leq f(j')$.*

So, following the philosophy that abstractions should be as simple as possible but no simplier, we henceforth use dependence differences rather than dependence relations whenever we are dealing exclusively with self dependences (i.e., in steps 2-4).

Step 2. Our next step is to characterize the set of linear functions that map all points in Δ to lexicographically non negative points. If we consider the linear functions as variable parts, this corresponds to characterizing the variable parts that are legal with respect to the self dependence differences in Δ. We know that all variable parts will be of the form: $a_1 i_1 + \ldots a_m i_m$ where i_1 is the first index variable, a_1 is a variable corresponding to the coefficient of the first index variable and so on. We want to compute a set $F(\Delta)$ of constraints on the a_i's such that

$$(a_1, \ldots, a_n) \in F(\Delta) \Leftrightarrow \forall (d_1, \ldots, d_n) \in \Delta, \sum_{i=1}^{n} a_i d_i \geq 0$$

There are various techniques we can use to generate $F(\Delta)$. The most complete, but also most expensive method is to use the affine form of Farkas Lemma [Sch86, Fea92a]:

Lemma 6.1 (Farkas) *Let the system $Ax \geq b$ of affine inequalities have at least one solution. An affine form ψ is non-negative for each x satisfying $Ax \geq b$ if and only if $\psi(x) \geq 0$ is a nonnegative affine combination of the inequalities in the system $Ax \geq b$.*

$\exists \lambda_0, \ldots, \lambda_m \geq 0$ s.t. $\forall x_1, \ldots, x_n$
$\psi(x) = a_1 x_1 \ldots + a_n x_n$
$= \lambda_0 + \lambda_1 (A_{11} x_1 \ldots + A_{n1} x_n - b_1) \ldots + \lambda_m (A_{1m} x_1 \ldots + A_{nm} x_n - b_m)$
$= (\lambda_0 - \lambda_1 b_1 \ldots - \lambda_m b_m) + (A_{11} \lambda_1 \ldots + A_{1m} \lambda_m) x_1 \ldots + (A_{n1} \lambda_1 \ldots + A_{nm} \lambda_m) x_n$

We apply Farkas lemma by noting that we can equate matching coefficients of the x_i's on each side of the equality and hence derive the following linear set of constraints:

$$\exists \lambda_0, \ldots, \lambda_m \geq 0 \text{ s.t.} \quad \begin{aligned} 0 &= \lambda_0 - \lambda_1 b_1 + \ldots - \lambda_m b_m \\ a_1 &= A_{11}\lambda_1 + \ldots + A_{1m}\lambda_m \\ &\vdots \\ a_n &= A_{n1}\lambda_1 + \ldots + A_{nm}\lambda_m \end{aligned}$$

By using Fourier variable elimination to eliminate the λ_i's, we can generate a set of constraints of the a_i's.

The Δ sets are represented internally as a disjunction of convex regions. Each of these convex regions is represented by a system of affine inequalities $A\delta \geq b$. Farkas Lemma is applied to each of these convex regions, with $\psi(\delta) \equiv a_1\delta_1 + \ldots + a_n\delta_n$, producing a convex system of linear inequalities on $a_1, \ldots, a_n$. The set of constraints $F(\Delta)$ is the intersection of each of these sets of constraints (and is therefore convex).

In practice, it is often the case that each of the systems of affine inequalities describing the Δ sets are very simple. In these cases, we can directly produce constraints on $a_1, \ldots, a_n$ without having to resort to applying Farkas Lemma.

Step 3. All of the constraints in $F(\Delta)$ are guaranteed to be linear, as opposed to just being affine (i.e., their constant terms are alway zero). Assume for the moment that one of these constraints is $f : (c_1 a_1 + \ldots + c_n a_n) \geq 0$. A constant dependence difference of $(c_1, \ldots, c_n)$ imposes exactly the same constraints on $a_1, \ldots a_n$ as does f. Therefore, we can generate a finite set of *constant* dependence differences Δ^c that impose exactly the same constraints on legal affine mappings as does Δ.

These new constant self dependence differences have the perhaps surprising property that they can be lexicographically negative. This unsettling situation can be reconciled by thinking of these arcs as ordering constraints rather than as data dependences. So, even if these lexicographically negative arcs induce cycles in the graph, there is no actual conflict. Although unsettling, cycles can be very beneficial. If two iterations are involved in a cycle, then we know that they must be mapped to the same point in time (at this level of the mapping). If such a cycle exists, it will greatly restrict the set of legal mappings for the statement, and may be propagated to induce dependence cycles in the iterations of other statements, greatly restricting the legal mappings of those statements.

Step 4. The ordering constraints in Δ^c represent a *minimal* set of ordering constraints that impose exactly the same set of constraints on the coefficients of legal variable parts as does the the original set of self dependences. To compute affine closure we want a *maximal* set of ordering constraints that impose exactly the same set of constraints. To do this we make use of the following property of affine functions:

Property 6.2 *If f is an affine function and i and j are two points such that $f(i) \geq 0$ and $f(j) \geq 0$, then $\forall \alpha, \beta \in \mathcal{R}^+, f(\alpha i + \beta j) \geq 0$*

We state without proof that the following computation produces the desired maximal set of ordering constraints:

$$\Delta^{\bullet} = \{a_1 d_1 + \ldots + a_m d_m \mid \exists a_1, \ldots, a_m \geq 0 \wedge \exists (d_1, \ldots d_m) \in \Delta^c\} \quad (3)$$

Step 5. It is then a simple matter to convert this maximal set of ordering constraints back into the form of a dependence relation:

$$R^{\bullet} = \{x \rightarrow x + d \mid d \in \Delta^{\bullet}\}$$

Note that even though the original relation R may have been a disjunction of a number of convex regions, the affine closure of that relation will always consist of a single convex region. This helps to keep down the number of disjunctions used to represent each dependence relation during the execution of the adapted Floyd-Warshall algorithm.

6.4 Affine Closure Example

The following is an example of the intermediate results obtained during an affine closure operation:

$$
\begin{aligned}
R = &\{ [i,j] \rightarrow [i',j'] \mid 1 \leq i < n \wedge 1 \leq j \leq m \wedge 1 \leq j' \leq m \wedge i' = i+1 \} \cup \\
&\{ [i,j] \rightarrow [i',j'] \mid 1 \leq i \leq n \wedge 1 \leq j < m \wedge i' = i \wedge j' = j+1 \} \\
\Delta = &\{ [d_1,d_2] \mid d_1 = 1 \} \cup \{ [d_1,d_2] \mid d_1 = 0 \wedge d_2 = 1 \} \\
F(\Delta) = &\{ [a_1,a_2] \mid 0 \leq a_1 \wedge 0 \leq a_2 \leq 0 \} \cap \{ [a_1,a_2] \mid 0 \leq a_2 \} \\
= &\{ [a_1,a_2] \mid 0 \leq a_1 \wedge 0 \leq a_2 \leq 0 \} \\
\Delta^c = &\{ [1,0], [0,1], [0,-1] \} \\
\Delta^{\bullet} = &\{ [d_1,d_2] \mid 0 \leq d_1 \} \\
R^{\bullet} = &\{ [i,j] \rightarrow [i',j'] \mid i \leq i' \}
\end{aligned}
$$

6.5 Closing the Entire Statement Graph

If we simply use $(d_{kk})^{\bullet}$ in place of $(d_{kk})^*$ in the adapted Floyd-Warshall algorithm, then we may not end up with a fixed point. This is because we are no longer simply performing a closure operation. Some of the edges added by affine closure are not in transitive closure of the original graph. Consider the program fragment and dependences shown in Figure 8. The self dependences for statement 2 will not be discovered until the last iteration of the k loop (when $k = 3$). Thus, the self dependences for statement 1 will not reflect the transitive dependences through these new self dependences of statement 2. We could however repeat the adapted Floyd-Warshall algorithm until we do reach a fixed point. We do not know of any upper bound on the number of times this process would need to be repeated before reaching a fixed point. We could easily stop after performing any number of passes. This might generate weaker constraints on the V_p's than iterating until we found a fixed point; on the other hand, even a single pass is stronger than transitive closure.

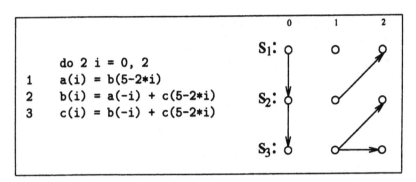

Fig. 8. Example program where multiple passes of affine closure are required

6.6 Characterizing Legal Variable Parts

Once we have closed the entire statement graph, we can now compute $V_p = F(\Delta^\oplus)$ for each statement p.

6.7 Characterizing Good Variable Parts

The techniques we use for characterizing legal mappings can also be used to assist in the selection of good mappings. The efficiency of the generated code depends largely on which loops are parallel. To generate a parallel loop, we must find variable parts that map all self dependence distances to 0. We can attempt this by trying to find variable parts that satisfy both $F(\Delta^\oplus)$ and $F(-\Delta^\oplus)$.

If we can not generate a parallel loop but are interested in parallelism, we might try to generate variable parts that map all self dependence distances to positive values. This will mean no dependences will remain for inner loops, which can therefore be run in parallel.

Doing this requires a relatively minor change to our application of Farkas lemma. Instead of setting $\psi(x) \equiv a_1 x_1 + \ldots + a_n x_n$, we set $\psi(x) \equiv a_1 x_1 + \ldots + a_n x_n - 1$. This will force all self dependence distances to be mapped to 1 or more.

6.8 Incorporating Mapping Decisions

We now consider the situation where we have already chosen variable parts for some of the statements. This additional knowledge allows us to further constrain the set of variable parts which can be used for the other statements. If we have already chosen variable part v_p for statement s_p, then we know that iteration i of statement s_p will be executed no later than iteration j of statement s_p if $v_p(i) \leq v_p(j)$. So, even if there is no actual data dependence from i to j, we can "pretend" that there is. We call such dependences *mapping dependences* since they can only be added because we know something about the mappings used. These newly introduced dependences are not useful by themselves, but they may allow us to transitively infer self dependences for other statements whose variable parts have not yet been chosen.

7 Characterizing Legal Constant Parts

Once we have a legal variable part v_p for each statement s_p, we must, if possible, select constant parts that align the variable parts.

We create a new variable c_p for each statement s_p. These new variables represent the constant offsets that must be added to the variable parts to make them align with one another. More precisely, this can be stated as $f_p = v_p + c_p$. We will construct a set of constraints involving these constant offset variables, such that any set of constant offset values that satisfy the constraints will properly align the variable parts.

We first consider the constraints on a pair of constant offset variables c_p and c_q, that are imposed by a single convex region d that is one of the disjunctions making up d_{pq}. We require that:

$$\forall i, j, Sym\ i \rightarrow j \in d \Rightarrow f_p(i) \leq f_q(j) \tag{4}$$

We substitute $v_p(i) + c_p$ for $f_p(i)$ and remove the quantification on Sym:

$$\forall i, j\ \text{ s.t. }\ i \rightarrow j \in d \Rightarrow v_p(i) + c_p \leq v_q(j) + c_q \tag{5}$$

This is the set of constraints on c_p, c_q and the symbolic constants that are imposed by d.

At this point, we could apply Farkas Lemma since Equation 5 is equivalent to requiring that the affine form $v_q(j) + c_q - v_p(i) + c_p$ is nonnegative at all points in the convex region described by d. We prefer however, to use the following methods, as we have found they are more efficient in practice. Our alternative approaches are not guaranteed to produce exact results in all situations, however we have not encountered any non-contrived programs where they do not produce satisfactory results. We start by rewriting Equation 5 as:

$$A : \quad \neg(\exists i, j\ \text{ s.t. }\ i \rightarrow j \in d \wedge v_p(i) + c_p > v_q(j) + c_q) \tag{6}$$

Unfortunately, the negation in Equation 6 usually produces a disjunction of several constraints. The conditions, D, under which the dependence exists are:

$$D : \exists i, j\ \text{ s.t. }\ i \rightarrow j \in d \tag{7}$$

Since $\neg D \Rightarrow A$, we can transform A as follows:

$$A \equiv \neg(D \wedge \neg A) \equiv \neg(D \wedge \text{gist } \neg A \text{ given } D) \equiv D \Rightarrow \neg\text{gist } \neg A \text{ given } D$$

Therefore Equation 6 is equivalent to Equation 8.

$$(\exists i, j\ \text{ s.t. }\ i \rightarrow j \in d) \Rightarrow$$
$$\neg(\text{gist } \exists i, j\ \text{ s.t. }\ i \rightarrow j \in d \wedge v_p(i) + c_p > v_q(j) + c_q \text{ given } \exists i, j\ \text{ s.t. }\ i \rightarrow j \in d) \tag{8}$$

Usually, the gist in Equation 8 will produce a single inequality constraint. If the gist produces a disjunction of inequality constraints, we could strengthen the condition by throwing away all but one of the inequalities produced by the gist. Unfortunately, Equation 8 also contains an implication operator. So, rather than constructing the set of constraints described by Equation 8, we construct a slightly stronger set of constraints by changing the antecedent to true, giving Equation 9.

$$\neg(\text{gist } \exists i,j \text{ s.t. } i \rightarrow j \in d \wedge v_p(i) + c_p > v_q(j) + c_q \text{ given } \exists i,j \text{ s.t. } i \rightarrow j \in d) \quad (9)$$

If an acceptable set of constant offset values can be found that satisfy these stronger constraints, these offsets must satisfy the weaker constraints, and therefore align the variable parts.

In practice, it is often the case that each of the convex regions d is very simple. In these cases we can directly produce constraints on the c_p's without resorting to the above gist calculation. For example, if d describes that there is a dependence between all iterations separated by a difference of x in direction i^m, then if both statements have variable part i^m, we can directly produce the constraint $c_p \leq c_q + x$.

For a given pair of statements s_p and s_q, we form a single set of constraints A_{pq} by combining the alignment constraints (Equation 9) resulting from all convex regions d between those two statements. We then combine the A_{pq} constraints one statement at a time, checking at each stage that the alignment constraints formed so far are satisfiable for all values of the symbolic constants.

Having obtained a set of alignment constraints, we can either return this set of constraints for use by an external system, or we can find a set of constant offset values that satisfy the alignment constraints. In finding this set of satisfying values, we could consider optimality criteria such as locality or lack of loop carried dependences.

8 Related Work

The framework of Unimodular transformations [Ban90, WL91] has the same goal as ours, in that it attempts to provide a unified framework for describing loop transformations. It is limited by the facts that it can only be applied to perfectly nested loops, and that all statements in the loop nest are transformed in the same way. It can therefore not represent some important transformations such as loop fusion, loop distribution and statement reordering. Most existing frameworks use dependence direction/difference vectors as a dependence abstraction rather than the dependence relations that we use. This is adequate for unimodular frameworks, but is not adequate to test the legality of the sorts of transformations that we can represent. Unimodular transformations are generalized in [LP92] to include mappings that are invertible but not unimodular. This allows the resulting programs to have steps in their loops, which can be useful for optimizing locality. Our mappings are not required to be unimodular and can therefore also generate steps.

Paul Feautrier [Fea92a, Fea92b] has independently developed a framework which is very similar to our own. It is similar in the following respects:

- He represents reordering transformations using schedules which are similar in form to our mappings.
- He generates a separate schedule for each statement.
- We both select mappings/schedules one level at a time, using the dependences that are not carried at outer levels to test legality.

However, we differ from Feautrier in the following respects:

- Unlike our mappings, Feautrier's schedules are not required to be 1-1. Instead, iterations that are to be executed in parallel are scheduled at the same point in time. Therefore, Feautrier's schedules (the time mapping) only partially specify the transformed code. In a separate decision process (the space mapping), parallel loops are generated to enumerate all the computations that need to be executed at each time point. This framework only allows the generation of innermost parallel loops; outer parallel loops are often desirable.
- His methods are designed to generate a schedule that produces code with a "maximal" amount of parallelism. He does this by generating a large set of constraints which describe all legal schedules. This set of constraints has a variable for each coefficient and each constant term of the schedule for each statement. For example, for the code from OLDA in Figure 2, the problem generated by Feautrier would have 6 variables for each statement: 3 each for the coefficients of p, q and i, 2 each for the coefficients of n and orb and 1 each for the constant term. He then introduces two linear functions of these variables, one representing the number of iterations that will be executed sequentially and a second representing how many dependences will be carried. These functions and constraints are then combined and transformed into a dual programming problem that is solved using Parametric Integer Programming (PIP). The net result of this process is that the schedule selected carries as many dependences as possible and among all such schedules, the one selected has as few sequential iterations as possible. These schedules will often not be optimal in practice because of issues such as granularity, data locality and code complexity. It is unclear if his method could be extended to include other criteria, such as good cache performance or parallel outer loops. We expect it would be difficult to encode such an optimization function for a code segment containing several statements.

Our approach differs fundamentally from Feautrier's in that at each stage we are "trying" specific mapping components. Working with actual mapping components, rather than with formulas describing mapping components, makes it much easier to analyze complex performance issues such as data locality.

9 Implementation Status

Prototype versions of many of the algorithms described in this paper are currently implemented in our extension of Michael Wolfe's `tiny` tool, and we are continuing to expand and strengthen our implementation. Our extension of `tiny` is available via anonymous ftp from `ftp.cs.umd.edu` in the directory `pub/omega`.

On a Sun Sparc 10/51, our current implementation requires 10 seconds to compute the affine closure of the yacobi code fragment described by Paul Feautrier [Fea91], which contains 34 assignment statements nested up to 4 loops deep. We require 3 seconds to analyze the cholsky routine from the NASA7 benchmark, which contains 11 statements nested up to 4 loops deep. Simplier programs, such as those shown in Figure 2, take less than 1/4 second to analyze. We hope to substantially improve these times.

10 Conclusions

We have presented a framework for unifying reordering transformations such as loop interchange, distribution, skewing, tiling, index set splitting and statement reordering. The framework is based on the idea that a transformation can be represented as a mapping from the original iteration space to a new iteration space.

We have described two basic techniques:

- Techniques that infer constraints on the legal mappings for individual statements. Using these methods, we can easily produce legal mappings. Other methods, such as those described in [KP93a], are required to determine which of the possible legal mappings are desirable.
- Techniques that given mappings for some statements can infer constraints on the legal mappings for the other statements. Without these techniques, we would often choose what appears to be a legal mapping for a statement, only to find out later that we can not find compatible mappings for the other statements.

We have described a variety of methods for deriving constraints on the sets of legal mappings. For most examples, applying all of these methods will be overkill. We hope to learn more about which combinations of these methods are cost effective in practice when we complete our implementation. One possibility is to vary the level of effort dynamically, as we encounter dead-ends or situations in which we have many reasonable choices that appear legal. In interactive environments where a user is guiding the optimization choices, a high level of effort is probably warranted.

References

[Ban90] U. Banerjee. Unimodular transformations of double loops. In *Proc. of the 3rd Workshop on Programming Languages and Compilers for Parallel Computing*, pages 192–219, Irvine, CA, August 1990.

[DR92]   Alain Darte and Yves Robert. Scheduling uniform loop nests. In *Proceedings of ISMN International Conference on Parallel and Distributed Computer Systems*, October 1992.

[Fea91]   Paul Feautrier. Dataflow analysis of array and scalar references. *International Journal of Parallel Programming*, 20(1), February 1991.

[Fea92a] Paul Feautrier. Some efficient solutions to the affine scheduling problem, Part I, One-dimensional time. *Int. J. of Parallel Programming*, 21(5), Oct 1992.

[Fea92b] Paul Feautrier. Some efficient solutions to the affine scheduling problem, Part II, Multidimensional time. *Int. J. of Parallel Programming*, 21(6), Dec 1992.

[KP93a]   Wayne Kelly and William Pugh. Determining schedules based on performance estimation. Technical Report CS-TR-3108, Dept. of Computer Science, University of Maryland, College Park, July 1993. to appear in Parallel Processing Letters (1994).

[KP93b]   Wayne Kelly and William Pugh. A framework for unifying reordering transformations. Technical Report CS-TR-3193, Dept. of Computer Science, University of Maryland, College Park, April 1993.

[KPR94]   Wayne Kelly, William Pugh, and Evan Rosser. Code generation for multiple mappings. Technical Report CS-TR-3317, Dept. of Computer Science, University of Maryland, College Park, July 1994. to appear at the 5th Symposium on the Frontiers of Massively Parallel Computation.

[LMQ91]   Herve Leverge, Christophe Mauras, and Patrice Quinton. A language-orientied approach to the design of systolic chips. *Journal of VLSI Signal Processing*, pages 173–182, Mar 1991.

[LP92]   Wei Li and Keshav Pingali. A singular loop transformation framework based on non-singular matrices. In *5th Workshop on Languages and Compilers for Parallel Computing*, pages 249–260, Yale University, August 1992.

[Nil80]   Nils J. Nilsson. *Principles of Artificial Intelligence*. Morgan Kaufmann Publishers, 1980.

[Pug91]   William Pugh. Uniform techniques for loop optimization. In *1991 International Conference on Supercomputing*, pages 341–352, Cologne, Germany, June 1991.

[Pug92]   William Pugh. The Omega test: a fast and practical integer programming algorithm for dependence analysis. *Communications of the ACM*, 8:102–114, August 1992.

[PW94]   William Pugh and David Wonnacott. Going beyond integer programming with the Omega test to eliminate false data dependences. *IEEE Transactions on Parallel and Distributed Systems*, 1994. To appear.

[Sch86]   A. Schrijver. *Theory of Linear and Integer Programming*. John Wiley and Sons, Chichester, Great Britain, 1986.

[ST92]   Vivek Sarkar and Radhika Thekkath. A general framework for iteration-reordering loop transformations. In *ACM SIGPLAN'92 Conference on Programming Language Design and Implementation*, pages 175–187, San Francisco, California, Jun 1992.

[WL91]   Michael E. Wolf and Monica S. Lam. A data locality optimizing algorithm. In *ACM SIGPLAN'91 Conference on Programming Language Design and Implementation*, 1991.

[Wol89]   M. J. Wolfe. *Optimizing Supercompilers for Supercomputers*. The MIT Press, Cambridge, MA, 1989.

A New Algorithm for Global Optimization for Parallelism and Locality

Bill Appelbe, Srinivas Doddapaneni and Charles Hardnett

College of Computing, Georgia Institute of Technology, Atlanta, GA 30332

Abstract. Converting sequential programs to execute on parallel computers is difficult because of the need to globally optimize for both parallelism and data locality. The choice of which loop nests to parallelize, and how, drastically affects data locality. Similarly, data distribution directives, such as DISTRIBUTE in High Performance Fortran (HPF), affects available parallelism and locality. What is needed is a systematic approach to converting programs to parallel form, based upon analysis that identifies opportunities for both parallelism and locality in one representation.

This paper presents a global framework for optimizing parallelism and locality, based upon constraint solving for locality between potentially parallel loop nests. We outline the theory behind the framework, and provide a global algorithm for parallelizing programs while optimizing for locality. We also give results from applying the algorithm to parallelizing the Perfect benchmarks, targeted at the KSR-1, and analyze the results. Unlike other approaches, we do not assume an explicit distribution of data to processors. The distribution is inferred from locality constraints and available parallelism. This approach works well for machines such as the KSR-1, where there is no explicit distribution of data. However, our approach could be used to generate code for distributed memory processors (such as generating HPF) with explicit data distribution.

1 Introduction

In order to effectively parallelize programs for distributed memory computers such as the Paragon or CM-5 or "shared memory" architectures such as the KSR-1 it is necessary to optimize for locality of reference. On distributed memory systems such as the Paragon, data must be explicitly passed between processors, so the communication costs are obvious, at least at the object program level. On shared memory machines, such as the KSR-1, the communication costs are "hidden" as cycle stalls due to fetches from non-local memory. Nevertheless, the communication costs are a significant overhead in practice, as the results in section 4 show. Shared memory machines introduce further problems due to false sharing.

Most previous work has focused upon subproblems such as optimizing locality for a single loop nest [12, 9, 10]. Other authors have focused upon the problem of scheduling loop iterations and transforming loops for maximum parallelism[5, 11] or optimizing data distribution[6].

All these approaches do not generalize easily to the problem of globally optimizing for both parallelism and locality. The fundamental insight to overcoming these limitations is that parallelism and locality cannot be optimized independently. What is needed is a program representation and associated analysis which captures global opportunities for both parallelism and locality, without restrictive assumptions. The model needs to be able to handle locality at both the processor and cache levels. Once the representation has been constructed, we can then systematically select sequences of program transformations and data distributions to parallelize the program and distribute data (using a machine dependent cost model when necessary).

Also, we do not want to preclude any parallelization transformations a priori, or apply any transformations before applying the global framework analysis, or restrict ourselves to any particular subset of transformations or data distributions initially.

This paper presents just such a general framework for Parallelism and Locality, PAL. In this paper we first define the PAL framework and its assumptions. We then show how it is applied to some "hard to parallelize" program fragments. We give a global algorithm for parallelization and data distribution using this model. Results of applying the algorithm to benchmarks are given, and the results discussed. Finally, we contrast our approach with other approaches to global parallelization strategies.

2   PAL Framework

Our approach is based on several underlying assumptions.

1. Available parallelism is at the loop-level. We want to find loops that can be executed in parallel, with different iterations mapped to different processors. Thus the our approach is not intended for fine-grain, instruction-level parallelism or for large-grain data-flow.

2. Dependence distances or directions are known. Of course, if a few dependences are not known then loop distribution can sometimes be used and loops containing only known dependences parallelized. For such loops it may not be possible to optimize at compile-time for locality of references. If not, the program may be amenable to parallelization by the inspector/executor model of runtime dependence testing.

3. The program is sequential, and no data distribution has been performed. This is hardly a restriction, as HPF permits data distributions to be ignored, and the model could either ignore parallel loop directives or constrain the solution space by these.

The input to our algorithm is a source program written in an imperative programming language such as Fortran, and we assume that syntactic and semantic analysis have been done. Thus, we are ignoring issues such as interprocedural data-flow analysis and so on.

Our approach can be summarized as a four stage process:

1. Determining available parallelism.
2. Determine the *locality constraints* upon the available parallelism.
3. Global optimization for locality.
   Construct the PAL graph, which represents all locality constraints and available parallelism. Then try to satisfy these constraints while still retaining as much as possible of the available parallelism. When all constraints cannot be met, break locality constraints that have the lowest cost (communication overhead).
4. Code Generation.
   Choose parallelization strategies that meet the remaining constraints and provide low overhead, minimize false sharing, and good load balancing. We use tiling, with tile sizes based upon the number of processors and problem size. Optimize communication, by overlapping it with computation using asynchronous messages (*prefetch* and *poststore* operations on the KSR).

Each of these steps are discussed in the following sections

2.1 Determining Available Parallelism

The goal of determining available parallelism is to classify each loop in each loop nest in the program as:

parallelizable no loop carried dependences, or parallelizable by statement transformations, or
skew-parallelizable two or more perfectly nested loops with recurrences, or
serial a loop with recurrences, not nested with other loops with recurrences.

For a loopnest $\mathcal{L}$, of depth d, the iteration space is denoted by $\mathcal{I}$, and consists of a set of iterations. Each iteration is identified by its index vector $\mathbf{i} = (i_1, i_2, i_3, ...i_d)$. The set of loop indices is denoted by $\mathcal{L}_{index}$, and the subset of these which are not serial is called the *parallel index* set, and denoted by $\mathcal{L}_{Par-index}$.

Thus, available parallelism simply means loops which are not serial. Loop carried dependences can be systematically removed by statement transformations (*alignment, replication, substitution*) [4] and by standard transformations for privatization of local variables. If there are no recurrences (more precisely, no cycles in the dependence graph for that loop level with all dependence directions positive), then all dependences can be removed, otherwise recurrences can be isolated in serial loops using loop distribution. These transformations can be applied to each level of a loop nest, including loops containing conditional statements[2].

An alternative approach is to remove dependences by skewing and other unimodular transformations (transforming the iteration space rather than statements). In an N-level loop this can result in N-1 levels of parallelism[11]. However, skewing introduces a communication overhead (which can later be minimized by block skewing).

Iteration space skewing introduces parallelism in nested loops with dependence cycles that cannot be broken by replication, such as the following stencil fragment:

```
FOR I = 2 TO N DO
    FOR J = 2 TO N DO
        A(I,J) = f(A(I-1, J-1), A(I, J-1), A(I-1, J))
```

Example 2: Stencil Program Fragment

Since there are cycles in both dimensions, statement transformations cannot be used to introduce parallelism. Instead, the iterations must be skewed, after blocking for locality. The iteration space after block skewing can be pictured as shown in figure 1:

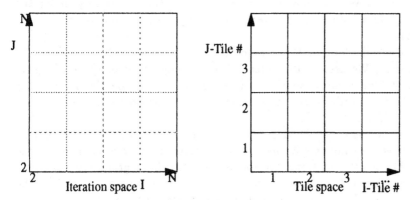

Figure 1 Tiling Iteration Spaces

Any tile (i, j) cannot be executed until tiles $(i - 1, j)$ and $(i, j - 1)$ have completed, and so on. However, tiles can be scheduled so that all tiles in a given row or column can be executed by the same processor without any degradation over a dynamic scheduling strategy. Once a processor completes execution of a tile (i, j), it can be allocated to execute either tile $(i + 1, j)$, or $(i, j + 1)$, or a new row or column of tiles. By allocating the same processor to a row or column of tiles, locality is improved, as data must always be transferred across tile boundaries in all tile dimensions. The choice of row or column parallelism is dictated either by compatibility for locality with other loop nests (explained below), or by cache considerations (e.g., row or column major array allocation).

Effectively, if a loop can be parallelized only by skewing the iteration space in k dimensions, then the same processor can be allocated to any $k - 1$ of these dimensions or a finer granularity of parallelism can be obtained by parallelizing in up to $k - 1$ dimensions.

In general, statement alignment *always* improves locality, and is preferable for removing dependences.[1] However, replication (for removing anti-dependences)

---

[1] More accurately, statement alignment can never degrade locality, as alignment shifts all accesses of an array variable to the same iteration, and hence the same processor. Even if the alignment is in a dimension that is not parallelized, some improvement in locality is likely due to cache level locality improvement.

has a computational overhead (making copies), although strip mining can be used to reduce copying[2]. Similarly, distribution introduces an overhead although it may improve parallelism in a given dimension. Hence, in our model we *identify* available parallelism rather than actually performing the transformations before analyzing for locality. Hence, in Example 1 above, we would identify the loop as parallelizable in the { I,J } dimensions by statement alignment in both dimensions.

3 Determining Locality Constraints

Locality occurs when the data accessed by a processor is resident in that processor's memory. We will now give a general definition of locality under the assumption that a data element is resident on only one processor (later this will be relaxed).

When a parallel loop nest $\mathcal{L}$ is executed, each iteration will be executed by some processor. We assume that there is an unbounded set or space of logical processors $\mathcal{P}$. The iteration space or set of iterations $\mathcal{I}$ of a parallel loop nest is *partitioned* into an ordered set of iterations executed by each processor:

$P(\mathcal{I}) = \{\mathcal{I}_1, ..., \mathcal{I}_p, ...\}, p \in \mathcal{P}$

The partition is constrained only by the requirement that there should be no loop carried dependences between two iterations in different elements of the partition. The finest partition, corresponding to the finest granularity of parallelism, is one in which each iteration in the iteration subspace spanned by the parallel index set $\mathcal{L}_{Par-index}$ is executed by a different processor. [2]

For an access of an array A, $A(\mathbf{f}(\mathbf{i}))$, within a parallel loop nest, the partition induces a set of elements of A accessed by a processor p: $A'_p = \{A(\mathbf{f}(\mathbf{i})) : \mathbf{i} \in \mathcal{I}_p\}$. Thus, any partition P of the iteration space $\mathcal{I}$ induces a *distribution* D of the data for the access A' to each processor p.

$D(A(\mathbf{f}(\mathbf{i})), P(\mathcal{I})) = \{A'_0, ... A'_p ...\}$

This must be a partition if there are any loop-carried dependences on A in this loop, as there cannot be dependences between partition elements.

For another access to the array A, $A'' = A(\mathbf{g}(\mathbf{j}))$, in this or another parallel loop nest $\mathcal{L}''$, there will be a corresponding distribution of the elements of A, based upon the iteration space partition used in that loop and the array subscript expression.

If there is a reaching dependence (either true or input) from $A(\mathbf{f}(\mathbf{i}))$ to $A(\mathbf{g}(\mathbf{j}))$ then we need to ensure locality (different processors do not access the same elements of A). This occurs if the two iteration space partitions P' and P'' satisfy the following locality constraint for the data distributions they induce on the accesses A' and A'':

---

[2] Strictly speaking, if levels are skew-parallelizable, then there there are dependences between elements in the finest partition. However, these can be ignored as they will be preserved by code generation later.

$$p, q \in \mathcal{P} : (A'_p \cap A''_q) \neq \emptyset \ \ implies \ \ that \ \ p = q \tag{1}$$

That is, there is no intersection between the elements of A accessed by different processors p and q in the set of processors $\mathcal{P}$.

This implies that there must be a 1-1 mapping between the subsets of the two partitions which access the same elements of A if they satisfy the locality constraint.

This mapping can be determined from the array subscript expressions, by equating them to determine the constraints on iterations which access the same array elements. If there is a reaching dependence from $A(\mathbf{f(i)})$ in loopnest $\mathcal{L}'$, to $A(\mathbf{g(j)})$ in loop nest $\mathcal{L}''$, and

$$\mathbf{f(i)} = (f_1(\mathbf{i}), f_2(\mathbf{i}), ...f_m(\mathbf{i})), \quad \mathbf{g(j)} = (g_1(\mathbf{j}), g_2(\mathbf{j}), ...g_m(\mathbf{j}))$$

Then, the *index constraints* for locality are:

$$\text{for each subscript } k \text{ in the range } 1..m, \ \ f_k(\mathbf{i}) = g_k(\mathbf{j}) \tag{2}$$

To satisfy locality between loop nest $\mathcal{L}'$, with iteration space $\mathcal{I}'$, and loop nest $\mathcal{L}''$ with iteration space $\mathcal{I}''$, the criteria is:

$$\mathbf{i} \in \mathcal{I}'_p \text{ and } \mathbf{j} \in \mathcal{I}''_q \text{ and } g_k(\mathbf{j}) = f_k(\mathbf{i}) \text{ for all } k \ \ implies \ \ that \ \ p = q \tag{3}$$

That is, if the same array element is accessed in the iteration $\mathbf{i}$ in $\mathcal{L}'$ and $\mathbf{j}$ in $\mathcal{L}''$, then these must be iterations executed by the same processor.

In general, the constraints cannot be solved unless we restrict the subscript expressions to simple forms. If we restrict the subscript expressions to be affine expressions of the loop indices, then any index constraint will be of the form:

$$\mathbf{F.i} + F_0 = \mathbf{G.j} + G_0 \tag{4}$$

where each of the F_i and G_i are integer constants.

If A is a one dimensional array, then $m = 1$ and there is just one index constraint. $\mathbf{F.i} + F_0$ and $\mathbf{G.j} + G_0$ each define a family of hyperplanes in the two iteration spaces.

One processor must execute all iterations in a hyperplane for locality. In effect, parallelism is in the direction normal to the hyperplane. This can be done in the source program by skewing the iteration space. For reasonable locality on shared memory machines like the KSR-1 it is necessary to tile (use a block distribution) at least in the column direction.

If any of the indices is a serial index then generally the constraint cannot be satisfied, as each processor will access a range of values even in the finest partition, and these ranges will overlap. For example,

```
A(I1) = ... /* in loop nest L': parallel index set = { I1 }
...
A(J1 + J2) = ... /* in loop nest L": parallel index set = { J1 }
```

If J2 takes on a range of values, then no partition of the iteration spaces will satisfy the locality constraint (assuming that the I1 and J1 loops have stride less than the range of J2).

3.1 Satisfying Multiple Constraints

Each index constraint potentially induces a partition of two iteration spaces at the source and sink of the dependence. As shown above, any single affine index constraint (of indices in the feasible parallel index set) can be satisfied if none of the indices in the constraint are scalar. In general, several affine index constraints can be satisfied provided that they are over disjoint sets of indices in the parallel index sets. Each constraint specifies that all points (iteration space vectors) in a hyperplance be executed by one processor. However, as noted below, hyperplanes which differ only by a constant value (alignment) can be partially satisfied by using a tiling strategy (communication occurs only at the boundary of tiles). In addition, by tiling the iteration space using several hyperplanes, communication costs can be reduced.

3.2 An Algorithm to Find Partitions

Finding partitions that preserve locality is trivial: merely have all iterations together in one partition element (serialize the program). However, we want to find the finest grain of partition. By aggregating elements of a finer partition we obtain coarser partitions corresponding to coarser parallelism. Of course, if a coarser partition is used in one loop nest, then a corresponding coarser partition is usually needed in other loop nests to preserve locality.

Ignoring locality, the finest partitions can be created by allocating one processor per iteration in all loops that are parallelizable. The finest partition is unique (under the assumption that no communication is allowed between processors). Given the finest partition of each loop nest (by identifying all loop that are parallelizable by statement transformations), the finest partition can be constructed by using the locality constraint as follows. Given the two subscript expressions for the array accesses $A(\mathbf{f}(\mathbf{i}))$ and $A(\mathbf{g}(\mathbf{j}))$, if $\mathbf{g}(\mathbf{j}) = \mathbf{f}(\mathbf{i})$ then $\mathbf{i}$ and $\mathbf{j}$ must be in the same partition. A partition of both loops which satisfies this constraint is the finest granularity of parallelism which satisfies locality.

For example:

```
FOR ALL I1 = 1 TO N DO
    FOR ALL I2 = 1 TO N DO
        Y(I1,N-I2) += X(I1,I2)
FOR ALL J1 = 1 TO N DO
    FOR J2 = 1 TO N DO
        Z(J1,J2) = Z(J1,J2-1) + Y(J2,J1-1)
```

Example 3: Adjacent Loop Nests

In this example, the first loop nest is parallel in both I1 and I2, whereas the second loop is parallel in J1. These give the initial partitions. Locality can be achieved for Y only if the two constraints I1 = J2 and N-I2 = J1-1 are satisfied. Since the second loop nest is serial in J2, the first constraint implies that the first loop nest must be serial in I1. The second constraint implies a mapping I2 ↦ N-J1+1.

Consider another example:

```
FOR I1 = 2 TO N DO
    FOR I2 = 2 TO N DO
        A(I1,I2) = f(A(I1-1, I2-1), A(I1, I2-1), A(I1-1, I2))
FOR J1 = 2 TO N DO
    FOR J2 = 2 TO N DO
        A(J1,J2) = g(A(J1, J2-1))
```

Example 4: Adjacent Loop Nests Parallelizable by Skewing

In this example, the first loop nest is parallelizable only by skewing, that is the dimensions I1 and I2 are pseudo-parallel. Since there are four accesses to A in the first loop, there are four constraints with the access in the second loop, which is parallel in the J1 dimension only. If we solve the constraints for the two assignments, it gives the solution that the first loop should be parallel in the I1 dimension, and the mapping between iterations should be I1 $\mapsto$ J1. Solving the second constraint gives the same parallel loops, but a different mapping I1 $\mapsto$ J1+1. Obviously, these two mappings cannot be simultaneously used. However, these mappings differ only by a constant: one is of the form $m(i)$ and the other is of the form $m(i) + k$. Then partial locality can be obtained by block decomposition of the iteration space. Partitioning the iteration spaces into blocks implies that the intersection between sets of array elements accessed by different processors is relatively small.

4 Global Optimization for Locality

Previous sections outlined how to solve constraints for a single dependence to obtain locality for that access. The key question is how to solve sets of constraints for the entire program, how to compromise when all constraints cannot be satisfied, and how to optimize communication.

Prior to global partitioning, we assume that a number of standard optimizations have been performed, and that symbolic analysis[8] has been done to simplify the program and determine the number of loop iterations. In practice, for the benchmarks below, we have used runtime traces to determine loop iterations. Also, we have used loop distribution to obtain perfect loop nests when possible and when inner loops were candidates for parallel execution.

The global algorithm for partitioning the iteration and data spaces, code generation, and communication optimization is as follows:

1. For each loopnest, $\mathcal{L}$, determine the candidate parallel index set $\mathcal{L}_{Par-index}$.
2. Determine the candidate *distributed array references*: any array access within a loopnest with a non-null candidate parallel index set, subscripted by an expression containing candidate parallel indices.
3. Determine the reaching dependences between all these distributed array references.
4. For each of these reaching dependences, determine the locality constraints as follows:

(a) Initialize copies of the parallel index sets for the source and sink of the dependence:
$$\mathcal{L}'_{Dep-Par-index} = \mathcal{L}'_{Par-index} \text{ and } \mathcal{L}''_{Dep-Par-index} = \mathcal{L}''_{Par-index}.$$

(b) Equate each of the subscript expressions, to obtain a set of constraints (equalities between subscript expressions), $C = \{c_1, c_2, ...c_{nc}\}$, where the initial number of constraints nc equals the number of dimensions of the array.

    i. remove any duplicate constraints and constraints with no indices in $\mathcal{L}'_{Dep-Par-index}$ and $\mathcal{L}''_{Dep-Par-index}$

    ii. if any remaining constraints contain indices not in either $\mathcal{L}'_{Dep-Par-index}$ or $\mathcal{L}''_{Dep-Par-index}$ (serial indices) remove this constraint and all indices in it from $\mathcal{L}'_{Dep-Par-index}$ and $\mathcal{L}''_{Dep-Par-index}$. Repeat until no further constraints removed.

(c) Annotate the reaching dependence with C.

Each subscript constraint c_k implies one or more mappings between parallel index sets and corresponding planes to parallelize in.

The end result of this stage is represented by the *PAL Graph*, which shows all parallelizable loop nests in the program, the constraints between them and the corresponding mappings between iteration spaces.

5. For each pair of loop nests $\mathcal{L}'$ and $\mathcal{L}''$ with locality constraints between them, determine the intersection of all these constraints. The intersection of two constraint sets $C' = \{c'_1, c'_2, ...c'_{nc'}\}$ and $C'' = \{c''_1, c''_2, ...c''_{nc''}\}$ is simply the set of identical constraints (or constraints which differ by a constant for partial locality using blocking).

If the intersection is empty, then locality cannot be obtained for all data. If constraints differ by a constant then partial locality can be obtained by block scheduling. Otherwise, scheduling can either be block or cyclic (though cache effects on shared memory multiprocessors generally favor block scheduling and allocation). If there is more than one constraint, locality can be obtained in more than one dimension provided that the constraints are over disjoint sets of indices.

If there is a constraint between $\mathcal{L}_1$ and $\mathcal{L}_2$, and another between $\mathcal{L}_2$ and $\mathcal{L}_3$ then this implies a constraint between $\mathcal{L}_1$ and $\mathcal{L}_3$ (which must be intersected with any direct constraint between $\mathcal{L}_1$ and $\mathcal{L}_3$).

6. Apply loop distribution when feasible and when it will improve locality: two conflicting constraints are from dependences between loopnests, whose sources (or sinks) within a loop nest have no loop carried dependences, or path of loop carried dependences between them.

7. Determine communication costs for breaking one or more locality constraints. Choose the lowest communication cost constraint to break. On the KSR, communication costs are simply the number of non-local memory references required to transfer data. This can be determined statically, although the expressions are a function of the loop bounds. In general, choose to break communication costs for read-only data first as this can be replicated.

5 Code Generation

After deciding which locality constraints to drop the final step is code generation. Code generation is highly dependent upon the target architecture, and our code generation algorithm is targeted at shared memory multiprocessors such as the KSR-1. There are three key steps in our code generation algorithm:

1. Blocking data structures to cache sizes and coalescing arrays
2. Scheduling loop iterations (mapping iterations to processors)
3. Generating parallel regions

We have applied the above algorithm to a range of benchmarks, including Perfect Benchmarks such as TRFD and FLO52 and NAS benchmarks including Scalar Pentadiagonal. The algorithm is broadly applicable to these benchmarks, excluding benchmarks such as SPICE which use sparse matrices. The discussion below focuses upon TRFD.

5.1 Blocking Data Structures

Blocking array row sizes to a multiple of the cache size is critical to performance on shared memory multiprocessors to avoid false sharing. In general, with large data structures and tiles, false sharing is a relatively small proportion of the overhead. In the TRFD benchmark, the overhead of false sharing was about 6% for the smaller iterations of the outermost scalar loop. This was removed by block aligning all arrays so that their column size was a multiple of the block size ([3] gives a global algorithm and feasibility criteria for global allocation of arrays on block boundaries).

On the NAS benchmark, blocking reduces execution time for a timestep from 2.54sec. to 2.23sec. for 30 processors. This can be done either at this stage or before analysis for locality, together will *array coalescing*. Coalescing takes k arrays with the same dimensions name(N, M, ...), accessed using the same subscript expressions in parallel loops, and replaces them by one array NAME(K, N, M, ...). This increases cache reuse and reduces the minimum tile size in the next dimension.

5.2 Scheduling Loop Iterations

In general, the strategy we used for loops with balanced loads was to tile in one or more dimensions (always including the row dimension to avoid false sharing) dividing the dimension(s) equally among the processors, one tile per processor (sized as a multiple of the 128 byte cache line). This calculation is done at runtime. However, in cases of triangular loops load balancing is needed.

Optimizations for Load Balancing Loop nest L4 and L5 in TRFD (Figure 3) present an opportunity for locality optimization and load balancing combined. The access patterns of L4 require a schedule where rows of X4 are assigned to individual processors. Ideally we want L5 to use the same schedule as L4. The algorithm finds the following constraints in L5:

    I5 = J5',   J5 = I5'

These constraints convey that the accesses occur in the upper and lower triangle of the matrix. It is only necessary to schedule the lower or upper triangle. Since we are scheduling a triangular access pattern it is important to consider load balancing. If we follow the schedule of L4 we would not have an even distribution of work when executing L5. Assuming there are P processors, and the the matrix is NxN, each processor would work on W tiles such that lower bound(P/2) $\leq$ W $\leq$ upper bound(P/2). Since each processor is assigned 1 tile on the main diagonal, W tiles are assigned to each processor from the lower triangle. Indirectly, W tiles are assigned from the upper triangle causing each processor to complete 2W + 1 tiles(see figure 4). This schedule guarantees that each processor will work on upper bound(P+1) and lower bound(P-1) tiles. Such optimizations are typically quite important. It often is not sufficient to obtain even locality and parallelism; load balancing must be considered too.

5.3 Generating Parallel Regions

As noted earlier, Barriers need to be inserted between any parallel loops which have a reaching dependence with an unsatisfied locality constraint after parallelization. Algorithms for minimizing the number of barriers have been developed by other authors (e.g., the Kennedy/Callahan algorithm[13]). The Kennedy/Callahan algorithm needs to be modified for our application, as it results in a barrier between any two parallel loops with a reaching dependence (as it assumes no processor to iteration mapping). We need to insert a barrier only if the resulting locality constraint is not satisfied.

The Kennedy/Callahan algorithm uses loop fusion of parallel loops to reduce the number of barriers needed. In our environment such fusion is unnecessary (although it is a minor optimization that reduces loop overhead and may improve cache locality).

The simple algorithm above for barrier insertion does not work when generating one large parallel region for the entire program (with serial sections executed by one processor). The problem is that execution of parallel loops may be control dependent on serial loops. This situation occurs several times in the Perfect benchmarks such as FLO52 (parallel loops within serial loops or branches from serial sections around parallel loops). The approach we have taken is to propagate the branch result outside the serial section. The alternative, small parallel regions rather than one large region, has a significant performance degradation on the KSR-1.

In our application the serial code is always executed by the same processor (processor 0).

The KSR-1 provides prefetch and poststore, which bring issue a non-blocking read/write of a cache line. These both have broadcast capability. The simplest strategy is to insert prefetches several iterations prior to the data being needed (the time for prefetch is about 150 cycles). On the NAS benchmark prefetches improved the performance of a timestep from 2.14sec. to 1.89sec. (about a 10% improvement). The KSR has several limitations on prefetch which prevent much better improvement.

6   Experimental Results

The program TRFD is about 500 lines of Fortran, and has an outer loop which iterates on the problem size which ranges from 10 to 40 in steps of 5. In TRFD there are 4 global shared arrays and seven loop nests within the outer loop that are potentially parallel (ignoring I/O and timing loops). The first step is to determine the available parallelism for each of these loop nests. Each loop nest is parallel in one or more dimensions. Some transformations were done to the program at this stage to increase available parallelism, such as: distribution to make loop nests perfectly nested, eliminating exits from loops, scalar expansion (privatization), eliminating auxiliary induction variables.

The next stage is constructing the PAL graph (figure 3, at the end of the paper).

All of the locality constraints cannot be satisfied, the graph indicates which constraints were selected to be satisfied to minimize communication.

For example, in loop nest L3 to loop L4, the candidate parallel index sets are $\{I_3\}$ and $\{I_4, J_4\}$ respectively

The locality constraints between L3 and L4 are:

X3: $X3(J_3, I_3) \rightarrow X3(K_4, I_4)$; $X3(K_3, I_3) \rightarrow X3(K_4, I_4)$

X4: $X4(J_3 \times (J_3 - 1) + K_3, \text{MRS}) \rightarrow X4(I_4 \times (I_4 - 1) + J_4, \text{MRS})$

Equating subscript expressions for the constraints on X3:
$J_3 = K_4$ $I_3 = I_4$ and $K_3 = K_4$ $I_3 = I_4$
leads to satisfying the locality constraint with I_3 and I_4 parallel, and the mapping $I_3 \rightarrow I_4$.

The non-linear constraint on X4 cannot be satisfied.

The locality constraints between loop nest L4 and L6 and L1, for X1 and X3, leads to J_4 being dropped from the candidate parallel index set for L4. Parallelizing, and hence distributing data, on I_4, leads to locality for X3, X2, and X1.

6.1   Performance

The table below summarizes the results obtained for a 10 processor KSR-1 for the last iteration of the outer scalar loop (largest problem size: N = 40). The result scale for more or fewer processors. All times are in secs., measured using KSR *pmon* timing routines on dedicated processors. The times given are for each of the 7 parallel loop nests and the entire program.

Loop Nest	Serial Time	Tiled Time 10 proc.	Parallel Time 10 proc.	(Min Pi time) 10 proc.
L1	0.01	0.03	0.00	0.00
L2	2.15	2.83	0.37	0.30
L3	75.50	47.80	7.47	7.43
L4	42.06	6.66	7.87	0.72
L5	1.41	0.46	0.26	0.20
L6	28.50	7.80	4.29	1.54
L7	21.17	15.40	2.92	0.56
Total	170.80	81.00	23.20	

The "tiled time" is the execution time using KSR TILE directives to parallelize each loop nest individually. This generally gives poor performance for across multiple loop nests because their is no control of the allocation of processors to tiles (hence locality is lost). KSR has a directive to allow sharing of schedules across loop nests (AFFINITY REGIONS), but we have found it of limited generality, and not as effective as explicit PARALLEL REGIONS and allocation of tiles to processors based upon processor ids.

For comparison, we parallelized the program using KSR KAP preprocessor/compiler. KAP can only generate TILE directives, and does no optimization for locality across loops. In addition, KAP uses very simple strategy to decide tile sizes and which loop nest to parallelize. On a KSR-2, TRFD took 69 sec. on 1 processor; when parallelized by KAP it took 102.5 sec. on 5 processors and 102 sec. on 10 processors.

Overall, our speedup for the parallel version with 10 processors was about 7.5. Some loops have poor load balancing, as illustrated by the column "Min Pi time", which gives the minimum execution time of the loop for each processor. We use static tiling of the iteration space, although our approach does not require static distribution of data. However, for several loops, particularly L4 and L7, there is an uneven workload distribution. The reason for this is triangular iteration space.

We also applied the algorithm to the NAS SP (Scalar Pentadiagonal) benchmark, which is a somewhat simpler benchmark with three parallel loop nests with communication between. In this case the scalar execution time for one time step was 35sec. With 31 processors, after communication optimizations described below, the time for one time step was 1.14 sec. (very close to linear speedup).

For the KSR-1, there is no need for explicit replication. In the benchmark example, the array X1 is implicitly replicated. Loop distribution and fusion are complementary. Loop fusion can be done as a pre or post pass. Loop distribution only improves potential locality when there are no dependences between the two loops that result from distribution (otherwise a locality constraint on the loop prior to distribution will be transformed into a locality constraint between the two loops after distribution).

7 Comparison with Other Work

Traditionally the problem of transforming a program to obtain parallelism and locality of reference is viewed as two independent subproblems. First, transform the program to expose the parallelism in the program. Next, analyze the array accesses in the parallel loops to determine the data and computation distributions that optimize the locality of reference (PARADIGM[7], and ADG[6]). But the optimality can only be obtained if subproblems are treated together[1]. Our approach brings both program transformations for parallel and determining distributions of data and computation to processors into a single framework.

The closest related work is that of Anderson and Lam[1]. They use explicit data distributions and iteration to processor mappings represented as linear transformation matrices. Unlike our approach, they rely upon iteration space transformations rather than initially using statement transformations. Our representation of partitions is more precise than theirs (which relies on basis vectors). However, in many cases both approaches would derive the same mappings. In addition, they use a communication graph corresponding to the PAL graph above. However, their communication graph is less precise (does not include dependences or constraints).

Other related work includes PARADIGM[7]. Their model is based upon explicit data distribution, and mesh decomposition. They use constraint solution, and do not have an explicit phase for identifying available parallelism. Other authors use graph representations for finding data distributions that optimize communication for a parallel program. The Alignment-Distribution Graph (ADG[6]) is similar in spirit to our PAL Graph. ADG is based on dataflow graph of a single assignment form of a given program, where as PAL graph is constructed by representing each loop nest as a node and dependences between the loop nests as edges labeled by constraints.

8 Conclusion & Future Work

We have presented a framework for analyzing for both parallelism and locality for distributed memory systems which is independent of any particular architecture. It is able to represent both locality and parallelism without relying on explicit data distributions or already parallelized programs. We have found that the PAL graph captures very succinctly both the available parallelism and locality. By itself, it is a useful program representation for programmers as well as program analysis.

Constraints on locality can be combined to determine global locality. We have applied the model to a range of benchmarks successfully by hand, are investigating implementing the algorithms as part of PAT, a tool for interactive parallelization. Current work is focusing upon a performance estimation model for the KSR to guide transformations and tiling strategies, and applying the algorithm to further benchmarks.

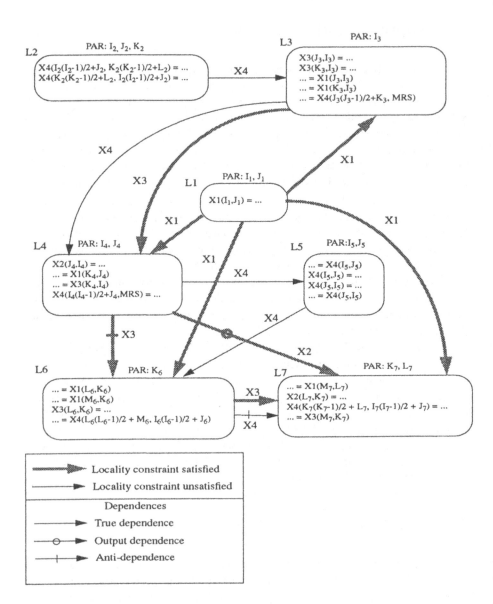

Figure 3: PAL Graph for TRFD Perfect Benchmark

References

1. ANDERSON, J., AND LAM, M. S. Global optimzations for parallelism and locality on scalable parallel machines. In *SIGPLAN Programming Language Design and Implementation* (1993), pp. 112–125.

2. APPELBE, B., DODDAPANENI, S., HARDNETT, C., AND SMITH, K. Determining transformation sequences for loop parallelization. Tech. Rep. GIT-ICS-92/59, Georgia Institute of Technology, Nov. 1992.

3. APPELBE, B., HARDNETT, C., AND DODDAPANENI, S. Aligning data structures for parallelism and locality. Tech. Rep. GIT-CC-94-20, Georgia Institute of Technology, Feb. 1994.

4. APPELBE, B., AND SMITH, K. Determining transformation sequences for loop parallelization. In *Fifth Workshop on Languages and Compilers for Parallel Computing* (July 1993).

5. CALLAHAN, D. *A Global Approach to Detection of Parallelism*. PhD thesis, Rice University, 1987. Rice Tech Report, COMP TR87-50.

6. CHATTERJEE, S., GILBERT, J., AND SCHREIBER, R. The alignment-distribution graph. In *Sixth Workshop on Languages and Compilers for Parallel Computing* (July 1993), pp. 234–252.

7. GUPTA, M., AND BANERJEE, P. Paradigm: A compiler for automatic data distribution on multicomputers. In *International Conference on Supercomputing* (June 1993), pp. 87–96.

8. HAGHIGHAT, M., AND POLYCHRONOPOULOS, C. Symbolic analysis for parallelizing compilers. Tech. rep., University of Illinois, 1994.

9. KENNEDY, K., AND MCKINLEY, K. Optimizing for parallelism and data locality. In *International Conference on Supercomputing* (July 1992), pp. 323–334.

10. RAMANUJAM, J., AND SADAYAPPAN, P. Tiling multidimensional iteration spaces for nonshared memory machines. In *Supecomputing '91* (Nov. 1991), pp. 111–121.

11. WOLF, M. E., AND LAM, M. S. A data locality optimizing algorithm. In *SIGPLAN Programming Language Design and Implementation* (1991), pp. 30–44.

12. WOLF, M. E., AND LAM, M. S. A loop transformation theory and an algorithm to maximize parallelism. *IEEE Transactions on Parallel and Distributed Systems* 2, 4 (October 1991), 452–482.

13. ZIMA, H., AND CHAPMAN, B. *Supercompilers for Parallel and Vector Computers*. ACM Press, New York, New York, 1990.

Polaris: Improving the Effectiveness of Parallelizing Compilers

William Blume, Rudolf Eigenmann, Keith Faigin, John Grout, Jay Hoeflinger, David Padua, Paul Petersen, William Pottenger, Lawrence Rauchwerger, Peng Tu and Stephen Weatherford

Center for Supercomputing Research and Development
Coordinated Science Laboratory
University of Illinois

Abstract. It is the goal of the Polaris project to develop a new parallelizing compiler that will overcome limitations of current compilers. While current parallelizing compilers may succeed on small kernels, they often fail to extract any meaningful parallelism from large applications. After a study of application codes, it was concluded that by adding a few new techniques to current compilers, automatic parallelization becomes possible. The techniques needed are interprocedural analysis, scalar and array privatization, symbolic dependence analysis, and advanced induction and reduction recognition and elimination, along with run-time techniques to allow data dependent behavior.

1 Introduction

Supporting standard programming languages on any kind of computer system is and has been an important issue in computer science. For parallel machine architectures this issue is not only more difficult but also crucial to make these machines easy to use. Parallel machines are more intricate and demand a deeper understanding from those users who have to exploit machine features through specific language constructs. As machine structures are evolving rapidly, these users would have to repeatedly learn new machine-specific features and language elements. These issues make the discipline of supporting standard languages, and thus automatic program transformations, an interesting and important research area.

For many years, the Center for Supercomputing Research and Development (CSRD) has been working toward the goal of making parallel computing a practical technology. Parallelizing compilers have been playing an important role in this quest. The present project has its early roots in a compiler evaluation effort of the late 80s, where we have found that despite the success on kernel benchmarks, available compilers were not very effective on large programs [EHLP91, BE92]. New measurements on a representative set of real programs were made possible, thanks to the Perfect Benchmarks® effort, which was initiated by CSRD, with participation from many other institutions [BCK+89].

Based on these observations, we have hand parallelized the program suite as a major new approach to identifying effective program transformations [EHLP91, EHJP92]. As a result we have found that not only can real applications be parallelized effectively, but the transformations can also be automated in a parallelizing compiler. One issue remained: we had not actually implemented these transformations and thus not delivered the final proof that parallelizing compilers can be improved dramatically.

To resolve this issue we have implemented a prototype of the Polaris compiler and have evaluated its effectiveness. The compiler consists of a sizable basic infrastructure for manipulating Fortran programs, which we describe in Section 2. The analysis and transformation techniques investigated in Polaris are discussed in Section 3. Finally, in Section 4 we present the current status of the Polaris prototype compiler.

---

[1] Research supported in part by Army contract DABT63-92-C-0033. This work is not necessarily representative of the positions or policies of the Army or the Government.

2 Internal Organization of the Compiler

The aim in the design of Polaris' internal organization [FHP+93] was to create an internal representation (IR) that enforced correctness, was robust and, through high-level functionality, easy to use.

Our view of the IR is that it is more than just the structure of the data within the compiler. We also view it as the operations associated with this data structure. Intelligent functionality can frequently go a long way toward replacing the need for complex data structures and is usually a more extensible approach. Thus, we have chosen to implement the data-portion of the IR in the traditional, straightforward form of an abstract syntax tree. On top of this simple structure, however, we can build layers of functionality which allow the IR to emulate more complex forms and provide higher-level operations.

We chose to implement Polaris in the object-oriented language C++ as it both allowed us structural flexibility and gave us the desired data-abstraction mechanisms. Operations built into the IR are defined such that the programmer is prevented from violating the structure or leaving it in an incorrect state at any point in a transformation. Transformations are never allowed to let the code enter a state that will no longer generate proper Fortran syntax. The system also guarantees that the control flow graph is consistent through automatic incremental updates of this information as a transformation proceeds. The automatic consistency maintenance has drastically decreased the time required to develop new optimizations within Polaris' production system.

Additional features that have been implemented in order to make the system robust and to maintain consistency include:

- A clear understanding of who is responsible for the deallocation of an object. The owner of an object is always responsible for its destruction. In Polaris we use the convention that a pointer is used to indicate ownership, and a reference is used to indicate that the object is not owned.

- The detection and reporting of aliased structures (structure sharing is not allowed) with a run-time error. For example, it would be an error to create a new expression and insert it into two different statements without first making a copy of the object.

- Detection of object deletion when that object is being referenced from another part of Polaris. If the deleted object is subsequently referenced, Polaris will abort with an internal consistency error. Furthermore, dangling pointers and their associated problems are avoided by the reference counting of all objects stored in collections.

- Extensive error checking throughout the system through the liberal use of assertions. Within Polaris, if any condition or system state is assumed, that assumption is specified explicitly in a **p_assert()** (short for "Polaris assertion") statement which checks the assumed condition and reports an error if the assumption is incorrect.

In our implementation, we have followed the usual object-oriented approach in that classes are used to represent the various program structures. These include programs, program units, statements, statement lists, expressions, symbols and symbol tables as well as a complete set of support structures which includes parameterized container and iterator classes. Each class provides extensive high-level functionality in the form of member functions used to manipulate the class instances.

Much of the implementation was intuitive and straightforward. The **Program** class, for instance, is little more than a collection of **ProgramUnits**. Among the included member functions are routines for reading complete Fortran codes as well as displaying them. There are also member functions for adding additional **ProgramUnits** as well as merging **Programs**.

The **ProgramUnit** class is, similarly, a holder for the various data structure elements that make up a Fortran program unit such as a statement list, a symbol table, common blocks, and equivalences.

Statements are simple, non-recursive structures kept in a list. There is no notion of statement blocks. However, we have made the implementation flexible enough that member functions which simulate the existence of statement blocks can easily be implemented on top of the current **Statement** class.

The data fields declared in the base **Statement** class (and which, therefore, exist in all statements) include sets of successor and predecessor flow links, sets of memory references, and an **outer** link that points to the innermost enclosing do loop. Whenever practical, we have implemented the member functions such that any modification to a statement results in the updating of affected data, in order to retain consistency.

Each derived statement class may declare additional fields. The **DoStmt**, for example, declares a **follow** field which points to its corresponding **EndDoStmt** as well as fields for the index of the loop and the initial, limit, and step expressions. Each statement class also declares a number of member functions such as a routine that returns an iterator which traverses all of the expressions contained in the statement. Along with similar member functions in the **Expression** class, this makes it easy, for instance, to traverse all the expressions in a loop body to examine expressions for dependence analysis.

Expressions and symbols are implemented in much the same way as statements in that an abstract base class declares structures common to all elements and specific classes are derived from the base. The base **Expression** class includes, for instance, member functions for such operations as retrieving type and rank information, simplification and structural equality comparison. Polaris has very powerful expression structural equality routines, as well as pattern-matching and replacement routines. These are based on an abstract **Wildcard** class, which is derived from Expression. To perform pattern matching, one simply creates a pattern expression (an expression that may contain wildcards anywhere in the tree) and compares this pattern to an expression using the equality matching member function. These functions have proven to be powerful and general and are used by the reduction recognition pass.

The **StmtList** class also contains much functionality which is frequently used during transformation passes. The **StmtList** class is, intuitively, a list of statements. In addition, it contains an extensive variety of high-level member functions for manipulating this list, all of which include automatic updating of control flow and loop-nesting information.

To maintain complete control of consistency inside the **StmtList** class, the manipulation of statements or statement lists are restricted by checks during the execution of Polaris. For example, the block to be processed must be entirely well-formed with regard to multi-block statements such as do loops and block-**if** statements. Another example is the restriction that deleting a block containing a statement which is referenced by a statement outside of the statement block being deleted is flagged as a run-time error during Polaris' execution. The programmer can also defer this consistency management by using a **List<Statement>** for the modification. In this way, we can create a section of code that is inconsistent during its creation and modification but which is checked for consistency when it is incorporated into the program. These safeguards create an environment where traditionally time-consuming errors are immediately recognized and correct code can be quickly created.

3 Transformations

In the following sections we will discuss many of the techniques that have been built into the current version of Polaris.

The first is the method of interprocedural analysis used for this stage of Polaris' development. We have chosen to implement inline expansion for several reasons: (1) it provides us with the most information possible, (2) it allows existing intraprocedural techniques to be used, (3) it allows the calling overhead of small routines to be eliminated. After we have gained more experience with the use of inline expansion in Polaris, we are planning on augmenting it with other forms of interprocedural analysis.

The second transformation is the recognition and removal of inductions and reductions. Generalized forms of these recurrences have been found to have an impact on the performance of the Perfect Benchmarks. The third technique is symbolic dependence analysis for the recognition of parallelism. Traditionally, dependence analysis has been numerical in nature. By exploiting the ability to reason about symbolic expressions we have shown that many previously intractable cases are now able to be automatically analyzed.

The fourth transformation is scalar and array privatization. This is one of the fundamental enabling transformations. Through advanced flow-sensitive analysis we can determine when arrays or even array sections can be replicated to reduce the storage that must be shared among the processors.

The final transformation discussed in this paper is a run-time technique for finding and exploiting parallelism. Even with the advanced symbolic analysis techniques and transformations that we have implemented, we find that sometimes the control flow of a region or the data dependence patterns are a function of the program input data. For these cases we are developing run-time methods for the recognition and implementation of parallelism. These techniques are not currently implemented in Polaris but will include inspector/executor [SMC91] style implementations as well as implementations based on speculative execution.

3.1 Inline Expansion

The Polaris inliner is designed to provide three types of services: complete inline expansion of subprograms for analysis, selective inline expansion of subprograms for code generation, and selective modification of subprograms.

Interprocedural analysis is a requirement for effective automatic parallelization. In Polaris, we chose to use complete inline expansion to allow full flow-sensitive interprocedural analysis, which is especially important for privatization. A driver routine is provided in the Polaris base to perform complete inline expansion for analysis.

For complete inline expansion, the inliner driver is passed a collection of compilation units: one is designated as the top-level program unit. The driver repeatedly expands subroutine and function calls in the top-level program unit. This allows the inliner to handle complex argument redimensioning and retyping by generating equivalences.

The first time a subprogram is to be expanded, the inliner creates a "template" object for each subprogram as it is represented within the top-level program (e.g., with subprogram variables renamed to avoid conflicts with top-level program symbols). At each individual call site, the inliner driver passes this template object back to the inliner, which makes a "work" copy of the object, makes on this copy call site-specific transformations, such as replacing references to formal parameters with actual parameters, and copying the statements and variables of the routine into the top-level program (eliminating the original CALL statement or function call).

In most cases, the inliner can map formal arrays directly into the corresponding actual array in the top-level program. Occasionally, a formal array must be mapped into an equivalent, linearized version of the actual array. In practice, the range test (Section 3.3) has been able to overcome the potential loss of dependence accuracy caused by linearization.

After the analysis of a completely inlined program, the template objects created during analysis can be used as a base for performing selective inline expansion of subprograms for code generation. Data collected using complete inline expansion for analysis can be used to guide selective modification of subprograms using such techniques as cloning, loop embedding, and loop extraction [HKM91].

All of the programs that we have tested were inlined successfully by Polaris. Some constructs are not easily expressible in Fortran after inline expansion. The constructs which are not fully supported involve the need for expressing an equivalence between non-conforming formal and actual parameters. An example is the passing of a REAL actual array to a COMPLEX formal array. This is handled automatically, but requires the favorable assumption that the variables are properly aligned in memory.

3.2 Induction Variable Substitution and Reduction Recognition

Induction and reduction variables form *recurrences*, which inhibit the parallel execution of the enclosing loop. Each loop iteration computes the value of the variable based on the value assigned in the previous iteration. In data dependence terms, this forms a cycle in the dependence graph, which serializes the loop.

Reduction variables most often accumulate values computed in each loop iteration, typically of the form sum = sum + <expression>. Because the "+" operation is commutative and distributive, partial sums can be accumulated on parallel processors and summed at the end of the loop. Due to the limited precision of Fortran variables, this transformation may introduce some inaccuracy, and therefore in most compilers the user has the option of disabling this transformation. However, we have not found this to be a problem for our benchmark suite.

Polaris uses a directive to flag potential reductions of the form:

$$A(\alpha_1, \alpha_2, \ldots, \alpha_n) = A(\alpha_1, \alpha_2, \ldots, \alpha_n) + \beta$$

where α_i and β are expressions that do not contain references to A, A is not referenced elsewhere in the loop, and α may be null (i.e., A is a scalar variable). The data-dependence pass later removes the flag if it can prove independence. The backend code generator for our target machine produces parallel code that implements flagged variables as reductions. More than one reduction statement can occur in a loop and they may sum into different array elements in different loop iterations. We are currently implementing a transformation to generate code for this case in Polaris.

Induction variables form arithmetic and geometric progressions which can be expressed as functions of the indices of enclosing loops. A simple case is the statement K=K+1, which can be deleted after replacing all occurrences of K with the initial value of K plus the loop index[2].

Current compilers are able to handle induction statements with loop invariant right-hand-sides in multiply nested "rectangular" loops. In our manual analysis of programs we have found two additional important cases: one, when induction variables appear in the (right-hand-side) increment of other induction variables (we will call these *coupled induction variables*), and two, when induction variables occur within *triangular* loop nests[3].

---

[2] Assuming a normalized loop

[3] In triangular loop nests, inner loop bounds depend on outer loop indices

The following example shows a triangular loop nest that contains a coupled induction variable. Polaris transforms this code into the parallelizable form shown (in Section 3.3 we will show how our dependence test investigates these non-linear subscript expressions). Notice that the use of coupled induction variables (K1 and K2) cause an unusually large code expansion.

```
K1 = 0
K2 = 0                      do I = 1, N
do I = 1,N                    do J = 1, I
   do J = 1,I                    X((I**4-2*I**3+3*I**2-2*I
      K1 = K1 + 1      ⇒     &        +(4*I**2-4*I)*J
      K2 = K2 + K1            &        +4*J**2+4*J)/8) = ...
      X(K2) = ...                   end do
   end do                     end do
end do
```

The Polaris induction variable substitution algorithm performs three steps in order to recognize and substitute induction variables:

1. Find candidate induction statements by recognizing recurrence patterns of scalar variables which are incremented by either a loop-invariant expression or an expression containing other candidate induction variables. The patterns we have encountered in our programs are relatively simple, and we have implemented a straightforward recognition scheme which finds dependence relationships between induction variables and detects cycles.

2. Compute the closed form of the induction variable at the beginning of each loop iteration (and the last value at the end of the loop) as functions of the enclosing loop indices. The total increment incurred by the induction variable in a loop body is first determined, and then this expression is summed across the iteration space of the enclosing loop. If an inner loop is encountered while computing this increment, the algorithm recursively descends into the inner loop and computes its closed form of the induction variable.

3. Substitute all occurrences of the induction variables. This step is the same as in other compilers. The substituted value is the closed form expression for the induction variable at the loop header plus any increments encountered up to the point of use in the loop body.

3.3 Symbolic dependence analysis

Data dependence analysis is crucial to determine what statements or loops can be safely executed in parallel. Two statement instances are data dependent if they both access the same memory location and at least one of these accesses is a write. If two statements do not have a chain of dependence relations connecting them, then they can be executed in parallel. Also, a loop can be executed in parallel, without the need for synchronization between iterations if there are no dependences between statement instances in different iterations.

There has been much research in the area of data dependence analysis. Because of this, modern day data dependence tests have become very accurate and efficient [PP93]. However, most of these tests require the loop bounds and array subscripts to be represented as a linear (affine) function of loop index variables; that is, the expressions must be in the form $c_0 + \sum_{j=1}^{n} c_j i_j$ where c_j are integer constants and i_j are loop index variables. Expressions not of this form are called *nonlinear* (i.e., they have a term of the form $n * i$ where n is unknown). Techniques have been developed to transform nonlinear expressions into linear ones (e.g., constant propagation and induction variable substitution), but they are not always successful.

In our experience with the Perfect Benchmarks, such nonlinear expressions do occur in practice. In fact, four of the twelve codes (i.e., DYFESM, QCD, OCEAN, and TRFD) that we hand-parallelized would exhibit a speedup of at most two if we could not parallelize loops with nonlinear array subscripts [BE94b]. For some of these loops, nonlinear expressions occurred in the original program text. For other loops, nonlinear expressions were introduced by the compiler. The two most common compiler passes that can introduce nonlinearities into array subscript expressions are induction variable substitution and array linearization. An example of how induction variable substitution can introduce nonlinear array subscripts is shown in Figure 1. This loop nest, taken from TRFD, accounts for about 70% of the code's sequential execution time.

```
X0 = 0
do I = 0, M-1                    do I = 0, M-1
    X = X0
    do J = 0, N-1                    do J = 0, N-1
        do K = 0, J-1                    do K = 0, J-1
            X = X+1
            A(X) = ...            ⇒              A((I*(N**2+N)+J**2-J)/2+K+1) = ...
        end do                           end do
    end do                           end do
    X0 = X0+(N**2+N)/2
end do                           end do
```

Fig. 1. Simplified version of loop nest OLDA/100 from TRFD, before and after induction variable substitution.

3.3.1 Range Test

To handle such nonlinear expressions, we have developed a symbolic dependence test called the *range test* [BE94a]. The range test is an extension of a symbolic version of Triangular Banerjee's Inequalities test [WB87, Ban88, HP91]. In the range test, we mark a loop as parallel if we can prove that the range of elements accessed by an iteration of that loop do not overlap with the range of elements accessed by other iterations. We determine whether these ranges overlap by comparing the minimum and maximum values of these ranges. To maximize the number of loops found parallel using the range test, we permute the visitation order of the loops in a loop nest when computing their ranges.

The computation of the minimum and maximum values of a symbolic array access expression can be quite involved. For example, the maximum value of the expression $f(i) = n * i$ for any value of i, where $a \le i \le b$, can be either $n * a$ or $n * b$, depending upon the sign of the value of n. So, to compute the minimum or maximum of an expression for a variable i, the range test first attempts to prove that the expression is either monotonically non-decreasing or monotonically non-increasing for i. The monotonicity of an expression, say f, is determined by computing the forward difference of the expression $(f(i+1) - f(i))$, then testing whether this expression is greater than or equal to zero, or less than or equal to zero. If $a \le i \le b$, then the maximum of expression $f(i)$ for any legal value of i is $f(b)$ if it is monotonically non-decreasing for i, $f(a)$ if it is monotonically non-increasing for i, and undefined otherwise. The computation of the minimum is similar.

As an example, we will show how to compute the minimum and maximum values of the subscript expression of array A for a fixed iteration of the outermost loop of the loop nest shown in Figure 1. Let $f(i,j,k) = (i * (n^2 + n) + j^2 - j)/2 + k + 1$ be the subscript expression for array A. To compute the minimum and maximum values of f for any legal value of the inner pair of loops, we will first determine the minimum and maximum values of f for the innermost loop, which has index k, then determine the minimum and maximum values that the middle loop, which has index j, can take for these minimum and maximum values. Since the forward difference for index k is positive (i.e., $f(i,j,k+1) - f(i,j,k) = 1$), f is monotonically non-decreasing for k. Thus, the maximum value (a_1) that f can take for any value of k is $a_1(i,j) = f(i,j,j-1) = (i * (n^2 + n) + j^2 - j)/2 + j$. Similarly, the minimum value (b_1) of f for index k is $b_1(i,j) = f(i,j,0) = (i * (n^2 + n) + j^2 - j)/2 + 1$. For the next loop, the index j is monotonically non-decreasing for both a_1 and b_1, since $a_1(i,j+1) - a_1(i,j) = j + 1 > 0$ and $b_1(i,j+1) - b_1(i,j) = j \ge 0$. So the maximum value (a_2) that f can take for any legal value of indices j and k is $a_2(i) = a_1(i,n-1) = (i * (n^2 + n) + n^2 - n)/2$ and the minimum value (b_2) is $b_2(i) = b_1(i,0) = (i * (n^2 + n))/2 + 1$.

By comparing these minimum and maximum values of array accesses, we can prove that there are no loop-carried dependences between these accesses. For example, there cannot be a loop-carried dependence from $A(f)$ to $A(g)$ for a loop with index i if the maximum value accessed by the jth iteration of index i for f is less than the minimum value accessed by the $(j+1)$th iteration of i for g, and if this minimum value of g is monotonically non-decreasing for i. See [BE94a] for other tests that use these minimum and maximum values of f and g.

Returning to the example for Figure 1, we will now apply the dependence test described above to prove that $A(f)$ does not carry any dependences for the outermost loop. From the previous example, we know that the maximum value that f can take for any legal value of indices j and k is $a_2(i) = (i * (n^2 + n) + n^2 - n)/2$ and the minimum value is $b_2(i) = (i * (n^2 + n))/2 + 1$. By the definition of the dependence test given above, if we can prove that $a_2(i) < b_2(i+1)$ and b_2 is monotonically non-decreasing for i, $A(f)$ cannot carry any dependences for the outermost loop. Since $b_2(i+1) - a_2(i) = n + 1 > 0$, $a_2(i)$ must be less than $b_2(i+1)$. Also, b_2 is monotonically non-decreasing since $a_2(i+1) - a_2(i) = n^2 + n > 0$.

Therefore, there are no carried dependences for the outermost loop and it can be executed in parallel. The same dependence test can be used to prove that the other loops from Figure 1 also do not carry dependences.

As the previous examples have shown, the range test requires the capability to compare symbolic expressions. For example, we needed to test whether $j > 0$ or $n^2 + n > 0$ in the previous examples. To provide such a capability, we have developed an algorithm called *range propagation*. Range propagation consists of two parts. One part determines symbolic lower and upper bounds, called ranges, for each variable at each point of the program. The other part uses these ranges to compare symbolic expressions. The next subsection will describe an efficient way in which these variable ranges may be computed from the program's control flow. Expression comparison using ranges is done by computing the sign of the minimum and maximum of the difference of the two expressions, using techniques similar to those described earlier.

A more complicated example is shown in Figure 2. This loop nest accounts for 44% of OCEAN's sequential execution time. (Interprocedural constant propagation and loop normalization were needed to transform the loop nest into the form shown.) Current data dependence tests would not be able to parallelize any of the loops in the nest because of the nonlinear term $258 * x * j$. The range test can prove all three loops as parallel. However, for it to do so, it must apply its tests on a temporary permutation of the loop nest, so that the outermost loop is swapped with the middle loop. This is necessary since the middle loop has a larger stride ($258 * x$) than the stride of the outermost loop (129). This causes an interleaving of the range of accesses performed by two distinct iterations of the outermost loop. By swapping the middle and outermost loops, the interleaving is eliminated, allowing all three loops to be identified as parallel.

```
do K = 0, X-1
  do J = 0, Z(K)
    do I = 0, 128
      A(258*X*J + 129*K + I + 1) = ···
      A(258*X*J + 129*K + I + 1 + 129*X) = ···
    end do
  end do
end do
```

Fig. 2. Simplified version of loop nest FTRVMT/109 from OCEAN

The range test subsumes Banerjee's Inequalities, which have been shown to be effective [PKK91] for real programs [PP93], in proving loops to be parallel with the assumption that they contain only linear subscript expressions. We expect the range test to be equally effective. In addition, the symbolic capabilities of the range test permit it to handle many of the symbolic expressions we have seen in the Perfect Benchmarks. Most current data dependence tests cannot handle symbolic subscripts [BE94b]. Our implementation of the range test in Polaris supports these claims. For the evaluation suite of codes for Polaris, described later, we have found that applying the range test alone was sufficient to identify all important loop nests as parallel for these codes.

3.4 Scalar and Array Privatization

Although symbolic dependence analysis will allow us to prove that more references in a loop nest are independent from each other, it will not allow a significantly greater number of important loops to be parallelized without additional transformations. In our experience, the most important of these transformations is *array privatization* [TP93].

Array privatization is used to eliminate memory-related dependences. It identifies scalars and arrays that are used as temporary work spaces by a loop iteration, and allocates a local copy of those scalars and arrays for that iteration.

To prove that a variable is privatizable, every use of that variable must be dominated by a definition of the variable in the same loop iteration. Determining the dominating definition for a scalar variable is straightforward, since a scalar is an atomic object that can only be read and written as a whole. However, since an array variable is a composite object that can be partially read and written, determining whether an array assignment dominates an array use needs an elaborate analysis of the array ranges. More specifically, the array privatizer must prove that the region of array elements referenced by the use is a subset of the region of array elements defined by the dominating assignment. Symbolic analysis techniques are often required for these region comparisons, since the regions often contain symbolic expressions.

In many cases, determining whether a region in a definition dominates a region in a use can be done using local information. However, in many other cases, it requires more elaborate symbolic analysis using global information.

```
S1 :   M = ...
       ...
S2 :   MP = M * P
       ...
       do I = 1, N
         do J = 1, MP
           A(J) = ...
         end do
         ...
         do K = 1, M
           do L = 1, P
             ...= A(M*(L-1)+K) ...
           end do
         end do
       end do
```

Fig. 3. Example for array privatization

A simple example where such analysis is necessary for array privatization is shown in Figure 3. To parallelize the I loop, array A must be privatized. Loop J defines the region A(1:MP), while loop K uses region A(1:M*P). Thus, to prove that A is privatizable, we only need to prove that $MP \geq M * P$. To prove this, we need to find out how the symbolic variables are related from their global *def-use* relations.

In Polaris, we use a demand-driven algorithm [TP94], based on a Static Single Assignment (SSA) representation, to obtain global information. To obtain the SSA form, program variables are renamed such that each time the variable is defined it is given a new name. Then, each time a variable is used, it is named according to which definition reaches it. In the program shown in Figure 3, each variable is assigned only once, so no renaming is necessary to obtain the SSA form. Our demand-driven algorithm proceeds backwards from use to definition. To prove that $MP \geq M * P$, the algorithm starts at loop J and backward-substitutes MP with M * P as defined in statement S_2. Because the goal is satisfied, the algorithm stops at this point and no further replacements are performed.

A more complicated example of the need for global information is shown in Figure 4, taken from the most time-consuming loop in BDNA. Several intermediate variables need to be privatized to parallelize the outermost loop in Figure 4. They are the scalar variables R, P, and M, and the arrays IND and A. Except for array A, it is easy to determine that these intermediate variables are privatizable.

To determine whether A is privatizable in loop I, it is necessary to determine the range of the use of A in loop L. By analyzing the subscript and the range of the loop L, it is easy to determine that the range is $\{A(IND(1)), A(IND(2)), \ldots, A(IND(P))\}$. The possible dominating definition for A is in loop J, where A is defined for the range A(1:I-1). To prove that the definition in loop J dominates all the uses in loop L, we need to prove that $\{A(IND(1)), A(IND(2)), \ldots, A(IND(P))\}$ falls in the range of A(1:I-1).

Our SSA based, demand-driven, sparse evaluation algorithm works well in situations like this where it is necessary to propagate values from complicated control structures with conditional assignments and statically assigned symbolic arrays. The demand-driven analysis determines how many elements of IND are defined in loop K making use of the fact that the subscript P for the assignment to IND(P) is a monotonically increasing variable with an initial value of 1 and step of 1. Using a monotonic variable identification technique similar to induction variable identification, the algorithm determines that all the elements in $\{IND(1), IND(2), \ldots, IND(L)\}$ are assigned in loop K.

Now that the algorithm knows the definition point for $\{IND(1), IND(2), \ldots, IND(P)\}$, it can substitute the loop variant terms in $\{A(IND(1)), A(IND(2)), \ldots, A(IND(P))\}$ with their values. Each of them takes on a value of loop index K. Because the value of K falls in the range [1:I-1], $\{IND(1), IND(2), \ldots, IND(P)\}$ will also fall in the same range. Hence all the uses of A fall within the range [1:I-1] and are therefore dominated by the definition A(1:I-1). Thus, the algorithm determines that the array A is privatizable in loop I.

```
do I = 2,N
    do J = 1, I - 1
        IND(J) = 0
        A(J) = X(I,J) - Y(I,J)
        R = A(J) + W
        if (R .LT. RCUTS) IND(J) = 1
    end do
    P = 0
    do K = 1,I - 1
        if (IND(K) .NE. 0) then
            P = P + 1
            IND(P) = K
        end if
    end do
    do L = 1,P
        M = IND(L)
        X(I,L) = A(M) + Z
    end do
end do
```

Fig. 4. Example from BDNA

3.5 Framework for Run-Time Analysis

The access pattern of some programs cannot be determined at compile time, either because of limitations in the current analysis algorithms or because the access pattern is a function of the input data. For example, compilers usually conservatively assume data dependences in the presence of subscripted subscripts. Although more powerful analysis techniques could remove this limitation when the index arrays are computed using only statically-known values, nothing can be done at compile-time when the index arrays are a function of the input data. Therefore, if data dependences such as these are to be detected, the analysis must occur at run-time. Because of the overhead involved, it is very important that run-time techniques be fast as well as effective.

3.5.1 Detecting data dependences at run-time

Consider a do loop for which the compiler cannot statically determine the access pattern of a shared array A that is referenced in the loop. Instead of executing the loop sequentially, the compiler could decide to speculatively execute the loop as a doall and generate code to determine at run-time whether the loop was, in fact, fully parallel. If the subsequent test finds that the loop was not fully parallel, then it will be re-executed sequentially.

To do this, it is necessary to have the ability to restore the original state when re-execution is needed. One strategy is to save the values of some arrays before starting the parallel execution of the loop and restore these values if the sequential re-execution is needed. However, in our implementation, some of

```
do I = 1, 8
    ...         = A(T(I))           T(1:8) = [2 2 2 10 8 8 8 10]
    A(U(I))     = ...               U(1:8) = [1 3 5  4 7 3 6 12]
    ...         = A(V(I))           V(1:8) = [1 3 2 10 7 3 8 12]
end do
```

	Position in shadow arrays												w_A	m_A
	1	2	3	4	5	6	7	8	9	10	11	12		
A_w	1	0	1	1	1	1	1	0	0	0	0	1	8	7
A_r	0	1	0	0	0	0	0	1	0	1	0	0		
A_{np}	0	0	0	0	0	0	0	0	0	0	0	0		
$A_w \wedge A_r$	0	0	0	0	0	0	0	0	0	0	0	0		

Fig. 5. The PD Test.

the values computed during the parallel execution are stored in temporary locations and then stored in permanent locations if the parallel execution was correct.

In order to implement such a strategy, we have developed a run-time technique, called the *Privatizing Doall test (PD test)*, for detecting the presence of cross-iteration dependences in a loop [RP94]. If there are any such dependences, this test does not identify them; it only flags their existence. In addition, if any variables were privatized for speculative parallel execution, this test determines whether those variables were, in fact, validly privatized. Our interest in identifying fully parallel loops is motivated by the fact that they arise frequently in real programs.

3.5.2 The PD test

The PD test is applied to each shared variable referenced during the loop whose accesses cannot be analyzed at compile-time. For convenience, we discuss the test as applied to only one shared array, say A. Briefly, the test traverses and marks shadow array(s) during speculative parallel execution using the access pattern of A, and after loop termination, performs a final analysis to determine whether there were cross-iteration dependences between the statements referencing A.

For each iteration, the first time an element of A is written during that iteration, the corresponding element in the write shadow array A_w is marked. If, during an iteration, an element in A is read, but never written, then the corresponding element in the read shadow array A_r is marked. Another shadow array A_{np} is used to flag the elements of A that *cannot* be privatized: an element in A_{np} is marked if the corresponding element in A is both read and written, and is read first, for any iteration.

A post-execution analysis determines whether there were any cross-iteration dependences between statements referencing A as follows. If $any(A_w(:) \cap A_r(:))^4$ is true, then there is at least one flow- or anti-dependence that was not removed by privatizing A. If $any(A_{np}(:))$ is true, then A is not privatizable (some element is read before being written in an iteration). The counter w_A records the total number of writes done to A_w by all iterations, and m_A is the total number of marks in A_w. If $w_A \neq m_A$, then there is at least one output dependence (some element is overwritten); however, if A is privatizable (i.e., if $any(A_{np}(:))$ is false), then these dependences were removed by privatizing A. The PD test is fully parallel and requires time $O(a/p + \log p)$, where p is the number of processors, and a is the total number of accesses made to A in the loop.

The PD test is illustrated using the loop shown in Figure 5. The access pattern is given by the subscript arrays T, V, and U. Since $A_w(:) \wedge A_r(:)$ and $A_{np}(:)$ are zero everywhere, the loop was a doall, but only after privatizing A since $w_A \neq m_A$.

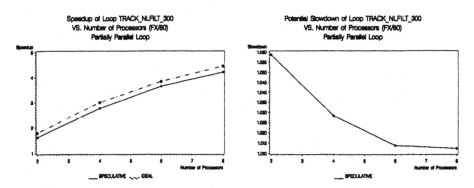

Fig. 6. Speedup and Potential Slowdown for NLFILT/300 from TRACK

3.5.3 Performance of run-time techniques

It can be shown that if the PD test passes, i.e., the loop is in fact fully parallel, then a significant portion of the ideal speedup of the loop is obtained. In particular, the speedups obtained range from nearly 100% of the ideal in the best case, to *at least* 25% of the ideal in the worst case (as derived from the parallel model). On the other hand, if the PD test fails, i.e., the loop is not fully parallel, then the sequential execution time will be increased by the time required by the failed parallelization attempt. Since the PD

---

4 **any** returns the "OR" of its vector operand's elements, i.e., $any(v(1:n)) = (v(1) \vee v(2) \vee \ldots \vee v(n))$.

test is fully parallel, this *slowdown* is proportional to $\frac{1}{p}T_{seq}$, where T_{seq} is the sequential execution time of the loop. If the target architecture is a MPP with *hundreds* or, in the future *thousands*, of processors, then the worst case potential speedups reach into the hundreds, and the cost of a failed test becomes a very small fraction of sequential execution time. Thus, speculating that the loop is fully parallel has the potential to offer large gains in performance, while at the same time risking only a small increase in the sequential execution time.

In Figure 6, we show experimental results of a Fortran implementation of the PD test on loop NLFILT/300 in a subroutine of TRACK. The measurements were made on an 8-processor Alliant FX/80 machine. The access pattern of the shared array in this loop cannot be analyzed by the compiler since the array is indexed by a subscript array that is computed at run-time. In addition, this loop is parallel for only 90% of its invocations. In the cases when the test failed, we restored state, and re-executed the loop sequentially. The speedup reported includes both the parallel and sequential instantiations. The potential slowdown reflects the increase in total execution time that would have resulted if the PD test had shown that the loop was not fully parallel: it is expressed as the ratio between $(T_{seq} + T_{pdt})$ and T_{seq}, where T_{pdt} is the time required for the PD test.

Our experimental results indicate that our techniques for loops with unknown iteration spaces usually yield significant speedups when compared to the available parallelism in the original loop. The experiments have also shown that the overhead associated with these techniques is generally very small. In addition, we have found that the additional memory requirements do not make these techniques impractical for the programs we have examined.

4 Evaluation of Polaris Parallelization

We place great importance on the evaluation of our work. When we began testing commercial parallelizers in the 1980s, we found that they performed well on small, synthetic loops, but when faced with actual scientific programs, they performed poorly. We analyzed them to determine the reasons for the deficiencies and identified several improvements that could be made in them. Now, we are implementing those improvements in the Polaris compiler, and once again we must evaluate where and how we have or have not succeeded.

4.1 The Benchmark Codes

The scientific programs that we used in our previous work were the Perfect Benchmarks®, which made it natural to use them to evaluate Polaris. We also included other scientific programs in order to demonstrate that our techniques apply to programs in general. We chose 6 of the 13 Perfect codes, plus two currently-in-use codes that we obtained from the National Center for Supercomputing Applications for our first evaluation efforts. We have determined that many of the other Perfect codes will require the use of some run-time techniques.

From the Perfect Benchmarks, we chose the programs ARC2D, BDNA, FLO52, MDG, OCEAN, and TRFD. Three of these codes (ARC2D, BDNA, and FLO52) have proven to be at least moderately parallelizable with traditional techniques. The other three (MDG, OCEAN, and TRFD) were poorly parallelized by traditional techniques. The two NCSA codes which we chose were CMHOG and CLOUD3D.

4.2 The Evaluation Metrics

Since we have focused our efforts on "finding parallelism" in this first year of the Polaris project, we devised a simple metric which attempts to quantify how well we achieved that. The metric is called *percent parallel coverage*. During the sequential execution of a program, we record how much time is spent executing each loop, determine the percentage of the overall running time of the sequential program, and call that figure the *percent coverage* of that loop. By adding up the coverages of each parallelized loop, we obtain the percent parallel coverage for the program. This gives us a single figure that portrays the quality of the parallelization. Even so, the percent parallel coverage is only a rough predictor of the eventual speedup that might be obtained from the code.

A second way of evaluating Polaris is to examine how well it does on loops ranked by running time. We ordered the loops in a program by average sequential running time per invocation, then divided the list into the longest-running 10%, the longest-running 50%, and finally all loops contributing at least 0.01% of the sequential running time. We tallied how many loops in each category required only "traditional" parallelization techniques, and how many required new Polaris techniques. The techniques found in the compilers we evaluated were scalar privatization, scalar reductions, recognition of induction variables in rectangular loop nests, and a simple subscript test. The major Polaris techniques were array privatization, array reductions, multi-site reductions, triangular inductions, the range test, and interprocedural analysis (as implemented through inline expansion).

4.3 The Results

Table 1 shows the resulting overall percent parallel coverage produced by the Polaris techniques for each of the eight benchmark codes, and what coverage could be gained by traditional techniques. In all cases, Polaris improved on the traditional techniques, and sometimes, quite dramatically, such as in the case of TRFD, where traditional techniques cover less than 1 percent, while Polaris found parallelism covering 99 percent of the sequential time.

We counted the number of loops in each category which were "intrinsically" serial (i.e., these could not be hand parallelized), how many required at least one of Polaris' techniques to be parallelized, how many could be parallelized by traditional techniques, and the total number of loops. These results were catalogued for the longest-running 10%, 50% and all loops (as described above). The results are displayed for each program in Table 2.

This table shows that in all percent brackets, Polaris' techniques are able to parallelize significantly more loops than traditional techniques. The fact that this ratio is most pronounced in the top 10% loops demonstrates the real impact of the new technology. Quite often we found that Polaris' techniques could parallelize the outer loop in a nest, while traditional techniques were sufficient only for the inner loops.

5 Conclusion

We have presented Polaris, a new parallelizing compiler, developed at the University of Illinois. Polaris includes a powerful basic infrastructure for manipulating Fortran programs and a number of improved analysis and transformation passes, notably subroutine inline expansion, symbolic analysis, induction and reduction variable recognition, data-dependence analysis, array privatization, and run-time analysis.

The current prototype of the Polaris compiler is able to parallelize our first evaluation suite of programs significantly better than available compilers. In many cases this is as good as the best manual parallelization.

Previous attempts at automatic parallelization were only successful for two of the programs in our test suite. Now we are successful in half of the Perfect Benchmarks and we expect to further increase this portion in the near future. This is a substantial improvement which expands the set of programs for which parallelizing compilers are successful from small and simple codes to medium sized and complicated. We have come a significant step closer to the goal of making parallel computing available to the broad user community.

Some remaining issues are the representativeness of our program suite and the machine model we are using. We believe that the Perfect Benchmarks plus the "NCSA suite" are a good starting point for a truly representative high-performance computer workload. The fact that our newly inspected programs have confirmed previous findings about effective parallelization techniques indicates that we are in fact converging in our search for the right compiler ingredients.

The output of Polaris is suitable for machines that provide a global address space. To use Polaris on message-passing machines one will need to develop complementing optimization techniques. We do not plan to develop these techniques since a number of such projects are currently underway. Furthermore, global address-based features will most likely be part of many parallel machines in the near term. This is already starting to happen as can be seen in the recent MPP announcements of Cray and Convex. However, it is important to note that Polaris' innovation is in improved recognition of parallelism, which is a necessary step for porting programs to any parallel machine available today.

References

[Ban88] Utpal Banerjec. *Dependence Analysis for Supercomputing*. Kluwer. Boston, MA, 1988.

[BCK+89] M. Berry, D. Chen, P. Koss, D. Kuck, L. Pointer, S. Lo, Y. Pang, R. Roloff, A. Sameh, E. Clementi, S. Chin, D. Schneider, G. Fox, P. Messina, D. Walker, C. Hsiung, J. Schwarzmeier, K. Lue, S. Orszag, F. Seidl, O. Johnson, G. Swanson, R. Goodrum, and J. Martin. The Perfect Club Benchmarks: Effective Performance Evalution of Supercomputers. *Int'l. Journal of Supercomputer Applications, Fall 1989*, 3(3):5–40, Fall 1989.

---

[5] CSRD reports are available via anonymous FTP from ftp.csrd.uiuc.edu:CSRD_Info, or the World Wide Web site http://www.csrd.uiuc.edu

[BE92]   William Blume and Rudolf Eigenmann. Performance Analysis of Parallelizing Compilers on the Perfect Benchmarks®Programs. *IEEE Transactions of Parallel and Distributed Systems*, 3(6):643–656, November 1992.

[BE94a]   William Blume and Rudolf Eigenmann. The Range Test: A Dependence Test for Symbolic, Non-linear Expressions. Technical Report 1345, Univ. of Illinois at Urbana-Champaign, Cntr. for Supercomputing Res. & Dev., April 1994.

[BE94b]   William Blume and Rudolf Eigenmann. Symbolic Analysis Techniques Needed for the Effective Parallelization of the Perfect Benchmarks. Technical Report 1332, Univ. of Illinois at Urbana-Champaign, Cntr. for Supercomputing Res. & Dev., January 1994.

[EHJP92] Rudolf Eigenmann, Jay Hoeflinger, G. Jaxon, and David Padua. The Cedar Fortran Project. Technical report, Univ. of Illinois at Urbana-Champaign, Cntr. for Supercomputing Res, & Dev., April 1992. CSRD Report No. 1262.

[EHLP91] Rudolf Eigenmann, Jay Hoeflinger, Zhiyuan Li, and David Padua. Experience in the Automatic Parallelization of Four Perfect-Benchmark Programs. *Lecture Notes in Computer Science 589. Proceedings of the Fourth Workshop on Languages and Compilers for Parallel Computing, Santa Clara, CA*, pages 65-83, August 1991.

[FHP+93] Keith A. Faigin, Jay P. Hoeflinger, David A. Padua, Paul M. Petersen, and Stephen A. Weatherford. The Polaris Internal Representation. Technical report, Univ. of Illinois at Urbana-Champaign, Cntr. for Supercomputing Res. and Dev., October 1993. CSRD Report No. 1317, UILU-ENG-93-8038.

[HKM91]   Mary W. Hall. Ken Kennedy, and Kathryn S. McKinley. Interprocedural transformations for parallel code generation. *Supercomputing'91*, pages 423–434, 1991.

[HP91]   Mohammad Haghighat and Constantine Polychronopoulos. Symbolic Dependence Analysis for High-Performance Parallelizing Compilers. *Parallel and Distributed Computing: Advances in Languages and Compilers for Parallel Processing, MIT Press, Cambridge, MA*, pages 310–330, 1991.

[PKK91]   K. Psarris, D. Klappholz, and X. Kong. On the accuracy of the Banerjee test. *Journal of Parallel and Distributed Computing*, 12(2):152–157, June 1991.

[PP93]   Paul M. Petersen and David A. Padua. Static and Dynamic Evaluation of Data Dependence Analysis. *Presented at ICS'93, Tokyo, Japan*, pages 107–116, July 19-23, 1993.

[RP94]   Lawrence Rauchwerger and David Padua. The PRIVATIZING DOALL Test: A Run-Time Technique for DOALL Loop Identification and Array Privatization . Technical Report 1329, Univ. of Illinois at Urbana-Champaign, Cntr. for Supercomputing Res. and Dev., January 1994.

[SMC91]   J. Saltz, R. Mirchandaney, and K. Crowley. Run-time parallelization and scheduling of loops. *IEEE Trans. Comput.*, 40(5), May 1991.

[TP93]   Peng Tu and David Padua. Automatic array privatization. In Utpal Banerjee, David Gelernter, Alex Nicolau, and David Padua, editors, *Proc. Sixth Workshop on Languages and Compilers for Parallel Com puting*, volume 768 of *Lecture Notes in Computer Science*, pages 500–521, Portland, OR, August 1993. Springer Verlag.

[TP94]   Peng Tu and David Padua. Demand-Driven Symbolic Analysis. Technical Report 1336, Univ. of Illinois at Urbana-Champaign, Cntr. for Supercomputing Res. & Dev., Febraury 1994.

[WB87]   Michael Wolfe and Utpal Banerjee. Data Dependence and its Application to Parallel Processing. *International Journal of Parallel Programming*, 16(2):137–178, 1987.

[Wea94]   Stephen Weatherford. High-Level Pattern-Matching Extensions to C++ for Fortran Program Manipulation in Polaris. Technical Report 1350, Univ of Illinois at Urbana-Champaign, Cntr. for Supercomputing Res. & Dev., May 1994.

PROGRAM	Polaris	traditional
MDG	99.95	68.54
ARC2D	99.94	69.96
TRFD	99.90	<0.01
FLO52	99.79	91.06
BDNA	97.95	32.33
OCEAN	95.42	32.58
CLOUD3D	84.55	43.09
CMHOG	81.93	17.11

Table 1. Percent coverage of the serial execution time of loops that can be parallelized with Polaris techniques and traditional techniques.

PROGRAM	top 10%			top 50%			all loops		
	serial	Pol/trad	total	serial	Pol/trad	total	serial	Pol/trad	total
ARC2D	1	7/3	8	8	32/28	40	10	70/64	80
FLO52	2	4/3	6	4	23/20	27	4	50/43	54
TRFD	0	0/0	1	0	2/0	3	0	4/0	6
MDG	1	2/0	3	3	10/3	14	3	23/16	28
BDNA	2	3/0	5	3	14/8	22	4	28/1	44
OCEAN	0	5/0	6	0	27/5	28	0	54/24	56
CLOUD3D	5	8/4	13	14	51/32	65	24	105/84	131
CMHOG	1	4/1	5	2	21/14	23	4	43/31	47

Table 2. Loop count in the categories: serial, needing Polaris/traditional techniques, total loops, for the evaluation codes. The loops were ordered by their average serial execution time, then divided into the groups: top 10%, top 50%, and all loops with 0.01% or more of the total serial time of the program.

A formal approach to the compilation of data-parallel languages

J.A. Trescher   L.C. Breebaart   P.F.G. Dechering*   A.B. Poelman*
J.P.M. de Vreught   H.J. Sips

Delft University of Technology, Faculty of Applied Physics
Email: BoosterTeam@cp.tn.tudelft.nl

Abstract. In this paper we describe an approach to the compilation of data-parallel programming languages based on a formally defined intermediate language, called *V-cal*. The calculus *V-cal* was designed to represent the semantics of data management and control primitives found in data-parallel languages and allows to describe program transformations and optimizations as semantics preserving rewrite rules.

Based on *V-cal* we propose a compiler design that meets two objectives: firstly, it provides a platform that allows compiler writers to construct different compilers from a set of implemented transformations and analyses using a modular construction set technique. Secondly, it structures the compilation process into three independent phases to facilitate the reuse of major parts of a compiler when porting it to a different target machine or architecture.

1   Introduction

It is widely recognized that the development of programs for distributed memory multi processors (DMMP) is a laborious, time-consuming and error-prone process. To support this process modern *data-parallel* languages provide a programming model with a single thread of control, thus supporting the familiar programming style of traditional imperative languages. To be able to adapt data-parallel programs automatically for efficient execution on a DMMP, data-parallel languages require the programmer to specify a mapping of data onto processors through *annotations*.

Experiences with some systems capable of automatically generating parallel code from data-parallel descriptions (a.o. Pandore [André 90], Fortran-D [Hiranandani 91], Vienna Fortran [Chapman 92]) have shown that this is a practical approach to exploit the power of DMMP while sustaining the (relative) ease of programming on sequential computer architectures. It also became clear that the current generation of parallelizing systems do not handle all applications equally well, and that much has to be learned before such systems will be able to deliver a reasonable performance for the full range of applications.

---

* Author is affiliated to N.W.O. and is sponsored by S.I.O.N.

Parallelizing compiler systems employ complex analysis and require a profound knowledge of the properties of a target architecture. In most systems this knowledge and analysis is hard coded into a large program. This makes it difficult to analyze the effect and interaction of different analysis and parallelizing techniques systematically. Additionally, it is difficult to upgrade such a system and it requires major efforts to transfer knowledge from one system to another. Therefore, while current parallelizing systems provide a proof of concept, they are of little use when trying to give answers to the questions that arise in the process of building more sophisticated systems [Pieper 93], such as

- how effectively are parallelizing compilers exposing parallelism?
- what is the contribution of each analysis and optimization technique?
- how do analysis and optimization techniques interact?
- how do optimization techniques interact?
- what additional analysis and optimization techniques would be helpful?
- how does language design influence analysis and optimization; and vice versa?

To explore possible answers to these questions, the data-parallel language *Booster* and an associated calculus *V-cal* that serves as a formal foundation of the compilation process have been defined [Paalvast 89] [Paalvast 91].

The language *Booster* provides a set of superscalar operations to express data-parallelism and introduces the *view* concept, a virtual data access mechanism that plays an important role in writing algorithms in *Booster* and in specifying annotations [Paalvast 91]. Another salient feature of *Booster* is the possibility to separate the descriptions of algorithms and the specification of annotations into different modules. By avoiding to scatter annotations through the source code the process of tuning becomes a matter of playing with different annotation modules and thus helps to identify the effects of annotations on the compilation process.

The semantics of *Booster* programs is formally defined using the notations of the calculus *V-cal* which was designed to represent the semantics of data management and control primitives found in data-parallel languages. In *V-cal* program transformations and optimizations are expressed by semantics preserving rewrite rules. Thus, *V-cal* provides a language-independent framework to express, to reason about, and to prove the correctness of the transformations involved in the compilation process of data-parallel languages. The first design of *V-cal*, presented in [Paalvast 92] proved unsatisfactory for a number of technical reasons. In this paper we present a redesign of *V-cal* that overcomes some difficulties encountered in the first attempt.

The rest of this paper is organized as follows: in Sections 2 and 3 we briefly introduce the concepts of *Booster* and *V-cal* necessary to understand the examples presented in the rest of this paper. Section 4 describes the general structure of compilers derived from our formal framework. In Section 5 we illustrate with a simple example how, using a modular construction set technique, different compilers can be derived from a set of implemented analyses and transformations.

Finally, we discuss the presented approach and outline our current research and development efforts.

2 Booster

Booster is an experimental language for the description of data-parallel algorithms. Data-parallelism is expressed through operations on superscalar data structures.

In parallel programming it is often important to identify sets of index values that refer to data upon which computations may be executed in parallel. In *Booster* this observation is acknowledged through the introduction of different language constructs for computations in the data and in the index domain.

For computations in the data domain *Booster* supports naturals, integers, reals, complex numbers, and *shapes*. A shape is *Booster*'s equivalent of a traditional array: a structured finite set of elements of a certain data type, accessed through indices. The ordered set of indices of a shape is called an *index set*. For computations on index sets *Booster* introduces *views*. A view is a function that takes an index set as an input, and returns another index set. Through the resulting index set of a view the data elements of the original shape can still be accessed. However, these data elements are now "viewed" through a different perspective.

Shapes and views

```
A: SHAPE {20} OF REAL;
B: SHAPE {3 # 10} OF COMPLEX;
V: VIEW {20};
W: VIEW;
```

Fig. 1. *Booster* declarations

In a *Booster* program view and shape identifiers are introduced by declarations as illustrated in Figure 1. The first statement declares A to be a vector of 20 data elements of type *real* – the *base type* of shape A. The index set of shape A is the ordered set $\{0,\ldots,19\}$. The shape B is declared to be a matrix of 3 by 10 data elements of type *real*. The index set for this shape is the ordered set $\{(0,0),(0,1),\ldots,(2,8),(2,9)\}$. A view may refer to the index set of shapes with arbitrary base types, therefore the declaration of view identifiers does not specify a base type. The declaration of the view identifier W even omits the specification of the cardinality of the index set that may be referred by W. As we will see this is in some cases desirable and renders views flexible and versatile.

View statements

View identifiers are defined by so-called *view statements*. The "identity" view

```
V <- A;
```

binds the view identifier V to the index set of the shape A. In Figure 2 we demonstrate how views can be used to select a subset of an index set, to permute index sets, or to change the dimensional form of an index set.

```
V: VIEW;
W: VIEW {20};
X: VIEW {4 # 5};
V <- A[\ 5..15];
W{i:_} <- A[19-i];
X{i:_, j:_} <- A[5*i+j] ;
```

Fig. 2. *Booster* view statements

In the first view statement the *set expression* \ 5..15 selects everything but the subrange $\{5, \ldots, 15\}$ of the index set of the shape A. After this statement the corresponding data elements of shape A may be referred through the index set $\{0, \ldots, 8\}$ of view V. In the second view statement a view on shape A is created that represents the index set of shape A in reverse order. The range of the variable i is defined to be the index set $\{0, \ldots, 19\}$ specified by the declaration of the view identifier W and the symbol _. In the last view statement the index set of the vector A is represented by a view with the form of a 4 by 5 matrix.

Content statements

```
A, B, C: SHAPE {n # n} OF REAL;
D: SHAPE {20} OF REAL;
E: SHAPE {10} OF REAL;
V: VIEW {10};

A := B + C;
A[2..6, 3..8] := C[4..8, 0..5];
A[i:_,j:_] := B[j, i];

V{i:_} <- A[2*i];
D[4] := 42;
V[2] := 42;

E := V;
```

Fig. 3. Some *Booster* statements

Content statements move and modify the data stored in shapes. Figure 3 shows some typical content statements. The first content statement makes an assignment to all elements of the shape A. In the second content statement the values of selected elements of the shape C are assigned to selected elements of shape A. The third content statement specifies that the shape A becomes the transpose of shape B.

The interaction between view and content statements is illustrated by the following three statements. After defining V the following content statements involving V and D have the same effect. Finally, the last statement shows how views can be utilized to emulate selective assignments known from *APL 2* [Brown 88].

Booster programs

In addition to the content and view statements, *Booster* also offers several control-flow constructs similar to those found in traditional imperative languages to express sequential, conditional, iterative, and repetitive execution. To structure source programs into modules *Booster* provides a module system similar to that of Modula-2 [Wirth 82].

```
MODULE LU;
FROM Data IMPORT M, Perm;
PROCEDURE Pivoting(IN V: VIEW {n # n};
  OUT PivRow: NATURAL; OUT P: VIEW {};
  OUT R,C: VIEW {n-1};
  OUT S: VIEW {n-1 # n-1});
  BEGIN
    PivRow := MAXINDEX(ABS (V[_,0]));
    P <- V[PivRow, 0];
    R <- V[PivRow,_];
    C <- V[\ PivRow,0];
    S <- V[\ PivRow,1..n];
END Pivoting;
VAR
  P,R,C,S: VIEW;
  PivRow: NATURAL; END;
BEGIN
  S <- M;
  WHILE SIZE(S) > 1 DO
    Pivoting(S, PivRow, P, R, C, S);
    Perm[n - SIZE(S[_, 0])] := PivRow;
    C[i:_] := C[i]/P;
    S[i:_,j:_] := S[i,j] - C[i]*R[j];
  END;
END LU.
```

Fig. 4. LU decomposition in *Booster*

We illustrate some of the concepts of *Booster* by means of a program that implements LU decomposition with partial pivoting. The algorithm presented in Figure 4 takes a non-singular $n \times n$ matrix M as input and returns a permutation matrix Perm and an upper and lower triangular matrix U and L both coded in M such that Perm M $= LU$. In each iteration of the algorithm the call of the procedure Pivoting identifies four areas of interest (cf. Figure 5): the pivot element P, the pivot row R, the pivot column C, and the remaining submatrix S. These areas are extracted from the view V by using partial pivoting on the first column (realized by a call to the intrinsic function MAXINDEX). The vector Perm represents an encoding of the permutation matrix by tracing the positions of the pivot elements.

Annotations

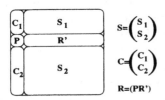

Fig. 5. Views defined by a call of the procedure Pivoting

Besides being used as virtual data access mechanism in the description of algorithms views also play an important role in the specification of annotations. The declared shapes of a *Booster* program define the amount of storage needed for the representation of the values the algorithm operates on. A shape, however, can be interpreted as a view on memory locations. In *Booster* the programmer can influence the representation of shapes by relating the shape to the memories of a virtual machine through a view. This principle is illustrated in Figure 6.

In its simplest form a virtual machine is described by a shape of "memory modules" without any topological information. This construction enables programmers to describe different memory mappings of a data structure by specifying an appropriate view. For instance, in the following program fragment the shape A is decomposed row-wise cyclic, column-wise cyclic and element-wise cyclic onto a vector of memory modules VM:

```
VM : SHAPE {n} OF PROCESSORS;
A  : SHAPE {k # m} OF REAL;
A{i:_,_}   <- VM[i MOD n];
A{_,j:_}   <- VM[j MOD n];
A{i:_,j:_} <- VM[(i*m+j) MOD n];
```

Returning to our example from Figure 4 two possible mappings are:

```
ANNOTATION MODULE LU;             ANNOTATION MODULE LU;
FROM Data IMPORT M;               FROM LU IMPORT S;
MACHINE                           MACHINE
   VM: SHAPE {n} OF PROCESSORS;      VM: SHAPE {n} OF PROCESSORS;
END;                              END;
BEGIN                             BEGIN
   M{i:_,_} <- VM[i MOD n];          S{i:_} <- VM[i MOD n];
END LU.                           END LU.
```

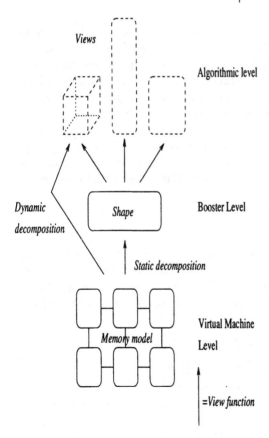

In the first case the shape M is decomposed row-wise over the different memory modules. If the owner-computes rule applies, this mapping implies that an increasing number of processors become idle as the algorithm proceeds. In the second case the mapping of data onto the machine model is done using the view identifier S. The effect of this *dynamic* decomposition on S, that represents the data on which all current calculation is performed, is load balancing at the expense of redistribution of data.

It is intended that the mapping of data to a machine model can be specified on different levels of abstraction. These range from a global partitioning of shapes or views (as shown above) to detailed machine specific (e.g. memory hierarchy) mapping onto processors and memories (see also [Thomas 92]).

Fig. 6. Data decomposition

3 V-cal

The calculus *V-cal* has been defined to provide a formal foundation for the compilation of data-parallel languages. It serves two purposes: firstly, it is used to describe the semantics of data-parallel languages. Secondly, it is used to describe the transformations of an optimizing compiler as semantics preserving rewrite rules.

A *V-cal* expression represents a function on *states*. In *V-cal* a state is an abstract representation of the information relevant to the execution of a program (i.e. values stored in memory locations, functions represented by view identifiers etc.). The denotational semantics of a *Booster*-program are defined by a syntactical mapping of *Booster* programs to *V-cal* expressions.

A complete formal introduction of *V-cal* is beyond the scope of this paper. However, this section will give sufficient details to demonstrate the principles underlying the presented approach and to understand the examples given in Section 5. A more comprehensive presentation of *V-cal*, *Booster*, and their relation can be found in [Breebaart 94].

Views and States

A view is a function on *index sets*. An index set $I = (\mathbf{l}, \mathbf{u}), \mathbf{l}, \mathbf{u} \in \mathcal{N}^d$ is a finite "rectangular" subset of $\mathcal{N}^d, d \geq 0$: $I \hat{=} \{(n_1, \ldots, n_d) \mid \exists n_i \in \mathcal{N} \bullet l_i \leq n_i \leq u_i, 1 \leq i \leq d\}$. Let IS be the set of all index sets, then a *view* is represented by a tuple $v = (dp, ip)$ with the *domain propagation* function $dp : IS \rightarrow IS$ which is defined exactly for one value is, and the *index propagation* function $ip : dp(is) \rightarrow is$.

In *V-cal* the set of memory locations an algorithm works on is represented by the index set Loc. Let $\mathcal{D}$ be the set of data values a memory location may contain, we then define the set of *data state functions* $D \hat{=} \{\delta \mid \delta : Loc \rightarrow \mathcal{D}\}$. Let ID be a set of identifiers and let $\mathcal{V}$ be the set of views, we then define the set of *view state functions* $V \hat{=} \{\varphi \mid \varphi : ID \rightarrow \mathcal{V}\}$. With these definitions we can define the set of *states* as $\Sigma \hat{=} D \times V$.

State functions

To motivate the definitions of the last paragraph we present in the following examples of *V-cal* expressions that are used to describe the semantics of declarations, view and content statements. In *V-cal* the effect of a declaration is described by a function that replaces the view state component of the current state by an appropriate function:

$$\mathcal{D}ecl : ID \times \mathcal{V} \rightarrow \Sigma \rightarrow \Sigma$$

$$\mathcal{D}ecl(id, v)((\delta, \varphi)) \hat{=} (\delta, \varphi \lhd \{(id, v)\})$$

The replacement operator $\lhd$ takes a function and an ordered set of value-result pairs as arguments and yields a function as result. Informally, it can be defined as:

$$(f \lhd (y, r))(x) \hat{=} \begin{cases} f(x) & \text{if } x \neq y \\ r & \text{otherwise} \end{cases}$$

$$(f \lhd \{(y_1, r_1), \ldots, (y_n, r_n)\})(x) \triangleq (\ldots (f \unlhd (y_1, r_1)) \unlhd \ldots \unlhd (y_n, r_n))$$

The semantics of the *Booster* declaration M: SHAPE {1000 # 1000} OF COMPLEX; may then be expressed by the *V-cal* expression $\mathcal{D}ecl(\text{M}, (dp_\text{M}, \mu_\text{M}))$ where $dp_\text{M} \triangleq \{(Loc_\text{M}, ((0,0), (999,999)))\}$, and $\mu_\text{M} : \{0, \ldots, 999\} \times \{0, \ldots, 999\} \rightarrow Loc_\text{M}$ for an index set $Loc_\text{M} \subseteq Loc$, is a mapping of the shape M to memory locations, such that Loc_M does not overlap with the range of the memory mapping of other declared shapes.

As with declarations, the effect of view statements is described by a function that changes the view state component of the current state:

$$View : ID \times ID \times \mathcal{V} \rightarrow \Sigma \rightarrow \Sigma$$

$$View(vid_1, vid_2, v)((\delta, \varphi)) \triangleq (\delta, \varphi \lhd \{(vid_1, v \bullet \varphi(vid_2))\})$$

where the infix operator $\bullet$ denotes the composition of views, defined as follows:

$$\bullet : \mathcal{V} \times \mathcal{V} \rightarrow \mathcal{V}$$

$$(dp_v, ip_v) \bullet (dp_w, ip_w) \triangleq (dp_v \circ dp_w, ip_w \circ ip_v)$$

We are now able to describe the semantics of the view statement

    C <- V[\ PivRow, 0];

in the procedure Pivoting of Figure 4 by the following *V-cal* expression:

$$View(\text{C}, \text{V}, (dp_\text{C}, ip_\text{C}))(\sigma)$$

$$dp_\text{C} \triangleq \{(((0,0), (\mathcal{A}_\sigma(\text{n}), \mathcal{A}_\sigma(\text{n}))), ((0), (\mathcal{A}_\sigma(\text{n-1}))))\}$$

$$ip_\text{C}(i) \triangleq \begin{cases} ip_{\varphi(\text{V})}(i, 0) & \text{if } i < \mathcal{A}_\sigma(\text{PivRow}) \\ ip_{\varphi(\text{V})}(i+1, 0) & \text{otherwise} \end{cases}$$

and $\mathcal{A}_\sigma$ is the semantic function that evaluates an expression in the state defined by the argument of the function $View$.

To define the *V-cal* expression that will be used to describe the semantics of content statements we must first introduce the concept of *parameter bindings*. A parameter binding "binds" a vector $\mathbf{v}$ of fresh (i.e. not used anywhere else) free variables to an index set $(\mathbf{l}, \mathbf{u})$ with the same dimension. Parameter bindings are denoted by $(\mathbf{v} \leftarrow (\mathbf{l}, \mathbf{u}))$ and imply that the variable v_i ranges over the set $\{l_i, \ldots, u_i\}$. Parameter bindings are necessary to refer to the instances of a superscalar operation.

The effect of content statements will be described in *V-cal* by a function that replaces the data state component of the current state by an appropriate function. Let $\mathcal{P}$ be the set of parameter bindings and let $\mathcal{E}(\mathbf{v})$ be the set of parametrized expressions (not defined in detail here), the corresponding *V-cal* expression is then defined as follows:

$$Content : \mathcal{P} \times \mathcal{V} \times \mathcal{E}(\mathbf{v}) \rightarrow \Sigma \rightarrow \Sigma$$

$$Content((i \leftarrow I), v, E(i))((\delta, \varphi)) \triangleq (\delta \lhd C, \varphi)$$

with the lexicographically ordered set $C \cong \{(ip_v(i), \mathcal{A}_{\delta_i}(E(i))) \mid i \in I\}$ and the sequence of data state functions $\delta_i \cong \delta \lhd \{c_j \mid c_j \in C, j < i\}$.

This scheme can easily be extended to work for lists of views and corresponding lists of expressions to represent the semantics of loops with several content statements in their body.

With these definitions the semantics of the statement

```
S[i:_,j:_] := S[i, j] - C[i]*R[j];
```

from our example in Figure 4 may be described by the following *V-cal* expression:

$$Content(((i, j) \leftarrow I), \varphi(\mathsf{S}), E(i, j))$$

$$I \cong \mathbf{range}(dp_{\varphi(\mathsf{S})})$$

$$E(i, j) \cong \delta_{(i,j)}(ip_{\varphi(\mathsf{S})}(i, j)) - \delta_{(i,j)}(ip_{\varphi(\mathsf{C})}(i)) * \delta_{(i,j)}(ip_{\varphi(\mathsf{R})}(j))$$

Building on these definitions it is straightforward to represent the semantics of data-parallel programs by means of a set of mutually recursive function definitions for the syntactic constructs of *Booster*, as illustrated below for the if and while statement, and statement lists:

$$\mathcal{I}\mathit{fstat} : B \times S\mathcal{L} \times S\mathcal{L} \to \Sigma \to \Sigma$$

$$\mathcal{I}\mathit{fstat}(b, S_1, S_2)(\sigma) \cong \begin{cases} Statlist(S_1)(\sigma) \text{ if } \mathcal{B}_\sigma(b) \\ Statlist(S_2)(\sigma) \text{ otherwise} \end{cases}$$

$$\mathcal{W}hile : B \times S\mathcal{L} \to \Sigma \to \Sigma$$

$$\mathcal{W}hile(b, S)(\sigma) \cong \begin{cases} (\mathcal{W}hilestat(b, S) \circ Statlist(S))(\sigma) \text{ if } \mathcal{B}_\sigma(b) \\ \sigma \qquad\qquad\qquad\qquad\qquad\qquad \text{ otherwise} \end{cases}$$

$$Statlist : S\mathcal{L} \to \Sigma \to \Sigma$$

$$Statlist((S_0, \dots, S_n))(\sigma) \cong \begin{cases} (Statlist((S_1, \dots, S_n)) \circ Stat(S_0))(\sigma) \text{ if } n > 0 \\ Stat(S_0)(\delta, \varphi) \qquad\qquad\qquad\qquad\qquad\quad \text{ otherwise} \end{cases}$$

where B, $\mathcal{B}$, and $S\mathcal{L}$ represent the set of boolean expressions, their evaluation function, and the set of statement lists, respectively.

Parallelism and communication

Booster provides a programming model that abstracts from parallelism, communication and synchronization. To be able to express optimizing program transformations in *V-cal* these concepts are made explicit by means of dedicated operators. For instance, the data-parallelism implicitly introduced in *Booster* by provision of superscalar operations, may be specified explicitly in *V-cal* using the $\mathcal{F}orall$-expression. The semantics of this expression is derived from the $Content$-expression as follows:

$$\mathcal{F}orall : \mathcal{P} \times V \times \mathcal{E}(\mathbf{v}) \to \Sigma \to \Sigma$$

$$\mathcal{F}orall((i \leftarrow I), v, E(i))(\sigma) \cong (\delta \lhd C, \varphi)$$

with the lexicographically ordered set $C \cong \{(ip_v(i), \mathcal{A}_\sigma(E(i))) \mid i \in I\}$.

From these definitions it is obvious that the "sequential" $\mathcal{C}ontent$-expression may be transformed to the "parallel" $\mathcal{F}orall$-expression, if there is no dependence of the values of the expressions $E(i)$ on values stored in memory locations referred to by ip_v.

Other optimizing program transformations may need to introduce synchronizations (e.g. do-across scheduling) or communication (e.g. array block transfer). For these purposes V-cal provides operators that introduce synchronization and data transport in a machine independent way.

4 A compiler design

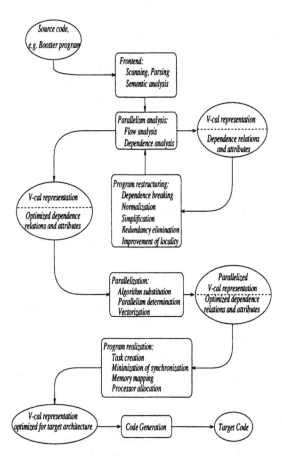

Fig. 7. Structure of a compiler using V-cal as intermediate language

The goal of a parallelizing compiler is to transform a program into a semantically equivalent representation that efficiently utilizes the target machines potential for parallel execution. The effectiveness of present compilers to exploit the potential parallelism of programs is mostly determined by the compiler writers' ability to choose the appropriate heuristics to guide the transformation process and his knowledge of the properties of the target architecture. However, as pointed out by others [Pieper 93] [Hulman 93], there is a lack of systematic research in this area and compiler writers are left to their own intuition and ingenuity.

Based on this observation we have two important goals we want to meet with the design of a compiler: first, there must be a flexible interface, that enables a compiler writer to study systematically the effects of different transformation sequences and heuristics employed by a parallelizing compiler. Second, it must be possible to reuse major parts of a compiler when porting it to a different target machine or architecture.

To meet the first design goal we propose a compiler design that provides a well defined interface to the transformation phases applied during program optimization. Transformations are implemented as modular and independent activities that may be applied in any order. This allows to construct different compilers with little overhead by defining different transformation sequences, and thus enables the compiler writer to explore the effect of different heuristics systematically.

To meet the second design goal we suggest to structure the compilation of data-parallel languages into three independent phases as depicted in Figure 7: first, a program is restructured with the goal to maximize the potential parallelism of an algorithm. In this phase only machine independent transformations are employed. Second, the program parts amenable to parallelization are substituted by their semantically equivalent parallel counterparts. Transformations in this phase will usually consider the general performance properties of the underlying architecture (e.g. distributed memory vs. shared memory architectures). Finally, the parallelized program is mapped to the target architecture in a way that makes efficient use of the given resources. The transformation sequence applied in this phase is geared to exploit the characteristics of a specific machine. When retargetting a compiler this part usually will be rewritten.

Dependence relations

The potential for parallel execution of a data-parallel program is determined by the dependence relations of the program parts. Therefore, the intermediate representation of a program and the representation of the data dependence relations form the scaffold of a parallelizing compiler determining which optimizations can be done and how easily.

Transformations may have effect on both the program structure and the dependence relations. To be able to implement transformations as independent activities in our compiler a *parallelism analysis* module is provided that allows transformations to acquire information about dependence relations and to update this information after a transformation. The following discussion gives a sketch of the functionality of a parallelism analysis module.

We distinguish three types of data dependence that constrain the potential parallel execution of two program components: *output dependence, anti dependence,* and *flow dependence* [Banerjee 88]. Let the set of *program components* C_P of a program P consist of the data references, expressions, content statements, view statements, procedure calls, and compound statements in P. In a compiler the dependence relations of P can then be represented as relations on program components: $\delta_P^o, \delta_P^a, \delta_P^f \subseteq C_P \times C_P$, respectively. Algorithms to compute approximations of the program dependence relations can be found in [Banerjee 88], [Wolfe 89], and [Zima 90].

For some program transformations it is useful to have more detailed information about the nature of a dependency, e.g. a distance vector or a run-time condition that verifies the existence of a dependency. Let ATTR be the set of those attributes, then this information can be represented in a compiler by functions: $f_{\delta_P^x}^A : \delta_P^x \rightarrow A, for\, A \in \mathrm{ATTR}, and\, x \in \{o, a, f\}$.

Transformations

According to the phases of a parallelizing compiler we classify the transformations applied by a parallelizing compiler into three categories: program restructuring transformations, parallelism determining transformations, and target dependent transformations.

The goal of program restructuring transformations is to improve the potential parallelism of a program by altering the control and data structures of the program to eliminate dependencies, e.g. scalar expansion, variable renaming, or statement splitting. Program restructuring transformations also include traditional compiler optimization techniques to remove redundant instructions, e.g. code motion or dead-code elimination.

The second category of transformations identifies the parts of a program that may be executed in parallel. Parallelism determining transformations include techniques that replace entire program fragments with an algorithm from a library of optimized algorithms for the particular target machine [Kessler 93], and those that replace sequential loops by parallel loops wherever possible.

Target dependent transformations utilize the knowledge about the underlying parallel software and hardware architecture to match the parallelized program to the target machine. The objective of these transformations is to introduce vectorization (e.g. loop unrolling, loop interchanging, strip mining), decrease synchronization time, and to minimize data access time (array decomposition and distribution, array block transfer, scalar expansion).

5   A simple transformation system

```
rule parallelize
  replace C [VcalExpr]
    'content P [ParameterBinding]
        V [list View] E [list Expression]
  where
    C [noDependence]
  by
    'forall P V E [updateDependencies]
end rule
```

Fig. 8. A simple TXL rule

In this section we define the optimization phase of a compiler that is able to perform some simple optimizing transformations on *V-cal* expressions. The examples we will use are loop distribution and logarithmic reduction replacement. The corresponding transformation rules are described using the tree transformation language TXL [Cordy 93]. The decision to use TXL to describe the transformations of a optimizing compiler was based on the experience gained defining and implementing a prototype of a rule based compiler system [Breebaart 92].

```
for i = 0, 99              for i = 0, 99
    A[i] = i;                  A[i] = i
    x = x + i              endfor;
endfor                     for i = 0, 99
                               x = x + i
                           endfor
```

(a) before distribution   (b) after distribution

Fig. 9. Loop distribution

A transformation rule in TXL consists of the specification of a *pattern*, a *replacement*, and an optional *condition*. A TXL transformation rule searches a tree for occurrences of its pattern, and, provided its condition succeeds, replaces the matched pattern by its replacement. The rule given in Figure 8 searches a tree for a *Content*-expression C and replaces it by a corresponding *Forall*-expression, provided there are no data dependences in C. After the replacement the dependence relations are updated appropriately. Note, in TXL a function is applied to its argument in postfix form, using the function name enclosed in square brackets.

Loop distribution allows to break a loop with a body of several statements into several smaller loops with the goal that some of the smaller loops are parallel. Consider the following *V-cal* expression

$$Content(((i) \leftarrow ((0),(99))), (\varphi(A),\varphi(x)), (i,\delta_i(ip_{\varphi(x)}) + i)) \tag{1}$$

which may be used to describe the semantics of the loop in Figure 9 (a). The first statement of this loop may be executed in parallel, while the second requires results from a preceding iteration, and therefore must be executed sequentially. However, since no dependence between these statements exists they may be split into two *Content*-expressions, from which one is amenable to parallelization.

A transformation rule that distributes *Content*-expressions is defined in Figure 10. This rule is applied only if one of the resulting *Content*-expressions is amenable to parallelization. This is expressed by the condition [?parallelize]. The result of an application of

```
rule distribute
  replace C [VcalExpr]
    'content P [ParameterBinding]
       V1 [View] V2 [View]
       E1 [Expression] E2 [Expression]
  construct C1 [VcalExpr]
    'content P V1 E1
  construct C2 [VcalExpr]
    'content P V2 E2
  where
    C [noDependence]
  where
    C1 [?parallelize]
    C2 [?parallelize]
  by
    'statlist((C1, C2)) [updateDependencies]
end rule
```

Fig. 10. Loop distribution in TXL

this rule to the *V-cal* expression (1) would be:

$$\mathcal{S}tatlist(Content(((i) \leftarrow ((0),(99))), \varphi(A), i),$$
$$Content(((i) \leftarrow ((0),(99))), \varphi(x), \delta_i(ip_{\varphi(x)}) + i)) \tag{2}$$

This *V-cal* expression corresponds to the pseudo code fragment in Figure 9 (b).

```
rule logarithmicStepSubstitution
  replace C [VcalExpr]
    'content P [ParameterBinding]
         V [lValue]
         R [rValue] O [Operator]
           E [Expression]
  construct Target [Ident]
    V [extractViewId]
  construct Source [VcalExpr]
    R [extractRefId]
  where
    Target [isScalar]
  where
    Target [= Source]
  where
    O [isCommutative]
  by
    'reduce P V O E [updateDependencies]
end rule
```

Fig. 11. Logarithmic step substitution

Another optimization for this *V-cal* expression would be to replace the second component of the statement list by a logarithmic step reduction. A rule that implements this optimization is presented below. The conditions of this rule require that the left hand side of the corresponding content statement is a scalar and the right hand side is an expression consisting of a binary commutative operator applied to this scalar and an arbitrary expression.

If this rule is applied to the *V-cal* expression (2) we obtain the expression:

$$\begin{aligned} Statlist(Content(((i) \leftarrow ((0),(99))),\varphi(\mathsf{A}),i), \\ Reduce(((i) \leftarrow ((0),(99))),\varphi(\mathsf{x}),+,i)) \end{aligned} \tag{3}$$

The optimization phase of a compiler that performs loop distribution, parallelization, and the logarithmic step reduction substitution may be defined by the simple rule depicted in Figure 12.

```
rule simpleOptimizer
  replace [program]
    P [program]
  by
    P [distribute]
      [logarithmicStepSubstitution]
      [parallelize]
end rule
```

Fig. 12. A simple optimizer

It is obvious how this scheme can be used to build more sophisticated transformation systems from a set of implemented transformation rules. Due to the modular nature of the transformation rules it is possible to study the effect of different transformation sequences by rearranging the corresponding rule applications.

6 Discussion

In this paper we have introduced a general approach to the compilation of data-parallel languages based on a formally defined calculus. We proposed to structure the compilation process in three phases, which allows to easily identify and reuse parts of a compiler when porting a compiler to a different target machine or architecture.

As a principal design issue we suggest to define program transformations and dependence analysis operations as modular and independent activities. This facilitates the construction of different compilers from a set of implemented transformations using a modular construction set technique. This process is supported by the expressiveness and functionality of the tree transformation language TXL. We hope that this research will enable compiler writers to explore the effect of heuristics used in parallelizing compilers systematically, and thus improve our understanding of the techniques which can be used in such a compiler effectively.

Currently, we are trying to define a weak type system for *V-cal* to enhance its usability. Our implementation efforts concentrate on the definition of an abstract data type that allows to efficiently compute, represent, and update the data dependence relations of *V-cal* expressions. It is also intended to extend *V-cal* by means to compute a set of alternative transformations and to compare the resulting expressions by means of a cost function.

References

[André 90] F. André, J. Pazat, H. Thomas *Pandore: A System to Manage Data Distribution*, in Proc. 1990 Intl. Conf. on Supercomputing, The Netherlands, 1990.

[Banerjee 88] U. Banerjee *Dependence Analysis for Supercomputing*, Kluwer Academic Publishers, 1988.

[Breebaart 92] L. Breebaart, P. Dornbosch *The rule language, syntax and semantics*, TNO-report, No. 92-TPD/zp-1024, October 1992.

[Breebaart 94] L. Breebaart, P. Dechering, A. Poelman, J. Trescher, H. de Vreught *The Booster Language Report*, TU Delft, Technical Report, *in preparation*.

[Brown 88] J. Brown, S. Pakin, R. Polivka *APL2 at a glance*, Prentice Hall, Englewood Cliffs, 1988.

[Chapman 92] B. Chapman, P. Mehrotra, H. Zima *Programming in Vienna Fortran*, Scientific Programming, 1(1):31-50, 1992.

[Cordy 93] J. Cordy, I. Carmichael *The TXL Programming Language, Syntax and Informal Semantics, Version 7*, Department of Computing and Information Science, Queens University at Kingston, txl@qucis.queensu.ca, 1993

[Hiranandani 91] S. Hiranandani, K. Kennedy, C.-W. Tseng *Compiler Support for Machine-Independent Parallel Programming in Fortran-D*, Technical Report RICE COMP TR91-149, Rice University, March 1991.

[Hulman 93] J. Hulman, S. Andel, B. Chapman, H. Zima *Intelligent Parallelization within the Vienna Fortran Compilation System*, in Proc. 4. Intl. Workshop on Compilers for Parallel Computers, Delft 1993, The Netherlands.

[Kessler 93] C. Kessler *Pattern Recognition Enables Automatic Parallelization of Numerical Codes*, in Proc. 4. Intl. Workshop on Compilers for Parallel Computers, Delft 1993, The Netherlands.

[Paalvast 89] E. Paalvast, H. Sips *A high-level language for the description of parallel algorithms*, in Proc. of Parallel Computing '89, North Holland Publ., 1989.

[Paalvast 91] E. Paalvast, A. van Gemund, H. Sips *Automatic Parallel Program Generation and Optimization from Data Decompositions* in Proceedings, 1991 International Conference Parallel Processing, St. Charles, USA.

[Paalvast 92] E. Paalvast *Programming for Parallelism and Compiling for Efficiency*, Ph.D. Thesis, TU Delft, 1992.

[Pieper 93] K. Pieper *Parallelizing Compilers: Implementation and Effectiveness*, Tech. Rep. Stanford University, Computer Systems Laboratory, CSL-TR-93-575, 1993.

[Thomas 92] H. Thomas, H. Sips, E. Paalvast *A Taxonomy of User-Annotated Programs for Distributed Memory Computers*, in Proceedings 1992 International Conference on Parallel Processing, 1992.

[Wirth 82] N. Wirth *Programming in Modula-2*, 3. Edition, Springer Heidelberg, 1982.

[Wolfe 89] M. Wolfe *Optimizing Supercompilers for Supercomputers*, MIT Press, Cambridge, Massachusetts, 1989.

[Zima 90] H. Zima with B. Chapman *Supercompilers for Parallel and Vector Computers*, ACM Press, New York, 1990.

The Data Partitioning Graph:
Extending Data and Control Dependencies
for Data Partitioning

Tsuneo Nakanishi[†], Kazuki Joe[†], Hideki Saito[*],
Constantine D. Polychronopoulos[*], Akira Fukuda[†] and Keijiro Araki[†]

[†] Graduate School of Information Science,
Nara Institute of Science and Technology
[*] Center for Supercomputing Research and Development,
University of Illinois at Urbana-Champaign

Abstract. Scalability and cost considerations suggest that distributed and distributed shared memory parallel computers will dominate future parallel architectures. These machines could not be used effectively unless efficient automatic and static solutions to the data partitioning and placement problem become available. Significant progress toward this end has been made in the last few years, but we are still far from having general solutions which are efficient for all classes of applications. In this paper we propose the data partitioning graph (DPG) as an intermediate representation for parallelizing compilers, which augments previous intermediate representations, and provides a framework for carrying out partitioning and placement of not only regular data structures (such as arrays), but also of irregular structures and scalar variables. Although recent approaches to task-graph-based intermediate representations focus on representing data and control dependencies between tasks, they largely ignore the use of program variables by the different tasks. Traditional data partitioning methods usually employ algorithm-dependent techniques, and are considered independently of processor assignments (which ought to be handled simultaneously with data partitioning). Moreover, approaches to data partitioning concentrate exclusively on array structures. By explicitly encapsulating the use of program variables by the task nodes, the DPG provides a framework for handling data partitioning as well as processor assignment in the same context. We also discuss the hierarchical data partitioning graph (HDPG) which encapsulates the hierarchy of the compiled programs and is used to map the hierarchy of computations to massively parallel computers with distributed memory system.

1 Introduction

Multiprocessor systems with hundreds and thousands of processors are slowly emerging as hardware technology continues to evolve. Due to limitations of memory access contention, hardware implementation technology and cost, these multiprocessor systems are almost exclusively implemented as distributed shared memory systems, or as message passing systems which can be configured to be significantly larger than distributed shared memory architectures.

On a distributed shared memory machine, each processor can access directly its local memory which is part of the shared address space, or any other remote memory modules at an increased latency. This increase in memory latency — which can be as large as 100 times the local memory access time — is perhaps the single most significant limiting factor of distributed shared memory architectures. Determining ways to reduce memory latency is therefore one of the central research problems in parallel processing. A combination of software and hardware techniques can be used to attack this bottleneck. In this paper we discuss a software solution based on the partitioning and allocation of data to local memories. The problem of data partitioning and allocation has been tackled by many in the parallel processing community, and although no universally acceptable solution exists, efficient heuristics have been proposed which work well only for specific classes of applications.

The cost of interprocessor communication in a message passing system is higher than that of a shared memory multiprocessor system. So is the cost of context switching. It is infeasible to apply process migration techniques for reducing interprocessor communication on a message passing system, though it is effective in shared memory systems. Therefore we need more efficient ways to partition data on message passing systems. The optimal data partitioning is an NP-complete problem. Usually programmers employ ad hoc or algorithm-dependent solutions. However, for automatic solutions via parallelizing compilers we need general algorithms for determining a near optimal partitioning. Many researchers have proposed various algorithms for data partitioning[6][7][8]. But several problems still remain. Some of the approaches find just a locally optimal solution, which is optimal only in a set of given loops. Many of them ignore the problem of processor allocation which is interwined with data partitioning.

In this paper, we propose a general framework for data partitioning which is independent of application problems. At first we discuss the case of distributed shared memory systems. In the future, we plan to extend this framework to message passing systems.

The new generation parallelizing compilers often use task graphs as an intermediate representation to analyze and optimize codes[3][4]. A task graph usually consists of nodes representing tasks and arcs representing control flow and/or dependencies between tasks. In this paper we introduce the Data Partitioning Graph (DPG), which is an extension of such a representation, namely the Control Data Dependence Graph (CDDG) proposed in [5]. We define the DPG by adding nodes which capture information about the use of program variables and arcs which express the access pattern to program variables on the CDDG. Using the DPG, we consider the problem of data partitioning as the problem of node clustering on the DPG. We also consider the problem of processor allocation in the same context. Later on we introduce the Hierarchical DPG (HDPG) which encapsulates the hierarchy of the compiled programs and is used to map this hierarchy on the hierarchy of the underlying architecture.

The paper is organized as follows. In Section 2, we review traditional task graphs. In Section 3, we introduce the DPG/HDPG and give a formal definition of the HDPG. In Section 4, we describe the data partitioning and the processor allocation approaches we have developed using the DPG/HDPG. In Section 5 we show an example of DPG. Finally Section 6 gives the conclusion of this paper.

2   Task Graphs

Task graphs are often used by parallelizing compilers to analyze or optimize a given sequential program. In this section, we give an overview of the Control Flow Graph (CFG), the Control Dependence Graph (CDG), the Data Dependence Graph (DDG) and the Control Data Dependence Graph (CDDG), which are used as the basis for deriving the DPG. For more details about the CFG, CDG,

DDG and CDDG please refer to [1] [3]. These graphs and their variants are commonly used as intermediate representations in sequential and parallelizing compilers.

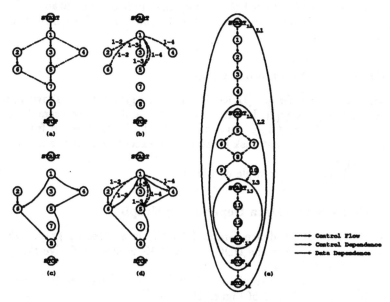

Fig. 1. Task Graphs

2.1 CFG: Control Flow Graph

The Control Flow Graph (CFG) is a directed graph which describes control flow such as loops and conditional branches. Optimizing compilers often employ CFG as a representation of programs[1]. Figure 1(a) shows an example of a CFG. A node of the CFG represents a task (basic block). Arcs show flow of program control, i.e., the relative execution order of tasks.

The CFG has two special nodes, *START* and *STOP*, each of which represents the starting and terminating point of program execution respectively. For each node in the CFG, there is a path from the *START* node to the node itself. Similarly, each of the nodes has a path from the node itself to the *STOP* node. There are no arcs directed either into the *START* node or out of the *STOP* node.

2.2 CDG: Control Dependence Graph

When there exists a conditional branch in a given program, tasks depending on the branch cannot be executed until the branch condition is evaluated. The dependence of tasks on the outcome of branch statements are called control dependencies. The Control Dependence Graph (CDG) is a directed graph which represents control dependencies between tasks. CDG is derived from the CFG using the postdominance relation[3]. In the CDG, nodes and arcs represent tasks and control dependencies between tasks respectively.

An arc (a, b), which is directed from node a to node b, has a label of the form $a - c$, where the node c is a node incident to node a. It may occur that $b = c$. An arc (a, b) labeled with $a - c$ implies that if the branch condition in node a is evaluated so that control flows from a to c, then node b is executable.

Figure 1(b) shows an example of a CDG, which is derived from the CFG shown in Figure 1(a).

2.3 DDG: Data Dependence Graph

The Data Dependence Graph (DDG) is a directed graph which shows data dependencies between tasks[2]. In the DDG, nodes and arcs represent tasks and data dependencies respectively. An arc (a, b) in the DDG directed from a node a to a node b, indicates that task b can not be executed until the execution of task a is completed.

Figure 1(c) shows an example of a DDG.

2.4 CDDG: Control Data Dependence Graph

The Control Data Dependence Graph (CDDG) is a directed graph which is derived from the CDG and the DDG. The CDDG is used to derive the general execution condition of tasks.

Figure 1(d) shows an example of a CDDG, which is derived from the CDG of Figure 1(b) and the DDG of Figure 1(c).

2.5 The Hierarchy of Task and Dependence Graphs

The Hierarchical Task Graph (HTG) is a hierarchical graph which explicitly captures the hierarchy of loops and functions in a program. This hierarchy allows any scope and parallelism of appropriate granularity to be easily handled. The definition, characteristics and the method to generate the hierarchy can be found in [3].

In the CFG a node generally represented a basic block. On the other hand, the HTG allows not only basic blocks but also loops and functions to be represented as nodes. A node representing a basic block is called a *simple* node, while nodes representing loops or function/subroutine calls are called *loop* or *compound* nodes respectively. Each *loop* or *compound* node has a CFG which shows control flows inside the corresponding loop or function. There are two special simple nodes in *loop* or *compound* nodes, a *start* node and *stop*, each of which represents the starting point and the terminating point of program execution respectively.

At each layer of an HDPG the CDDG is derived by combining of the DDG and the CDG which is derived from CFG. Finally, the Hierarchical CDDG (HCDDG) is obtained from the CDDG. Figure 1(e) shows an example of an HTG.

3 HDPG : The Hierarchical Data Partitioning Graph

3.1 The Overview of DPG

In this section we give an overview of the DPG and formally define the hierarchical data partitioning graph or HDPG. In conventional representations of task graphs nodes correspond to computations or tasks and arcs represent data or other precedence constraints between tasks. CDDG is an example of such a task graph. To approach the data partitioning problem on a task graph, DPG is defined by having a new type of nodes and arcs appended to the CDDG. The new nodes represent sets of variables, and the arcs between the new nodes and the CDDG nodes represent references to these variables. A formal definition of the new nodes and arcs is given later in this section. Figure 2 is an example of a DPG.

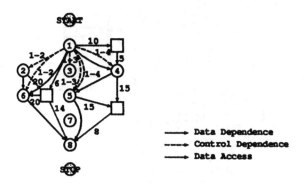

Fig. 2. Data Partitioning Graph (DPG)

In the DPG variables are divided into two classes: private or shared. If a variable *var* is accessed by only one task *t*, it is a private variable of *t*. On the other hand, if *var* is accessed by two or more tasks it is a shared variable.

There are two types of nodes in the DPG: C–nodes or D–nodes. A C–node represents a task; these are the nodes of the CDDG. In addition, C–nodes have two attributes, execution time of the task and the set of private variables of that task. C–nodes are shown as circular nodes in Figure 2.

A D–node represents a set of shared variables with information of tasks which access them; it also includes information about the access type (Read or Write) and the cost of accessing each shared variable from within a specific task node of the CDDG. D–nodes are shown as square nodes in Figure 2. The way to classify shared variables into D–nodes is described in Section 3.2 where a more formal definition of D–nodes is given.

There are three types of arcs in a DPG: i) arcs connecting C–nodes, ii) arcs from C–nodes to D–nodes, and iii) arcs from D–nodes to C–nodes.

Arcs between C–nodes are identical to those of the corresponding CDDG including their attributes. They represent control or data dependencies.

An arc between a C–node and a D–node indicates that a statement (computation) within the C–node reads or writes the variables of the D–nodes. When a task corresponding to a C–node *cv* reads a variable in a D–node *dv*, an arc from *dv* to *cv* is introduced in the DPG. Similarly, an arc from *cv* to *dv* is included when *cv* writes a variable in *dv*. In either case, estimated cost to accessing variables is given as an attribute. The definition of the access cost is discussed in Section 3.2.

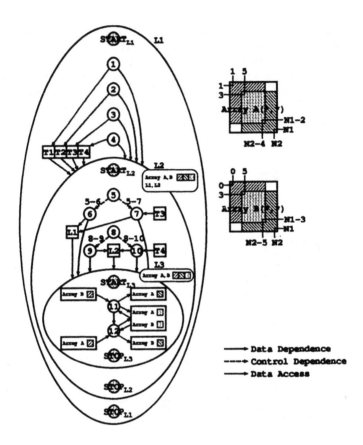

Fig. 3. Hierarchical Data Partitioning Graph (HDPG)

3.2 A Formal Definition of the HDPG

As described above, each CFG of an HTG is combined with the DDG to construct the corresponding CDDG. Incorporating the hierarchy into a CDDG is described in [5]. HCDDG denotes a CDDG with explicit specification of the hierarchy of the computation in terms of loops and subroutine calls. The HDPG (Hierarchical DPG) can be obtained from the corresponding HCDDG by converting each CDDG in the HCDDG to DPG.

The definition of the HDPG is similar to that of the DPG, with the exception of the definition of private/shared variables. In an HTG, the definition of private/shared variables depends on their scope level.

In order to establish our notation we give a formal definition of an HDPG. An HDPG is obtained from an HCDDG. HDPG and HCDDG are denoted as $HDPG(\{HCV, HDV\}, \{HCE_c, HCE_d, HDE_r, HDE_w\})$, and $HCDDG(HV, \{HE_c, HE_d\})$ respectively. In the case of HDPG, HCV denotes a set of C–nodes, HDV a set of D–nodes, HCE_c a set of control dependence arcs, HCE_d a set of data dependence arcs, HDE_r a set of arcs from D–nodes to C–nodes (Read access), and HDE_w a set of arcs from C–nodes to D–nodes (Write access) respectively. In the case of HCDDG, HV is the set of HCDDG nodes, HE_c is the set of control dependence arcs, and HE_d is a set of data dependence arcs.

We will use the term "task" interchangeably with nodes of an HCDDG and C–nodes of an HDPG, since both of them are in one-to-one correspondance with tasks. We show Figure 3 as an example of an HDPG of the program shown in below.

```
L 1:        DO K = 1, NM, LAMBDA
S 1:           T1 = K DIV M + 3
S 2:           T2 = (K + LAMBDA) DIV M + 3
S 3:           T3 = K MOD M + 5
S 4:           T4 = (K + LAMBDA) MOD M + 5 - 1
L 2:           DO I = T1, T2
S 5:              IF I <> T1
S 6:                 THEN L1 = 5
S 7:                 ELSE L1 = T3
S 8:              IF I <> T2
S 9:                 THEN L2 = N2
S10:                 ELSE L2 = T4
L 3:              DO J = L1, L2
S11:                 A(I, J) = B(I - 3, J - 5)
S12:                 B(I, J) = A(I - 2, J - 4)
                  EndDO
               EndDO
            EndDO
```

The Hierarchical Structure of HCDDG For any node $hv \in HV$, we define $DESCENDANTS(hv)$ a set of nodes contained in hv, $CHILDREN(hv)$ a set of nodes directly contained in hv, $ANCESTORS(hv)$ a set of nodes containing hv, and $parent(hv)$ a node directly containing hv. For example, in the HCDDG obtained from Figure 1(e), variable $DESCENDANTS$, $CHILDREN$, $ANCESTORS$, $parent$ of loop node $L2$ are shown in below.

$$DESCENDANTS(L2) = \{START_{L2}, 5, 6, 7, 8, 9, 10, L3,$$
$$START_{L3}, 11, 12, STOP_{L3}, STOP_{L2}\}$$
$$CHILDREN(L2) = \{START_{L2}, 5, 6, 7, 8, 9, 10, L3, STOP_{L2}\}$$
$$ANCESTORS(L2) = \{L1\}$$
$$parent(L2) = L1$$

Shared and Private Variables We represent a set of variables referenced by tasks hv and $DESCENDANTS(hv)$ as $VAR(hv)$. The definition of private/shared variables in the hierarchical graph is shown below.

For any variable var we define the following relation $\mathcal{R}_{var}$, which represents the hierarchy of nodes referencing var in HCDDG.

$$\mathcal{R}_{var} = \{(hv_1, hv_2) : hv_1 = parent(hv_2),$$
$$var \in VAR(hv_1), var \in VAR(hv_2)\}$$

Relation $\mathcal{R}_{var}$ constructs a tree graph $T_{\mathcal{R}_{var}}(TV, TE)$. Obviously elements in HV and TV are in one–to–one correspondence. The function $g_{HV \to TV}$ express this correspondence. We represent TV_L as the minimum element in TV which has two or more children on this tree. If $g_{HV \to TV}(hv)$ is equal or less than TV_L where $hv \in HV$ contained in $\hat{hv} \in HV$ directly (namely $hv \in CHILDREN(\hat{hv})$), we define that var is private at hv. If $g_{HV \to TV}(hv)$ is greater than TV_L, we define *var* as shared in $\hat{hv}$. If there does not exist a path from the root of the tree to $g_{HV \to TV}(hv)$, it means *var* is not referred to by hv.

For instance, in Figure 2 variable $A(5,\ 3)$ is referred to by tasks 11 and 12 shows a tree (solid line) as in Figure 4. We can see that $A(5,\ 3)$ is shared in node $L3$ and private at $L3$, $L2$, and $L1$ from this tree.

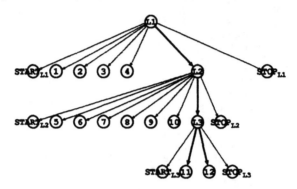

Fig. 4. shared/private variables

Thus, we define $PVAR_{\hat{hv}}(hv)$ as a set of private variables at $hv \in CHIL$-$DREN(\hat{hv})$ and $SVAR_{\hat{hv}}$ as a set of shared variables in $\hat{hv} \in HV$.

The Definition of HCV, HCE_c, HCE_d Elements of HV and HCV are in one–to–one correspondence. The function $g_{HV \to HCV}$ expresses this relation.[1] The element in HCV which corresponds to $hv \in HV$ is $g_{HV \to HCV}(hv)$. Using this function, we can redefine HCV, HCE_c, HCE_d from HV, HE_c, HE_d as follows.

$$HCV = \{g_{HV \to HCV}(hv) : hv \in HV\}$$
$$HCE_c = \{(hcv_1, hcv_2) : (hv_1, hv_2) \in HE_c,$$
$$hcv_1 = g_{HV \to HCV}(hv_1),$$
$$hcv_2 = g_{HV \to HCV}(hv_2)\}$$
$$HCE_d = \{(hcv_1, hcv_2) : (hv_1, hv_2) \in HE_d,$$
$$hcv_1 = g_{HV \to HCV}(hv_1),$$
$$hcv_2 = g_{HV \to HCV}(hv_2)\}$$

A node $hcv \in HCV$ has an execution cost of the task $hv = g_{HV \to HCV}^{-1}(hcv)$, and a set of variables $PVAR_{\hat{hv}}(hv)$ where $\hat{hv} = parent(hv)$. By definition, each element of HCE_c or HCE_d corresponds to an element of HE_c or HE_d respectively. Namely any arcs in HCE_c or HCE_d inherit the same attributes from arcs in the corresponding HE_c or HE_d.

Here we can define $DESCENDANTS$, $CHILDREN$, $ANCESTORS$ and *parent* for elements in HCV as well as HV.

---

[1] Note that there is an inverse function $g_{HV \to HCV}^{-1}$ of $g_{HV \to HCV}$ because the relation between HV and HCV is one–to–one.

$$DESCENDANTS(hcv) = \{hcv' \in HCV :$$
$$hv' \in DESCENDANTS(g^{-1}_{HV \to HCV}(hcv)),$$
$$hcv' = g_{HV \to HCV}(hv')\}$$
$$CHILDREN(hcv) = \{hcv' \in HCV :$$
$$hv' \in CHILDREN(g^{-1}_{HV \to HCV}(hcv)),$$
$$hcv' = g_{HV \to HCV}(hv')\}$$
$$ANCESTORS(hcv) = \{hcv' \in HCV :$$
$$hv' \in ANCESTORS(g^{-1}_{HV \to HCV}(hcv)),$$
$$hcv' = g_{HV \to HCV}(hv')\}$$
$$parent(hcv) = g^{-1}_{HV \to HCV}(parent(g^{-1}_{HV \to HCV}(hcv)))$$

Besides we can define $PVAR$ and $SVAR$ for elements in HCV.

$$PVAR_{\hat{hcv}}(hcv) = PVAR_{g^{-1}_{HV \to HCV}(\hat{hv})}(g^{-1}_{HV \to HCV}(hcv))$$
$$SVAR_{\hat{hcv}} = SVAR_{g^{-1}_{HV \to HCV}(\hat{hcv})}$$

The Definition of Access Costs Data partitioning is applied to variables which are shared by tasks. Therefore one of the most important aspects of data partitioning is to quantify the cost of accessing shared variables. In DPG and HDPG, each arc between C–nodes and D–nodes has a total cost for accessing variables of the D–node by tasks in the C–node. The access cost should not be confused with a communication cost. A communication cost involves the hardware architecture. Furthermore the cost cannot be estimated unless a processor allocation is given. On the other hand, the access cost can be expressed as some quantity derived from software rather than hardware.

Let $\omega_r(hcv, var)$ and $\omega_w(hcv, var)$ be the total access cost when each task hcv reads from and writes to shared variables $var \in SVAR_{\hat{hv}}$ where $\hat{hv} = parent(hv)$ respectively. If hcv is a *simple* node, $\omega_r(hcv, var)$ and $\omega_w(hcv, var)$ are defined as follows.

$$\omega_{\{r|w\}}(hcv, var) = n \times r$$

where n is the size of the accessed variable and r is the possible number of accesses. On the other hand, if hcv is a *loop* node or a *compound* node, $\omega_r(hcv, var)$ and $\omega_w(hcv, var)$ are defined as the sum of access costs from all tasks in hcv. Namely,

$$\omega_{\{r|w\}}(hcv, var) = \sum_{hcv' \in CHILDREN(hcv)} \omega_{\{r|w\}}(hcv', var)$$

If hcv does not do read or write access var, we define $\omega_r(hcv, var) = 0$ or $\omega_w(hcv, var) = 0$ respectively.

In the DPG we already pointed out that variables are classified by considering the tasks which access them, the type of accesses and their access costs. Using those policies, it may happen that the number of D–nodes swells immoderately because of the wide range of access costs. To avoid the above problem, we apply a clustering method to access costs. It allows the range of access costs to be reduced and as a result we have the appropriate number of D-nodes. We now define $f(\omega)$ as a function which returns a representative value where access cost is ω in the corresponding class. Figure 5 is an example of function $f(\omega)$.

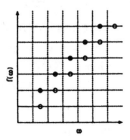

Fig. 5. Function $f(\omega)$

The Definition of Access Patterns Let $ap_{\hat{hcv}}(var)$ be an access pattern for variable var shared in $\hat{hcv} \in HCV$. $ap_{\hat{hcv}}(var)$ is expressed as a triplet.

$$ap_{\hat{hcv}}(var) = \{(hcv, r, w) : hcv \in CHILDREN(\hat{hcv}),$$
$$r = f(\omega_r(hcv, var)),$$
$$w = f(\omega_w(hcv, var))\}$$

Let $AP_{\hat{hcv}}$ be a set of access patterns for all shared variables in $\hat{hcv}$. $AP_{\hat{hcv}}$ is defined as follows.

$$AP_{\hat{hcv}} = \{ap_{\hat{hcv}}(var) : var \in SVAR_{\hat{hcv}}\}$$

Note that there are not equal access patterns in $AP_{\hat{hcv}}$ since $AP_{\hat{hcv}}$ is a set. For any elements $ap \in AP_{\hat{hcv}}$, we define $RD_{\hat{hcv}}(ap)$, $WR_{\hat{hcv}}(ap)$ and $SVAR_{\hat{hcv}}(ap)$ as follows.

$$RD_{\hat{hcv}}(ap) = \{hcv : (hcv, r, w) \in ap, r > 0\}$$
$$WR_{\hat{hcv}}(ap) = \{hcv : (hcv, r, w) \in ap, w > 0\}$$
$$SVAR_{\hat{hcv}}(ap) = \{var \in SVAR_{\hat{hcv}} : ap(var) = ap\}$$

The Definitions of HDV, HDE_r and HDE_w Any $ap \in AP_{\hat{hcv}}$ has one-to-one correspondence with a D-node $hdv \in HDV_{\hat{hcv}}$ which is involved in $\hat{hcv}$. This corresponding relation is denoted by $g_{AP \rightarrow HDV_{\hat{hcv}}}$ [2]. Now $HDE_{r\hat{hcv}}$ and $HDE_{w\hat{hcv}}$ are redefined as the followings.

---

[2] Note that there is an inverse function $g^{-1}_{AP \rightarrow HDV_{\hat{hcv}}}$ of $g_{AP \rightarrow HDV_{\hat{hcv}}}$ because each element of $AP_{\hat{hcv}}$ has one-to-one correspondence with $dv \in HDV_{\hat{hcv}}$.

$$HDV_{\hat{hcv}} = \{g_{AP \to HDV_{\hat{hcv}}}(ap) : ap \in AP_{\hat{hcv}}\}$$

$$HDE_{r\,\hat{hcv}} = \{(hdv, hcv) : hcv \in HCV, hdv \in HDV_{\hat{hcv}},$$

$$hcv \in RD_{\hat{hcv}}(g_{AP \to HDV_{\hat{hcv}}}^{-1}(hdv))\}$$

$$HDE_{w\,\hat{hcv}} = \{(hcv, hdv) : hcv \in HCV, hdv \in HDV_{\hat{hcv}},$$

$$hcv \in WR_{\hat{hcv}}(g_{AP \to HDV_{\hat{hcv}}}^{-1}(hdv))\}$$

Any $hdv \in HDV_{\hat{hcv}}$ represents a set of shared variables, $SVAR_{\hat{hcv}}(ap)$, which have an access $ap = g_{AP \to HDV}^{-1}(hdv)$.

And any $hde_r = (hdv, hcv) \in HDE_{r\,\hat{hcv}}$ has a total cost

$$\sum_{var \in SVAR_{\hat{hcv}}(g_{AP \to HDV}^{-1}(hdv))} \omega_r(hcv, var)$$

where $\hat{hcv} = parent(hcv)$ as its attribute when a task hcv reads variables in hdv.

In the same way, any $hde_w = (hcv, hdv) \in HDE_{w\,\hat{hcv}}$ has a total cost

$$\sum_{var \in SVAR_{\hat{hcv}}(g_{AP \to HDV}^{-1}(hdv))} \omega_w(hcv, var)$$

where $\hat{hcv} = parent(hcv)$ as its attribute when a task hcv writes to variables in hdv.

Finally HDV, HDE_r and HDE_w are defined as the followings.

$$HDV = \bigcup_{\hat{hcv} \in HCV} HDV_{\hat{hcv}}$$

$$HDE_r = \bigcup_{\hat{hcv} \in HCV} HDE_{r\,\hat{hcv}}$$

$$HDE_w = \bigcup_{\hat{hcv} \in HCV} HDE_{w\,\hat{hcv}}$$

4 Data Partitioning and Processor Assignment

As we mentioned above, data partitioning and processor assignment can be dealt with as a problem of node classification. In this section we describe an approach to data partitioning and processor assignment using the DPG/HDPG. We assume a cluster-based shared memory parallel computer as in Figure 6 as the target architecture. We next discuss the developement of data partitioning/processor assignment algorithms and we also show their application.

We attempt to classify C–nodes and D–nodes respectively, and assign each of them to appropriate clusters, namely data partitioning and processor assignment (cluster assignment in a strict sense). Suppose a group consisting of C–nodes and D–nodes is assigned to a cluster C. It means that tasks of C–nodes in the group

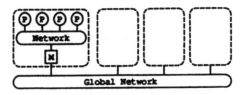

Fig. 6. cluster-base shared memory parallel computer

are executed in C, and that private variables of C–nodes and shared variables of D–nodes in the groups are assigned to C.

We consider the following terms for classification of DPG nodes.

1. Parallelism
2. Communication cost
3. Network topology

Here we show an example of data partitioning and processor assignment using the DPG of Figure 7(a). Although it is ideal to do data partitioning and processor assignment simultaneously, we assume that the processor assignment is already given, for simplicity.

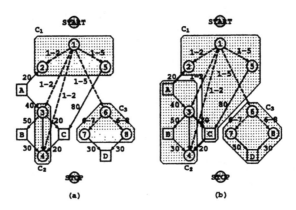

(a)   (b)

Fig. 7. Data Partitioning in DPG

Suppose that C–node groups $\{1, 2, 5\}$, $\{3, 4\}$ and $\{6, 7, 8\}$ are assigned to clusters C_1, C_2 and C_3 respectively. Since D–nodes B and D are only accessed by C_2 and C_3, they should be assigned to C_2 and C_3. And A is accessed by C_1 with cost 20 and by C_2 with cost 40. Therefore D–node A should be assigned to C_2. Similarly, D–node C is assigned to C_1. Consequently we get data partitioning as shown in Figure 7(b). This means that variables whose access patterns are same to ones in D–node C and private variables in C–nodes 1, 2, and 3 are assigned to the cluster C_1. It is similar about assignments to C_2 and C_3. Accesses to a variable which cause interprocessor communication are ones corresponding to thick edges in Figure 7(b). Their communication costs are given as functions of access costs attached to their edges.

4.1 Data Partitioning and Processor Assignment in HDPG

In this section we consider processor assignment in an HDPG. Processor assignment in HDPG is performed at each layer at a time. In higher layers, C-nodes represent coarser tasks such as loops and functions. Usually these tasks are executed in parallel on multiple processors. Therefore in higher layers of the HDPG we assign a set of C-nodes to groups of processors (clusters) instead of to a single processor.

On the other hand we assign C-nodes to processors in lower layers. Assigned processors are in clusters which were assigned at higher layers. When we can follow dependency between tasks statically, we can assign processors. Otherwise, we assign C-nodes only to clusters and apply dynamic allocation such as self scheduling for the assignment to processors. Generally speaking, dynamic factors such as run-time dependencies tend to appear in lower layers while static factors such as compile-time dependence tend to appear in higher layers. We apply data partitioning to each layer of HDPG from high layer to low layer as is applied to DPG.

Furthermore there are two cases about data partitioning. One is the case that data relocation (data migration) is required, and another is the case that an initial data location is kept during execution of a given program.

When we do not assume data migration, we must assign D-nodes in the lowest layer to a specific cluster. In HDPG, D-nodes which belong to different loop/compound nodes, in other words, D-nodes whose scopes are different, may correspond to same variables. Therefore we need to keep consistency among them.

When we assume data migration, we can assign D-nodes which correspond to same variables to different clusters. In the case of that, we have to regulate timings of data migration and it should be decided during processor assignment of C-nodes. No matter whether we assume data migration or not, it is important to keep consistency of cluster assignment of variables.

When we do data partitioning and processor assignment in an HDPG, we need not to assign C-nodes and D-nodes to clusters exclusively. We should rather assign a C-node or a D-node to multiple clusters. For example, there may exist a situation that a C-node is a loop node which represents a parallel-executable loop. If the number of processors required to execute the loop exceeds the number of processors in the cluster, we should assign the C-node to multiple clusters. A set of variables which is attached to a D-node in a particular layer can be split and construct other D-nodes in lower layers. Once such new D-nodes are created, these variables can be assigned to different clusters. Considering these cases, it is appropriate to assign a D-node to several clusters. Similar situation can raise when private variables in a C-node at some layer can change into shared variables, namely change into variables attached to new D-nodes at lower layers.

4.2 Algorithms for Data partitioning and Processor Assignment

When we investigate algorithms for data partitioning/processor assignment in HDPG, we consider two factors: i) whether the processor assignment is static and ii) whether the data migration is required. As for i), it depends on the interaction between data partitioning and processor assignment. In short, the main factor may be characteristics of a given program. As for ii), it depends on architectures of targeted machine. In the system with (global) cache memory, communication

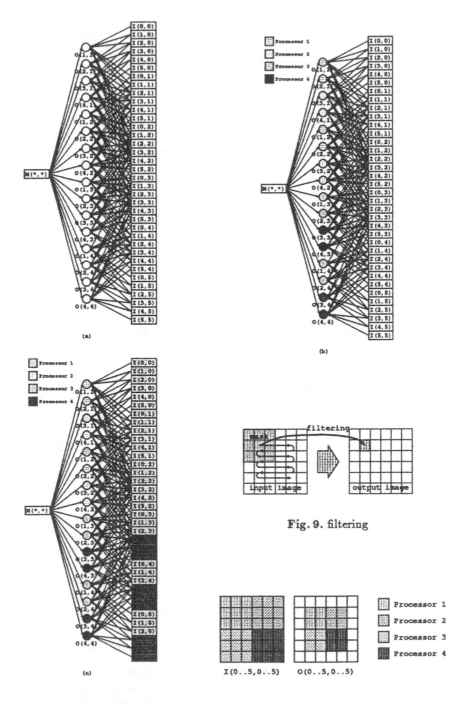

Fig. 8. DPG for filtering

Fig. 9. filtering

Fig. 10. Data Partitioning for filtering

penalties may be hidden by only one cache miss without data migration. In the system without such cache memory, explicit data migrations would be required unless complete data partitioning is given or the programming model is such as data parallel one.

By using static processor assignment, we can focus on data partitioning. Thus the above complex problem results in a problem of clustering D–nodes. And we have a lot of candidate algorithms such as heuristics.

If we do not use static processor assignment, algorithms which give simultaneous solutions for data partitioning and processor assignment are required. Furthermore use of data migration may restrict the algorithms.

We introduce some possible approaches. One of the candidates is a matrix representation. If we obtain a matrix which is represented by an HDPG, we can apply successive permutation operations to rows and/or columns of the matrix and obtain a blocked form matrix. Each block of the matrix represents a group of D–nodes and C–nodes which should be assigned to a cluster. For example, an HDPG is considered as a subset of Hasse diagram of a power set where the set consists of all D–nodes and C–nodes in given HDPG. In general, a matrix representation under Fussy semi-ordering is available for subsets of Hasse diagram. Another candidate can be a conventional pattern recognition technique. By introducing some kind of similarity to D–nodes and C–nodes in HDPG, we can apply clustering algorithms such as K-means or LVQ.

In either case, the original problem is converted into an optimization problem, and we need significant computation in order to get a local optimal solution.

5 Example

In this section we show an example of DPG. We take a filtering for image processing as an example.

Suppose we have an input image and a mask of which size are 6×6 and 3×3 respectively. The input image is represented as 6×6 array $I(0..5, \ 0..5)$. Also the mask is represented as 3×3 array $M(-1..1, \ -1..1)$ whose element has a value used for a convolution operation. The mask scans an input image with applying convolution operations at every point inside of the input image and write results to 6×6 array $O(0..5, \ 0..5)$ which represents an output image. (See Figure 9)

At each point (x, y) of the image the following calculation is applied.

$$O(x, \ y) = \sum_{dy=-1}^{1} \sum_{dx=-1}^{1} I(x + dx, \ y + dy) * M(dx, \ dy)$$

We show the program of the filtering bellow.

```
DO Y = 1, 4
   DO X = 1, 4
      O(X, Y) = ( I(X - 1, Y - 1) * M(X - 1, Y - 1)
                + I(X    , Y - 1) * M(X    , Y - 1)
                + I(X + 1, Y - 1) * M(X + 1, Y - 1)
                + I(X - 1, Y    ) * M(X - 1, Y    )
                + I(X    , Y    ) * M(X    , Y    )
                + I(X + 1, Y    ) * M(X + 1, Y    )
                + I(X - 1, Y + 1) * M(X - 1, Y + 1)
                + I(X    , Y + 1) * M(X    , Y + 1)
```

$$+ I(X + 1, Y + 1) * M(X + 1, Y + 1))$$

    EndDO
    EndDO

The DPG for the program is shown in Figure 8(a). Note that we unroll loops in the program since we have not decided the representation of D–nodes in loops yet, and let each unrolled loop body be a task.

Suppose we have 4–processors multiprocessor and assign processors like in Figure 8(b). Obviously there exists no control or data dependencies between tasks, and a task makes an access to each corresponding variable. Therefore every edge in Figure 8(b) represents accesses to variables whose costs are 1. Considering above facts we can partition data like in Figure 8(c) on the DPG shown in Figure 8(b). Each element of M(*, *) is accessed by all tasks with the same access cost (namely 1). We can assign them to our favorite processors, moreover we had better duplicate them and assign their copies to all the processors since M(*, *) are read only variables. Results of partitioning I(*, *) and O(*, *) are shown in Figure 10.

6   Conclusion

In this paper we propose the Data Partitioning Graph (DPG) as a representation for handling data partitioning. Moreover we propose the Hierarchical Data Partitioning Graph (HDPG) which exploits the hierarchy of actual programs and parallel computer architectures. In DPG/HDPG, data partitioning as well as processor assignment is dealt with as a problem of graph partition. Therefore DPG/HDPG can deal with data partitioning and processor assignment simultaneously which is a more effective approach than independently solving each problem.

Future work will focus on the data partitioning algorithms for DPG/HDPGs and implementation as a frontend of an actual parallelizing compiler.

References

1. A.V.Aho, R.Sethi and J.D.Ullman: "Compilers", Addison Wesley, 1986.
2. U.Banerjee: "Dependence Analysis for Supercomputing", Kluwer Academic Publishers, 1988.
3. M.B.Girkar: "Functional Parallelism Theoretical Foundations and Implementations ", Ph.D Thesis No.1182, Center for Supercomputing Research and Development, University of Illinois at Urbana-Champaign, 1991.
4. H.Kasahara, H.Honda, A.Mogi, A.Ogura, K.Fujiwara and S.Narita: "A Multi-grain Parallelizing Compilation Scheme on OSCAR", Proc. 4th Workshop on Languages and Compilers for Parallel Computing, pp. 283–297, Aug. 1991.
5. M.B.Girkar and C.D.Polychronopoulos: "Automatic Extraction of Functional Parallelism from Ordinary Programs", IEEE Trans. on Parallel and Distributed Systems, Vol. 3, No. 2, pp. 166–178, Mar. 1992.
6. M.Gupta and P.Banerjee: "Demonstration of automatic data partitioning techniques for parallelizing compilers on multicomputers", IEEE Trans. on Parallel and Distributed Systems, vol.3, pp.179–193, Mar. 1992.
7. P.D.Holvland and L.M.Ni: "A Model for Automatic Data Partitioning", Proc. of Int'l Conf. on Parallel Processing, 1993.
8. T.S.Chen and J.P.Sheu: "Communication-Free Data Allocation Techniques for Parallelizing Compilers on Multicomputers", Proc. of Int'l Conf. on Parallel Processing, 1993.

Detecting Value-Based Scalar Dependence [*]

Eric Stoltz and Michael Wolfe

Department of Computer Science and Engineering
Oregon Graduate Institute of Science & Technology
Portland, OR 97291-1000
{stoltz,mwolfe}@cse.ogi.edu

Abstract. Precise value-based data dependence analysis for scalars is useful for advanced compiler optimizations. The new method presented here for flow and output dependence uses Factored Use and Def chains (FUD chains), our interpretation and extension of Static Single Assignment. It is precise with respect to conditional control flow and dependence vectors. Our method detects dependences which are independent with respect to arbitrary loop nesting, as well as loop-carried dependences. A loop-carried dependence is further classified as being carried by the previous iteration, with distance 1, or by any previous iteration, with direction $<$. This precision cannot be achieved by traditional analysis, such as dominator information or reaching definitions. To compute anti- and input dependence, we use Factored Redef-Use chains, which are related to FUD chains. We are not aware of any prior work which explicitly deals with scalar data dependence utilizing a sparse graph representation.

1 Introduction and Problem Statement

Data dependence analysis is usually presented in terms of array references in nested loops. A great deal of work has also been done to find dependence due to pointer aliasing. Little has been written about data dependence analysis for scalar references, except to refer to standard data flow analysis [13], to treat a scalar as a degenerate array [7], or to use simple methods based on the dominator relationship or the syntactic structure of the program.

In this paper, we present a new approach to finding data dependence for scalars. Our approach has several features, one of which is that it computes value-based dependence, not just address-based dependence. Value-based dependence is a more precise definition [10]; using value-based dependence reduces the number of dependence relations and may allow more optimizations. Another feature is that our method computes precise dependence distance, when precision is possible, or imprecise dependence vectors otherwise. Precise dependence distance is important for many optimizations, such as instruction scheduling, software pipelining and parallelization. For instance, knowing that the dependence distance is precisely one may simplify communication address calculation

---

[*] Supported in part by NSF grant CCR-9113885 and a grant from Intel Corporation and the Oregon Advanced Computing Institute.

on a parallel machine, since the source and sink of the dependence are likely nearest neighbors. In other cases, *privatization* of scalar variables is possible when they are detected as being involved in only loop-independent dependences [3, 13].

We employ standard terminology for *data dependence*. The common address-based definitions of flow, output, anti-, and input dependence can be found in many references [1, 15, 16].

Value-based dependence relations are a subset of the address-based dependence relations [10]. The difference is explained by a simple example:

$$
\begin{aligned}
S_1: &\quad \text{A = B - 1} \\
S_2: &\quad \text{B = A + 1} \\
S_3: &\quad \text{A = B + C} \\
S_4: &\quad \text{B = B / A}
\end{aligned}
$$

The address-based definition of dependence includes $S_1\ \delta^f\ S_4$ for A and $S_1\ \delta^a\ S_4$ for B. Since A is assigned a new value in S_3, statement S_4 cannot use the value assigned in S_1. Similarly, since S_2 assigns a new value to B, the assignment in S_4 cannot overwrite the value that was used in S_1. Thus, these two dependence relations are unnecessary.

We define value-based dependence relations as follows: A flow dependence appears between a definition of a variable and a use of that variable when the definition precedes the use in execution, and the use fetches the value that was stored at the definition. An output dependence appears between two definitions of a variable when one definition precedes the other in execution, and the second overwrites the value stored at the first. An anti-dependence appears between a use and a definition of a variable whenever the use precedes the definition in execution, and the definition overwrites the value that was fetched at the use. An input dependence appears between two uses of a variable, if there is no killing definition of that definition between the two uses. Essentially, a value-based dependence cannot reach past a killing definition of a variable. As always, the compiler can only compute an approximation to the actual value-based dependence relations.

Using value-based dependence relations is especially important within loops. Most dependence representations in loops use some abstraction to describe the iterations where the source and target of the dependence occur. As usual, we assume each iteration is identified by an *iteration vector* of integers (often the index variable values). One common abstraction is a distance vector, which is the vector difference between the iteration vectors of the source and target iterations; if there is dependence from iteration $\mathbf{i}^s$ to iteration $\mathbf{i}^t$, the dependence relation has distance $\mathbf{d}$ if $\mathbf{i}^s + \mathbf{d} = \mathbf{i}^t$. Sometimes an exact distance cannot be computed; in that case, a less precise abstraction is used, called a direction vector [15]. The direction vector is a vector of relations from the set $\{<, =, >, \leq, \neq, \geq, \star\}$; if there is dependence from iteration $\mathbf{i}^s$ to iteration $\mathbf{i}^t$, the dependence relation has direction Θ if $i_k^s\ \theta_k\ i_k^t$, for loop nest level k. We allow a generalized *dependence vector*, where each element is either an integer value, if the exact distance for that loop nest level is known, and a direction relation if not.

The detection of scalar dependences within a loop requires careful analysis to get the precise dependence vector. We explain using the following loop:

```
S₁:   T = 0
S₂:   I = 1
S₃:   loop
S₄:       I = I + 1
S₅:       C[I] = V + T
S₆:       if TEST[I] then
S₇:           T = B[I+1]
S₈:           V = T + 1
S₉:       else
S₁₀:          V = B[I]
S₁₁:      endif
S₁₂: endloop
```

There is a *loop-carried* flow dependence relation $S_7 \ \delta^f \ S_5$ for variable T, and two more *loop-carried* flow dependence relations $S_8 \ \delta^f \ S_5$ and $S_{10} \ \delta^f \ S_5$ for variable V. However, the dependence distance for the V dependences is exactly one; since V is assigned on every iteration, any loop carried dependence relation must come from the previous iteration. For the T dependence carried by the loop, however, the distance can be any positive integer, since T might not be assigned on every iteration. The flow dependence $S_1 \ \delta^f \ S_5$ for T is not carried by any loop. It is *loop independent*. A dependence within the same loop, but not carried by any loop, such as $S_7 \ \delta^f \ S_8$ for T, is also loop independent. We denote a loop independent dependence using δ_∞, such as $S_1 \ \delta^f_\infty \ S_5$.

Simple dominator-based analysis will find precise dependence relations when the assignment dominates the use in the body of the loop (to give loop-independent dependence) or when the assignment dominates the back edge (to give loop-carried dependence with distance one). In this example, however, neither S_8 nor S_{10} dominates the loop back edge, so such simple analysis will fail. We will show this situation occurs frequently in our benchmark programs.

Our analysis is based on Factored Use and Definition chains (FUD chains). FUD chains are our implementation and interpretation of the Static Single Assignment (SSA) form [6] of a program, with extensions. We have previously described how to use FUD chains for other scalar analysis methods, such as induction variable detection and constant propagation [8, 12]. The concepts of FUD chains are described in Section 2. Other intermediate representations, such as dependence flow graphs [9] or the program dependence web [2], could also be used with similar algorithms; these representations contain enough information to find the actual dependences, though they do not represent the dependence relations explicitly. We note that reaching definitions is not sufficient, since it does not take into account how definitions on conditional branches are carried by loops.

The algorithm for finding flow dependence starts at a use and follows the

FUD chains to all reaching definitions. We want more information than just the reaching definitions; we also want the most precise dependence distance information possible. This method is described in Section 3, along with experimental data from common scientific benchmarks. As with other work, we modify the flow graph so each natural loop has a unique preheader and postbody; the loop header will thus have exactly two predecessors, the preheader (which collects multiple non-loop predecessor edges) and the postbody (which collects multiple back edges).

The algorithm to find output dependence is essentially the same as that for flow dependence. The only difference is that the initial call is from definition sites, rather than usage sites, of a variable. This algorithm is presented in Section 4.

However, the algorithm to find anti- and input dependence cannot use FUD chains. The information needed for these dependences is the set of uses that are overwritten by a definition. We modify the FUD chain construction algorithm to create Factored Redef-Use (FRDU) chains. FRDU chains link each definition to the most recent downward exposed use, and that use to the next most recent downward exposed use. This is described in Section 5.

2 Intermediate Representation

2.1 FUD Chains and Graph Preliminaries

The algorithms to convert a program into FUD form are based upon the *Control Flow Graph* (CFG), which is a graph $G = <V,E,Entry,Exit>$, where V is a set of nodes representing basic blocks in the program, E is a set of edges representing sequential control flow in the program, and *Entry* and *Exit* are nodes representing the unique entry point into the program and the unique exit point from the program. *Branch* nodes have their outgoing edges determined by a predicate. After a program has been converted into FUD form, it has two key properties:

1. Every use and definition of a variable in the program has exactly one reaching definition, and
2. At confluence points in the CFG, pseudo-assignments called ϕ-*functions* are introduced. A ϕ-function for a variable merges the values of the variable from distinct incoming control flow paths (in which a definition occurs along at least one of these paths), and has one argument for each control flow predecessor. We refer to the nth argument of ϕ-function f as $f[n]$. The ϕ-function is itself considered a new definition of the variable for chaining purposes, but its reaching definitions are accessed via its arguments, which are treated as variable uses.

We provide these semantics by inserting at each use and definition of a variable a pointer to the unique reaching definition for the variable at that point. This pointer will be to either a definition site or to a ϕ-function. In this way, use-def and def-def chains *factor* the graph into a sparse representation for each variable. This gives rise to the FUD chains referred to in the previous section.

For theoretical details on SSA graph construction the reader is referred to the paper by Cytron et al. [6], while details of FUD chain construction are provided in an earlier paper [11].

2.2 Reference Chaining

The general process of providing pointers (links) between arbitrary pairs of definition sites and usage sites of a variable is called *reference chaining*. Typically, for a particular problem such as constant propagation or finding dependences as addressed in this paper, the CFG is traversed to insert pointers to maintain a desired property, such as described above.

After inserting these pointers, links can be followed along the desired chain. *Chain(u)* corresponds to the end of a reference pointer from u. For clarity, we assume that a statement-based program is being processed. Each variable site will be a reference (**ref**) for variable v in one of the following two ways:

- $\mathbf{D}_n^v$ – a definition of v at statement n in the program.
- $\mathbf{U}_n^v$ – a use of v at statement n in the program.

We use the following functions to extract information from a given reference d, where $d = \mathbf{ref}_n^v$:

- $num(d) = n$
- $var(d) = v$

For the current work, we employ the following reference chains: use-def, def-def, redef-use, and use-use.

2.3 Classification of ϕ-functions

It is critical to distinguish between two "flavors" of ϕ-functions: those at the header of a loop (referred to as loop-header ϕ's), and all other ϕ-functions. Loop-header ϕ-functions merge the value which reaches from outside the loop and the last reaching definition from inside the loop. Due to unique loop preheaders and post-bodies as described in Section 1, each loop-header ϕ-function will have exactly two arguments. For convenience, the first argument always points to the unique reaching definition from outside the loop, while the second argument points to the last definition within the loop body.

Since ϕ-functions are placed at *dominance frontiers* [6] of variable definition sites, and the loop-header basic block dominates all blocks contained within the loop, we note a crucial property of loop-header ϕ-functions: a loop-header ϕ-function for variable v exists *iff* there is a definition of v within the loop.

3 Flow Dependence Algorithm

3.1 Necessary Ingredients

At first glance, it may appear that scalar flow dependence information could be gathered by applying traditional data-flow techniques, *e.g.* dominator analysis

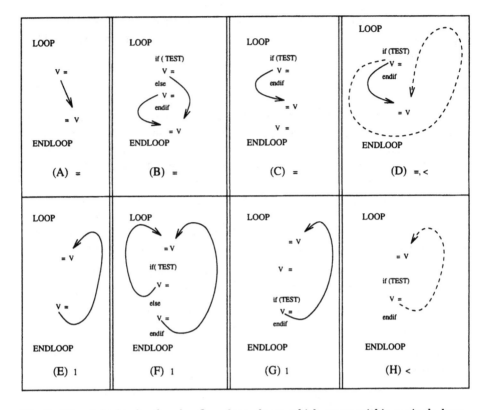

Fig. 1. The eight kinds of scalar flow dependence which occur within a single loop, grouped by related pairs. Solid lines represent loop-independent(=) or loop-carried(1) dependences, while a dotted line represents a loop-carried(<) dependence.

and reaching definitions. When the source of the dependence dominates the sink, or the loop postbody does not lie on any path from the definition to the use, the dependence must be in the current loop iteration, hence it would be loop-independent. If the definition dominates the postbody, the distance would be 1, while remaining cases would indicate a distance of < or unknown.

However, these observations are not sufficient to capture either precise distance nor correct classification. Referring to the second example presented in the introduction, and represented graphically but in simplified form for variable V as Figure 1(F), we notice that the flow dependence distance from either definition of V to the use of V is precisely 1. We also note that in this example neither definition of V dominates the postbody, but since all paths through the postbody contain a definition to V, the distance must be 1.

Thus, to correctly classify flow dependences, we follow the chain from each use, which will lead to either a definition or ϕ-function. When encountering a non-loop-header ϕ-function, we follow the chains of each argument. Intuitively, a loop-independent flow dependence will be discovered by following use-def links in the current loop body (or to a definition site outside the loop in which the use occurs), while loop-carried dependences must always flow through the loop-header ϕ-function.

When a chain reaches a loop-header ϕ-function, we conceptually continue to follow the links around the loop. To prevent infinite cycling, each loop-header ϕ-function has a flag, *self* (initially set to *false*), which indicates whether following chains around the loop can reach back to that loop-header ϕ-function. If the *self* flag gets set to *true*, a non-loop-header ϕ-function (or a non-killing definition) must have been encountered while following chains for that loop instance; this indicates a conditional branch which may or may not be taken during any particular iteration, but where on at least one of the branches there exists a chain which can reach the loop-header ϕ-function without encountering a killing definition. Thus, while the dependence is loop-carried, we do not know its precise distance, so we denote its direction as $(<)$. If the *self* flag remains *false*, then all paths must encounter a killing-definition for the variable being analyzed; this means that the flow dependence must be to the subsequent iteration, and its distance is 1.

3.2 Algorithm 1: Precisely Detecting Scalar Flow Dependence

An algorithm for detection of scalar flow dependences within a single loop has been presented previously [11]. To extend this algorithm for nested loops, several issues need to be addressed. First, we must provide a recursive routine, to allow arbitrary nesting. Second, distance and/or direction of the dependence must be accurate in terms of all loops which contain the dependence. This second point implies that a dependence relation between two references may in fact be more than one dependence: it can be a dependence with respect to an inner loop as well as another dependence with respect to an outer loop.

Data Structures. We use the following data structures for our algorithms:

- loop-header ϕ-functions:
  - *self*: a flag representing whether a loop-header ϕ can transitively reach itself (Initialized to *false*)
  - *Reaching_set*: a set of definitions which can be reached by following *chain(ϕ)*[2] (Initialized to $\emptyset$)
- loops:
  - *nest(loop)*: returns the nest level of *loop*
  - *loop(ref)*: returns the innermost loop containing *ref*
  - *nl(ref)*: returns *nest(loop(ref))*
  - *common(ref1,ref2)*: returns the most deeply nested loop which contains both *ref1* and *ref2*
- references:
  - *marked(ref)*: *marked(ref)* = *u* indicates *ref* has already processed use *u* in **Find_Dependence**. Initialized to $\emptyset$
  - *Reached(ref)*: $r \in$ Reached(*ref*) indicates *ref* has already processed loop-header ϕ *r* in **Find_Reaching**. Initialized to $\emptyset$

For each dependence (excluding loop independent dependences) we build a *dependence vector* to describe the most precise information available for all loops, from the outermost loop containing the dependence to the most deeply nested loop containing both references of the dependence. A *nest level* is associated with each loop, starting at 1 for outermost loops.

When building the dependence vector, we must first find the most deeply-nested loop (*com*) which contains both the source and sink of the dependence, since we do not consider loops at a nest level greater than *com*. Next, the nest level of *com* is compared to the nest level of the loop containing the ϕ-function being processed (*phi_loop*), since all loop-carried dependences are as a result of processing loop-header ϕ-functions, as noted above. If the nest levels of *com* and *phi_loop* are equal, then the *phi_loop* will carry the dependence. If the nest level of *com* is greater than the nest level of *phi_loop*, *phi_loop* still carries the dependence, but loops between *phi_loop* and *com* have unknown information, and their entry into the dependence vector is denoted $\star$. Finally, if the nest level of *phi_loop* is greater than the nest level of *com*, *phi_loop* clearly does not carry the dependence, hence the dependence is independent(∞).

Algorithm 1. Figures 2 and 3 presents the complete algorithm for detecting scalar flow dependences within loops.

Algorithm 1 operates as follows:

Given: A program converted to FUD chain form
             Auxiliary data structures initialized

Do: $\forall$ scalar uses U in the program,
             Find_Dependence(*chain(U)*, U, f)

Output: A list of statement based flow dependences, and a dependence
             vector for any dependence which is not loop independent

3.3   Discussion of Algorithm 1

Algorithm 1 first calls **Find_Dependence** on a scalar use, its use-def link, and the type f (flow dependence). Encountering scalar definitions result in loop independent dependences, while non-loop-header ϕ-functions result in recursive calls on the links from each argument. When loop-header ϕ-functions are encountered, the set of references which can be reached within that loop are calculated with an on-demand call to **Find_Reaching**, which determines what definitions of a particular variable can flow around the loop. Then, each element in this set results in a dependence with a dependence vector computed by **Build_Vector**.

Since loop-header ϕ-functions are distinguished from ϕ-functions which occur at other merge points in the control flow graph, cycles in the call graph for **Find_Dependence** are fairly rare. However, redundant calls may occur in two ways. First, there may be an irreducible flow graph, and second, a non-killing

194

Procedure: **Scalar Dependence Detection**

```
 1:  Find_Dependence( d, u, t )

 2:      if marked( d ) = u then return endif
 3:      marked( d ) = u
 4:      if d is a loop-header φ then
 5:          Find_Dependence( Chain(d)[1], u, t )
 6:          if Reaching_Set(d) ≠ ∅ then
 7:              Find_Reaching( Chain(d)[2], d )
 8:          endif
 9:          for c ∈ Reaching_Set( d ) do
10:              if self( d ) = true then
11:                  dep_vec = Build_Vector( d,c,u,< )
12:              else
13:                  dep_vec = Build_Vector( d,c,u,1 )
14:              endif
15:              output S_num(c) δᵗ_(dep_vec) S_num(u)
16:          endfor
17:      else if d is a φ-function then
18:          for each argument j of d do
19:              Find_Dependence( Chain(d)[j], u, t )
20:          endfor
21:      else
22:          output S_num(d) δᵗ_∞ S_num(u)
23:          if d is a non-killing definition then
24:              Find_Dependence( Chain(d), u, t )
25:          endif
26:      endif

27: End Find_Dependence
```

Lines 11, 13, 15, 22 contain math:

11: $dep\_vec = \textbf{Build\_Vector}(\ d,c,u,<\ )$

13: $dep\_vec = \textbf{Build\_Vector}(\ d,c,u,1\ )$

15: output $S_{num(c)}\ \delta^t_{(dep\_vec)}\ S_{num(u)}$

22: output $S_{num(d)}\ \delta^t_\infty\ S_{num(u)}$

Fig. 2. Identifying Scalar Flow or Output Dependences within multiple loops

definition along one branch of a conditional for the variable being processed may result in repetitious calls to **Find_Dependence** for the same use of that variable. Since **Find_Dependence** processes one use of a variable at a time, we have included a *marked* field associated with each reference point. By checking this field, we eliminate extra calls due to non-killing definitions and potential infinite loops as a result of irreducible flow graphs.

The situation is similar for the routine **Find_Reaching**, except that the *Reaching_Set* is associated with particular loop-header φ-functions, and not in terms of a processed usage site. In this case we keep, for each definition site, a list of loop-header φ-functions which have already processed that site.

We illustrate Algorithm 1 with the following example. We number variable definitions and uses for readability; since in fact no new names are added to

Procedure: **Calculate Reaching Set**

```
1: Find_Reaching( d, f )

2:        if d = f then
3:            self( f ) = true
4:            return
5:        endif
6:        if f ∈ Reached( d ) then return endif
7:        Reached( d ) = Reached( d ) ∪ f
8:        if  d is a loop_header φ function then
9:            Find_Reaching( Chain(d)[1], f )
10:           Find_Reaching( Chain(d)[2], d )
11:           add Reaching_Set( d ) to Reaching_Set( f )
12:       else if d is a φ-function then
13:           for each argument j of d do
14:               Find_Reaching( Chain(d)[j], f )
15:           endfor
16:       else
17:           add d to Reaching_Set( f )
18:           if d is a non-killing definition then
19:               Find_Reaching( Chain(d), f )
20:           endif
21:       endif

22: End Find_Reaching
```

Procedure: **Build Dependence Vector**

```
1: Build_Vector( func,def,ref,entry )

2:        com = common( def, ref )
3:        if nest(com) = nl(func) then
4:            dep_vec[1 ... nl(func) - 1] = 0
5:            dep_vec[nl(func)] = entry
6:        else if nest(com) > nl(func) then
7:            dep_vec[1 ... nl(func) - 1] = 0
8:            dep_vec[nl(func)] = entry
9:            dep_vec[nl(func) + 1 ... nest(com)] = ⋆
10:       else
11:           dep_vec = ∞
12:       endif

13: End Build_Vector
```

Fig. 3. Procedures for Reaching Definition Sets and Building Dependence Vectors

the symbol table, subscripts represent the semantics of FUD chains, not the implementation. In this example (in which we assume the exit is at the top of each loop) :

$$
\begin{array}{ll}
S_1: & \text{V}_1 \ =\\
S_2: & \text{loop1}\\
S_3: & \quad \text{V}_3 \ = \ \phi(\text{V}_1, \text{V}_5)\\
S_4: & \quad \text{loop2}\\
S_5: & \quad\quad \text{V}_5 \ = \ \phi(\text{V}_3, \text{V}_9)\\
S_6: & \quad\quad \text{if TEST then}\\
S_7: & \quad\quad\quad \text{V}_7 \ =\\
S_8: & \quad\quad \text{endif}\\
S_9: & \quad\quad \text{V}_9 \ = \ \phi(\text{V}_5, \text{V}_7)\\
S_{10}: & \quad\quad\quad = \ \text{V}_9\\
S_{11}: & \quad \text{endloop2}\\
S_{12}: & \text{endloop1}
\end{array}
$$

the only use of V occurs at S_{10}. Thus, we make the call **Find_Dependence**(*chain*(U_{10}^V), U_{10}^V, f), which is equivalent to **Find_Dependence**(D_9^V, U_{10}^V, f). Since D_9^V is a ϕ-function, recursive calls are made to **Find_Dependence**(D_5^V, U_{10}^V, f) and **Find_Dependence**(D_7^V, U_{10}^V, f). From the second of these calls we get the loop-independent dependence

$$S_7 \ \delta_\infty^f \ S_{10}$$

from line 22 of Figure 2.

The other call, **Find_Dependence**(D_5^V, U_{10}^V, f), is a reference to a loop-header ϕ-function, thus **Find_Dependence**(D_3^V, U_{10}^V, f) is called on the first argument in S_5, while the second argument invokes a call to **Find_Reaching**(D_9^V, D_5^V), setting the *self* flag for D_5^V and discovering its *Reaching_Set* $= \{D_7^V\}$. Lines 9 - 11 and 15 of Figure 2 give us the dependence

$$S_7 \ \delta_{(0,<)}^f \ S_{10}$$

Finally, **Find_Dependence**(D_3^V, U_{10}^V, f) is also a reference to a loop-header ϕ-function, thus **Find_Dependence**(D_1^V, U_{10}^V, f) is called on the first argument in S_3, and **Find_Reaching**(D_5^V, D_3^V) is called by the second argument, setting the *self* flag for D_3^V and discovering its *Reaching_Set* $= \{D_7^V\}$ (by merging with the *Reaching_Set* of D_5^V). We then output these last two dependences:

$$S_7 \ \delta_{(<,*)}^f \ S_{10} \text{ and } S_1 \ \delta_\infty^f \ S_{10}$$

3.4 Measuring Algorithm 1 on Scientific Benchmarks

How often do the cases in Figure 1 occur? To discover the usefulness of our method, we ran our algorithm over the scientific benchmarks contained in the Perfect Club [5], RiCEPS, and Mendez suites. In order to keep the investigation at a level which is easy to analyze, this set of data only counted flow dependences

routine	lines	# loop-independent				# loop-carried (<)		# loop-carried (1)	
		A	B	C	D	D	H	E	F & G
PERFECT club									
adm	6106	3439	163	1	92	92	2302	149	16
arc2d	3965	2600	6	0	2	2	193	8	0
bdna	3978	3465	27	6	6	6	57	112	8
dyfesm	7609	929	7	11	129	129	103	82	0
flo52	1987	1620	20	10	2	2	81	180	44
mdg	1239	728	4	1	1	1	106	157	2
mg3d	2813	1625	19	7	4	4	124	1420	4
ocean	4344	1421	23	3	310	310	1509	118	3
qcd	2277	570	50	0	0	0	339	191	0
spec77	3886	1807	36	5	24	24	263	780	9
spice	18522	10456	3184	38	907	907	1810	2075	435
track	3785	624	20	0	3	3	72	26	3
trfd	486	197	9	0	0	0	10	39	0
RiCEPS									
boast	8068	5499	598	21	330	330	1188	582	40
ccm	23557	5286	142	4	12	12	555	1200	11
hydro	13050	1667	167	6	0	0	221	31	0
linpackd	798	165	0	0	0	0	26	20	0
simple	1314	1065	6	1	0	0	11	23	1
sphot	1145	480	43	0	0	0	216	13	27
wanal1	2110	925	16	0	253	253	113	125	6
wave	7521	3919	57	6	24	24	162	288	8
Mendez									
baro	984	416	0	0	0	0	17	44	0
euler	1202	484	48	0	6	6	45	37	2
mhd2d	928	359	0	0	0	0	3	23	6
shear	916	561	3	6	0	0	5	34	4
vortex	711	495	14	0	7	7	116	19	0
Total	123301	50802	4662	126	2112	2112	9647	7776	620

Table 1. A count of the different kinds of scalar flow dependences detected in scientific codes, classified according to the type of loop structure from Figure 1. The source and sink of the dependence are within the same inner loop.

in which the source and sink of the dependence were within the same inner loop. More complicated cases occur, and are handled correctly by our methods, but space limitations preclude their discussion in this paper. As shown in Figure 1, there are eight categories of dependences within a single loop, although cases F and G are statistically grouped together since they are semantically equivalent. We show F and G in Figure 1 separately because the eight cases form a coherent pattern of matching pairs.

Table 1 shows the result of our analysis. The case in question from §3.1, F, comprises 7% of all loop-carried(1) dependences where the source and sink of the dependence lie within the same inner loop. In some codes, such as spice and flo52 from the PERFECT Club suite or sphot from the RiCEPS suite, the percentage ranges from 17% to 68%. This demonstrates that simple analysis is not sufficient to achieve the precision which we capture with our algorithms.

Note that D is the case that will result in both a loop-independent and loop-carried($<$) dependence. This case is correctly analyzed by our algorithm, since a ϕ-function for V will be placed immediately after the endif statement, resulting in recursive calls to the **Find_Dependence** routine; one will discover the loop-independent flow dependence, and the other will discover the loop-carried($<$) flow dependence. An examination of Table 1 reveals that some codes possess structure in which this class of dependence is quite significant.

4 Output Dependence - Algorithm 2

Figures 2 and 3 also give the complete algorithm for computing scalar output dependence. The differences are that definitions are used for input, and we pass the dependence type o (output dependence) to **Find_Dependence**. Computing output dependence for scalars is a fairly trivial modification to Algorithm 1 since def-def chains have been inserted as a component of FUD chains. Algorithm 2 operates as follows:

Given: A program converted to FUD chain form
              Auxiliary data structures initialized

Do: $\forall$ scalar defs D in the program
              Find_Dependence(chain(D), D, o)

Output: A list of statement based output dependences, and a dependence
              vector for any dependence which is not loop independent

The algorithm to detect scalar output dependence has successfully been implemented, but due to space limitations we do not report the results of those experiments here.

5 Anti- and Input Dependence

FUD chains do not contain the necessary information to find anti- or input dependence relations; a method to determine what uses are redefined by each definition is required. Another reference chain, similar to FUD chains but linked in a different manner, can be used for this purpose. This structure, which we call *factored redef-use chains* (FRDU chains) links each definition to the closest preceding downward-exposed use. FRDU chains are built with the same methods used to build FUD chains, except uses are treated like definitions and definitions are treated like uses (additionally, a definition kills all previous downward-exposed uses). The ϕ-placement algorithm [6] is used (with slight modifications) to place Υ-functions wherever two or more downward-exposed uses or definitions merge. (To be precise, Υ-functions are placed wherever two basic block nodes with non-identity transfer functions for "reaching uses" meet, similar to the technique employed by sparse evaluation graphs [4].) The chaining algorithm (originally called "renaming") is modified to keep a stack of current uses for each variable (instead of a stack of current definitions), and employs Υ-functions instead of ϕ-functions. At *Entry*, the "current use" is set to $\perp$, meaning there is no current use. When a use is reached, it is linked to the current use of that variable, and this use becomes the new current use by pushing it onto the stack of uses. When a definition is reached, it is also linked to the current use. If it is a killing definition, $\perp$ is pushed onto the current use stack for that variable, meaning that there is no downward-exposed use on that path. To find anti-dependences, we use a method similar to Algorithm 2, where we start at all variable definitions, but follow FRDU chains to reaching uses.

Input dependence is computed in the same way as anti-dependence, except that we start at variable uses and chain to reaching uses. Detecting value-based input dependence can be useful for optimizing locality of reference, achieving better memory-hierarchy (i.e. cache) performance [14]. We have successfully implemented FRDU chains and the algorithms to detect anti- and input dependences. Lack of space precludes reporting our results here.

6 Extensions and Conclusion

We are developing several extensions to the scalar dependence analysis presented. For example, the inclusion of path-sensitive analysis (if available at compile time) may be possible, such as using tripcount information on loops or conditional constant propagation, to eliminate extra recursive calls at ϕ-function sites. Also, extracting precise information may be available for dependences which flow into or out of a loop: we can sometimes determine that a dependence flowing out of a loop must be from the last iteration or that a dependence flows into a loop only on its first iteration.

We are not aware of any previous work which explicitly deals with scalar dependence analysis using a sparse graph representation. We have presented new algorithms to detect and classify value-based flow, output, anti-, and input dependences for all references in a program, providing precise distance vectors where available, and direction vectors otherwise. Preliminary results have been provided for common scientific codes.

Acknowledgements

We would like to gratefully acknowledge the reviewers, whose thorough reading and suggestions definitely improved the quality of this paper.

References

1. John R. Allen and Ken Kennedy. Automatic translation of Fortran programs to vector form. *ACM Trans. on Programming Languages and Systems*, 9(4):491–542, October 1987.

2. Robert A. Ballance, Arthur B. Maccabe, and Karl J. Ottenstein. The Program Dependence Web: A representation supporting control-, data-, and demand-driven interpretation of imperative languages. In *Proc. ACM SIGPLAN '90 Conf. on Programming Language Design and Implementation*, pages 257–271, White Plains, NY, June 1990.

3. Michael Burke, Ron Cytron, Jeanne Ferrante, and Wilson Hsieh. Automatic generation of nested, fork–join parallelism. *The Journal of Supercomputing*, 3(2):71–88, July 1989.

4. Jong-Deok Choi, Ron Cytron, and Jeanne Ferrante. Automatic construction of sparse data flow evaluation graphs. In *Conf. Record 18th Annual ACM Symp. Principles of Programming Languages*, pages 55–66, Orlando, Florida, January 1991.

5. George Cybenko, Lyle Kipp, Lynn Pointer, and David Kuck. Supercomputer performance evaluation and the Perfect Benchmarks. In *International Conference on Supercomputing*, pages 254 – 266, March 1990.

6. Ron Cytron, Jeanne Ferrante, Barry K. Rosen, Mark N. Wegman, and F. Kenneth Zadeck. Efficiently computing Static Single Assignment form and the control dependence graph. *ACM Trans. on Programming Languages and Systems*, 13(4):451–490, October 1991.

7. Paul Feautrier. Dataflow analysis of array and scalar references. *International Journal of Parallel Programming*, 20(1):23–54, 1991.

8. Michael P. Gerlek, Eric Stoltz, and Michael Wolfe. Beyond induction variables: Detecting and classifying sequences using a demand-driven SSA form. *To appear in TOPLAS*.

9. Richard Johnson and Keshav Pingali. Dependence-based program analysis. In *Proc. ACM SIGPLAN '93 Conf. on Programming Language Design and Implementation*, pages 78–89, Albuquerque, NM, June 1993.

10. Vadim Maslov. Lazy array data-flow dependence analysis. In *Conf. Record 21st Annual ACM Symp. Principles of Programming Languages*, pages 311–325, Portland, OR, January 1994.

11. Eric Stoltz, Michael P. Gerlek, and Michael Wolfe. Extended SSA with factored use-def chains to support optimization and parallelism. In *Proc. of 27th Annual Hawaii International Conference on System Sciences*, pages 43–52, January 1994.

12. Eric Stoltz, Michael Wolfe, and Michael P. Gerlek. Constant propagation: A fresh, demand-driven look. In *Symposium on Applied Computing*, Phoenix, AZ, March 1994. ACM SIGAPP.

13. Chau-Wen Tseng. An optimizing Fortran D compiler for MIMD distributed-memory machines. PhD Dissertation TR93-199, Rice University, Dept. of Computer Science, January 1993.

14. Michael E. Wolf. Improving locality and parallelism in nested loops. PhD Dissertation COMP TR. CSL-TR-92-538, Stanford Univ., Dept. Computer Science, August 1992.

15. Michael Wolfe. *Optimizing Supercompilers for Supercomputers*. Research Monographs in Parallel and Distributed Computing. Pitman Publishing, London, 1989. (also available from MIT Press).

16. Michael Wolfe and Utpal Banerjee. Data dependence and its application to parallel processing. *International J. Parallel Programming*, 16(2):137–178, April 1987.

Minimal Data Dependence Abstractions
for Loop Transformations

Yi-Qing Yang, Corinne Ancourt, François Irigoin*

Ecole des Mines de Paris/CRI

Abstract. Many abstractions of program dependences have already been proposed, such as the Dependence Distance, the Dependence Direction Vector, the Dependence Level or the Dependence Cone. These different abstractions have different precision. The *minimal* abstraction associated to a transformation is the abstraction that contains the minimal amount of information necessary to decide when such a transformation is legal. The minimal abstractions for loop reordering and unimodular transformations are presented. As an example, the dependence cone, that approximates dependences by a convex cone of the dependence distance vectors, is the minimal abstraction for unimodular transformations.

Introduction

The aim of dependence testing is to detect the existence of memory access conflicts in programs. When two statements have a conflicting access to a datum, the *dependence* establishes that the execution order of the two statements cannot be modified without possible changes to the program semantics. A transformation can be applied if dependence relations are still preserved after the transformation. Many transformations require more than a simple dependent/independent information to be legally applied on a set of statements. Dependence relations are represented by finite dependence abstractions that contain the data flow dependences of the statement set.

Many dependence abstractions have already been proposed, such as the Dependence Distance [17], the Dependence Direction Vector [23], the Dependence Level [1] or the Dependence Cone [10]. These different abstractions have different precisions. They are presented in Sections 2 and 3. Depending on their precisions, the abstractions contain either not enough or sufficient or too much information to decide if a transformation T can be legally applied or not. Section 4 describes the conditions that must be satisfied to legally perform T and the minimal information that must contain an abstraction to be used by the legality test of T. Among the *valid* abstractions, one contains the *minimal* information necessary to decide when T is legal. Section 5 gives the minimal abstraction associated to reordering transformations such as loop reversal, loop permutation, unimodular transformations, partitioning and parallelization. This notion of minimality is interesting when the compiler/parallelizer needs an *exact* answer to the question *could T be legally applied ?* from the simplest representation of the dependences.

---

* E-mail: <yang,ancourt,irigoin@cri.ensmp.fr>

1 Notations

The notations used in the following sections are:
- $\vec{i}^n$ is an element of the loop nest iteration set I^n;
- $\ll$ denotes the lexicographic order, while $\prec$ is the execution order;
- $S(\vec{i})$ is the $\vec{i}$-th iteration of Statement S.
- $\delta_{\mathcal{A}}^*$ is the dependence relation represented by Abstraction $\mathcal{A}$.

2 Different Abstractions

Many finite abstractions have been designed to represent infinite sets of dependences in nested loops. They describe the data dependences with more or less effective accuracy. Depending on their precision, these abstractions contain either not enough, minimal or too much information to decide if a transformation can be legally applied. The different abstractions and their precisions are illustrated on example in Figure 1.

```
DO I = 1, n
  DO J = 1, n
S:      T(I,J) = T(3I,J+1)
```

$$\left\{ \begin{array}{llll} 1 \le i \le n & 1 \le i' \le n & 3i = i' \\ 1 \le j \le n & 1 \le j' \le n & j+1 = j' \end{array} \right.$$

Fig. 1. Program 1 and Dependence system 1

The dependence test must decide the satisfiability of the dependence system 1 in Figure 1. The equalities characterize possible data access conflicts between T(I,J) and T(3I,J+1), while the inequalities represent the constraints on the loop indices.

2.1 Dependences between Iterations

The abstraction $DI(L)$ is exactly the set of dependent iterations between the statement instances of a loop nest L: $DI(L) = \{(\vec{i}, \vec{i'}) | \exists S_1, S_2 \in L, S_1(\vec{i})\delta^* S_2(\vec{i'})\}$. $DI(L)$ is obtained by solving an exact integer linear programming system for each couple of array references belonging to the nested loops.
For Program 1, DI represents in Figure 2(a) all the solutions of the dependence system. A parametric version of the dependent iterations can be expressed as: $DI(P1) = \{((i,j),(3i,j+1)) \mid 1 \le i \le n, 1 \le j \le n\}$.
Since no approximation is made on the exhaustive list of dependent iterations, this abstraction cannot be used for infinite set of dependences. Thus, abstractions approximating this exact set have been suggested. We quickly review the most important dependence abstractions, used for optimizing and parallelizing programs, in the following sections.

2.2 The Distance Vector

Dependence distance vectors are used to relatively characterize a set of dependent iterations: $D(L) = \{\vec{d} \mid \exists(\vec{i}, \vec{i'}) \in DI(L), \vec{d} = \vec{i'} - \vec{i}\}$
Taking Program 1, the dependence system 1 may be rewritten in terms of distance vectors:
$$\left\{ \begin{array}{lll} d_i = 2i, & 1 \le i \le n & 1 \le i + d_i \le n \\ d_j = 1, & 1 \le j \le n & 1 \le j + d_j \le n \end{array} \right.$$

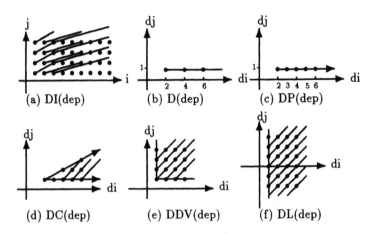

Fig. 2. DI, D, DP, DC, DDV, DL for Program 1

The dependences represented in Figure 2(b) are specified by:
$D(P1) = \{(2k, 1) \mid 1 \leq k \leq n\}$. When comparing with the representation of DI
in Figure 2(a), note the different space: (i, j) is replaced by (d_i, d_j).
Compared to DI, the use of D reduces the amount of memory needed to store
uniform dependences[2]. However, in many cases, the dependence distance is not
constant. So, abstractions approximating D like the *Dependence Polyhedron*, the
Dependence Cone, the *Dependence Direction Vector* and the *Dependence Level*
have been designed to cope with these cases.

2.3 The Dependence Polyhedron

The dependence polyhedron $DP(L)$ approximates the set of distance vectors
$D(L)$ with the set of points that are convex combinations of $D(L)$ vectors. It
constrains the set of integer points of the $D(L)$'s convex hull.
$$DP(L) = \{\vec{v} = \sum_1^k \lambda_i \vec{d_i} \in Z^n \mid \vec{d_i} \in D(L), \lambda_i \geq 0, \sum_{i=1}^k \lambda_i = 1\}$$
The polyhedron $DP(L)$ can be concisely described by its *generating system* [20],
which is a triplet made of three sets of vertices, rays and lines, $(\{\vec{v_i}\}, \{\vec{r_j}\}, \{\vec{l_k}\})$.
Even if $DP(L)$ approximates $D(L)$, it keeps all the information useful to legally
apply reordering transformations as abstraction D. Figure 2(c) illustrates $DP(L)$
for Program 1. The convex hull contains new vectors: $(3, 1), (5, 1)$, etc...

2.4 The Dependence Cone

The dependence cone $DC(L)$ approximates $D(L)$ with the set of points that are
positive linear combination of $D(L)$ vectors. It is defined as:
$$DC(L) = \{\vec{v} = \sum_{i=1}^k \lambda_i \vec{d_i} \in Z^n \mid \vec{d_i} \in D(L), \lambda_i \geq 0, \sum_{i=1}^k \lambda_i \geq 1\}$$
The main advantage of Abstractions DP and DC is that, in many cases, only
one structure (a polyhedron) is necessary to the representation of the information contained in $D(L)$. The memory space gain is notable especially when the
dependence set is not finite or is large with non-uniform dependences. DP and
DC are easier to use than $D(L)$ for computing loop partitioning [11].

---

[2] usually known as *constant* dependences

Abstractions DP and DC can be automatically computed and accurately so when array subscript expressions are affine. Algorithms for computing $DP(L)$ and $DC(L)$ are described in [10] and [26]. They use techniques as the simplex or the Fourier-Motzkin algorithm that have an exponential time complexity. However, as remark [18] and [26], these techniques have shown a polynomial behavior in practice in this context.

2.5 The Dependence Direction Vector

Abstractions $DP(L)$ and $DC(L)$ represent approximated sets of $D(L)$. These three abstractions contain the information useful to legally apply transformations that reorder iteration sets. However, transformations such as loop interchange or permutation, that only modify the sign or the order of the dependence distance vector, do not need the actual distance information. So, abstractions like $DDV(L)$ [23] and $DL(L)$ [1] relating only the sign or the level of dependence vectors have been suggested. Each Dependence Direction Vector element is one of $\{<,=,>\}$. Other elements like $\leq, \geq, *$ may be used to summarize two or three DDV's. The $DDV(L)$ abstracting the dependences for a loop nest L is defined as: $DDV = \{ (\psi_1, \psi_2, ..., \psi_n) \mid \exists S_1, S_2 \in L,\ S_1(\vec{i})\ \delta^*\ S_2(\vec{i'}),$
$$i_k\ \psi_k\ i'_k\ (1 \leq k \leq n), \psi_i \in \{<,=,>\}\}.$$
For Program 1, $DDV(P1) = \{(<, <)\}$. It is represented in Figure 2(e).

2.6 The Dependence Level

The dependence level DL has been introduced by Allen & Kennedy [1] for the vectorization and parallelization of programs. It gives the nest level of the outermost loop l that carries dependences, when dependence vector component is positive. To preserve the program semantics, Loop l must be kept sequential. Then, the lexico-positivity of the loop dependences are preserved and all inner loops may be parallelized if no other dependence exists. $DL(L)$ is defined as:
$$DL(L) = \{k \mid \exists (\psi_1, ..., \psi_n) \in DDV(L), 1 \leq i \leq k-1\ \wedge \psi_i\ is\ =\ \wedge\ \psi_k\ is\ <\}.$$
For Program 1, $DL(P1) = \{1\}$. Dependences are represented in Figure 2(f).

3 Abstraction Precision

The six abstractions of dependences surveyed in the Section 2 have different precisions as was shown in Figure 2. Abstraction DI enumerates all the dependent iterations when the other abstractions express or approximate the dependence distance vectors of the loop nest.

To determine the precision of these abstractions, we define a minimal comparison set of dependent iterations $\widetilde{DI}_A$ for each abstraction $\mathcal{A}$. $\widetilde{DI}_A$ is the set of dependent iterations corresponding to the dependences represented by abstraction $\mathcal{A}$. $\widetilde{DI}_A = \{ (\vec{i}, \vec{i} + \vec{d}) : \vec{i}, \vec{i} + \vec{d} \in I^n,\ \vec{d} \in \tilde{D}_A \}$ where $\tilde{D}_A$ is the set of dependence Distance vectors corresponding to the dependences represented by abstraction $\mathcal{A}$. To compare two ordinary abstractions $\mathcal{A}1$ and $\mathcal{A}2$, the two sets $\widetilde{DI}_{A1}$ and $\widetilde{DI}_{A2}$ are analyzed.

Definition 1
$\mathcal{A}1$ is more precise than $\mathcal{A}2$ (noted $\mathcal{A}1 \supset \mathcal{A}2$) if $\widetilde{DI}_{A1} \subseteq \widetilde{DI}_{A2}$.

To compare abstractions approximating D, the sets $\tilde{D}_{A1}$ and $\tilde{D}_{A2}$, having a lower memory cost than $\tilde{DI}$, could be used [3]. According to Definition 1, the hierarchy of abstraction precisions is: $DI \supseteq D \supseteq DP \supseteq DC \supseteq DDV \supseteq DL$. Figure 2 illustrates this hierarchy.

4 Transformations

In order to exploit the implicit parallelism contained in programs, loop transformations are applied on program loop nests. These transformations reorder statements and iterations in order to explicit parallelism.

In the following sections, we distinguish three classes of transformations:

A program restructuring transformation reorders the statements and iterations of the program. It transforms the statement $S(\vec{i}^n)$ in a new one $S'(\vec{j}^m)$. As an example of this kind of transformations, loop distribution distributes the statements of a loop nest into different loop nests having the same iteration set as the initial code.

A reordering transformation is a particular program restructuring transformation that only reorders loop iterations without changing the order of statements in the loop nest. It is a bijection between two iteration sets that might have different dimensions. It transforms the statement $S(\vec{i}^n)$ into a new one $S(\vec{j}^m)$ where n might be different from m. Strip mining, that reorders by partitioning the iteration set into several iteration blocks, belongs to this class of transformations.

A unimodular transformation is a particular reordering transformation that is a bijection between two iteration sets having the same dimension. Loop interchange belongs to this class.

The conditions that must be verified, for any class of transformations, for legally applying the transformation are presented.

4.1 Legal Transformation

A transformation is *legal* if the program has the same semantics after transformation than before. The new execution of statement instances must preserve all the loop nest lexico-positive dependences [4].

Program Restructuring Transformation

Definition 2 *Performing a restructuring transformation T on a loop nest L is legal and is noted $legal(T, L)$ if and only if: for any dependence $S_1(\vec{i}^n) \, \delta^* \, S_2(\vec{i'}^n)$ of L such that $T(S_1(\vec{i}^n)) = S'_1(\vec{j}^m)$ and $T(S_2(\vec{i'}^n)) = S'_2(\vec{j'}^m)$, the condition $S'_1(\vec{j}^m) \prec S'_2(\vec{j'}^m)$ is verified.*

Definition 2 ensures that the lexico-positivity of the dependences is preserved after transformation. When an abstraction A different from DI is used, Definition 3 gives the conditions for testing the legality of the transformation. The dependences are expressed here in function of $\tilde{DI}_A$, the set of dependent iterations corresponding to the dependences of A.

---

[3] Proof is given in [26]

Definition 3 *Performing a restructuring transformation* T_A *on a loop nest* L *is legal, which is noted* $legal(T, L, A)$ *if and only if: for any dependence* $S_1(\vec{i}^n) \, \delta^* \, S_2(\vec{i'}^n)$ *of* L *such that* $\forall \, (\vec{i}, \vec{i'}) \in \widetilde{DI}_A$, $T(S_1(\vec{i}^n)) = S_1'(\vec{j}^m)$ *and* $T(S_2(\vec{i'}^n)) = S_2'(\vec{j'}^m)$, *the condition* $S_1'(\vec{j}^m) \prec S_2'(\vec{j'}^m)$ *is verified.*

If the application of T is legal according to the condition of Definition 3 then the condition of Definition 2 is also verified. The opposite proposition is not true.

Theorem 1 *Let* T *be a restructuring transformation.* $legal(T, L, A) \implies legal(T, L)$

Proof: Assuming that T_A is legal according to the condition of Definition 3, then: $\forall(\vec{i}, \vec{i'}) \in \widetilde{DI}_A$ with $T(S_1(\vec{i}^n)) = S_1'(\vec{j}^m)$ and $T(S_2(\vec{i'}^n)) = S_2'(\vec{j'}^m)$, the condition $S_1'(\vec{j}^m) \prec S_2'(\vec{j'}^m)$ is verified. Because DI is the most precise dependence abstraction, we have $DI \subseteq \widetilde{DI}_A$ that means that: $\forall(\vec{i}, \vec{i'}) \in DI \implies (\vec{i}, \vec{i'}) \in \widetilde{DI}_A$. It implies that $\forall(\vec{i}, \vec{i'}) \in DI$ such that $T(S_1(\vec{i}^n)) = S_1'(\vec{j}^m)$ and $T(S_2(\vec{i'}^n)) = S_2'(\vec{j'}^m)$, the condition $S_1'(\vec{j}^m) \prec S_2'(\vec{j'}^m)$ is also verified. $\square$

Reordering Transformation
Reordering transformations only reorder the iteration set of a loop nest. So, the dependences $S_1(\vec{i}^n) \, \delta^* \, S_2(\vec{i'}^n)$ between references S_1 and S_2 correspond to dependences $\vec{i}^n \, \delta^* \, \vec{i'}^n$ between iterations. Such dependences can be simply represented using dependent iterations $\vec{i} \prec_\delta \vec{i'}$. All the dependences between the different statements of L can be characterized by a single set $DI(L)$ defined as:
$DI(L) = \{(i_1, i_2) | i_1 \prec_\delta i_2 \Leftrightarrow \exists S_1(i_1) \, \delta^* \, S_2(i_2) \wedge i_1 \neq i_2 \}$
The legality condition for a reordering transformation, translating the preservation of the lexico-positivity constraints, follows:

Definition 4 *Performing a reordering transformation* T *on a loop nest* L *is legal, and is noted* $legal(T, L)$, *if and only if:* $\forall \, (\vec{i}^n, \vec{i'}^n) \in DI(L)$ *such that* $T(\vec{i}^n) = \vec{j}^m$ *and* $T(\vec{i'}^n) = \vec{j'}^m$ *the condition* $\vec{j}^m \prec \vec{j'}^m$ *is verified.*

As for restructuring transformations, when an abstraction A different from DI is used, a definition using dependences in function of $\widetilde{DI}_A$ is derived from Definition 4.

Unimodular Transformation
An unimodular transformation [3], [22], [15] is a bijection between two iteration sets I^n and I'^n having the same dimension. It corresponds to an unimodular change of basis M with $\vec{I'} = M \times \vec{I}$. The test of legality is: if $\vec{i_1} \delta^* \vec{i_2}$, then $i_1' \ll i_2'$ must be verified after the transformation defined as $i_1' = M \times i_1$ and $i_2' = M \times i_2$. This condition can be expressed in terms of dependence distance vectors as: $\vec{d'} \gg 0$ must be verified after transformation, with $\vec{d} = i_2 - i_1$, $\vec{d'} = i_2' - i_1'$ and $\vec{d'} = M \times \vec{d}$.
Because the unimodular transformations reorder iteration sets only, a single set: $D(L) = \{\vec{d} \mid \vec{d} = \vec{i_2} - \vec{i_1}, \, \vec{i_1} \delta^* \vec{i_2} \wedge \vec{i_1} \neq \vec{i_2} \}$ can be used to characterize all loop nest dependences. The following definitions and theorem describe the legality tests for unimodular transformations:

Definition 5 *Performing an unimodular transformation T on a loop nest L is legal if and only if: $\forall \vec{d^n} \in D(L)$ such that $T_{unimod}(\vec{d^n}) = \vec{d'}^n$, the condition $\vec{d'}^n \gg 0$ is verified.*

As for reordering transformations, when an abstraction A different from D is used, a definition using $\widetilde{D}_A$ is derived from Definition 5.

4.2 Valid and Minimal Abstraction

The tests of legality for restructuring, reordering and unimodular transformations have been introduced in Section 4.1. These tests use the abstractions that are derived from the dependent iteration set [4] or from the dependence distance vector set [5] to verify the validity of a transformation. However, the information contained in these abstractions is often too rich, and other abstractions less precise and having a lower computation or memory cost, could be used.

We define a *valid* abstraction associated to a transformation T as an approximate abstraction containing enough information to decide the legality of T. Among the abstractions, DI is the most precise. So, if an abstraction A (different from DI) contains the same information as DI to decide that the transformation T is legal, then this abstraction A is *valid* for T.

Definition 6 *Let A be an abstraction less precise than DI and T a restructuring transformation. If for any loop nest L, $legal(T, L, DI) \implies legal(T, L, A)$, then the abstraction A is valid for testing the legality of the transformation T.*

Several valid abstractions associated to a transformation may exist. In fact, all abstractions more precise than a valid abstraction are also valid.

Theorem 2 *Let A be a valid abstraction for testing the legality of a transformation T. Any abstraction A_i such that $A_i \supseteq A$ is also a valid abstraction for testing the legality of T.*

Proof: We know that A is a valid abstraction for $T(L)$ and that $A_i \supseteq A$. Then, in accordance with Definition 6: $legal(T, L, DI) \implies legal(T, L, A)$.
Definition 3 gives the equivalence: $legal(T, L, A) \iff [\forall (\vec{i}, \vec{i'}) \in \widetilde{DI}_A$ with $T(S_1(\vec{i}^n)) = S_1'(\vec{j}^m)$ and $T(S_2(\vec{i'}^n)) = S_2'(\vec{j'}^m)$ then $S_1'(\vec{j}^m) \prec S_2'(\vec{j'}^m)]$. By hypothesis $A_i \supseteq A$, so $\forall (\vec{i}, \vec{i'}) \in \widetilde{DI}_{A_i}$ then $(\vec{i}, \vec{i'}) \in \widetilde{DI}_A$. By combining this hypothesis with the previous equivalence, the following assertion is verified: $\forall (\vec{i}, \vec{i'}) \in \widetilde{DI}_{A_i}$ with $T(S_1(\vec{i}^n)) = S_1'(\vec{j}^m)$ and $T(S_2(\vec{i'}^n)) = S_2'(\vec{j'}^m)$, then $S_1'(\vec{j}^m) \prec S_2'(\vec{j'}^m)$. That is equivalent to: $legal(T, L, A) \implies legal(T, L, A_i)$, and implies $legal(T, L, DI) \implies legal(T, L, A_i)$. $\square$

Among the valid abstractions associated to a transformation, there is one that contains the *minimal* information necessary to decide whether the transformation is legal. This abstraction is called *minimal* and is defined by the following Definition:

---

[4] DI or $\widetilde{DI}_A$ when A is different from DI
[5] D or $\widetilde{D}_A$ when A is different from D

Definition 7 *Let $\mathcal{A}1$ be a valid abstraction for the transformation T and $\mathcal{A}2$ be a another abstraction such that $\mathcal{A}1 \supseteq \mathcal{A}2$ and $\neg \exists \mathcal{A}3 / \mathcal{A}1 \supseteq \mathcal{A}3 \supseteq \mathcal{A}2$. If $\exists L$ such that $legal(T, L, \mathcal{A}1) \wedge \neg(legal(T, L, \mathcal{A}2))$, then abstraction $\mathcal{A}1$ is minimal for testing the legality of the transformation T.*

Minimality is relative to a particular set of abstractions. The minimal abstractions associated to the reordering transformations that are presented in the next section are minimal for the set of six abstractions DI,D,DP,DC,DDV and DL. To broaden this study to another abstraction, the new abstraction $\mathcal{A}$ must be first classified in the precision hierarchy of the abstractions. Let's assume that $D_1 \supseteq \mathcal{A} \supseteq D_2$ where D_1 and D_2 are one of the previously studied abstractions. Let T_1, T_2 and T_3 be the sets of transformations for which respectively (1) Abstraction D_1 is not valid (2) Abstraction D_2 is valid (3) Abstraction D_1 is valid when Abstraction D_2 is not valid. Then the characteristics of $\mathcal{A}$ are the following ones:

- $\mathcal{A}$ is not valid for each transformation of T_1
- $\mathcal{A}$ is valid for each transformation of T_2
- if $\mathcal{A}$ is valid according to Definition 7 for a transformation T of T_3 then it is minimal for T de facto.

5 Minimal Abstraction and Transformation

Dependence abstractions and loop transformations are linked. The dependences are used to test the legality of a transformation when it changes the program dependences. Because the abstractions have different precisions, a transformation may be declared illegal or legal depending on the abstraction which is used. Thus, choosing a valid abstraction associated to a transformation is important for programs.

Among the valid abstractions associated to a transformation, one is the *minimal* abstraction. It contains the minimal information necessary to decide if the transformation can be applied legally or not. This section focuses on the minimal abstraction associated to the following transformations: loop reversal, loop permutation, unimodular transformation, partitioning and parallelization.

For any T among these transformations, a section presents the effect of T on the dependences, the minimal[6] abstraction associated to T and the legality test applied to T. The theoretical proofs of minimality of abstractions associated to these transformations are given in [26]. Each proof proceeds in two steps: (1) proves that the abstraction is valid for the transformation, (2) according to definition 7, gives a counter example which shows that an abstraction less precise than the minimal abstraction does not contain enough information to decide the transformation legality. Due to space limitation, only a counter example illustrating the transformation is presented in this section.

5.1 Loop Reversal

A loop reversal transformation $Invers_k$ $(l_1, l_2, ..., l_n)$ applied on a n-dimensional loop nest reverses the execution order of loop l_k. The effect of the transformation on the dependence distance vector $\vec{d} = (d_1, .., d_k, .., d_n)$ is $Invers_k (\vec{d}) =$

---

[6] among those presented in this paper

```
DO I = 2, n                          DO I = 2, n
  DO J = 2, n                          DO J = 2, n
    DO K = 2, n                          DO K = n,2,-1
  A(I,J,K)=A(I-1,J,2K)+A(I,J-1,2K)      A(I,J,K)=A(I-1,J,2K)+A(I,J-1,2K)

       Program 2                             Program 3
```

$(d_1, ..., -d_k, ..., d_n)$. So, the lexico-positivity of the dependences is preserved after transformation if the following condition is verified:

$legal(Invers_K, L) \Longleftrightarrow \forall \vec{d} \in D(L), (d_1, ..., -d_k, ..., d_n) \gg 0.$

Theorem 3 *The minimal abstraction for the loop reversal transformation is the Dependence Level DL.*

An example illustrating the previous assertion: In Program 2, the loop nest has two data flow dependence relations that are expressed with the following dependence abstractions: • $D = \{(1, 0, -k), (0, 1, -k) | 2 \le k \le n\}$,
• $DDV = \{(<, =, >), (=, <, >)\}$ and $DL = \{1, 2\}$
Abstraction DL asserts that the 3-rd loop can be reversed because the constraints on the lexico-positive dependences are still preserved after reversing $K : 3 \notin DL \Longrightarrow DL = \{1, 2\}$ after transformation. Now, imagine a dependence abstraction $\mathcal{A}$ less precise than DL and giving only a general dependent/independent information on the set of statements on which the transformation must be applied. Then, not enough information is contained in $\mathcal{A}$ to verify if reversing the 3-rd loop is legal or not. In doubt, the loop reversal is declared illegal. Using DL, loop K can be reversed. The new loop nest is figured in Program 3.

All abstractions DI, D, DC, DP, DDV and DL are *valid* for a loop reversal transformation. The test of legality associated to the minimal abstraction DL is:

$legal(Invers_k, L) \Longleftrightarrow k \notin DL(L) \Longleftrightarrow projection(DL(L), k) = \emptyset.$

5.2 Loop Permutation

A loop permutation transformation [2] $Perm_P (L)$ performs permutation P on the n-dimensional iteration set of the loop nest $L = (l_1, l_2, .., l_n)$. The new loop nest L' is defined by $L' = (l_{p[1]}, l_{p[2]}, ..., l_{p[n]})$ where $\{p[1], p[2], .., p[n]\}$ is a permutation of $\{1, 2, ..n\}$. The effect of the transformation on the dependence distance vector $\vec{d} = (d_1, .., d_k, .., d_n)$ is: $\vec{d'} = Perm_P (\vec{d}) = (d_{p[1]}, ..., d_{p[k]}, ..., d_{p[n]})$. So, the lexico-positivity of the dependences is preserved after transformation if the following condition is verified:

$legal(Perm_P, L) \Longleftrightarrow \forall \vec{d} \in D(L), (d_{p[1]}, ..., d_{p[k]}, ..., d_{p[n]}) \gg 0$

Theorem 4 *For loop permutations, the minimal abstraction is the Dependence Direction Vector DDV.*

An example illustrating the previous assertion: The dependences of Program 3 can be represented using the D, DDV and DL abstractions:
• $D = \{(1, 0, k), (0, 1, k) \mid 2 \le k \le n\}$ • $DDV = \{(<, =, <), (=, <, <)\}$
• $DL = \{1, 2\}$.

```
DO I = 1,n                          DO I = 1,n
  DO J = 1,n                          DO J = 1,n
    A(I,J) = A(I,2J) + A(2I,J-I+1)       A(I,J) = A(2I,J+1) + A(2I,I+J)


      Program 4                           Program 5
```

The use of abstraction DDV allows to verify that the permutation of the (I, J, K) loops into (K, I, J) loops is legal, because $Perm\ _P((<, =, <), (=, <, <)) = \{(<, <, =), (<, =, <)\}$. This is $\gg 0$, since the first element, different from "=", is $<$ which enforces the lexico-positivity of the dependences. In contrast, the use of DL [7] does not allow to conclude the legality of this permutation, because no dependence information is known on the 3-rd loop which will be the outmost loop after permutation.

All abstractions DI, D, DC, DP and DDV are *valid* for a loop permutation transformation. The test of legality associated to the minimal abstraction is then: $legal(Perm_P, L) \iff \forall \overrightarrow{ddv} \in DDV(L), Perm_P(\overrightarrow{ddv}) \gg 0$.

5.3 Unimodular Transformation

An unimodular transformation $TU_M\ (L)$ performs an unimodular change of basis M on the iteration set I of the loop nest L. After transformation, the iteration set becomes $I' = M \times I$. The determinant of M is equal to 1 or -1.

The effect of the transformation on the dependence distance vector $\vec{d}$ is $\vec{d'} = TU_M\ (\vec{d}) = M \times \vec{d}$. In order to preserve the lexico-positivity constraints of the dependences, the following condition must be verified:
$legal(TU_M,\ L) \iff \forall \vec{d} \in D(L),\ M \times \vec{d} \gg 0$

Theorem 5 *The minimal abstraction for an unimodular transformation is the Dependence Cone DC.*

An example illustrating the previous assertion: The program 4 loop nest contains two dependence relations. The first one characterizes data access conflicts between the two references $A(I, 2J)$ and $A(I, J)$. The corresponding dependence system is $S = \{di = 0, dj = j, 1 \le j \le n\}$.

Abstractions D, DC and DDV represent these dependences in the following manner: $\bullet\ D(dp1) = \{(0, x) \mid 1 \le x\}$ $\bullet\ DC(dp1) = (\{(0, 1)\}, \{(0, 1)\}, \emptyset)$
 $\bullet\ DDV(dp1) = \{(=, <)\}$

The second dependence relation represents data access conflicts between two references $A(2I, J - I + 1)$ and $A(I, J)$. The corresponding dependence system is $S = \{di = i, di + dj = 1, 1 \le i \le n\}$.

Abstractions D, DC and DDV represent these dependences as:
 $\bullet\ D(dp2) = \{(x, -x+1)\} \mid 1 \le x\}$ $\bullet\ DC(dp2) = (\{(1, 0)\}, \{(1, 0), (1, -1)\}, \emptyset)$
 $\bullet\ DDV(dp2) = \{(<, >)\}$

Before testing the legality of the transformation, the union of dependences must be computed. The definitions of union for the different abstractions are given in [10],[25] and [26]. Using the same abstractions, this union is expressed as:

---

[7] DL is the abstraction just under DDV in the abstraction precision order

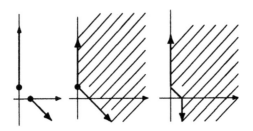

Fig. 3. D(L), DC(L) and DDV(L)

- $D(L) = D(dp1) \cup D(dp2) = \{(0, x), (x, -x + 1) \mid 1 \leq x\}$
- $DC(L) = convex\_hull(DC(dp1) \cup DC(dp2)) = (\{(0, 1)\}, \{(0, 1), (1, -1)\}, \emptyset)$
- $DDV(L) = DDV(dp1) \cup DDV(dp2) = \{(\leq, <), (<, >)\}$.

Figure 3 illustrates these dependences.

Let's assume that we would like to know if the unimodular change of basis M is legal or not, with : $M = \begin{pmatrix} 1 & 1 \\ 0 & 1 \end{pmatrix}$. The computation of the lexico-positivity constraints having to be preserved amounts to:

- $M \times D(dp1) = (x, 0)$ and $M \times D(dp2) = (1, x)$, which are $\gg 0$
- $M \times DC(L) = (\{(1, 1)\}, \{(1, 1), (0, 1)\}, \emptyset)$, which is $\gg 0$ and
- $M \times DDV(L) = M \times DDV(dp1) \cup M \times DDV(dp2)$

As we can see, abstractions D and DC allow to decide that the unimodular transformation can be applied legally, while the DDV abstraction cannot conclude since $M \times DDV(dp2) = (< + >, <)$ is not necessary lexico-positive.

All abstractions DI, D, DP and DC are *valid* for an unimodular transformation. The test of legality associated to the minimal abstraction is:

$legal(TU_M, L) \iff \wedge_{1 \leq i \leq k}(M \times DC_i \gg 0)$ with $DC(L) = (\cup_{1 \leq i \leq k} DC_i)$.

5.4 Partitioning

A partitioning transformation [13], [14], [11] $Part_H$ applied on a n-dimensional loop nest splits the iteration space into blocks of some regular shape by using p families of parallel hyperplanes. The shape and size of the partitioned blocks are defined by the partitioning vector $H = (\vec{h_1}, \vec{h_2}, ..., \vec{h_p})$, where the p families of hyperplanes are respectively orthogonal to $\vec{h_i}$ vectors. This transforms the iteration space I^n into a new one I^{p+n}.

Two iterations i_1 and i_2 of the initial iteration space belong to the same partitioned block if [11]:

$(\lfloor \vec{h_1} \times \vec{i_1} \rfloor, \lfloor \vec{h_2} \times \vec{i_1} \rfloor, ..., \lfloor \vec{h_n} \times \vec{i_1} \rfloor) = (\lfloor \vec{h_1} \times \vec{i_2} \rfloor, \lfloor \vec{h_2} \times \vec{i_2} \rfloor, ..., \lfloor \vec{h_n} \times \vec{i_2} \rfloor)$

According to the results of [11], performing a partitioning H is legal if the following condition is verified: (1) $\quad \forall \vec{d} \in D(L) \quad H \cdot \vec{d} \geq \vec{0}$

For an abstraction $\mathcal{A}$ different from D, the polyhedron characterizing the dependences represented in $\mathcal{A}$ is noted $P_{\mathcal{A}}$. $P_{\mathcal{A}}$ is described by its generating system: $(\{\vec{v_i}\}, \{\vec{r_j}\}, \{\vec{l_k}\})$. Condition (1) can be expressed in terms of $\mathcal{A}$ in the following way: $\quad H \cdot P_{\mathcal{A}} \geq \vec{0} \Longrightarrow legal(Part_H, L, \mathcal{A})$

where $H \cdot P_{\mathcal{A}} \geq \vec{0}$ is equivalent to $[\forall v_i, r_j, l_k \in P_{\mathcal{A}}(L) \quad H \cdot v_i \geq \vec{0}, H \cdot r_j \geq \vec{0}, H \cdot l_k = \vec{0}]$.

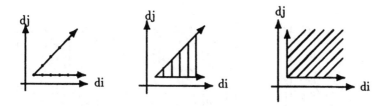

Fig. 4. D, DC and DDV for Program 5

Theorem 6 *The minimal valid abstraction associated to a partitioning transformation is DC.*

An example illustrating the previous assertion: Program 5 contains two anti-dependences. The first one characterizes data access conflicts between the two references $A(2I, J + 1)$ and $A(I, J)$. Its dependence system is $S = \{di = i, dj = 1, 1 \leq i \leq n\}$. The dependence can be represented using D, DC and DDV:

- $D(dep1) = \{(x, 1) \mid 1 \leq x\}$,
- $DC(dep1) = (\{(1, 1)\}, \{(1, 0), (1, 1)\}, \emptyset)$
- $DDV(dep1) = (<, <)$

The second anti-dependence characterizes data access conflicts between the two references $A(2I, I + J)$ and $A(I, J)$.

Its dependence system is $S = \{di = dj, di \geq 1\}$. Its representations by D, DC and DDV is:

- $D(dep2) = \{(x, x) \mid 1 \leq x\}$
- $DC(dep2) = (\{(1, 1)\}, \{(1, 1)\}, \emptyset)$
- $DDV(dep2) = (<, <)$

The union of the two dependences is expressed as:

- $D(L) = D(dep1) \cup D(dep2) = \{(x, 1), (x, x) \mid 1 \leq x\}$.
- $DC(L) = convex\_hull(DC(dep1) \cup DC(dep2)) = (\{(1, 1)\}, \{(1, 0), (1, 1)\}, \emptyset)$.
- $DDV(L) = DDV(dep1) \cup DDV(dep2) = (<, <)$.

$D(L)$, $DC(L)$ and $DDV(L)$ are illustrated by Figure 4.

Let's assume that we would like to partition the iteration space according to the partitioning vector $H = (h_1, h_2)$ where $h_1 = (\frac{1}{3}, -\frac{1}{3})$ and $h_2 = (\frac{1}{3}, 0)$. The lexico-positivity constraints for abstractions D, DC and DDV are expressed as follows:

- $H \cdot D(dep1) = (\frac{x-1}{3}, \frac{x}{3})$ and $H \cdot D(dep2) = (0, \frac{x}{3})$. Since $x \geq 1 \Longrightarrow$ $H \cdot D(dep1) \geq \vec{0}$ and $H \cdot D(dep2) \geq \vec{0}$, $Part_H^D(L)$ is legal with respect to D.

- $H \cdot DC(L) = (\{(0, \frac{1}{3})\}, \{(\frac{1}{3}, \frac{1}{3}), (0, \frac{1}{3})\}, \emptyset)$ Since $s_i, r_j \in H \cdot DC(L) \geq \vec{0}$ and $d_k = \emptyset$, we have $H \cdot DC(L) \geq \vec{0} : Part_H^{DC}(L)$ is legal with respect to DC.

- Since $DDV(L) = \{(<, <)\}$, $P(DDV(L)) = (\{(1, 1)\}, \{(1, 0), (0, 1)\}, \emptyset)$ and $H \cdot DDV(L) = (\{(0, \frac{1}{3})\}, \{(\frac{1}{3}, \frac{1}{3}), (-\frac{1}{3}, 0)\}, \emptyset)$. Since $s_1 = (0, \frac{1}{3}) \geq \vec{0}$ and $r_2 = (-\frac{1}{3}, 0) \leq \vec{0} \Longrightarrow \neg(H \cdot DDV(L) \leq \vec{0}) \wedge \neg(H \cdot DDV(L) \geq \vec{0})$, $Part_H^{DDV}(L)$ is illegal.

Figure 5 shows the H partitioning associated to the D, DC and DDV dependences. We can see that with D there is no dependence cycles between partitioned blocks. Note that the additional dependence distance vector belonging

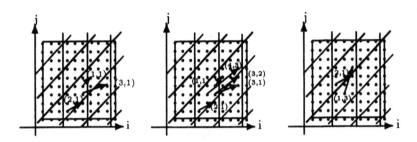

Fig. 5. Partitioning H with D, DC and DDV

to DC does not introduce additional dependence relations between partitioned blocks. But two dependences represented by $DDV(L)$: $(1,3)$ and $(2,1)$ give a cycle between two blocks. Then, $Part_H^{DDV}(L)$ is illegal.

DC allows to conclude the legality of $Part_H$, because condition (1) is verified. On the contrary, abstraction DDV cannot conclude because the set of points described by: $\{s_1 = (0, \frac{1}{3}) \geq \vec{0} \wedge r_2 = (-\frac{1}{3}, 0) \leq \vec{0}\}$ does not verify (1).

In conclusion, all abstractions DI, D, DP and DC are *valid* for a loop partitioning transformation. The test of legality associated to the minimal abstraction is:
$(\wedge_{1 \leq i \leq k}(H \cdot DC_i \geq \vec{0})) \vee (\wedge_{1 \leq i \leq k}(H \cdot DC_i \leq \vec{0})) \Longrightarrow legal(Part_H, L)$
Irigoin and Triolet detail in [11] the algorithm for computing hyperplane partitionings, that is a generalization of strip-mining with no restriction on the stripe direction, using DC.

5.5 Parallelization

Performing a parallelization $Paral$ on a loop nest L along the parallelizing vector $\overrightarrow{pv}$ transforms each loop i with $\overrightarrow{pv}(i) = 0$ in a parallel loop.

$$\overrightarrow{pv}(k) = \begin{cases} 0 \ the \ k-th \ loop \ is \ parallel \\ 1 \ the \ k-th \ loop \ is \ sequential \end{cases}$$

The effect of the parallelization on $\vec{d} = (d_1, .., d_k, .., d_n)$ is $projection(\vec{d}, \overrightarrow{pv}) = (d_{i_1}, d_{i_2}, ...d_{i_m})$ where i_k are the sequential loop indices. As the loop reversal transformation, the parallelization modifies the iteration execution order only in internal loop levels. Thus to preserve the lexico-positivity constraints, the loop levels being parallelized must not affect the initial lexico-positivity dependences. The following condition have to be verified to legally apply a parallelization :
$legal(Paral(\overrightarrow{pv}), L) \iff \forall \vec{d} \in D(L)$ such that $d_k = 0$ $(1 \leq k \leq j - 1) \wedge$
$d_j > 0 \wedge projection(\vec{d}, \overrightarrow{pv}) = (d_{i_1}, d_{i_2}, ...d_{i_m})$ then $d_j \in \{d_{i_1}, d_{i_2}, ...d_{i_m}\}$.
To legally parallelize a loop nest, the minimal abstraction is DL.

Program 6:
```
DO I = 1, n
   DO J = 1, n
      A(I,J) = A(I-1,J-1)
```

An example illustrating the previous assertion: Taking Program 6, the dependences can be represented using D and DL: $D = \{(1,1)\}$ and $DL(L) = \{1\}$ Let's assume that we would like to know if the parallelization of the 2-nd loop is legal. Then $\overrightarrow{pv}$ is equal to $(1, 0)$. The lexico-positivity constraint is expressed as: $projection(\{1\}, (1, 0)) = \{1\}$

DL permits to conclude that the parallelization of loop J is legal because the lexico-positivity constraints have been preserved after parallelization. An abstraction less precise giving, for example, only a general dependent/independent information on the set of statements would not contain enough information for the legality test.

All abstractions DI, D, DC, DP, DDV and DL are *valid* for a loop parallelization transformation. Since the parallelization modifies the iteration execution order only in internal loop levels, the lexico-positivity constraints are preserved if the parallelized loop levels do not appear in the dependence levels. So the test of legality associated to the minimal abstraction is:

$$legal(Paral(\overrightarrow{pv}), L) \Longleftarrow projection(DL(L), \vec{1} - \overrightarrow{pv}) = \emptyset$$

6 Related Work

Most dependence abstractions have originally been developed for particular transformations. As such examples, the dependence direction vector was proposed by M. Wolfe for loop interchanging [23] and the dependence level by Allen & Kennedy for the vectorization and the parallelization of programs [1]. The dependence direction vector has been the most popular dependence abstraction, because it has been successfully used for some important transformations such as loop interchanging and loop permutation. Moreover, its computation is easy and its representation in the dependence graph handy. Most compiler systems have implemented distance and direction vector abstractions. A lot of work has been done on developing more advanced transformations, but few effort has been spent on studying the valid and minimal dependence abstraction for a loop transformation.

In [24], M. Wolfe has arisen a similar question "What information is necessary to decide when a transformation is legal?". A review of the related work on loop transformations and dependence abstractions, including some particular dependence information such as crossing threshold and cross-direction, is presented. A table gives the valid dependence abstraction supporting each considered transformation. However, some important abstractions, such as the dependence cone, and some advanced transformations, such as unimodular transformations and loop partitioning, were not considered.

V. Sarkar & R. Thekkath [19] developed a general framework for applying reordering transformations. They used the *dependence vector* abstraction whose element is either a distance value, in case of constant dependence, or a direction value, in the other cases. For each considered transformation, the rules for mapping dependence vectors, loop bound expressions and the loop nest are defined. These mapping rules were developed from the *dependence vector* abstraction. However, the dependence vector does not contain sufficient information to legally apply advanced transformations, such as unimodular transformations and loop tiling, without some risks of loosing precision.

M. E. Wolf & M. S. Lam [21] introduced a new type of dependence vector for applying unimodular transformations and loop tiling. In their definition, each component d_i of the dependence vector can be an infinite range of integers, represented by $[d_i^{min}, d_i^{max}]$. This new dependence vector is more precise than

V. Sarkar's dependence vector, and overcomes some drawbacks of the direction vector by using the value range of d_i instead of its sign. On the other hand, it is less precise than the dependence cone DC because it is only the projection of DC on the d_i axis. The test of legality based on this dependence vector is approximative because the addition, subtraction and multiplication operations defined on this dependence vector are conservative.

Our study deals with abstractions that are derived from the dependence distance vectors. But, abstraction such as the information given by array data flow analysis [6], [16] provides more precise information about dependencies than the dependence distance vectors. The results of transformations such as the privatization [16] or linear scheduling computation [7], [8] depend on the dependence analysis precision. So, abstractions providing more precise information than the dependence distance vectors have to be introduced to deal with those transformations.

Conclusion

The precision criteria for abstractions DI, D, DP, DC, DDV, and DL have been presented in this paper and report that the precision hierarchy of the abstractions is $DI \supseteq D \supseteq DP \supseteq DC \supseteq DDV \supseteq DL$.

The minimal abstraction associated to a transformation, that contains the minimal information necessary to decide when such a transformation is legal, is defined for three different class of transformations. The minimal abstraction for the reordering transformations: loop reversal, loop permutation, unimodular transformation, partitioning and parallelization have been identified and is respectively DL, DDV, DC, DC and DL. According to the definition, all the abstractions that are more precise than the minimal abstraction associated to the transformation are valid for such a transformation.

This paper shows that the dependence cone DC carries enough information for testing the legality of some advanced transformations such as unimodular transformations and loop partitioning. Moreover, [26] shows that this representation allows to obtain the same set of valid linear schedules, both one- and multidimensional, than with abstraction D without any loss.

Acknowledgments

We wish to give special thanks to P. Jouvelot for his constructive remarks and critical reading of this paper.

References

1. R. Allen, K. Kennedy, "Automatic Translation of FORTRAN Programs to Vector Form", *ACM Transactions on Programming Languages and Systems*, Oct. 1987.
2. U. Banerjee, "A Theory of Loop Permutations", *2nd Workshop on Languages and compilers for parallel computing*, 1989
3. U. Banerjee, "Unimodular Transformation of Double Loops", *3rd Workshop on Programming Languages and Compilers for Parallel Computing*, Irvine, 1990
4. U. Banerjee, "Loop transformations for restructuring compilers: the foundations", *Kluwer Academic Editor*, 1993

5. A. J. Bernstein, "Analysis of Programs for Parallel Processing", *IEEE Transactions on Electronic Computers*, Vol. EC-15, No. 5, Oct. 1966.
6. P. Feautrier, "Dataflow Analysis of Scalar and Array References", *Int. Journal of Parallel Programming*, Vol. 20, No 1,February,1991, pp 23-53.
7. P. Feautrier, "Some Efficient Solutions to the Affine Scheduling Problem, Part I, One-Dimensional Time", *Int. Journal of Parallel Programming*, Vol 21, 1992.
8. P. Feautrier, "Some Efficient Solutions to the Affine Scheduling Problem, Part II, Multi-Dimensional Time", *Int. Journal of Parallel Programming*, Vol 21, 1992.
9. F. Irigoin, "Loop Reordering With Dependence Direction Vectors", In *Journées Firtech Systèmes et Télématique Architectures Futures: Programmation parallèle et intégration VLSI*, Paris, Nov. 1988.
10. F. Irigoin, R. Triolet, "Computing Dependence Direction Vectors and Dependence Cones with Linear Systems", *Rap.Int. CAI87E94 Ecole des Mines de Paris,*
11. F. Irigoin, R. Triolet, "Supernode Partitioning", In *Conference Record of Fifteenth ACM Symposium on Principles of Programming Languages*, 1988.
12. F. Irigoin, R. Triolet, "Dependence Approximation and Global Parallel Code Generation for Nested Loops", In *International Workshop Parallel and Distributed Algorithms*, Bonas, France, Oct. 1988.
13. R. Karp, R. Miller and S. Winograd, "The Organization of Computations for Uniform Recurrence Equations", *Journal of the ACM*, v. 14, n. 3, pp. 563-590, 1967
14. L. Lamport, "The Parallel Execution of DO Loops", *Communications of the ACM 17(2)*, pp. 83-93, 1974
15. W. Li, K. Pingali, "A singular loop transformation framework based on non-singular matrices", In *Languages and Compilers for Parallel Computing*, Yale University, August 1992.
16. D. Maydan, S. Amarasinghe, M.Lam, "Array Data Flow Analysis and its use in Array Privatization", *Stanford Report*, 1993
17. Y. Muraoka, "Parallelism Exposure and Exploitation in Programs", *PhD thesis*, Dept. of Computer Science, University of Illinois at Urbana-champaign, Feb. 1971.
18. William Pugh, "A Practical Algorithm for Exact Array Dependence Analysis", *Communications of the ACM* , August 1992, pp.102-114
19. V. Sarkar, R. Thekkath, "A General Framework for Iteration-Reordering Loop Transformations", In *Programming Language Design and Implementation*, San Francisco, June 1992.
20. A. Schrijver, *Theory of Linear and Integer Programming*, John Wiley & Sons 1986.
21. M.E. Wolf, M.S. Lam, "Maximizing Parallelism via Loop Transformations", In *Programming Languages and Compilers for Parallel Computing*, Aug. 1-3, 1990.
22. M.E. Wolf, M.S. Lam, "A Loop Transformation Theory and an Algorithm to Maximize Parallelism", *Transactions on Parallel and Distributed Systems*, Oct. 1991.
23. M. Wolfe, "Optimizing Supercompilers for Supercomputers", *PhD Thesis, Dept. of Computer Science*, University of Illinois at Urbana-Champaign, October 1982.
24. M. Wolfe, "Experiences with Data Dependence and Loop Restructuring in the Tiny Research Tool", *Technical Report*, No. CS/E 90-016, Sep. 1990.
25. M. Wolfe, "Experiences with Data Dependence Abstractions", In *Proceedings of the 1991 ACM International Conference on Supercomputing*, Germany, June 1991.
26. Y.Q. Yang, "Tests de Dependance et Transformations de programme", *PhD of University Pierre et Marie Curie* , November 93.

Differences in Algorithmic Parallelism in Control Flow and Call Multigraphs

Vincent Sgro and Barbara G. Ryder*

Rutgers University

Abstract. Our parallel hybrid analysis methods facilitate the parallelization of the analysis phase of a software transformation system, by enabling deeper semantic analyses to be accomplished more efficiently than if performed sequentially. Our previous empirical studies profiled these hybrid techniques on the Reaching Definitions problem [LMR91, LR92a, LR92b]. Recently, we have applied our method to the Interprocedural May_Alias Problem for Fortran programs in a prototype implementation. The interpretation of our results suggested further performance studies, comparing our region partition algorithms (both Bottom_Up and Forward partitioning [LRF94]) on call multigraphs and control flow graphs. These comparisons yielded statistically significant differences in performance of our graph partitioning techniques applied to these two graph populations. This research is part of a larger effort to calculate the modification side effects problem (MOD) for Fortran programs using our parallel hybrid techniques.

1 Introduction

Data flow analysis is a compile-time technique that gathers semantic information about a program from its source code. Many software applications can use more precise data flow information than is practically available with sequential data flow algorithms today; often precision is sacrificed for analysis speed. Seldom is information calculated across procedure boundaries; however, many software transformation tools need such information to be most effective. These include debuggers, data-flow-based testers, optimizing sequential compilers, parallelizing compilers, program slicers, semantic program browsers and semantic change analyzers [Ryd89]. Our parallel hybrid data flow analysis algorithms are aimed at speeding up time-consuming analysis calculations by utilizing multiple processors that soon will be found in desktop workstations.

Our parallel hybrid algorithms are general-purpose data flow solution procedures, based on the family of sequential hybrid data flow algorithms [MR90]. These algorithms decompose a flow graph into regions, solve local problems on

* The work presented here was supported, in part, by ARPA contract DABT-63-93-C-0064 and by the National Science Foundation grants CCR92-13518 and CCR90-23628. The content of the information herein does not necessarily reflect the position of the Government and official endorsement should not be inferred.

each region and stitch together their solutions to find the global solution on the entire graph. These algorithms are an amalgam of fixed point iteration (i.e., within the regions) and elimination methods (i.e., propagation from region to region). Previously, we profiled the performance of the original parallel hybrid algorithm on the Reaching Definitions problem [ASU86] on a distributed memory machine, an iPSC/2 at the Cornell Theory Center. We published empirical results for this unoptimized algorithm for Reaching Definitions on Fortran procedures from *Linpack* and *BCF*, a curve-fitting program [LMR91]. Subsequently, we developed the *region partition* optimization and presented empirical results [LR92a, LR94] comparing optimized and unoptimized parallel hybrid algorithm performance on a larger data set, using the same Reaching Definitions problem. These newer studies included flow graph characteristics for our data that proved to be significant to algorithm performance. In [LR92b], we offered an initial look at these flow graph properties for SPICE, one program in the Perfect Benchmarks, and also presented improvements in algorithm performance for the SPICE procedures. These properties impacted the effectiveness of our region partition optimization and revealed *algorithmic parallelism* in our solution process.

Previously, we have discussed three sources of possible parallelism in data flow analysis: *separate-unit* parallelism gained from processing distinct program constructs separately (e.g., loops, procedures etc.); *independent-problem* parallelism gained from solving more than one data flow problem on the same flow graph; and *algorithmic* parallelism gained from finding possible parallelism in the solution procedure itself [LR92a]. Our parallel hybrid algorithms decompose the flow graph of a program into regions, perform local analyses on these regions, do a global propagation of information between regions and then propagate global information within regions. A good decomposition must strike a balance between the amount of parallelism and an appropriate grain size for computation. Thus, the ability of the region partitioning algorithms to determine a good grain size for computation is crucial to the success of our approach, especially on distributed memory machines. The performance of these partitioning techniques proved most significant in interpreting the results of algorithm performance on an interprocedural data flow problem versus an intraprocedural problem.

This paper describes our experiences with an implementation of the Interprocedural May_Alias problem for Fortran. The disappointing speedups obtained led us to subsequent study of the effectiveness of our region partitioning methods on call multigraphs as compared to control flow graphs. We developed two metrics, *Region_Size* and *Interregion_Communication*, to measure the relative goodness of a given decomposition and then used these metrics to compare the effectiveness of both of our *Bottom_Up* and *Forward* partitioning techniques [LRF94, LR94] on call multigraphs and control flow graphs. After statistical analyses of these measures on two data sets of 34 call multigraphs and 696 control flow graphs, we found a significant difference in the structure of these two graph populations that influenced the decompositions induced. This work is an important step toward optimizing our parallel hybrid algorithms to work on interprocedural problems, and eventually, to solve the family of problems in Fortran MOD. By design, hybrid algorithms exemplify algorithmic parallelism. By using all three forms of parallelism mentioned above, we believe we can effectively parallelize the entire analysis phase of a software tool; this is the eventual goal of our research.

In the rest of the paper, we briefly define necessary data flow analysis concepts and describe our parallel hybrid algorithms in Section 2. Then, we detail our experiences with our implementation of the Interprocedural May_Alias problem on an iPSC/2 at the Cornell Theory Center in Section 3. The performance metrics we developed and the data collected on them from our call multigraph and control flow graph populations also are explained. We discuss related work in parallel data flow analysis in Section 4. Finally, we present our conclusions and plans for future work in Section 5.

2 Background

2.1 Parallel Hybrid Data Flow Algorithm

There are three families of general-purpose solution procedures for data flow analysis: *iterative, elimination* and our *hybrid* technique [MR90], the latter an amalgam of the first two approaches.[2] An *iterative* algorithm, based on fixed-point iteration, starts with a safe, initial solution, and then proceeds to a maximum fixed point for the equations; this technique requires that the data flow equations be *monotone* [Hec77]. An *elimination* algorithm has two phases and is conceptually similar to Gaussian elimination [RP86]. In the *elimination* phase, local data flow information within each interval is summarized and collected for all the intervals. In the *propagation* phase, the collected, relevant, global data flow information is propagated into each interval.

A *hybrid* data flow algorithm uses the strongly connected component (SCC) decomposition to divide a flow graph into single-entry node regions [MR90]. Intuitively, the hybrid algorithm solves local data flow problems defined within regions iteratively and then propagates global information on the condensed region graph in an elimination-like manner. The hybrid algorithm is applicable to *factorable* data flow problems; most interesting intraprocedural and interprocedural problems have been shown to be factorable [MR90, Mar89, MR91], although constant propagation is not.

Our parallel hybrid data flow analysis algorithms are fashioned from the sequential hybrid algorithm described briefly above by finding algorithmic parallelism in the solution process. The parallel hybrid algorithm is organized in a *master-worker* model of parallelism. A master task performs problem initialization and task creation. The worker tasks are associated with each region;

---

[2] In addition, there is a family of data flow solution procedures for specific intraprocedural problems called the *partitioned variable technique (PVT)*; these partition the solution of a data flow problem by variables and find the relevant information for a single variable, one at a time [Zad84].

some tasks are *independent,* while others, associated with propagation of global information through the condensed flow graph, are *interdependent.*

The phases of the parallel hybrid algorithm[3] are [LMR91]:

1. *Flow graph condensation.* Construct the flow graph and find its strongly connected components. Find a topological order for the strongly connected component condensation, whose nodes represent flow graph regions.
2. *Problem setup.* Determine local information from flow graph nodes (e.g., variables, value-setting statements), setup the local data flow problem lattice on each region and set up the global problem lattice.
3. *Local solution.* In each region, iterate the local data flow problem to solution.
4. *Global propagation.* In topological order on the condensed graph, propagate the global data flow information. For each region, combine the local problem solution with incoming global information at the region entry node to obtain global information at region exit edges.
5. *Local propagation.* Use the local problem solutions to compute global data flow information for every node in every region.

The master tasks are flow graph condensation and problem setup; each region spawns one worker task each for local solution, global propagation and local propagation. The interdependences of tasks associated with different regions are captured by the edges of the condensed flow graph. Tasks associated with the same region must be performed in the following order: local solution, global propagation, local propagation.

Our algorithm design was targeted for distributed memory architectures. A simple mapping strategy was used; all tasks associated with a region were mapped to the same processor to insure data locality. In addition, a compile-time mapping strategy estimated the work per region and statically allocated tasks to attempt to load balance the processors and avoid run-time overhead. We built local dynamic schedulers on each processor, using the following task priorities: (highest to lowest): global propagation, local solution, local propagation.

Initially, we used the sequential hybrid algorithm directly as a model for our parallel data flow method, but there were too many trivial components in the strongly connected component decompositions. The computation in these regions was too fine-grained, and diminished the savings we obtained by parallelizing the solution process. Therefore, we designed two region partition techniques, *Forward* and *Bottom_Up,* to design more effective parallelism in our graph decompositions; both preserve the necessary single-entry node property (i.e, the *entry constraint*) of our regions [LMR91, LR94, LRF94]. The Forward clustering technique is based on Allen/Cocke intervals [AC76], tempered with a maximal size (i.e., the *size constraint*).[4] The Forward method forms regions by proceeding along the direction of execution flow on flow graph edges. The entry constraint

---

[3] applied to a forward data flow problem in which information is propagated along the direction of execution [Hec77].

[4] This will be represented as *S.*

is satisfied, since we include a node in a region only if all of its immediate predecessors are already in the region. The size constraint is satisfied since we include a node in a region only if the resulting region has its size no larger than S. The advantages of the Forward algorithm are efficiency and ease of implementation; however, it uses no knowledge of the graph structure and proceeds in an oblivious manner. This can result in very poor partitioning for a graph with many leaf nodes (i.e., nodes with no successor), for example, a balanced tree with every leaf a region.

The Bottom_Up method uses the dominator tree of the flow graph to direct the clustering and a topological order on the flow graph to prevent multiple-entry regions from being formed. In this algorithm, children are merged with parents in the dominator tree as long as the single-entry condition is not violated and the maximal size is not exceeded. Because of nested control structures, there may be paths from one dominator tree sibling to another in the flow graph. If we use a topsort order on the flow graph to order sibling nodes, we can show that the entry constraint will be maintained.

We have shown that finding a minimal region partition for a fixed maximal region size is *NP hard* [Lee92], so our techniques are actually approximation algorithms. Both of these techniques are *greedy* in that they try to make the region as large as possible without violating the size constraint.

2.2   May_Alias Problem Definition

The solution to the interprocedural *May_Alias* problem lists pairs of variables which refer to the same storage location during some execution of each procedure. The May_Alias problem is important for calculation of side effects in a program because aliases mean that variables which don't explicitly appear in a value-setting statement may still suffer side effects from the statement. There are solutions for this problem for languages like Fortran where call by reference parameter passing methods are the only sources for dynamic aliasing [CK89]. These are formulated on the call multigraph representing possible procedure calls in a program. Algorithms for Fortran May_Alias depend on the following observations:

Alias Introduction: There are specific constructs a program that introduce aliases:

1. A single variable occurs in more than one position in a call. The corresponding formals in the called procedure will be aliased during that call.

2. A global variable occurs as an actual in a call. The corresponding formal in the called procedure will be aliased to that global during that call.

Alias Propagation: Once an alias is created, there are specific constructs that propagate these aliases to other procedures. Assume $< x, y >$ are aliased in procedure M at a call of procedure N :

1. If x and y are formal parameters of M used as actuals in the call to procedure N, then the corresponding formals of procedure N will be aliased on entry to N.

2. If x is a formal parameter of procedure M is used as an actual in the call to procedure N, and y is global to N, then the formal corresponding to x in N and the global y will be aliased on entry to N.

3. If x is a formal parameter of procedure M, y is global to procedure N, and both are used as actuals in the call to procedure N, then the corresponding formals of procedure N will be aliased on entry to N.

2.3   May_Alias Problem Formulation for Hybrid Algorithm

The hybrid algorithm solution for this problem requires the definition of four local problems on each region [MR91]:

Restricted Problem - R: This is the May_Alias problem restricted to the region; that is, we solve for May_Alias as though the region were the entire program. For this we use the same formulation as was described above, with alias introduction and propagation.

The Formal Pair Problems - F: This is a set of problems that solve for possible aliases between 2 formal parameters of a procedure within the region, induced by an assumed alias between two region entry node formals. Each F problem corresponds to a different entry node formal alias pair. Alias propagation rule 1 is used to propagated these aliases through the region.

The Head Global Problems - H: This is a set of problems that solve for aliases between a formal within the region and a global variable. Each problem assumes that a representative global variable is aliased to a region entry node formal. These aliases are propagated by alias propagation rule 2 throughout the region.

The Internal Global Problem - I: This is a set of problems that correspond to the situation in alias propagation rule 3, namely when a formal is aliased to a global and both that formal and that global are used as arguments in a procedure call. Given an instance of this situation involving formal f and global g, we use the H problem for f to initialize the corresponding I problem, by substituting g for the representative global and using alias propagation rule 3 to propagate this alias into alias pairs involving the corresponding two formals of the called procedure. Then, alias propagation rule 1 is used to further propagate these aliases.

As can be seen, these local problems are rather complex, although not difficult to solve. The example problem and its solution in Table 3 shows May_Alias formulated with our sequential hybrid algorithm.

3 Investigations

3.1 May_Alias Implementation

A team of undergraduate students coded a solution to the May_Alias problem as previously described in [CK89] on call multigraphs using Bottom_Up partitioning on an iPSC/2. Discouragingly, the reasonable speedups realized on control flow graphs were not obtained from our experiments with call multigraphs. There are many possible reasons why this speed increase was not realized, but it is difficult to calculate which was the most significant. The implementors of the algorithm used good software engineering methods for ordinary platforms; however, they did not translate very well to a distributed, parallel machine environment. For the most part, the problems were the result of using object oriented programming techniques. These techniques, though they lend themselves to well organized and maintainable code, put a level (or more) of abstraction between the programmer and the machine architecture. More appropriate data structures and operations could have been chosen, but were not, since they existed in a different abstraction level than the programmers were coding. Examples of these include:

Solution Representation. The hybrid algorithms for Reaching Definitions were formulated as *bit vector* problems; the May_Alias problem, on the other hand, was not. The data flow information, sets of pairs of variable names, was kept as unencoded strings, a form that was far less efficiently manipulated. The equality test used was a simple string comparison which introduced context switching overhead. Performing set unions and membership tests required quite a lot of work.

Message Encoding. Since the processors existed on a distributed machine, the method of information transfer was through message passing. The data communicated was a representation of flow graph structure. The machine was designed to pass arrays of information as messages. If the low-level representation had been some sort of array structure (e.g., an adjacency matrix), then the message encoding would have been straightforward; however, the graphs were represented as structures and pointers, which had to be translated twice every time a message needed to be passed.

Heap Manipulation. There were several places where blocks of memory were allocated and immediately freed within a tight loop. It was not evident that this was happening since it was buried deep in the object structure.

In addition to the problems already cited, there are differences between call multigraphs and flow graphs that may have had an influence on the performance of the analysis algorithms. Since the May_Alias problem involved call multigraphs, and the programs being analyzed in the experiments were Fortran programs which had no recursion, the graphs had only trivial strongly connected components. Thus, in the absence of loops in the graph, there was no need to do iteration. One topologically ordered pass through a region was enough to obtain a local solution. These local tasks contain little computation and thus, the communication between processors probably dominated all computation. In comparison, the control flow graphs did contain many loops, so there were many non-trivial components on which iteration was necessary to solve the Reaching Definitions problem.

Also, the *shapes* of control flow graphs and call multigraphs are quite different. Control flow graphs have nodes with no more than two (usually) edges leaving them. Call multigraphs, on the other hand, may have many edges leaving and entering them. This difference in shape may affect the performance of the graph partitioning algorithms.

The work required by the data flow problems that we profiled was quite different. It is not clear that the quantity of information being manipulated in the control flow and call multigraph problems was the same.

3.2 Metrics

The performance differences cited above clearly pointed to graph structure as a possible major discriminant between the two experiments. Therefore, we focused our attention on measuring the heuristic performance of the two graph partitioning algorithms.

Algorithm Constraints and Desirada. A well distributed parallel execution would be characterized by regions of moderately balanced size (i.e. tasks) and minimal inter-region communication. Having regions of approximately equal size helps to simplify task assignment. Since the Fortran call multigraphs did not have any cycles, the size of the region was directly related to the amount of computation required for finding local solutions and doing local propagation. In distributed memory machines, the cost of communication is quite high. If the solution found by a partitioning algorithm has a great many edges between the regions, then there is a risk that cross-processor communication will dominate the computation; then parallelization of the analysis will only increase the total processing time.

Though the size constraint designed into the partitioning algorithms is closely related to the idea of balanced region size, it is not clear whether an algorithm that fulfills the size constraint will fulfill the balanced region criterion optimally. Also, the entry constraint does not guarantee to minimize the number of edges between regions. In fact, the balanced region criterion and communication constraint may interfere with each other, a possible source of trouble with the implementation of the parallel hybrid aliasing algorithm. To test the significance of this difference, some metrics were developed and used to compare the performance of the Forward and Bottom_Up algorithms on control flow and call multigraphs.

Region Size Metric. The primary reason for performing graph partitioning is to identify convenient sets of graph nodes that can be processed separately, thus creating parallel tasks. However, once the number of regions exceeds the number of processors being used on the parallel machine, mapping multiple regions to the same processor needs to be done. In such a situation, load balancing can become a problem particularly with regions that have cycles since, in the presence of cycles, the amount of work needed to process a region becomes unpredictable. However, in our experiment, aliasing analysis was performed on the call multigraphs of Fortran 77 programs for which recursion was not supported. Therefore, there were no cycles to complicate the estimation.

We want regions corresponding to tasks that are easily mapped to processors. To evaluate the effectiveness of the partitioning algorithms to perform this task, a *quality measure* was needed. The partitioning algorithms have a parameter that represents maximal region size. Presumably, this parameter is chosen based on the number of processors available to the algorithm. It was, therefore, assumed that the best an algorithm could do was to divide the call multigraph into regions each exactly the size specified. (Of course, one may have to be smaller.) Using this assumption, the difference between the number of regions actually formed and the best the algorithm could have done, produces a useful measure of algorithm quality with respect to region sizing. Therefore, the Region_Size metric is:

$$Region\_Size = 1 - \frac{(a - \frac{n}{S})}{n - \frac{n}{S}}$$

where a is the number of regions actually formed by the partitioning algorithm, n is the number of call multigraph nodes in the graph being processed, and S is the maximum size parameter. The numerator is the distance between the optimal partitioning with respect to size and the partitioning obtained. The denominator is a normalization factor. Subtracting the normalized difference from one provides a more intuitive measure, in that the closer Region_Size is to one, the better the algorithm performed.

It may be argued that the standard deviation of the sizes of the regions may be better to use for this measure. However, there are situations where the standard deviation discerns too strictly. For example, assume there is a call multigraph with twelve nodes and that there are three processors available. The maximum region size is chosen to be $S = 4$ in the hopes that there will be three regions of four nodes each, giving each processor one region, as in Figure 1. However, the algorithms are very unlikely to actually produce such a partitioning. They may also produce five regions of varying sizes. Figure 1 shows two such possible suboptimal partitionings. It will take more work to decide on a processor mapping in the two cases with five regions than when there are three. However, the actual work done in the two five region cases is equivalent, ignoring that of context switching between regions. The standard deviation would differentiate between the two, incorrectly showing suboptimal 2 to be superior over suboptimal 1. Our Region_Size metric will not make that distinction.

Minimizing Communication. Since communication throughput is a known bottleneck in parallel processing, it is also an objective of the partitioning algorithms to form regions that will cause the tasks that they represent to have as little data interdependence as possible. Since aliases are propagated through function and procedure calls, the number of call multigraph edges into a region provide a good estimate of the degree that each region depends on information from sources outside that region.

To simplify, we will measure how well each algorithm does with respect to inter-region communication by counting the number of inter-region call multigraph edges. The worst either algorithm can do is to have every edge be an inter-region edge. Therefore, the quality measure is:

$$Interregion\_Communication = 1 - \frac{a}{e}$$

where, a is the actual number of inter-region edges and e is the total number of edges in the call multigraph. As with the Region_Size quality measure, the normalized value is subtracted from one to provide a more intuitive value. The closer Interregion_Communication is to one, the better the algorithm performance in reducing the inter-region communication.

3.3 Experiments

The two partitioning methods, Forward and Bottom_Up, were tested against each other on the same set of graphs to show if, in general, one performs better than the other. Then, each method was tried on both control flow graphs and call multigraphs to see if the graph type affects their performance.

Data Set Quality. First, all the analyses are being performed on a limited set of Fortran programs, mostly scientific applications and libraries.[5] The application area may have a strong impact on the structure of the graphs and, therefore, possibly the performance of the partitioning algorithms. It should be noted that the results given here may or may not be extendable across a range of applications. However, this data does explain the differences in performance we experienced between the Reaching Definitions and May_Alias implementations, since the graphs used here are those generated in these experiments.

Second, the number of control flow graphs available vastly outnumbered the number of call multigraphs.[6] The t-test used in this section is normally rather stable so this should not matter much. Nonetheless, although the results shown are for the entire sample, the tests were verified on random sub-samples of control flow graphs chosen so that the sample sizes would be equal.

Methods. The statistical methods involved summarizing the results of the tests and expressing the differences that these summaries show.[7] The first step in the tests was to apply each partitioning method to each call multigraph and control flow graph while varying the size parameter S that each method uses, from two to half the number of nodes in each graph. Then, the two metrics were calculated for each partitioning. Thus, we obtained a set of performance results for each method on each graph. For example, the leftmost plot of Figure 2 shows the performance of the Bottom_Up partitioning algorithm, as S is varied from two to half the graph size. Notice how the data points are not linear.

---

[5] We have found it difficult to obtain a broad range of applications through user solicitation and investigation of repositories on the Internet.

[6] The data set size difference was due to the fact that any one program may contain many control flow graphs, but only one call multigraph.

[7] The methods used were suggested by Dr. Javier Cabrera of the Rutgers University Statistics Department.

The next step was to find a way to summarize the results of the test so that simple statistical tests could be performed on the data. It was decided that the data would first be *transformed* so that the results be as close to a linear relationship to the size parameter S as possible. The transformation used was: $q/(1-q)$, where q was the value of the quality measure. A regression was applied to the resulting linearized data and the x-intercept and slope of the fitted lines were used as the summary information. The x-intercept is a rough estimate of how the algorithms perform in the lower values of S and the slope expresses the improvement of the algorithms as the S parameter increases. For example, the rightmost plot of Figure 2 shows the same data as the leftmost plot, after it has been transformed. Notice how the data is closer to the regression line.

Scatter plots of the x-intercept against slope showed clusters of points that seemed differentiated in some way. This was especially true for the Region_Size metric. For example, Figure 3 is a scatter plot of the results of the Region_Size metric calculated from partitionings obtained by the Bottom_Up algorithm on both the control flow graphs and the call multigraphs. The differences in the data points of the plot in Figure 3 are almost linearly separable. Other plots were not as clean, but the means of the clusters were significantly different.

To show the significance of the separation, a t-test was used on the means of the intercepts and the means of the slopes. For this test, the null hypothesis is:

$$H_0 : \mu_1 - \mu_2 = 0$$

where μ_1 and μ_2 are the population means we are testing. Since we will always assign the higher mean to μ_1, the alternative hypothesis is:

$$H_a : \mu_1 - \mu_2 > 0$$

What is being done is a test for a significant difference of the means. If we *do not reject* the null hypothesis, then there is insufficient evidence to indicate that the means are different. If we *reject* the null hypothesis, then we can conclude that there is a significant difference and, further, that μ_1 is the greater of the two.

In all of the analyses, the statistical confidence parameter α was chosen to be $\alpha = .025$, except when otherwise noted. This means that if we conclude that there is a significant difference in the population means, then there is a .025 probability that we do so erroneously.

3.4 Results

The most dramatic of the differences can be seen in the analysis of the Bottom_Up and Forward partitioning methods across the two types of graphs. In each of the cases, the null hypothesis is rejected and a significant difference is found. It may be concluded with some measure of confidence that both the algorithms perform better on control flow graphs than they do on call multigraphs. The results can be seen in Table 1.

The performance difference between the Bottom_Up and Forward methods on the same type of graph is less dramatic and can be seen in Table 2. In each case, the slope is significantly better for the Bottom_Up method. This seems to imply that, with some measure of confidence, the Bottom_Up algorithm improves faster than the Forward method as the size limit parameter S increases. On the other hand, there was insufficient evidence to conclude that either method did better on the x–intercept. In fact, in the first case, the Forward algorithm seems to have done better.[8]

4 Related Work in Parallel Data Flow Analysis

Previous work by others on parallel data flow algorithms was reported in [Zob90, GPS90, KGS94] Kramer *et al.* presented an approach based on parallel prefix operation (i.e., scan). Although interesting in approach, this can only handle reducible flow graphs as formulated; a "by hand" comparison is offered on the effectiveness of graph decomposition by this algorithm and our unoptimized algorithm [LMR91]. Both Zobel and Gupta *et al.* designed parallel elimination algorithms. Zobel parallelized Allen-Cocke interval analysis [AC76] and reported some empirical experiences for the available expressions problem on five C functions [Zob90].[9] Since her approach had no control over the flow graph partitioning, very large intervals limited parallelism and caused load imbalance. If a flow graph is acyclic, this approach offers no parallelism at all. In their parallel elimination method, Gupta *et al.* attempted to partition a reducible flow graph into single-entry, single-exit regions instead of intervals using a syntax-directed method [GPS90]. Although their approach had some control over the size of regions in flow graph partitioning, the restriction that regions must be *Single-entry and single-exit* required the corresponding program to be well-structured. Thus, in practice, this technique is not sufficiently effective. Additionally, there were no experimental results reported.

5 Future Work and Conclusions

Because of the homogeneity of the data studied, it might make sense to repeat our tests using a more heterogeneous data set. If our results are corroborated, then some obvious directions emerge. The statistics showed that the partitioning algorithms do not perform as well on call multigraphs as they do on control flow graphs. Methods of improving this performance should be investigated. Currently, we are working on improving the Bottom_Up algorithm by using heuristics to choose which of the children of a node in the dominator tree will

---

[8] Here, the Forward algorithm had the higher mean and the null hypothesis was rejected, implying that it may have done significantly better.

[9] The Available Expressions problem involves information necessary for common subexpression elimination [ASU86].

be merged into its region. Hopefully, our heuristics will lower the amount of communication between regions and obtain better load balancing.

Addressing the larger problem of "What went wrong with our aliasing implementation?" it may be that the May_Alias problem has a small amount of work required at each graph node, unlike Reaching Definitions. If this is so, then there may not be enough work for the processors to do in each worker task that would allow them to overcome the communication bottleneck. We hypothesize that adding other problems to be solved in conjunction with the May_Alias analysis will improve the situation. As stated previously, we intend to investigate the concurrent solution of several interprocedural data flow problems in the context of an implementation of the Fortran MOD problem [LR92a]. Parallelizing the entire data flow analysis phase of a software translation tool is appealing, in that it holds promise of generating enough work for overcoming the communication to computation cost ratio.

Another possible avenue for future investigation is to implement our parallel hybrid algorithm on a shared address space architecture. This might uncover different performance problems which can be addressed.

To summarize our accomplishments delineated in this paper, we built an initial implementation of our parallel hybrid algorithm applied to an interprocedural data flow problem on a distributed memory machine, and discovered an essential difference in the structure of control flow graphs versus call multigraphs. This difference, corroborated by the statistical analyses detailed here, affected how well our region-finding algorithms could decompose these call multigraphs for effective parallel computation. By better tuning the partitioning algorithms to program calling structures, we hope to attain useful speedups in our next round of experiments with our parallel hybrid algorithms.

Acknowledgments: Our colleagues Richard Martin and David Hunter, two Rutgers seniors at the time they were involved with our research, were responsible for the May_Alias implementation; without their diligent efforts, we would not have been able to make the observations in this paper. These students were supported by funds provided by the National Science Foundation under its Research Experiences for Undergraduates program and an Undergraduate Research Internship sponsored by the Rutgers University Provost's Office. We also thank Dr. Javier Cabrera for suggesting the statistical methods used in this study.

References

[AC76] Frances E. Allen and John Cocke. A program data flow analysis procedure. *Communications of the ACM*, 19(3):137–147, 1976.

[ASU86] A. V. Aho, R. Sethi, and J. D. Ullman. *Compilers: Principles, Techniques, and Tools.* Addison-Wesley, 1986.

[CK89] Keith Cooper and Ken Kennedy. Fast interprocedural alias analysis. In *Conference Record of the Sixteenth Annual ACM Symposium on Principles of Programming Languages*, pages 49–59, January 1989.

[GPS90] Rajiv Gupta, Lori Pollock, and Mary Lou Soffa. Parallelizing data flow analysis. In *Proceedings of the Workshop on Parallel Compilation*, Kingston, Ontario, Canada, May 1990.

[Hec77] Matthew S. Hecht. *Flow Analysis of Computer Programs.* Elsevier North-Holland, Amsterdam, Netherlands, 1977.

[KGS94] Robert Kramer, Rajiv Gupta, and Mary Lou Soffa. The combining DAG: A technique for parallel data flow analysis. *IEEE Transactions on Parallel and Distributed Systems,* August 1994. to appear.

[Lee92] Yong-fong Lee. *Performing Data Flow Analysis in Parallel.* PhD thesis, Department of Computer Science, Rutgers University, May 1992.

[LMR91] Yong-fong Lee, Thomas J. Marlowe, and Barbara G. Ryder. Experiences with a parallel algorithm for data flow analysis. *The Journal of Supercomputing,* 5(2):163–188, October 1991.

[LR92a] Yong-fong Lee and Barbara G. Ryder. A comprehensive approach to parallel data flow analysis. In *Proceedings of the ACM International Conference on Supercomputing,* pages 236–247, July 1992.

[LR92b] Yong-fong Lee and Barbara G. Ryder. Parallel hybrid data flow algorithms: A case study. In *Conference Record of 5th Workshop on Languages and Compilers for Parallel Computing, Yale University,* pages 296–310, August 1992. *Springer-Verlag Lecture Notes in Computer Science, Number 757.*

[LR94] Yong-fong Lee and Barbara G. Ryder. A framework for parallel compile-time analyses. *The Journal of Supercomputing,* 1994. in press.

[LRF94] Yong-fong Lee, Barbara G. Ryder, and Marc E. Fiuczynski. Region analysis: A parallel elimination method for data flow analysis. In *Proceedings of the IEEE Conference on Computer Languages,* pages 31–42, May 1994.

[Mar89] Thomas J. Marlowe. *Data Flow Analysis and Incremental Iteration.* PhD thesis, Rutgers University, August 1989.

[MR90] Thomas J. Marlowe and Barbara G. Ryder. An efficient hybrid algorithm for incremental data flow analysis. In *Conference Record of the Seventeenth Annual ACM Symposium on Principles of Programming Languages,* pages 184–196, January 1990.

[MR91] Thomas J. Marlowe and Barbara G. Ryder. Hybrid incremental alias algorithms. In *Proceedings of the Twentyfourth Hawaii International Conference on System Sciences, Volume II, Software,* January 1991.

[RP86] Barbara G. Ryder and Marvin C. Paull. Elimination algorithms for data flow analysis. *ACM Computing Surveys,* 18(3):277–316, September 1986.

[Ryd89] Barbara G. Ryder. Ismm: Incremental software maintenance manager. In *Proceedings of the IEEE Computer Society Conference on Software Maintenance,* pages 142–164, October 1989.

[Zad84] F. Kenneth Zadeck. Incremental data flow analysis in a structured program editor. In *Proceedings of the ACM SIGPLAN '84 Symposium on Compiler Construction,* pages 132–143. ACM Press, June 1984. Montreal, Canada.

[Zob90] Angelika Zobel. Parallel interval analysis of data flow equations. In *Proceedings of the 1990 International Conference on Parallel Processing, Vol.II,* pages 9–16. The Penn State University Press, August 1990.

Between Control Flow and Call Multigraphs		Intercept	Slope
Bottom_Up / Communication	Threshold	1.96420	
	t statistic	2.71985	4.09056
	Conclusion	**reject**	**reject**
Bottom_Up / Region	Threshold	1.96464	
	t statistic	3.76389	3.060471
	Conclusion	**reject**	**reject**
Forward / Communication	Threshold	1.96420	
	t statistic	6.51384	4.79076
	Conclusion	**reject**	**reject**
Forward / Region	Threshold	1.96464	
	t statistic	3.75678	2.86510
	Conclusion	**reject**	**reject**

Table 1. Control flow graphs had the higher mean.

Between Bottom_Up and Forward		Intercept	Slope
Control Flow / Communication	Threshold	1.96223	
	t statistic	2.09734	3.20279
	Conclusion	*reject*	**reject**
Control Flow / Region	Threshold	1.96248	
	t statistic	1.57803	4.71373
	Conclusion	**not reject**	**reject**
Call / Communication	Threshold	2.00488	
	t statistic	0.21242	2.78743
	Conclusion	*not reject*	**reject**
Call / Region	Threshold	2.00488	
	t statistic	0.73695	3.50183
	Conclusion	**not reject**	**reject**

Table 2. Bottom_Up had the highest mean except where the conclusion is italicized.

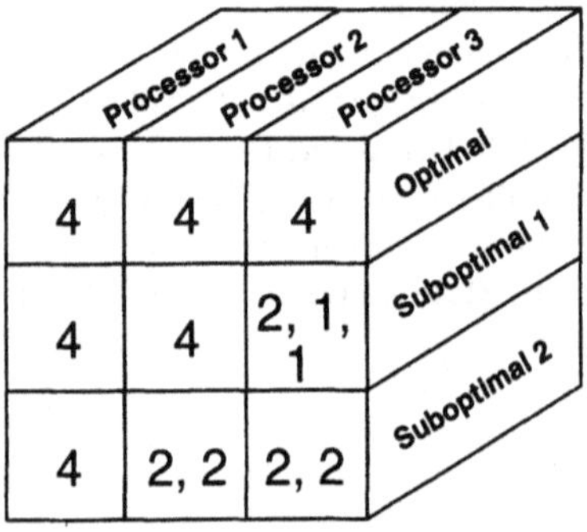

Fig. 1. An optimal and two suboptimal partitionings with $S = 4$ and a call multigraph of twelve nodes.

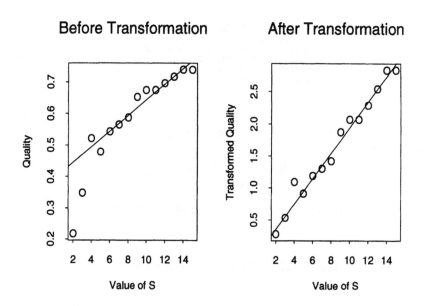

Fig. 2. A plot of the performance of the Bottom-Up algorithm on a *single* call multigraph as S is varied. The second plot is the same information after it is transformed.

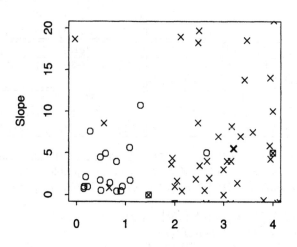

Fig. 3. Scatter plot showing call multigraphs (O) and control flow graphs (X).

In procedure P1 (f1, f2, f3) we have
    a: P2 (f1,f2);
In procedure P2 (x1, x2) we have a local
variable y1 and b: P3 (x1, x2, y1);
In procedure P3 (x3, x4, x5) we have
    c: P1 (x3, x3, g1);
    d: P2 (x4, x5);

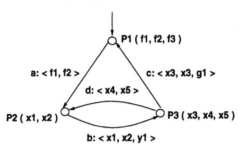

Fig. 4. Call multigraph with relevant code

R	**H**$\langle G1, f1 \rangle$
$(P1): \{(g1, f3), (f1, f2)\}$ $(P2): \{(x1, x2)\}$ $(P3): \{(x3, x4)\}$	**R** $\cup$ $(P1): \{(G1, f1), (G1, f2)\}$ $(P2): \{(G1, x1), (G1, x2)\}$ $(P3): \{(G1, x3), (G1, x4)\}$
F$\langle f1, f2 \rangle$	**H**$\langle G2, f2 \rangle$
R since $(f1, f2) \in \mathbf{R}(P1)$	**R** $\cup$ $(P1): \{(G2, f1), (G2, f2)\}$ $(P2): \{(G2, x1), (G2, x2)\}$ $(P3): \{(G2, x3), (G2, x4)\}$
F$\langle f1, f3 \rangle$	**I**$\langle g1, f3 \rangle$
R $\cup (P1): \{(f1, f3)\}$ and same for **F**$\langle f2, f3 \rangle$, **H**$\langle G3, f3 \rangle$	**H**$\langle G3, f3 \rangle [G3 \leftarrow g1] = $ **R**
I$\langle g1, f1 \rangle$	**I**$\langle g1, f2 \rangle$
H$\langle G1, f1 \rangle [G1 \leftarrow g1] \cup$ $(P1): \{(f1, f3), (f2, f3)\}$	**H**$\langle G2, f2 \rangle [G2 \leftarrow g1] \cup$ $(P1): \{(f1, f3), (f2, f3)\}$

If set of external bindings is $\{(f1, f3), (g1, f2), (g2, f3)\}$, then the alias solution at Pi will be the union of the problems **R**, **F**$\langle f1, f3 \rangle$, and the **I** problem **I**$\langle g1, f2 \rangle$, and the two instantiated **H** problems, **H** $\langle G2, f2 \rangle [G2 \leftarrow g1]$ and **H** $\langle G3, f3 \rangle [G3 \leftarrow g2]$. Thus,

$$Alias(P1) = \{(g1, f2)(f1, f2)\} \cup \{(f1, f3)\} \cup \{(g1, f1), (g1, f2)\}$$
$$\cup \{(g2, f3)\} \cup \{(f1, f3), (f2, f3)\}$$
$$= \{(f1, f2), (g1, f3), (f1, f3), (g1, f1), (g1, f2), (f2, f3), (g2, f1), (g2, f2)\}$$
$$Alias(P2) = \{(x1, x2), (g1, x1), (g1, x2), (g2, x1), (g2, x2)\}$$
$$Alias(P3) = \{(x3, x4), (g1, x3), (g1, x4), (g2, x3), (g2, x4)\}$$

Table 3. Alias Solution for above call multigraph

Flow-Insensitive Interprocedural Alias Analysis in the Presence of Pointers

Michael Burke, Paul Carini, Jong-Deok Choi
IBM T. J. Watson Research Center

Michael Hind
State University of New York at New Paltz
IBM T. J. Watson Research Center

Abstract. Data-flow analysis algorithms can be classified into two categories: *flow-sensitive* and *flow-insensitive*. To improve efficiency, flow-insensitive interprocedural analyses do not make use of the intraprocedural control flow information associated with individual procedures. Since pointer-induced aliases can change within a procedure, applying known flow-insensitive analyses can result in either incorrect or overly conservative solutions. In this paper, we present a *flow-insensitive data-flow analysis algorithm* that computes interprocedural pointer-induced aliases. We improve the precision of our analysis by (1) making use of certain types of *kill* information that can be precomputed efficiently, and (2) computing aliases generated in each procedure instead of holding at the exit of each procedure. We improve the efficiency of our algorithm by introducing a technique called *deferred evaluation*.

Interprocedural analyses, including alias analysis, rely upon the *program call graph* (*PCG*) for their correctness and precision. The *PCG* becomes incomplete or overly imprecise in the presence of function pointers. This paper also describes a method for constructing the *PCG* in the presence of function pointers.

1 Introduction

Data-flow analysis computes information about the potential behavior of a program in terms of the definitions and uses of data objects. Such data-flow information is important in providing compiler and run-time support for the parallel execution of programs originally written in sequential languages [2, 3, 25, 14]. It is also important for compilers and programming environment tools [2, 10, 21]. Data-flow analysis for programs written in languages with only static data structures (i.e., arrays), such as FORTRAN, enjoys numerous techniques developed for it. However, data-flow analysis for programs written in languages with dynamically-allocated data structures, such as C, C++, LISP, and Fortran 90, has been less successful due to pointer-induced aliasing.

Aliasing occurs when there exists more than one *access path* [24] to a storage location. Access paths are l-value expressions that are constructed from variables, pointer indirection operators, and structure field selection operators. In C these expressions would include the '*' indirection operator, and the '—>' and '.' field select operators. Two access paths are *must-aliases* at a statement S if they refer to the same storage location in all execution instances of S. Two access paths are *may-aliases* at S if they refer to the same storage location in some execution instances of S. This paper addresses the computation of may-aliases, of which must-aliases are a subset. We will refer to may-aliases as aliases, whenever the meaning is clear from context. For example, consider statement S_1 in Figure 1. After the statement is executed, $*p$ and r refer to the same storage location and thus become aliases of each other, which we express as the *alias relation* $<*p, r>$. In the figure, we denote the alias relations holding *after* each statement by placing it on the same line with the statement.

```
SubA() {          Flow-Sensitive                        Flow-Insensitive
  S₁:p = &r;      {<*p,r>}                  {<*p,r>,<*q,s>,<*q,r>,<*q,t>}
     if (...)
  S₂: q = p;      {<*p,r>,<*q,r>}           {<*p,r>,<*q,s>,<*q,r>,<*q,t>}
     else
  S₃: q = &s;     {<*p,r>,<*q,s>}           {<*p,r>,<*q,s>,<*q,r>,<*q,t>}
  S₄:...          {<*p,r>,<*q,s>,<*q,r>}  {<*p,r>,<*q,s>,<*q,r>,<*q,t>}
  S₅:q = &t;      {<*p,r>,<*q,t>}           {<*p,r>,<*q,s>,<*q,r>,<*q,t>}
}
```

Fig. 1. Example Program Segment and Its Aliases

Data-flow analysis algorithms can be classified into two categories: *flow-sensitive* and *flow-insensitive* [4, 28]. Flow-sensitive algorithms consider intraprocedural control flow information during the analysis and, in general, are more precise than flow-insensitive algorithms. Flow-insensitive algorithms do not make use of intraprocedural control flow information during the analysis. As such, they can be more efficient than flow-sensitive algorithms and have been used primarily for the class of problems for which flow-sensitive algorithms do not provide increased precision. There exists, however, a range of trade-offs between efficiency and precision [9]. Flow-insensitive analysis can also be used to improve efficiency, at the potential cost of precision, for the class of problems for which flow-sensitive analysis can yield better precision. Pointer-induced aliasing is a problem in this class.

In this paper, we present a flow-insensitive interprocedural algorithm that computes may-aliases in the presence of general pointers for languages like C, C++, LISP, and Fortran 90, and that can provide information with comparable precision to flow-sensitive analyses. The algorithm, which has been implemented in a Fortran 90 research prototype, is based on the general framework for flow-insensitive analysis described in [9] without algorithmic elaborations. We also present a method for constructing the *program call graph* (*PCG*) in the presence of function pointers. The method accommodates function pointers precisely and efficiently in the framework of pointer-induced alias analysis. It is applicable to both flow-sensitive and flow-insensitive frameworks for computing pointer-induced aliases.

Consider the example in Figure 1, which illustrates the major difference between flow-sensitive and flow-insensitive analyses. Assume that no aliases hold before S_1 and that S_4 does not modify any pointer variables. Flow-sensitive analysis [9] will compute alias relations $< *p, r >$ and $< *q, t >$, but not $< *q, r >$ or $< *q, s >$, as holding immediately after S_5.[1] Since no intraprocedural control information is used in a flow-insensitive analysis, it does not distinguish the execution order among statements within a procedure. As shown in the third column, it will thus compute all four aliases as holding at each point in the procedure, except at the procedure entry. This example shows that for pointer-induced aliasing, flow-sensitive analysis can provide better precision than flow-insensitive analysis.

However, the difference in precision between the two analyses can be negligible for certain programs. Consider the effect of the if statement in Figure 1. If we exclude statement S_5, the same three alias relations are computed to hold immediately after S_4 in both a flow-sensitive and a flow-insensitive analysis. Branches and loops tend to diminish the difference in precision between the two analyses. Further, when a flow-sensitive analysis produces a large number of alias relations, our flow-insensitive analysis can provide a more efficient alternative.

Notice that in Figure 1 the assignment to q at S_5 *kills* any alias relations of $*q$ arriving at S_5. A flow-sensitive analysis makes use of this kill information in computing the alias relations holding after S_5. This is possible since it can determine what nodes follow S_5 using control flow information. In Section 3, we show how to improve the precision of our flow-insensitive analysis, without incurring the full overhead of flow-sensitive interprocedural analysis, by making use of certain types of kill information that can be computed efficiently.

For correctness and precision, interprocedural data-flow analyses make use of the *PCG*. Figure 2 illustrates the *PCG* for an example program segment, where nodes represent procedures and edges represent call sites. In the presence of function pointers and parameters, the *PCG* of a program is incomplete, resulting in either an incorrect or overly conservative analysis. Call site c3 illustrates how this can occur. Without precise knowledge of the aliases of *funcPtr(), a *PCG* edge must be inserted to each *PCG* node for correctness. Our method constructs the *PCG* of a program in the presence of function pointers precisely and efficiently in the framework of pointer-induced alias analysis. The precision of the method is the same as the precision of the underlying pointer-induced alias analysis method.

The rest of the paper is organized as follows. Section 2 defines terminology used in the paper and describes the background context. Section 3 describes the framework for our flow-insensitive interprocedural analysis of pointer-induced

---

[1] We do not include the alias relation $< *p, *r >$ holding at S_2, since it can be inferred by the alias relations $< *p, r >$ and $< *q, r >$ holding there (Section 2).

237

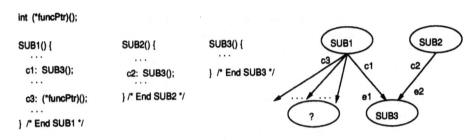

Fig. 2. Example Program Segment and Its *PCG*

aliasing. Section 4 gives further details concerning the intraprocedural component of our analysis. Using *deferred evaluation*, we show how to reduce the number of statements that are considered during the iteration step of the intraprocedural component. Section 5 describes how to accommodate function pointers in the framework of alias analysis. Section 6 compares our work with others, and Section 7 draws conclusions.

2 Background

We ignore the computation of *static* aliases that occur due to the C union construct and Fortran EQUIVALENCE statement. Static aliases do not change within a program and can be computed by the front-end of the compiler. In this paper, we focus on computing pointer-induced aliasing, while ignoring parameters (reference, call-by-value, or copy-in-copy-out). Complete discussions on the interactions between parameters and pointer-induced aliasing can be found in [23, 9].

Fig. 3. Example Alias Graph

Pointer-induced alias relations determine a directed graph, called an *alias graph*, as shown in Figure 3: $< *p, q >$ implies that there is a (de-referencing) edge from object p to object q. Likewise, $< **p, r >$ implies that there exists an object q such that there is an edge from p to q and one from q to r. Our method assumes that every memory location which is referenced or dereferenced has a unique name. Each named object that participates in a pointer-aliased relation is associated with a single node in the directed graph. Although we have proposed a method for naming dynamically allocated objects (malloc sites) in [9], any naming method may be employed.

The *exhaustive* list of aliases holding for the example is $\{< *p, q >, < *q, r >, < **p, r >, < **p, *q >\}$. Notice that $< **p, r >$ and $< **p, *q >$ can be inferred from $\{< *p, q >, < *q, r >\}$, which corresponds to the *transitive reduction* [1] of the directed graph. This *compact representation* [9], which we utilize in our pointer-induced alias analysis method, combines two techniques to reduce the size of the alias sets. It discards alias pairs that do not have at least one named object or that involve more than one level of dereferencing. This representation enables deferred evaluation to be used during the intraprocedural component of our flow-insensitive analysis. A discussion of this technique is provided in Section 4. Tradeoffs between this representation and a more exhaustive approach [23] are discussed in [27].

3 Flow-Insensitive Interprocedural Alias Analysis

To improve efficiency, a flow-insensitive analysis does not rely on intraprocedural control flow information. Instead, the effects of a procedure are captured in a summarized form and associated with either a node or edge of the *PCG*. In the computation of pointer-induced aliasing, the information directly generated at a node is dependent not only on the statements in the procedure, but also on the information that is propagated along the *PCG* edges to and from that node. Thus, we cannot determine the direct effects of a procedure without interprocedural information. Instead, the set of pointer-assignment statements in a procedure is associated with each node. Their effect on alias information will be computed during the analysis. The information describing how parameters are passed at a call site is once again associated with each edge.

With the above information as input, the flow-insensitive interprocedural alias analysis computes $PGen_p$, the set of alias relations *generated* by the invocation of procedure p, for each procedure in the program. This approach differs from previous approaches for flow-sensitive analysis, which summarize alias information of a procedure by capturing what *holds* on exit from the procedure [23, 9].

When the summarized procedure information for flow-insensitive analysis is the set of aliases that *hold* on exit of the procedure, alias information can be propagated along *unrealizable* control paths. The advantage of our approach for flow-insensitive analysis is that only the aliases that are generated in the procedure are propagated back to a call site which invokes the procedure.

For the example in Figure 2, aliases propagated from $Sub1$ to $Sub3$ along $e1$ can be propagated, if not killed in $Sub3$, not only to call site $c1$ in $Sub1$, but also to call site $c2$ in $Sub2$ via $e2$, yielding conservative information. Using our approach, only aliases that are generated in $Sub3$ are propagated back to $Sub2$. This does not entirely eliminate the unrealizable control path problem, since aliases generated by a procedure can depend on the aliases that hold in that procedure. (Section 3.3 provides further details.) Techniques that handle this problem can be incorporated into our algorithm to handle these indirect effects and further refine precision [9, 23].

In addition to $PGen_p$, we compute the following sets:

$Entry_p$: the set of alias relations that hold upon entry to procedure p,

$Holds_p$: the set of alias relations that are presumed to hold at each point in p, except at the entry of p,

$IGen_p$: the set of alias relations *generated* by the pointer-assignment statements[2] of procedure p,

$CSGen_p$: the set of alias relations *generated* by call sites in the procedure p.

In this section, we describe the relationship among these sets and provide a set of data-flow equations representing this relationship. We classify these five sets according to the manner in which information is propagated when computing them. Two categories of sets exist: *interprocedural* ($Entry_p$ and $CSGen_p$) and *intraprocedural* ($IGen_p$, $Holds_p$, and $PGen_p$).

$Entry_p$ represents the alias information that *holds* upon entry to p. It is captured by propagating the alias information that holds at a call site of p *forward* along the corresponding PCG edge. This information is unioned with the alias information propagated from other call sites which invoke p.

$CSGen_p$ represents the alias information *generated* at the call sites in p. This information is computed by propagating the $PGen$ of the procedures called in p *backward* along the corresponding PCG edges. Since information is propagated forward and backward along the PCG edges, pointer-induced aliasing over the PCG is a *bi-directional* problem.

In flow-sensitive analyses *kill* information is used to reduce the size of alias sets propagated forward and backward along the PCG edges as well as within each procedure [23, 9]. In Section 3.4, we describe how to improve the precision of the interprocedural sets by selectively utilizing kill information without incurring the full overhead of flow-sensitive interprocedural analysis.

3.1 Overview of the Algorithm

Figure 4 shows a high-level description of our algorithm for interprocedural alias analysis.[3] The major characteristic of the algorithm is the *interleaving* of the intraprocedural (Steps S_6 and S_7) and interprocedural phases (Steps S_8 and S_9). Each phase is followed by the other, which uses the results of the previous phase as its input. The intraprocedural phase can be flow-sensitive or flow-insensitive. The algorithm that we present here is flow-insensitive. This interleaving removes the requirement that the iterations alternate topological directions when solving the bi-directional problem. An interleaving paradigm similar to this is used in our previous work for flow-sensitive analysis of interprocedural aliasing [9].

During an intraprocedural phase, the following three *intraprocedural sets* are computed for each procedure p: $PGen_p$, $Holds_p$, and $IGen_p$. In computing these intraprocedural sets, the two interprocedural sets, ($Entry_p$ and $CSGen_p$) computed during the previous interprocedural phase, are used. Computing the interprocedural sets in turn uses the intraprocedural sets computed during the

---

[2] We regard storage allocation and deallocation statements for pointers, such as malloc and free in C, as pointer assignment statements.

[3] In the presence of PCG cycles, topological order is defined by the removal of *back edges* [20].

S_1: foreach procedure p in the PCG
S_2:   set $Entry_p = STATIC\_ALIASES$;
S_3:   set $CSGen_p = \{\}$;
S_4: build initial PCG;
S_5: repeat
S_6:   foreach procedure p in the PCG
S_7:   compute intraprocedural alias sets of p, using interprocedural alias sets;
S_8:   foreach procedure p in the PCG
S_9:   compute interprocedural alias sets of p, using intraprocedural alias sets;
S_{10}:until aliasing converges;

Fig. 4. Algorithm to Compute Interprocedural Aliasing

previous intraprocedural phase. The iterations over the PCG (Steps S_5 through S_{10}) handle this mutual dependence between the inter- and intraprocedural sets.

The basic algorithm presented in Figure 4 can be enhanced in a number of ways. The interprocedural computation, Steps S_8 and S_9, can be incorporated into the intraprocedural phase. This can be accomplished by performing the update of the interprocedural information of each procedure, Step S_9, as soon as the relevant intraprocedural information is computed at S_7. Using this enhancement, a topological traversal of the PCG is generally more efficient than visiting procedures in arbitrary order.[4] Finally, the iterative algorithm can be implemented with a worklist to improve efficiency.

In the following sections, we describe how to compute the interprocedural and intraprocedural sets. These descriptions would require no modifications to incorporate the enhancements described above.

3.2   Interprocedural Phase

With the intraprocedural sets computed, the interprocedural sets can be computed as follows:

$$Entry_p = \bigcup_c ForwardBind_c(HoldsBefore_c), \text{where call site } c \text{ calls } p \quad (1)$$

$$CSGen_p^c = BackwardBind_c(PGen_q), \text{where } p \text{ calls } q \text{ at call site } c \quad (2)$$

$$CSGen_p = \bigcup_{c \in p} CSGen_p^c \quad (3)$$

$Entry_p$ is computed by propagating information along all call sites to p. *Forward-Bind$_c$* maps the set of alias relations holding at call site c (referred to as

---

[4] Alternating iterations between topological and reverse-topological order may further improve efficiency.

HoldsBefore$_c$) into alias relations holding in the called routine, using the arguments of *c*. With flow-insensitive analysis, *HoldsBefore$_c$* for a call site *c* in *q* is the same as *Holds$_q$*. *BackwardBind$_c$*, which is similar to *ForwardBind$_c$*, maps alias relations holding at the called routine into alias relations holding immediately following the call site *c*, using the arguments of *c*. (Details of these mapping mechanisms are given in [9].)

3.3 Intraprocedural Phase

With the interprocedural sets computed, the intraprocedural sets can be computed by solving the following equations:

$$Holds_p = Entry_p \cup CSGen_p \cup IGen_p \tag{4}$$

$$IGen_p = \bigcup_s IGen_s(Holds_p), \text{where statement } s \text{ in } p \text{ is a ptr. assignment} \tag{5}$$

$$PGen_p = CSGen_p \cup IGen_p \tag{6}$$

The cyclic dependences between equations (4) and (5) require iteration over the set of pointer-assignment statements in *p*. Since our flow-insensitive analysis does not use control flow information, it must, for correctness, reflect all possible paths that can be constructed by the set of statements associated with *p*. Thus, we treat each procedure as a single (potentially large) loop consisting of all the pointer-assignment statements of the procedure in some arbitrary order. Figure 5 illustrates our technique. The control flow graph on the left (Figure 5-A) represents the original program. The graph in the middle (Figure 5-B) illustrates the manner in which we capture the effect of all possible paths. The order in which statements are chosen in this graph is arbitrary, and for this example is the worst possible order. A total of three iterations are required to construct the eight alias relations that result from this graph [7].

Figure 6 specifies our intraprocedural algorithm. Initially, we assume aliases that reach *p* interprocedurally via *Entry$_p$* and *CSGen$_p$* are in *Holds$_p$* (S_1). We also assume *IGen$_p$* is empty (S_2). The loop from S_4 to S_6 traverses each pointer assignment statement, adding alias relations generated by each statement to the *Holds$_p$* and *IGen$_p$* sets for the procedure of interest. Since the aliases generated depend on *Holds$_p$*, this traversal is repeated until no new aliases are generated. Note that computing *PGen$_p$* is not part of the iteration; *PGen$_p$* is computed upon convergence. Where kill information is not considered, this method is equivalent to considering all possible paths. Section 4 describes how to identify certain types of pointer-assignment statements that need not be considered during the iteration (Steps S_4 to S_6).

In [9], the effect of a pointer-assignment statement *s* on aliasing is described in terms of its alias *transfer function* (*TF$_s$*) as follows:

$$HoldsAfter_s = TF_s(HoldsBefore_s),$$

where *HoldsBefore$_s$* and *HoldsAfter$_s$* are the aliases holding immediately before and after *s*, respectively. *IGen$_s$* in Equation 5 can be derived from *TF$_s$*.

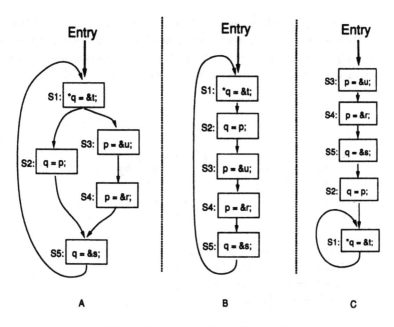

Fig. 5. Intraprocedural Example

S_1: $Holds_p = Entry_p \cup CSGen_p$
S_2: $IGen_p = \{\}$
S_3: repeat
S_4:   foreach pointer assignment statement, s, in p
S_5:   compute the set, $A = IGen_s(Holds_p)$
S_6:   add A to $Holds_p$ and $IGen_p$
S_7: until aliasing converges;
S_8: $PGen_p = CSGen_p \cup IGen_p$

Fig. 6. Intraprocedural Algorithm

With flow-insensitive analysis, $Holds_p$ is the alias information assumed to hold at each point in p, including immediately before and after s. Thus, when a fixed point is reached, the following equation is satisfied by $Holds_p$:

$$Holds_p = TF_s(Holds_p), \text{for all } s \text{ in } p.$$

3.4 Using Kill Information

In this section, we describe how to improve the interprocedural precision by utilizing precomputed kill information. Consider Figure 7, where procedure r

calls procedure p at S_2, and the assumed values for $Entry_r$ and $CSGen_p^{S_2}$ are provided in the figure. By Equation 1, the alias relations that are propagated to $Entry_p$ from S_2 are those that hold at S_2. From our discussion above, this is $Holds_r$, which is: $\{<*x, a_1>, \ldots, <*x, a_n>, <*x, y>, <*x, z>\}$.

```
r() {                        p() {
   S1:   x = &y;                S1:   x = &y;
   S2:   p();                   S2:   q();
   S3:   x = &z;                S3:   x = &z;
}                            }
```

$Entry_r = \{<*x, a_1>, \ldots, <*x, a_n>\}$
$IGen_r = \{<*x, y>, <*x, z>\}$
$IGen_p = \{<*x, y>, <*x, z>\}$
$CSGen_p^{S_2} = \{<*x, b_1>, \ldots, <*x, b_n>\}$

Fig. 7. *ForwardKill* and *BackwardKill* Example

Although this is correct, one can improve the precision of this solution by selectively using kill information to limit the alias relations that are propagated interprocedurally [9]. We adopt this approach by defining for each call site c, contained in procedure r, $ForwardKill_c$, which represents alias relations that are killed along all paths from the entry point of r to c. We use $ForwardKill_c$ to remove alias relations from $Entry_r$ and then factor in any aliases that are generated by r ($IGen_r \cup CSGen_r$), for correctness, in computing the aliases to be propagated at c. In the example of Figure 7, $\{<*x, y>, <*x, z>\}$ is propagated to p, but not $\{<*x, a_1>, \ldots, <*x, a_n>\}$.

Below we give the updated equation for $Entry_p$ (Equation 1 of Section 3.2). Along with the addition of kill information, $HoldsBefore_c$ has been expanded.

$$Entry_p = \bigcup_c ForwardBind_c(Entry_r - ForwardKill_c \cup IGen_r \cup CSGen_r),$$

where call site c, located in r, calls p

The computation of $ForwardKill_c$ can be performed before the interprocedural propagation (S_6 of Figure 4), and used when needed. This allows the interprocedural algorithm to remain flow-insensitive, as no control flow information is required during the propagation. A pointer variable is killed when it appears without any indirection operations on the left side of an assignment statement or in a malloc or free function call.[5] Killing a pointer variable via indirection, i.e. $*x = \ldots$ requires must alias information for $*x$. Thus, for kill information to be used for this kind of statement, must-alias information is required.

In an analogous manner this technique can be used to improve the precision of information during the backward PCG propagation. Information is interprocedurally propagated from a called routine to a calling routine p at call site c via $CSGen_p^c$. To improve the precision of this set, we define the *BackwardKill* set for a call site c in p, $(BackwardKill_c)$ to represent alias relations that are killed along all paths from c to the *exit* node of p. We use this set when constructing $PGen_p$, by removing all alias relations from $CSGen_p^c$ that are killed after the call. If any of these aliases are generated elsewhere in p, they are included in $PGen_p$ for correctness.

Below we give the updated equation for $PGen_p$ (Equation 6 of Section 3.3). We divide $CSGen_p$ into its call site components to allow the addition of kill information.

$$PGen_p = \bigcup_{c \in p}(CSGen_p^c - BackwardKill_c) \cup IGen_p$$

Figure 7 also gives an example where using the *BackwardKill* information improves the precision of $PGen_p$. Without kill information we have,

$$PGen_p = CSGen_p \cup IGen_p = \{<*x, b_1>, \ldots, <*x, b_n>, <*x, y>, <*x, z>\}.$$

By using the new equation for $PGen_p$, we get

$$PGen_p = \{<*x, y>, <*x, z>\}.$$

Like $ForwardKill_c$, $BackwardKill_c$ can be computed as a preprocessing step before the flow-insensitive iteration over the PCG has begun. A spectrum of killing criteria, based on the amount of control flow information required, can be employed when computing these sets. The computation of kill using only dominator trees is described in [9].

4 Deferred Evaluation

Section 3.3 describes how to capture the effect of all possible intraprocedural paths by treating a procedure as a single loop consisting of the pointer-assignment statements of the procedure in some arbitrary order. In this section we improve the efficiency of the intraprocedural phase by identifying certain types of pointer assignments that need not be considered during the intraprocedural iteration. For example, consider statements S_3, S_4, and S_5 of Figure 5. Since the alias relations generated by these statements can be computed independently of the alias relations that hold before executing them, these statements need not be

---

[5] It is possible to broaden this definition, and improve precision, by allowing user function calls to kill pointer variables [7].

included in the iteration.[6] These statements have a constant *IGen* set; they only contribute to the procedure *IGen* set and do not depend on what aliases hold. Statements with a constant *IGen* set can be treated like *ForwardKill* and *BackwardKill* information, in that the alias relations they generate can be precomputed prior to the interprocedural propagation (S_5 of Figure 4). This enhancement reduces the number of intraprocedural iterations required for convergence from three to two.

Determining the alias relations generated by statements S_1 and S_2 requires information about the alias relations holding at these statements. In statement S_1 the aliases of $*q$ are required. In particular, for every x such that $< *q, x >$ holds, we will create an alias relation $< *x, t >$. Statement S_2 requires the aliases of $*p$. It will create alias relations $< *q, y >$ for all y where $< *p, y >$ holds. Thus, it appears that both types of statements must be included in our intraprocedural iteration.

However, for the aliases generated by statement S_2, the dereference component is known: i.e., $*q$. Furthermore, q is the *source* node of the edges that represent these aliases in the alias graph. Therefore, our algorithm is able to defer the evaluation of statement S_2 until after the intraprocedural iteration has completed, when the aliases of $*p$ are known. This is accomplished by creating a *deferred alias relation* from q to p, with a *deferred value* of 0. This signifies that $*q$ will be aliased to all objects that p can reach via a path of length 1 over the alias graph. If aliases of $*q$ are required during the iteration, we infer the alias relations the deferred alias relation represents. In this example, it represents edges from q to whatever p points to, i.e. $\{< *q, y > \mid$ for all y such that $< *p, y >\}$.

Thus, only statement S_1 remains in the intraprocedural iteration. If the procedure does not contain any statements of this type, no intraprocedural iteration is required. After the intraprocedural iteration has completed, deferred alias relations are expanded into full alias relations without a loss of precision. We refer to this approach as *deferred evaluation*.

Figure 5-C shows how the example program would be processed using deferred evaluation. Notice that only one statement is contained in the loop and thus, only one iteration would be required for aliasing to converge. This compares favorably to the original analysis, where three iterations are required before convergence. (See [7] for more details.)

We generalize the previous example by classifying pointer-assignment statements into three categories listed below. Type 1 statements have a constant *IGen* function and are processed first. For Type 2 statements we create deferred alias relations with a *deferred value* of r. This is performed before the iteration and then expanded after the iteration converges. We iterate over Type 3 statements.

Type 1: $p = \&q$;
Type 2: $p = \underbrace{*\ldots*}_{r} q; r \geq 0$

---

[6] This is not the case with *exhaustive representations* [23], which, assuming $< *s, p >$ holds, would include $< ** s, u >$ as holding after considering S_3.

Type 3: $\underbrace{*\ldots*}_{l}p = \underbrace{*\ldots*}_{r}q; l \geq 1, r \geq -1$, "$r = -1$" is equivalent to $\&q$.

Below we summarize the enhanced intraprocedural algorithm using deferred evaluation. This algorithm decreases the number of pointer assignment statements considered in S_4 of Figure 6, by considering some statements at S_2 and expanding deferred alias relations after S_8. This reduces the number of statements considered during the intraprocedural iteration, which can also reduce the number of iterations required for convergence of this phase. No precision is lost using this technique.

1. Add alias relations from Type 1 statements to $IGen_p$ (S_2)
2. Create deferred alias relations for Type 2 statements (S_2)
3. Iterate over Type 3 statements only (S_4)
4. Expand deferred alias relations (after S_9)

5 Incremental Analysis for Function Pointers

In this section, we describe a method for constructing the PCG in the presence of function parameters, variables, and pointers. Our method accommodates function parameters and arbitrary levels of function pointers by using the framework of pointer-induced aliasing. When embedded in the alias analysis, which generally occurs before any other phases that need the PCG, the method incurs minimal overhead. Although we focus on flow-insensitive analysis in this paper, the techniques described in this section to accommodate function pointers can also be applied to flow-sensitive analysis. We will use the term "function pointers" to refer to function parameters, function variables, and function pointers. Likewise, we will use "regular pointers" to refer to pointers that are not function pointers.

Recall from Figure 4 the *interleaving* of the intraprocedural (Steps S_6 and S_7) and interprocedural phases (Steps S_8 and S_9). Interleaving these two phases makes our algorithm particularly well suited for accommodating function pointers via *incremental* interprocedural data-flow analysis. Incremental data-flow analysis addresses the issue of updating data-flow information, without a full recomputation, when part of the program is changed [26, 6]. In our case, the program itself does not change, but its graphical representation, the PCG, changes as the analysis proceeds. Such changes in the representation of the program warrant the use of incremental analysis for efficiency.

Incremental alias analysis in the presence of function pointers is achieved by first handling function pointers the same way as regular pointers during the intraprocedural phase of the analysis (Steps S_6 and S_7), and then identifying new PCG edges from the alias information as the computation proceeds. This way, our method *does not* compute aliasing from scratch as new PCG edges are found. Instead, it adds these new edges to construct the new PCG and incrementally continues the alias computation, using the alias information computed with the previous PCG as the initial condition.

Formally, this amounts to computing an additional *interprocedural* set of procedures, which is the set of aliases of a function pointer, fp, invoked at call site, c, as follows:[7]

$$FuncAlias_c = \{\, proc \mid < *fp, proc > \in HoldsBefore_c,\ *fp \text{ is invoked at } c \}.$$

The algorithm then incrementally updates the PCG with the newly added edges identified from $FuncAlias_c$. These two steps are performed as the first step of an interprocedural phase.

Alias analysis generally occurs before any other phases that need the PCG, and the embedded PCG construction will incur minimal overhead. When applied only to function pointers, our algorithm still constructs the same PCG without incurring the overhead of full alias analysis. This way, it can be used as a general method to construct the PCG, independently of any other data-flow analysis such as the alias analysis of regular pointers described in this paper. More details are provided in [7].

6 Related Work

Larus [25] gives a flow-insensitive intraprocedural algorithm to compute aliases in LISP programs. This algorithm uses alias graphs, which are similar to ours, but serve both as values propagated to solve data-flow equations and as representations of statements' effects on propagated values [25]. He uses the fastness closure technique of Graham and Wegman [15] to correctly process the alias graphs.

Flow-sensitive interprocedural algorithms for pointer-induced aliases are given in [23, 9, 12, 13]. They utilize kill information and can provide improved precision over a flow-insensitive analysis that does not utilize kill information during the analysis. Our flow-insensitive algorithm utilizes precomputed kill information to improve interprocedural precision. Complete discussions on the interactions between reference parameters and pointer-induced aliasing are also given in [9].

A framework for flow-insensitive interprocedural analysis of pointer-induced aliasing is described in [9] without algorithmic elaborations. The algorithm described in this paper is based on that framework.

Methods for constructing the PCG in the presence of function parameters and function variables are given in [34, 5, 8, 16, 22]. Our method accommodates function parameters and arbitrary levels of function pointers. As such, it is more general than methods for constructing the PCG in the presence of function parameters [5, 31, 8] or function variables [16, 22]. By using the framework of pointer-induced aliasing, it is also more precise than Weihl's method, which performs transitive closure of the alias relations [34].

Emami, Ghiya, and Hendren [13] independently proposed an algorithm similar to ours for constructing the PCG for the same programming model we consider. Also, a similar problem to constructing the PCG is performing control

---

[7] If fp is a function parameter or variable, the '*' is not required.

248

flow analysis in functional languages, where functions are first class objects [33]. Solutions to this problem are given in [33, 32, 19, 29, 11, 30]

Hall and Kennedy [16] suggested a method, similar to Lakhotia's method [22], to improve Weihl's approach. Lakhotia performs interprocedural constant propagation analysis over the *system dependence graph* [18]. We believe his method for handling *label variables* can be easily incorporated into our algorithm. Our algorithm can be easily extended to use a work list, as done in [23, 16]. It can also be extended to build the *Interprocedural Control Flow Graph* (ICFG) [8, 17, 23], instead of the *PCG*.

7 Conclusions

In this paper, we have presented a flow-insensitive algorithm that computes interprocedural pointer-induced aliases. We enhance the precision of the interprocedural phase of our algorithm by (1) utilizing precomputed kill information, and (2) computing aliases generated in each procedure rather than aliases holding at the exit of each procedure. We preserve correctness during the intraprocedural phase of the algorithm by iterating over those statements that are dependent on the current alias relations. A technique called deferred evaluation is introduced to improve the efficiency of the intraprocedural phase by identifying a class of pointer-assignment statements that can be excluded from the intraprocedural iteration.

We have also presented a method for constructing the *PCG* in the presence of function pointers. This method can be applied to either a flow-sensitive or flow-insensitive analysis. It uses incremental analysis and is based on our alias analysis framework.

Our flow-insensitive alias analysis algorithm has been implemented in a Fortran 90 research prototype. We plan to measure the efficiency and precision of our algorithms on Fortran 90, C, and C++ programs.

Acknowledgements

We thank the referees for their helpful comments and Laureen Treacy for her careful proofreading.

References

1. A. V. Aho, M. R. Garey, and J. D. Ullman. The transitive reduction of a directed graph. *SIAM Journal on Computing*, 1(2):131–137, 1972.
2. Frances Allen, Michael Burke, Philippe Charles, Ron Cytron, and Jeanne Ferrante. An overview of the ptran analysis system for multiprocessing. *Proceedings of the ACM 1987 International Conference on Supercomputing*, 1987. Also published in The Journal of Parallel and Distributed Computing, Oct., 1988, 5(5) pages 617-640.

3. Randy Allen, David Callahan, and Ken Kennedy. Automatic decomposition of scientific programs for parallel execution. *Conference Record of the Fourteenth Annual ACM Symposium on Principles of Programming Languages*, pages 63–76, January 1987.

4. John Banning. An efficient way to find the side effects of procedure calls and the aliases of variables. *6th Annual ACM Symposium on the Principles of Programming Languages*, pages 29–41, January 1979.

5. Michael Burke. An interval-based approach to exhaustive and incremental interprocedural data flow analysis. Technical report, IBM Research, August 1987. Report RC12702.

6. Michael Burke. An interval-based approach to exhaustive and incremental interprocedural data-flow analysis. *ACM Transactions on Programming Languages and Systems*, 12(3):341–395, July 1990.

7. Michael Burke, Paul Carini, Jong-Deok Choi, and Michael Hind. Efficient flow-insensitive alias analysis in the presence of pointers. Technical report RC 19546, IBM T. J. Watson Research Center, September 1994.

8. D. Callahan, A. Carle, M. W. Hall, and K.Kennedy. Constructing the procedure call multigraph. *IEEE Transactions on Software Engineering*, 16(4):483–487, April 1990.

9. Jong-Deok Choi, Michael Burke, and Paul Carini. Efficient flow-sensitive interprocedural computation of pointer-induced aliases and side effects. *Conference Record of the Twentieth Annual ACM Symposium on Principles of Programming Languages*, January 1993.

10. Jong-Deok Choi and Jeanne Ferrante. Static slicing in the presence of GOTO statements. *ACM Transactions on Programming Languages and Systems*, 1994. To appear.

11. Alain Deutsch. On determining lifetime and aliasing of dynamically allocated data in higher-order functional specifications. In *17th Annual ACM Symposium on the Principles of Programming Languages*, pages 157–168, San Francisco, January 1990. ACM Press.

12. Alain Deutsch. Interprocedural may-alias analysis for pointers: Beyond k-limiting. In *SIGPLAN '94 Conference on Programming Language Design and Implementation*, 1994.

13. Maryam Emami, Rakesh Ghiya, and Laurie J. Hendren. Context-sensitive interprocedural points-to analysis in the presence of function pointers. In *SIGPLAN '94 Conference on Programming Language Design and Implementation*, 1994.

14. Dennis Gannon, Vincent A. Guarna, Jr., and Jenq Kuen Lee. Static analysis and runtime support for parallel execution of C. *Proceedings of the Second Workshop on Languages and Compilers for Parallel Computing*, August 1989.

15. Susan L. Graham and Mark Wegman. A fast and usually linear algorithm for global flow analysis. *Journal of the Association for Computing Machinery*, 23(1):172–202, January 1976.

16. Mary W. Hall and Ken Kennedy. Efficient call graph analysis. *ACM Letters on Programming Languages and Systems*, 1(3):227–242, September 1992.

17. Mary Hean Harrold and Mary Lou Soffa. Efficient computation of interprocedural definition – use chains. *ACM Transactions on Programming Languages and Systems*, 16(2):175–204, March 1994.

18. Susan Horwitz, Thomas Reps, and David Binkley. Interprocedural slicing using dependence graphs. *ACM Transactions on Programming Languages and Systems*, 12(1):26–60, January 1990.

19. W. L. Harrison III. The interprocedural analysis and automatic parallelisation of Scheme programs. *Lisp and Symbolic Computation*, 2(3):176–396, October 1989.
20. John B. Kam and Jeffrey D. Ullman. Global data flow analysis and iterative algorithms. *JACM*, 23,1:158–171, January 1976.
21. K. Kennedy, K. S. McKinley, and C. Tseng. Interactive parallel programming using the parascope editor. *IEEE Transactions on Parallel and Distributed Systems*, 2(3):329–341, July 1991.
22. Arun Lakhotia. Constructing call multigraphs using dependence graphs. In *20th Annual ACM SIGACT-SIGPLAN Symposium on the Principles of Programming Languages*, pages 273–284. ACM, January 1993.
23. William Landi and Barbara G. Ryder. A safe approximate algorithm for interprocedural pointer aliasing. *Proceedings of the ACM SIGPLAN '92 Conference on Programming Language Design and Implementation*, pages 235–248, June 1992.
24. J. R. Larus and P. N. Hilfinger. Detecting conflicts between structure accesses. *Proceedings of the ACM SIGPLAN '88 Conference on Programming Language Design and Implementation*, 23(7):21–34, July 1988.
25. James Richard Larus. *Restructuring Symbolic Programs for Concurrent Execution on Multiprocessors*. PhD thesis, University of California, 1989. Technical Report No. UCB/CSD 89/502.
26. T. J. Marlowe and B. Ryder. An efficient hybrid algorithm for incremental data flow analysis. *17th Annual ACM Symposium on the Principles of Programming Languages*, pages 184–196, January 1990.
27. Thomas Marlowe, William Landi, Barbara Ryder, Jong-Deok Choi, Michael Burke, and Paul Carini. Pointer-induced aliasing: A clarification. *SIGPLAN Notices*, 28(9):67–70, September 1993.
28. T.J. Marlowe, B.G. Ryder, and M.G. Burke. Defining flow-sensitivity in data flow problems. *In Preparation*, 1994.
29. Torben Æ Mogensen. Binding time analysis for polymorphically typed higher-order languages. In *Proceedings TAPSOFT*, volume 352 of *Lecture Notes in Computer Science*, pages 298–312. Springer Verlag, 1989.
30. A. Neirynck, P. Panangaden, and A. J. Demers. Effect analysis in higher-order languages. *International Journal of Parallel Programming*, 18(1):1–17, 1989.
31. Barbara Ryder. Constructing the call graph of a program. *IEEE Software Engineering*, May 1979.
32. Peter Sestoft. Replacing function parameters by global variables. In *Conference on Functional Programming Languages and Computer Architecture*, pages 39–53, London, September 1989. ACM Press.
33. Olin Shivers. Control flow analysis in Scheme. In *SIGPLAN '88 Conference on Programming Language Design and Implementation*, pages 164–174, June 1988.
34. William Weihl. Interprocedural data flow analysis in the presence of pointer, procedure variables and label variables. *Conf. Rec. Seventh ACM Symposium on Principles of Programming Languages*, 1980.

Incremental Generation of Index Sets for Array Statement Execution on Distributed-Memory Machines

S. D. Kaushik, C.-H. Huang, and P. Sadayappan

Department of Computer and Information Science

The Ohio State University

Columbus, OH 43210

Abstract. In compiling array statements for distributed-memory machines, efficient generation of local index sets and communication sets is important. Several techniques for enumerating these sets for block-cyclically distributed arrays have been presented in the literature. When sufficient compile-time information is not available, generation of the structures which facilitate efficient enumeration of these sets, is performed at run-time. In this paper, we address the incremental generation of local index sets and communication sets to reduce the runtime cost of array statement execution. We develop techniques for performing the incremental generation using the virtual processor approach for execution of array statements involving block-cyclically distributed arrays.

Keywords: Array statements, Distributed-memory machine, High Performance Fortran, Data distribution, Data communication.

1 Introduction

Languages such as High Performance Fortran (HPF) [5], Fortran-D [6], Vienna Fortran [3], and pC++ [1] provide a programming environment which allows annotation of single address space programs with distribution directives specifying the mapping of arrays to processors on a distributed-memory machine. The compiler is responsible for partitioning the arrays and generating node code for the annotated program. Array statements are used to express data parallelism in these languages. Consider the array statement:

$$B(l_2 : u_2 : s_2) = \mathcal{F}(A(l_1 : u_1 : s_1)) \tag{1}$$

The array section $A(l_1 : u_1 : s_1)$ consists of elements of A with indices $\{l_1 + i * s_1 \mid 0 \leq i \leq \lfloor (u_1 - l_1)/s_1 \rfloor\}$. In the array statement, the result of $\mathcal{F}(A(l_1 + i * s_1))$ is assigned to $B(l_2 + i * s_2)$. Under the *owner-computes* rule, the processor on which $B(l_2 + i * s_2)$ is allocated performs the computation and the assignment $B(l_2 + i * s_2) = \mathcal{F}(A(l_1 + i * s_1))$. Since the computation performed on a processor may involve array elements resident on other processors, all non-local data is fetched into temporary arrays in a processor's local memory using interprocessor communication. Thus the processor must determine which elements of $B(l_2 : u_s : s_2)$ are allocated to it, the order in which these elements are located in its local memory, the processors from which it must receive non-local data and

252

```
for k = 1, time
    /* Compute red points */
    S1: a(1 : n − 1 : 2, 1 : n − 1 : 2) = F(a(1 : n − 1 : 2, 0 : n − 2 : 2),
        a(0 : n − 2 : 2, 1 : n − 1 : 2), a(1 : n − 1 : 2, 0 : n − 2 : 2),
        a(2 : n : 2, 1 : n − 1 : 2), a(1 : n − 1 : 2, 1 : n − 1 : 2))
    S2: a(2 : n − 1 : 2, 2 : n − 1 : 2) = · · ·
    . . .
```

Fig. 1. Red-Block Successive Over Relaxation.

---

the location of the non-local data in local memory. The determination of the following sets for each processor p reduces the indexing and communication overhead.

- Local index set of p: set of local memory indices on p whose value will be evaluated by the array statement.
- Send processor set of p: set of processors to which p has to send data.
- Send data index set of p to processor q: local indices of the array elements resident on p but needed by processor q.
- Receive processor set of p: set of processors from which p has to receive data.
- Receive data index set of p from processor q: local indices of the array elements needed by p but resident on q.

If the arrays have only block or cyclic distributions, then the data index sets and the processor sets can be characterized using regular sections for closed forms [8, 10]. However, for the general block-cyclic distribution, closed form characterization of these sets using simple regular sections is not possible.

Several approaches have addressed the efficient execution of array statements involving block-cyclically distributed arrays. A *virtual processor approach* to efficiently enumerate the data index sets and processor sets is presented in [7, 8]. The approach is based on viewing a block-cyclic distribution as a block (or cyclic) distribution on a set of virtual processors, which are cyclically (or block-wise) mapped to physical processors. Closed forms developed for block and cyclically distributed arrays are used in the virtual processor domain. The problem of local index set identification was addressed by Chatterjee et al. [4] using a *finite-state machine* (FSM) to traverse the local index space. Stichnoth et al. [11] address the problem of index set and processor set identification. The formulation proposed has similarities to an instance of the virtual processor approach. The implementation of the Fortran-D compiler at Rice University is being extended to handle arrays with block-cyclic distributions [9]. An approach similar to the FSM approach [4] for determining the local memory access sequence is used and efficient algorithms for computing the FSM for frequently occuring cases are presented.

In general, all the schemes proposed in the literature require computation of additional information at runtime for the efficient execution of the array statements. In this paper, we present methods for reusing previously calculated index and communication sets to reduce the runtime cost of calculating additional index and communication sets. The methods are developed in the context of the virtual processor approach [7, 8]. For example, consider a portion of the code segment for red-black SOR in Fig. 1. Statement $S1$, can be expressed in terms of four simple array statements $S1_1$, $S1_2$, $S1_3$, and $S1_4$ of the form shown in Eq. 1. Once the communication sets for $S1_1$ have been evaluated, the communication sets for $S1_2$, $S1_3$, and $S1_4$ can be incrementally evaluated. The local index set for section $a(2 : n - 1 : 2, 2 : n - 1 : 2)$ in $S2$ can be incrementally evaluated from the local index set for $a(1 : n - 1 : 2, 1 : n - 1 : 2)$ in $S1$. Thus techniques for incremental evaluation of index and communication sets are of significant importance.

The paper is organized as follows. Section 2 briefly describes the communication sets and the local index sets for the array statement. In Section 3, the virtual processor approach for handling block-cyclic distributions is described. Techniques for incrementally generating local index sets for the virtual processor approach are presented in Section 4. The incremental generation of communication sets is addressed in Section 5. Conclusions and directions for future work are presented in Section 6.

2 Data Distributions and Array Statements

In this section, we describe the compilation of array statements involving regularly distributed arrays. Consider an array $A(0 : n - 1)$ distributed onto P processors. In a *block-cyclic* distribution, specified as *cyclic(b)*, blocks of size b are allocated to the processors in a cyclic fashion. The array A is split into P local arrays residing in the local memories of the processors. The local array segment is referred to as A_loc in the node program. An element $A(i)$ of the array A has a *global* and a *local* index. The global index i is the index in array A, as referenced in a HPF program. The index of element $A(i)$ in A_loc is its local index. The relations between the global index i, local index l, and processor index p for the block-cyclic distribution are

$$i = (l \ div \ b)bP + bp + l \ mod \ b, \quad l = (i \ div \ Pb)b + i \ mod \ b, \quad p = (i \ div \ b) \ mod \ P$$

Let arrays $A(0 : n_1 - 1)$ and $B(0 : n_2 - 1)$ be distributed on P_1 and P_2 processors using a *cyclic(b_1)* and *cyclic(b_2)* distribution, respectively. Consider the array assignment statement in Eq. 1. The semantics of the array assignment require that the entire section $A(l_1 : u_1 : s_1)$ is read, the result of $\mathcal{F}$ on each element of the section evaluated and written to the corresponding element of $B(l_2 : u_2 : s_2)$. This corresponds to copying $A(l_1 : u_1 : s_1)$ to a temporary array section Tmp, computing the function $\mathcal{F}$ on the elements of Tmp and assigning the resulting values to $B(l_2 : u_2 : s_2)$. The node code for a processor consists of the following three segments: send out all the data required by other processors, receive data from other processors required for local computation, and perform local computation. Hence, for the array section $A(l_1 : u_1 : s_1)$, each processor

```
/* Sending phase */
for q ∈ PSend(p)
    pack A_loc(DSend(p, q)); send to q;

/* Receiving phase */
for q ∈ PRecv(p)
    recv Buf from q; Tmp(DRecv(p, q)) = Buf(0 : |DRecv(p, q)| − 1)

/* Execution phase */
for i ∈ LIndex(p)
    B_loc(i) = F(Tmp(i))
```

Fig. 2. Node program on processor p, for $B(l_2 : u_2 : s_2) = \mathcal{F}(A(l_1 : u_1 : s_1))$.

---

p, $0 \leq p < P_1$ has to evaluate the following information for every other processor q, $0 \leq q < P_2$.

- Local indices of the data elements that p owns and are required by q. Processor p has to send this set of elements to processor q. The set is referred to as $DSend(p, q)$.

Similarly, for the array section $B(l_2 : u_2 : s_2)$, each processor p, $0 \leq p < P_2$ has to evaluate the following information for every other processor q, $0 \leq q < P_1$.

- Local indices of the data elements that p needs and are located on q. Processor p will receive this set of data elements from q. The set is referred to as $DRecv(p, q)$.

For the array section $B(l_2 : u_2 : s_2)$, each processor p, $0 \leq p < P_2$ has to evaluate the following information.

- Local indices of the elements of $B(l_2 : u_2 : s_2)$ that p owns. Processor p has to compute new values for this set of elements. This local index set is referred to as $LIndex(p)$.

Note that $DSend$ and $DRecv$ are expressed in terms of the local indices on the corresponding processors. Two additional sets of processor indices are defined as follows

- $PSend(p) = \{q \mid DSend(p, q) \neq \phi, 0 \leq q < P_2\}, 0 \leq p < P_1$,
- $PRecv(p) = \{q \mid DRecv(p, q) \neq \phi, 0 \leq q < P_1\}, 0 \leq p < P_2$.

Using these sets, the node program pseudo-code for the execution of the array statement is as shown in Fig. 2. Since the send and receive data and processor sets are integral to the execution of array assignments, efficient schemes for enumerating these sets are important. For block and cyclic distributions, the send and receive data index and processor sets can be expressed as simple regular sections [7]. However, for block-cyclic distributions, these sets cannot be expressed as simple regular sections. In [7], a virtual processor approach is used to combine these forms for block-cyclic distributions.

The code for statements involving multiple right hand side array sections is generated by repeating the simple array assignment. Let T_1 and T_2 be temporary arrays with identical distribution as A. The evaluation of $A(l_1 : u_1 : s_1) = B(l_2 : u_2 : s_2) + C(l_3 : u_3 : s_3)$ is performed as:

$$
\begin{aligned}
S_1 : \quad & T_1(l_1 : u_1 : s_1) = B(l_2 : u_2 : s_2) \\
S_2 : \quad & T_2(l_1 : u_1 : s_1) = C(l_3 : u_3 : s_3) \\
S_3 : \quad & A(l_1 : u_1 : s_1) = T_1(l_1 : u_1 : s_1) + T_2(l_1 : u_1 : s_1).
\end{aligned}
$$

The code for S_1 and S_2 can be generated as shown in Fig. 2. Since T_1 and T_2 are identically distributed and aligned as A, statement S_3 requires only the execution phase. We now describe the virtual processor approach for handling block-cyclic distributions.

3 Virtual Processor Approach

In this section, we briefly describe the *virtual processor approach* for efficient execution of array statements involving block-cyclically distributed arrays. For details the reader is referred to [8, 7]. For an array statement of the form $B(l_2 : u_2 : s_2) = \mathcal{F}(A(l_1 : u_1 : s_1))$, the virtual processor approach involves:

1. Viewing a $cyclic(b_1)$ distribution of A as a block (or cyclic) distribution on VP_1 virtual processors which are cyclically (or block-wise) mapped to P processors. These views are referred to as *virtual-block* or *virtual-cyclic* views depending on whether a block or cyclic distribution is used in the virtual processor domain. The $cyclic(b_2)$ distribution of B is also viewed as a block or cyclic distribution on VP_2 virtual processors.

2. The communication and computation required to perform the array statement is determined by using the closed forms for block and cyclic distributions in the virtual processor domain. Each physical processor is responsible for performing the computation and communication for the virtual processors mapped to it.

We now describe the two virtualization views - the virtual block view and the virtual cyclic view.

3.1 Virtual-Block View

Let array $A(0 : n - 1)$ be distributed using a $cyclic(b)$ distribution on P processors. In the *virtual-block view*, A is assumed to be block distributed on $VP = \lceil n/b \rceil$ virtual processors. These virtual processors are assigned to P processors in a cyclic fashion. The set of virtual processors on processor p is $(p : VP : P)$. Fig. 3(a) illustrates the virtual-block view of a $cyclic(4)$ distribution of $A(0 : 15)$ on two processors. The array has a block distribution on four virtual processors

v_0 to v_3, which are cyclically allocated to the two processors p_0 and p_1, i.e., v_0 and v_2 are mapped to p_0, while v_1 and v_3 are mapped to p_1. The index l denotes the local index of the array element on the virtual processor.

Using closed form expressions developed for the block and cyclic distributions data index sets are evaluated in terms of the local indices of the array elements on the virtual processors. These local indices are not the same as the local index on the processor to which they are mapped. For instance, in Fig. 3(a), element $A(8)$ has a local index of 4 in A_loc on processor p_0, but a local index of 0 on virtual processor v_2. Since the physical processor p performs the computation and communication for the virtual processor v mapped to it, it is necessary to determine the translation from the virtual processor's local index space to the physical processor's local index space. If the virtual processor v is mapped to processor p, then the array element with local index j on v has a local index $(v \ div \ P) * b + j$ on processor p. Under the virtual-block view, a stride of s in the local index space of a virtual processor on processor p remains unchanged in the local index space of p.

Proc. 0					Proc. 1				
l	0	1	2	3	l	0	1	2	3
$v0$	0	1	2	3	$v1$	4	5	6	7
$v2$	8	9	10	11	$v3$	12	13	14	15

Proc. 0					Proc. 1				
l	$v0$	$v1$	$v2$	$v3$	l	$v4$	$v5$	$v6$	$v7$
0	0	1	2	3	0	4	5	6	7
1	8	9	10	11	1	12	13	14	15

(a) (b)

Fig. 3. Array $A(0 : 15)$ with *cyclic*(4) distribution on two processors. (a) Virtual-block view, (b) Virtual cyclic view.

Consider the array section $A(l : u : s)$. Under the virtual-block view not all virtual processors necessarily own elements of the array section. We refer to virtual processors that own array section elements as being *active*. A closed form characterization of the active virtual processors on a physical processor will reduce the indexing overhead on the physical processor. If $s \leq b$, then each virtual processor $v \in (l \ div \ b : u \ div \ b)$ has at least one element of the array section. Let $v_l = l \ div \ b$ and $v_u = u \ div \ b$. Since the set of virtual processors on processor p is $(p : VP : P)$, the active virtual processors on p for array A, denoted by $VAct(p)$, are given by

$$VAct(p) = (v_l : v_u) \cap (p : VP : P) = (v_f : min(v_u, VP) : P),$$

where $v_f = max(v_l + (p - v_l) \ mod \ P, p)$. If $s > b$ then each active virtual processor has exactly one element of the array section. The active virtual processors are given by $((l : u : s) \ div \ b) \cap (p : VP : P)$. Each active virtual processor in $(l : u : s) \ div \ b$ is scanned and a check performed to determine if it is located on processor p.

3.2 Virtual-Cyclic View

Under the *virtual-cyclic* view, array $A(0 : n-1)$ distributed using a *cyclic(b)* distribution is assumed to have a cyclic distribution on $VP = min(P * b, n)$ virtual processors. These virtual processors are block distributed on the P processors. Thus, the set of virtual processors on a processor p is $(p*b : min(p*b+b-1, n-1))$. Fig. 3(b) illustrates the virtual-cyclic view of a *cyclic(4)* distribution of $A(0 : 15)$ on two processors. The array has a cyclic distribution on eight virtual processors. These eight virtual processors are allocated to the two processors in a block fashion, i.e., v_0 through v_3 are mapped to p_0, while v_4 through v_7 are mapped to p_1.

The array element with local index j on a virtual processor v, has a local index $(v \bmod b) + b*j$ on the processor to which it is mapped. A stride of s in the local index space of a virtual processor corresponds to $s*b$ in the processor's local index space. Thus the array section $(l : u : s)$ in the local index space of a virtual processor v is mapped to the section $((v \bmod b) + b * l : (v \bmod b) + b * u : s * b)$ in the local index space of the processor it is mapped to.

Consider the array section $A(l : u : s)$. The elements of A located on a virtual processor v have indices $(v : n : P * b)$. Thus v is active if the intersection $(v : n : P * b) \cap (l : u : s)$ is not empty, i.e. the linear diophantine equation $v + cP = l + is$ has got a solution. Hence, a virtual processor v is active if $gcd(s, P * b)|(v - l)$ and the first element of the intersection lies in the array section [2]. The first element can be found by solving the Diophantine equation $i * s - c * P * b = v - l$. Let i_1 and c_1 be the solution such that i_1 is the smallest non-negative integer for which the corresponding c_1 is non-negative. If $l + i_1 * s \leq u$ then the virtual processor v is active. If the first active virtual processor on processor p is v_f, then the active virtual processors on p are

$$V Act(p) \in (v_f : min(u, p * b + b - 1) : gcd(s, P * b)).$$

Note that not every processor in $(v_f : min(u, p * b + b - 1) : gcd(s, P * b))$ will have an element of the array section. The first virtual processor v_f is given by $v_f = ((-p * b + l) \bmod gcd(s, P * b)) + p * b$.

4 Incremental Generation of Local Index Set

In this section, we address the incremental generation of local index sets. Consider an array $A(0 : n - 1)$ distributed using a *cyclic(b)* distribution on P processors and the array statements

$$
\begin{aligned}
S_1 : \quad & A(l : u : s) = f_1(A(l : u : s)) \\
S_2 : \quad & A(l + c : u' : s) = f_2(A(l + c : u' : s)).
\end{aligned}
$$

Both S_1 and S_2 do not require communication. The node code for processor p is shown in Fig. 4(a). $V Act(S, p)$ denotes the set of active virtual processors on processor p corresponding to the left hand array section of statement S. The

```
int ll(n/Pb), lu(n/Pb), ls(n/Pb)
float A_loc(n/P)
```

```
int ll(n/Pb), lu(n/Pb), ls(n/Pb);
float A_loc(n/p);
```

```
Evaluate VAct(S_1, p)
for v ∈ VAct(S_1, p)
    ll(v) = LLx(S_1, v, p);
    lu(v) = LUx(S_1, v, p);
    ls(v) = Ls(S_1, v, p);
    for i = V(ll(v)), V(lu(v)), V(ls(v))
        A_loc(i) = f_1(A_loc(i));
Evaluate VAct(S_2, p);
for v ∈ VAct(S_2, p)
    ll(v) = LLx(S_2, v, p);
    lu(v) = LUx(S_2, v, p);
    for i = V(ll(v)), V(lu(v)), V(ls(v))
        A_loc(i) = f_2(A_loc(i));
```

```
Evaluate VAct(S_1, p);
for v ∈ VAct(S_1, p)
    ll(v) = LLx(S_1, v, p);
    lu(v) = LUx(S_1, v, p);
    ls(v) = Ls(S_1, v, p);
    for i = V(ll(v)), V(lu(v)), V(ls(v))
        A_loc(i) = f_1(A_loc(i));
Inc_Eval(S_1, S_2, VAct(S_1, p)
    VAct(S_2, p), ll[], lu[], ls[]);
for v ∈ VAct(S_2, p)
    for i = V(ll(v)), V(lu(v)), V(ls(v))
        A_loc(i) = f_2(A_loc(i));
```

(a) (b)

Fig. 4. Node program on p. (a) Direct evaluation of local index set, (b) Incremental evaluation.

---

local index set $LIndex(S, v, p) = (LLx(S, v, p) : LUx(S, v, p) : Ls(S, v, p))$ is evaluated at run-time. The functions $LLx()$, $LUx()$, and $Ls()$ correspond to the lower bound, upper bound and stride of the local index set on virtual processor v. These functions depend on the virtualization view and are developed in the following sections. The function V translates the index and stride from the index space of the virtual processor to that of the physical processor on which it is located as described in Section 3. The independent evaluation of the local index sets at runtime for S_1 and S_2 is shown in Fig. 4(a). This will require separate evaluation of the lower and upper bounds and stride for every active virtual processor on p. The overhead can be reduced by incrementally evaluating the local index sets for S_2 as shown in Fig. 4(b). Note that $Inc\_Eval()$ also evaluates the new active virtual processor set. We now develop the procedure $Inc\_Eval()$ for the incremental evaluation of the local index sets for the virtual block view.

4.1 Virtual Block View

Consider array $A(0 : n - 1)$ distributed on P processors using a $cyclic(b)$ distribution and the array section $S1 : A(l : u : s)$. Let A be viewed under a virtual block view. Consider virtual processor v and let $A(l + i_1 s)$ and $A(l + j_1 s)$ be the first and the last elements of $A(l : u : s)$ located on v. We obtain i_1 and j_1 as follows:

$$i_1 = \left\lceil \frac{vb - l}{s} \right\rceil, \quad j_1 = \left\lfloor \frac{vb + b - 1 - l}{s} \right\rfloor.$$

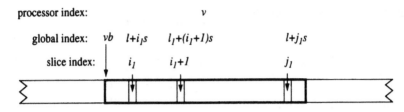

processor index: v

global index: vb $l+i_1s$ $l_1+(i_1+1)s$ $l+j_1s$

slice index: i_1 i_1+1 j_1

Fig. 5. Determination of local index sets.

From Fig. 5, it follows that:

$$LLx(S_1, v, p) = l + i_1 s - vb, \quad LUx(S_1, v, p) = l + j_1 s - vb, \quad Ls(S_1, v, p) = s.$$

Consider the array $A(0:55)$ distributed on $P = 2$ processors using a *cyclic(7)* distribution and the array sections $A(0:55:4)$ and $A(1:55:4)$ as shown in Fig. 6. The lower and upper bounds of the local index set for each virtual processor are marked. It is observed that the virtual processors can be split into two groups based on the difference between the lower bounds of the local index sets of the two array sections. For the first group, the lower bound of the local index set for array section $A(1:55:4)$ is obtained by incrementing the corresponding lower bound for $A(0:55:4)$ by one. For the second group the lower bound for $A(1:55:4)$ is obtained by decrementing the lower bound for $A(0:55:4)$ by three. If these virtual processors groups can be efficiently enumerated then the new lower bounds of the local index set can be enumerated using a single addition operation. We formally state this as follows.

Theorem 1. *Consider array $A(0:n-1)$ distributed on P processors using a cyclic(b) distribution and sections $S1 : A(l : u : s)$ and $S2 : A(l + c : u' : s)$. Let $c_2 = c \bmod s$. Under the virtual block view, for virtual processor v which is located on p and is active for $S1$ and $S2$ we have*

$$LLx(S_2, v, p) = \begin{cases} LLx(S_1, v, p) + c_2 & \text{if } (vb - l) \bmod s = 0, \\ LLx(S_1, v, p) + c_2 & \text{if } c_2 < (vb - l) \bmod s, \\ LLx(S_1, v, p) + c_2 - s & \text{if } c_2 \geq (vb - l) \bmod s > 0. \end{cases} \quad (2)$$

Proof: Array A is distributed on $VP = \lceil n/b \rceil$ virtual processors using a block distribution. Consider virtual processor v located on p. Let $A(l + i_1 s)$ and $A(l + i_2 s)$ be the first elements of $A(l : u : s)$ and $A(l + c : u' : s)$ located on v, respectively. Let $c = c_1 s + c_2$, $0 \leq c_2 < s$ and $vb - l = v_1 s + v_2$. We have

$$i_1 = \left\lceil \frac{vb - l}{s} \right\rceil = \left\lceil \frac{v_2}{s} \right\rceil + v_1, \quad i_2 = \left\lceil \frac{vb - l - c}{s} \right\rceil = \left\lceil \frac{v_2 - c_2}{s} \right\rceil + v_1 - c_1.$$

Since $0 \leq c_2, v_2 < s$, it follows that

$$i_1 = \begin{cases} v_1 + 1 & \text{if } v_2 > 0, \\ v_1 & \text{if } v_2 = 0, \end{cases} \quad i_2 = \begin{cases} v_1 - c_1 & \text{if } c_2 \geq v_2, \\ v_1 - c_1 + 1 & \text{if } c_2 < v_2. \end{cases}$$

Array Section: $A(0:55:4)$

		Proc. 0									Proc. 1					
	0	1	2	3	4	5	6		0	1	2	3	4	5	6
v0	[0]	1	2	3	[4]	5	6	v1	7	[8]	9	10	11	[12]	13
v2	14	15	[16]	17	18	19	[20]	v3	21	22	23	[24]	25	26	27
v4	[28]	29	30	31	[32]	33	34	v5	35	[36]	37	38	39	[40]	41
v6	42	43	[44]	45	46	47	[48]	v7	49	50	51	[52]	53	54	55

Array Section: $A(1:55:4)$

		Proc. 0									Proc. 1					
	0	1	2	3	4	5	6		0	1	2	3	4	5	6
v0	0	[1]	2	3	4	[5]	6	v1	7	8	[9]	10	11	12	[13]
v2	14	15	16	[17]	18	19	20	v3	21	22	23	24	[25]	26	27
v4	28	[29]	30	31	32	[33]	34	v5	35	36	[37]	38	39	40	[41]
v6	42	43	44	[45]	46	47	48	v7	49	50	51	52	[53]	54	55

Fig. 6. Incremental Evaluation of local index set for virtual block view

---

Combining the above inequalities we have

$$i_2 = \begin{cases} i_1 - c_1 & \text{if } c_2 < v_2, \\ i_1 - c_1 - 1 & \text{if } c_2 \geq v_2 > 0, \\ i_1 - c_1 & \text{if } v_2 = 0. \end{cases}$$

Theorem. 1 follows by evaluating $LLx(S_2, v, p)$ and $LLx(S_1, v, p)$ from i_1 and i_2, respectively. $\qquad\square$

Thus the lower bound of the local index set for virtual processor v for the array section in S_2 can be incrementally evaluated using a single addition if we can efficiently enumerate the set of virtual processors in the inequalities in Eq. 2. The key idea is to note that the qualifying inequalities in Eq. 2 can be represented as a set of simple regular sections. Consider the example in Fig. 6. We have

$$LLx(S_2, v, p) = \begin{cases} LLx(S_1, v, p) + 1 & \text{if } 1 < 7v \bmod 4, \\ LLx(S_1, v, p) - 3 & \text{if } 1 \geq 7v \bmod 4 > 0, \\ LLx(S_1, v, p) + 1 & \text{if } 7v \bmod 4 = 0. \end{cases}$$

The inequality $1 < 7v \bmod 4$ corresponds to the set of simple regular sections $\{(1 : 7 : 4), (2 : 7 : 4)\}$, $7v \bmod 4 = 0$ corresponds to $\{(0 : 7 : 4)\}$, and $1 \geq 7v \bmod 4 > 0$ corresponds to $\{(3 : 7 : 4)\}$. On processor $p = 0$, the virtual processors given by $\{(0 : 7 : 4), (2 : 7 : 4)\}$ determine the new lower bound by incrementing the old lower bound by one. On processor $p = 1$, the virtual processors $\{(1 : 7 : 4)\}$ determine the new lower bound by incrementing the old bound by one while $\{(3 : 7 : 4)\}$ determine the new lower bound by decrementing the old bound by three. We express the inequalities as a set of regular sections and project the regular sections onto the active virtual processor set of each processor. Once the set of sections representation is developed the lower bound of the local index sets can be incremental evaluated as follows.

$$\textbf{for } i = 0, num\_sects - 1$$
$$\textbf{for } v = Sect[i].l, Sect[i].u, stride$$
$$ll(v) = ll(v) + Sect[i].disp$$

We now describe the method for construction of the set of sections representation. We express each inequality as a set of linear diophantine equations, determine simple regular sections as solutions to the diophantine equations and project the sections of virtual processors onto the active virtual processor set of the processor.

Consider the inequality $c_2 < (vb - l) \bmod s$. We can rewrite the inequality $c_2 < (vb - l) \bmod s$ as a set of $s - c_2 - 1$ linear diophantine equations in variables v and k

$$\{(vb - l) \bmod s = m \ : \ c_2 < m < s\} \equiv \{vb - ks = m + l : \ c_2 < m < s\}. \quad (3)$$

The linear diophantine equation $vb - ks = m + l$ has solutions only for those values of $m + l$ that are divisible by $gcd(s, b)$. The general solution to a solvable linear Diophantine equation $vb - ks = m + l$ is found as follows. Let $g_1 = gcd(s, b) = u_1 b - k_1 s$, where u_1, k_1, and g_1 are found using the extended Euclid algorithm [2]. The parameterized solution for v is given by $v = \frac{m+l}{g_1} u_1 - \frac{s}{g_1} t$, $t \in \mathcal{Z}$. Let v_f be the smallest non-negative solution for v. Then the set of virtual processors $(v_f : VP : \frac{s}{g_1})$ are solutions to the equation $vb - ks = m + l$. A similar regular section can be evaluated for every solvable diophantine equation in the set in Eq. 3 by determining the first virtual processor v_{fi} of the section. Let this set of regular sections be denoted by $LSect = \cup_i \{LSect_i\}$, where $LSect_i = (v_{fi} : VP : \frac{s}{g_1})$. We are interested in estimating the new local index set of virtual processors located on processor p which are active for both S_1 and S_2. Projecting the section $LSect_i$ to the virtual processors on p which are active for both S_1 and S_2, is equivalent to determining the intersection $LSect_i \cap VAct(S_1, p) \cap VAct(S_2, p)$. For the case when $s \leq b$ all the virtual processors in $(l/b : u/b) \cap ((l + c)/b : u'/b) = (v : u)$ are active for both S_1 and S_2. The intersection can be computed by determining $(v_{fi} : VP : P) \cap (v : u) \cap (p : VP : P)$. The algorithm for construction of the set of sections when $s < b$ is provided in Fig. 7

If $s > b$ then each virtual processor has at most one element of the array section. In this case a direct evaluation of the local index sets is performed for all the new active processors. A direct evaluation is also performed for all virtual processors in $VAct(S_2, p) - VAct(S_1, p)$.

The incremental evaluation requires a single addition for evaluation of the lower bound of the local index set as opposed to three multiplies, five additions and 2 divisions for the direct approach. However, the construction of the set of sections requires a large overhead directly proportional to the stride which is small and fixed.

Algorithm 1 (Generation of Sections for incremental index set evaluation)

Input:

1. Array section l, u, s, processors P, block size b, processor p, offset c.
2. $VAct(S_1) = (v_o : u_o)$ and $ll(), lu(), ls()$ for $A(l : u : s)$ for virtual processors on p.
3. $(g_1, u_1, k_1) \leftarrow Extended\_GCD(b, s)$; $(g_2, u_2, k_2) \leftarrow Extended\_GCD(P, s/g_1)$;

Output:

1. $VAct(S_2) = (v_n : u_n)$
2. Set of sections $LSect$ for incremental evaluation of lower bound of local index set.

Method:

$len \leftarrow 0$; $c_2 = c \bmod s$; $stride = \frac{s*P}{g_1*g_2}$;
/* Evaluate $VAct(S_2) = (v_n : u_n)$ */
$v_n = (l + c)/b$; $u_n = u'/b$; $v = max(v_n, v_o)$; $u = min(u_n, u_o)$;

/* Express the inequalities as a set of simple regular sections */
for $i = l$ **to** $l + s - 1$
    /* Determine v_{fi} and if $(v_n : u_n) \cap (p : VP : P) \cap (v_{f_i} : VP : \frac{s}{g_1})$ is non-empty */
    if $(i \bmod g_1 == 0) \wedge ((p - \frac{i}{g_1}u_1) \bmod g_2 == 0)$ **then** /* non-empty */
        $v_f = \frac{i}{g_1}u_1 - \frac{s}{g_1}(\lfloor \frac{iu_1}{s} \rfloor)$; $v_f = v_f + \frac{s}{g_1}\left(\lceil \frac{v_n - v_f}{s/g_1} \rceil\right)$;
        $lsect[len].l = max(v_f, p) + \left(\left(\frac{(s/g_1)v_2(p - v_f)}{g_2} + v_f\right) - max(v_f, p)\right) \bmod stride$;
        $lsect[len].u = u$; $lsect[len].s = stride$;
        if $(i == l \vee i > l + c_2)$ **then**
            $lsect[len].disp = c_2$;
        else
            $lsect[len].disp = c_2 - s$;

Fig. 7. Incremental Evaluation of local index set for virtual block view

---

5 Incremental Generation of Communication Sets

In this section, we address the incremental evaluation of the communication sets. Consider the array statements

$$S_1 : \quad B(l_2 : u_2 : s_2) = A(l_1 : u_1 : s_1) \tag{4}$$
$$S_2 : \quad B(l_2 + d : u_2 + d : s_2) = A(l_1 + c : u_1 + c : s_1) \tag{5}$$

The node code (only communication) for the array statement S_1 using the virtual processor approach is shown in Fig. 8. The sets $VPSnd(), VPRcv(), VDSnd()$, and $VDRcv()$ are equivalent to $PSend(), PRecv(), DSend()$, and $DRecv()$, respectively in the virtual processor domain. To distinguish between the active virtual processor sets corresponding to the sections of arrays A and B, the active virtual processor sets are tagged as $VAct_A()$ and $VAct_B()$, respectively. Before performing the actual communication, the sets $VPSnd(), VPRcv(), VDSnd()$, and

$VDRcv()$ have to converted into the equivalent $PSend()$, $PRecv()$, $DSend()$, and $DRecv()$ sets. This conversion depends on the virtual views at the source and target block-cyclic distribution and is described in [7]. In Fig. 8, we refer to

```
/* Send phase 1 for proc p */          /* Receive phase 1 for proc p */
for v_p ∈ VAct_A(S_1, p)                for v_p ∈ VAct_B(S_1, p)
    Evaluate VPSnd(S_1, v_p)               Evaluate VPRcv(S_1, v_p)
    for v_q ∈ VPSnd(S_1, v_p)              for v_q ∈ VPRcv(S_1, v_p)
        Evaluate VDSnd(S_1, v_p, v_q)          Evaluate VDRcv(S_1, v_p, v_q)

Convert VPSnd(S_1, v_p), to PSend(S_1, p)   Convert VPRcv(S_1, v_p) to PRecv(S_1, p),
and VDSnd(S_1, v_p, v_q), DSend(S_1, p, q)  and VDRcv(S_1, v_p, v_q) to DRecv(S_1, p, q)

/* Send phase 2 for proc p */          /* Receive phase 2 for proc p */
for q ∈ PSend(S_1, p)                   for q ∈ PRecv(S_1, p)
    Pack (A_loc(DSend(S_1, p, q)), tmp);    Recv (q, tmp)
    Send (q, tmp)                          Unpack (tmp, A_loc(DRecv(S_1, p, q)));
```

Fig. 8. Node code for statement S_1 for processor p.

the communication sets in terms of virtual processors at the end of the sending and receiving phase one as $VSendInfo(S,p)$ and $VRecvInfo(S,p)$. The code for S_2 can incrementally evaluate $VSendInfo(S_2,p)$ and $VRecvInfo(S_2,p)$ from $VSendInfo(S_1,p)$ and $VRecvInfo(S_1,p)$, respectively, perform the conversion to $PSend()$ and $DSend()$ sets and then perform the communication in phase two.

We present techniques for the incremental construction of the communication sets. We consider the case when array $A(0 : n_1 - 1)$ is viewed under a virtual block view and $B(0 : n_2 - 1)$ under a virtual cyclic view and evaluate the send data and processor sets.

5.1 Virtual Block to Virtual Cyclic

Consider the sequence of array statements in Eq. 4 and Eq. 5 and the arrays $A(0 : n_1 - 1)$ and $B(0 : n_2 - 1)$ distributed using a $cyclic(b_1)$ and $cyclic(b_2)$ distibutions on P_1 and P_2 processors respectively. $A(0 : n_1 - 1)$ is viewed under a virtual block view while $B(0 : n_2 - 1)$ is viewed under a virtual cyclic view.

We evaluate the send communication sets. Consider virtual processor v_p and let $A(l_1 + i_1 s_1)$ and $A(l_1 + j_1 s_1)$ be the first and last elements of the section $A(l_1 : u_1 : s_1)$ located on v_p. Similarly let $A(l_1 + i'_1 s_1)$ and $A(l_1 + j'_1 s_1)$ be the first and last elements of the section $A(l_1 + c : u_1 + c : s_1)$ located on v_p. Let

$c = c_1 s_1 + c_2$. As shown in [7], we have

$$VPSnd(S_1, v_p) = (l_2 + (i_1 : min(j_1, i_1 + \frac{lcm(s_2, P_2)}{s_2} - 1) * s_2)) \bmod P_2 b_2,$$

$$VPSnd(S_2, v_p) = (l_2 + d + (i'_1 : min(j'_1, i'_1 + \frac{lcm(s_2, P_2)}{s_2} - 1) * s_2)) \bmod P_2 b_2.$$

In Section 4, we have developed a set of sections representation characterizing the virtual processors for which $i'_1 = i_1 - c_1$, or $i'_1 = i_1 - c_1 - 1$, and $j'_1 = j_1 - c_1$, or $j'_1 = j_1 - c_1 - 1$. Let v_p belong to the set for which $i'_1 = i_1 - c_1$ and $j'_1 = j_1 - c_1$. A similar analysis can be performed for the remaining cases. Thus we have

$$VPSnd(S_2, v_p) = (l_2 + (d - c_1 s_2) +$$
$$(i_1 : min(j_1, i_1 + \frac{lcm(s_2, P_2 b_2)}{s_2} - 1) * s_2)) \bmod P_2 b_2$$

Thus in the general case $VPSnd(S_2, v_p)$ and $VPSnd(S_1, v_p)$ may not be identical and $VPSnd(S_2, v_p)$ is directly evaluated. However, the data send sets can be incrementally evaluated from $VDSnd(S_1, v, p)$. We note that for each processor v_q in $VPSnd(S_1, v_p)$, there exists a corresponding first array section slice index k_1 in $(i_1 : min(j_1, i_1 + lcm(s_2, P_2 b_2)/s_2 - 1))$. The indices of all the array section slices sent by v_p to v_q can be determined as $(k_1 : j_1 : lcm(s_1, P_s)/s_2)$ (refer [7]). Since $VDSnd(S_1, v_p, v_q)$ consists of the local indices of these slices on v_p we have

$$VDSnd(S_1, v_p, v_q) = (l_1 + k_1 * s_1 - v_p b_1 : l_1 + j_1 * s_1 - v_p b_1 :$$
$$lcm(s_2, P_2 b_2) * s_1/s_2).$$

Let v'_q be the virtual processor in $VPSnd(S_2, v_p)$ corresponding to slice $k_1 - c_1$. Following a similar argument we have

$$VDSnd(S_2, v_p, v'_q)$$
$$= (l_1 + c + k_1 * s_1 - v_p b_1 - c_1 s_1 : l_1 + j_1 * s_1 - v_p b_1 - c_1 s_1 :$$
$$lcm(s_2, P_2 b_2) * s_1/s_2)$$
$$= VDSnd(S_1, v_p, v_q) + c - c_1 s_1 = VDSnd(S_1, v_p, v_q) + c_2.$$

Thus the virtual processor data send sets corresponding to S_2 can be incrementally evaluated using a single addition for the upper and lower bound. The virtual processors v_q and v'_q have the same index position in $VPSnd(S_1, v_p)$ and $VPSnd(S_2, v_p)$, respectively.

6 Conclusion

We have addressed the incremental evaluation of local index sets and communication sets using the virtual processor approach for execution of array statements involving block-cyclically distributed arrays. Incremental evaluation and reuse of these sets is important for reducing the runtime execution cost of array statements.

Incremental evaluation of local index sets and communication set when the two array sections have different strides has not been considered. While shifts of array sections occur frequently in scientific codes, stride changes are not as frequent. It is also not yet clear if incremental evaluation of the local index and communication sets will provide significant benefits compared to separate independent evaluation when different strides are involved. Work in this direction is currently in progress.

References

1. F. Bodin, P. Beckman, D. Gannon, S. Yang, S. Kesavan, A. Malony, and B. Mohr. Implementing a parallel C++ runtime system for scalable parallel systems. In *Supercomputing '93*, pages 588–597, 1993.
2. D. Burton. *Elementary Number Theory*. Allyn and Bacon, Inc, Boston, revised printing edition, 1984.
3. B. M. Chapman, P. Mehrotra, and H. P. Zima. Vienna Fortran – a Fortran language extension for distributed memory multiprocessors. In J. Saltz and P. Mehrotra, editors, *Language, Compilers and Runtime Environments for Distributed Memory Machines*, pages 39–62. 1992.
4. S. Chatterjee, J. R. Gilbert, F. J. E. Long, R. Schreiber, and S.-H. Teng. Generating local addresses and communication sets for data parallel programs. In *Proc. of ACM Symposium on Principles and Practices of Parallel Programming*, pages 149–158, May 1993.
5. High Performance Fortran Forum. High Performance Fortran langauge specification version 1.0. Technical Report CRPC-TR92225, Rice University, May 1993.
6. G. Fox, S. Hiranandani, K. Kennedy, C Koelbel, U. Kremer, C.-W. Tseng, and M. Wu. Fortran-D Language Specification. Technical Report TR-91-170, Dept. of Computer Science, Rice University, Dec. 1991.
7. S. K. S. Gupta, S. D. Kaushik, C.-H. Huang, and P. Sadayappan. On compiling array expressions for efficient execution on distributed-memory machines. Technical Report OSU-CISRC-4/9-TR19, Department of Computer and Information Science, The Ohio State University., April 1994.
8. S. K. S. Gupta, S. D. Kaushik, S. Mufti, S. Sharma, C.-H. Huang, and P. Sadayappan. On compiling array expressions for efficient execution on distributed-memory machines. In *Proc. of Intl. Conf. on Parallel Processing*, volume II, pages 301–305, 1993.
9. S. Hiranandani, K. Kennedy, J. Mellor-Crummey, and A. Sethi. Advanced compilation techniques for Fortran D. Technical Report CRPC-TR-93-338, Center for Research on Parallel Computation, Rice University, Oct. 1993.
10. C. Koelbel. Compile-time generation of communication for scientific programs. In *Supercomputing '91*, pages 101–110, Nov. 1991.
11. J. M. Stichnoth. Efficient compilation of array statements for private memory multicomputers. Technical Report CMU-CS-93-109, School of Computer Science, Carnegie Mellon University, Feb. 1993.

A Unified Data-Flow Framework for Optimizing Communication

Manish Gupta, Edith Schonberg and Harini Srinivasan

IBM T. J. Watson Research Center
P. O. Box 704
Yorktown Heights, NY 10598

Abstract. This paper presents a framework, based on global array data-flow analysis, to reduce communication costs in a program being compiled for a distributed memory machine. This framework applies techniques for partial redundancy elimination to *available section descriptors*, a novel representation of communication involving array sections. With a single framework, we are able to capture numerous optimizations like (i) vectorizing communication, (ii) eliminating communication that is redundant on any control flow path, (iii) reducing the amount of data being communicated, (iv) reducing the number of processors to which data must be communicated, and (v) moving communication earlier to hide latency, and to subsume previous communication. Further, the explicit representation of availability of data in our framework allows processors other than the owners also to send values needed by other processors, leading to additional opportunities for optimizing communication. Another contribution of this paper is to show that the bidirectional problem of eliminating partial redundancies can be decomposed into simpler unidirectional problems, in the context of communication as well.

1 Introduction

Distributed memory architectures are becoming increasingly popular as a viable and cost-effective method of building massively parallel computers. However, the absence of global address space, and consequently, the need for explicit message passing among processes makes these machines very difficult to program. This has motivated the design of languages like High Performance Fortran (HPF) [6], that allow the programmer to write sequential or shared-memory parallel programs that are annotated with directives specifying data decomposition. The compilers for these languages are responsible for partitioning the computation, and generating the communication necessary to fetch values of non-local data referenced by a processor. A number of such prototype compilers have been developed [14, 24, 16, 18, 15, 3, 11, 20].

Since the cost of interprocessor communication is usually orders of magnitude higher than the cost of accessing local data, it is extremely important for the compilers to optimize communication. The most common optimizations include message vectorization [14, 24], using collective communication [10, 16], and overlapping communication with computation [14]. However, most compilers perform little global analysis of the communication requirements across different loop nests. This precludes general optimizations, such as redundant communication elimination, or carrying out extra communication inside one loop nest if it subsumes communication required in the next loop nest.

There have been some efforts towards using data-flow analysis to optimize communication. Granston and Veidenbaum [8] use data-flow analysis to detect redundant accesses to global memory in a hierarchical, shared-memory machine. However, they do not explicitly represent information about the availability of data on processors. Instead, they rely on simplistic assumptions about scheduling of parallel loops, which are often not applicable. Amarasinghe and Lam [3] use the *last write tree* framework to perform optimizations like eliminating redundant messages. Their framework does not handle general conditional statements, and they do not eliminate redundant communication due to different references in arbitrary statements (for instance, statements appearing in different loop nests). Von Hanxleden et al. [23, 22] have developed a data flow framework for generating communication in the presence of indirection arrays. Their work focuses on irregular subscripts, and therefore does not attempt to obtain more precise information about array sections. Gong et al. [7] describe a data-flow procedure that unifies optimizations like vectorizing communication and removing partially redundant communication. They only handle programs with singly nested loops and unidimensional arrays, and with very simple subscripts.

This paper presents a framework, based on global array data-flow analysis, to reduce communication in a program. We apply techniques for partial redundancy elimination, discussed in the context of eliminating redundant computation by Morel and Renvoise [17], and later refined by other researchers [5]. The conventional approach to data-flow analysis regards each access to an array element as an access to the entire array. Previous researchers [9, 8, 19] have applied data-flow analysis to array sections to improve its precision. However, using just array sections is insufficient in the context of communication optimizations. There is a need to represent information about the processors where the array elements are available, or need to be made available. For this purpose, we use a new kind of descriptor, the *Available Section Descriptor* (ASD) [12]. We use ideas from the interval analysis method [2, 9] to develop a procedure for obtaining global data-flow information, that is recorded using the ASDs. With the resultant framework, we are able to capture a number of optimizations, such as:

- vectorizing communication,
- eliminating communication that is redundant in any control flow path,
- reducing the amount of data being communicated,
- reducing the number of processors to which data must be communicated, and
- moving communication earlier to hide latency, and to subsume previous communication.

We do not know of any other system that tries to perform all of these optimizations, and in a global manner. Further, the explicit representation of availability of data in our framework allows processors other than the owners also to send values needed by other processors, leading to additional opportunities for optimizing communication. Following the results presented in [5] for partially redundant computations, we show that the bidirectional problem of eliminating partial redundancies can be decomposed into simpler unidirectional problems, in the context of communication represented using ASDs as well.

Available section descriptors were first presented in [12], which describes ASD operations needed to solve dataflow equations and an algorithm to eliminate fully redundant communication. That algorithm does not remove partially redundant communication and also does not deal with the problem of hiding the latency. This paper extends [12], by presenting a unified solution to all of the communication optimization problems outlined above. An advantage of our approach is that the analysis is performed on the original program form, before any communication is introduced by the compiler. Thus, communication optimizations based on data availability analysis need not depend on a detailed knowledge of explicit communication representations.

2 Motivating Example

Before proceeding with the data flow algorithm for the various communication optimizations mentioned in Section 1, we illustrate these optimizations using an example. Figure 1(a) shows an HPF program and a high level view of communication that would be generated by a compiler following the *owner-computes* rule [14, 24], which assigns each computation to the processor that owns the data being modified. The HPF directives specify the alignment of each array with respect to a two-dimensional virtual processor template VPROCS. The variables a and z are two-dimensional arrays aligned with VPROCS, and d, e, and w are one-dimensional arrays aligned with the first column of VPROCS. The notation $x(i) \rightarrow VPROCS(i, j)$ (we omit the range of i and j for saving space in the figure) means that the value of $x(i)$ is sent to the virtual processor position $VPROCS(i, j)$, for all $1 \leq i \leq 100$, $1 \leq j \leq 100$. The communication shown in Figure 1(a) already incorporates message vectorization, a commonly used optimization to move communication out of loops. While message vectorization is captured naturally by our framework as we shall explain, in this paper we focus on other important optimizations that illustrate the power of this framework. Reduced communication after global optimization is shown in Figure 1(b). We consider optimizations performed for each variable d, e, and w.

There are two identical communications for e in Figure 1(a), which result from the uses of e in statements 10 and 26. In both cases, e(i) must be sent to VPROCS(i, j), for all values of i, j. However, because of the assignment to e(1) in statement 13, the second communication is only *partially redundant*. Thus, we can eliminate the second communication, except for sending e(1) to VPROCS(1, j), for all values of j. This reduced communication is *hoisted* to the earliest possible place after statement 13 in Figure 1(b).

In Figure 1(a), there are two communications for d, resulting from uses of d in statements 16 and 26. In Figure 1(b), the second communication has been

```
HPF align (i, j) with VPROCS(i,j) :: a, z
HPF align (i) with VPROCS(i,1) :: d, e, w
```

1:	`do i = 1, 100`	`do i = 1, 100`
5:	`    e(i) = d(i) * w(i)`	`    e(i) = d(i) * w(i)`
6:	`    d(i) = d(i) + 2 * w(i)`	`    d(i) = d(i) + 2 * w(i)`
7:	`end do`	`end do`

$$e(i) \rightarrow VPROCS(i,j) \qquad\qquad e(i), d(i) \rightarrow VPROCS(i,j)$$

8:	`do i = 1, 100`	`do i = 1, 100`
9:	`    do j = 1, 100`	`    do j = 1, 100`
10:	`        z(i,j) = e(i)`	`        z(i,j) = e(i)`
11:	`    end do`	`    end do`
12:	`end do`	`end do`
13:	`e(1) = 2 * d(1)`	`e(1) = 2 * d(1)`

$$e(1) \rightarrow VPROCS(1,j)$$

14:	`if (s ≠ 0) then`	`if (s ≠ 0) then`

$$d(i), w(i) \rightarrow VPROCS(i,100) \qquad w(i) \rightarrow VPROCS(i,100)$$

15:	`    do i = 1, 100`	`    do i = 1, 100`
16:	`        z(i,100) = d(i) / w(i)`	`        z(i,100) = d(i) / w(i)`
17:	`    end do`	`    end do`
18:	`else`	`else`
19:	`    do i = 1, 100`	`    do i = 1,100`
20:	`        z(i,100) = m`	`        z(i, 100) = m`
21:	`        w(i) = m`	`        w(i) = m`
22:	`    end do`	`    end do`

$$w(i) \rightarrow VPROCS(i,100)$$

23:	`end if`	`end if`

$$e(i), d(i) \rightarrow VPROCS(i,j)$$
$$w(i) \rightarrow VPROCS(i,100)$$

24:	`do j = 1, 100`	`do j = 1, 100`
25:	`    do i = 1, 100`	`    do i = 1, 100`
26:	`        a(i,j) = a(i,j) +`	`        a(i,j) = a(i,j) +`
	`            (d(i) * e(i))/z(i,j)`	`            (d(i) * e(i))/z(i,j)`
27:	`    end do`	`    end do`
28:	`    z(j,100) = w(j)`	`    z(j,100) = w(j)`
29:	`end do`	`end do`

(a)	(b)

Fig. 1. Program before and after communication optimizations.

hoisted to the earliest possible place, after statement 7, where it *subsumes* the first communication, which has been eliminated.

Finally, there are two communications for w, resulting from uses of w in statements 16 and 28. The second, *partially redundant*, communication is hoisted inside the two branches of the if statement, and is eliminated in the then branch. The assignment to w(i) at statement 21 prevents the communication in the else branch from being moved earlier.

The result of this collection of optimizations leads to a program in which communication is performed as early as possible, and the total communication volume has been reduced.

3   Overview of Available Section Descriptors

The Available Section Descriptor is an extended version of an array section descriptor, that also records information about the availability of data items on processors. It is defined as a pair $\langle D, M \rangle$, where D is an array section descriptor, and M is a descriptor of the function mapping elements in D to virtual processors. We use the term *mapping* to convey the availability (as a result of prior communication), or the intended availability (to implement a particular communication), of data at processors.

We use the *bounded regular section descriptor* (BRSD) [13] to represent array sections. A BRSD is represented as an expression $A(S)$, where A is the name of an array variable, S is a vector of subscript values such that each of its elements is either (i) an expression of the form $\alpha * k + \beta$, where k is a loop index variable and α and β are invariants, (ii) a triple $l : u : s$, where l, u, and s are invariants (the triple represents the expression discussed above expanded over a range) , or (iii) $\perp$, indicating no knowledge of the subscript value. For example, given a 100 x 100 array A, the BRSD $A(2 : 100 : 2, 1 : 100)$ represents every even-numbered row of that array.

The processor space is regarded as an unbounded grid of virtual processors. The abstract processor space is similar to a *template* in High Performance Fortran (HPF) [6], which is a grid over which different arrays are aligned. The mapping function descriptor M is a pair $\langle P, F \rangle$, both P and F being vectors of length equal to the dimensionality of the processor grid. The ith element of P (denoted as P_i) indicates the dimension of the array A that is mapped to the ith grid dimension, and F_i is the mapping function for that array dimension, i.e., $F_i(j)$ returns the position(s) along the ith grid dimension to which the jth element of the array dimension is mapped. We represent a mapping function as

$$F_i(j) = (c * j + l) : (c * j + u) : s,$$

where c, l, u and s are invariants. The parameters c, l and u may take rational values, as long as $F_i(j)$ evaluates to a range over integers, over the data domain. The above formulation allows representation of one-to-one mappings (when $l = u$), one-to-many mappings (when $u \geq l + s$), and also constant mappings (when $c = 0$). The one-to-many mappings expressible with this formulation are more

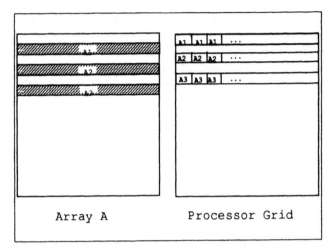

Fig. 2. ASD Illustration

general than the replicated mappings for ownership that may be specified using HPF [6].

If an array has fewer dimensions than the processor grid, clearly there is no array dimension mapped to some of the grid dimensions. For each such grid dimension i, P_i takes the value m, which represents a "missing" array dimension. In that case, F_i is no longer a function of a subscript position. It is simply an expression of the form $l : u : s$, and indicates the position(s) in the ith grid dimension at which the array is available.

Example. Consider a 2-D virtual processor grid VPROCS, and an ASD $\langle A(2 : 100 : 2, 1 : 100), \langle [1, 2], [F_1, F_2] \rangle \rangle$, where $F_1(i) = i - 1, F_2(j) = 1 : 100$. The ASD represents an array section $A(2 : 100 : 2, 1 : 100)$, each of whose element $A(2*i, j)$ is available at a hundred processor positions given by VPROCS$(2 * i - 1, 1 : 100)$. This ASD is illustrated in Figure 2. Figure 2(a) shows the array A, where each horizontal stripe A_i represents $A(2 * i, 1 : 100)$. Figure 2(b) represents the mapping of the array section onto the virtual processor template VPROCS, where each subsection A_i is replicated along its corresponding row.

4 Data Flow Analysis

In this section, we present a procedure for obtaining data-flow information for a structured program. We are able to perform a collection of communication optimizations within a single framework, based on the following observations. Determining the *data availability* resulting from communication is a similar problem to determining available expressions in classical data flow analysis. Thus, optimizations like reducing and hoisting communications are similar to eliminating redundant expressions and code motion. Furthermore, applying partial redundancy elimination techniques at the granularity of sections of arrays and processors enables not merely elimination, but also reduction in the volume of communication in different control flow paths.

The bidirectional data-flow analysis for suppression of partial redundancies, introduced by Morel and Renvoise [17], and refined subsequently [5], defines a framework for unifying common optimizations on available expressions. We adapt this framework to solve the set of communication optimizations described in Section 2. This section presents the following results.

- Section 4.1 reformulates the refined data-flow equations from [5] in terms of ASDs. We have incorporated a further modification that is useful in the context of optimizing communication.
- Section 4.2 shows that the bidirectional problem of determining the possible placement of communication can be solved by obtaining a solution to a backward problem, followed by a forward correction.
- In contrast to previous work, solving these equations for ASDs requires array data-flow analysis. In Section 4.3, we present the overall data-flow procedure that uses interval analysis.

As with other similar frameworks, we require the following edge-splitting transformation to be performed on the control flow graph before the analysis begins: any edge that runs directly from a node with more than one successor, to a node with more than one predecessor, is split [5]. Thus, in the transformed graph, there is no direct edge from a branch node to a join node.

4.1 Data Flow Equations for Partial Redundancy Elimination

We use the following definitions:

$ANTLOC_i$: communication in node i, that is not preceded by a definition of any data being communicated.

$CGEN_i$: communication in node i, that is not followed by a definition of any data being communicated.

$KILL_i$: data being killed (on all processors) due to a definition in node i.

$AVIN_i/AVOUT_i$: availability of data at the entry/exit of node i.

$ANTIN_i/ANTOUT_i$: communication anticipated at the entry/exit of node i.

$PPIN_i/PPOUT_i$: communication that may be placed at entry/exit of node i.

$INSERT_i$: communication that should be inserted at the exit of node i.

$REDUND_i$: communication in node i that is redundant.

Local Data Flow Variables For an assignment statement, both $ANTLOC$ and $CGEN$ are set to the communication required to send each variable referenced on the right hand side (rhs) to the processor executing the statement. That depends on the compute-rule used by the compiler in translating the source program into SPMD form. The procedure for determining $CGEN$ corresponding to the *owner computes* rule is described in [12]. We shall just illustrate it here with an example. Consider the program segment shown below:

HPF ALIGN $A(i,j)$ WITH VPROCS(i,j)
$A(i,j) = \ldots B(2*i, j-1) \ldots$

The communication for this statement is obtained as $CGEN = \langle B(2*i, j-1), \langle [1,2], [F_1, F_2] \rangle \rangle$, where $F_1(i) = i/2$, and $F_2(j) = j+1$. The dimension mapping $P = [1,2]$ specifies that the first and the second array dimension are mapped respectively to the first and the second dimension of the virtual processor grid. The mapping functions F_1 and F_2 together specify that the element $B(2*i, j-1)$ is mapped onto VPROCS(i,j). The $KILL$ variable for the statement is set to $\langle A(i,j), \mathcal{U} \rangle$, signifying that $A(i,j)$ is killed on all processors. The procedure for determining $CGEN$, $ANTLOC$, and $KILL$ for nodes corresponding to program intervals shall be discussed in Section 4.3.

Global Data Flow Variables The data flow equations, as adapted from [5], are shown below.[1] Both $AVIN$ and $PPIN$ are defined as $\emptyset$ for the entry node, while $PPOUT$ and $ANTOUT$ are defined as $\emptyset$ for the exit node.

$$AVOUT_i = [AVIN_i - KILL_i] \cup CGEN_i \tag{1}$$

$$AVIN_i = \cap_{p \in pred(i)} AVOUT_p \tag{2}$$

$$ANTIN_i = [ANTOUT_i - KILL_i] \cup ANTLOC_i \tag{3}$$

$$ANTOUT_i = \cap_{s \in succ(i)} ANTIN_s \tag{4}$$

$$PPIN_i = [ANTLOC_i \cup (PPOUT_i - KILL_i)]$$
$$\cap [\cap_{p \in pred(i)} (AVOUT_p \cup PPOUT_p)] \tag{5}$$

$$PPOUT_i = \cap_{s \in succ(i)} PPIN_s \tag{6}$$

$$INSERT_i = [PPOUT_i - AVOUT_i] - [PPIN_i - KILL_i] \tag{7}$$

$$REDUND_i = PPIN_i \cap ANTLOC_i \tag{8}$$

The problem of determining the availability of data ($AVIN_i / AVOUT_i$) is similar to the classical data-flow problem of determining *available expressions* [1]. The first equation ensures that any data overwritten inside node i is removed from the availability set, and data communicated during node i (and not overwritten later) is added to the availability set. The second equation indicates that at entry to a join node in the control flow graph, only the data available at exit on each of the predecessor nodes can be considered to be available.

The computation of anticipatability of communication ($ANTIN/ANTOUT$) proceeds in the backward direction, and is employed to determine $ANTLOC$, as will be shown in Section 4.3. Equation 3 shows that any data with a definition

---

[1] The original equation in [5] for $PPIN_i$ has an additional term, corresponding to the right hand side being further intersected with $PAVIN_i$, the partial availability of data at entry to node i. This term is important in the context of eliminating partially redundant computation, because it prevents unnecessary code motion that increases register pressure. However, moving communication early is useful even if it does not lead to a reduction in previous communication, because it helps hide the latency. Hence, we drop that term in our equation for $PPIN_i$.

is removed from the anticipatable (upward exposed) communication at entry to node i, and any communication not preceded by a definition is added to that set. Equation 4 shows that only communication that is anticipated at entry to each successor node to i can be anticipated at exit from node i.

The term $[ANTLOC_i \cup (PPOUT_i - KILL_i)]$ in Equation 5 denotes the part of communication occurring in node i or hoisted into it that can legally be moved to the entry of node i. A further intersection of that term with $[\cap_{p \in pred(i)}(AVOUT_p \cup PPOUT_p)]$ gives an additional property to $PPIN_i$, namely that all data included in $PPIN_i$ must be available at entry to node i on every incoming path due to original or moved communication. $PPOUT_i$ is set to communication that can be placed at entry to each of the successor nodes to i, as shown by Equation 6. Thus, $PPOUT_i$ represents communication that can legally and *safely* appear at the exit of node i. The property of safety implies that the communication is necessary, regardless of the flow of control in the program.

Finally, $INSERT_i$ represents the communication that should be inserted at the exit of node i as a result of the optimization. Given that $PPOUT_i$ represents safe communication at that point, as shown in Equation 7, $INSERT_i$ consists of $PPOUT_i$ minus the following two components: (i) data already available at exit of node i due to original communication: given by $AVOUT_i$, and (ii) data available at entry to node i due to moved or original communication, and which has not been overwritten inside node i: this component is given by $(PPIN_i - KILL_i)$. Following the insertions, any communication in node i that is not preceded by a definition of the data (i.e., $ANTLOC_i$) and which also forms part of $PPIN_i$ becomes redundant. Thus, in Equation 8, $REDUND_i$ represents the communication in node i that can be deleted.

The union, intersection, and difference operations on ASDs are described in [12], and will not be discussed here. The ASDs are not closed under these operations (the intersection operation is always exact, except in the special case when two mapping functions, of the form $F_i(j) = c*i+l : c*i+u : s$, for corresponding array dimensions have different values of the coefficient c). Therefore, it is important to know for each operation whether to underestimate or overestimate the result, in case an approximation is needed. In the above equations, each of $AVIN_i, AVOUT_i, PPIN_i, PPOUT_i$, and $REDUND_i$ are *underestimated*, if necessary. On the other hand, $INSERT_i$ is *overestimated*, if needed. This ensures that the compiler does not incorrectly eliminate communication that is actually not redundant. Even though $INSERT_i$ is potentially overestimated, our framework guards against inserting extra communication by never overestimating $PPIN_i$ and $PPOUT_i$. The Morel-Renvoise framework [17] and its modified versions ensure that $PPIN_i$ and $PPOUT_i$ represent safe placements of computation. Correspondingly, in the context of our work, $PPIN_i/PPOUT_i$ represents no more communication than necessary at the entry/exit of node i.

4.2 Decomposition of Bidirectional Problem

Dhamdhere et al. [5] prove some properties about the bidirectional problem of eliminating redundant computation, and also prove that those properties are

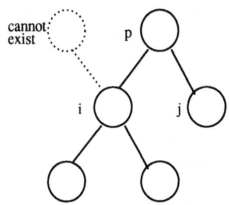

Fig. 3. Proving the decomposition of the bidirectional problem

sufficient to allow the decomposition of that problem into two unidirectional problems. One of those properties, distributivity, does not hold in our case, because we represent data-flow variables as ASDs rather than bit strings, and the operations like union and difference are not exact, unlike the boolean operations. However, we are able to prove directly the following theorem:

Theorem 1. *The bidirectional problem of determining $PPIN_i$ and $PPOUT_i$, as given by Equations 5 and 6, can be decomposed into a backward approximation, given by Equations 9 and 10, followed by a forward correction, given by Equation 11.*

$$BA\_PPIN_i = ANTLOC_i \cup (PPOUT_i - KILL_i) \qquad (9)$$

$$PPOUT_i = \cap_{s \in succ(i)} BA\_PPIN_s \qquad (10)$$

$$PPIN_i = BA\_PPIN_i \cap [\cap_{p \in pred(i)}(AVOUT_p \cup PPOUT_p)] \qquad (11)$$

Proof: BA_PPIN_i represents a *backward approximation* to the value of $PPIN_i$. We will show that the correction term $(\cap_{p \in pred(i)}(AVOUT_p \cup PPOUT_p))$ applied to a node i to obtain $PPIN_i$ cannot lead to a change in the value of $PPOUT$ for *any* node in the control flow graph, and that in turn implies that the $PPIN$ values of other nodes are also unaffected by this change.

The correction term, being an intersection operation, can only lead to a reduction in the value of the set $PPIN_i$. Let $X = BA\_PPIN_i - PPIN_i$ denote this reduction, and let x denote an arbitrary element of X. Thus, $x \in BA\_PPIN_i$, and $x \notin PPIN_i$. Hence, there must exist a predecessor of i, say, node p (see Figure 3), such that: $x \notin AVOUT_p$ and $x \notin PPOUT_p$. Therefore, p must have another child j such that $x \notin BA\_PPIN_j$, otherwise x would have been included in $PPOUT_p$. Now let us consider the possible effects of removal of x from $PPIN_i$. From the given equations, a change in the value of $PPIN_i$ can only affect the value of $PPOUT$ for a predecessor of i (which can possibly lead to other changes). Clearly, the value of $PPOUT_p$ does not change because $PPOUT_p$ already does not include x. But node i cannot have any predecessors other than

p because p is a branch node, and by virtue of the edge splitting transformation on the control flow graph, there can be no edge from a branch node to a join node. Hence, the application of the correction term at a node i cannot change the $PPOUT$ value of any node: this implies the validity of the above process of decomposing the bidirectional problem.

4.3 Overall Data-Flow Procedure

Thus, our data flow analysis procedure consists of three passes over the control flow graph of the program. The first pass is a forward pass that determines $AVOUT_i$ and $AVIN_i$ for different nodes. The second pass goes backwards, determining the values of BA_PPIN_i and $PPOUT_i$. Finally, there is a forward correction pass that determines $PPIN_i$. During the final pass, $INSERT_i$ and $REDUND_i$ are also determined for each node. We now describe how we use interval analysis to handle loops in the program.

INTERVAL ANALYSIS Interval analysis is precisely defined in [4]. The analysis is performed in two phases, an *elimination phase* and a *propagation phase*, that are explained below. We use Tarjan intervals [21], which correspond to program loops. Given a structured program, each interval has a unique header node h. As a further restriction, we require each interval to have a single loop exit node l. The edge-splitting transformation, discussed earlier, adds a node b to split the back-edge $\langle l, h \rangle$ into two edges, $\langle l, b \rangle$ and $\langle b, h \rangle$.

Elimination Phase The elimination phase processes the program intervals in a bottom-up (innermost to outermost) traversal. The nodes of each interval are visited in a forward or backward traversal, depending on whether the data-flow problem is forward or backward. After each interval has been processed, its dataflow information is summarized and is associated with its header node, and the interval is logically collapsed. We now describe how the values of local data-flow variables, $ANTLOC$, $CGEN$, and $KILL$ are summarized for nodes corresponding to program intervals. These values are used in the computations of global data-flow variables, in the propagation phase.

The computation of $ANTLOC$ proceeds in the backward direction. The anticipatability of communication at exit from the last node, $ANTOUT_l$, is initialized to $\emptyset$. Then the transfer functions given by Equations 3 and 4 are applied to each statement during the backward traversal of the interval. Finally, $ANTOUT_h$ represents the anticipatability of communication for the interval body for a single loop iteration. The communication for the entire interval that precedes the data definition is summarized by "expanding" on $ANTOUT_h$, and subtracting the ASD corresponding to the expanded form of all definitions, FD, that are sources of a flow dependence carried by the loop (since those definitions correspond to data communicated in later iterations of the loop):

$$ANTLOC_h = \text{expand}(ANTIN_h, k, low : high) - (\cup_{FD}\text{expand}(FD, k, low : high))$$

Definition. For an ASD set S, and a loop with index k varying from *low* to *high*, *expand*$(S, k, low : high)$ is a function that replaces all single data item references $\alpha * k + \beta$ used in any array section descriptor D in S by the triple $(\alpha * low + \beta : \alpha * high + \beta : \alpha)$, and any mapping function of the form $F_i(j) = c * k + o$ by $F_i(j) = c * low + o : c * high + o : c$.

The forward computations of $KILL$ and $CGEN$ for the collapsed interval are obtained in a similar manner. Those are described in [12], and summarized below:

$$KILL_h = \text{expand}(K_l, k, low : high)$$
$$CGEN_h = \text{expand}(AVOUT_l, k, low : high) - (\cup_{AD}\text{expand}(AD, k, low : high))$$

where K_l and $AVOUT_l$ respectively represent the data killed and the data made available by the loop body in one iteration, and AD represents each definition that is the target of an anti-dependence carried by the loop.

Propagation Phase The propagation phase processes the program intervals in a top-down (outermost to innermost) traversal, and the nodes of each interval are visited in a forward or backward traversal. Thus, data flow information from outside is propagated to nodes inside the interval. During this node traversal, any inner interval is treated as a single node represented by its header. Our analysis calculates the data flow information for a loop iteration k. For the first pass obtaining the forward solution of $AVIN/AVOUT$, and the second pass obtaining the backward solution of $BA\_PPIN/PPOUT$, the values of $AVIN_h$ and $PPOUT_l$ at the beginning of the kth loop iteration are given by:

$$AVIN_h^k = [AVIN_h^{low} - \text{expand}(K_l, k, low : k - 1)] \cup$$
$$[\text{expand}(AVOUT_l, k, low : k - 1) - (\cup_{AD}\text{expand}(AD, k, low : k - 1))]$$
$$PPOUT_l^k = [PPOUT_l^{low} - \text{expand}(K_l, k, low : k - 1)] \cup$$
$$[\text{expand}(ANTIN_h, k, low : k - 1) - (\cup_{FD}\text{expand}(FD, k, low : k - 1))]$$

Explanation $AVIN_h^{low}$ represents the data that is available at entry to the header before the loop is entered. The data available at the beginning of iteration k consists of:

1. The data made available before the loop is entered which is not killed in iterations $low : k - 1$, and
2. The data made available on all previous iterations $low : k - 1$, which has not been killed before iteration k.

The two terms unioned together in the above equation for $AVIN_h^k$ correspond to these two components. The equation for $PPOUT_l^k$ is obtained in a similar manner.

The transfer functions given by Equations 1 and 2, and by Equations 9 and 10 are then respectively applied in the two passes to obtain data flow information for the remaining nodes. Finally, during propagation phase of the third pass, the forward correction as given by Equation 11 is applied to $PPIN_i^k$ for each node i using the values of $AVOUT_i^k$ and $PPOUT_i^k$ computed earlier.

5 Communication Optimizations

Following the determination of $INSERT$ and $REDUND$ for each node, communications corresponding to the values of $INSERT$ are placed at the exits of nodes, and the values of $REDUND$ are used to delete redundant communication. We now describe how different optimizations are captured by the data flow procedure that we have described. Message vectorization is accounted for by the computation of $ANTLOC$ for an entire interval, as it characterizes the communication that can be moved outside a loop. Since message vectorization is a well-understood optimization implemented by most distributed memory compilers based on data-dependence [24, 18, 14, 16, 15, 11], we shall focus on other important optimizations that require the generality of data-flow analysis.

Both of the equations for determining $INSERT$ and $REDUND$ inherently capture the elimination of redundant communication. When communication is moved and inserted at some other place, the available data ($AVOUT$) and the communication corresponding to ($PPIN - KILL$) is subtracted from it, as shown by Equation 7. $REDUND$ refers not only to communication made redundant by the availability of data due to some other communication, but also serves to wipe out original communication that has been moved to a different point and which appears in the $INSERT$ term at its new place.

During the remainder of our discussion, we shall refer to the original communication being optimized as $COMM = \langle D_1, M_1 \rangle$ and to the redundant part of the communication being deleted as $DELETE = \langle D_2, M_2 \rangle$. This redundant part could correspond to $REDUND$ or to the communication being subtracted in the equation for $INSERT$. We shall use the notation $D \rightarrow VPROCS(M(D))$ to represent the communication $\langle D, M \rangle$.

5.1 Elimination of redundant communication

If $COMM \subseteq DELETE$, i.e., if $D_1 \subseteq D_2$, and $M_1(D_1) \subseteq M_2(D_1)$, the communication of D_1 to processors $M_1(D_1)$ is redundant because the data is already available at those processors under the mapping function M_2. Hence, $COMM$ can be eliminated.

For example, in Figure 1(a), the communication for d just before statement (15) is $COMM = d(i) \rightarrow VPROCS(i, 100), i = 1 : 100$. From our data flow procedure, $PPIN = d(i) \rightarrow VPROCS(i, 1 : 100), i = 1 : 100)$ at this point in the program. Hence, $DELETE$ corresponds to $REDUND = d(i) \rightarrow VPROCS(i, 100), i = 1 : 100$. Since $COMM = DELETE$, this communication can be completely eliminated.

5.2 Reduction in volume of communication

Even if $COMM \nsubseteq DELETE$, a non-empty $DELETE$ can still lead to a reduction in the volume of communication. The reduced amount of communication is given by:

$$COMM^{new} = \langle D_1, M_1 \rangle - \langle D_2, M_2 \rangle$$
$$= \text{list}(\langle D_1 - D_2, M_1 \rangle, \langle D_1, M_1 - M_2 \rangle) \tag{12}$$

Under different conditions, this reduction could mean that the amount of data being communicated is reduced, or the number of processors to which data is sent could be reduced.

Reduction in amount of data The second term in Equation 12 evaluates to null and the new communication involves a reduced amount of data being sent to the same processors if $M_1(D_1) \subseteq M_2(D_1)$, but $D_1 \not\subseteq D_2$. Intuitively, this case implies that D_1 does not include all of D_2, but the set of processors, to which any element common to D_1 and D_2 has to be sent under communication $\langle D_1 \cap D_2, M_1 \rangle$, is a subset of the set of processors where that element is already available under the mapping function M_2. Hence, the amount of data being communicated can be reduced from D_1 to $D_1 - D_2$.

For example, in Figure 1(a), the communication of e just before statement 24 is $COMM = e(i) \rightarrow VPROCS(i, 1 : 100), i = 1 : 100$. Our algorithm moves this communication to the point just after statement 13. The computation of $INSERT$ for e subtracts the availability of data at this point, which is $e(i) \rightarrow VPROCS(i, 1 : 100), i = 2 : 100$, *i.e.*, all but the first element of the vector e are already available on the columns of VPROCS. Hence, the new communication inserted at this point is: $COMM^{new} = e(1) \rightarrow VPROCS(1, 1 : 100)$, which represents a reduction of data.

Reduction in number of processors involved The first term in Equation 12 evaluates to null and the new communication involves the same data being sent to fewer processors if $D_1 \subseteq D_2$, but $M_1(D_1) \not\subseteq M_2(D_1)$. This case arises when the data to be communicated is a subset of the data that is available, though it is available at fewer processors than needed. Thus, the data D_1 can be sent to just the extra processors, $M_1(D_1) - M_2(D_1)$, where it is not available.

This is illustrated in Figure 4: after message vectorization, the communication for variable d at the point just before statement 5 is $d(i) \rightarrow VPROCS(i, 1 : 100), i = 1 : 25$. Our data flow procedure moves it before statement 1. The data already available $(AVOUT)$ at this point is $d(i) \rightarrow VPROCS(i, 1 : 50), i = 1 : 100$. On subtracting this component from the communication being moved, the inserted communication is determined to be $COMM^{new} = d(i) \rightarrow VPROCS(i, 51 : 100), i = 1 : 25$. Thus, data is sent to fewer processors.

A possible negative side-effect of reducing the volume of communication by subtracting the redundant component is that a single communication may be broken into a number of smaller communications, which may not be desirable. However, this side-effect can always be controlled because the result of the difference operation in Equation 12 can always be overestimated to give back $\langle D_1, M_1 \rangle$, the original communication. While in some cases such as the ones illustrated above, the optimization will definitely reduce the cost of communication, in general the compiler needs a cost estimator to guide these decisions.

```
     HPF align (i, j) with VPROCS(i,j) :: a, z
     HPF align (i) with VPROCS(i,1) :: d, w
```
$d(i) \rightarrow VPROCS(i, 1:50), i = 1:100$ $d(i) \rightarrow VPROCS(i, 1:50), i = 1:100$

                                                $d(i) \rightarrow VPROCS(i, 51:100), i = 1:25$

```
1:   do i = 1, 100                     do i = 1, 100
2:      do j = 1, 50                       do j = 1, 50
3:         a(i,j) = a(i,j) * d(j)             a(i,j) = a(i,j) * d(j)
4:      end do                             end do
5:   end do                            end do
```
$d(i) \rightarrow VPROCS(i, 1:100), i = 1:25$
```
6:   do i = 1, 25                      do i = 1, 25
7:      do j = 1, 100                      do j = 1, 100
8:         z(i,j) = a(i,j-1) * d(i)           z(i,j) = a(i,j-1) * d(i)
9:      end do                             end do
10:  end do                            end do
```

            (a)   (b)

Fig. 4. Example illustrating reduction in number of processors

5.3 Movement of communication for subsumption and for hiding latency

Since our framework moves communications as early as legally possible, subsumption of communication placed earlier in the original program is naturally taken care of by the data-flow equations. For example, going back to Figure 1, $INSERT$ for d before statement (8) is determined to be $d(i) \rightarrow VPROCS(i, 1 : 100), i = 1 : 100$, i.e, our analysis procedure hoists this communication from statement (24) to (8). As explained earlier, since $REDUND$ for d at statement (15) is $d(i) \rightarrow VPROCS(i, 100), i = 1 : 100$, the communication of d at this point is *subsumed*.

Our data flow analysis procedure moves communications as early as legally possible and avoids introducing unnecessary communication, thus handling conditional control flow effectively. Traditionally, researchers have proposed inserting sends ahead of receives to help hide the latency of communication. In the context of our framework, a better approach would be to place *non-blocking* receives and *blocking* sends[2] at the point of insertion of communication, and inserting a wait at the reference to non-local data for the receive to be over before reading that data. This leads to the initiation of communication at the earliest possible point (under the constraint that there is no speculative communication), and waiting for the data to arrive only when it is needed. Thus,

---

[2] Blocking send can also be used, but in that case the compiler has to insert a wait for the send to be over before overwriting that data.

for communication that can be moved significantly further ahead, much of the latency can be hidden.

6 Conclusions

We have presented a data-flow framework for reducing communication costs in a program. This framework provides a unified algorithm for performing a number of optimizations that eliminate redundant communication and that reduce the volume of communication, by reducing both the data and the number of processors involved. The algorithm also determines the earliest point at which communication can legally be moved, without introducing extra communication. That helps hide the latency of communication. This algorithm is quite general, it handles control flow and performs optimizations across loop nests. An advantage of our approach is that the analysis is performed at the granularity of sections of arrays and processors, that significantly enhances the scope of optimizations based on eliminating partial redundancies. We prove that in the context of an ASD representation also, the bidirectional problem of determining placement can be decomposed into a backward problem followed by a forward correction.

Future work will involve extending the data flow framework to perform interprocedural optimizations, and developing algorithms for additional optimizations that exploit the fact that processors other than the owners can also send values to processors that need them. Also, experience is needed with the ASDs, to determine the effectiveness and the cost of this analysis in practice.

References

1. A. V. Aho, R. Sethi, and J. D. Ullman. *Compilers: principles, techniques, and tools.* Addison-Wesley, 1986.
2. F. E. Allen and J. Cocke. A program data flow analysis procedure. *Communications of the ACM*, 19(3):137–147, March 1976.
3. S. P. Amarasinghe and M. S. Lam. Communication optimization and code generation for distributed memory machines. In *Proc. ACM SIGPLAN '93 Conference on Programming Language Design and Implementation*, Albuquerque, New Mexico, June 1993.
4. M. Burke. An interval-based approach to exhaustive and incremental interprocedural data-flow analysis. *ACM Transactions on Programming Languages and Systems*, 12(3):341–395, July 1990.
5. D. M. Dhamdhere, B. K. Rosen, and F. K. Zadeck. How to analyze large programs efficiently and informatively. In *Proc. ACM SIGPLAN '92 Conference on Programming Language Design and Implementation*, San Francisco, CA, June 1992.
6. High Performance Fortran Forum. High Performance Fortran language specification, version 1.0. Technical Report CRPC-TR92225, Rice University, May 1993.
7. C. Gong, R. Gupta, and R. Melhem. Compilation techniques for optimizing communication in distributed-memory systems. In *Proc. 1993 International Conference on Parallel Processing*, St. Charles, IL, August 1993.

8. E. Granston and A. Veidenbaum. Detecting redundant accesses to array data. In *Proc. Supercomputing '91*, pages 854–965, 1991.

9. T. Gross and P. Steenkiste. Structured dataflow analysis for arrays and its use in an optimizing compiler. *Software - Practice and Experience*, 20(2):133–155, February 1990.

10. M. Gupta and P. Banerjee. A methodology for high-level synthesis of communication on multicomputers. In *Proc. 6th ACM International Conference on Supercomputing*, Washington D.C., July 1992.

11. M. Gupta, S. Midkiff, E. Schonberg, P. Sweeney, K.Y. Wang, and M. Burke. PTRAN II: A compiler for High Performance Fortran. In *Proc. 4th Workshop on Compilers for Parallel Computers*, Delft, Netherlands, December 1993.

12. M. Gupta and E. Schonberg. A framework for exploiting data availability to optimize communication. In *Proc. 6th Workshop on Languages and Compilers for Parallel Computing*, Portland, OR, August 1993.

13. P. Havlak and K. Kennedy. An implementation of interprocedural bounded regular section analysis. *IEEE Transactions on Parallel and Distributed Systems*, 2(3):350–360, July 1991.

14. S. Hiranandani, K. Kennedy, and C. Tseng. Compiling Fortran D for MIMD distributed-memory machines. *Communications of the ACM*, 35(8):66–80, August 1992.

15. C. Koelbel and P. Mehrotra. Compiling global name-space parallel loops for distributed execution. *IEEE Transactions on Parallel and Distributed Systems*, 2(4):440–451, October 1991.

16. J. Li and M. Chen. Compiling communication-efficient programs for massively parallel machines. *IEEE Transactions on Parallel and Distributed Systems*, 2(3):361–376, July 1991.

17. E. Morel and C. Renvoise. Global optimization by suppression of partial redundancies. *Communications of the ACM*, 22(2):96–103, February 1979.

18. A. Rogers and K. Pingali. Process decomposition through locality of reference. In *Proc. SIGPLAN '89 Conference on Programming Language Design and Implementation*, pages 69–80, June 1989.

19. C. Rosene. *Incremental Dependence Analysis*. PhD thesis, Rice University, March 1990.

20. E. Su, D. J. Palermo, and P. Banerjee. Automating parallelization of regular computations for distributed memory multicomputers in the PARADIGM compiler. In *Proc. 1993 International Conference on Parallel Processing*, St. Charles, IL, August 1993.

21. R. E. Tarjan. Testing flow graph reducibility. *Journal of Computer and System Sciences*, 9(3):355–365, December 1974.

22. R. v. Hanxleden and K. Kennedy. A code placement framework and its application to communication generation. Technical Report CRPC-TR93337, Rice University, October 1993.

23. R. v. Hanxleden, K. Kennedy, C. Koelbel, R. Das, and J. Saltz. Compiler analysis for irregular problems in Fortran D. In *Proc. 5th Workshop on Languages and Compilers for Parallel Computing*, New Haven, CT, August 1992.

24. H. Zima, H. Bast, and M. Gerndt. SUPERB: A tool for semi-automatic MIMD/SIMD parallelization. *Parallel Computing*, 6:1–18, 1988.

Interprocedural Communication Optimizations for Distributed Memory Compilation

Gagan Agrawal and Joel Saltz

Department of Computer Science,
University of Maryland, College Park
MD 20742
{gagan,saltz}@cs.umd.edu

Abstract. Managing communication is a difficult problem in distributed memory compilation. When the exact data to be communicated cannot be determined at compile time, communication optimizations can be performed by runtime routines which generate *schedule* for communication. This leads to two optimization problems: placing communication so that data once communicated can be reused if possible and placing *schedule calls* so that the result of runtime preprocessing can be reused for communicating as many times as possible. In large application codes, computation and communication is spread across multiple subroutines, so acceptable performance cannot be achieved without performing these optimizations across subroutine boundaries. In this paper, we present an Interprocedural Analysis Framework for these two optimization problems. Our optimizations are based on a program abstraction we call *Control & Call Flow Graph*. This extends the *call graph* abstraction by storing the control flow relations between various call sites within a subroutine. We show how communication placement and schedule call placement problems can be solved by data-flow analysis on *Control & Call Flow Graph* structure.

1 Introduction

In recent years, there have been major efforts in developing language and compiler support for programming distributed memory machines. High Performance Fortran (HPF) has recently been proposed as a Fortran extension for programming these machines [20]. To obtain good performance on distributed memory parallel machines, it is important to efficiently manage communication between processors. Parallel programming languages like HPF allow the programmer to specify data distribution; a good choice of data distribution can reduce the total volume of communication between processors. Still, because of large communication latencies and a relatively small bandwidth offered by current day machines, the communication costs can become a significant factor in many applications.

---

[1] This work was supported by NSF under grant No. ASC 9213821 and by ONR under contract No. N00014-93-1-0158. The authors assume all responsibility for the contents of the paper.

It is important for the compiler to make use of communication optimizations like message vectorization, message coalescing and message aggregation [21] to keep the communication overheads low.

Making communication efficient is a major challenge for the compilers for distributed memory machines. It is often not possible to determine the exact communication required at compile time. This may happen because data distribution may not be known at compile time, exact loop bounds and strides may not be compile time constants or the data may be accessed through indirection arrays whose contents are not known at compile time. In these cases, it may not be possible for the compiler to ensure optimized communication. The compiler can, however, insert calls to runtime primitives which can determine the exact data to be communicated and obtain optimized communication performance. PARTI/CHAOS runtime system for irregular [9] and regular [2, 30] applications provides routines with these functionalities. In this approach, a *schedule* building primitive is called at runtime which computes the exact communication required. *Datamove* primitives can use the *schedule* generated to communicate between processors.

The compiler now needs to insert calls to appropriate runtime primitives to optimize communication. Compiler techniques have been developed for recognizing data access patterns at compile time and inserting calls to appropriate primitives [1, 3, 17]. Runtime optimization primitives can be expensive, so it is important to reuse the result of runtime preprocessing whenever possible. For example, if the set of data elements to be accessed does not change over multiple iterations of a loop, then the schedule generated by the first iteration can be reused by the successive ones. Similarly, if the same data elements need to be accessed by several different loops in the program, then the same schedule can be used across these loops. It is also possible that data once communicated may still be valid while executing a later loop and may therefore not have to be communicated again.

Large application programs typically involve large numbers of procedures or subroutines. Therefore, it is important to perform compiler analysis and optimizations for schedule calls and communication placement across subroutine boundaries. Techniques for optimized communication placement have been developed [18] but are restricted to a single subroutine level.

In this paper we present interprocedural analysis framework for communication and schedule call placement optimizations in distributed memory compilation. Traditionally, interprocedural analysis has been based upon a program abstraction *call graph* [15, 16]. A call graph is a directed graph whose nodes represent procedures or subroutines in the program and a directed edge represents procedure invocation. We have found this abstraction to be insufficient for performing interprocedural analysis and optimizations for communication and schedule call placement. For our purpose, we use a program abstraction we call *Control & Call Flow Graph (C&CFG)*. This program abstraction captures the control flow relationships between various call sites within a subroutine. We show how communication placement and schedule call placement can be optimized by data-flow analysis over a *C&CFG*.

The rest of this paper is organized as follows. In Section 2, we further discuss distributed memory compilation and formalize the optimization problems. In Section 3, we define *Control & Call Flow Graph*, which is the basis for our analysis. Interprocedural analysis and transforms are presented in Section 4. In Section 5, we compare our scheme with other approaches. We conclude in Section 6.

2 Distributed Memory Compilation

In this section we discuss distributed memory compilation. We discuss how runtime preprocessing can be used for optimizing communication in a number of cases when the exact set of data to be communicated cannot be determined at compile time. We discuss this in context of two different sets of codes: regular and irregular. In this paper, by irregular codes we mean codes in which data is accessed through indirection arrays in parallel loops. Codes which do use an indirection array while accessing data are regular codes.

2.1 Compiling Regular Codes

In a parallel loop,if data is accessed without using indirection arrays, all loop bounds and strides are compile time constants and data distribution is known at compile time; then the compiler can determine new loop bounds on each processor and the exact set of data elements to be communicated. In this case, the compiler can perform various communication optimizations [22]. However, if all information is not available at compile time, then the compiler may need to insert symbolic calculations in the generated code to determine new loop bounds and data sets to be communicated. This can become very complicated, especially when the data is not block distributed, data distribution is not known or there are (possibly) non-unit strides. The compilation task can be simplified by inserting calls to runtime primitives which can determine new loop bounds, exact data sets to be communicated and can perform communication optimizations. In practice, application codes are written to execute on varying problem sizes or problem instances and therefore loop bounds and strides may not be compile time constants, or data distribution may not be known at compile time.

2.2 Compiling Irregular Codes

Irregular codes are codes which access data through indirection arrays. In Figure 1, we show a parallel loop in which array *y* is accessed through an indirection array *ia*. The elements of the array *y* that need to be communicated depends upon the contents of array *ia*. Often it may be beneficial to distribute the array *y* based upon the contents of array *ia* [27]. This distribution can only be carried out at runtime after the contents of array *ia* have been read in or have been computed.

```
        Real   X(m), Y(m)      ! data arrays
        Integer IA(n)          ! indirection array

C    ORIGINAL HPF CODE
        forall i =  1, n  X(i)  =  X(i) + Y(IA(i))

C    COMPILED CODE
C    Build the required schedule
        Sched   =  Irreg_Sched(.. parameters ..)
C    Commnicate data using the schedule build above
        Call Data_Move(Y,Sched)

C    Actual Loop
        do 10  i =   1, n_local
        X(i) =  X(i) +  Y(IA_local(i))
10    continue
```

Fig. 1. Compiling a HPF irregular loop

Runtime preprocessing can be used to optimize communication. CHAOS primitives for irregular problems [9] provide such functionality. In Figure 1, we also show how SPMD code can be generated for the given irregular loop. A communication schedule is generated by a call to *Irreg_Sched*, which analyzes the contents of array *ia* to determine the exact communication required. The required data are sent or received by the *Data_Move* primitive.

2.3 Optimization Problems

In both regular and irregular applications, runtime preprocessing can be used to optimize communication whenever the data set to be communicated cannot be determined at compile time. Runtime preprocessing (i.e. calls to routines *Reg_Sched* or *Irreg_Sched*) can be expensive. Large application programs often present opportunities for reusing schedule several times [9]. Large scientific and engineering computations are often iterative in nature, which means that there is a main time step loop to iterate over a set of routines performing the computation. It is often possible to use the same set of schedules over different iterations. Also, many computational loops, possibly spread over several subroutines, may require the same set of data elements to be communicated. In this case, same schedule can be used again and the overhead of runtime preprocessing can be reduced. In some cases, the data communicated may not have been modified, so a loop executed later may just use the data communicated for executing an earlier loop.

We can, therefore, formulate two different optimization problems for distributed memory compilation. *Schedule Call Placement* means optimized placement of schedules and their reuse to reduce the overhead of runtime preprocessing. *Communication Placement* means optimized placement of communication and avoiding redundant communication. Clearly, each of these placement problems has associated safety requirements.

In previous work, techniques have been developed for optimized communication placement within a single subroutine [18]. Schedule call placement within a single subroutine can be addressed using methods for Partial Redundancy Elimination [11, 25]. However, no efforts have been made to perform these optimizations across subroutine boundaries. Without optimized schedule call placement and communication placement across subroutine boundaries, it will not be possible to obtain reasonable performance on large applications.

3 Control & Call Flow Graph

In traditional interprocedural analysis, program is abstracted by a *call graph* [15, 16]. In a call graph $G = (V, E)$, V is the set of subroutines and directed edge $e = (i, j)$ ($e \in E$) represents a call site in which subroutine i invokes subroutine j. The limitation of call graph is that no information is available about control flow relationships between various call sites within a subroutine. This information is important for schedule call placement and communication placement problems. For reusing schedules over computational loops which are in different subroutines, we need to know the relationship between call sites invoking these subroutines. We, therefore, define a new program abstraction *Control & Call Flow Graph* (*C&CFG*), which stores control flow relationships between call sites within a subroutine. Our program abstraction is similar to Callahan's program abstraction, Program Summary Graph, which includes intraprocedural edges based upon reaching definitions [5]. This abstraction was defined for interprocedural reaching definitions analysis. In Section 5, we compare our abstraction *C&CFG* with Callahan's Program Summary Graph.

3.1 Definitions

We focus on imperative languages. In our discussion, we refer by subroutine any separate program unit, i.e. procedures or functions in Pascal, subroutines or functions in Fortran or functions in C, including main function or procedure. We assume, for convenience, that a subroutine can only be invoked through a separate call statement. Invocation of any subroutine ends by execution of a return statement. Every subroutine has one or more return statements. To explain the abstraction *C&CFG*, we use the following definitions:

Definition 1: Call Restricted Basic Block (*CRBB*) is a sequence of consecutive statements in a subroutine, excluding any call or return statement, in which the flow enters at the beginning and leaves at the end without possibility of branching except at the end.

A *CRBB* is a basic block [4] with the restriction that no call or return statement is allowed within it. A subroutine can be partitioned into a set of *CRBBs*, a set of call statements and a set of return statements. For the purpose of our discussion, we further assume that each subroutine has a unique *start* node.

Definition 2: Extended Control Flow Graph (*ECFG*) of a subroutine is a directed graph $G = (V, E)$, where the set of nodes V consists of a start node, all *CRBBs*, call statements and return statements in the subroutine. An edge $e \in E$, $e = (i, j)$ represents possible flow of control from node i to node j. If node i is a call statement, then edge e represents possible control flow from return of the subroutine invoked by this call statement. If node j is a return statement, then edge e represents possible flow of control from node i to the end of invocation of the subroutine.

An *ECFG* is a control flow graph [4] in which call statements and return statements are considered as separate nodes. The start node has no incoming edge and nodes for return statements have no outgoing edges.

Definition 3: Control & Call Flow Graph (*C&CFG*) of a program is a directed multigraph $G = (V, E)$, where the set of nodes V consists of an entry node and a return node for each subroutine in the program, and the edges are of two types: **Invocation** edges and **Flow** edges. Associated with every flow edge $e \in E$, there is a list l of *CRBBs*. This list l consists of *CRBBs* which may be visited during flow of control between source and sink of the edge, without visiting any other call statement.

For subroutine i, the entry node is denoted by e_i and the return node is denoted by r_i. If subroutine i possibly invokes subroutine j, then invocation edge (e_i, e_j) exists. Flow edges are inserted in the following cases:

1. Subroutines i and j are invoked by subroutine k, and there is path p in *ECFG* of k from a call site invoking i to a call site invoking j which does not include any other call statements. Flow edge (r_i, e_j) exists in this case. The list l consists of *CRBBs* of subroutine k, which may occur in path p from call to i to call to j such that path p does not include any other call statements.

2. Subroutine i invokes subroutine j and there is path p in *ECFG* of i from the *start* node of subroutine i to a call site invoking j which does not include any other call statements. In this case, flow edge (e_i, e_j) exists. The list l consists of *CRBBs* of subroutine i, which may occur in in path p from *start* node of i to call for j such that path p does not include any other call statements.

3. Subroutine j invokes subroutine i and there is path p in *ECFG* of j from a call site invoking i to a return statement within subroutine j which does not include any other call statements. In this case, flow edge (r_i, r_j) exists. The list l consists of *CRBBs* of subroutine j, which may occur in path p from call to i to a return statement such that path p does not include any other call statements.

In Figure 2, we show an irregular code. This is actually a much striped down version of an Euler equation solver on an irregular mesh [9]. The *C&CFG* for this code is shown in Figure 3.

```
        Program Euler
        Real X(nnodes), Y(nnodes)
        Integer IA(nedges), IB(nedges)

C       Input data ...
        do 10 i = 1, nsteps
        Call Dflux(X,Y,IA,IB)
        Call Eflux(Y,IA)
        if (nt .gt. 0) then
        Call Psmoo(Y,IB)
        endif
        do 10 j = 1, nedges
        IB(j) = .. IB(j) ..
10      continue
        return
        end

        Subroutine Dflux(A,B,C,D)
        if (nfac .gt. 0) then
        do 20 i = 1, nedges
        A(i) = A(i) + B(C(i))
20      continue
        endif
        do 30 i = 1, nedges
        A(i) = A(i) + B(D(i))
30      continue
        return
        end

        Subroutine Eflux(Y,IA)
        if (nfac .gt. 0) then
        do 40 i = 1, nedges
        Y(i) = Y(i) + Y(IA(i))
40      continue
        endif
        return
        end

        Subroutine Psmoo(A,B)
        do 50 i = 1, nedges
        A(i) = A(i) + A(B(i))
50      continue
        return
        end
```

Fig. 2. An Irregular Code

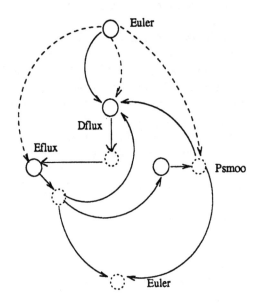

○ Entry Node

◌ Return Node

── Flow Edge

---· Invocation Edge

Fig. 3. *C&CFG* for program Euler

4 Interprocedural Analysis

In this section, we discuss the interprocedural analysis framework for optimizing schedule call and communication placement. We assume that a schedule call or runtime preprocessing is placed as a single statement (possibly call to a library routine) in the subroutine. We also assume that in the code generated after intraprocedural compilation, communication is placed in form of calls to a collective communication routine (similar to *Data_Move* primitive we presented in our examples in Section 2). The implementation of such routine typically includes calls to sends and receives. We do not consider the possibility of separating sends and receives. By considering sends and receives part of the same statement, we can treat schedule calls and communication statements in identical fashion, keeping our scheme simple. For the purpose of our discussion, we refer to a communication statement or schedule call statement, which is a candidate for interprocedural optimization, a *candidate*. A candidate is a call to a library or message passing routine, and we will refer to the actual arguments passed to it as the *parameters* of the candidate.

Our algorithm has three phases: an initial local analysis, an interprocedural propagation phase and a final local placement phase. The initial local analysis collects candidates for interprocedural redundancy elimination. The interprocedural analysis phase solves redundancy elimination problem on a *C&CFG*. The final local placement phase is required for final exact placement of the candidate inside the subroutine after the interprocedural propagation phase has determined which subroutine each candidate has to be placed in. Our scheme is applicable on an arbitrarily shaped *C&CFG*, so it can handle recursive procedures. We have not considered the possibility of aliasing in our current work. Before discussing the details of the three phases of algorithm, we briefly review the classical redundancy elimination techniques.

4.1 Intraprocedural Redundancy Elimination

The problem of candidate placement comprises of two different optimization problems: eliminating redundant candidates and hoisting loop invariant candidates. These two optimization problems were solved intraprocedurally in a common framework by Morel and Renvoise [25], calling it partial redundancy elimination. This scheme has been further extended and refined by Dhamdhere [11], Drechsler [12], Knoop et. al. [24] and Sorkin [29].

Partial redundancy elimination is modeled as a data-flow problem on an arbitrarily shaped control flow graph of a subroutine. It considers single statements, which have some *computation* associated with them, as the unit for placement. Data-flow analysis is done for each statement to determine the earliest possible placement. The analysis is based upon three properties: *transparency* of a basic block, which means that the variables involved in the computation are not modified in the basic block; *availability* at a point in the control flow graph which means that if the computation is placed at this point, it will deliver the same result as the last computation made before this point and *anticipability* at a point in the control flow graph, which means that the computation placed at this point will have the same result as the first computation after this point. Availability and anticipability are computed over the flow graph by data-flow analysis, using the transparency information available for the basic blocks. Using availability and anticipability, placement of the computation is determined. We do not present the details of the algorithm and data-flow equations here.

A redundancy elimination technique, like Morel's scheme, can only eliminate computations which are lexically identical. Other techniques have been developed for eliminating unnecessary pieces from the program, even if they are not in the form of lexically identical computations. Value numbering [28] is such a technique for determining when two computations are equivalent. We use a hybrid version between Morel's redundancy elimination and value numbering technique for interprocedural redundancy elimination. For each candidate for placement, we determine its program slice [31] with respect to the subroutine. In comparing communication and schedule calls placed in the different subroutines, we consider their slices with respect to the subroutines within which they were initially placed.

4.2 Initial Local Analysis

Consider any subroutine. In the local analysis phase, an intraprocedural redundancy elimination scheme removes redundant communication and schedule calls within a subroutine and places them as early as possible [25, 18]. The following analysis is carried out for each candidate in the subroutine. We compute slice of the subroutine with respect to the parameters of candidate at the point in the subroutine where candidate is called. A program (subroutine) slice is defined as a program comprising of a set of statements which contribute, either directly or indirectly, to the value of certain variables at a certain point in the program [10, 31]. This set of variables and the point in the program is together refered to as the slicing criterion. For our purpose, the slicing criterion used is the set of parameters of candidate, at the point in the program where candidate is invoked.

After computing the slice, we identify all global variables and formal parameters of the subroutine which contribute, either directly or indirectly, to the value of any of the parameters of the candidate. (These are simply the global variables and formal parameters which appear in the slice). This set of global variables and formal parameters is called *influencers* of the candidate. For simplicity, we treat arrays as scalar, which means that any array which is a global variable or a formal parameter, either contributes to the value of parameters of candidate or does not, individual elements of the array or regular sections [19] are not considered.

Note that if we were interested in determining only the influencer set, we do not need to compute slices, it can be done just with SSA Graph [8]. The purpose of using a program slice is that we are interested in moving not just the candidate, but the entire slice associated with the candidate.

```
      Program Euler
      Real X(nnodes), Y(nnodes)
      Integer IA(nedges), IB(nedges)
C     Input data ...
      do 10 i = 1, nsteps
      Call Dflux(X,Y,IA,IB)
      Call Eflux(Y,IA)
      if (nt .gt. 0) then
      Call Psmoo(Y,IB)
      endif
      do 10 j = 1, nedges_local
      IB(j) = .. IB(j) ..
10    continue

      Subroutine Dflux(A,B,C,D)
      Sched2 = Irreg_Sched(D)
      if (nfac .gt. 0) then
      Sched1 = Irreg_Sched(C)
      Call Data_Move(B,Sched1)
      do 20 i = 1, nedges_local
      A(i) = A(i) + B(C_local(i))
20    continue
      endif
      Call Data_Move(B,Sched2)
      do 30 i = 1, nedges_local
      A(i) = A(i) + B(D_local(i))
30    continue
      Subroutine Eflux(Y,IA)
      if (nfac .gt. 0) then
      Sched3 = Irreg_Sched(IA)
      Call Data_Move(Y,Sched3)
      do 40 i = 1, nedges_local
      Y(i) = Y(i) + Y(IA_local(i))
40    continue
      endif
      Subroutine Psmoo(A,B)
      Sched4 = Irreg_Sched(B)
      Call Data_Move(A,Sched4)
      do 50 i = 1, nedges_local
      A(i) = A(i) + A(B_local(i))
50    continue
```

Fig. 4. Result of Intraprocedural Compilation

```
      Program Euler
      Real X(nnodes), Y(nnodes)
      Integer IA(nedges), IB(nedges)
C     Input data ...
      if (nfac .gt. 0) then
      Sched1 = Irreg_Sched(IA)
      endif
      do 10 i = 1, nsteps
      Sched2 = Irreg_Sched(IB)
      if (nfac .gt. 0) then
      Call Data_Move(Y,Sched1)
      endif
      Call Dflux(X,Y,IA,IB)
      Call Eflux(Y,IA)
      if (nt .gt. 0) then
      Call Psmoo(Y,IB)
      endif
      do 10 j = 1, nedges_local
      IB(j) = .. IB(j)..
10    continue
      Subroutine Dflux(A,B,C,D)
      if (nfac .gt. 0) then
      do 20 i = 1, nedges_local
      A(i) = A(i) + B(C_local(i))
20    continue
      endif
      Call Data_Move(B,Sched2)
      do 30 i = 1, nedges_local
      A(i) = A(i) + B(D_local(i))
30    continue
      Subroutine Eflux(Y,IA)
      if (nfac .gt. 0) then
      do 40 i = 1, nedges_local
      Y(i) = Y(i) + Y(IA_local(i))
40    continue
      endif
      Subroutine Psmoo(A,B)
      Call Data_Move(A,Sched2)
      do 50 i = 1, nedges_local
      A(i) = A(i) + A(B_local(i))
50    continue
```

Fig. 5. Code after Interprocedural Optimizations

An interesting case is the presence of subroutine calls in control flow from the start of the subroutine to schedule call or communication statement. It is possible to construct slices across subroutines [23], but this may be too expensive. For each such subroutine call in the control flow path of candidate, we just examine if any of the variables which contribute to the value of any parameters of the candidate, is modified by the subroutine call [7]. If so, we do not consider this candidate for hoisting outside the subroutine.

All subroutine entry nodes of $C\&CFG$ are marked with the set of candidates for placement, with lists of their influencers and their slices within the subroutine. Other information collected during initial local analysis phase is Mod and Ref set for each $CRBB$ in each subroutine. Mod set for a $CRBB$ means the set of variables which are modified, or are given a new definition in the $CRBB$. Ref set for a $CRBB$ means the set of variables which are referred to in the Call Restricted Basic Block. Mod and Ref information within subroutines is commonly computed for various intraprocedural optimizations in compilers [4]. This information is used during interprocedural propagation phase for determining safety of hoisting candidates across subroutines.

4.3 Interprocedural Propagation

Interprocedural propagation phase is based upon Morel's redundancy elimination [25]. We do not give the detailed set of data-flow equations for this redundancy elimination, but point to the differences which appear in applying Morel's algorithm on a $C\&CFG$ rather than a control flow graph.

A $C\&CFG$ has edges of two types: flow edges and invocation edges. In applying the data-flow analysis, we only consider flow edges. Consider a node i which has a candidate C marked for placement. This candidate has a set of influencers and a program slice associated with it. We need to determine its availability at successors of i and its anticipability at predecessors of i. Let a flow edge e connect node i to its successor j and l be the list of $CRBBs$ associated with the edge e. Suppose that e is the only incoming edge to j. Let k be the subroutine in which the $CRBBs$ in l are (k could be i or j also). In determining availability of C at node i's successor node j, we make use of the Mod and Ref information available for $CRBBs$ in l. In this, we need to take into account the renaming of variables across subroutine boundaries. If the node i is a subroutine entry node, (in this case, k is i), then we do need to do any renaming while examining $CRBBs$ in l. If node i is a subroutine return node, then the subroutine i is invoked from subroutine k. In invocation of subroutine i from subroutine k, there is a set of actual variables corresponding to the formal variables in subroutine i. We replace the formal parameters in the influencer set of C with the the corresponding actual parameters in invoking i. Similarly, in the program slice computed for the candidate C, formal parameters are replaced by actual parameters in invocation of subroutine i.

We then examine all the $CRBBs$ in l if any of the members of influencer set is modified or referred. If candidate C is a schedule call, it will be available at j only if none of its influencer is modified by any $CRBB$ in l. If candidate C is a communication, it will be available at j only if none of its influencer is modified by any $CRBB$ in l and the data it moves is not referred to in any of the $CRBBs$.

Renaming may need to be done again while marking a candidate available at node j. If node j is a subroutine return node, no renaming is required. Otherwise, if any member of the influencer set for candidate C is an actual parameter while invoking j, then it is replaced by the corresponding formal parameter of j.

If candidate C has been found to be available at node j, we compare C with candidates available at node j. By comparing the slices available for candidates, we can determine if any of the candidates at j is equivalent to candidate C. If so, these candidate(s) can be dropped from further consideration.

A $C\&CFG$ is a multigraph, whereas a Control Flow Graph is always a graph. A node a may have more than one outgoing flow edge to the same node b. This may happen because two or more subroutines invoke both subroutines a and b and there is a control flow path from statement calling a to statement calling b in both subroutines. In this case, while determining availability of candidate C at node b, we check the Mod information along lists of $CRBBs$ associated with all the directed edges from node a to node b.

4.4 Final Local Placement

When the data-flow analysis on $C\&CFG$ terminates, each candidate is associated with a node , possibly different from the node where it initially was. This node could be a subroutine entry node or a subroutine return node. If candidate C is associated with return node r_i, then C can be placed inside subroutine i. Intraprocedural data-flow analysis can be done to determine where exactly in subroutine i, C can be placed. If C is associated with a subroutine entry node e_i, then there are two possibilities. C can be placed inside subroutine i, at the earliest, or C can be placed before each invocation to i, in the subroutines invoking i. The second alternative is preferable in cases when i is not invoked from several different sites because intraprocedural data-flow analysis can again be used to place C as early as possible (possibly outside a loop). In placing C, entire slice corresponding to C is placed. For this, all variables written into in the slice (prior to the computation of the candidate) are privatized, i.e., a new name is given to them. While removing the code from the original subroutine, only the candidate is removed. Entire slice is not removed, since the results of the computations in the slice may contribute to other computations in the subroutine.

Example: In Figure 4, we show the result of intraprocedural compilation on an irregular code shown in Figure 2. *Irreg_Sched* and *Data_Move* calls are inserted, as discussed in Section 2. In Figure 5, we show the code after interprocedural optimizations. *Sched1* and *Sched3* are found to be equivalent, since array IA is not modified between calls to Dflux and Eflux and they are surrounded by the same if condition and nfac is not modified in the program. More over, since IA and nfac are never modified, Sched1 can be hoisted out of time step loop. Similarly, *Sched2* and *Sched4* are found to be equivalent, since array IB is not modified between calls to Dflux and Eflux. But array IB is modified in main subroutine, so this *Sched* cannot be hoisted out of time step loop. The array Y is not modified between Dflux and Eflux, so the *Data_Move* in Eflux is found equivalent to *Data_Move* in Dflux using *Sched1*. However, since Y is modified in Eflux, *Data_Move* in Psmoo is not equivalent to second *Data_Move* in Dflux, even though they use equivalent schedules.

5 Related Work

We briefly present the rational behind our program abstraction *C&CFG*. We compare it with Callahan's Program Summary Graph and other approaches to interprocedural optimization.

We are interested only in certain high-payoff optimizations, i.e. placement of schedule calls and communication statements. We basic premise in our work is that in real applications, only a relatively small number of subroutines form the major computational work, and need placement of schedule calls and communication.

Callahan's Program Summary Graph was intended to solve reaching definitions problem interprocedurally. It has separate call, entry, exit and return nodes for each parameter to a subroutine call. There are intraprocedural edges corresponding to data-flow of actual parameters between call sites. Intraprocedural edges are inserted by solving reaching definitions problem within each routine. In our framework, we are interested in placement of candidates, which have a number of influencers (global variables and formal parameters) associated with it. We do not create separate nodes for each parameter and edges for reaching definitions associated with each of them. Only two nodes, an entry node and a return node, are created for each call site and intraprocedural edges are based upon control flow between call sites and not data-flow of individual actual arguments.

Framework for Interprocedural Analysis and Transforms (FIAT) [16] has recently been proposed as a general environment for interprocedural analysis. This is based up Call Graph program abstraction but supports general annotations at nodes, which can be used to store control flow graphs of individual subroutines. We chose to store explicit control flow edges between nodes and using the enhanced graph for data-flow analysis.

Inlining is an approach for performing interprocedural transformations or optimizations by replacing each call statement by code for the subroutine [15]. While inlining appears to be a conceptually simple scheme, it can cause an explosion in the size of resulting code and has been found to cause many side-effects as well [6]. Note that if a Control Flow Graph is constructed for the inlined code, the number of nodes in the CFG can also increase substantially, because same subroutine may be inlined at several different call sites. In *C&CFG*, there is no increase in the number of nodes in the graph if subroutine is invoked several times. Data flow analysis on *C&CFG* can also determine when procedure cloning will help in improving quality of code, thus offering same benefit that inlining can possibly offer but without the same overheads. Myer has suggested concept of SuperGraph [26] which is constructed by linking control flow graphs of subroutines by inserting edges from call site in the caller to start node in callee. The total number of nodes in SuperGraph can get very large and consequently the solution may take much longer time to converge. $C\&CFG$ helps in keeping the intraprocedural and interprocedural analysis phases separate so that neither of the analysis may have to be performed on a large structure.

Certain other approaches have also been suggested for performing useful interprocedural transformations. Notion of Loop Extraction and Loop Embedding has been suggested for automatic parallelization in shared-memory compiling [14]. In this approach, subroutines which are enclosed by (possibly) parallel loops are either inlined or the loop headers are included in the subroutine for ease in parallelization. Such an approach can be used for hoisting loop invariant candidates but it does not give sufficient information to be able to reuse schedule generated or data communicated when two subroutines are always invoked one after another. Augmented Call Graph (ACG) has been introduced for various optimizations in distributed memory compilation [13]. This abstraction records any loop(s) enclosing a subroutine call. Again, this abstraction does not allow to look for redundant schedule calls or communication in adjacent subroutines. Interprocedural analysis for reaching data decomposition and managing overlap cells was presented in [13], but schedule call placement and communication placement were not considered. Hanxleden and Kennedy have suggested a framework for placing communication in distributed memory compilation [18], which considers sends and receives separately but is restricted to analysis within a subroutine.

6 Conclusions

This paper deals with two problems associated with compilation for distributed memory parallel machines. They are: *schedule call placement* and *communication placement*. We have outlined an interprocedural analysis framework for solving these two placement problems. The basis for our analysis is a new program abstraction, called *Control & Call Flow Graph* ($C\&CFG$) which extends the previously used abstraction call graph by storing control flow relationship between different call sites in a subroutine. We presented an algorithm for construction of $C\&CFG$. We outlined an interprocedural analysis strategy for these placement problems. Our method consists of three phases, an initial local analysis, an interprocedural propagation phase and final local placement phase. Our approach is based upon intraprocedural redundancy elimination schemes. We actually use a hybrid between lexical redundancy elimination techniques and value numbering based techniques for determining equivalent computations. For each candidate for placement (communication or schedule call), a slice within its current subroutine is extracted. Redundant schedules or communication can be determined by comparing these slices extracted from different subroutines. We are currently working on several details of our scheme and examining properties of the scheme.

Acknowledgements

We thank Bill Pugh for critically reading earlier versions of this paper and suggesting several improvements to the scheme and its presentation. We will like to acknowledge Paul Havlak for numerous discussions we had with him on this topic. We are implementing this scheme as a part of the D system being developed under the leadership of Ken Kennedy at Rice university. We gratefully acknowledge our debt to the implementers of the interprocedural infrastructure (FIAT) and the existing Fortran D compiler.

References

1. Gagan Agrawal, Alan Sussman, and Joel Saltz. Compiler and runtime support for structured and block structured applications. In *Proceedings Supercomputing '93*, pages 578–587. IEEE Computer Society Press, November 1993.
2. Gagan Agrawal, Alan Sussman, and Joel Saltz. Efficient runtime support for parallelizing block structured applications. In *Proceedings of the Scalable High Performance Computing Conference (SHPCC-94)*, pages 158–167. IEEE Computer Society Press, May 1994.
3. Gagan Agrawal, Alan Sussman, and Joel Saltz. An integrated runtime and compile-time approach for parallelizing structured and block structured applications. *IEEE Transactions on Parallel and Distributed Systems*, 1994. To appear. Also available as University of Maryland Technical Report CS-TR-3143 and UMIACS-TR-93-94.
4. Alfred V. Aho, Ravi Sethi, and Jeffrey D. Ullman. *Compilers: Principles, Techniques, and Tools*. Addison-Wesley, 1986.
5. D. Callahan. The program summary graph and flow-sensitive interprocedural data flow analysis. In *Proceedings of the SIGPLAN '88 Conference on Program Language Design and Implementation*, Atlanta, GA, June 1988.
6. K. Cooper, M. W. Hall, and L. Torczon. An experiment with inline substitution. *Software—Practice and Experience*, 21(6):581–601, June 1991.
7. K. Cooper, K. Kennedy, and L. Torczon. The impact of interprocedural analysis and optimization in the rn programming environment. *ACM Transactions on Programming Languages and Systems*, 8(4):491–523, October 1986.
8. Ron Cytron, Jeanne Ferrante, Barry K. Rosen, Mark N. Wegman, and F. Kenneth Zadeck. Efficiently computing static single assignment form and the control dependence graph. *ACM Transactions on Programming Languages and Systems*, 13(4):451–490, October 1991.
9. R. Das, D. J. Mavriplis, J. Saltz, S. Gupta, and R. Ponnusamy. The design and implementation of a parallel unstructured Euler solver using software primitives. *AIAA Journal*, 32(3):489–496, March 1994.
10. Raja Das, Joel Saltz, and Reinhard von Hanxleden. Slicing analysis and indirect access to distributed arrays. In *Proceedings of the 6th Workshop on Languages and Compilers for Parallel Computing*, pages 152–168. Springer-Verlag, August 1993. Also available as University of Maryland Technical Report CS-TR-3076 and UMIACS-TR-93-42.
11. D.M. Dhamdhere. Practical adaptation of the global optimization algorithm of Morel and Renvoise. *ACM Transactions on Programming Languages and Systems*, 13(2):291–294, April 1991.

12. K. Drechsler and M. Stadel. A solution to a problem with Morel and Renvoise's "Global optimization by suppression of partial redundancies". *ACM Transactions on Programming Languages and Systems*, 10(4):635–640, October 1988.

13. M. W. Hall, S. Hiranandani, K. Kennedy, and C. Tseng. Interprocedural compilation of Fortran D for MIMD distributed-memory machines. In *Proceedings of Supercomputing '92*, Minneapolis, MN, November 1992.

14. M. W. Hall, K. Kennedy, and K. S. McKinley. Interprocedural transformations for parallel code generation. In *Proceedings of Supercomputing '91*, Albuquerque, NM, November 1991.

15. Mary Hall. *Managing Interprocedural Optimization*. PhD thesis, Rice University, October 1990.

16. Mary Hall, John M Mellor Crummey, Alan Carle, and Rene G Rodriguez. FIAT: A framework for interprocedural analysis and transformations. In *Proceedings of the 6th Workshop on Languages and Compilers for Parallel Computing*, pages 522–545. Springer-Verlag, August 1993.

17. Reinhard v. Hanxleden. Handling irregular problems with Fortran D - a preliminary report. In *Proceedings of the Fourth Workshop on Compilers for Parallel Computers*, Delft, The Netherlands, December 1993. Also available as CRPC Technical Report CRPC-TR93339-S.

18. Reinhard v. Hanxleden. Give-n-take: A balanced code placement framework. Technical Report CRPC-TR94388-S, Center for Research on Parallel Computation, Rice University, March 1994.

19. P. Havlak and K. Kennedy. An implementation of interprocedural bounded regular section analysis. *IEEE Transactions on Parallel and Distributed Systems*, 2(3):350–360, July 1991.

20. High Performance Fortran Forum. High Performance Fortran language specification. *Scientific Programming*, 2(1-2):1–170, 1993.

21. S. Hiranandani, K. Kennedy, and C. Tseng. Evaluation of compiler optimizations for Fortran D on MIMD distributed-memory machines. In *Proceedings of the Sixth International Conference on Supercomputing*. ACM Press, July 1992.

22. Seema Hiranandani, Ken Kennedy, and Chau-Wen Tseng. Compiling Fortran D for MIMD distributed-memory machines. *Communications of the ACM*, 35(8):66–80, August 1992.

23. Susan Horwitz, Thomas Reps, and David Binkley. Interprocedural slicing using dependence graphs. *ACM Transactions on Programming Languages and Systems*, 12(1):26–60, January 1990.

24. J. Knoop, O. Rüthing, and B. Steffen. Lazy code motion. In *Proceedings of the ACM SIGPLAN '92 Conference on Program Language Design and Implementation*, San Francisco, CA, June 1992.

25. E. Morel and C. Renvoise. Global optimization by suppression of partial redundancies. *Communications of the ACM*, 22(2):96–103, February 1979.

26. E. Myers. A precise interprocedural data flow algorithm. In *Conference Record of the Eighth ACM Symposium on the Principles of Programming Languages*, pages 219–230, January 1981.

27. Ravi Ponnusamy, Joel Saltz, and Alok Choudhary. Runtime-compilation techniques for data partitioning and communication schedule reuse. In *Proceedings Supercomputing '93*, pages 361–370. IEEE Computer Society Press, November 1993. Also available as University of Maryland Technical Report CS-TR-3055 and UMIACS-TR-93-32.

28. B. K. Rosen, M. N. Wegman, and F. K. Zadeck. Global value numbers and redundant computations. In *Conference Record of the Fifteenth ACM Symposium on the Principles of Programming Languages*, pages 12–27, San Diego, CA, January 1988.

29. A. Sorkin. Some comments on "A solution to a problem with Morel and Renvoise's 'Global optimization by suppression of partial redundancies'". *ACM Transactions on Programming Languages and Systems*, 11(4):666–668, October 1989.

30. Alan Sussman, Gagan Agrawal, and Joel Saltz. A manual for the multiblock PARTI runtime primitives, revision 4.1. Technical Report CS-TR-3070.1 and UMIACS-TR-93-36.1, University of Maryland, Department of Computer Science and UMIACS, December 1993.

31. Mark Weiser. Program slicing. *IEEE Transactions on Software Engineering*, 10:352–357, 1984.

Analysis of Event Synchronization in Parallel Programs

J. Ramanujam and **A. Mathew**

Department of Electrical and Computer Engineering
Louisiana State University, Baton Rouge, LA 70803
(jxr@gate.ee.lsu.edu)

Abstract. The increase in the number and complexity of parallel programs has led to a need for better approaches for synchronization error detection and debugging of parallel programs. This paper presents an efficient and precise algorithm for the detection of nondeterminacy (race conditions) in parallel programs. Nondeterminacy exists in a program when the program yields different outputs for different runs with the same input. We limit our attention to nondeterminacy due to errors in synchronization and to race conditions due to these unsynchronized accesses to shared variables. A directed acyclic graph called a task graph is used to represent the accesses to shared variables in a parallel program with edges representing guaranteed ordering. The algorithm proposed here constructs an augmented task graph, and then uses a modification of depth-first search to classify the edges in the augmented task graph. The edges are analyzed and the nodes that are guaranteed to execute before an event are linked to these events by edges representing guaranteed ordering among events. This ordering is used to detect any race conditions in parallel programs.

1 Introduction

The difficulty of writing and debugging parallel programs is becoming apparent with the increase in the number and the complexity of parallel programs. Debugging parallel programs is considerably more difficult than debugging sequential programs, because of potential nondeterminacy. Nondeterminacy is the possibility that a parallel program yields different outputs for different runs with the same input data. Such nondeterminacy may be intentional; in this paper, we limit our attention to nondeterminacy caused by synchronization errors. Race conditions arise when the synchronization operations do not guarantee ordering among two or more accesses to the same memory location, when at least one of these accesses is a write.

Debugging of parallel programs requires specialized tools and algorithms to detect race conditions. In recent years, work in this area has led to better definition of various forms of race conditions and improved algorithms, but much remains to be done. The objective of this paper is to present an algorithm for race detection in parallel programs. The algorithm uses the task graph of the parallel program as input; it constructs an augmented task graph by adding a directed edge from every post on an event to every wait on the same event. It should be noted that while the task graph is acyclic, the augmented task graph may contain cycles. The algorithm uses a modification of depth-first search to classify the edges of the augmented task graph, using a heuristic to decide the order in which nodes are visited. Based on the classification of edges and further analysis, the guaranteed ordering among the nodes is obtained. This information is used to identify possible race conditions and nondeterminacy in the program.

This paper is organized as follows. In Section 2, we present the necessary background for this paper, including the program model and constructs for which the techniques presented in this paper apply; in addition, we review related work. Section 3 describes the improved algorithm that is used in trace analysis of parallel programs using event

---

[1] Supported in part by an NSF Young Investigator Award CCR–9457768, an NSF grant CCR–9210422, and by the Louisiana Board of Regents through contract LEQSF (1991-94)-RD-A-09.

synchronization without `clears`. Section 4 illustrates the use of the algorithm on sample program segments. Section 5 concludes with a summary and a discussion of approaches to extending the work to parallel programs that use `clears`.

2 Background and Related Work

We consider parallel programs consisting of tasks running on the processors of shared address space machines. Sequential programs due to their sequential semantics, guarantee ordering between accesses to shared memory. In parallel programs, this ordering can be enforced by either the sequential semantics of events within a task, or by explicit synchronization between events in different tasks that may execute concurrently. Incorrect synchronization leads to incorrect ordering between events and accesses to shared memory.

A *determinate* program produces the same output for different runs with the same input. Sequential programs are determinate. A *nondeterminate* program is one that produces different output for different runs with the same input and code. Parallel programs usually exhibit nondeterminacy due to errors in synchronization, but the nondeterminacy may be intentional as in the case of asynchronous parallel algorithms.

Race conditions are time-dependent errors that occur due to lack of ordering of accesses (at least one of which is a write access) to shared data by different processes. Bernstein [3] presents the requirements that must be true for a program to be determinate. A *conclusive* race is a race that is not dependent on the input data, whereas an *input-dependent* race is one that is dependent on the input data, and which may manifest itself for certain input data but not for others. Inaccurate race detection algorithms may report races that are not genuine and these are called *spurious* races.

2.1 Language Model

We assume a language with parallel constructs and synchronization primitives similar to those in CEDAR Fortran [1] and other dialects of parallel Fortran that support programming on a shared address space. The following parallel constructs and synchronization primitives are considered.

An *event* is a synchronization variable that can have only two states, posted or cleared. A `post(x)` on an event x sets the state of the event x to posted. A `post` does not change the state of an event that has already been posted; the event continues to remain posted. A `wait(x)` on an event x whose state is not posted, suspends the task that called it till the event is posted. A `clear(x)` on an event x resets the state of the variable x to cleared. The event may be reused after a clear on the event; the next `post(x)` sets the state of x to posted.

2.2 Race Detection

Most approaches to detection of races in parallel programs are a combination of static analysis and dynamic methods, since neither of the two provide sufficient information when used alone. Static analysis is faster, but may report nondeterminacy where one may not exist. Trace analysis is usually more accurate than static analysis. Static analysis is valid for a wider range of data as compared to trace analysis that is just valid for the input data used in a particular execution. Practical approaches to race detection therefore usually use static analysis to determine ranges of input data which might exhibit races (and therefore identify potential races) and use trace analysis to examine these cases one by one and pinpoint the sources of nondeterminacy.

2.3 Related Work

Model for Reasoning About and Characterizing Race Conditions: A formal model that characterizes the actual, observed and potential behaviors of programs was first proposed by Netzer [17, 20]. This model provides a conceptual framework on which the theoretical and practical aspects of dynamic race detection and debugging for shared-memory parallel programs can be based.

Netzer defines actual behavior of parallel programs as that which precisely represents program execution, observed behavior as the partial information that can be recorded and potential behavior as the alternate executions possibly allowed by the nondeterminism in the program. These behaviors of a parallel program are used to characterize the races into general and data races. General races generally apply to programs intended to be deterministic. Data races apply to nondeterministic parallel programs that contain critical sections.

Static and Dynamic Analysis: Static analysis methods use the program listing to detect races and assume that all the execution paths through the program are possible. Explicit synchronization in the program is used to determine the potential ordering in the program. Two basic approaches to static analysis are generally used. In the first approach, all possible states that the program can exist in are traversed and a graph of the state space is constructed either explicitly [15] or implicitly. In the second approach, dataflow analysis is used to detect potential event orderings [2, 5]. In general, dataflow methods are less accurate, but have better time and space complexity than state-space methods.

Static analysis is used to augment dynamic analysis [1, 6, 7, 8, 9, 14, 22]. Dynamic analysis detects races for a particular execution of the program; these methods generally differ in the way the information that is used in the analysis is collected and analyzed. The two approaches used are: post-mortem [1, 6, 7, 8, 9, 12, 13, 18] and on-the-fly [14, 18, 22] analysis. Allen and Padua [1] describe a method for the post-mortem analysis of Fortran programs in a shared-memory parallel machine. They use static analysis to reduce the trace information collected. Choi, Miller and Netzer [6] describe the techniques used in the debugging parallel programs using flowback analysis. For C programs using counting semaphores and the fork/join construct, Miller and Choi [16] present a parallel debugger using post-mortem data race analysis. These methods typically detect data races and not general races. Helmbold, McDowell and Wang [12, 13] present models and algorithms to find possible event orderings in traces of programs that use anonymous synchronization.

On-the-fly analysis techniques for detecting data races in programs using fork/join and arbitrary synchronization have been developed by Schoenberg [22]. A technique for detecting data races in Fortran programs using parallel do loops and synchronization using send and wait primitives, is described by Hood, Kennedy and Mellor-Crummey [14].

Algorithms That Compute Guaranteed Ordering: Emrath, Ghosh and Padua [7, 8, 9] present methods for detecting general races in programs using event synchronization. They present two algorithms for post-mortem analysis, namely, the Exhaustive Pairing Algorithm (EPA) and the Common Ancestor Algorithm (CAA) to compute guaranteed orderings, which are described next.

Common Ancestor Algorithm (CAA): Emrath, Ghosh and Padua [7, 8] have proposed an algorithm that computes the guaranteed ordering for programs containing the synchronization operations post, wait and clear. The algorithm is based on the property that a node that precedes all the posts that might trigger a wait necessarily precedes the wait node. Arcs are added not from all the ancestors of the posts that may trigger the wait, but from the closest common ancestor of those nodes. The CAA works in polynomial time but has the disadvantage that it may miss out on some of the guaranteed ordering even for program that do not use `clears`.

Exhaustive Pairing Algorithm (EPA): Emrath, Ghosh and Padua [8] propose an algorithm that computes every possible execution ordering due to the synchronization operations `post`, `wait` and `clear`. The algorithm produces an execution graph for each of the possible pairings, and detects the feasible execution graphs; it computes the transitive closure of the execution graphs to determine the feasibility of the execution graph. The intersection of the transitive closures of all feasible execution graphs is computed to yield the result. The exhaustive-pairing algorithm works in exponential time and always computes ordering accurately.

Netzer and Ghosh Algorithm: Netzer and Ghosh [18] present a precise and efficient algorithm for trace analysis of programs with post-wait synchronization, without `clears`; the complexity of their algorithm is $O(np)$ where n is the number of synchronization events and p is the number of processes.

3 Depth-First Search Algorithm for Event Ordering

The algorithm presented in this paper computes the ordering for a trace of a parallel program using synchronization with events. The algorithm is based on depth-first search (DFS) [10, 23] and traverses the augmented task graph containing synchronization and task edges. The order in which the edges are traversed is determined by a heuristic. The edges are then classified based on the DFS algorithm. Some edges are discarded and a final graph is constructed from the remaining edges. This graph is used to determine ordering between events.

3.1 Necessary Conditions for an Ordering to be Feasible

Ghosh [8, 11] notes that with regard to the Exhaustive Pairing Algorithm (EPA), that the following conditions are true for every feasible execution ordering of a parallel program using explicit event synchronization (`post`/`wait` synchronization) without `clears`.

- Operations within the same task are sequential and are hence ordered.
- Every `wait` that is triggered is preceded by at least one `post` on the event.
- These two requirements must be satisfied by the execution order without leading to any cycles in the order.

3.2 Task Graphs

A task graph is a directed acyclic graph that represents the ordering among the nodes that represent coordination operations; coordination operations are those operations that determine ordering (which comprise of task spawning, task merging and synchronization operations) and those that represent accesses to shared memory. The arcs represent the guaranteed ordering between the nodes in the same process. A unique root node represents the start of the parallel program; there is a directed edge from the root node to the first nodes in each process. Task graphs are acyclic.

3.3 Depth-First Search Algorithm for Event Ordering

The algorithm computes the guaranteed ordering and gives all possible ordering for a program that uses event synchronization using `post`, `wait` and no `clears`. The graph showing guaranteed ordering for a program is built based on the three conditions given above that are guaranteed to hold in every feasible ordering. The algorithm uses an augmented task graph. The augmented task graph is constructed from a task graph by adding an edge from every post on an event to every wait on the same event. All operations within a task are connected by directed arcs, the direction of the arcs representing the sequential execution within a task. The edges of the task graph can be classified into two types:

Task edges: These edges join two operations within the same task and represent the sequential execution ordering of the operations within a task.

Synchronization edges: These edges represent the synchronization between two tasks. For synchronization using post/wait without clears, the only valid synchronization edges are those from a post on an event to a wait on the event.

Even though task graphs are acyclic, the augmented task graph may contain cycles. The algorithm presented next performs a depth-first search of the augmented task graph, classifies edges, and then computes guaranteed ordering. Fig. 1 defines the notation used in the algorithm. Note that we do not present pseudocode for the procedures, *discard_edges()*, *compute_ordering()*, *delete_synchronization_edges()*, and *new_edge_discovered()*.

$n \in N$	≡ Set of nodes in the task graph.
$e \in E$	≡ Set of edges in the task graph.
	$n_1^{t_i} \xrightarrow{e} n_2^{t_k}$
$n_1^{t_i}$	≡ Source node of the edge (Belongs to task t_i).
$n_2^{t_k}$	≡ Destination node of the edge (Belongs to task t_k).
R	≡ Root node for the task graph.
$seq\_num(n)$	≡ Sequence number assigned to the node; it is the order in which the nodes are visited by the algorithm.
seq_num	≡ Global sequence number.
$f(n)$	≡ Father of node n.
$last(t_i)$	≡ Last node of task t_i that has already been processed
$type(e)$	≡ Type of Edge
	Unused : Edge has not been visited.
	Tree : Edge e was used to discover destination node n_2.
	Forward : Edge e where $seq\_num(n_1) \leq seq\_num(n_2)$.
	Back : Edge e where $seq\_num(n_1) > seq\_num(n_2)$ AND n_2 is an ancestor of n_1.
	Cross : Edge e where $seq\_num(n_1) > seq\_num(n_2)$ AND n_2 is not an ancestor of n_1.

Fig. 1. Notation used in the algorithm

The procedure $init()$ (see Fig. 2) initializes the sequence number of all nodes to zero and the father of all the nodes to UNDEFINED. These parameters are assigned their proper values by the algorithm. All edges including synchronization edges are initialized to edge type UNUSED. The search is started with the root node of the augmented task graph as the source node and with the global sequence number of zero, as no nodes have

procedure $init()$ {
$\forall$ e $\in$ E $\quad$ $type(e)$ $\longleftarrow$ UNUSED
$\forall$ n $\in$ N $\quad$ $seq\_num(n)$ $\longleftarrow$ 0; $f(n)$ $\longleftarrow$ UNDEFINED ;
t_i $\longleftarrow$ 0 ; $n_1^{t_i}$ $\longleftarrow$ R ; /* root node */
$df\_order(n_1^{t_i}, 0)$;
$discard\_edges()$;
$compute\_ordering()$;
$delete\_synchronization\_edges()$; }

Fig. 2. The init procedure

procedure $df\_order(n_1^{t_i}, seq\_num)$ {
$\quad$ seq_num++; $seq\_num(n_1^{t_i})$ $\longleftarrow$ seq_num;
$\quad$ $process\_edge(n_1^{t_i}, seq\_num)$; }

Fig. 3. The df_order procedure

procedure $process\_edge(n_1^{t_i}, seq\_num)$ {
$\quad$ **while** $(((n_1^{t_i} \longrightarrow n_2^{t_k}) \longleftarrow unused\_incident\_edge(n_1^{t_i})) \neq$ NULL) {
$\quad\quad$ $type(e)$ $\longleftarrow$ USED
$\quad\quad$ **if** $(seq\_num(n_2^{t_k}) \neq 0)$ {
$\quad\quad\quad$ $new\_edge\_discovered(e)$
$\quad\quad\quad$ continue }
$\quad\quad$ **else** {
$\quad\quad\quad$ **if** $((perform\_synchronization\_operation(n_2^{t_k}) \neq$ WAIT)
$\quad\quad\quad\quad$ &&$(prev\_nodes\_of\_task\_already\_processed(t_k)))$ {
$\quad\quad\quad\quad$ $new\_edge\_discovered(e)$
$\quad\quad\quad\quad$ $f(n_2^{t_k})$ $\longleftarrow$ $n_1^{t_i}$; $\quad$ $last(t_k)$ $\longleftarrow$ n_2; $\quad$ $n_1^{t_i}$ $\longleftarrow$ $n_2^{t_k}$
$\quad\quad\quad\quad$ $df\_order(n_1^{t_i}, seq\_num)$ }
$\quad\quad\quad$ **else** {
$\quad\quad\quad\quad$ $new\_edge\_discovered(e)$
$\quad\quad\quad\quad$ continue } } }
$\quad$ **if** $(f(n_1^{t_i}) \neq$ UNDEFINED) {
$\quad\quad$ $n_1^{t_i}$ $\longleftarrow$ $f(n_1^{t_i})$
$\quad\quad$ $process\_edge(n_1^{t_i}, seq\_num)$ }
$\quad$ **else if** (there exists an $n_2^{t_k}$ such that $seq\_num(n_2^{t_k}) > 0$) {
$\quad\quad$ $n_1^{t_i}$ $\longleftarrow$ $n_2^{t_k}$
$\quad\quad$ $df\_order(n_1^{t_i}, seq\_num)$ } }

Fig. 4. The process_edge procedure

been visited by the algorithm. The root node belongs to task 0 and the rest of the nodes belong to tasks 1 to total number of tasks in the augmented task graph.

The procedure $df\_order(n_1^{t_i}, seq\_num)$ (Fig. 3) is a recursive procedure that is invoked each time a new node is visited. This procedure calls the procedure $process\_edge$ to differentiate between discovery of a node and visit of a node; a node could be discovered but not visited. When a node is discovered (or rediscovered), but not visited, the node is not assigned (or reassigned) a sequence number, but the edge used to discover the node is marked USED or assigned a edge type. The sequence number of a node is the the global sequence number when the node was visited for the first time. After the node is assigned a sequence number the node is further processed by the procedure $process\_edge(n_1, seq\_num(n_1^{t_1}))$.

The procedure $process\_edge(n_1^{t_i}, seq\_num)$ (Fig. 4) processes all incident edges from the source node, $n_1^{t_i}$. The procedure $unused\_incident\_edge(n_1^{t_i})$ returns unused incident edges based on a heuristic. The heuristic assigns weights to the edges depending on the type of source node and the type of the destination node. The edge with the greatest weight is returned by the procedure.

An edge that is returned by the $unused\_incident\_edge(n_1^{t_i})$ procedure is marked USED. If the sequence number of the destination node $n_2^{t_k}$ is not zero *i.e.*, the node has already been visited and hence assigned a sequence number, the procedure continues to the next unused edge if any. If the sequence number of the destination node $n_2^{t_k}$ is zero, *i.e.*, the node has not been visited, then the node is examined to determine if the node is a synchronization node or an ordinary node. If the node is a synchronization node, the synchronization operation is performed on the event. If the operation is a post on the event, the event is posted. The algorithm keeps track of the order in which events become posted during depth-first search in the array *sigorder;* the event variable that becomes posted at the ith position is stored in *sigorder*[i]. If the operation is a wait then the node can be visited only if the event is posted. This ensures the second necessary condition for a feasible ordering is satisfied. The algorithm also checks if all previous nodes of the task t_k have been processed which ensures that the first condition for a feasible ordering is satisfied. If the first two conditions have been satisfied, the destination node $n_2^{t_k}$ is visited.

If the algorithm visits the destination node $n_2^{t_k}$, the father of the destination node is the source node $n_1^{t_i}$. The destination node $n_2^{t_k}$ is then assigned to the last node processed for the task t_k. The destination node $n_2^{t_k}$ becomes the source node $n_1^{t_i}$ and the procedure $df\_order(n_1^{t_i}, seq\_num)$ is invoked. If the destination node has not yet been visited but cannot be visited in this iteration of the algorithm because one one of the two conditions is not satisfied, the algorithm processes any other unused incident edge for the source node $n_1^{t_i}$.

If all the incident edges from the source node have been processed, the procedure $process\_edge$ $(n_1^{t_i}, seq\_num)$ checks if the father of the source node $n_1^{t_i}$ is defined. If so, the procedure backtracks by assigning the father of the source node $f(n_1^{t_i})$ as the source node $n_1^{t_i}$ and recursively calling itself. If all the incident edges from the source node have been processed and the father of the source node is not defined, the algorithm checks if there are any unvisited nodes in the augmented task graph *i.e.*, any node which has its sequence number undefined. If the augmented task graph is weakly connected, *i.e.*, the underlying undirected graph is connected, the presence of nodes whose sequence numbers are undefined indicate potential deadlocks in the program. If the augmented task graph is not weakly connected, then procedure $df\_order(n_1^{t_i}, seq\_num)$ is invoked with $n_1^{t_i}$ equal to a node whose sequence number is undefined, and which has no incoming edges.

It should be noted that while the task graph is a directed acyclic graph, the augmented task graph may contain cycles. depth-first search of directed graph that results in *back edges* indicates the presence of cycles. Since cycles are impossible in event orderings, back edges discovered by DFS can be discarded. After termination of the algorithm the modified DFS tree obtained is further processed to determine guaranteed ordering between the accesses to shared memory. The following rules are used to process the modified DFS tree obtained by the routine *discard_edges()*.

- All back edges are discarded. (Lemma 1 in Section 3.5)
- All task edges that are forward edges are discarded. (Lemma 2 in Section 3.5)
- Forward edges from the root node can be discarded.
- All other edges *i.e.*, tree, cross and forward that have not been discarded are considered as they represent ordering or potential ordering.

After the termination of the modified DFS, the edges that can be discarded are discarded. The remaining edges are analyzed to determine potential races and nondeterminism by the routine *compute_ordering()*. The procedure *compute_ordering()* adds the Guaranteed to Execute Before (GEB) edges to the task graph based on the classification of the edges remaining in the augmented task graph after the termination of the modified DFS and *discard_edges()*. The procedure *delete_synchronization_edges()* deletes all synchronization edges that are not GEB edges from the task graph.

If more than one edge terminates on a wait of an event, these edges represent possibly *different* execution paths that may be taken by the program; such multiple paths represent possible nondeterministic behavior due to shared memory accesses along these paths. If the set of edges ending at a wait node, say wait(X), contains a tree edge, and either a cross-edge or an undiscarded forward edge, then there is no guaranteed ordering between any post(X) and that wait(X). Otherwise, there is a guaranteed ordering from post(X) to wait(X). The procedure *compute_ordering()* first adds all such guaranteed edges. For all events Y for which no guaranteed ordering exists from post(Y) to wait(Y), the procedure uses the array *sigorder* to find the guaranteed ordering edges as follows. Let k be an integer such that $sigorder[k] = Y$. Find the largest index $j (j < k)$ such that $sigorder[j] = Z$ is an event for which there is a guaranteed ordering from post(Z) to wait(Z). Add an edge from the node post(Z) to wait(Y). If no such Z exists, there are no events in the program that are guaranteed to execute before Y (except the root node and all nodes preceding it in within the same process).

3.4 Heuristic Used in the Algorithm

Table 1. Assignment of weights to task edges by heuristic

	WAIT(A)	POST(A)	X	WAIT(B)	POST(B)
POST(A)	$\gg \mathcal{N}$	$> \mathcal{N}$	$\mathcal{N}$	$< \mathcal{N}$	$> \mathcal{N}$
WAIT(A)	$< \mathcal{N}$	$> \mathcal{N}$	$\mathcal{N}$	$< \mathcal{N}$	$> \mathcal{N}$
X	$< \mathcal{N}$	$> \mathcal{N}$	$\mathcal{N}$	$< \mathcal{N}$	$> \mathcal{N}$
R	$< \mathcal{N}$	$> \mathcal{N}$	$\mathcal{N}$	$< \mathcal{N}$	$> \mathcal{N}$

$\mathcal{N}$ denotes a Normal weight. R denotes the root node. X denotes a node which corresponds to a local (non-synchronization) operation in a task.

The heuristic assigns the weights to the edges based on the tables (See Table 1 and Table 2). The rows denote the type of source nodes and the columns indicate the types of destination nodes for each edge. The entry in the table denotes the weight assigned to the edge; if an edge can not exist, it is denoted by an asterisk. The heuristic is used by the routine *unused_incident_edge* to determine the next edge to be returned to the modified DFS of the algorithm. The heuristic is biased to ensure that coordination edges are processed before task edges.

3.5 Correctness of DFS Algorithm for Event Synchronization without `Clears`

In order to prove that correctness of the algorithm, we make the following observations regarding the DFS.

Observation 1: A DFS always traverses an edge of a given digraph in any direction only once.

Observation 2: A DFS traverses all edges of a digraph that is at least minimally connected.

Observation 3: A forward and cross edge with respect to one DFS tree of a digraph can be a tree edge with respect to another DFS tree of the digraph.

Observation 4: If $i \xrightarrow{f} j$ is a forward edge, then there exists a path composed of tree edges of length $n > 1$, $i \longrightarrow k_1 \longrightarrow k_2 \longrightarrow \cdots \longrightarrow k_{n-1} \longrightarrow j$.

The algorithm presented here is a modification of DFS and preserves the properties of the DFS. The four observations regarding DFS hold true here as well. Since, there is an edge from the root node to the first node in each task and since the search is always started at the root, there is a single DFS tree in the case of weakly connected task graphs. The algorithm only modifies the order in which the edges of the task graph are traversed. The routine *unused_incident_edge* returns an unused edge according to a heuristic. This routine also ensures that the two factors that determine ordering are always met while the task graph is being traversed by the algorithms. The two conditions that determine ordering that are enforced by the routine *unused_incident_edge* are:

1. The ordering of operations within a task is sequential. The ith operation of a task t always executes before operation $(i + 1)$ of task t;
2. A `wait` on an event cannot continue until there has been at least one `post` on that event.

Lemma 1. All edges that are designated as back edges by the modified DFS of the algorithm can be ignored.

Proof: If b is a back edge of a DFS tree such that $i \xrightarrow{b} j$ then,

- The DFS sequence number of i is greater the that of j. The DFS sequence number is the DFS sequence number that represents the order in which the nodes were discovered by the DFS. Back edges are edges in a DFS tree, from node that were discovered later on in the search to those discovered earlier.
- Node i is an ancestor of node j.

Back edges can not be task edges. A back edge b can only be a synchronization edge, specifically a synchronization edge from a `post` in a task to a `wait` in another task. From the definition of a back edge this indicates that the `wait` node j executed before the `post` node i. Considering the semantics of `post`/`wait` synchronization this implies that the `wait` was triggered by another `post` that executed before the `post` i. Since a `post` on an event has no effect on an event that has already been posted, the `post` i may be ignored and the back edge b may be ignored. Also a back edge in a DFS tree can never a tree edge in a different DFS tree of the same digraph. □

Lemma 2. Task edges are either tree or forward edges. Forward task edges may be ignored in the analysis of the task graph.

Proof: If T is a task edge of a DFS tree such that $i \xrightarrow{T} j$ then,

- The DFS sequence number of node i is lower than that of node j, since *unused_incident_edge* ensured that a node earlier in a task is discovered earlier by the modified DFS than one later on.
- The node j is always an descendant of node i.

It has been already proved in Lemma 1 that tree edges cannot be back edges.

The destination node of a task edge is a descendant of the source node and therefore there exists an ancestor/descendant relationship between the two node, since no such relationships can exist between the nodes of a cross edge, task edges cannot be cross edges.

If a task graph is a forward edge then it may be ignored in the analysis of the task graph. This follows from observation 4 on DFS trees. Any ordering information that may be obtained from a forward task edge $i \xrightarrow{T_f} j$ about potential ordering between the nodes i and j and other nodes can be obtained by considering the path(s) $i \longrightarrow k_1 \longrightarrow \cdots \longrightarrow k_{n-1} \longrightarrow j$ composed of either tree or tree and cross edges. The ordering information that can be obtained from the forward task graph is a subset of the information that can be obtained from the alternate path. The forward tree edge contains information regarding the sequential execution within the task only, whereas the alternate path contains information regarding ordering involving other tasks as well. □

Lemma 3. After the termination of the modified DFS and after deletion of unwanted edges by *discard_edges()* , there exists a synchronization edge $n_1^{t_i} \xrightarrow{S} n_2^{t_j}$ if the edge is a triggering synchronization edge TSE, $n_1^{t_i} \xrightarrow{TSE} n_2^{t_j}$ i.e., the synchronization edge is traversed and the post corresponding to the edge is the first post to trigger the wait, in any one of the possible execution orderings.

Proof: To aid in the proof, the concept of a Triggering Synchronization Edge (TSE) is introduced. A TSE is a synchronization edge from a post on an event to a corresponding wait, which first sets the state of the event to posted. All other other posts and therefore their corresponding edges have no effect on the event since the event is already posted (and remains posted since clears on the event are not allowed). An edge $n_1^{t_i} \xrightarrow{TSE} n_2^{t_j}$ is a TSE iff the edge is executed at least in one of the possible executions and if the edge triggers the event *i.e.*, the first to set the event to posted. To prove that if an edge is a TSE it is present as a synchronization edge in the modified DFS tree after the algorithm terminates and after unnecessary edges are deleted by *discard_edges()*.

Observation 2 on the DFS states that all edges of a digraph are traversed if the digraph is minimally connected. Since the the original task graph has an edge from each post on an event to all waits on the same event, all these edges are traversed by the modified DFS. These edges are classified by the search into tree, cross, forward and back edges. The set of all TSE is a subset of the set of edges that the search traverses, therefore all TSE are processed by the algorithm. Since the only synchronization edges that are discarded are back edges, proof that no TSE are back edges will complete the proof that if an edge is a TSE, the synchronization edge will be present in the modified DFS tree. Assume that the edge TSE is a TSE such that $n_1^{t_i} \xrightarrow{TSE} n_2^{t_j}$ then $n_1^{t_i}$ is a post on an event and $n_2^{t_j}$ is the wait that is triggered for the first time, by the post. If TSE were to be a back edge this would imply that the DFS sequence number of $n_2^{t_j}$

would be greater than DFS sequence number of $n_2^{t_j}$, and therefore imply that $n_2^{t_j}$ has been already visited by the modified DFS. Since $n_2^{t_j}$ is a wait this would imply that the wait has already been posted, therefore the edge would not be a TSE. This violates our original assumption, and therefore a TSE cannot be a back edge.

Assume that a synchronization edge is not a TSE. Then for every possible execution, the node $n_2^{t_j}$ or the wait node is always triggered before the synchronization edge. $\square$

Theorem 4. After the termination of the algorithm, for all nodes in the task graph there exists a path from n_1 to n_2, only if, $n_1^{t_i} \xrightarrow{\text{GEB}} n_2^{t_j}$.

Proof: After the termination of the algorithm the only paths that exist are the paths within a task and the GEB arcs. Since task paths are sequential, portions of the path between n_1 and n_2 that are along tasks obey the GEB property. We have to prove that the begin and end nodes of every GEB arc added by the algorithm obey the GEB property, since these are the only arcs that remain between tasks after the algorithm terminates.

For every event in the task graph, after the algorithm ensures that all TSE remain (Lemma 3). The procedure *compute_ordering()* using the array *sigorder* adds GEB arcs from the closest common node that executes before all the TSE; therefore, the source node of the GEB must execute before the destination node of the GEB, which is the event. This is true for all events in the graph.

Since both the sequential path within tasks and the GEB arcs both obey the GEB property and these are the only two type of paths that remain in the task graph, any combination of the two would obey the GEB property. $\square$

Table 2. Assignment of weights by heuristic to synchronization edges

	WAIT(A)	POST(A)	X	WAIT(B)	POST(B)
POST(A)	$\gg \mathcal{N}$	*	*	*	*
WAIT(A)	*	*	*	*	*
X	*	*	*	*	*
R	$< \mathcal{N}$	$> \mathcal{N}$	$\mathcal{N}$	$< \mathcal{N}$	$> \mathcal{N}$

An asterisk denotes that the edge cannot exist. $\mathcal{N}$ denotes a Normal weight. R denotes the root node. X denotes a node which corresponds to a local (non-synchronization) operation in a task.

Within each task, we only need to consider the first operation (either a post or a wait) on any event variable, because of the GEB edges within each task. The complexity of the algorithm presented here is $O(ep)$ where e is the number of event variables and p is the number of processes [21]. From this algorithm, one can derive an $O(e)$ algorithm for detecting deadlocks and infinite waits [21]. The reader is referred to [21] for details.

4 Application of the Algorithm on Sample Program Segments

This section shows the application of the DFS-based heuristic to sample program segments that have been used in the literature. Consider program segment 1 in Fig. 5 from [18]. On a cursory examination, this segment appears to be race-free. The program when analyzed by the algorithm, shows the existence of a race between the accesses to S in task 2 and task 3 *i.e.*, $I = S$ and $S = I$ respectively. The access task 1 is ordered with respect to the other two accesses, and does not constitute a race. The augmented task

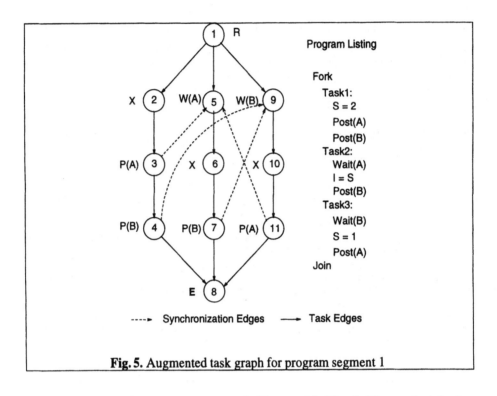

Fig. 5. Augmented task graph for program segment 1

graph representing the program segment is illustrated in Fig. 5. The synchronization edges are added from all `posts` on an event to all `waits` on the same event. The modified DFS traverses the task graph and terminates. The tree generated by the search is illustrated in Fig. 6. The tree edges are then examined and all forward edges within a task and all back edges are discarded, by the routine *discard_edges()*. These edges are marked with an asterisk in Fig. 6. The procedure *compute_ordering()* then examines the remaining edges and computes the closest common edge to each event in the graph.

In the task graph the only edge that could potentially trigger the event *A* is that from node 3 (edge [3,T] in Fig. 6), since the only other edge that could trigger event *A* is the back edge [9,B] that is discarded. Therefore, node 3 is guaranteed to execute before node 5. When we consider the wait on event *B* (node 9), there are two `posts` (nodes 4 and 7) that could trigger it; there are two edges that terminate at the node in the DFS tree, namely [6,T] and [13,C]. Thus, there is no guaranteed from either node 4 or node 7, to node 9. Since *sigorder*[1] is A and *sigorder*[2] is B and we have a GEB edge from node 3 to node 5, we add an edge from node 3 to node 9.

There is no guaranteed order between the accesses that lie along any of the paths with any access on the other path, or with an access along the path that follows the event. Therefore there is no ordering between the access at node 6 and that node 10. These accesses represent a race condition and is reported. The access at node 2 is ordered with respect to the other two orders. The graph showing the guaranteed ordering, and the GEB edges is illustrated in Fig. 7.

Program Segment for which the Common Ancestor Algorithm Generates Spurious Races
The second program segment (shown in Fig. 8) is one for which the *common ancestor algorithm* generates spurious races, as is shown by Emrath, Ghosh and Padua [8]. The algorithm proposed gives the correct ordering and does not report a spurious race for the program segment. The algorithm uses an augmented task graph with edges added as in Fig. 8. The DFS tree produced by the algorithm is shown in Fig. 9; the discarded edges are marked with asterisks.

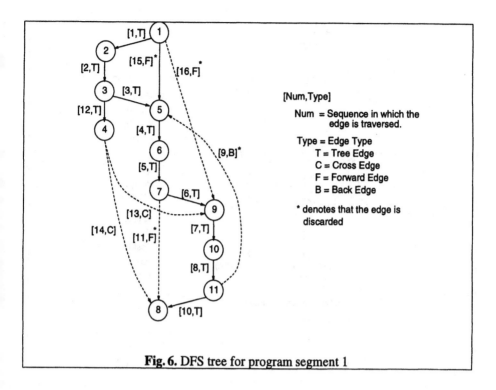

Fig. 6. DFS tree for program segment 1

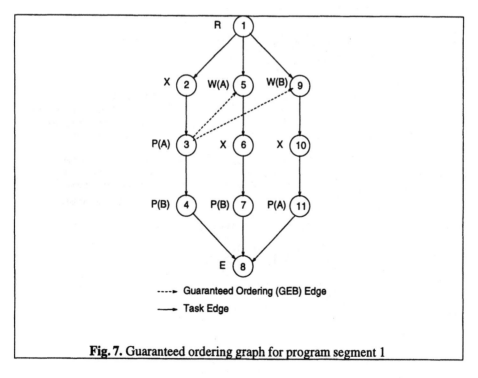

Fig. 7. Guaranteed ordering graph for program segment 1

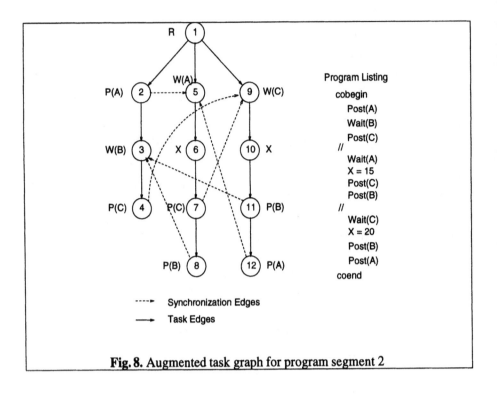

Fig. 8. Augmented task graph for program segment 2

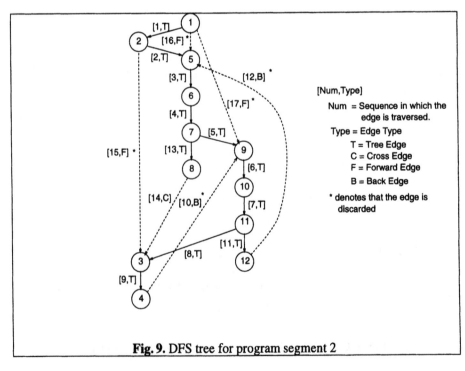

Fig. 9. DFS tree for program segment 2

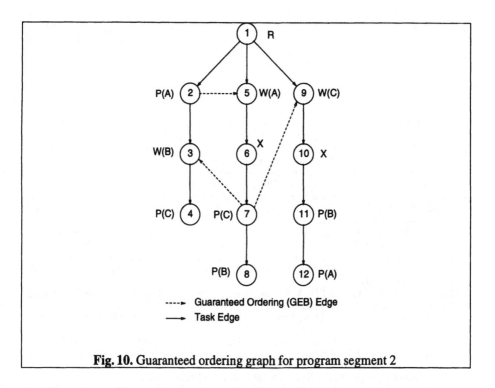

Fig. 10. Guaranteed ordering graph for program segment 2

The procedure *compute_ordering()* then examines the remaining tree, cross and forward edges and computes the closest common node for each event. In this program segment, the closest common node for event A is node 2, since the back edge from node 12 is discarded and the only TSE is [2,T]. For event C the only TSE is [5,T] since the other edge [17,F] is a forward edge in a task. For the event B there are two possible execution paths [14,C] and [8,T], since the forward edge [15,F] is discarded, the closest common node is the node where the paths containing the two possible TSE originate, node 7. This is because the events are triggered in the order A, C and then B, and both events A and C have GEB edges from posts to waits. Since a path exists between the two shared memory accesses *i.e.*, nodes 6 and 10, the accesses are ordered and no race is detected by the algorithm.

5 Summary

This paper presents an $O(ep)$ (e is the number of event variables and p is the number of processes) algorithm that computes guaranteed ordering for parallel programs using post/wait synchronization without clears. The algorithm first constructs an augmented task graph by adding a directed edge from every post on an event to every wait on the same event. The algorithm then uses a modification of depth-first search to classify the edges of the augmented task graph. While the task graph is acyclic, the augmented task graph may contain cycles. The order in which the edges are traversed is determined by a heuristic. Depending on the classification, some of the edges are discarded. The remaining edges are used to construct a graph representing the guaranteed ordering between events. This graph is then used to detect nondeterminacy in the program.

For programs that use post/wait synchronization with clears, the problem of detecting guaranteed ordering is NP-complete [8, 11]. In such cases, we use a heuristic [21] to recognize certain structures in the graph such as a clear (X) followed by a

315

`wait(X)` within the same process (where X is an event), or a `wait(X)` followed by a `clear(X)` within the same process. Work is also in progress in deriving a DFS-based algorithm for semaphore synchronization.

References

1. Allen, T. R. and D. A. Padua, "Debugging Fortran on a Shared Memory Machine," *Proc. Intl. Conf. Parallel Processing*, pp. 721-727, St. Charles, IL, Aug. 1987.
2. Balasundaram, V. and K. Kennedy, "Compile-time Detection of Race Conditions in a Parallel Program," *Proc. 3rd Intl. Conf. Supercomputing*, pp. 175-185, Jun. 1989.
3. Bernstein, A. J., "Analysis of Programs for Parallel Processing," *Proc. IEEE Trans. on Electronic Computers*, EC-15(5), pp. 757-763, Oct. 1966.
4. Callahan, D., K. Kennedy and J. Subhlok, "Analysis of Event Synchronization in a Parallel Programming Tool," *Proc. 2nd Symposium on the Principle and Practice of Parallel Programming*, pp. 21-30, Mar. 1990.
5. Callahan D. and J. Subhlok, "Static Analysis of Low-Level Synchronization," *Proc. SIGPLAN Workshop on Parallel and Distributed Debugging*, pp. 100-111, May. 1988.
6. Choi, J., B. P. Miller and R. H. B. Netzer "Techniques for Debugging Parallel Programs with Flowback Analysis," *ACM Trans. Programming Languages and Systems*, pp. 491-530,Vol. 13, No. 4, Oct. 1991.
7. Emrath, P. A., S. Ghosh and D. A. Padua, "Event Synchronization Analysis for Debugging Parallel Programs," *Proc. Supercomputing 89*, ACM Press, New York pp. 580-588, 1989.
8. Emrath, P. A., S. Ghosh and D. A. Padua, "Detecting Nondeterminacy in Parallel Programs," *IEEE Software*, pp. 69-77, Jan. 1992.
9. Emrath, P. A. and D. A. Padua, "Automatic Detection of Nondeterminacy in Parallel Programs," *Proc. SIGPLAN Workshop on Parallel and Distributed Debugging*, pp. 89-99, May. 1988.
10. Even, Shimon, *Graph Algorithms*, Computer Science Press, 1976.
11. Ghosh, S., "Automatic Detection of Nondeterminacy and Scalar Optimizations in Parallel Programs," *Ph.D. Thesis*,, Dept. of Computer Science, University of Illinois at Urbana-Champaign, 1992.
12. Helmbold, D. P., C. E. McDowell and J. Wang, "Analyzing Traces for Anonymous Synchronization," *Proc. Intl. Conf. Parallel Processing*, pp. 70-77, St. Charles, IL, Aug. 1990.
13. Helmbold, D. P., C. E. McDowell and J. Wang, "Determining Possible Event Orders by Analyzing Sequential Traces," *IEEE Trans. Parallel and Distributed Systems*, pp. 827-839, Vol. 4, No. 7, Jul. 1993.
14. Hood, R., K. Kennedy and J. Mellor-Crummey, "Parallel Program Debugging with On-the-fly Anomaly Detection," *Proc. Supercomputing 90*, New York pp. 74-81, Nov. 1990.
15. McDowell, C. E. and D. P. Helmbold, "Computing Reachable States of Parallel Programs," *Proc. ACM/ONR Workshop on Parallel and Distributed Debugging*, pp. 89-99, May. 1991.
16. Miller, B. P. and J. Choi, "A Mechanism for Efficient Debugging of Parallel Programs," *Proc. ACM SIGPLAN Conf. on Programming Lang. Design and Implementation*, pp. 135-144, Jun. 1988.
17. Netzer, R. H. B., "Race Condition Detection for Debugging Shared-Memory Parallel Programs," *Ph.D. Thesis*, Dept. of Computer Science, University of Wisconsin-Madison, 1991.
18. Netzer, R. H. B. and S. Ghosh, "Efficient Race Condition Detection for Shared-Memory Programs with Post/Wait Synchronization," *Proc. Intl. Conf. Parallel Processing*, Aug. 1992.
19. Netzer, R. H. B. and B. P. Miller, "On the Complexity of Event Ordering for Shared-Memory Parallel Program Executions," *Proc. Intl. Conf. Parallel Processing*, II-93-II-97, Aug. 1990.
20. Netzer, R. H. B. and B. P. Miller, "What are Race Conditions? Some Issues and Formalizations," *ACM Letters on Programming Languages and Systems*, Vol. 1 No. 1, Mar. 1992.
21. Ramanujam, J. and Ashvin Mathew, "Detection of Nondeterminacy in Parallel Programs," *Technical Report* 94-01-03, Department of Electrical and Computer Engineering, Louisiana State University, Baton Rouge, Jan. 1994.
22. Schonberg, E., "On-the-fly Detection of Access Anomalies," *Proc. ACM SIGPLAN Conf. on Programming Lang. Design and Implementation*, pp. 285-297, Jul. 1989.
23. Tarjan, R., "Depth-First Search and Linear Graph Algorithms," *SIAM Journal on Computing*, Vol. 1, pp. 146-160, 1972.

Computing Communication Sets for Control Parallel Programs

Jeanne Ferrante[1], Dirk Grunwald[2] and Harini Srinivasan[2]

[1] IBM, T.J Watson Research Center, PO Box 704
Yorktown Heights, NY 10598
Email:ferrant@watson.ibm.com
[2] Department of Computer Science
Univ of Colorado, Boulder, CO 80309-0430,
Email:(grunwald, harini) @cs.colorado.edu

Abstract. Data flow analysis has been used by compilers in diverse contexts, from optimization to register allocation. Traditional analysis of sequential programs has centered on scalar variables. More recently, several researchers have investigated analysis of *array sections* for optimizations on modern architectures. This information has been used to distribute data, optimize data movement and vectorize or parallelize programs. As multiprocessors become more common-place, we believe there will be considerable interest in explicitly parallel programming languages. In this paper, we extend traditional analysis to array section analysis for parallel languages which include additional control and synchronization structures.

1 Introduction

Parallel computer architectures are becoming more common as computational demands increase and these new machines become more cost effective. Programming such machines using sequential languages has had only limited success [13, 5]. It is recognized that to achieve good performance on such machines, new parallel algorithms need to be developed [38]. Explicitly parallel programming languages such PCF Fortran [30], IBM Parallel Fortran [25], CC++ [7, 8], Parallel SETL [24], The Force [26], and Occam [32] allow the direct expression of such algorithms, and so are finding increasingly wider use.

Common control parallel (or task parallel) constructs found in a number of explicitly parallel programming languages [30, 25, 21, 24, 26] are *co-begin,co-end* and *parallel loops*. Co-begin, co-end parallelism allows multiple blocks to execute in parallel. These languages commonly contain synchronization primitives to coordinate processes. Commonly, co-begin, co-end blocks execute in a data-independent manner, except where synchronization is used. Some languages, such as The Force [26], specify the data that have to be synchronized by explicit *produce* and *consume* notation (*data-oriented synchronization*). Other languages such as PCF FORTRAN and IBM Parallel FORTRAN [30, 25] use event variables and Post and Wait primitives. Event variables do not specify the data that needs to be synchronized. Matching Post and Wait statements require that *all* shared variables in the waiting processor be made consistent with those in the posting processor. In the case of this event synchronization, the programmer specifies "control-oriented" synchronization, *i.e.*, precedence constraints between threads. Our analysis techniques gain the benefits of data-oriented synchronization for parallel programs written with control-oriented synchronization. They accomplish this by conservatively estimating the data that must be propagated between threads during such synchronization.

Recent work [18, 19] has investigated analysis of *array sections* for optimizations on modern architectures. Gross and Steenkiste[19] have a general framework for forward and backward array section and scalar analysis of sequential programs. Granston and Veidenbaum [18] extended [19] to analyze array sections in programs containing statically scheduled doall parallelism without synchronization. In this paper, we extend our previous scalar analysis [11] of explicitly parallel programs with cobegin/co-end parallelism and event synchronization to compute data flow information on *array sections* for the same programs.

We also show one application of our analysis in this paper: partitioning parallel programs. The parallel constructs provided by these languages allow the programmer to specify the 'ideal' parallelism in their applications. It is left to the compiler to determine the *useful* parallelism. In particular, partitioning parallel programs at compile-time to a granularity that fits the particular execution architecture has been shown to be a successful approach to achieving useful parallelism [27, 31, 37, 6, 17, 29, 35, 15, 43, 42, 36].

Previous work such as [37, 42] assume execution time estimates of the nodes and communication cost estimates on the edges of a graph to aid in partitioning decisions; nodes with costly communication between them can be merged to decrease the communication cost and thus the overall execution time. These communication cost estimates can be obtained from analysis of sequential programs, as in PTRAN [2], by explicit representation in the input parallel language, as in Jade [34], or by execution profiling [35]. However, if not just the communication cost, but the actual variables that need to be *sent* and *received* are known as a result of data flow analysis, this information can be used to further help partitioning. To our knowledge, no other previous work [37, 6, 17, 29, 35, 15, 43, 42, 36] considered the use of data flow information to aid partitioning.

In this paper, we extend array section analysis (in particular, the Reaching Definitions and Live Definitions problems) to include explicitly parallel programs with a limited form of event synchronization. We also generalize our previous work on scalar analysis for parallel programs to include programs not only with co-begin, co-end parallelism and some event variable synchronization, but also doall loops. We then show how the results of our analysis can be used to compute *Communication sets* for these parallel programs. This information allows us to communicate only the "needed"data at synchronization points, instead of communicating all shared data. Finally, we show how the results of such analysis can yield better execution time estimates when partitioning explicitly parallel programs on the KSR [33].

We have found very little related work. Duesterwald *et al* present a data flow framework for array reference analysis that exploits fine-grained parallelism [12]. Maydan *et al* [10] used *Last Write Trees* to analyze nested loops for array dataflow information. Gupta and Schonberg [20] present a data flow framework for computing data availability information in programs based on the framework in [19]. None of this work considers control parallelism or explicit synchronization. Cytron *et al* [9] used data flow analysis of automatically parallelized sequential programs to implement compiler-directed caching. Although similar information is computed, our analysis is more difficult due to explicit parallel and synchronization constructs.

The rest of the paper is organized as follows: Section 2 describes the control parallelism and synchronization constructs and the motivation for the data flow analysis of programs that exhibit these constructs; Section 3 describes the data flow analysis techniques to compute *reaching definitions* and *live definitions* information in control parallel programs. Section 4 describes the computation of *communication sets* using the information from the analysis in Section 3. Section 5 presents some experimental results for the example program in this paper. Finally, in Section 6, we give conclusions and some directions for future work.

2 Control Parallelism and Synchronization

We consider control parallel programs that exhibit cobegin/coend parallelism (a limited form of task parallelism) and doall, *i.e.*, loop parallelism. A cobegin/coend construct specifies parallelism among different sections of code. Each such section of code corresponds to a *thread* in the parallel construct. In the case of parallel loops, the different iterations can execute in parallel; hence, each iteration of a parallel loop corresponds to a specific thread.

Our programming model assumes that these different threads must be data independent, except where an appropriate synchronization mechanism is used. Synchronization can be specified using event counters or sequence counters and Post and Wait statements. A post(ev) "posts" the boolean event variable ev and the execution of a wait(ev) is suspended if the event variable has not been posted until this posting occurs. Languages such as PCF Fortran [30] that support event and sequence synchronization require that the shared variables used and modified by the program are made consistent at both Post and Wait statements in the program. We assume *copy-in/copy-out* semantics in our analysis of parallel programs, where at thread creation points, each thread gets its own copy of the shared variables and the global memory is updated with the local copies from the different threads only at coend and Wait statements. We refer the reader for details of our *copy-in/copy-out* assumption to our earlier papers [11, 40].

The rest of this section illustrates the control parallel and synchronization constructs using an example and motivates the need for data flow analysis of such programs using this example.

2.1 Motivating Example

Consider the program in Figure 1: threads T0, T1 and T2 correspond to the three sections of code in the cobegin/coend parallel block that can execute in parallel. The threads T0 and T2 synchronize with T1 via the event variables, ev and ev' respectively. The iterations of the parallel loop used to initialize arrays A and X execute in parallel.

Without data flow analysis, all shared variables must be communicated at the synchronization points. Data flow analysis will infer that

- the use of A(j) in T1 comes from the definition of A(i) in thread T0, where $i = j$. This is the only value that need be communicated when ev is posted in T0.
- the definition of Y(k) in T2 is the value used in T1. This is the only value that need be communicated when ev' is posted in T2.
- at the cobegin node, only arrays A and B need to be sent to thread, T0; arrays A, X, C to thread T1 and arrays X, Y, D to thread T2.

Moreover, such data flow analysis, when combined with other analyses, can make more optimization possible. In our example, the function sin(X(j)) is called in both threads T1 and T2. Using interprocedural analysis to determine the call has no side effects, and data flow analysis to determine each function call uses the same data in both threads, it is possible to merge these two threads and avoid evaluating the function twice.

Even further, the results of such data flow analysis can be used to guide a partitioner which is responsible for merging and scheduling threads for available parallelism. If two processors are available for the three threads, there are three possible schedules for this parallel program: {T0-T1} and T2; {T0-T2} and T1; and {T1-T2} and T0, where { } in each of the schedules indicates a merged thread to be executed on a single processor.

We assume the partitioner uses execution and communication time costs to make its decisions. For this purpose, suppose we make the simple assumptions that a function call costs 100 time units, an assignment statement costs 1 unit, and a communication of a single element 1 unit. The execution time for each of the above cases is computed as the sum of the total computation time and the total communication and synchronization time. Thus the computation time for T0, T1 and T2 are all dominated by the function call in their respective loops, i.e., approximately 10K units each.

Both schedules 1 and 2 increase the computation time of the merged thread, T, since T executes two distinct function calls sequentially. On the other hand, in schedule 3, one of the function calls is redundant and can be eliminated. Since after this optimization there is only a single function call in the merged thread in schedule 3, the computation time of this merged thread is still approximately 10K units.

Schedule 2 does not reduce the data movement in the program since synchronization is not eliminated by this schedule. Schedule 1 eliminates the synchronization between T0 and T1 and hence, array A is local to the processor executing T1 and need not be moved between processors during program execution. Schedule 3 gives a similar outcome and eliminates the movement of array Y between threads T2 and T1. In addition, schedule 3 also results in fewer data being communicated at the cobegin – array X is used in T1 and T2 and has to be propagated to the local memory of only one processor in this schedule. A reduction in data movement between processors corresponds to a reduction in the *communication* time.

Hence, based on the above arguments for reduction in computation and communication times for the three possible schedules, it is clear that schedule 3 is the most preferred.

```
doall i = 1, 100        /* Initialize */
    A(i) = ;   X(i) =
end doall
while (not converged) loop
    Cobegin
        T0:  do  i = 1, 100
                A(i) = A(i)*5
                post(ev(i))
                B(i) = cos(A(i))
            end do
      //
        T1: do  j = 1, 100
                g = sin(X(j))
                wait(ev(j))
                g = g * A(j)
                wait(ev'(j))
                C(j) = g + X(j)*Y(j)
            end do
      //
        T2:  do k = 1, 100
                Y(k) =
                post(ev'(k))
                D(k) = sin(X(k))
             end do
    Coend
end while /* end of convergence loop */
End
```

Fig. 1. Example Illustrating the use of data flow information in scheduling

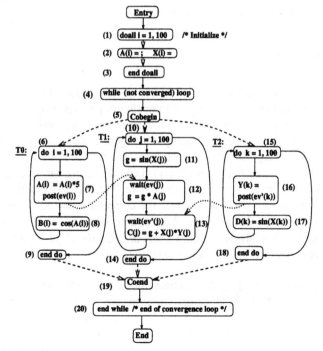

Fig. 2. Parallel Control Flow Graph

The efficiency of scheduling this simple (and admittedly contrived) parallel program is greatly influenced by the variables used within each thread and the variables "passed" between synchronizing processors. Communication costs alone would not provide the necessary information for analyzing these schedules. For scalable, shared-address space architectures, such as the KSR1, the Convex SPP or the Cray T3D, knowing the actual data that is moved can tip the scheduling decision in an unexpected direction. This information on what data is used can also influence scheduling for other parallel architectures, such as multithreaded architectures[4]. In order to determine the actual data and its interactions, it is necessary to compute which definitions of variables are used and defined in specific threads in the program and also, which definitions are "propagated" between specific threads at "consistency points", *i.e.* cobegin and Wait points.

Existing sequential analysis techniques do not handle parallelism and synchronization and hence can not be used to compute this information. Our previous work [11] discusses analysis of scalar variables in parallel programs and points out the inadequacy of sequential analysis techniques for analyzing parallel programs. Since arrays are commonplace in scientific and numerical computation, it is essential to perform array analysis for explicitly parallel programs as well. We use data flow analysis to determine the set of definitions of both array elements and scalars to be communicated between different points in a parallel program. We use *reaching definitions* information to compute the *live definitions* at each point in the parallel program; these are definitions that may be needed in subsequent execution. This information is used to compute the *Send* and *Receive* sets, or the set of variables a thread may send (receive) to (from) another thread. The *send* and *receive* sets may be used to guide particular partitioning or scheduling decisions as illustrated above.

3 Data Flow Analysis

In this section, we briefly overview the data flow analysis necessary to compute *reaching definitions* and *live definitions* information in explicitly parallel programs that exhibit event or sequence synchronization. We explain these two data flow problems in the context of parallel programs using the example in Figure 1. The details of the data flow equations and analysis algorithms for scalar variables and without including doall loops can be found in our earlier paper [11]. [14] contains more details of the reaching definition analysis for the programs considered here. The reaching definitions and live definitions information are used to compute the communication sets, *i.e.*, the set of definitions passed between threads at synchronization and thread creation points in the program. Our data flow analysis techniques use the *Parallel Flow Graph* (PFG) data structure: a node in the PFG can be any of the following:

- an *extended basic block* representing a basic block with at most one Post statement at the beginning of the basic block or at most one Wait statement at the end of the basic block.
- cobegin, coend representing a cobegin and coend statement respectively.
- doall, enddoall representing a doall and enddoall statement respectively.
- *Entry, Exit* representing the unique entry and exit of the program respectively.

and edges represent either parallel control flow, sequential control flow or synchronization. Figure 2 shows the PFG for the program in Figure 1; the dashed edges represent parallel control flow edges and the dotted edges represent the synchronization edges. The solid edges represent sequential control flow edges.

3.1 Reaching Definitions Analysis

We are interested in computing the set of definitions of scalar and array section variables that may reach any point p in the parallel program.

We use the set, *Gen* (n), that represents the set of definitions generated in node n. While computing reaching definitions information, it is necessary to keep track of the set of definitions that must be invalidated by other definitions in the program. A definition of a variable 'v' that is invalidated in a node n does not reach the exit of the node since it is overridden by a new definition of 'v' in n. Traditional sequential analysis techniques to compute reaching definitions information use the *Kill* set at each node for this purpose. In sequential programs, *Kill* (n) for any node n is a local property of n. This is not the case for the parallel programs considered here, and part of the difficulty in computing such sets.

In the context of parallel programs, data is propagated differently along sequential, parallel and synchronization edges. For a parallel control flow edge, $a \rightarrow b$, whenever a executes, b *must* execute. Hence, any definition that is invalidated at the exit of a must always be invalidated at the entry to b. This invalidation information is important in computing the set of definitions that reach b from all its parallel predecessors. Similarly, for a synchronization edge $p \rightarrow w$ where p is the posting node and w the waiting node, if p is the only Post node that triggers the execution of w, then any definition invalidated in p must be invalidated in w. This information is important in computing the set of definitions that reach w from all its predecessors. Event synchronization, however, gives rise to synchronization edges that need not always be executed. For example, it is possible to post an event conditionally. As long as the parallel program is deadlock free, at least one of the Posts for a Wait must execute whenever the Wait executes.

The data flow equations for parallel programs are extensions to the sequential data flow equations. However, in the presence of array sections, we have extended the interval-based algorithms in [19] for array data flow analysis of sequential programs to accommodate our data flow equations for parallel programs. We refer the reader to [14] for the data flow equations and algorithms.

Example: We now describe the results of our analysis using the example in Figure 2. We represent array sections using the *Bounded Regular Section Descriptors* (BRSD) [22]. This representation allows subsections of arrays $M(S)$, where M is the name of the array and S is a vector of subscript values such that each element is: (a) an expression of the form $a * k + b$, where k is the induction variable (b) a triple, $l : u : s$ where l is the lower bound, u the upper bound and s is the stride; or (c) $\perp$ indicating no knowledge of the subscript type.

Figure 3 gives the results of our reaching definitions analysis for the cobegin nodes, its successors and the Post and Wait nodes in Figure 2. In this figure, we have

Node	ParIn	ParOut
(5)	$\{A_2(1:100), X_2(1:100)\}$	$\{A_2(1:100), X_2(1:100)\}$
(6)	$\{A_2(1:100), X_2(1:100)\}$	$\{A_7(1:100), B_8(1:100), X_2(1:100)\}$
(10)	$\{A_2(1:100), X_2(1:100)\}$	$\{A_7(1:100), C_{13}(1:100), X_2(1:100),$ $Y_{16}(1:100), B_8(1:99), D_{17}(1:99), g_{12}\}$
(15)	$\{A_2(1:100), X_2(1:100)\}$	$\{A_2(1:100), X_2(1:100), Y_{16}(1:100),$ $D_{17}(1:100)\}$
(7)	$\{A_7(1:i-1), B(1:i-1), A_2(i:100),$ $X_2(1:100)\}$	$\{A_7(1:i), B(1:i-1), A_2(i+1:100),$ $X_2(1:100)\}$
(16)	$\{A_2(1:100), X_2(1:100), Y_{16}(1:k-1),$ $D_{17}(1:k-1)\}$	$\{A_2(1:100), X_2(1:100), Y_{16}(1:k),$ $D_{17}(1:k-1)\}$
(12)	$\{A_7(1:i), B(1:i-1), A_2(i+1:100),$ $X_2(1:100), C_{13}(1:i-1), g_{11}\}$	$\{A_7(1:i), B(1:i-1), A_2(i+1:100),$ $X_2(1:100), C_{13}(1:i-1), g_{12}\}$
(13)	$\{A_7(1:i), B(1:i-1), A_2(i+1:100),$ $X_2(1:100), C_{13}(1:i-1), Y_{16}(1:i), g_{11}\}$	$\{A_7(1:i), B(1:i-1), A_2(i+1:100),$ $X_2(1:100), Y_{16}(1:i), C_{13}(1:i-1), g_{12}\}$

Fig. 3. Results of Reaching Definitions Analysis at nodes of interest

augmented the BRSD representation with the node number to distinguish definitions of the same variable in different nodes in the PFG.

Since our data flow equations take the semantics of parallelism and synchronization into account, our analysis for parallel programs correctly infers that $A_7(1:j)$ and $A_2(j+1:100)$ reach the entry to node (12) in iteration j of the loop in thread T1 and that $A_2(1:j)$ is always invalidated by the time node (12) in iteration j of this loop executes. Since we have extended array section analysis to handle parallelism and synchronization, we are able to compute specific array elements that reach any point in the program. Our analysis is however restricted to normalized loops and simple array subscripts.

3.2 Live Definitions Analysis

In the *live definitions* problem [23], a definition d of a variable v is *live* at a point p in a program if definition d will be used after p and before any redefinitions of variable v. The data flow sets used to compute live definitions information are:

DDefs(n): the set of definitions in n.
DUses(n): the set of definitions that are used in block n before the corresponding variable is redefined.
LiveIn(n) : the definitions live at the entry to a node.
LiveOut(n) : the definitions live at the exit of a node.

The computation of live definitions information at a node uses the reaching definitions information at this node. In particular, we use the set of definitions reaching the entry to a node n in computing *DUses* (n). The basic data flow equations to compute the *LiveIn* and *LiveOut* information at any node are:

Node	LiveIn	LiveOut
(5)	$\{A_2(1:100), X_2(1:100)\}$	$\{A_2(1:100), X_2(1:100)\}$
(6)	$\{A_2(1:100)\}$	$\{\}$
(10)	$\{X_2(1:100)\}$	$\{\}$
(15)	$\{X_2(1:100)\}$	$\{\}$
(7)	$\{A_2(i:100)\}$	$\{A_7(i), A_2(i+1:100)\}$
(16)	$\{Y_{16}(1:i-1), X_2(i:100)\}$	$\{Y_{16}(1:i), X_2(i:100)\}$
(12)	$\{A_7(i), X(i:100)\}$	$\{X_2(i:100)\}$
(13)	$\{A_7(i+1:100), X(i:100), Y_{16}(i)\}$	$\{A_7(i+1:100), X_2(i+1:100)\}$

Fig. 4. Results of Live Definitions Analysis

$$LiveIn(n) = (LiveOut(n) - DDefs(n)) \cup DUses(n)$$

$$LiveOut(n) = \bigcup_{s \in Succ(n)} (LiveIn(s) \cap ParIn(s))$$

While computing *LiveIn* (n) and *LiveOut* (n) for a node n in the PFG that is within a parallel construct, we also compute *LocalLiveIn* (n) and *LocalLiveOut* (n) sets: these sets represent the live definitions information local to the specific thread in the parallel construct in which n appears.

The details of the algorithm to compute live definitions for explicitly programs with cobegin, doall parallelism and array sections are given in [14]. The live definitions results at the cobegin node and its successors and the Post and Wait nodes in Figure 1 are given in Figure 4. Since we use interval analysis to compute *LiveIn* and *LiveOut* information for array sections, the *LiveOut* sets for nodes (6), (10) and (15) are the live definitions information at the exit of the corresponding loops. Since we accommodate synchronization semantics in our equations, our analysis is able to infer that the definition $A_7(j)$, and not $A_2(j)$ is live at the entry to node (12). Also since $X_2(j)$ is live at the entry to both nodes (11) and (17), it is possible to infer that the expression evaluated on the RHS of the assignment statements in both these nodes are identical. Note that although $B_8(1:i-1)$ reaches the exit of (7), it is not in the live definitions set at (7) or (12) since this data is not used later on. Thus, live definitions information in parallel programs can also be used to eliminate dead-code in these programs.

We have implemented the iterative and interval-based algorithms to compute reaching definitions and live definitions in parallel programs using the SETL prototyping language. We used this implementation to compute the reaching definitions results and live definitions results in Figures 3 and 4 respectively. Note that in the presence of array section variables, the set operations, union, intersection and minus are on sets of array section definitions. These operations are on BRSD's and explained in [28]. We use similar algorithms in our implementation of the set operations. Our algorithms for these set operations also consider the node numbers in the BRSD representation to accommodate definitions of variables.

4 Communication Sets

We now present the data flow equations to compute *send/receive* sets. These equations use the reaching definitions and live definitions data flow information computed for parallel programs. For the programs that we consider, we compute these sets at those points in the program where memory consistency operations take place: cobegin, doall nodes and their immediate successors; coend, enddoall nodes and their immediate predecessors; and corresponding Post/Wait nodes.

At a cobegin node, the data that must be sent to each forked thread consists of those definitions of variables that are used in the forked thread. The set of definitions that must be received by any thread at a fork node, *i.e.*, the *receive* set of a successor of a cobegin node is that subset of *send*(cobegin) that is used locally within this thread:

$$send(\text{cobegin}) = LiveOut(\text{cobegin}), \quad receive(s) = LocalLiveIn(s)$$

where s is a successor of the cobegin node.

The data that should be sent to the coend node are all definitions of variables that reach the coend and used in subsequent nodes. This includes definitions sent from the predecessors of coend and definitions sent from the cobegin: $receive(\text{coend}) = LiveIn(\text{coend})$

The *send* at a predecessor, p, of a coend is computed as: $send(p) = LiveOut(p) - send(\text{cobegin})$, *i.e.*, the set of definitions that are live at the exit of p and that are not directly propagated to the coend node from the corresponding cobegin node. This ensures that only the variables defined or communicated to the thread in which p appears need to be communicated to the coend node.

The *send* and *receive* sets at doall and enddoall nodes are:

$$send(\text{doall}) = LiveOut(\text{doall}), \quad receive(\text{enddoall}) = LiveIn(\text{enddoall})$$

The *receive* set at the successor s of a doall node is: $receive(s) = LiveIn(s)$. The *send* set at the predecessor p of an enddoall node is: $Send(p) = LiveOut(p)$

Similarly, the *send* and *receive* sets at posting and waiting nodes can be computed based on the live definitions and reaching definitions information at these nodes. A definition is in the *send* set of a posting node if it is in the *LiveIn* set of at least one of its synchronization successors in the Parallel Flow Graph and *reaches* the exit of the posting node. A definition is in the *receive* set of a waiting node if it is in the *send* set of at least one of its synchronization predecessors. For a posting node p and a waiting node q, $send(p)$ and $receive(q)$ are defined as follows:

$$send(p) = (\bigcup_{s \in SynchSucc(p)} LiveIn(s)) \cap ParOut(p)$$

$$receive(q) = \bigcup_{s \in synch\_pred(q)} send(s)$$

where *SynchSucc*(p) are the synchronization successors of p and *synch_pred*(q) are the synchronization predecessors of q. The different semantics of post-wait synchronization and parallel control flow at cobegin, coend nodes accounts for the slight difference in the computation of the *send/receive* sets at these nodes. Using the above data flow equations to compute communication sets, we infer the following *send* and *receive* sets for the parallel program in Figure 1:

Node	send	receive
(5)	$\{A_2(1:100), X_2(1:100)\}$	
(6)		$\{A_2(1:100)\}$
(10)		$\{X_2(1:100)\}$
(15)		$\{X_2(1:100)\}$
(7)	$\{A_7(i)\}$	
(16)	$\{Y_{16}(i)\}$	
(12)		$\{A_7(i)\}$
(13)		$\{Y_{16}(i)\}$

Note that even though array B is defined in thread T0, only the elements of A defined in this thread are used in T1. Hence, B is not communicated to T1 via the synchronization thread. Similarly, only Y (and not D) is communicated from T2 to T1.

5 Experimental Results

The data flow information computed in this paper can be used to perform classical code optimizations such as redundant code elimination and code motion, to improve the parallelism in explicitly parallel programs and to partition programs at compile-time. In this section, we show some results of using the data flow information in explicitly parallel programs for compile-time program partitioning. We use the communication sets, computed using the data flow equations given in section 4, in estimating the communication costs in parallel programs. We incorporate these costs into a well-understood algorithm in the literature for partitioning parallel programs [36]. The algorithm in [36] attempts to partition the tasks in the parallel program, balancing parallelism and overhead. In general, this optimization problem is NP-complete and a number of heuristics have been proposed. This algorithm iteratively merges tasks based on the following two heuristics: choose task T_1 that results in the maximum average decrease in overhead; then, merge T_1 with the task that results in the lowest critical path length.

The critical path and the overhead costs are computed from a knowledge of both the computation cost and the cost of overheads such as Post, Wait and Fork. The details of the algorithm can be found in [36]. Our aim is not to develop another partitioning algorithm, but to suggest improvements to the algorithm in [36]. These improvements are based on data flow analysis of parallel programs. The rest of this section briefly overviews our approach. The details of our modifications to the algorithm by Sarkar can be found in [39].

Communication Costs

According to the KSR manual [33], the latency incurred in accessing a single cache line (128 bytes) from a different processor in the same ring takes approximately 7 microsecs (μs). Therefore, it takes approximately 4375 μs to access a 100x100 array of floating point values. By comparison, the time for fork is 2,500μs, and the times to post and wait for a signal are 32μs and 34μs, respectively. Thus, the data movement or communication cost is significantly greater than the other overhead costs on the KSR. Therefore, knowledge of the communication costs in the parallel program should provide additional information for partitioning these programs. The communication sets can be used to estimate the communication costs which contribute to the total execution time of a task and the critical path length of a partition. These costs can also be used to determine the decrease in overhead due to overlapping communication sets between tasks. In addition, our data flow information can also be used to perform code optimizations such as common sub-expression elimination and code hoisting. The resulting decrease in execution time due to these optimizations also contribute to the criteria for merging tasks. We incorporated the effect of communication sets and the other data flow information into the partitioning algorithm in [36].

Experimental Design and Results

To illustrate our approach, we used a parallel program generated by the PTRAN analysis system for multiprocessing [3]. PTRAN generates parallel programs with Parallel Cases and parallel loops. The Parallel Cases construct is analogous to the cobegin,coend construct discussed in this paper. We used the parallel program, NEWRZ generated by the PTRAN compilation system to illustrate our approach. NEWRZ is a subroutine from program SIMPLE. This routine calculates the new velocities, coordinates, the density and change in specific volume used in the computational fluid dynamics and heat flow code of SIMPLE [16]. The original PTRAN generated program expresses the maximum possible parallelism in the program. Based on the partition from the algorithm in [36] and our modified version of this algorithm, we obtained two different parallel programs. We implemented the two partitions for NEWRZ obtained from the two versions of the partitioning algorithm described above.

The implementation used the KSR pthread run-time system. This run-time system provides function calls for thread creation (pthread_create()), barrier synchronization (pthread_barrier()) and locks (pthread_mutex_lock(), pthread_mutex_unlock()). We used pthread_mutex_lock() and pthread_mutex_unlock() to implement the event synchronization primitives on the KSR. We used the pthread_barrier functions along with pthread_create to implement the Parallel Cases and Parallel Loop constructs. The execution time was measured as the average of 20 runs for each of the two partitions. For the partition that uses data flow information, the execution time of the parallel program is 25.29 secs. For the partition of that does not use data flow information, the corresponding execution time is 30.35 secs. Thus, knowledge of data flow information and subsequent optimizations in this case gives a partition that is 16.6% faster. The performance gain for NEWRZ suggests the applicability of our data flow analysis results in an existing partitioning algorithm.

We remark that the model that we use does not exactly fit the KSR memory consistency implementation. The KSR implements an invalidation protocol in hardware:

whenever a write to a memory location occurs, the write operation can not commit unless any copies of this data on other processors have been invalidated. However, our cost model assumes that a write operation does not wait for the invalidation to be completed. We assume communication costs at a `Wait` node and not at a `Post` node. Our cost model is more appropriate for a weak memory consistency implementation where invalidations can occur at any point after a write to a location occurs. Thus writes can be pipelined causing less delay in the process issuing the write. In order to completely model a strong consistency implementation, it may be necessary to compute additional data flow sets that model the invalidation protocol.

6 Conclusions

Data flow information can be used to obtain better estimates of the computation and communication costs in explicitly parallel programs. These costs can be used to obtain efficient schedules of such programs. In this paper, we have shown how to compute communication sets that can be used to estimate the cost of data movement during the execution of a parallel program. We have illustrated how such communication information is useful in making scheduling decisions.

We use reaching definitions and live definitions information in computing the communication sets at synchronization points in a parallel program. The analysis necessary to compute these data flow properties in explicitly parallel programs are significant extensions to the corresponding analysis for sequential programs. We have illustrated how the reaching definitions and live definitions information can be used to schedule computations in explicitly parallel programs.

Acknowledgements: This work was funded in part by NSF grant No. ASC-9217394 and an IBM Graduate Fellowship.

References

1. Frances Allen, Michael Burke, Philippe Charles, Ron Cytron, and Jeanne Ferrante. An overview of the PTRAN analysis system for multiprocessing. In *Proc. 1987 International Conf. on Supercomputing*, pages 194–211, Athens, Greece, June 1987.
2. Frances Allen, Michael Burke, Philippe Charles, Ron Cytron, and Jeanne Ferrante. An overview of the PTRAN analysis system for multiprocessing. *J. Parallel and Distributed Computing*, 5(5):617–640, October 1988.
3. Frances Allen, Michael Burke, Philippe Charles, Ron Cytron, and Jeanne Ferrante. An overview of the PTRAN analysis system for multiprocessing. *J. Parallel and Distributed Computing*, 5(5):617–640, October 1988. (update of [1]).
4. Robert Alverson, David Callahan, Daniel Cummings, Brian Koblenz, Allan Porterfield, and Burton Smith. The Tera Computer System. In *Proc. 17th Annual Symposium on Computer Architecture, Computer Architecture News*, pages 1–6, Amsterdam, Netherlands, June 1990. ACM, ACM.
5. W. Blume. Success and limitations in automatic parallelization of the perfect benchmark programs. Technical report, U. of IL-Center for Supercomputing Research and Development, July 1992. CSRD Rpt. No. 1249.

6. Shahid H. Bokhari. Partitioning problems in parallel, pipelined, and distributed computing. *IEEE Transactions on Computers*, C-37:48–57, January 1988.

7. K.M. Chandy and C.F. Kesselman. Compositional C++: Compositional parallel programming. In *Proceedings of the Fourth Workshop on Parallel Computing and Compilers*. Springer-Verlag, 1992.

8. K.M. Chandy and C.F. Kesselman. *Research Directions in Object Oriented Programming*, chapter CC++: A Declarative Concurrent Object Oriented Programming Notation. MIT Press, 1993.

9. Ron Cytron, Steve Karlovsky, and Kevin P. McAuliffe. Automatic management of programmable caches (extended abstract). *Proceedings of the 1988 International Conference on Parallel Processing*, August 1988. Also available as CSRD Rpt. No. 728 from U. of Ill.-Center for Supercomputing Research and Development.

10. D. E. Maydan, S. Amarasinghe and M. S. Lam. Array data flow analysis and its use in array privatization. In *Conf. Record 20th Annual ACM Symp. Principles of Programming Languages*, Charleston, South Carolina, January 1993.

11. Dirk Grunwald and Harini Srinivasan. Data Flow Equations for Explicitly Parallel Programs. In *Conf. Record ACM Symp. Principles and Practice of Parallel Programming*, San Diego, California, May 1993.

12. E. Duesterwald, Rajiv Gupta, and Mary Lou Soffa. A practical data flow framework for array reference analysis and its use in optimizations. *Proceedings of the SIGPLAN 93 conference on programming language design and implementation*, pages 68–77, June 1993.

13. R. Eigenmann and W. Blume. An effectiveness study of parallelizing compiler techniques. *Proceedings of the International Conference on Parallel Processing*, August 1991.

14. Jeanne Ferrante, Dirk Grunwald, and Harini Srinivasan. Array Section Analysis for Control Parallel Programs. Technical Report CU-CS-684-93, University of Colorado at Boulder., November 1993.

15. A. Gerasoulis, Venugopal, and T. Yang. Clustering task graphs for message passing architectures. *Proceedings of the 4th ACM Inter. Conf. on Supercomputing (ICS 90)*, pages 447–456, June 1990.

16. J. E. Gilbert. An Investigation of the Partitioning Algorithms Across an MIMD Computing System. Technical Report Technical Report 176, Stanford University, Computer Systems Laboratory, May 1980.

17. Milind Girkar and Constantine Polychronopoulos. Partitioning programs for parallel execution. Technical report, U. of IL-Center for Supercomputing Research and Development, July 1988. CSRD Rpt. No. 765 Also in Proc. of ACM 1988 Int'l. Conf. on Supercomputing, St. Malo, France, July 4-8, 1988, pp. 216-229.

18. E. Granston and A. Veidenbaum. Detecting Redundant Accesses to Array Data. In *Proc. of Supercomputing 1991*, pages 854–965, Albuquerque, NM, November 1991.

19. Thomas Gross and Peter Steenkiste. Structured Dataflow Analysis for Arrays and its Use in an Optimizing Compiler. *Software - Practice and Experience*, 20(2):133–155, February 1990.

20. Manish Gupta and Edith Schonberg. A Framework for Exploiting Data Availability to Optimize Communications. In *Proc. of the Sixth Workshop on Languages and Compilers for Parallel Computing* [41].

21. P. Brinch Hansen. The Programming Language Concurrent Pascal. *IEEE Transactions on Software Engineering*, 1(2):199–206, June 1975.

22. P. Havlak and K. Kennedy. An Implementation of Interprocedural Bounded Regular Section Analysis. *IEEE Trans. on Parallel and Distributed Systems*, 2(3):350–360, July 1991.

23. Matthew S. Hecht. *Flow Analysis of Computer Programs*. North Holland, New York, 1977.

24. S. Flynn Hummel and R. Kelly. A rationale for massively parallel programming with sets. *Journal of Programming Languages*, 1993. Published by Chapman and Hall. To appear.
25. IBM. *Parallel Fortran Language and Library Reference*, March 1988. Pub. No. SC23-0431-0.
26. Harry F. Jordan, Muhammad S. Benten, Gita Alaghband, and Ruediger Jakob. The force: A highly portable parallel programming language. In Emily C. Plachy and Peter M. Kogge, editors, *Proc. 1989 International Conf. on Parallel Processing*, volume II, pages II–112 – II–117, St. Charles, IL, August 1989.
27. B. W. Kernighan and S. Lin. An efficient heuristic procedure for partitioning graphs. *The Bell System Technical Journal*, pages 291–307, February 1970.
28. C. Koelbel. Compiling Programs for Nonshared Memory Machines. Technical report, Purdue University, August 1990.
29. C. McCreary and H. Gill. Automatic determination of grain size for efficient parallel processing. *CACM*, 32(9):1073–1078, September 1989.
30. Parallel Computing Forum. PCF FORTRAN. *FORTRAN Forum*, 10(3), September 1991. special issue.
31. Jih-Kwon Peir. *Program Partitioning and Synchronization on Multiprocessor Systems*. PhD thesis, University of Illinois at Urbana-Champaign, March 1986. Report No. UIUCDCS-R-86-1259.
32. Dick Pountain and David May. A tutorial introduction to OCCAM Programming. March 1987.
33. Kendall Square Research. Technical summary. Technical report, Kendall Square Research, 1992.
34. M. Rinard, D. Scales, and M. Lam. Heterogeneous Parallel Programming in Jade. In *Proc. of IEEE Supercomputing 92*, pages 245–258, Nov. 1992.
35. Vivek Sarkar. *Partitioning and Scheduling Parallel Programs for Multiprocessors*. Pitman, London and The MIT Press, Cambridge, Massachusetts, 1989. In the series, Research Monographs in Parallel and Distributed Computing. This monograph is a revised version of the author's Ph.D. dissertation published as Technical Report CSL-TR-87-328, Stanford University, April 1987.
36. Vivek Sarkar. Automatic Partitioning of a Program Dependence Graph into Parallel Tasks. *IBM Journal of Research and Development*, 35(5/6):779–804, September/November 1991.
37. Vivek Sarkar and John Hennessy. Partitioning parallel programs for macro-dataflow. *ACM Conference on Lisp and Functional Programming*, pages 202–211, August 1986.
38. L. Snyder. Type architecture, shared memory, and the corollary of modest potential. *Annual Review of Computer Science*, pages 289–318, 1986.
39. Harini Srinivasan. *Optimizing Explicitly Parallel Programs*. PhD thesis, University of Colorado, Aug 1994. in preparation.
40. Harini Srinivasan and Michael Wolfe. Analyzing programs with explicit parallelism. In Utpal Banerjee, David Gelernter, Alexandru Nicolau, and David A. Padua, editors, *Languages and Compilers for Parallel Computing*, pages 405–419. Springer-Verlag, 1992.
41. *Proc. of the Sixth Workshop on Languages and Compilers for Parallel Computing*, Portland, OR, August 1993.
42. T. Yang and A. Gerasoulis. Pyrros: Static task scheduling and code generation for message passing multiprocessors. In *Proc. of 6th ACM Inter. Conf. on Supercomputering (ICS 92)*, pages 428–437, July 1992.
43. T. Yang and A. Gerasoulis. A Fast Static Scheduling Algorithm for DAGs on an Unbounded Number of Processors. In *Proc. of IEEE Supercomputing 91*, pages 633–642, Nov. 1991.

Optimizing Parallel SPMD Programs

Arvind Krishnamurthy and Katherine Yelick*
{arvindk,yelick}@cs.berkeley.edu

University of California at Berkeley

Abstract. We present compiler optimization techniques for explicitly parallel programs that communicate through a shared address space. The source programs are written in a single program multiple data (SPMD) style, and the machine target is a multiprocessor with physically distributed memory and hardware or software support for a single address space. Unlike sequential programs or data-parallel programs, SPMD programs require *cycle detection*, as defined by Shasha and Snir, to perform any kind of code motion on shared variable accesses. Cycle detection finds those accesses that, if reordered by either the hardware or software, could violate sequential consistency. We improve on Shasha and Snir's algorithm for cycle detection by providing a polynomial time algorithm for SPMD programs, whereas their formulation leads to an algorithm that is exponential in the number of processors. Once cycles and local dependencies have been computed, we perform optimizations to overlap communication and computation, change two-way communication into one-way communication, and apply scalar code optimizations. Using these optimizations, we improve the execution times of certain application kernels by about 20-50%.

1 Introduction

Optimizing explicitly parallel shared memory programs requires *cycle detection* analysis to ensure proper parallel program semantics. Consider the parallel program fragment in Figure 1. The program is indeterminate in that the read of Y may return either 0 or 1, and if it is 0, then the read to X may return either 0 or 1. However, if 1 has been read from Y, then 1 must be the result of the read from X. Intuitively, the parallel programmer relies on the notion of *sequential consistency*, which says the parallel execution must behave as if it is an interleaving of the sequences of memory operations from each of the processors [9]. As a more useful program example, assume that X is a data structure being produced by processor 2 and Y is a "presence" bit to denote that it has been produced.

If the two program fragments in Figure 1 were analyzed by a sequential compiler, it might determine that the reads or writes could be reordered, since there

* This work was supported in part by the Advanced Research Projects Agency of the Department of Defense monitored by the Office of Naval Research under contract DABT63-92-C-0026, by Lawrence Livermore National Laboratory, by AT&T, and by the National Science Foundation (award numbers CDA-8722788 and CCR-9210260). The information presented here does not necessarily reflect the position or the policy of the Government and no official endorsement should be inferred.

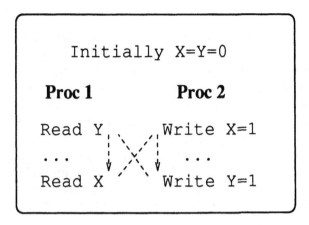

Fig. 1. If the read of Y returns 1, then the read of X must as well.

are no dependencies in either case. If either pair of the accesses is reordered, the execution in which Y is 1 and X is 0, might result. Alternatively, imagine that the program is executed in a distributed memory environment in which X is located on a third processor, and Y is located on processor 1. If the writes are non-blocking, i.e., the second one is initiated before the first is complete, then again sequential consistency could be violated. Similar scenarios exist for systems in which the network reorders messages or the compiler keeps copies of shared data in registers.

The cycle detection problem is to detect access cycles, such as the one designated by the figure-eight in Figure 1. In addition to observing local dependencies within a program, a compiler must ensure that accesses issued by a single processor in a cycle take place in order. Cycle detection is necessary for basic optimizations in shared memory programs, whether they run on physically shared or distributed memory and whether they have dynamic or static thread creation. Cycle detection is not necessary for automatically parallelized sequential programs or data parallel programs with sequential semantics, because every pair of accesses has a fixed order. In the example, the semantics would determine that either the write or read to X (similarly Y) must appear in particular order.

In spite of the semantic simplicity of deterministic programming models, in practice, many applications are written in an explicitly parallel model. In this paper, we consider the common special case of Single Program Multiple Data (SPMD) programs, where multiple copies of a uniprocessor program communicate either through a shared address space [5] or through messages. This model is popular for writing libraries like ScaLapack and runtime systems for high level languages like HPF [6] and pC++ [3]. The uniprocessor compilers that analyze and compile the SPMD programs are ill-suited to the task, because they do not have information about the semantics of the communication and synchronization mechanisms. As a result, they miss opportunities for optimizing communication and synchronization, and the quality of the scalar code is limited by the inability to move code around parallelism primitives [11].

Cycle detection requires finding *conflicts* between concurrent code blocks, which are pairs of accesses to the same location from two different processors where at least one is a write. Cycle detection requires alias information, and is therefore similar to dependence analysis in parallelizing compilers. However, our goal in optimizing SPMD is more modest: the main source of parallelism has been exposed by the application programmer, so our job is to optimize the parallel code by making better use of local processor and network resources.

Cycle detection was first described by Shasha and Snir [15] and later extended by Midkiff, Padua, and Cytron to handle array indices. Their formulation gives an algorithm that is exponential in the number of processors and requires $PROCS$ (the number of processors) copies of the program. We give a polynomial time algorithm for the restricted version of the problem arising in SPMD programs.

Our target machine is a multiprocessor with physically distributed memory and hardware or software support for a global address space. A remote reference on such a machine has a long latency, from roughly 80 cycles on a Cray T3D [13] to 400 cycles on a CM5 using Active Messages [16]. However, most of this latency can be overlapped with local computation or with the initiation of more communication, especially on machines like the J-Machine and *T, with their low overheads for communication startup.

Two important optimizations for these multiprocessors are communication overlap and the elimination of round-trip message traffic. The first optimization, *message pipelining*, changes remote read and write operations into their split-phase analogs, *get* and *put*. In a split-phase operation, the initiation of an access is separated from its completion [5]. The operation to force completion of outstanding split-phase operations comes in many forms, the simplest of which (called *sync* or *fence*) blocks until all outstanding accesses are complete. To improve communication overlap, *puts* and *gets* are moved backwards in the program execution and *syncs* are moved forward. The second optimization eliminates acknowledgement traffic, which are required to implement the *sync* operation. In some cases global synchronization information can be used to eliminate the acknowledgement.

Other optimizations are also enabled by our analysis, but are not discussed in detail in this paper. These include improved scalar optimizations, making local cached copies of remote values, and storing a shared value in a register. The last two fall into the general class of optimizations that move values up the memory hierarchy to keep them closer to the processor [1].

The primary contribution of this paper is a new polynomial time algorithm for cycle detection in SPMD programs. This improves on the running time of the algorithm by Shasha and Snir, which is exponential in the number of processors. This analysis is used to perform optimizations such as message pipelining by using the portable Split-C runtime system as an example backend [5].

We describe the compilation and optimization problem for a simple shared memory language. The target language is Split-C, which is described in section 2. We present basic terminology needed for the analysis in section 3 and the analysis itself in section 5.1. Section 6 gives a basic code generation algorithm. Section 7 estimates the potential payoffs of our approach by optimizing a few application kernels. Related work is surveyed in section 8, and conclusions drawn in section 9.

2 The Target Language

Our target language is Split-C, a SPMD language for programming distributed memory machines [5]. Split-C provides a global address space through two mechanisms: a global distributed heap and distributed arrays. Values allocated in the global heap can be accessed by any processor using a *global pointer*; they can be accessed by the processor that owns that portion of the heap using a local pointer. Global pointers can be stored in data structures and passed in and out of functions using the same syntax as normal (local) pointers. Dereferencing a global pointer is more expensive than dereferencing a local one: it involves a check (in software on the CM5) to see whether the value is on the current processor or not, and if not, a message is sent to the owning processor. Split-C also provides a simple extension to the C array declaration to specify *spread arrays*, which are spread across the entire machine. Each index in the spread dimensions is placed on a different processor, mapping them linearly from zero to PROCS, wrapping as needed.

Our source language is almost a subset of Split-C, and has the essential components necessary to present our approach. For simplicity, the source language has shared global variables rather than heap-allocated objects. The shared variables have sequentially consistent semantics. A sample program is given in Figure 2. Shared variables are designated with the keyword shared: the variable flag and the array result are shared, while copies of i and sum exist on each processor. All processor begin executing the main procedure together, although they may execute different code in a data-dependent fashion. The pseudo-constant PROCS denotes the total number of processors and MYPROC denotes the executing processor's identity.

The source language can be trivially compiled into Split-C by allocating shared values in the distributed heap, and turning the shared variable accesses into global pointer dereferences. The shared array construct is directly mapped into a Split-C spread array declaration. The problem of choosing layouts to reduce communication is orthogonal; layout information could come from the programmer, as in HPF or Split-C [6, 5], or from a separate analysis phase [4].

The most important feature of the Split-C language is its support for split-phase memory operations. Given global pointers src1 and dest2, and local values src2 and dest1 of the same type, the split-phase operations are expressed simply as:

```
dest1 := *src1;
*dest2 := src2;
/* Unrelated computation */
sync();
```

In the first assignment statement, a get operation is performed on src1, and in the second, a put is performed on dest2. Neither of these operations are

```
shared event flag;
shared int result[10];

main() {

    int i, sum = 0;
    if (MYPROC == 0) {
        for (i=0; i<10; i++) result[i] = i;
        post(flag);
    }
    wait(flag);
    for (i=0; i<10; i++) sum += result[i];
    barrier();

}
```

Fig. 2. Shared Memory SPMD Program

guaranteed to complete (the values of dest1 and dest2 are undefined) until after the sync statement.

This mechanism allows for communication overlap, but the sync construct provides less control than one might want, because it groups together all outstanding puts and gets from a single processor. Split-C also provides finer grained mechanisms in which a sync object (implemented by a counter) is associated with each memory operation. A family of get_ctr and put_ctr operations are provided to initiate accesses, along with a sync_ctr operation to wait for completion of an access. The signatures, in this case for double word values, are shown below:

```
void d_get_ctr (double *dest, double *global src, Counter *ctr);
void d_put_ctr (double *global dest, double *src, Counter *ctr);
void sync_ctr (Counter *ctr)
```

The computation from the earlier example can therefore be written:

```
d_get_ctr (&dest1, src1, ctr);
d_put_ctr (dest2, &src2, ctr);
/* Unrelated computation */
sync_ctr (ctr);
```

To separate the completion of the get from that of the put, two separate counters could be used. In general, this makes it possible to synchronize on a set of accesses, which is useful when two computations (for example two iterations of a loop) are overlapped.

Split-C also provides a store operation that is a variant of the put operation. A store operation generates a write to a remote memory location, but does not acknowledge when the write operation completes. It exposes the efficiency of one-way communication in those cases where the communication pattern is well understood.

Split-C runs on top of Active Messages on the CM5, and there are prototype implementations for the Paragon, SP-1, and a workstation network [10]. It defines a portability layer with fast, non-blocking remote accesses that, unlike large message passing systems, can be implemented without message buffering on both ends [16]. It blurs the distinction between machines with a hardware global address space and those without, making it a good choice for an abstract machine language.

3 Cycle Detection

A parallel execution on n processors is given by n sequences of instruction executions $P_1, \ldots, P_n$. We can ignore the local computation and local accesses, and therefore take each P_i to be the sequence of reads and writes to shared variables. Given an execution $P_i = a_1, \ldots, a_n$, we associate with P_i a graph, $(Vert, Edge)$, with vertices $Vert = \{a_1, \ldots, a_n\}$ and directed edges $Edge = \{[a_1, a_2], [a_2, a_3], \ldots, [a_{n-1}, a_n]\}$. The *program order*, P, is defined to be the union of these P_i's. A parallel execution will order accesses to shared variables. Such an ordering of accesses is *consistent* if the read/write behavior is observed, i.e., if reads always return value of the latest preceding write. We assume the following guarantee is made by the architecture:

System Contract 1 *Let V_v be the set of accesses initiated by the processors to the variable v. Then there exists a total order, E_v, of accesses in V_v that is consistent.*

On a distributed memory machine without hardware caching, each of the E_v's are totally ordered by the processor that owns the variable. With caching, it is the hardware designer's responsibility to ensure this semantics through a cache coherence protocol. The union of these E_v's defines the *execution order*, E, which is partial. Figure 3 illustrates these concepts using solid arrows for P edges and dashed arrows for E edges.

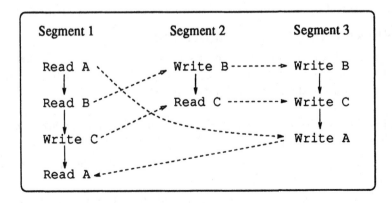

Fig. 3. P and E for a particular execution

The first part of our system contract is very weak—it says nothing about the order in which accesses take place relative to the program order. In a sequentially consistent machine, we would require that there be a single total order that is a superset of the program order, or equivalently, $P \cup E$ is acyclic.

Our target machine does not necessarily keep the accesses from a single program segment in order. The put and get operations specifically permit hardware reordering. To generate code for such a machine and allow for code motion during optimization, we need to determine which of the "happens after" paths in the program order P can be ignored, and which must be enforced. We augment our program to mark those orderings in P^+, the transitive closure of P, that must be observed. A *delay set*, D, for P is a subgraph of P^+. We now extend our system contract to make sure that the delay set is observed:

System Contract 2 *Given a program order P with delay set D, $D \cup E$ is acyclic.*

Note that if we take D to be P, this forces our machine to produce a sequentially consistent execution. Our goal during analysis, however, is to find a much smaller D that still ensures sequential consistency. We say that a delay set D is *sufficient* for program order P if, on any machine that satisfies the system contracts, $P \cup E$ is acyclic, i.e., the execution is sequentially consistent.

P and E are defined for a particular execution of a program, but we would like our analysis to work with a compile-time representation. We therefore approximate P and E (conservatively) by some superset of each. We approximate P by the control flow graph (CFG) of the program segment. Since there are loops in the control flow graph, CFG is no longer a total order on accesses. Also, the notion of an access is replaced by that of an *access instruction* that could initiate multiple accesses to a particular memory location during the execution of the program. At compile time, the runtime ordering of accesses to a variable is also not known. Hence, we approximate E by undirected versions of the E edges, which are called *conflict edges*, C. In general, the conflict edges may be further approximated if our alias analysis is imperfect. The only restriction necessary for correctness of our compiler is $E \subseteq C$ for any execution of the program.

4 Shasha and Snir's Algorithm

Shasha and Snir proved that there exists a minimum delay set, D, that can be defined by considering cycles in $P^+ \cup C$. We present their result in a slightly different form using the following kinds of paths.

Definition 1. A path $[a_1, \ldots, a_n] \in P^+ \cup C$ is *simple*, if for any access a_i in the path, if a_i is an access on processor P_k, then the following hold:

1. If access a_{i+1} is also in P_k, then for all other accesses a_j ($a_j \neq a_i$ and $a_j \neq a_{i+1}$), a_j is not in P_k.
2. If a_{i-1} and a_{i+1} exist ($i \neq 1$ and $i \neq n$) and $[a_{i-1}, a_i] \in C$ and $[a_i, a_{i+1}] \in C$, then for all $a_j \neq a_i$, a_j is not in P_k.

Thus, a simple path is one that visits each processor at most once, with at most two adjacent accesses on a processor. The following special case of simple paths defines the existence of a potential violation of sequential consistency.

Definition 2. Given an edge $[a_n, a_1]$ in some P_k^+, a path $[a_1, \ldots, a_n] \in P^+ \cup C$ is called a *back-path*, for $[a_n, a_1]$ if $[a_1, \ldots, a_n]$ is a simple path.

Shasha and Snir use the notion of a *simple cycle*, which is given by an edge in P^+ along with its back-path. The two are clearly equivalent, but ours lends itself more naturally to an algorithm presentation. We define a particular delay set, $D_{S\&S}$, to be the those edges in P^+ possessing back-paths:

$$D_{S\&S} = \{[a_i, a_j] \in P^+ \| [a_i, a_j] \text{ has a back-path in } P^+ \cup C\}$$

Shasha and Snir proved that if $D_{S\&S}$ is observed, the execution will be sequentially consistent:

Theorem 3. *[15] $D_{S\&S}$ is sufficient.*

They also proved that $D_{S\&S}$ in some sense characterizes the *minimal* delays: in any execution in which an edge in $D_{S\&S}$ executes out of order, there could be a violation of sequential consistency. This notion of minimality is not as strong as we would like, because it ignores the existence of control structures and synchronization that can prevent reorderings from happening even though the cycles exist statically.

5 Shasha and Snir's Algorithm is Exponential

Although Shasha and Snir do not specify the details of an algorithm for computing back-paths, they claim [15] there is a polynomial time algorithm for detection of backpaths in a program that "consists of a fixed number of serial program segments." In practice, one does not (typically) compile a program for a fixed number of processors: either the language contains constructs for dynamically creating parallel threads, or there is a single program that will be compiled for an arbitrary number of processors. We can show that if PROCS is taken as the problem size, the computation needed for the Shasha and Snir formulation is NP-complete[2].

Theorem 4. *Given a directed graph G with n vertices, we can construct a parallel program P for n processors such that there exists a Hamiltonian path in G iff there exists a simple cycle in P.*

5.1 Cycle Detection for SPMD Programs

In this section we present an efficient algorithm for computing the minimum delay set in an SPMD program. The algorithm is based on the idea of backpaths, but uses only two copies of the SPMD code, rather than one for each processor. It eliminates the condition that a back-path must pass through each program segment at most once. For SPMD programs, the delay edges computed by our algorithm is still minimal.

---

[2] The construction and the proof for the following theorem is in [8]

We first describe a transformation of the given control flow graph and then present an algorithm for detecting back-paths in the resulting graph. We show that the delay edges computed for the transformed graph are the same as in Shasha and Snir's approach.

The Transformed Graph

In an SPMD program graph $P = \{P_1, ..., P_n\}$, all P_i are identical. Let V be the set of vertices in some P_i and E be the set of directed edges in P_i. The conflict edges are bi-directional, so we write (u, v) for the pair of edges $[u, v]$ and $[v, u]$. We define a conflict set, C_{SPMD} as the set of edges in P such that at least one of the accesses in the edge is a write.

We generate a new graph P_{SPMD} with nodes V_{SPMD} and edges E_{SPMD}, defines as follows. V_{SPMD} is two copies of the accesses in G, which we label L and R for left and right.

$$V_{SPMD} = \{< v, L >, \; < v, R > \; | \; v \in V\}$$
$$T_1 = \{(< u, L >, < v, R >), \; (< v, L >, < u, R >) \; | \; (u, v) \in C_{SPMD}\}$$
$$T_2 = \{(< u, R >, < v, R >) \; | \; (u, v) \in C_{SPMD}\}$$
$$T_3 = \{(< u, R >, < v, R >) \; | \; [u, v] \in P\}$$
$$E_{SPMD} = T_1 \cup T_2 \cup T_3$$

This transformed graph has two copies of the original program. A backpath will have endpoints in the left part of P_{SPMD} and internal path nodes in the right part. The T_1 edges connect the left and right nodes. The T_2 edges are conflict edges between right nodes. The T_3 edges are program edges that link the right nodes. The left nodes have no internal edges. Therefore, a path from $< v, L >$ to $< u, L >$ is composed of a T_1 edge, followed by a series of T_2 and T_3 edges and terminated with a T_1 edge. Figure 4 illustrates the construction for a simple program.

For every edge $[< u, L >, < v, L >] \in P$, we check whether there exists a path from $< v, L >$ to $< u, L >$ in the graph G'. We construct the set D_{SPMD} that consists of all edges $[u, v]$ having a path from $< v, L >$ to $< u, L >$. Our algorithm runs in polynomial time: if n is the number of accesses in the program, the delay set can be computed in $O(n^3)$ time. Our algorithm has nearly the same sufficiency property as Shasha and Snir's, but is slightly more conservative if there are very long backpaths. The *length* of a backpath is defined as the number of conflict edges in the path.

Theorem 5. *Given an SPMD program for which the longest backpath P_{SPMD} is less than or equal to $PROCS$, $D_{SPMD} = D_{S\&S}$.*
Proof: *Omitted for brevity.*

Our algorithm is correct regardless of the assumption on the longest backpath. To see why ours is more conservative in the (probably rare) case in which the program contains a long backpath, consider such a program. Our algorithm, as described, will compute a delay set for an arbitrary number of processors. If a program with a backpath of length n is run on $PROCS < n$ processors, the

Code:
```
while (turn != MYPROC);
numTrans++;
fund += giftAmt;
turn++;
```

Transformed Graph:

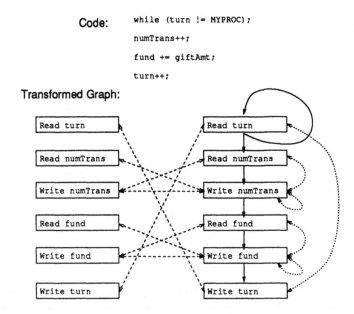

Fig. 4. Cycle detection using two copies of the original program

execution order identified by that backpath has insufficient number of processors to actually take place. Thus, the delay edge added for that backpath is unnecessary. Even this difference between the algorithms is not fundamental: if the value of $PROCS$ is known at compile time, our backpath detection algorithm can search for backpaths shorter than $PROCS$.

6 Code Generation

In this section, we describe how the delay set information is used to generate Split-C style code and some of the trade-offs that arise during this process. The formulation of a delay set from the previous section is quite general, and can be used on a variety of memory models. Our presentation of Split-C code generation is simply one concrete example of such code generation.

The input to code generation is the control flow graph, the delay graph computed by the back-path recognition algorithm, and the *use-def* graph for local variables (as obtained through standard sequential compiler analysis). In code generation process, we need to satisfy the following constraints:

1. Delay constraints are observed.
2. Before every use of a local variable, the corresponding definition is complete.

Consider the program shown in figure 5. The solid line is the delay edge, and the dashed line is a def-use edge for the local variable x.

6.1 A Simple Code Generation Module

We describe a code generation strategy that is simple, but not optimal, and then describe some improvements for it.

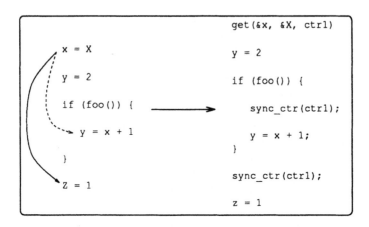

Fig. 5. Code Generation

A simple strategy is to generate a temporary counter for every remote access statement. One should bear in mind that an access statement might initiate multiple accesses during a program's execution. The counter can be used to ensure completion of all the accesses that have been initiated by the access statement. A Split-C code generated for a sample program is shown in figure 5. The counter variable is generated by the compiler. A split-phase get operation is initiated to fetch the value of X into the local variable x. A later sync_ctr operation on $ctr1$ ensures completion of all accesses initiated by the access statement.

The sync_ctr operation waits until the accesses are complete by waiting for the counter value to be reset. A property that makes code generation easy is that a sync_ctr operation behaves like a *null* operation if the program has already executed a sync_ctr on the same counter. In other words, a particular control path through the program can encounter multiple sync_ctr operations on the same counter. This suggests the following simple scheme for code generation.

Let a be an access statement in the program. Let $[a, b_1]$, $[a, b_2]$,..., $[a, b_k]$ be the set of delay constraints on this statement, and if a is a remote read operation, let $[a, c_1]$, $[a, c_2]$,..., $[a, c_l]$ be the set of def-use edges for the local variable being defined by the statement. The compiler converts a into a split-phase operation, and inserts a sync_ctr operation just in front of the access statements b_1, b_2,..., b_k, c_1, c_2,..., c_l. If, however, a **write** access does not have any delay constraints, we transform the **write** access into a **store** access, which is more efficient since it avoids acknowledging the completion of the access.

6.2 Pragmatics of Code Generation

The primary drawback of the simple code generation algorithm is the excessive use of the sync_ctr operation. Certain obvious improvements can be made to the simple scheme. However, it is not clear whether an optimal compile-time technique exists for code generation. As we will discover in this section, the code generation problem is similar in spirit to other compile-time techniques that need profiling information to generate near-optimal code.

Even though correctness of the program's execution is not violated by introducing extra sync_ctr operations, we would like to minimize their use since there is a cost attached to executing a sync_ctr operation. The first step is to reduce the number of program points at which sync_ctr operations are introduced.

Here is the modified algorithm for introducing sync_ctr operations:

1. Every remote access operation a is split into two operations: the corresponding split-phase initiate and a sync_ctr operation.

2. Let s be the sync_ctr operation associated with the split-phase initiate statement i. Rules are used for propagating s through the control flow graph in order to increase the number of instructions between i and s.

   (a) If s is ahead of b in a basic block in the control flow graph and if there are no delay or def-use constraints of the form $[i, b]$, then move s past b. If there are delay or def-use constraints of the form $[i, b]$, s comes to a halt in front of b.

   (b) If s is at the end of a basic block, propagate s to all the successors of the basic block, and continue the motion of the different copies of s.

   (c) If s is ahead of another copy of s, merge the two s operations into a single s operation.

This algorithm propagates the sync_ctr operations as far away from the initiation as possible. Also, if the access a is constrained to complete before the set of access statements b_1, b_2,..., b_k and if for some statement b_l there is no possible flow of control that hits b_l without encountering one of the other b_i statements, then the algorithm does not introduce a sync_ctr operation ahead of b_l. The simple algorithm would have incurred the penalty of an extra sync_ctr operation.

However, the algorithm still suffers from two drawbacks. First, there could be still certain control paths that execute more than one sync_ctr operation (as in figure 5). Second, if there is a delay constraint in which the initiation and the sync_ctr are nested within different conditionals and loops, our algorithm could execute unnecessary sync_ctr operations.

For example, given a delay constraint $[a, b]$ where b appears inside a loop, but a does not, we would not want to introduce a sync_ctr operation inside the loop since that would require the operation to be executed as many times as the loop would be executed. All but the first sync_ctr operation would be redundant. To avoid the cost of unnecessary sync operations, we could employ a loop-unrolling technique. We could separate the first iteration of the loop from the other iterations and introduce the sync_ctr operation only in the code for the first iteration.

The opposite problem occurs for a delay $[a, b]$ where a appears inside a conditional, but b does not. It is not clear where the sync_ctr operation should be introduced to ensure optimal performance. If we have the sync_ctr operation just ahead of b, we could suffer the penalty of executing the operation even when a a access had not been executed. Note that this does not affect the correctness of the code due to the nature of Split-C counters. On the other hand, if we introduce the sync_ctr operation at the end of the conditional containing a, we might be hiding only part of the latency by prematurely waiting for its completion. Static analysis cannot help in choosing between the two alternatives. Relative costs of remote accesses and local memory operations (for updating counters) could be used as an heuristic for code generation.

7 Potential Benefits

We quantify the benefits of our approach by studying the effect of the optimizations on a set of computational kernels. The four applications in our benchmark suite:

1. **FFT:** Computing the fast-fourier transform.

2. **Stencil:** 4-point stencil computation on a regular grid.

3. **Cg:** Computing the conjugant gradient of a sparse matrix.

4. **Em3d:** Solving Maxwell's equations on an irregular grid.

The prototype compiler automatically introduces the message pipelining and one-way communications optimizations for *FFT* and *Stencil*. For *Cg* and *Em3d*, the loops appearing in the benchmarks were manually unrolled before invoking the compiler[3]. The execution times of these applications were improved by 20-50% through message-pipelining and one-way communication optimizations. These were measured on the CM5 multiprocessor. The relative speedups should be even higher on machines with lower communication startup costs or longer relative latencies (when the fraction of the latency that can be overlapped is higher).

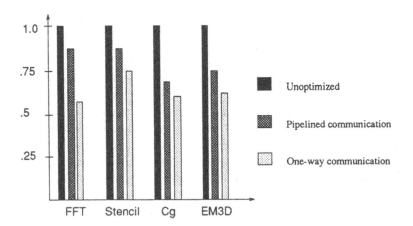

Fig. 6. Normalized Execution Times

---

[3] The loop-unrolling transformation is done as a pre-processing transformation that enlarges the size of basic blocks, thereby increasing the scope of prefetching and pipelining.

Figure 6 gives the performance results of these experiments. The figure gives the execution times, normalized so that the unoptimized execution time is 1. Thus, a relative speed of 0.5 corresponds to a factor of 2 speedup. Other optimizations, such as caching remote values, are also enabled by our analysis, and result in additional performance improvements on some of these applications [8].

8 Related Work

Most of the research in optimizing parallel programs has been for data parallel programs. In the more general control parallel setting, Midkiff and Padua[11] describe eleven different instances where standard optimizations (like code motion and dead code elimination) cannot be directly applied. Analysis for these programs is based on the pioneering work by Shasha and Snir[15], which was later extended by Midkiff et al[12] to handle array based accesses. However, their analysis technique is computationally expensive even for programs with a small degree of parallelism since both the minimal cycle detection problem and the array subscript analysis problem have exponential running times. The algorithm presented in this paper for SPMD programs does not deal with array analysis, but we believe their techniques for handling array subscripts could be incorporated into our SPMD framework.

Compilers and runtime systems for data parallel languages like HPF and Fortran-D[7] implement message pipelining optimizations. The Parti runtime system and associated HPF compiler uses a combination of compiler and runtime analysis to generate code for overlapping communication, aggregating groups of messages, and other optimizations [2]. These optimizations have also been studied in the context of parallelizing compilers[14]. However, as discussed earlier, compiling data parallel programs is fundamentally different than compiling SPMD programs. First, it is the compiler's responsibility to map parallelism of degree n (the size of a data structure) to a machine with PROCS processors, which can sometimes lead to significant runtime overhead. Second, the analysis problem for data parallel languages is simpler, because they have a sequential semantics resulting in directed conflict edges. Standard data-dependence techniques can be used in data parallel language to determine whether code-motion or pipelining optimizations are valid.

9 Conclusions

We have presented analysis techniques and optimizations for SPMD programs on distributed memory multiprocessors. The potential payoff of a few of these optimizations is estimated using hand optimizations on a small set of applications. The performance improvements are as high as a factor of two on the CM5, with even better performance expected on future architectures with lower communication startup.

The new form of analysis that is needed for explicitly parallel programs in a general (not data-parallel) execution model, is cycle detection, as introduced by Shasha and Snir. We showed that their formulation of the analysis led to an NP-complete problem and, therefore, an algorithm that was exponential in the number of processors. Applied to an SPMD program, their algorithm relied on analyzing PROCS copies of the code. We improved on their basic algorithm by giving an alternate formulation that uses only two copies of the code and computes nearly the same set of cycles in polynomial time. Finally, we showed how to use this analysis to generate code for an abstract machine language, Split-C.

References

1. B. Alpern, L. Carter, and E. Feig. Uniform memory hierarchies, Oct. 1990.
2. H. Berryman, J. Saltz, and J. Scroggs. Execution time support for adaptive scientific algorithms on distributed memory multiprocessors. *Concurrenty: Practice and Experience*, pages 159–178, June 1991.
3. F. Bodin, P. Beckman, D. Gannon, S. Yang, S. Kesavan, A. Maloney, and B. Mohr. Implementing a parallel C++ runtime system for scalable parallel system. In *Supercomputing '93*, pages 588–597, Portland, Oregon, November 1993.
4. S. Chatterjee, J. Gilbert, R. Schreiber, and S.-H. Teng. Optimal evaluation of array expressions on massively parallel machines. In *Workshop on Languages, Compilers and Run-Time Environments for Distributed Memory Multiprocessors*, pages 68–71, 1993.
5. D. E. Culler, A. Dusseau, S. C. Goldstein, A. Krishnamurthy, S. Lumetta, T. von Eicken, and K. Yelick. Parallel programming in Split-C. In *Supercomputing '93*, pages 262–273, Portland, Oregon, November 1993.
6. High Performance Fortran Forum. High Performance Fortran language specification version 1.0. Draft, Jan. 1993.
7. S. Hiranandani, K. Kennedy, and C.-W. Tseng. Compiler optimziations for Fortran D on MIMD distributed-memory machines. In *Proceedings of the 1991 International Conference on Supercomputing*, 1991.
8. A. Krishnamurthy. Optimizing explicitly parallel programs. Technical Report CSD-94-835, University of California, Berkeley, September 1994.
9. L. Lamport. How to make a multiprocessor computer that correctly executes multiprocess programs. *IEEE Transactions on Computers*, C-28(9):690–691, September 1979.
10. S. Luna. Implementing an efficient global memory portability layer on distributed memory multiprocessors. Master's thesis, University of California, Berkeley, May 1994.
11. S. Midkiff and D. Padua. Issues in the optimization of parallel programs. In *International Conference on Parallel Processing - Vol II*, pages 105–113, 1990.
12. S. P. Midkiff, D. Padua, and R. G. Cytron. Compiling programs with user parallelism. In *Languages and Compilers for Parallel Computing*, pages 402–422, 1990.
13. W. Oed. The Cray research massively processor system: T3D. Ftp from ftp.cray.com, Nov. 1993.
14. A. Rogers and K. Pingali. Compiling for distributed memory architectures. *IEEE Transactions on Parallel and Distributed Systems*, march 1994.
15. D. Shasha and M. Snir. Efficient and correct execution of parallel programs that share memory. *ACM Transactions on Programming Languages and Systems*, 10(2):282–312, April 1988.
16. T. von Eicken, D. E. Culler, S. C. Goldstein, and K. E. Schauser. Active Messages: a Mechanism for Integrated Communication and Computation. In *International Symposium on Computer Architecture*, 1992.

An Overview of the Opus Language and Runtime System

Piyush Mehrotra and Matthew Haines

Institute for Computer Applications in Science and Engineering
[pm,haines]@icase.edu

Abstract. We have recently designed a set of Fortran language extensions, called *Opus*, that allow for integrated support of task and data parallelism. The language introduces a new mechanism, *shared data abstractions (SDAs)* for communication and synchronization among these data parallel tasks. In this paper we present an overview of the language and describe the thread based runtime systems that we are implementing to support the language.

1 Introduction

Data parallel language extensions, such as High Performance Fortran (HPF) [13] and Vienna Fortran [3], are adequate for expressing and exploiting the data parallelism in scientific codes. However, there are a large number of scientific and engineering codes which exhibit multiple levels of parallelism. *Multidisciplinary optimization* (MDO) applications are a good example of such codes. These applications, such as weather modeling and aircraft design, integrate codes from different disciplines in a complex system in which the different discipline codes can execute concurrently, interacting with each other only when they need to share data. In addition to this outer level of task parallelism, the individual discipline codes often exhibit internal data parallelism. It is desirable to have a single language which can exploit both task and data parallelism, providing control over the communication and synchronization of the coarse-grain tasks.

We have recently designed a new language, called *Opus*, which extends HPF to provide the support necessary for coordinating the parallel execution, communication, and synchronization of such codes [4]. Along with extensions to manage independently executing tasks, we have introduced a new mechanism, called *Shared Data Abstractions* (SDAs), which allows these tasks to share data with each other. SDAs generalize Fortran 90 modules by including features from both *objects* in object-oriented languages and *monitors* in shared memory languages. The result is a data structure mechanism that provides a high-level, controlled interface for large grained parallel tasks to interact with each other in a uniform manner.

---

[1] This research supported by the National Aeronautics and Space Administration under NASA Contract No. NASA-19480, while the authors were in residence at ICASE, MS 132C, NASA Langley Research Center, Hampton, VA 23681.

The runtime system that we are designing to support the features of Opus is divided into two portions: a language-dependent and a language-independent subset. The language-independent portion of the runtime system is based on our lightweight threads package called Chant. This provides an interface for lightweight, user-level threads which have the capability of communication and synchronization across separate address spaces. The language-dependent portion of the runtime system provides support for management of tasks and SDAs running on parallel and heterogeneous environments.

The remainder of the paper is organized as follows: Section 2 briefly outlines the Opus language; Section 3 outlines the runtime support necessary for supporting the task and shared data abstraction extensions in Opus; and Section 4 discusses related research.

2 The Opus Language

In Opus, a program is composed of a set of asynchronous, autonomous tasks that execute independently of one another. These tasks may embody nested parallelism, for example, by executing a data parallel HPF program or by spawning other tasks. A set of tasks interact by creating an SDA object of an appropriate type and making the object accessible to all tasks in the set. The SDA executes autonomously on its own resources, and acts as a data repository. The tasks can access the data within an SDA object by invoking the associated SDA public methods, which execute asynchronously with respect to the invoking task. However, the SDA semantics enforce exclusive access to the data for each call to the SDA. This is done by ensuring that only one method of a particular SDA is active at any given time. This combination of task and SDA concepts forms a powerful tool for hierarchically structuring a complex body of parallel code.

We presume that High Performance Fortran (HPF) [13] is to be used to specify the data parallelism in the codes. Thus, the set of extensions described here build on top of HPF and concentrate on management of asynchronous tasks and their interaction through SDAs.

2.1 Task Management

Opus tasks are units of coarse-grain parallelism executing in their own address space. Tasks are spawned by explicit activation of *task programs* (entities similar to HPF subroutines, where the keyword TASK CODE replaces SUBROUTINE) using the spawn statement:

$$\textbf{SPAWN } \textit{task-code-name } (\textit{arg, } ...) \; [\; \textbf{ON } \textit{resource-request} \;]$$

The semantics of the spawn statement are similar to that of a Unix *fork* in that the spawning task continues execution past the spawn statement, independent (and potentially in parallel) of the newly spawned task. A task *terminates* when its execution reaches the end of the associated task program code, or is explicitly killed.

Tasks execute on a set of system resources specified by the *resource request* in the optional ON clause of the spawn statement. The resource request consists of a machine specification indicating the physical machine to be used for its execution. If the task embodies nested data parallelism using HPF constructs, a processor specification as part of the resource request selects a set of processors for its execution. In the latter case, the compiler will generate the appropriate SPMD code to be executed on the selected processors.

2.2 Shared Data Abstractions

Shared Data Abstractions (SDAs) allow independently executing tasks to interact with each other in a controlled yet flexible manner. An SDA specification, modeled after the Fortran 90 *module*, consists of a set of data structures and an associated set of methods (procedures) that manipulate this data. The data and methods can be public or private, where public methods and data are directly accessible to tasks which have access to an instance of the SDA type. Private SDA data and methods can only be used by other methods within the SDA.

An instance of an SDA also executes in its own address space. In addition, all method arguments are passed using call-by-value or call-by-value-return ensuring that an SDA has no direct access to any other data. A task can create and instance of an SDA type which can then be passed to other tasks at the time of creation or through other SDA method calls. A set of tasks can thus share data and interact by making method calls to shared instances of SDAs.

As stated before, access to SDA data is exclusive, thus ensuring that there are no conflicts due to the asynchronous method calls. That is, only one method call associated with an SDA object can be active at any time. Other requests are delayed and the calling task is blocked until the currently executing method completes. In this respect, SDAs are similar to monitors.

Figure 1 presents a code fragment that specifies the SDA *stack* which can be used to communicate integers between tasks in a last-in-first-out manner. The SDA is comprised of two parts, separated by the keyword **CONTAINS**. The first part consists of the internal data structures of the SDA, which in this case have all been declared private, and thus cannot be directly accessed from outside the SDA. The second part consists of the procedure declarations which constitute the methods associated with the SDA.

Each procedure declaration can have an optional *condition clause* using the keyword **WHEN**, which "guards" the execution of the method. The condition clause consists of a logical expression, comprised of the internal data structures and the arguments to the procedure. A method call is executed only if the associated condition clause is true at the moment of evaluation, otherwise it is enqueued and executed when the condition clause becomes true. For example, the *put* method can be executed only when *count* is less than *max* and the *get* method can be executed only when *count* is greater than zero.

Similar to HPF procedure declarations, each SDA type may have an optional resource request directive, which allows the internal data structures of the SDA to be distributed across these processors. This is useful (or perhaps necessary) for

```
SDA TYPE  stack (max)
   INTEGER max
   INTEGER lifo(max)
   INTEGER count
   PRIVATE lifo, count, max

   . . .
CONTAINS
   SUBROUTINE get (x)  WHEN (count . gt. 0)
      INTEGER x
      x = lifo(count)
      count = count - 1
   END

   SUBROUTINE put (x)  WHEN (count . lt. max)
      INTEGER x
      count = count + 1
      lifo(count) = x
   END

   INTEGER FUNCTION cur_count
      cur_count = count
   END
   . . .
END stack
```

Fig. 1. Code fragment specifying the *stack* SDA

SDAs that comprise large data structures. The dummy arguments of the SDA methods can also be distributed using the rules applicable to HPF procedure arguments.

In this section, we have briefly described the main features of Opus; a more detailed description of the language features, including SDA type parameterization and persistence, can be found in [4]. A more concrete example using the features of Opus to encode a simplified application for the multidisciplinary design of an aircraft can also be found in [4].

3 Opus Runtime Support

As specified in the previous section, an Opus program is potentially constructed of three types of parallel entities: parallel tasks, data parallel statements, and SDA method tasks. There are several reasons for wanting to map several of these entities onto a single physical processor: to allow for more parallel entities than physical processing elements; to increase locality of SDA data by placing an SDA on the same processor as a parallel task or data parallel statement;

or to minimize the idle time for a processor by overlapping the execution of various parallel entities with blocking instructions. To allow for parallel entities that are independent of the physical processing resources, Opus employs the well known concept of a *lightweight thread* to represent its unit of parallelism in all cases. Lightweight threads have several advantages over the traditional approach of using operating system processes for representing parallel tasks: they contain only a minimal context to allow for efficient support of fine-grain parallelism and latency-tolerance techniques; they provide explicit control over scheduling decisions; and they provide the ability to execute tasks on parallel systems that do not support a full operating system on each node. One should note that most of the current lightweight threads packages typically assume a single address space as their execution environment. However, Opus requires underlying support for lightweight threads that are capable of execution and communication in a distributed memory environment.

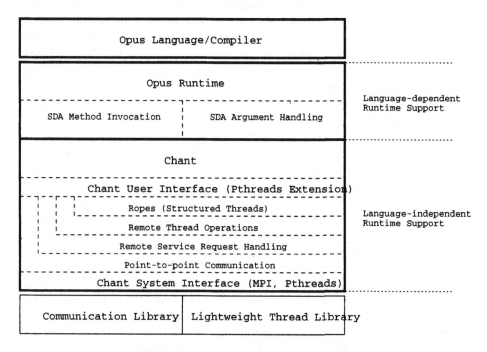

Fig. 2. Runtime layers supporting Opus

As depicted in Figure 2, the runtime system is divided into two essential layers: *Opus Runtime*, which provides support for task and SDA management, and *Chant*, which provides underlying support for lightweight threads in a distributed memory environment. Since Chant does not assume any particular knowledge of the Opus language, we refer to this layer as the language-independent layer, whereas Opus Runtime clearly represents the language-dependent layer. This layered approach allows us to build on a large collection of existing runtime work in the areas of lightweight threads and communication systems. In cooperation with other researchers in this field, we are in the process of attempting to define a standard language-independent runtime interface (at the level of Chant) for parallel languages, called *PORTS*. By using a modular design for the Opus runtime system, we are in the position to take advantage of such a system when it emerges.

We now provide a description of both Chant and Opus Runtime, focusing on some of the basic issues that must be addressed to obtain an efficient implementation of the language. Previous work on Chant [11] and Opus Runtime [12] provides a more detailed description of these systems.

3.1 Chant

Despite their popularity and utility in uniprocessor and shared memory multiprocessor systems, lightweight thread packages for distributed memory systems have received little attention. This is unfortunate: in a distributed memory system, lightweight threads can overlap communication with computation (latency tolerance), emulate virtual processors, and also permit dynamic scheduling and load balancing. However, there is no widely accepted implementation of a lightweight threads package that supports direct communication between two threads, regardless of whether they exist in the same address space or not. Chant has been designed to fill this need.

Chant extends the POSIX pthreads standard for lightweight threads [14] by adding a new object called a **chanter** thread, which supports the functionality for both point-to-point and remote service request communication paradigms, as well as remote thread operations. Point-to-point communication primitives (i.e. *send/receive*) are required to support most existing explicit message passing programs. Remote service request communication primitives are needed to support RPC-style communications [21], as well as client-server applications and *get/put* primitives. Remote thread operations are necessary to support threads in a global environment, such as creating a thread on another processor. Ropes, also based on **chanter** threads, are used for implementing parallel computations which are inherently structured, such as SPMD data parallel codes. Ropes provide a an indexed naming scheme for the threads, as well as a scope for global communication, reduction, and synchronization operations.

Chant is built as a layered system (as shown in Figure 2), where point-to-point communication provides the basis for implementing remote service requests, which in turn provides the basis for implementing global thread operations. Our design goals center on portability, based on existing standards for lightweight threads and communication systems, and efficiency, based on supporting point-to-point message passing without interrupts or extra message buffer copies.

Point-to-Point Communication: Point-to-point communication is characterized by the fact that both the sending thread and receiving thread agree that a message is to be transferred from the former to the latter. Although there are various forms of send and receive primitives, their defining aspect is that both sides are knowledgeable that the communication is to occur. As a result of this understanding, it is possible to avoid costly interrupts and buffer copies by registering the receive with the operating system before the message actually arrives. This allows the operating system to place the incoming message in the proper memory location upon arrival, rather than making a local copy of the message in a system buffer. Chant ensures that no message copies are incurred for point-to-point communication that wouldn't otherwise be made by the underlying communication system, which is tantamount to reasonable efficiency on low-latency/high-bandwidth machines.

To support message passing from one thread to another, Chant must provide solutions to the problems of naming global threads within the context of an operating system entity (process), delivering messages to threads within a process, and polling for outstanding messages.

To enable the use of the underlying thread package for all thread operations local to a given processing element, a **chanter** thread is defined in relation to a particular processing element, which in turn is composed of a process group identifier and a process rank within the group. The group/rank paradigm can be matched to most parallel systems, and also corresponds directly to the MPI standard for representing processing elements [6]. Therefore, a global Chant thread is defined by a 3-tuple, composed of a group identifier, a rank within the group, and a local thread identifier. The type of the local thread identifier is determined by the thread type of the underlying thread package and, although this will vary for different thread packages, allows the global threads to behave normally with respect to the underlying thread package for operations not concerned with global threads.

Most communication systems support delivery to a particular context within a particular processor, but do not provide direct support for naming entities within the context, namely a thread. All message passing systems, however, support the notion of a message header, which is used by the operating system as a *signature* for delivering messages to the proper location (process). Messages also contain a body, which contains the actual contents of the message. In order to ensure proper delivery of messages to threads, and without having to make intermediate copies, the entire global thread name (group, rank, thread) must appear in the message header. Some communication systems, such as MPI, provide a mechanism by which thread names can easily be integrated into the message header. MPI accomplishes this using the *communicator* (i.e. group) field. However, for systems which do not provide support for message delivery to entities within a process, we must overload one of the existing fields in the message header, typically the user-defined tag field. This approach has the disadvantage of reducing the number of tags allowed, but the alternative approach, placing the thread identifier in the message body, would force an intermediate thread to receive all incoming messages, decode the body, and forward the remaining message to the proper thread. In addition to being time consuming, this method would require the message body to be copied for both sending (to insert the thread id) and receiving (to extract the thread id).

The problem of waiting for a message is solved by polling for incoming messages, either by the operating system or user-level code. Operating system polls either block the entire processor while the operating system spins and waits, or allows the process to continue execution and generates an interrupt when a message arrives. Neither of these solutions are desirable, since blocking the entire processor disables the opportunity to execute other (ready) threads, and interrupts are very expensive, causing cache disruptions and mutual exclusion problems. Therefore, in Chant, message polling does not involve the operating system and is done either by the thread which initiates the receive request or by the scheduler. The *thread-polls* method has the advantage of not having to register receive operations with the scheduler, and will work for any underlying thread package, but will cause context switching overheads in the case when a thread is re-scheduled but cannot complete the receive operation. The *scheduler-polls* method requires all threads to register a receive with the scheduler, and then are removed from the ready queue and placed on a blocking queue until the message arrives. This avoids the overhead of scheduling a thread that is not really ready to run, but forces the scheduler to poll for outstanding messages on each context switch, and may not be supported by some lightweight thread libraries. An analysis of these policies is given in [11].

An initial implementation of the Chant point-to-point communication layer for the Intel Paragon was found to introduce only a 6% overhead (on average) for a 1K byte message when compared to the same operations using Paragon processes [11]. These initial performance numbers are encouraging as they demonstrate that thread-based communication introduce little overhead.

Remote Service Requests: Having established a mechanism by which lightweight threads located in different addressing spaces can communicate using point-to-point mechanisms, we now address the problem of supporting remote service requests, which builds on our design for point-to-point message passing. Remote service request messages are distinguished from point-to-point messages in that the destination thread is not expecting the message. Rather, the message details some request that the destination thread is to perform on behalf of the source thread. The nature of the request can be anything, but common examples include returning a value from a local addressing space that is wanted by a thread in a different addressing space (*remote fetch*), executing a local function (*remote procedure call*), and processing system requests necessary to keep global state up-to-date (*coherence management*).

Most remote service requests require some acknowledgment to be sent back to the requesting thread, such as value of a remote fetch or the return value from a remote procedure call. To minimize the amount of time the source thread remains blocked, we wish to process the remote service request as soon as possible on the destination processor, but without having to interrupt a computation thread prematurely. Interruptions are costly to execute and can disrupt the data and code caches which, as processor states increase, will continue to have a detrimental effect on the efficiency of a program. Also, the MPI standard [6] does not support interrupt-driven message passing, thus utilizing interrupts in a design would preclude the use of the MPI communications layer. Therefore, we need a polling mechanism by which remote service requests can be checked without having to prematurely interrupt a computation thread when such a request arrives.

Since the main problem with remote service requests is that they arrive at a processor unannounced, we simply introduce a new thread, called the *server thread*, which is responsible for receiving all remote service requests. Using one of the polling techniques outlined in Section 3.1, the server thread repeatedly issues nonblocking receive requests for any remote service request message, which can be distinguished from point-to-point messages by virtue of being sent to the designated server thread rather than a computation thread. When a remote service request is received, the server thread assumes a higher scheduling priority than the computation threads, ensuring that it is scheduled at the next context switch point.

If the underlying architecture supports a low-latency remote service request mechanism, such as Active Messages [21], in addition to the point-to-point primitives, then Chant would ideally shortcut the remote service request mechanism just described to take advantage of these primitives.

Remote Thread Operations: As well as adding communication primitives to a lightweight thread interface, Chant must support the existing lightweight thread primitives that are inherited from the underlying thread package. These primitives provide functionality for thread management, thread synchronization, thread scheduling, thread-local data, and thread signal handling. We divide these primitives into two groups: those affected by the addition of global thread identifiers in the system, and those not affected. For example, the thread creation primitive must be capable of creating remote threads, but the thread-local data primitives are only concerned with a particular local thread. Our goal in designing Chant is to provide an integrated and seamless solution for both groups of primitives. This is accomplished in two ways.

1. Since a global thread identifier contains a local thread id, it is possible to extract this identifier (using the **pthread_chanter_thread** primitive) and use it as an argument for thread primitives concerned only with local threads, such as manipulating the thread-specific data of a local thread.
2. Thread primitives that are affected by the global identifiers either take a thread identifier as an argument (such as join) or return a thread identifier (such as create). In either case, the primitive must handle the situation of a thread identifier that refers to a remote thread.

Having described the details of how Chant supports remote service requests, we can now utilize this functionality in the form of a remote procedure call. Similar to the manner in which Unix creates a process on a remote machine [22],

Chant utilizes the server thread and the remote service request mechanism to implement primitives which may require the cooperation of a remote processing element.

Ropes: Threads represent task parallelism and the general concept of MIMD programming, where one thread is created for each parallel task that is desired, and execution of the threads is independent and asynchronous. However, data parallelism represents a particular specialization of MIMD programming (often termed SPMD programming), in which all tasks execute the same code but on separate data partitions. Therefore, what is required is a group of threads that captures this behavior better than a collection of otherwise unrelated threads. Specifically, a *rope* is defined as a collection of threads, each executing the same code segment, and participating in certain global communication and coordination operations, where the scope of these global operations is defined as the threads within the rope. This allows for data parallel tasks to mix with unrelated tasks on the same processor, yet restrict all global communication and synchronization operations to those threads that are participating in the data parallel task.

Chant supports ropes by introducing a new object, called a **rope**, which corresponds to a data parallel thread. In addition to the attributes of a global thread, a **rope** thread contains a index relative to the threads within that rope so that all threads within a rope may refer to each other using this index rather than the global thread identifier. This rope index naming scheme is maintained using a local translation table on each processor, which translates a rope identifier and index into a global thread identifier. In addition, new primitives for collective communication and reduction are available to **rope** threads.

3.2 Opus Runtime

In the last subsection, we presented Chant, the language-independent part of the runtime system. We now describe the design of the runtime system required to support the features of Opus that differ from HPF: tasks and SDAs. The two major issues in the Opus runtime system are the management of the execution and interaction of tasks and SDAs. In the initial design, we have concentrated on the interaction and have taken a simplified approach to resource management. We presume that all the required resources are statically allocated and the appropriate code is invoked where necessary. We will later extend the runtime system to support the dynamic acquisition of new resources.

The interaction between tasks and SDAs requires runtime support for both method invocation and method argument handling. These issues are explored in the following subsections.

SDA Method Invocation: The semantics of SDAs place two restrictions on method invocation:

1. each method invocation has *exclusive* access to the SDA data (i.e. only one method for a given SDA instance can be active at any one time), and
2. execution of each method is guarded by a *condition clause*, which is an expression that must evaluate to true before the method code can be executed.

We can view an SDA as being comprised of two components: a control structure, which executes the SDA methods in accordance with the stated restrictions, and a set of SDA data structures.

At this point, our design only supports a centralized SDA control structure, represented by a single *master* thread on a specified processor. All remaining SDA processors will host *worker* threads, which take part in the method execution when instructed by the master thread. The first restriction, mutually-exclusive access to the SDA, is guaranteed by the fact that the SDA control structure is centralized. Allowing for distributed control of an SDA would require implementing distributed mutual exclusion algorithms to guarantee the monitor-like semantics of SDAs, and is a point of interest for future research.

Having established the master-worker organization of the SDA control structure, we can now describe a simple mechanism for ensuring that the second restriction, conditional execution of the methods, is enforced. When an SDA master thread receives a request to execute a method, its condition function is first evaluated to see if the condition is true and, if not, the method is enqueued and another request is handled. Whenever a condition function evaluates to true, the associated method is invoked, after which the condition functions for any enqueued methods are examined to see if their conditions have changed. Starvation is prevented by ensuring that any enqueued method whose condition has changed, is processed before a new method request is handled.

Details of a prototype implementation of this method invocation mechanism, along with preliminary experiments measuring the overhead of the method invocation design can be found in [12]. Our initial experiments show that our design adds only a small amount of overhead to a raw RPC call across a network of workstations.

SDA Method Argument Handling: Opus supports the exploitation of data parallelism within tasks. For example, an Opus task may be an HPF code with the data structures distributed across a set of processors. On the other hand, SDAs may also embody data parallelism and have their internal data structures mapped to a set of processors. Since a task and the SDA with which it is interacting, may be executing on independent set of resources, the method arguments will have to be communicated and remapped before the method code is executed. In this section, we discuss the issues of handling distributed method arguments.

To illustrate the issues, let's consider the situation of a task, `main` distributed across M processors and an SDA instance, S, distributed on N processors. Let us consider the issues that arise with different values of M and N.

If M and N are both greater than 1, then both `main` and S along with their data structures are distributed. We will assume that `main` and S are each represented by a set of threads distributed over the processors, and that each contains a *master* thread among the set, which is responsible for external coordination of the thread group. When `main` invokes a method of `S`, the actual argument, say `A`, distributed across `M` processors will have to be copied into the formal argument, say `B`, distributed across `N` processors. To execute the method, we have the following options:

1. The master thread from `main` collects the elements of `A` into a local scratch array, then sends it to the master thread for `S`, which distributes the values among `S`'s remaining threads, such that each thread updates its portion of `B`. This provides the simplest solution in terms of scheduling data transfers, since only one transfer occurs, from master thread of `main` to master thread of `S`. However, two scratch arrays and two gather/scatter operations are required, consuming both time and space.

2. The master thread from `main` collects the elements of `A` into a local scratch array, then negotiates with the master thread of `S` to determine how the scratch array is to be distributed among the threads of `S`, taking `B`'s distribution into account. After the negotiation, `main`'s master thread distributes the scratch array directly to `S`'s threads. This approach eliminates one scratch array and the scatter operation, but introduces a negotiation phase that is required to discern `B`'s distribution.

3. The master thread from `main` negotiates with the master thread of `S`, then informs the other threads in `main` to send their portion of `A` to `S`'s master thread. When the master thread from `S` has received all of the messages and formed a local scratch array, the array is distributed among the remaining threads in `S`. As with the previous scenario, this approach eliminates a one scratch array and a gather operation at the expense of a negotiation phase.

4. The master thread from `main` negotiates with the master thread of `S`, then informs the other threads in `main` to send their portion of `A` to the appropriate threads in `S`, according to the distribution of `B`. This approach eliminates both scratch arrays and gather/scatter operations, but requires all threads from `S` and `main` to understand each others array distribution.

This level of complexity in data structure management is necessary to accommodate the various modules which comprise an Opus code, since each module will typically be developed independently of the others and may view the same data in a different format or distribution. In addition to remapping a data structure from one distribution to another, the SDA may be required to change the dimensionality of a data structure or to filter the data using some predefined filter. The methods outlined above will accommodate all of these requests.

The choice of which method to use will be dependent on various factors and may sometimes be made statically at compile time. However, we presume that in most cases the negotiation will occur at runtime and the choice made based on the current set of circumstances. We have started an initial implementation of the above design and will experiment with the various choices in order to characterize the overheads involved with each of them.

4 Related Research

Other language projects that focus on the integration of task and data parallelism include Fortran-M [7], DPC [18] and FX [19]. Fortran-M and DPC support mechanisms for establishing message pathways between tasks, and all communication between the tasks is transmitted via these pathways. Fortran-M uses the concept of "channels" for establishing its pathways, and DPC uses concepts similar to C file structures. In FX, tasks communicate only through arguments at the time of creation and termination. In contrast, Opus allows communication between tasks in the form of SDAs, which are data structures that resemble C++ objects with monitor-like semantics and conditions placed on method invocation.

Orca [1] and Ada 9x both provide object models similar to SDAs in that all provide encapsulated shared data, mutually exclusive access, and conditional synchronization. However, the application domains for these systems are different: distributed programming (Orca), real-time applications (Ada 9x), and integration of task and data parallelism (Opus/SDAs). Accordingly, the implementation strategies are different for the three approaches: Orca objects are replicated, Opus SDAs are distributed, and Ada 9x assumes shared memory.

Thread-based runtime support for parallel languages is common in the realm of shared memory multiprocessors [2, 9, 15, 16, 17, 23]. One lightweight thread system for shared memory multiprocessors, *pthreads++*, supports the notion of ropes for data parallel execution of threads [20]. However, lightweight thread systems for distributed memory multiprocessors are far less common. In addition to several application-specific runtime systems that support distributed memory threads in a rather ad-hoc fashion [5, 10], there are two systems which provide a general interface for lightweight threads capable of communication in a distributed memory environment: Nexus and NewThreads. Nexus [8] supports a remote service request mechanism between threads, based the asynchronous remote procedure call provided in Active Messages [21]. However, standard send/receive primitives are not directly supported, and the overhead required to provide this functionality atop a remote service request mechanism is currently unknown. In addition, the cost of selecting, verifying, and calling the correct message handling routine without hardware and operating system support is expensive on most machines. Chant takes the opposite approach by providing a basis for efficient point-to-point communication (using well-known libraries), on top of which a remote service request mechanism is provided. NewThreads provides communication between remote threads using a "ports" naming mechanism, where a port can be mapped onto any thread, and thus requires a global name server to manage the unique port identifiers. Chant uses a thread identifier that is relative to a given process and processor, thus eliminating the need for a global name server for basic point-to-point communication, and also supports the POSIX standard pthreads interface for the lightweight thread operations.

5 Conclusions

Opus extends the HPF standard to facilitate the integration of task and data parallelism. In this paper we have provided an overview of the runtime system necessary to support the new extensions on a variety of parallel and distributed systems. The runtime system is divided into a language-dependent layer atop a language-independent layer. The language-dependent layer, called Opus Runtime, provides the functionality necessary for supporting tasks and SDAs. The language-independent layer, called Chant, provides lightweight threads that support point-to-point communication, remote service requests, and remote thread operations in a distributed memory environment. In addition, Chant provides a mechanism for grouping threads into collections called ropes for the purpose of performing data parallel operations. Chant is built atop standard lightweight thread and communication libraries, and adds relatively little overhead to either of these layers. In addition to supporting Opus Runtime, Chant can provide support for other projects which can benefit from the use of lightweight threads, such as distributed simulations and load balancing.

Preliminary experiments with various parts of the Opus runtime system indicate that the overhead introduced by our design is fairly small. We are currently enhancing our prototype and will report on the performance of Opus Runtime and Chant in future papers.

References

1. Henri E. Bal, M. Frans Kaashoek, and Andrew S. Tanenbaum. Orca: A language for parallel programming of distributed systems. *IEEE Transactions on Software Engineering*, 18(3):190–205, March 1992.
2. Brian N. Bershad, Edward D. Lazowska, Henry M. Levy, and David B. Wagner. An open environment for building parallel programming systems. Technical Report 88-01-03, Department of Computer Science, University of Washington, January 1988.
3. Barbara Chapman, Piyush Mehrotra, and Hans Zima. Programming in Vienna Fortran. *Scientific Programming*, 1(1):31–50, 1992.
4. Barbara M. Chapman, Piyush Mehrotra, John Van Rosendale, and Hans P. Zima. A software architecture of multidisciplinary applications: Integrating task and data parallelism. In *Proceedings Conpar '94, Lecture Notes in Computer Science*, Springer-Verlag, Vol. 854 pages 664–676, September 1994.
5. D. E. Culler, A. Sah, K. E. Schauser, T. von Eicken, and J. Wawrzynek. Fine-grain parallelism with minimal hardware support: A compiler-controlled threaded abstract machine. In 4th *International Conference on Architectural Support for Programming Languages and Operating Systems*, 1991.
6. Message Passing Interface Forum. *Document for a Standard Message Passing Interface*, draft edition, November 1993.
7. I. T. Foster and K. M. Chandy. Fortran M: A language for modular parallel programming. Technical Report MCS-P327-0992 Revision 1, Mathematics and Computer Science Division, Argonne National Laboratory, June 1993.

8. Ian Foster, Carl Kesselman, Robert Olson, and Steven Tuecke. Nexus: An interoperability layer for parallel and distributed computer systems. Technical Report Version 1.3, Argonne National Labs, December 1993.

9. Dirk Grunwald. A users guide to AWESIME: An object oriented parallel programming and simulation system. Technical Report CU-CS-552-91, Department of Computer Science, University of Colorado at Boulder, November 1991.

10. Matthew Haines and Wim B¨ohm. An evaluation of software multithreading in a conventional distributed memory multiprocessor. In *IEEE Symposium on Parallel and Distributed Processing*, pages 106–113, December 1993.

11. Matthew Haines, David Cronk, and Piyush Mehrotra. On the design of Chant: A talking threads package. ICASE Report 94-25, Institute for Computer Applications in Science and Engineering, NASA Langley Research Center, Hampton, VA 23681, April 1994. (To appear in Supercomputing '94).

12. Matthew Haines, Bryan Hess, Piyush Mehrotra, John Van Rosendale, and Hans Zima. Runtime support for data parallel tasks. ICASE Report 94-26, Institute for Computer Applications in Science and Engineering, NASA Langley Research Center, Hampton, VA 23681, April 1994. (To appear in Frontiers '95).

13. High Performance Fortran Forum. *High Performance Fortran Language Specification*, version 1.0 edition, May 1993.

14. IEEE. *Threads Extension for Portable Operating Systems (Draft 7)*, February 1992.

15. Jeff Kramer, Jeff Magee, Morris Sloman, Naranker Dulay, S. C. Cheung, Stephen Crane, and Kevin Twindle. An introduction to distributed programming in REX. In *Proceedings of ESPRIT-91*, pages 207–222, Brussels, November 1991.

16. Frank Mueller. A library implementation of POSIX threads under UNIX. In *Winter USENIX*, pages 29–41, San Diego, CA, January 1993.

17. Bodhisattwa Mukherjee, Greg Eisenhauer, and Kaushik Ghosh. A machine independent interface for lightweight threads. Technical Report CIT-CC-93/53, College of Computing, Georgia Institute of Technology, Atlanta, Georgia, 1993.

18. B. Seevers, M. J. Quinn, and P. J. Hatcher. A parallel programming environment supporting multiple data-parallel modules. In *Workshop on Languages, Compilers and Run-Time Environments for Distributed Mmeory Machines*, October 1992.

19. J. Subhlok, J. Stichnoth, D. O'Hallaron, and T. Gross. Exploiting task and data parallelism on a multicomputer. In *Proceedings of the 2nd ACM SIGPLAN Symposium on Principles and Practice of Parallel Programming*, San Diego, CA, May 1993.

20. Neelakantan Sundaresan and Linda Lee. An object-oriented thread model for parallel numerical applicaitons. In *Proceedings of the Second Annual Object-Oriented Numerics Conference*, pages 291–308, Sunriver, OR, April 1994.

21. Thorsten von Eicken, David E. Culler, Seth Copen Goldstein, and Klaus Erik Schauser. Active messages: A mechanism for integrated communications and computation. In *Proceedings of the 19th Annual International Symposium on Computer Architecture*, pages 256–266, May 1992.

22. W. E. Weihl. Remote procedure call. In Sape Mullender, editor, *Distributed systems*, chapter 4, pages 65–86. ACM Press, 1989.

23. Mark Weiser, Alan Demers, and Carl Hauser. The portable common runtime approach to interoperability. *ACM Symposium on Operating Systems Principles*, pages 114–122, December 1989.

SIMPLE Performance Results in ZPL

Calvin Lin and Lawrence Snyder

University of Washington

Abstract. This paper presents performance results for ZPL programs running on the Kendall Square Research KSR-2 and the Intel Paragon. Because ZPL is a data parallel language based on the Phase Abstractions programming model, these results complement earlier claims that the Phase Abstractions model can lead to portability across MIMD computers. The ZPL language and selected aspects of the compilation strategy are briefly described, and performance results are compared against hand-coded programs.

1 Introduction

In 1991 the authors claimed that programs written in languages founded on the CTA machine model and the Phase Abstractions programming model would be portable across the major families of MIMD parallel computers [6, 8]. The evidence offered to support this claim was the observed performance of the SIMPLE computational fluid dynamics program on five parallel machines that represented the MIMD machines then available: the Sequent Symmetry, BBN Butterfly, Intel iPSC/2, nCUBE/7 and a Transputer array machine; see Figure 1. It was noted that this program achieved at least P/2 speedup on all platforms, and it met or exceeded all published performance for the SIMPLE computation.[2] Though no comparable degree of machine independence had previously been reported, the results did not represent any language or compiler support: The SIMPLE program was written in pseudocode and hand translated to C code that made calls to a message passing library. The problem is that although the hand translation used no exotic analysis and assumed no sophisticated compiler technology, the possibility existed that high level languages and their compilers would be unable to produce the same high quality object code for these disparate computers. This paper addresses this problem by repeating the previous experiment on two modern machines, the Intel Paragon and the Kendall Square Research KSR-2—this time using a high level language called ZPL.

The first goal of this paper is to present evidence that a compiler *can* perform the necessary translations to achieve portability for the SIMPLE program.

[1] This research was supported in part by Office of Naval Research Contract N00014-92-J-1824 and NSF Contract CDA-9211095

[2] Figure 1 compares against results from Hiromoto *et al.*'s hand coded results on the Denelcor HEP [4] and Pingali and Rogers' compiled Id program on the iPSC/2 [11].

Though the evidence is not yet complete—the compiler has only been targeted to two MIMD machines—it is stronger in one sense: The original pseudocode represented a very low level language, so while the pseudocode used powerful concepts from the Phase Abstractions programming model, it did not exploit any high level abstractions such as the data parallel facilities of ZPL. A second goal of this paper is to compare the performance of small ZPL programs with hand coded programs written in C with message passing. These results give an indication of the compiler's effectiveness at producing efficient code. Together, the data presented here supports the claim that the CTA and Phase Abstractions are a conceptual foundation on which portable parallel programs can be written.

This paper is organized as follows. Section 2 provides background by reviewing the Phase Abstractions programming model. Sections 3 and 4 then describe the ZPL language and the ZPL compiler. Our experiments are presented in Section 5, followed by concluding remarks.

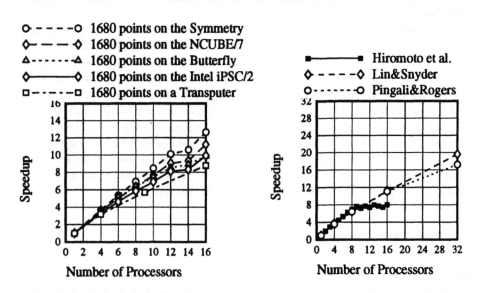

Fig. 1. (a) SIMPLE Speedup on Various Machines   (b) SIMPLE with 4096 points

2 Background: Phase Abstractions

The Phase Abstractions programming model serves as the basis for both our earlier results and the current language-based results. This section briefly reviews the salient features of the Phase Abstractions. A more complete description can be found elsewhere [1, 3, 14].

The Phase Abstractions programming model identifies three levels of parallel programming: the X level, the Y level, and the Z level. The Z level specifies a program's overall control logic and the sequential invocation of *phases* to solve the overall problem. Phases are defined at the Y level, which isolates the explicitly parallel aspects of a parallel program. A phase is a parallel algorithm that typically uses a single pattern of communication; examples include parallel implementations of FFT, Gaussian Elimination, and global maximum. Phases are composed of multiple processes, and these are programmed at the X level. X level processes are defined by sequential code that can communicate with other processes through some message passing mechanism.

The Y level deals with explicit parallelism, so new abstractions are provided to help manage this parallelism. In a non-shared memory model, each process consists of local data, local code, and some local interface to the overall communication structure. In the Phase Abstractions model these three components are encapsulated in a *section*, which is a logical unit of concurrency. Each section can be independently assigned to a processor for execution, and the degree and granularity of parallelism is controlled by increasing or decreasing the number of sections.

The notion of *ensembles* is used to partition each phase's data, code and communication structure. A *data ensemble* specifies how global data is partitioned across the different sections. A *code ensemble* assigns a piece of code to each section, and a *port ensemble* defines ports that connect the section with other sections; these ports are used by X level processes when communicating with other processes. A given section typically consists of multiple data ensembles, a single code ensemble, and a single port ensemble[3]: the code specified by the code ensemble manipulates the local data as defined by the data ensembles, and communicates with other processes as defined by the port ensembles. By describing all aspects of a section through the common notion of an ensemble, all aspects of parallelism can scale in a coherent fashion.

3 The ZPL Language

For the sake of performance, low level languages can be built upon the Phase Abstractions, and, in fact, such languages have been proposed [8, 9]: Orca C is a low level non-shared memory language that extends the programming model with modest conveniences. Thus, Orca C is a MIMD language that gives programmers control over the performance-sensitive aspects of their programs. However, for regular data parallel computations, such control is typically not as critical to performance and such a language can be unnecessarily tedious. ZPL is a subset of Orca C that aims to provide conciseness, convenience, and clarity for

---

[3] In sophisticated computations a section can comprise multiple code ensembles—for example, Kung and Leiserson's systolic matrix multiplication algorithm [5] ideally consists of two processes per processor, one to move data and one to compute new local products—and may comprise multiple port ensembles.

data parallel computations. By addressing a restricted domain the language and compiler design are simplified and good performance can be attained.

ZPL may seem somewhat limited in its expressiveness when compared to other data parallel languages, and these in turn are limited relative to the requirements of full MIMD computation. However, the limitations of ZPL are not a concern because ZPL is a subset of Orca C. Z level programs in Orca C consist of ZPL code mixed with invocations of programmer-defined phases. Thus, computations not easily expressed in ZPL can be written using the full power of Orca C, while those naturally expressible in ZPL can exploit the convenience of ZPL.

3.1 Language Features

As a Z level language, ZPL provides a global view of the computation, so the programmer sees a single address space and all parallelism is implicitly specified. The principal concepts of ZPL are briefly enumerated below:

Regions. The primary mechanism for expressing data parallel computation is through regions. A region is an index set, and can be defined as follows: R = [1..n, 1..n]. Executing a statement containing array references in the context of a region name causes the statement to be instantiated for and executed with each index value of the region.

Array computations. By using regions, expressions involving arrays can be performed without tedious indexing. For example, the following statement finds for all index values of R the difference between the elements of A and B.

[R] C := A-B;

The operations are performed elementwise and provide the user with a clear and succinct means of expressing concurrency.

Directions. Directions are used to express offsets and translate index sets. For example, for a two dimensional array, the northern direction can be used to translate a position to the row above it. The northern direction might be defined as follows: north = [-1, 0].

At. The At operator (@) is used with directions to provide relative indexing. For example, the averaging of the four nearest neighbors required in the Jacobi iteration is given by the following statement:

[R] (A@north+A@east+A@west+A@south)/4;

Of. The Of operator uses a direction to define the boundary regions adjacent to some base region. Thus, the "extra" 0th row of A, required when shifting array A north, is defined and initialized as with one statement: [north of R] A := 0.

Wrap and *Reflect*. Special statements, **wrap** and **reflect**, support mirrored and periodic boundary conditions.

Control structures. ZPL includes the usual control constructs, including **if**, **for**, **repeat**, **while**, **exit**, **continue**, and **return**, along with function calls.

Promotion. Scalar values can be used in array expressions in ZPL as if they were arrays of the proper dimension and size. Thus, in the expression **2*A**, the scalar is promoted to conform to the region in which it is executed, and in effect matches the portion of the array operand with which it is executed.

Masks. It is possible to apply operations selectively to the elements of an array according to a boolean condition. For example, **[R with mask]** specifies the indices of **R** for which the value of **mask** is true (non-zero).

Reduce and *Scan*. The usual reduction and scan operators are provided, including sum, product, logicals, bitwise logicals, minimum, and maximum. For example, **max\ A** reduces **A** to its largest element.

ZPL has several other interesting features that, although worthy of mention, are rather involved and not needed in the programs discussed in the experiments below. These are described in the literature [10, 15].

The above summary of ZPL should allow the Jacobi program of Figure 2 to be easily understood. The program begins with declarations, first for the region R, then for two array variables, **A** and **Temp**, then for a scalar, **error**, and finally for a set of directions. The next block of code defines and initializes the boundary regions, assigning zeros to the array and all boundaries except the southern boundary, which is set to **1.0**. The body of the program, executed in the context of the region specifier, **[R]**, iterates until convergence: The values of the next iteration are found by averaging the four nearest neighbors at each point. In the statement, **error := max\(abs(Temp - A))**, the absolute difference of the elements of the two iterations is computed by promoting the scalar function, **abs()**, to apply to the elements of its array argument; the maximum reduction is then performed to find the greatest error that will be used to test for termination.

3.2   Parallel Foundation for ZPL

Although its language semantics are implicitly parallel, ZPL's parallel execution is made explicit by exposing the Phase Abstractions as its underlying programming model. This is a necessity because ZPL is a sublanguage of an explicitly parallel language. The parallelism is formulated in terms of the CTA [13], an abstract machine on which the program is logically thought to be executed. Programmers, knowing the general characteristics of the parallel execution, can thus assess the performance implications of alternate program implementations.

Logically, the ZPL program should be thought of as a sequence of phase invocations, with the ZPL compiler producing the X and Y level code that implements these phases. In the parlance of the Phase Abstractions, ZPL's arrays

```
program Jacobi;

config var  N: integer = 100;
direction   east  = [0, 1];
            west  = [0,-1];
            north = [-1,0];
            south = [1, 0];

region      R = [1..N, 1..N];

constant    epsilon: real = .01;
var         A, Temp: [R] real;
            error  : real;

procedure Jacobi();
begin
  [east of R]  A := 0.0;
  [west of R]  A := 0.0;
  [north of R] A := 0.0;
  [south of R] A := 1.0;
  [R]          A := 0.0;

  [R]          repeat
                   Temp := (A@east + A@west + A@north + A@south)/4;
                   error := max\ (abs(Temp-A));
                   A := Temp;
               until error < epsilon;
end;
```

Fig. 2. ZPL Program for the Jacobi Iteration.

are data ensembles that by default are distributed across the processors in a 2D blocked fashion,[4] and scalars are Z level control variables that are replicated across all processors. The code ensemble generated for each of these lightweight phases is the object C code produced by the ZPL compiler for the particular ZPL statement. The port ensemble for each phase, while implicit to the user, is explicit to the compiler: The @ and wrap operators specify connectivity between neighboring sections and the scan and reduce operators specify a machine-specific tree connectivity.

The use of the Phase Abstractions model and the CTA abstract machine is crucial because it provides the compiler with a single view of all MIMD computers. In particular, the model leads to a single compiler that produces identical object code for both the shared address space KSR-2 and the non-shared memory Intel Paragon.[5]

---

[4] The decomposition can be changed through Orca C's Y level ensemble declarations.

[5] We currently perform no machine-specific optimizations.

4   The ZPL Compiler

We have modified the Parafrase-2 source-to-source translator [12] to compile ZPL programs to SPMD C code with calls to machine-specific communication routines. We rely on each machine's native C compiler to complete the translation to machine code.

Space limitations prevent a full description of the compilation process, but three significant tasks are the insertion of communication, the implementation of array statements, and the representation of ensembles. Communication is explicitly represented in our AST as Send and Receive nodes. In the naive case these communication nodes are inserted wherever the At operator is used. Array statements are implemented by creating *Mloops* in the AST. Mloops represent the region that applies to a given ZPL statement, and Mloops are converted to nested **for** loops in the object code. The use of Mloops differentiates loops derived from array operations from loops defined by users, a distinction that can be useful because of the restricted nature of Mloops. Finally, ensembles are implemented as arrays with additional descriptors that describe their size, shape, and amount of *fluff*, where fluff is a cache used for holding neighboring array values.

The current ZPL compiler performs only a small number of optimizations. One optimization concerns the elimination of redundant communication operations, an effect that is similar to common subexpression elimination. Each local section of an ensemble maintains a cache to hold data from neighboring sections, and these caches are updated only when Def-Use analysis detects that it is necessary. This optimization is explained in more detail in Appendix A.

We currently perform conservative Mloop fusion that reduces the number of Mloops in SIMPLE from about 165 to about 100. More aggressive fusion that looks for optimal loop iteration orders is being explored.

5   Experiments

Our primary result compares the performance of a compiled ZPL implementation of the SIMPLE benchmark against earlier implementations written in C. This result completes earlier claims that the Phase Abstractions model can be used to create portable programs. We then present a second set of results involving the Jacobi iteration. By looking at a small program that is essentially a subset of the SIMPLE computation, this experiment provides a more detailed look at the performance difference between ZPL programs and hand-coded C programs.

Hardware. The Intel Paragon is a distributed memory computer with 18 nodes arranged in a mesh structure. Each node consists of an Intel i860 processor and 16 MB of local memory, and runs the OSF Mach operating system.

The Kendall Square Research KSR-2 has 56 processors connected by two levels of rings. A coherent cache-only memory structure provides a global address space. Each custom processor runs at 40 Mhz and can issue both integer and floating point instructions on each cycle. Each processor has a 256 KB instruction cache, a 256KB data cache, and 32 MB of local memory.

5.1 SIMPLE Results

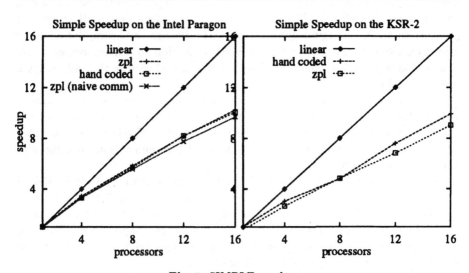

Fig. 3. SIMPLE results.

Figure 3 compares the speedup of SIMPLE written in ZPL against our hand-coded version written in C with messages passing [6]. Ten iterations were run for a problem with 256×256 data points (all C programs were compiled with optimizations at level -O2). The graph on the left shows that on the Paragon the speedup of our ZPL program (the curve labeled "zpl") is very close to that of the hand-coded program. Note that the P=1 time for "hand coded" is a sequential program with no unnecessary overhead for parallelism, and the ZPL program running on one processor was still 1.9% faster. On the Paragon, the better node performance of the ZPL program is due to our use of "walkers" and "bumpers," described below.

At P=4 the ZPL program is 4.1% faster than hand-coded, but as the number of processors increases the hand-coded program does relatively better. For example, at P=16 the ZPL program is 3.9% slower. This performance difference appears to be due to the slightly higher overhead of the ZPL object code, and as P grows the cost of this overhead becomes a larger percent of the execution time. For example, the ZPL compiler produces code for communication between two neighbors that works for any processor and any region. By contrast, the hand-coded program hard codes some of this information, knowing, for example, that a process on the west edge of the computation has no western neighbors to send messages to.

ZPL's superior performance at P=1 is surprising because the ZPL program has all of the overhead mentioned above. However, a detailed examination of the cost of Mloops versus the cost of hand-coded nested loops shows that our use of walkers and bumpers is a big win on the Paragon: Walkers are pointers that are used to iterate over arrays in Mloops; walkers are advanced at each iteration by bumpers. Of course, the hand-coded program could also use walkers and bumpers, but this would be extremely tedious. Note that if all arrays were declared to reside contiguously in memory, the Paragon's C compiler could use induction variable elimination and strength reduction to achieve better performance than our walkers and bumpers, but this would require that all arrays be statically defined.

The curve labeled "zpl (naive comm)" represents a naive communication insertion strategy where sends and receives are emitted for every statement that contains an ⊙. Figure 3 shows that the performance difference between "naive comm" and "zpl," which uses our Def-Oriented communication insertion algorithm, is considerable.

The graph on the right of Figure 3 shows the performance on the KSR-2. At P=1 the ZPL program is 27.9% slower than hand-coded. For P greater than one the performance of the two programs is very close, with the hand-coded program being about 10% faster. Interestingly, these trends are completely reversed from the Paragon. Further analysis is needed to explain this behavior and an anomaly at P=8, where the ZPL program is slightly faster.

5.2 Jacobi Results

In addition to SIMPLE, we also compare a ZPL implementation of Jacobi against a hand-coded message-passing implementation [7] for a 512×512 problem that converged at 279 iterations. (See Figure 4.) At P=1 the ZPL program is 5.2% slower than hand-coded. For more than one processor the overhead is between 5.4% (P=4) and 1.8% (P=16). The discontinuity at P=8 of the hand-coded curve is an artifact of the program's data partitioning. For a 512×512 problem size, the number of cache misses in the inner loop is roughly halved as we double the number of processors from P=1 to 2 and from 2 to 4. However, after P=8 no further reduction of caches misses occurs because the number of columns per processor remains unchanged. That is, each processor has 128 columns for P=8 (256×128), P=12 (170×128) and P=16 (128×128).

Figure 4 also shows a curve labeled "naive access," which shows the importance of using walkers and bumpers. The "naive access" curve represents a straightforward approach where each array access is computed independently. The high cost of these array accesses is due to the fact that each array may have different amounts of fluff, and many aspects of ZPL arrays—such as their dimension and the size of each element—may not be known at compile time.

Strangely, the ZPL program is faster than hand-coded on the KSR. We suspect the difference is due to data alignment and caching effects, but further

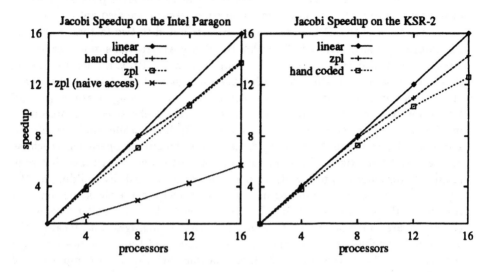

Fig. 4. Jacobi results.

investigation is required. These results contrast with the SIMPLE results where the ZPL program was faster than hand-coded on the Paragon but slower on the KSR. We observe that the Paragon's node compiler is more robust than the KSR's and appears to perform superior optimizations. If we assume that the hand-coded programs do not benefit as much from scalar optimizations, we observe that the Paragon's superior compiler is likely to have little impact on straightforward programs such as Jacobi, and larger impact on more complicated programs such as SIMPLE. Thus, the Paragon's native C compiler improves the ZPL performance of SIMPLE (relative to hand-coded) more than it improves the ZPL performance of Jacobi. On the KSR, however, the node compiler has less effect.

While some of the results in this section have not been fully explained, one conclusion is clear: The ZPL programs are extremely competitive with hand-coded C programs.

6 Conclusion

This paper complements earlier Phase Abstractions portability experiments by showing performance results for a SIMPLE program written in ZPL, a high level language that is based upon the Phase Abstractions. The present data shows good performance results for two very different parallel computers, the Intel Paragon and the Kendall Square Research KSR-2. Additional optimizations are underway that will concentrate on eliminating overhead of high level data parallel operations. For example, array temporaries can be expensive and should be eliminated, re-used, or converted to scalars whenever possible. Further optimizations to reduce or hide communication latency are also anticipated.

The success of the ZPL compiler can be attributed to two factors. First, the ZPL language was designed to fit within the Phase Abstractions model as part of Orca C, and this design simplifies the compiler's task. ZPL is a Z level language that can focus on well-studied parallel abstractions such as data parallel array operations and reduction operations. Although some language features (not all features were discussed in this paper) cause non-trivial obstacles and interesting implementation problems, the separation from MIMD parallelism is beneficial. For example, communication only comes from structured operations such as **@, wrap**, and reductions; this contrasts sharply with other languages that may require communication for arbitrary array accesses. Second, by building on the Phase Abstractions programming model the compiler can use the same concepts that make Phase Abstractions applicable to a wide class of parallel computers: the non-shared memory view of the machine that encourages data locality, the notion of ensembles that parameterizes grain size, and the decomposition of a program into phases that makes ZPL compatible with the other components of Orca C.

Acknowledgments. We thank those who have helped implement ZPL—Ruth Anderson, Bradford Chamberlain, Sung-Eun Choi, George Forman, E Chris Lewis, Kurt Partridge, and W. Derrick Weathersby. We are particularly grateful to E Lewis for his critical role in acquiring the experimental data presented here.

References

1. Gail Alverson, William Griswold, Calvin Lin, David Notkin, and Lawrence Snyder. Abstractions for portable, scalable parallel programming. Technical Report 93–12–09, Department of Computer Science and Engineering, University of Washington, submitted to *IEEE Trans. on Parallel and Distributed Systems*, 1993.
2. S. Amarasinghe and M. Lam. Communication optimization and code generation for distributed memory machines. In *Proceedings of the SIGPLAN'93 Conference on Program Language Design and Implementation*, June 1993.
3. William Griswold, Gail Harrison, David Notkin, and Lawrence Snyder. Scalable abstractions for parallel programming. In *Proceedings of the Fifth Distributed Memory Computing Conference*, 1990. Charleston, South Carolina.
4. R. E. Hiromoto, O. M. Lubeck, and J. Moore. Experiences with the Denelcor HEP. In *Parallel Computing*, pages 1:197–206, 1984.
5. H. T. Kung and C.E. Leiserson. *Introduction to VLSI Systems*. Addison-Wesley, Reading, MA, 1980. Section 8.3, by C. Mead and L. Conway.
6. Jinling Lee, Calvin Lin, and Lawrence Snyder. Programming SIMPLE for parallel portability. In Uptal Banerjee, David Gelernter, Alexandru Nicolau, and David Padua, editors, *Languages and Compilers for Parallel Computing*, pages 84–98. Springer-Verlag, 1992.
7. Calvin Lin and Lawrence Snyder. A comparison of programming models for shared memory multiprocessors. In *Proceedings of the International Conference on Parallel Processing*, pages II 163–180, 1990.

8. Calvin Lin and Lawrence Snyder. A portable implementation of SIMPLE. *International Journal of Parallel Programming*, 20(5):363–401, 1991.
9. Calvin Lin and Lawrence Snyder. Data ensembles in Orca C. In Uptal Banerjee, David Gelernter, Alexandru Nicolau, and David Padua, editors, *Languages and Compilers for Parallel Computing*, pages 112–123. Springer-Verlag, 1993.
10. Calvin Lin and Lawrence Snyder. ZPL: An array sublanguage. In Uptal Banerjee, David Gelernter, Alexandru Nicolau, and David Padua, editors, *Languages and Compilers for Parallel Computing*, pages 96–114. Springer-Verlag, 1993.
11. Keshav Pingali and Anne Rogers. Compiler parallelization of SIMPLE for a distributed memory machine. Technical Report 90–1084, Cornell University, 1990.
12. Constantine Polychronopolous, Milind Girkar, Mohammad Reza Haghighat, Chia Ling Lee, Bruce Leung, and Dale Schouten. Parafrase-2: An environment for parallelizing, partitioning, synchronizing, and scheduling programs on multi-processors. In *Proceedings of the International Conference on Parallel Processing*, volume 2, pages 39–48, August 1989.
13. Lawrence Snyder. Type architecture, shared memory and the corollary of modest potential. In *Annual Review of Computer Science*, pages I:289–318, 1986.
14. Lawrence Snyder. Foundations of practical parallel programming languages. In *Proceedings of the Second International Conference of the Austrian Center for Parallel Computation*. Springer-Verlag, 1993.
15. Lawrence Snyder. A ZPL programming guide. Technical report, Department of Computer Science and Engineering, University of Washington, 1994.
16. Reinhard v. Hanxleden and Ken Kennedy. A code placement framework and its application to communication generation. Technical Report CRPC-TR93337, Center for Research on Parallel Computation, Rice University, October 1993.

A Communication Insertion

We employ Def-Use analysis to insert communication nodes into the AST: Send nodes are placed after arrays are modified and Receive nodes are placed before arrays are read. Here we distinguish between standard Defs and Uses that indicate data dependencies and the subset of these that induce communication. Henceforth we restrict our attention to the latter. Communication is induced when a pair of array references have different direction vectors for their Def and their Use. For example, the following pairs of statements induce communication:

```
A := ...          /* Def of A */
... := A@east;    /* Use of A */

B@east := ...     /* Def of B */
...    := B;      /* Use of B */
```

The following pairs of statements do not produce communication.

```
A := ...          /* Def of A */
... := A;         /* Use of A */

B@east := ...     /* Def of B */
...    := B@east; /* Use of B */
```

Note that as opposed to standard scalar Def-Use (DU) chains, each of the above DU chains represents the transmission of an entire fluff area of an array whenever the direction vectors for the Def and Use differ.

Multiple direction vectors can map to the same processor direction. For example, the direction vectors [0,1] and [0,2] both map to the **east** processor direction. To see the importance of using processor directions, consider the following example where a single message consisting of two columns can satisfy both Uses of the variable **A**.

```
A := ...
... := A@east;          /* insert single Receive before this statement */
... := A@east2;
```

If our algorithm considered only direction vectors, **east** and **east2** would be distinct and require separate communication. Our solution will instead send two columns by inserting a single message before the reference to **A@east**.

Def-Oriented Insertion Algorithm Our initial algorithm uses a "Def-oriented" approach and is shown in Figure 6. The goal of the algorithm is to identify the first DU chain corresponding to each processor direction and insert a Send node and Receive node for this DU chain.

The algorithm traverses the set of DU chains emanating from a single Def node (the *source node*) and maintains a **visited** table (see Figure 5) that has one record per processor direction (there are eight for 2D block decompositions), with the **mark** bits initially set to 0. Each time a DU chain is traversed, the **mark** bit for the appropriate processor direction is set to 1, the **insertion_point** is set to point to the statement that corresponds to the Use (or end of basic block), and the **size** field is set to the magnitude of the Use's direction vector. Once the **mark** and **insertion_point** fields have been set they are never changed, but if we encounter a variable whose vector length is greater than the value in the table, the **size** field is set to the larger value. When the last of the DU chains for the source node has been traversed, communication nodes are created: A pair of nodes is created for each processor direction whose mark bit is 1. The Send is inserted after the Def and the Receive is inserted at the specified insertion point.

The algorithm is similar for the case that an **@** appears on the left hand side of an assignment, except we then look for *any* Use of the same array on the right hand side. An additional bit is used to differentiate **@**'s that appear on the left hand side from those that appear on the right.

Control flow can complicate the insertion of communication because corresponding Send and Receive operations must either both execute or both not execute. Hence, our algorithm places Send nodes immediately after Defs and places the corresponding Receives as late as possible within the same basic block. Finally, we point out that the above algorithm operates on a per-region basis, so there is a separate **visited** table for each region, and messages are never combined for fluff that corresponds to different regions.

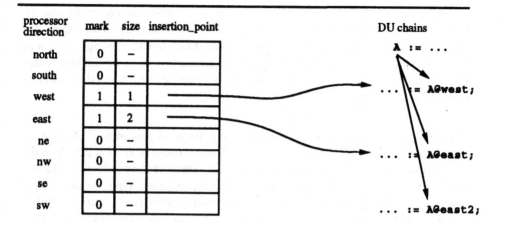

Fig. 5. The Def-Oriented insertion algorithm's visited table.

```
for each Def of an array in the dependency graph
{
    Clear the visited table;
    Traverse all DU chains emanating from the current Def;
    {
        if Def has no @
            Look for references to the array with @'s on rhs;
        else Def has an @
            Look for any reference to the array on rhs;
        for each such array reference found
        {
            if mark is 0 for this chain's processor direction
            {
                Set mark to 1 for this processor direction;
                Set insertion_point to statement corresponding to Use;
                Set size according to the direction vector;
            }
            else
            {
                (this processor direction already visited)
                Update size if this Use's direction vector > size;
            }
        }
    }
}
```

Fig. 6. The Def-Oriented communication insertion algorithm.

There are many other possible communication insertion algorithms.[2, 16] A *Use-Oriented* approach would insert Receives immediately before Uses and place Sends as early as possible within the same basic block. This approach may be better than Def-oriented in terms of combining messages for different variables. Much work remains in comparing and developing communication insertion algorithms.

Diagonal Directions Communication along diagonal processor directions results in communication with up to three different processes since a 2D block decomposition is used. For example, a reference to **A@northeast** induces communication with the neighbors to the north, northeast, and east. Thus, we decompose diagonal processor directions into their component pieces (see Figure 7). Notice that each orthogonal component direction—in this case the North and East components—spans an entire dimension of the region. Although **A@northeast** does not require the left element, we include this value (only if we also see **A@north**) to reduce the number of messages. For example, if the North Component did not include the "missing corner," the following code fragment would require four messages: one to send each of the three components of **A@northeast**, and one to satisfy **A@north**.

```
A := ...
... := A@northeast;      /* send North, East and NE Components */
... := A@north;          /* send North Component */
```

Our implementation, however, sends a single message to update both **A@north** and the North Component of **A@northeast**.

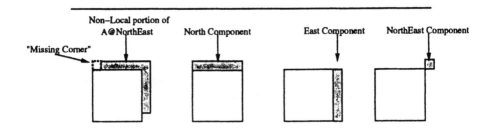

Fig. 7. Diagonal communication is broken into component pieces.

Cid: A Parallel, "Shared-memory" C for Distributed-memory Machines

Rishiyur S. Nikhil

Digital Equipment Corporation, Cambridge Research Laboratory

Abstract. *Cid* is a parallel, "shared-memory" superset of C for distributed-memory machines. A major objective is to keep the entry cost low. For users– the language should be easily comprehensible to a C programmer. For implementors– it should run on standard hardware (including workstation farms); it should not require major new compilation techniques (which may not even be widely applicable); and it should be compatible with existing code, run-time systems and tools. Cid is implemented with a simple pre-processor and a library, uses available C compilers and packet-transport primitives, and links with existing libraries.

Cid extends C with MIMD threads and global objects and a common "join-variable" mechanism for dealing with asynchronous actions. The number of threads is arbitrary and may vary dynamically. Any C object can be registered as a global object; the resulting "global pointer" may be used to access the object from any PE (processing element) in a locked, coherent, cached manner. Combining locking with cacheing reduces communication traffic. Being entirely in software, there is the opportunity to vary coherence protocols to suit the application. Distributed data structures may built by linking across PEs with global pointers, or by using Cid's distributed array primitives.

The programmer does no explicit message-passing, but Cid exposes some abstractions of the distributed memory machine. PEs have separate address spaces; threads may be forked to different PEs, but a thread does not span PE boundaries. Threads access remote data only *via* thread arguments and results, and global objects. Finally, several Cid operations are made explicitly asynchronous, in recognition of the underlying communication and synchronization costs.

In this paper, we describe the language, our first, multi-threaded implementation, some preliminary results, and compare with related systems.

1 Introduction

Distributed memory parallel computers, such as the Thinking Machines CM-5, Intel Paragon, and workstation farms, are now becoming commonplace. So far, their primary programming model is explicit message-passing, with their "multicomputer" nature visible to the programmer. It is now widely conceded

---

[1] One Kendall Square, Bldg. 700, Cambridge MA 02139, USA; nikhil@crl.dec.com

that this is too difficult for routine programming, and there is a search for simpler, shared-memory parallel programming models. HPF (High Performance Fortran) [11] is one such model, but seems limited to computations involving simple loop-level parallelism on dense rectangular arrays (although there is much active research to go beyond this, see for example [8]).

One approach is to restore completely the original "SMP" threads-plus-locks shared memory programming model, relying on transparent, global, consistent cacheing that is supported by a combination of hardware and systems software (*e.g.*, the KSR-1, DASH [14] and FLASH [13] at Stanford, *T-ng [2] and Alewife [1] at MIT, Tempest and Typhoon [20, 17] at Wisconsin, *etc.*). Some potential obstacles to widespread availability of these approaches include: cost (because of special hardware); inflexibility (because of false-sharing, or because sharing protocols may not easily be changed to suit different applications); and effectiveness (may require sophisticated compiler analysis, and often the user's main control over locality is to ride the (non-trivial) coherence mechanisms expertly).

In contrast, Cid^2 has much lower expectations about system infrastructure. It is a purely software approach, can run on any distributed memory machine (including workstation farms), and requires no modifications to C compilers or operating systems. There are a few language extensions (all handled by simple preprocessing) and some library calls. Cid can use any, possibly unreliable, packet transport system, from PVM to UDP to raw network packets. Cid code can be linked with existing code and libraries, and use existing program-development tools such as profilers and debuggers.

Cid extends C with four features. The first three are MIMD threads, global objects and distributed arrays, and the fourth is a common *join variable* mechanism to deal with asynchronous thread, object and array operations. A Cid thread is simply an asynchronous call to a C function. Any existing C variable (scalar, struct/union or array; static, automatic or heap-allocated) can be registered as a Cid global object, and there are facilities for locked, coherent, cached access to such objects from any PE (processing element). Cid provides facilities to allocate arbitrary n-dimensional arrays, with any one dimension distributed across the PEs (with distribution specifications borrowed from HPF). A thread on any PE has locked, coherent, cached access to any element of such an array, and can iterate over the elements of an array that are "local" to its PE. A thread can fetch data towards its PE, or it can fork a thread to run on the data's PE. The programmer can control forking and thread placement precisely, or leave it up to an automatic system (this also means he can control data distribution precisely, or leave it to automatic decisions).

Unlike other MIMD shared-memory approaches, Cid does not attempt completely to hide from the programmer the underlying distributed memory system and cost of communication. For example, although threads can be forked from any PE to any PE, each thread is always entirely local to a PE and does not migrate. A thread on one PE can access data from another PE only *via* thread

---

[2] The name derives from C, and from the Id parallel programming language [15], our multi-threaded implementation of which inspired many ideas in Cid [16].

arguments and results, or *via* the global object and distributed array mechanisms. A global object never spans multiple PEs. All potentially long-latency events— forking a thread and waiting for its result, or gaining access to a global object or array element, or allocating a distributed array— are couched as asynchronous events: a thread initiates the operation and associates it with a join variable, and later explicitly waits for completion of the operation, using that join variable. This allows us to express "futures", pre-fetches and post-stores, barrier synchronizations, *etc.* By combining lock acquisition with remote data access, Cid reduces communication traffic, and makes shared data access not much more verbose than conventional SMP code. Cid's asynchronous operations are exploited in the implementation which is *multi-threaded* and overlaps computation with the long latencies of remote operations and synchronization waits.

One consequence of our design philosophy is that Cid may not satisfy the language purist. In the spirit of C itself, and of various SMP extensions to C, Cid provides expressive functionality, but leaves the "proper" use of this functionality up to programmer-convention and discipline. The advantage is that Cid has a low, incremental entry cost, making it easily approachable for the user and the implementor. We believe that this feature distinguishes Cid from some other parallel C's for distributed memory machines.

We describe the programming model for Cid in Section 2. We provide an overview of the implementation, and the current implementation status in Section 3. In Section 4, we discuss related work, notably Split-C [6], Olden [4], Charm [12] and Threaded-C [9]. Section 5 is a brief conclusion.

2 Cid

Cid is basically C, plus threads and global objects, plus a *join* mechanism for asynchronous thread and object operations.

2.1 Threads and Joins

Forking a thread in Cid is an asynchronous function call. A function must be declared forkable by preceding its declaration with the cid_forkable keyword. It can then be invoked in a cid_fork statement:

    cid_fork (*join-var*; *pe*) *lhs* = f (*arg1*, ..., *argN*);

where *join-var*, *pe*, and "*lhs* =" are all optional.

The simplest method of synchronization in Cid is a *join*. A thread initiates N asynchronous actions, associating each one with a *join variable*. As each action completes, it *signals* the variable. The initiating thread *waits* at the variable, and may proceed only after N signals have been given. Consider this parallel Fibonacci function:

```
cid_forkable
int fib (int N)
{
```

```
        int fibN1, fibN2;
        cid_initialized_jvar(jv);    /* Macro declares and inits join var jv */

        if (N < 2) return N
        else {
            cid_fork (jv;) fibN1 = fib(N-1);    /* in another thread */
            fibN2 = fib(N-2);                   /* in this thread */
            cid_jwait(&jv);                     /* wait for forked call */
            return fibN1 + fibN2;
        }
    }
```

The cid_fork statement forks the function call to run in a separate, parallel thread; the current thread goes on to compute fib(N-2). When the forked call completes, the result is automatically deposited into fibN1, and the join-variable jv is signalled. The current thread waits, if necessary, at cid_jwait().

A single join variable may be used to wait for several forked events (the number may be dynamic). For example:

```
    while (...)
        if (...)
            cid_fork (jv;) x = loop_body(j, ..);
    cid_jwait(&jv);
```

In each iteration of the loop, if the if-condition is true, an instance of loop_body() is forked. The cid_jwait outside the loop waits for the right number of forks to complete. Some of the forked calls may signal before the cid_jwait is executed, or before forks later in the loop are even initiated. Join variables can be re-used; for example:

```
    for (i = 0; i < M; i++) {
        cid_jinit(&jv);
        for (j = 0; j < N; j++)
            cid_fork  (jv;) X[i,j] = loop_body(i, j, ..)
        cid_jwait(&jv);
    }
```

The outer loop is sequential. Each iteration re-initializes jv before performing the parallel inner loop, which uses jv for a "barrier" synchronization.

Join variables are just a pre-defined struct type; they may be embedded in other data structures, passed as arguments, returned as results, dynamically allocated, etc.

The cid_fork statement is related to Multilisp futures [10]. Here, we unbundle the synchronization variable from the result variable, so that it is possible for more than one forked call to share synchronization variables. This uses fewer synchronization variables, allows us to re-use them, and is more efficient– a thread waiting for N results does not have to suspend and resume N times by touching N futures— it suspends at most once on the join variable.

2.2   Forking to other PEs (processing elements)

A distributed memory platform consists of N PEs ("processing elements"); these
are referred to by logical PE numbers $0 \ldots N - 1$.[3] The cid_fork statement can
name a specific PE on which to run the forked function:

        cid_fork (jv; pe) x = f(...);

Here, pe is an integer-valued expression. The value should either be in the range
0 to $N - 1$ to specify a particular PE, or it should be:

- CID_ANY, allowing the runtime system to choose the PE; or
- CID_OPT, specifying that forking is optional– the runtime system may choose to
  fork or to execute it as a normal function call (and signal the join variable).
  If forked, it also chooses the PE. (Omitting the pe field is equivalent to
  specifying CID_OPT.)

CID_ANY and CID_OPT have different deadlock behavior— in CID_OPT, the programmer must avoid any synchronization dependence from the current thread to the
forked function. In both these cases, load-balancing considerations may be used
to distribute threads. CID_OPT allows dynamic thread-granularity control– the
system may avoid forking if all PEs are busy.

2.3   Global objects and pointers

A global "pointer" is a name for an object that is valid across all PEs; it may
be used by a thread on any PE to refer to the object. All global pointers are of
type gptr.[4] Given an arbitrary C pointer lp to an object on the current PE, a
corresponding global pointer may be constructed using:

        gp = cid_to_global (lp, size);

This "registers" the object in a *global object table* in the current PE (each PE
has its own table). The table entry contains not only the local pointer lp, but
also the size of the object, a lock for the object, and related information. (If lp
is NULL, cid_to_global immediately returns NULL.) gp is represented as a C
integer type with bit fields containing the current PE number and an integer
unique to that PE. Thus, gp is unique across all PEs, and is used by Cid as a
lookup key in global object tables (the object may subsequently have entries in
other PEs' object tables due to cacheing). A global pointer is not a pointer in
the C sense– it does not support pointer arithmetic or dereferencing, nor does
it have any duality with arrays. This example program constructs a distributed
full binary tree of a given depth:

```
typedef struct tree_s {
    int   info;
    gptr  left, right;
} tree, *tree_p;
```

---

[3] Each PE may itself be a shared-memory multiprocessor that runs multiple Cid
threads concurrently.

[4] Unfortunately, this loses type information. If we implement/modify a C type-checker,
we could improve this notation, as is done in Split-C[6].

```
cid_forkable
gptr make_tree (int depth)
{
    tree_p t;
    cid_initialized_jvar(jv);

    if (depth == 0)
        t = NULL;
    else {
        t = (tree_p) malloc(sizeof(tree));    /* alloc this node */
        t->info = ... ;                        /* fill info */
        cid_fork (jv;)                         /* fork construction */
            t->left = make_tree(depth - 1);    /*    of left */
        t->right = make_tree(depth - 1);       /* construct right */
        cid_jwait(&jv);                        /* wait for left */
    }
    return cid_to_global(t);
}
```

It forks a thread to construct the left sub-tree and constructs the right sub-tree itself. This happens recursively, so the entire tree is constructed in parallel. Since the forked call does not specify a PE, the actual distribution of the tree will follow distribution choices made by the runtime system. Of course, the programmer is free to specify PEs precisely, to control how the tree is distributed.

The PE number encoded in a global pointer can be extracted using:

```
pe = cid_to_pe(gp)
```

This merely involves extracting a bit field from gp, and requires no communication. If gp is NULL, cid_to_pe returns the current PE. One may obtain a local pointer to a global object using:

```
lp = cid_to_local(gp)
```

This may involve copying the object from its "home" PE (details in the next section, where we discuss cid_get_obj(), of which cid_to_local() is only a special case). The function cid_to_pe() is often used to fork a function to the PE where a particular object resides. For example, this function recursively adds up the information in the nodes of our binary tree:

```
cid_forkable
int tree_add (gptr gp)
{
    int sl, sr;
    tree_p lp;
    cid_initialized_jvar(jv);

    lp = cid_to_local(gp);
    if (lp == NULL)
        return 0;
    else {
        cid_fork (jv; cid_to_pe(lp->left))  sl = tree_add(lp->left);
        cid_fork (jv; cid_to_pe(lp->right)) sr = tree_add(lp->right);
        cid_jwait(&jv);
```

```
        retutn lp->info + sl + sr;
    }
}
```

In the initial call to tree_add, the root node may be copied to that PE, by cid_to_local. However, each subsequent recursive call on a sub-tree is forked to the PE that holds the root of that sub-tree, avoiding any further object copying. The computation "follows" the tree around the PEs. This illustrates how the user has a fair degree of control over locality even though the actual data distribution may be dynamic.

2.4 cid_get_obj: Accessing remote objects

In addition to sending work close to data, it is also necessary to bring data close to work. For example, a function that traverses two trees with different distributions can follow one tree around the PEs, but will need to "pull" nodes from the other tree. The function for accessing a remote object is:

        cid_get_obj (&jv, &lp, gp, *access_mode*)

This initiates an action to assign, to lp, an ordinary C pointer to a local copy of the object named by gp. The local copy may be the original object itself (if this PE is its home); an existing copy of the object that was fetched by some previous call to cid_get_obj, or a fresh copy now obtained by the runtime system from the home of the object. Since this is a potentially long-latency operation, it is asynchronous– the call returns immediately and the the thread may do other work, but it must eventually cid_jwait(&jv) before it can safely dereference lp. Conceptually, this is a "pre-fetch" of the object, with the join variable indicating completion. *Access_mode* is an integer specifying the nature of this access, and causes appropriate locking and consistency-maintenance mechanisms to be invoked. For example, multiple threads, perhaps on different PEs, may access an object simultaneously with CID_READ, while CID_WRITE ensures exclusive access. CID_COPY is useful for read-only data, allowing Cid to avoid keeping track of the object for maintaining coherence. Similarly, other access modes permit simpler, cheaper, specialized coherence mechanisms.

There is no operation to "put back" an object. Instead, when a thread has finished accessing a global object, it just announces this with:

        cid_release (gp)

The run time system decides if, when and how the object is returned to its home PE (there may be other threads on this PE that are still using the object, and some access modes make it unnecessary to return the object, or even a release notification). The user can explicitly "unregister" a global object using:

        cid_free(gp)

with all the usual caveats about dangling pointers. The "lp = cid_to_local(gp)" call can now be explained as an abbreviation for:

```
{   cid_initialized_jvar(jv);
    cid_get_obj(&jv, &lp, gp, CID_WRITE);  cid_jwait(&jv);
}
```

2.5 Distributed Arrays

The global objects described in the previous sections do not span PE boundaries (although it is of course possible to build distributed data structures with components on different PEs and linked with global pointers). Further, the granularity of locking and cacheing (communication) is the entire object itself. In contrast, a distributed array is a conceptually monolithic object that can span PE boundaries. The granularity of locking and cacheing is the individual array element (which may be arbitrarily large).

We discuss 2-dimensional arrays here, for example, but Cid has facilities for arbitrary n-dimensional arrays. Distributed array allocation is asynchronous:

```
cid_alloc_2d (&jv, &gp, NI, NJ, sizeof_elem, dist, block_size)
```

NI, NJ are the dimensions, and the size of elements is specified explicitly. dist specifies the distribution: BLOCK or CYCLIC, on ROW or COL, and the last argument specifies the blocking factor (with the same meanings as in HPF, from which these concepts are borrowed). In general, for an n dimensional array, any one dimension may be distributed across Cid's linear "processor array". The allocator returns a global pointer gp asynchronously (signalled in jv).

An array element can be accessed from any PE, and then released, using:

```
cid_get_2d      (&jv, &lp, gp, I, J, access_mode)
cid_release_2d ( gp, I, J)
```

which are exactly analogous to cid_get_obj and cid_release described earlier. In addition, Cid provides an iteration macro:

```
for_my_2d (gp, I, J)
```

This expands into a C for-loop header that iterates I and J over the indices of the array gp that happen to be allocated on the current PE. This allows us to write SPMD-style "owner-computes" array code.

3 Implementation Details

3.1 Pre-processor

Cid has just two syntax extensions: the cid_forkable keyword immediately preceding a function declaration, and the cid_fork statement. The pre-processor uses the cid_forkable keyword to generate request and response handlers for that specific function. The handlers are just C functions that take messages as arguments. This pre-processor activity is similar to conventional RPC stub generation. When the pre-processor encounters a cid_fork statement, it expands it into a block that constructs and sends a request message for a remote invocation of that function. All generated code sequences know the exact layout of the messages they handle, and there is no general-purpose message parsing, packing or unpacking.

3.2 Threads

Cid threads are always local to a PE, and there are no references across PE boundaries. Each PE may contain many threads, but all multi-threading is done by the Cid run-time system– to Unix, each PE looks like a single process with a single thread. Each Cid thread has its own stack, which is allocated when the thread begins execution, not when it is forked. Stacks are allocated off the dynamic heap; we amortize this cost by getting them in chunks and maintaining our own free-list of stacks, so that stack allocation and deallocation are normally cheap. Further, when one thread completes, we try to reuse its stack for another thread if possible, before deallocating it. The Cid runtime system uses a small piece of hand-written assembler for stack-switching (about 40 lines of straight-line code). Except for the fact that a Cid thread does not use the "standard" stack, it runs like a normal Unix program. In fact, we freely use standard C libraries, as well as standard Unix debuggers such as dbx.

A suspended thread (during a cid_jwait) is represented just by its stack pointer, with all its saved state sitting on top of the stack. The saved state consists of callee-save register values and a continuation PC value.

3.3 Forking

The Cid runtime system is basically a message-driven, non-preemptive, multi-threaded system. Each PE has three queues. The *ready queue* is a list of stack pointers of runnable threads (woken up at a cid_jwait). The *stealable queue* is a list of messages representing forked functions that may be run on any PE. The *fixed queue* is a list of messages representing forked functions that must be run on this PE. Thus, fork-request messages do double-duty as closures on the stealable and fixed queues. A top-level dispatch loop repeatedly takes work from one of these queues and executes it to completion. We first describe forking a function to a specific PE:

```
cid_fork (jv; j) x = f(..args..);
```

This expands into code that increments a join count in jv and sends a message to PE j, which (eventually) causes f to be run there. Then, a message is sent back which causes the result to be deposited in x and jv to be signalled.

All messages are *active messages* [19], *i.e.*, they contain a pointer to a C function (called a *handler*) that is directly called with the message itself as argument. Incoming messages are executed at any time, as they arrive, on top of whatever stack happens to be active at the time. This is safe because message handlers never suspend, *i.e.*, they will always return to the previous activity. In our example, the message sent to PE j has the form:

```
ptr to enqueue_on_fixed_queue_handler()    /* handler */
ptr to f_req()                             /* not f itself! */
i                                          /* PE return addr */
ptr to jv
ptr to x
... args ...
```

At PE j, the enqueue-on-fixed-queue handler simply pushes the message on the fixed queue. Later, the main dispatch loop initiates the thread_root function on a new stack, with a pointer to this message as argument. This calls f_req with a pointer to the message as argument. f_req is the pre-processor-generated function for f that efficiently unmarshalls the arguments from the message and calls f. When f returns (eventually), f_req constructs and sends back the following message to PE i:

```
ptr to f_resp()                          /* handler */
ptr to jv
ptr to x
result
```

When this message arrives, f_resp is executed as the handler. This is another pre-processor-generated function for f; it efficiently unmarshalls the message, copies the result into x and signals jv.

3.4 Join synchronization

A join variable is a structure containing a counter, initially zero, and a stack pointer, initially NULL. Each asynchronous action (e.g., cid_fork, cid_get_obj) increments the count, and each signalling action decrements it. If a signalling action decrements it to zero and there is a non-NULL stack pointer present, the stack pointer is put on the ready queue.

A cid_jwait() that finds the counter equal to zero just falls through (no pending signals). Otherwise, the callee-save register state and PC are saved on the stack, the stack pointer is saved in the structure, and it jumps to the main dispatch loop after changing the stack pointer to a reserved, "standard" scheduler stack.

3.5 Scheduling

The top-level loop of each PE looks at the ready queue, fixed queue, and stealable queue, in that order. If a stack pointer is available on the ready queue, it restores the register state (saved at top of the stack) and jumps to the saved PC. For a message dequeued off the fixed or stealable queues, it calls thread_root() on a new stack, passing it the message as argument, as explained above.

Stealable threads and dynamic granularity management When the main loop of a PE has no other work, it send a message to a *steal handler* on another PE (choosing other PEs in a round-robin fashion). The steal handler on that PE, if it finds the stealable queue empty, simply registers a pending steal request. Otherwise, it pops a message off the stealable queue and sends it to the requesting PE, with the handler procedure set to the enqueue-on-stealable-queue-handler. Thus, a stealable message simply moves from one PE's stealable queue to another PE's stealable queue and, thus, may be stolen again. There is absolutely no reformatting or extra copying of this message as it migrates across PEs.

A cid_fork statement specifying a PE always sends a fork request message to that PE. A cid_fork specifying CID_ANY adds a fork message to the local stealable queue, except when there is a pending unsatisfied steal request, in which case it is sent immediately to the requesting PE. A CID_OPT specification is the same, except that it also decides whether to fork or not based on whether there is a pending steal request and on the length of the stealable queue. In both cases, a PE does not voluntarily send a stealable-fork message unless asked for work; it may get around to executing the fork itself, and thus avoid the communication.

3.6 Global pointers and remote object access

A global pointer to an object x is an integer type, with bit fields encoding the PE on which x resides, and a unique integer (unique within that PE) for x. The cid_to_pe() operation simply does some bit-manipulation. Each PE maintains a table, keyed on global pointers, both for objects that it owns and for objects for which it has temporary "cache copies". Each table entry holds the ordinary C pointer to the local copy of the object, the size of the object, a reference count, and state for consistency-maintenance. The cid_to_global() operation makes a new entry in the table and returns the new global pointer. Let us first ignore access-mode considerations in describing the action of:

    cid_get_obj (&jv, &lp, gp, access_mode)

The join count is incremented and the local table is checked for an entry for gp. If present, either because it is owned locally or because it has been previously cached here, its reference count in the object table is incremented, lp is set to point at the object, jv is signalled, and we return. If there is no entry in the object table, we send a request message to the object's home PE, and return.

The remote object-request handler replies (eventually) with a message containing a copy of the object. On arrival, the response handler allocates a local copy, enters it in the table with key gp, sets its reference count in the table to one, points lp at the object, and signals jv.

When the corresponding cid_release(gp) is executed, the object's reference count in the table is decremented. Even if the reference count is zero, we do not immediately return the object or notify its home PE, unless space is tight or the home PE has asked for it back. A subsequent cid_get_obj may find the object still here, and thus avoid communication.

To handle access modes, we maintain additional state information in each object table entry, and invoke additional protocol code to regulate availabilty of each object. For example, when an object is currently being accessed on several PEs in CID_READ mode, its entry in the object table on its home PE contains a list of the PEs that hold copies. If a CID_WRITE request now arrives at the home PE, it queues the request on the object table entry and sends a request to each of the reading PEs, asking to be notified when all readers have released the object. When it has received all these notifications, it sends the write-copy to the requesting PE. This is essentially a directory-based coherence mechanism similar to many that are well discussed in the literature [5]. We expect to experiment with many variations.

3.7 Implementation status and preliminary results

We have recently completed our first implementation of Cid, on Digital Alpha/OSF1 workstation farms (with a Gigaswitch FDDI crossbar interconnect).

We can use any, possibly unreliable, non-blocking, packet-transport layer; for now, we use UDP sockets. We have successfully run several trivial parallel programs (nfib, make_tree, blocked matrix multiplication), and a parallel version of the Barnes-Hut n-body simulation. Compared to the original sequential C Barnes-Hut code, out Cid version runs runs about 13% slower on one machine, about 6% faster on two machines, and about 300% faster on 8 machines.

4 Related work

Other researchers have worked on tailoring software-based coherence protocols to the nature of sharing; on tying coherence mechanisms to program-level objects (rather than architectural units such as pages or cache lines), and on combining synchronization with data access (*e.g.*, [3], [15], [20], [18]. However, the languages that seem most closely related to Id are discussed below.

4.1 Split-C

The first main difference between Split-C[6] and Cid is that Cid has an MIMD model, whereas Split-C has an SPMD model. In Cid, execution begins with one thread on PE 0, which forks threads under program control; the number of threads may vary dynamically, and there may be many threads per PE. In Split-C, there is precisely one thread per PE, *ab initio*, and this stays constant throughout the computation. This also leads to different synchronization models. Split-C's SPMD model leads it more naturally towards anonymous, "barrier-like" synchronization operations where a PE's single thread waits for *all* outstanding split-phase operations to complete. Cid's MIMD model leads us more naturally towards synchronization based on explicit join variables.

Second, Cid and Split-C have very different object models. In Split-C, global pointers are true C-like pointers, supporting pointer arithmetic. Remote objects are directly addressed and accessed, there is no object-level synchronization, and there is no implicit object movement or cacheing. Thus, while Cid's cid_get_obj() operation is superficially similar to Split-C's split-phase remote fetches, they are very different in their cacheing behavior, in how they signal completion, and in their approach to synchronizing multiple accesses to the same object. A remote Split-C object must be explicitly "put back", whereas a Cid object is merely released locally, and is eventually pulled back by the home PE. Finally, Cid's distributed arrays have a very different flavor to Split-C's "spread arrays".

An explicit goal in Split-C is to follow C's example in that the programmer has a relatively clear cost model for each primitive. This is achieved because the communication costs of each primitive is roughly predictable. In Cid, the object cacheing and dynamic distribution of work and data make the communication costs less predictable.

4.2 Olden

Olden is a parallel C from Princeton [4]. A long term goal is for the programmer to use ordinary, sequential C, with opportunities for MIMD parallelism exposed automatically through analysis by the compiler (the designers introduce parallelism manually for now, while concentrating on runtime system implmentation issues). Olden appears to be geared mainly at codes for tree-structured data— as yet there are no language facilities (such as locking mechanisms) for dealing with graph data structures that have shared substructures.

Unlike Cid, which distinguishes between ordinary pointers and global pointers, Olden uniformly uses global pointers, which are used like ordinary C pointers. Also unlike Cid, an Olden thread (a stack) can span PE boundaries– migration of a thread is automatic, based on attempts to dereference a global pointer that points at another PE. A problem yet to be addressed adequately is what to do when a function dereferences pointers to two global objects on different PEs, since the automatic function migration mechanism will cause it to thrash between the two PEs. From this point of view, Cid is a lower level language in which the user manages this kind of locality explicitly– he explicitly forks the function to run near one object and accesses the other object remotely.

A consequence of Olden's implementation, which can automatically migrate parts of a stack to other PEs and can move stack frames locally, is that Olden disallows the user from creating pointers to stack variables. This is a restriction on normal C programming style. Olden also requires a fair number of changes to existing C compilers, which we explicitly avoid.

4.3 Charm, Threaded-C, TAM and P-RISC

Charm [12] and Threaded-C [9] are message-driven parallel C's for distributed memory machines. The fundamental difference between these two languages and Cid, Split-C and Olden is that they require a "continuation-passing style" of programming. For example, a normal C function that performs a remote data access must be split into two functions: the first one initiates the access and the second one executes when the access is complete. Any of the normal C function's local variables that are needed by both halves must be passed explicitly (in a separate data structure in Threaded-C, and in a Chare instance in Charm).

Continuation-based programming (also seen in "Actors" systems) seems quite tricky for humans (it is fine as an intermediate language). We believe this is because it is difficult to *modularize* continuation-passing style, causing it to pervade the whole program: if a function F calls a function G which has to be split due to a remote data access, then F also has to be split at the call to G, and this happens transitively. Recognising this difficulty, the designers of Charm are attempting to develop a simpler, graphical notation called Dagger.

Berkeley's TAM [7], and the author's own P-RISC [16] are both message-driven models used for implementing the Id programming language. Both have split-phase actions for latency tolerance, and both use join counters to wait for n long-latency events. However, they are both very low-level, continuation-based models that are not well suited for user-level programming, nor do they mesh well with existing C code (Threaded-C was inspired by these models and attempts to fix this).

5 Conclusion

We have described Cid, a shared-memory parallel C for shared- and distributed-memory machines. It is not a pure shared memory model— the programmer is aware that a particular object may reside on a different PE, and must access it either by forking a thread to run on that PE or by using special remote object access operations. The latency of communication and synchronization is visible to the programmer in the form of asynchronous, split-phase operations whose completion is signalled explicitly in join variables. Nevertheless, there are mechanisms for automatic distribution of work and data, and for automatic granularity control.

Cid is a low-entry-cost language: it consists of a simple pre-processor and a portable library, can use any ANSI C compiler and any (possibly unreliable) packet-transport layer, can link with existing code, and can use standard tools such as debuggers and profilers. A C programmer can use Cid constructs incrementally– sequential code unrelated to parallelism is unchanged.

We have outlined our recently-completed first implementation, which runs on workstation farms, and presented initial results from one non-trivial application. In the coming months we expect to implement several more applications, implement faster message-passing underneath Cid, and to port it to other platforms.

Acknowledgements: Thanks to my colleagues at CRL and MIT, and to the anonymous referees, whose comments helped improve the presentation in this paper. Thanks also to Aman Singla who, as a summer intern at CRL, contributed greatly to Cid implementation and produced the Cid Barnes-Hut code.

References

1. A. Agarwal, D. Chaiken, G. D'Souza, K. Johnson, D. Kranz, J. Kubiatowicz, K. Kurihara, B.-H. Lim, G. Maa, D. Nussbaum, M. Parkin, and D. Yeung. The MIT Alewife Machine: A Large-Scale Distributed-Memory Multiprocessor. In *Proc. Wkshp. on Multithreaded Computers, Supercomputing '91, Albuquerque NM*, November 1991.
2. Arvind, B. S. Ang, and D. Chiou. StarT the Next Generation: Integrating Global Caches and Dataflow Architecture. In *Proc. ISCA '92 Dataflow Workshop, Hamilton Island, Australia*, 1994 (expected).
3. B. N. Bershad, M. J. Zekauskas, and W. A. Sawdon. The Midway Distributed Memory System. Technical Report CMU-CS-93-119, School of Computer Science, Carnegie Mellon University, March 1993.
4. M. C. Carlisle, A. Rogers, J. H. Reppy, and L. J. Hendren. Early Experience with Olden. In *Proc. 6th Ann. Wkshp. on Languages and Compilers for Parallel Computing, Portland OR, Springer-Verlag LNCS 768*, pages 1–20, August 12-14 1993.

5. D. Chaiken, C. Fields, K. Kurihara, and A. Agarwal. Directory-based Cache Coherence in Large-Scale Multiprocessors. *IEEE Computer*, 23(6):49–59, June 1990.

6. D. E. Culler, A. Dusseau, S. C. Goldstein, S. Lumetta, T. von Eicken, and K. Yelick. Parallel Programming in Split-C. In *Proc. Supercomputing 93, Portland OR*, November 1993.

7. D. E. Culler, A. Sah, K. E. Schauser, T. von Eicken, and J. Wawrzynek. Fine-grain Parallelism with Minimal Hardware Support: A Compiler-Controlled Threaded Abstract Machine. In *4th Intl. Conf. on Architectural Support for Programming Languages and Operating Systems*, pages 164–175, April 1991.

8. R. Das, M. Uysal, J. Saltz, and Y.-S. Hwang. Communication Optimizations for Irregular Scientific Computations on Distributed Memory Architectures. Technical Report CS-TR-3163, U. Maryland Computer Science, October 1993.

9. M. Halbherr, Y. Zhou, and C. F. Joerg. MIMD-style Parallel Programming Based on Continuation-Passing Threads. Technical Report CSG Memo 355, MIT Laboratory for Computer Science, March 7 1994.

10. R. H. Halstead. Multilisp: A Language for Concurrent Symbolic Computation. *ACM Trans. on Programming Languages and Systems*, 7(4):501–539, October 1985.

11. High Performance Fortran Forum. *High Performance Fortran: Language Specification, Version 1.0*, May 3 1993. Anonymous ftp: titan.cs.rice.edu.

12. L. V. Kale. Parallel Programming with CHARM: An Overview. Technical Report 93-8, Dept. of Computer Science, University of Illinois at Urbana-Champaign, 1993.

13. J. Kuskin, D. Ofelt, M. Heinrich, J. Heinlein, R. Simoni, K. Gharachorloo, J. Chapin, D. Nakahira, J. Baxter, M. Horowitz, A. Gupta, M. Rosenblum, and J. Hennessy. The Stanford FLASH Multiprocessor. In *Proc. ISCA 94, Chicago IL*, April 1994.

14. D. Lenoski, J. Laudon, K. Gharachorloo, W.-D. Weber, A. Gupta, J. Hennessy, M. Horowitz, and M. S. Lam. The Stanford DASH Multiprocessor. *IEEE Computer*, pages 63–79, March 1992.

15. R. S. Nikhil. Id (Version 90.1) Reference Manual. Technical Report CSG Memo 284-2, MIT Laboratory for Computer Science, 545 Technology Square, Cambridge MA 02139, USA, July 15 1991.

16. R. S. Nikhil. A Multithreaded Implementation of Id using P-RISC Graphs. In *Proc. 6th Ann. Wkshp. on Languages and Compilers for Parallel Computing, Portland, Oregon, Springer-Verlag LNCS 768*, pages 390–405, August 12-14 1993.

17. S. K. Reinhardt, J. R. Larus, and D. A. Wood. Tempest and Typhoon: User-Level Shared Memory. In *Proc. ISCA 94, Chicago IL*, April 1994.

18. B. Totty and D. A. Reed. Dynamic Object Management for Distributed Data Structures. In *Proc. Supercomputing 92*, pages 692–701, November 1992.

19. T. von Eicken, D. E. Culler, S. C. Goldstein, and K. E. Schauser. Active Messages: a Mechanism for Integrated Communication and Computation. In *Proc. 19th. Ann. Intl. Symp. on Computer Architecture, Australia*, pages 256–266, May 1992.

20. D. A. Wood, S. Chandra, B. Falsafi, M. D. Hill, J. R. Larus, A. R. Lebeck, J. C. Lewis, S. Mukerjee, S. Palacharla, and S. K. Reinhardt. Mechanisms for Cooperative Shared Memory. In *Proc. 21st ISCA, San Diego, CA*, May 1993.

EQ: Overview of a New Language Approach for Prototyping Scientific Computation*

Thomas Derby, Robert Schnabel, and Benjamin Zorn**

University of Colorado at Boulder

Abstract. This research investigates a new paradigm for scientific programming, which focuses on the direct representation of user concepts and the use of standard mathematical notation. We apply these ideas to the problem of designing a language for prototyping numerical computations. In the process, we arrive at a language (EQ) that does not fit into standard language categories such as imperative or functional, but has features of both paradigms. This paper presents an overview of the EQ language, focusing on how our design goals lead to the language features present in EQ. Two detailed examples are given, followed by performance results from our experimental prototype. These timings indicate that EQ programs can be competitive with those written in C. Finally, we briefly discuss the impact of our design on the optimization of EQ programs.

1 Introduction

Despite the rich history of algorithmic developments for scientific computation and the widespread use of scientific codes for practical problem solving, the history of programming languages for use in scientific computation does not show a similar development. FORTRAN was the first high-level language designed specifically for numerical programming, and is still the de facto standard. APL was the first language based around array computations, and had some impact on scientific programming, although today it is used relatively infrequently [7]. MatLab is a modern interpretive environment that is gaining an increasing following, especially for use in prototyping work [9]. Fortran90 is the latest in this line of languages, and adds many new features to FORTRAN [6].

Each of these languages is based around a fundamentally imperative (or procedural) paradigm; a sequence of statements is executed one after another, with control structures such as GOTO used to alter this order. The imperative paradigm was originally designed for numerical computation, and has been quite successful for it. This paradigm does have significant limitations, however, such as the inability to directly correspond to the style and content of equations that scientists write in describing their algorithms in papers, and the tendency to be far longer than the scientist's description. These difficulties include significant difficulties in using the imperative paradigm for parallel computations. For these

---

* Research supported by NSF grant ASC-9307315

** Department of Computer Science, Campus Box 430, University of Colorado, Boulder, Colorado, 80309, U.S.A. (zorn@cs.colorado.edu)

reasons, as well as others, many attempts have been made to find new languages that alleviate these problems.

Many of the new languages that have been proposed for use in numerical programming have been attempts to show that other paradigms (such as object-oriented or functional programming) can be successfully used for numerical work, with a suitable set of libraries or additional language constructs [1] [3]. The success of these new languages in the scientific community has been very limited so far. Since these languages are based around computing paradigms not particularly designed for scientific computation, this result does not seem surprising.

An area where we feel that fundamental improvements can be made in scientific programming is in languages for prototyping. In particular, we feel that much prototyping work could benefit from support for language constructs that match the way scientists and mathematicians specify algorithms informally. These new constructs include unordered equational and definitional specifications of algorithms, and basic notation that supports iteration. At the same time, support for fundamental imperative constructs is also necessary. Finally, it is important that the language produce code that is sufficiently efficient that reliable measurements and comparisons can be made from it. Efficiency is an area where currently popular prototyping tools are deficient.

To meet these objectives, we feel that a new language paradigm is needed. This paradigm should be designed with the particular needs of scientific programming in mind, but without some of the limitations of the imperative paradigm. This paper describes a language, EQ, that is a first step in our investigation of new paradigms for scientific programming. EQ provides a language that we feel improves the ease of production and understanding of prototype numerical programs for optimization and linear algebra, and provides sufficient efficiency that comparative timing measurements can be used to compare algorithms.

This paper presents our preliminary results in developing and implementing the EQ language. Sections 2 and 3 describe our ideas about how a programming language for prototyping scientific computations in optimization and linear algebra should be designed. Section 4 contains two example EQ programs, with line-by-line explanations. Section 5 summarizes the results of our implementation efforts to date. Section 6 contrasts our work in language design with related work. Finally, we describe in section 7 the future of this research, and present our conclusions in section 8.

2 Design Principles

In order to design a language for scientific computation that is truly an improvement over current languages, we feel that there are two important design principles that should be kept in mind, and used to guide the design throughout.

First, the language should directly represent the objects and concepts that the programmer uses to understand the algorithm, such as matrices and ranges of indices. The language should not require one to think in terms of abstractions that are not already a part of the way a user visualizes a problem. For example, an LU decomposition is not generally thought of as a recurrence, and so it should not be coded that way. Languages designed with this principle in mind should be easier to use than ones that are not, and programs should be shorter and easier to understand as well. Note that both standard imperative languages and functional languages fail to follow this design principle, but each in different ways. For example, imperative languages force the user to think about the ordering of their computation; in many cases, this is extra information that is irrelevant to the correctness and efficiency of the algorithm. Purely functional languages describe computations in terms of recursive function invocations; this is not the way in which simple loops are thought of by programmers of scientific codes.

Second, the language should mimic standard mathematical notations wherever possible. This principle is in many ways a consequence of the first principle, as the way mathematics and algorithms are written down for human understanding is a good guide towards people's understanding of those algorithms. As an example, the multiplication operation between two matrices in standard mathematics does not compute element-by-element multiplications; neither, therefore, should a language for scientific computations. A second example is notation for iteration; mathematics tends to use subscripts in notation such as a_k or a_+ to indicate position within a sequence, rather than imperative assignment statements such as "x = x + 1," which have no meaning from a mathematical viewpoint.

3 Features of EQ

The EQ language is composed of two parts. First, it provides a set of definitional features for defining new values in terms of old ones. These include unordered equations, the if statement, range variables, and matrix operations. The other main part of EQ is its unique support for iterative constructs: explicit notations for change, the followed-by operator, and the do loop.

3.1 Unordered Equations

Mathematical notations, in general, are not ordered; a set of equations is given. Typical examples have extra words between these equations; "x = sin y, where y = ..." and "let y = ... in x = sin y" are common examples. To model these kinds of notation more simply, EQ provides a simple unordered model. For example,

```
a = 4;
b = a + correction;
correction = sqrt (a);
```

would compute a = 4, correction = 2, and b = 6. This "unordered" paradigm allows the programmer much greater flexibility, and is similar to the "natural" way of expressing algorithms; statements that logically belong together can be placed in proximity, even if they cannot be executed consecutively.

In addition, unordered equations correspond to a "proof-oriented" view of the program; each equation can be thought of as a fact about the values the program computes, rather than a computational rule. These facts can then be

used to prove properties about programs. From this point of view, it is convenient
to be able to view these statements as unordered.

EQ is a "single assignment" language; this means that the same variable
cannot be defined twice. EQ insists on this property even for arrays; the code
fragment

```
a[1] = 1;
a[2] = 2;
```

is not permitted in EQ. By permitting only one assignment to an array variable,
EQ avoids the problem of determining if any element of the array is defined
twice at run time, and greatly simplifies the dependency analysis necessary for
efficient compilation. It is, however, sometimes desirable to be able to write
code fragments such as the above; we show how to achieve the effect of multiple
assignments in section 3.6.

3.2 Conditionals - the If Statement

Conditional computations in EQ are handled in a very similar way to that used
in imperative languages:

```
if (x >= y) {
    maximum = x;
    minimum = y;
}
else {
    maximum = y;
    minimum = x;
}
```

computes both the minimum and maximum of x and y. Although there are
multiple assignments to variables here, each "branch" of the conditional must
assign a variable only once.

By providing a conditional statement (as opposed to the conditional expression used by functional languages,) we have avoided the need to have records
or tuples.[3] Adding such types to EQ would not be difficult, but would be a
violation of our "direct representation" design principle. More importantly, the
conditional statement permits the programmer to assign to a variable in only
ONE of the branches of an if statement; this will have a well defined (and important) meaning when used with EQ's iterative statements.

3.3 Computation over Sets - the Range Variable

Performing computations over a set of values is a very common activity in programming. In numerical computations, typically these are sets of subscripts.
Using loop notation (as is required in languages such as FORTRAN) obscures

---

[3] Use of a conditional expression to assign two values such as minimum and maximum
would involve a notation using tuples such as "(maximum, minimum) = if (x>=y)
then (x, y) else (y, x)."

the intent and potential parallelism of the program, in addition to expanding code volume. To address these issues, EQ provides the range variable: a variable that takes on a consecutive set of integer values. Definition statements that involve a range variable are performed for each possible value of the variable. For example:

```
i = 1..20;
a[i] = 0;
```

makes a length 20 vector of zeros. Range variables are also used in many other contexts, including reduction operations. For example:

```
i = 1..20;
s = sum [i]: a[i];
```

adds up the elements of array a. Combining different uses of range variables can yield tremendous expressive power:

```
i,j,k = 1..10;
c[i,k] = sum[j]: a[i,j] * b[j,k]
```

is a matrix multiplication program for 10x10 matrices.

We note that range variables cannot be used to define recurrences; statements such as

```
x[i] = x[i-1] + 1;
```

are considered circular (x is defined in terms of itself) and are not permitted in EQ. These kinds of computations are expressed in EQ using its "over" loops; see section 3.8.

3.4 Matrix Operations

For notational convenience, EQ provides matrix operations that closely correspond with those used in standard mathematics. Thus, A * B, where A and B are two dimensional matrices, represents a standard matrix-matrix multiplication, not the element-by-element computation which it would in APL or Fortran90. We feel that element-by-element multiplication is more clearly expressed using subscripting and range variables:

```
i,j = 1..n;
C[i,j] = A[i,j] * B[i,j];
```

Currently, EQ supports addition ("+"), subtraction ("-"), and multiplication ("*") of matrices, in addition to transposition, which is represented by the postfix "~" operator. We hope eventually to support less "computational" operations (such as matrix inverse) efficiently; see section 7.

3.5 Explicit Notations for Change

In an unordered notation, each name can represent only a single value; thus, a FORTRAN-style assignment statement such as "x = x + 1" is not meaningful in such a context. To express such relationships in EQ, we turn once again to notation used for writing down algorithms that have iteration as a major component. In areas such as numerical optimization, one often finds notation such as:

$$x_+ = x_c + x_p$$

where the subscripts +, c, and p stand for the next value, current value, and previous value, respectively. EQ models this notation very closely:

```
next x = x + prev x;
```
is a statement that would be used in a program to compute a Fibonacci series. This notation corresponds more closely to the algorithmic ideas than FORTRAN code for the same computation, which would require a temporary to be introduced (and assignment statements carefully placed) to express this computation.

In general, the "next" and "prev" prefixes allow references to past and future values of a variable. For convenience, the notation "x'" can be used as an abbreviation for "next x." Multiple prefixes can be used to reference values in the distant past or future (although this is rarely done.) We show how to use these constructs in sections 3.6 and 3.7.

3.6   Followed-by Operator

In order to use the "next" and "prev" notation, there must be a way to move "forwards" in time, so that the value that used to be called "next x" becomes "x", "x" becomes "prev x", and so on. EQ provides two mechanisms for incrementing the "time step." The first is the "followed-by" operator "=>", which moves forwards one unit in time. An example of this is:

```
a = 5 =>
a = prev a * 2;
```
which computes the value a = 10.

Generally, if we have the statement A => B, then the variables defined by A are accessible within B, but with one extra "prev" (or one fewer "next") if B redefines that variable. The variables defined by A which are redefined by B are not accessible outside the followed-by statement (in the previous example, the value "5" is not visible outside the followed-by statement.)

One additional aspect of the followed-by operator is important. If the statements in B make a "partial" definition of a variable (either by only defining some elements of an array or by defining a variable in only one branch of a conditional,) then the undefined portions of that variable default to the value defined in A for the variable. This rule allows the followed-by operation to be used when an array must be built up out of several parts, because multiple definitions of the same array are not allowed. For example, one way of defining an n by n identity matrix is:

```
a = 1..n; b = 1..n;
I[a,b] = 0 =>
I[a,a] = 1;
```
The first definition of I gives each element the value zero, and the second assigns ones to the diagonal. Since the second definition of I doesn't define all of I's elements, the values from the first definition are used to fill in the undefined spaces.

3.7   Approximation Loops - the "do" Statement and "once" Clause

Most loops in numerical codes iterate over a fixed set of integer values (like FORTRAN's DO loops.) These loops are best described using EQ's range variables.

Of the remaining loops in scientific computation, almost all fall into the category of approximation loops; these loops iterate, improving an initial approximation to some quantity on each execution of the loop, until either an adequate approximation to the answer is achieved, or the approximation process fails. These loops often have multiple exit conditions, with different code that needs to be run for each exit case, and are not well modeled by standard while or repeat loops.

EQ supports approximation loops directly with its "do" statement. Each iteration of the loop advances time by one step. We give a simple example.

```
x = n/2;
do {
    next x = (x + n/x) / 2;
    once (|next x - x| < 1e-7)) sqrt = next x;
}
```

This program computes the square root of a number x, and stores it in the variable sqrt. The first equation initializes our loop. The do statement continues to compute values for "next x" and time-shift them back into "x" until the boolean expression of the once statement becomes true, at which time sqrt is assigned the last computed approximation, which is "next x" (not x.)

In general, a do loop body consists of an unordered set of statements that include one or more once clauses. The do loop repeatedly executes its body until one of its once clauses is triggered (has its condition become true.) When this happens, the body of the once clause is executed, and the loop is finished. If multiple once clauses are used, their conditions are tested in order; the lexically first once clause that has a true condition is the one that is used. This is the only case in EQ where the order of statements can change the semantics of a program.

3.8 More Uses for Range Variables: the "at" and "over" Statements

We discuss two more statements which illustrate the power of range variables. Unfortunately, neither of these is implemented in the current prototype (see section 5.)

The first of these is the "at" statement. This statement is often used in code which finds a minimum or maximum element:

```
i = 1..10;   j = 1..20;
...
at max[i,j]: c[i,j] {
  next c[i,j] = 0;
}
```

sets the maximal element of c to zero. In general, the at statement takes a "min" or "max" expression, and runs the following statements for the one value of the range variables which maximizes (minimizes) the expression. If there is more than one maximizer (minimizer), EQ chooses the first one it finds. Note that within the body of the at statement, the range variables maximized (minimized) over behave like ordinary variables with fixed values.

This construct more naturally expresses the programmer's intentions than using a loop like FORTRAN would require. We feel it is also more elegant than using a "location of maximum" reduction operator[4].

The second statement which uses range variables in a unique way is the "over" statement. This statement can be used to write an ordered loop (similar to the do loop) which loops over the values in the range variable. This allows one to write recurrence-like programs:

```
x = 3..100;
fib [1] = 1 =>
fib [2] = 2 =>
over x: {
    fib [x] = prev fib [x - 1] + prev fib [x - 2];
}
```

computes the first 100 elements of the fibonacci sequence. The over statement runs its body as if were a do loop; after each iteration, a time-shift is done, and i is changed to the next value in the range.

By default, the over statement loops through the values of the range variable from smallest to largest; to reverse this direction, the keyword "rev" is placed before the variable name.

4 Example Programs

We present two examples of EQ programs, with explanations and observations about the EQ constructs used. The first emphasizes the use of range variables, while the second emphasizes iteration and matrix operations. Both examples include statements not implemented in the current EQ prototype (see section 5.)

4.1 LU Decomposition Example

The following EQ code computes an LU decomposition with partial pivoting. The input matrix a is of size 1..n x 1..n, and the decomposition is computed "in place," being returned in a' (where a' is the abbreviation for "next a"). The vector of pivoting information is stored in p'. For simplicity of presentation, our algorithm contains no singularity detection. The lines have been numbered so we can refer to them later.

```
(1)     k = 1..n;
(2)     p[k] = k;
(3)     over k: {
(4)         i, j = k+1..n;
(5)         piv = k..n;
```

---

[4] In order to use this sort of reduction style, tuples would have to be introduced. For example, the above example might read "let (ii, jj) = maxloc (c [i,j] for i = 1..10, j = 1..20) in ..."

```
(6)        at max [piv]: |a[piv, k]| {
(7)           t1 = p[k] => p'[k] = p[piv] => p'[piv] = t1;
(8)           t2 = a[k,] => a'[k,] = a[piv,] => a'[piv,] = t2;
           } =>
(9)        a'[i,k] /= a[k,k] =>
(10)       a'[i,j] -= a[i,k] * a[k,j];
           }
```

Line (1) sets up a range variable to loop over the entire matrix. Line (2) defines
the initial state of the pivot vector p: each row is in its original location. The
assignment is done for each possible value of k. Line (3) begins the main loop.
The **over** statement loops through each of the values of the range variable k,
going from 1 to n. Unlike normal usage of a range variable, in an over statement
the values are used sequentially. Each of lines (4) through (10) is executed once
for each value of k, starting with 1 and going through n. These statements
perform the pivoting and elimination steps. Lines (4) and (5) set up needed range
variables for the computations at a single iteration of the LU decomposition; piv
will be used to perform the pivot step, and i and j will perform the rank one
update to a. Line (6) searches for the proper row to pivot with, using the **at**
statement, which goes through all of the values of piv, searching for the row
with the biggest element in column k. Lines (7) and (8) perform the required
exchanges, using the fixed value of piv that was computed by the at statement.
Line (7) exchanges the pivoting information, and (8) exchanges rows of the
matrix. The followed-by operator is used because each set of three steps must
be done in the specificed order. Line (9) computes the multipliers, storing them
in place. Note that this must be done after the pivoting, thus the followed-by
operator is again used. Line (10) does the rank one update. Range variables are
used to perform this operation without the use of loops. Since this operation
uses the multipliers, the followed-by operator is placed between it and line (9).

This example makes very little use of one of the most important features of
EQ, the ability to specify equations in an unordered manner. It does, however,
illustrate the simplicity that comes from the index range features of EQ.

4.2 BFGS Example

The EQ code given below solves the n variable unconstrained minimization problem minimize f(), using a simple version of the popular BFGS Gauss-Newton
method. It takes as inputs the function f() and its gradient gradf(), as well
as an initial estimate to the solution, start_point. The algorithm updates the
inverse hessian, H, and uses a simple quadratic interpolation line search.

```
           %Initialize the algorithm
(1)        iter = 1;
(2)        x = start_point;
(3)        fx = f(x);
(4)        gx = gradf(x);
```

```
(5)      i = 1..n;  j = 1..n;
(6)      H[i,j] = 0 => H[i,i] = 1;

(7)      do {

         % Inverse Hessian update
(8)      s = x' - x;  y = gx' - gx;
(9)      H' = H + ((s - H*y) * s~ + s * (s - H*y)~) / s~*y
               - s*s~*(s - H*y)~*y/(s~*y)^2;

         % Step length computation
(10)     lambda = 1;
(11)     do {
(12)       trial_x = x - lambda*H*gx;
(13)       trial_fx = f (trial_x);

(14)       slope = -gx~*H*gx;
(15)       trial_lambda = -lambda * slope /
                     2 * (trial_fx - fx - lambda * slope);
(16)         lambda' = max (trial_lambda, lambda / 10);

(17)         once (trial_fx < fx + 1e-4 * slope) {
(18)           x' = trial_x;  fx' = trial_fx;  gx' = gradf (x');
             }
         }

         % Termination conditions
(19)     once (fx' - fx < 1e-8) {
(20)         answer = x';  success = TRUE;
         }

(21)     iter' += 1;
(22)     once (iter > 500) {
           success = FALSE;
         }
       }
```

We note the heavy use of matrix notation in this algorithm. Lines (1) through (5) initialize the algorithm. The only use of range variables in this algorithm is in lines (5) and (6), to initialize H to the identity matrix. Lines (7) through (22) form the main loop, which produces better and better approximations to the minimizer of f.

Lines (8) and (9) compute the BFGS update. Note that they can be written at this point because EQ uses unordered equations. These lines will be evaluated by EQ only after the computations in line (18) have been completed.

Lines (10) through (18) form the line search, which is again a loop which produces better and better approximations – this time to an acceptable step length lambda. Lines (12) and (13) compute the x and fx values for our current step length. Lines (14) through (16) compute the new trial step length. Line (17) checks the termination condition, and once the condition is satisfied, makes the trial values official in line (18).

Finally, we have the termination conditions for our main loop, of which there are two. The first, at lines (19) and (20), checks for small changes in function value. If this occurs, the algorithm is successful, and we return our answer. The second termination test, in lines (21) and (22), checks for excessive iterations.

We feel this example illustrates the convenience and elegance of EQ's approximation loop facilities. Of particular note is the lack of variables for holding "old" values of variables; the programmer was simply able to refer to x' and x at the same time. This would not be possible in other languages we know of. The example also shows the value of simple matrix operations, although that is not a feature unique to EQ.

5 Implementation Results

A prototype compiler for the EQ language has been implemented, that translates an EQ program into an equivalent C program, for compilation using a standard C compiler. We present some typical timing results comparing EQ programs with hand-coded C versions of our PLU and BFGS algorithms[5]. Since the prototype EQ implementation does not currently support all of the EQ constructs used within the examples (in particular, the "at" and "over" statements,) we have been forced to use alternative EQ versions of the examples which do not use these statements. We plan to add these constructs to our prototype in the future; see section 7. For the PLU algorithm, we computed 100 50x50 decompositions. For BFGS, we minimized a simple function of 64 variables - taking about 150 iterations of the main loop.

Problem	Optimization	EQ	C	Ratio
PLU	OFF	9.0	3.4	2.6
	ON	4.7	0.8	5.9
BFGS	OFF	1.8	1.4	1.3
	ON	0.7	0.4	1.8

Table 1. Timing of sample EQ programs, in seconds

The first column in Table 1 contains the base C times, both with and without C compiler optimization turned on. We then give the corresponding times for the raw EQ generated programs. The EQ programs are slower by a factor of 1.3 to 5.9, which we feel is reasonable for a first implementation of a prototyping system. There is clearly room, however, for improvements in the efficiency of generated EQ programs.

---

[5] These measurements were taken on a DECstation 5000/260 using its standard cc compiler, but we received similar performance ratios on other machines.

402

Further investigation revealed that a large amount of the additional time required by the EQ version was caused by the calls to memcpy() [6], which are produced by the EQ compiler. These calls are generated when a time step occur in the EQ program (followed-by operations and do loops,) and are used to copy the value of a variable into its "previous" variable. Many, however, were totally unnecessary and could be removed entirely. Others could be reduced in size to only one dimension. To examine the potential effects of "copy elimination" optimization, we removed the memcpy() calls by hand from the code output by the EQ compiler, giving the results shown in Table 2.

Problem	Optimization	EQ	C	Ratio
PLU	OFF	4.8	3.4	1.4
	ON	1.0	0.8	1.3
BFGS	OFF	1.7	1.4	1.2
	ON	0.5	0.4	1.3

Table 2. Timing of sample EQ programs with memcpy()'s removed, in seconds

In the optimized case, these EQ times are within thirty percent of the hand-written C code. This suggests that EQ programs can produce efficiency very close to that of optimized C code, provided that the problem of copy elimination can be suitably solved. Recent results with SISAL suggest this can be done effectively. [2]

6 Related Work

In this section, we consider other programming languages which are related to EQ or to scientific programming. These can be divided into several broad categories, and we discuss each of them below.

Imperative languages are those languages which use the assignment statement ($x = x + 1$) as their primary computational mechanism. These languages are commonly used in scientific programming, and include various versions of FORTRAN (including Fortran90 [6],) C [8], and interpreted languages such as MATLAB [9] and APL [7], as well as many languages of only historical interest [11]. These languages are good at representing the change or update of a value, which explains their relative ease of use and popularity for scientific coding. However, the imperative paradigm has problems expressing relationships which should be maintained throughout a computation, such as norm_of_y = norm(y);, which should cause norm_of_y to be updated when y is.

Object-oriented languages such as C++ [12] are used mostly as a language extension tool; classes are used to construct objects such as matrices that are

---

[6] The C library function memcpy() copies a block of memory from one location to another.

useful to scientific programming. Thus, C++ can be used to create some limited forms of language extension, but the end-user is still programming in the imperative model.

Functional languages are often defined as all non-imperative languages, but we refer here to languages based upon single-assignment and an "expression" model of computation (i.e., everything is an expression.) These languages include Haskell [5] [4], SISAL [1], and Id [10], among others. These languages are single-assignment, which makes them good at expressing invariants such as `norm_of_y = norm(y);`. However, their inability to express change simply can make their use in scientific programming very complex. SISAL and Id have some primitive looping abilities, but cannot express the change of part of an object such as an array.

In the category of "dataflow" languages are languages such as EPL [13] and Lucid [14]. EPL is an equation-based language, using a construct very similar to EQ's range variables, but with no control structures. Instead, computations are written using recurrences, which become increasingly complex and confusing for large algorithms. The ability to write arbitrary recurrences also causes significant difficulties for efficient execution. Lucid is also equation based, and uses an algebra based on streams of values to specify computation. This seems to us confusing and difficult to read when compared with EQ's notation.

7 Future Work

The prototype EQ implementation we currently have does not support constructs such as "at" and "over"; correcting these deficiencies will be one of the top priorities for our future work in this area. Once this is done, it will be possible to do further examples of EQ programming, of a more lengthy and complex nature than those given here. We hope to use these experiences to continue to evolve and change the constructs of the EQ language.

Another area of interest is the efficient support for more complex matrix operations such as matrix inversion, and support for some kinds of sparse matrices, such as triangular and diagonal matrices. We hope to be able to add these kinds of constructs to EQ, using compile-time analysis to avoid any loss of efficiency.

Additionally, a study and implementation of optimizations (in particular, the rank reduction optimization) is important to obtain a clearer understanding of the impact of the EQ language on both space and time efficiency. In addition to efficiency, we plan to do a study of dependability as well, examining what various transformations to EQ programs (such as the introduction of temporary variables) do to the efficiency of the resulting executable code.

Finally, a detailed study of the opportunities for parallelism in EQ is justified. EQ has much potential data parallelism exposed directly to the user of the language, through its range variables, and its unordered equations express "functional" parallelism. We plan to continue research into both implicit and explicit models of parallelism in EQ. We also feel that parallel versions of this language could be quite natural, since the unorderedness of EQ statements and range variables imparts an inherent parallelism to the semantics of the language.

8 Conclusion

This goals of this research are to explore a new paradigm for scientific computation that emphasizes a direct representation of user concepts. In order to limit the scope of the work, we have focused on optimization and dense linear algebra problems. Another target of the EQ project is to produce a prototyping system which is sufficiently efficient to permit timing measurements to be used to compare different algorithms.

Our new language paradigm is based on a single-definition system of unordered equations. We feel that this corresponds to the way in which mathematicians and scientists think about problems – how and what is computed, not when. In order to support such an unordered system, unique features had to be added to allow modification and change to be expressed in EQ. This was done by providing an explicit notation for change (through the "next" and "prev" prefixes,) and building control structures such as the "do" loop on top of this. To this basic structure we added the range variable, a powerful implicit looping construct. The majority of loops appearing in a FORTRAN program can be reduced to uses of this construct, which more closely agree with mathematical notation than looping notation does.

The goal of comparative timings means that special attention must be given to optimization. In particular, the goal must be to blend efficiency with dependability: the ability to "count" on the compiler making optimizations. Many standard optimizations, such as common subexpression elimination, are more easily accomplished in EQ than in other paradigms. However, languages such as EQ require optimizations not needed in other paradigms. A particular example of this is the rank reduction. This optimization is very general, and can take the place of optimizations such as copy elimination.

We feel that the benefits of our new notation are that EQ expresses algorithms in numerical optimization more naturally and elegantly than other language paradigms available. Programs written in EQ for our limited problem domain tend to express direct user concepts, rather than programming language concepts. Where this is not the case, we will continue development of the EQ language. A preliminary implementation indicates that EQ can be expected to produce very reasonable efficiency for a prototyping language. We feel these initial results are very encouraging.

Further work will undoubtedly yield further refinements and improvements of the programming model proposed in this paper. But we feel that this work shows that investigations into new languages specifically focused on scientific computations can provide interesting and useful alternatives to the standard imperative paradigm.

References

1. A. P. W. Bohm, R. R. Oldehoeft, D. C. Cann, and J. T. Feo. *SISAL Reference Manual, Language Version 2.0.*
2. David Cann. RETIRE FORTRAN? a debate rekindled. *Communications of the ACM*, 35(8):81 – 89, August 1992.
3. Paul N. Hilfinger and Phillip Collela. FIDIL: A language for scientific programming. In Robert Grossman, editor, *Symbolic Computation: Applications to Scientific Computing*, chapter 5, pages 97–138. SIAM, 1989.
4. Paul Hudak et al. Report on the programming language Haskell: A non-strict, purely functional language version 1.2. *SIGPLAN Notices*, 27(5):R–1–R–164, May 1992.
5. Paul Hudak and Joseph Fasel. A gentle introduction to Haskell. *SIGPLAN Notices*, 27(5):T–1–T–53, May 1992.
6. ISO. *Fortran 90 Standard ISO/IEC 1539: 1991(E)*.
7. Kenneth E. Iverson. *A Programming Language*. Wiley, New York, New York, 1962.
8. Brain W. Kernighan and Dennis M. Ritchie. *The C Programming Language*. Prentice-Hall, 1978.
9. Math Works Inc. *MATLAB User's Guide*, 1992.
10. Rishiyur S. Nikhil. Id language reference manual, version 90.1. Postscript available via FTP from Massachusetts Institute of Technology, July 1991.
11. Jean E. Sammet. *PROGRAMMING LANGUAGES: History and Fundamentals*, chapter IV, pages 128–313. Prentice-Hall, Engelwood Cliffs, New Jersey, 1969.
12. Bjarne Stroustrup. *The C++ Programming Language*. Addison-Wesley, Reading, Mass., 1986.
13. Boleslaw K. Szymanski. EPL – parallel programming with recurrent equations. In Boleslaw K. Szymanski, editor, *Parallel Functional Languages and Compilers*, chapter 3, pages 51 – 104. ACM Press, New York, New York, 1991.
14. William W. Wadge. *Lucid, the Dataflow Programming Language*. Academic Press, London, 1985.

Reshaping Access Patterns for Generating Sparse Codes*

Aart J.C. Bik, Peter M.W. Knijnenburg and Harry A.G. Wijshoff

High Performance Computing Division
Department of Computer Science, Leiden University
P.O. Box 9512, 2300 RA Leiden, the Netherlands
ajcbik@cs.leidenuniv.nl

Abstract

In a new approach to the development of sparse codes, the programmer defines a particular algorithm on dense matrices which are actually sparse. The sparsity of the matrices as indicated by the programmer is only dealt with at compile-time. The compiler selects appropriate compact data structure and automatically converts the algorithm into code that takes advantage of the sparsity of the matrices. To achieve efficient sparse codes, the compiler must be able to reshape some access patterns before a data structure is selected. In this paper, we discuss a reshaping method that is based on unimodular transformations.

1 Introduction

Because of the inherent complexity of sparse codes, it is worthwhile to consider whether sparse codes can be generated automatically. In [7, 9] we have proposed an approach in which the algorithm is defined on dense matrices and automatically converted into sparse code. This implies that all operations are defined on two dimensional arrays, which re-

duces the complexity of sparse codes development and maintenance, and enables more standard compiler optimizations [6]. Annotations are used to identify which of the declared dense data structures are actually sparse. Matrices which are actually sparse are referred to as **implicitly sparse matrices**, because the programmer does not have to deal with the sparsity explicitly. This burden is placed on the compiler which, in order to exploit the sparsity as much as possible, selects a compact data structure and generates corresponding sparse code. This approach can be used for sparse matrices with arbitrary nonzero structures, but if the matrices are available on file, compile-time analysis of these matrices [10] or some kind of annotation can be used to enable the compiler to take advantage of certain properties of the nonzero structures.

However, as alluded to in previous work, the application of standard program transformations is essential for the generation of efficient sparse codes. Because the input program operates on two-dimensional arrays that support direct access, the programmer is free to use all kind of access patterns through the arrays. In some cases, preference is given to a particular kind of access patterns. For instance, column-wise access is often used in FORTRAN to enable vectorization or to improve the spatial locality of the program. However, in general, all kind of access patterns through the implicitly sparse matrices can occur. Sparse data structures usually only support efficient gener-

* Support was provided by the Foundation for Computer Science (SION) of the Netherlands Organization for the Advancement of Pure Research (NWO) and the EC Esprit Agency DG XIII under Grant No. APPARC 6634 BRA III.

ation of entries along one kind of access patterns. This is caused by the fact that these data structures do not only consists of primary storage to store numerical values, but also of overhead storage used to access these values and to reconstruct the structure of the matrix. Supporting several kind of access patterns would require data structures in which the savings in storage for numerical values is diminished by the required amount of overhead storage, or for which the maintenance overhead would increase the execution time considerably. Therefore, before an organization for the sparse data structure is selected, reshaping the access patterns can resolve conflicts between different kind of access patterns. This can improve the performance of the resulting sparse code considerably.

The outline of the rest of this paper is as follows. In section 2, we give a motivation for the necessity of reshaping techniques in order to generate efficient sparse codes. In section 3 we give an outline of unimodular transformations, which will be used for the reshaping techniques. These techniques are discussed in section 4. We give some examples in section 5. Finally, in section 6, conclusions and issues for future research are stated.

2 Importance of Reshaping

Below, we illustrate that reshaping access patterns for implicitly sparse matrices is essential for the automatic generation of efficient code.

2.1 Definitions

Most occurrences of an implicitly sparse matrix A appear in a nested loop of degree n. We assume that the subscript functions of each occurrence can be represented by a single mapping $F_A(\overline{I}) : \mathbf{Z}^n \rightarrow \mathbf{Z}^2$ of the form $F_A(\overline{I}) = \overline{m} + M \cdot \overline{I}$, where $\overline{I}$ denotes the surrounding loop indices, that is $\overline{I} = (I_1, \ldots, I_n)^T$:

$$F_A(\overline{I}) = \begin{pmatrix} m_{10} \\ m_{20} \end{pmatrix} + \begin{pmatrix} m_{11} \ldots m_{1n} \\ m_{21} \ldots m_{2n} \end{pmatrix} \cdot \overline{I}$$

Each occurrence induces **access patterns**, consisting of the index sets of the elements that are referenced in one execution of the innermost loop. The **direction** of an access pattern is defined as $\overline{d}_A = (m_{1n}, m_{2n})$. If either m_{1n} or m_{2n} is zero, the access patterns are called **row-** and **column-wise** respectively. All other nonzero directions are referred to as **diagonal-wise**. Access patterns for which $\overline{d}_A = \overline{0}$ holds are called **scalar-wise**. For the latter kind of access patterns, a direction is usually induced at a higher level i, for which m_{1i} or m_{2i} is nonzero. Two directions $\overline{d}$ and $\overline{d}'$ are called **linearly dependent** if $\overline{d} = \lambda \cdot \overline{d}'$ for some $\lambda \in \mathbf{R}$.

2.2 A Naive Approach

Consider, for example, the following fragment, where an operation $\overline{c} \leftarrow A \cdot \overline{b}$ is followed by an accumulation of particular elements in an implicitly sparse matrix:

```
        DO I = 1, M
          DO J = 1, N
S1:         C(I) += A(I,J) * B(J)
          ENDDO
        ENDDO
        DO J = 1, N / 2
          DO I = 1, M / 2
S2:         ACC += A(2*I,2*J)
          ENDDO
        ENDDO
```

In [9] we have shown that statements S_1 and S_2 only have to be executed for entries, i.e. elements that are stored explicitly in the compact data structure of A. If the organization of the selected data structure is consistent with the access pattern in these statements, a special construct can be generated that will iterate over all entries along a certain access pattern at run-time.

Since S_1 and S_2 induce respectively row- and column-wise access patterns through A, one of the following fragments would result after selection of the data structure (see [7, 9] for details on the data structure and code generation):

row-wise storage of A:
```
DO I = 1, M
    DO A = LW(I), HGH(I)
        J = IND(A)
S1:     C(I) += VAL(A) * B(J)
    ENDDO
ENDDO
DO J = 1, N / 2
    DO I = 1, M / 2
        A = LKP(IND,LW(2*I),HGH(2*I),2*J)
S2:     IF (A != _|_) ACC += VAL(A)
    ENDDO
ENDDO
```

column-wise storage of A:
```
DO I = 1, M
    DO J = 1, N
        A = LKP(IND,LW(J),HGH(J),I)
S1:     IF (A != _|_) C(I) += VAL(A) * B(J)
    ENDDO
ENDDO
DO J = 1, N / 2
    DO A = LW(2*J), HGH(2*J)
        I = IND(A)
S2:     IF (MOD(I,2) = 0) ACC += VAL(A)
    ENDDO
ENDDO
```

In the first fragment, a construct that iterates over entries can be used for S_1. This construct can also be used for S_2 in the second fragment, although a test is required because only the entries $a_{i,2*j}$ in a column for which $i \bmod 2 = 0$ holds, are operated on in the original dense fragment. If row-wise storage is selected, a lookup is required for S_2 to fetch the elements in the matrix. The value $\perp$ is returned if this element is not an entry. Consequently, we can skip the operations for these zero elements, although this test does not reduce the execution time [23].

Similarly, a lookup results for S_1 if column-wise storage is selected. These lookups are unwanted for two reasons. First, each lookup induces substantial overhead because in the worst case all entries in a whole row or column must be scanned in order to obtain the address of an entry, or to conclude that the element to be fetched is not an entry. Second, no reduction in the number of iterations is obtained. For example, S_1 is executed $M \cdot N$ times in the second fragment, but only NZ times in the first, where NZ indicates the total number of entries in A.

2.3 Reshaping for Consistency

The problems arising in the previous section are caused by the inconsistency of access patterns of occurrences of the same matrix, i.e. the access patterns induced by the occurrences of A in S_1 and S_2 overlap and have linearly independent directions $(0,1)$ and $(2,0)$ respectively. Since the organization of the data structure can only support the storage of entries along access patterns in one direction, lookups must be generated for all occurrences inducing access patterns that are inconsistent with this data structure organization.

However, in some cases, reshaping techniques can be used to obtain consistency. For the previous fragment, interchanging the loops that surround S_3 converts the direction of the access patterns through A into $(0,2)$. Consequently, if sparse row-wise storage is selected for A, code in which a construct iterates over entries can be generated for both S_1 and S_2. In table 1, we present some timings of the two versions of the previous section and the reshaped variant on one CPU of a CRAY C98/4256 for some matrices of the Harwell-Boeing Sparse Matrix Collection [17] in the appropriate storage format. The row-wise variant is preferable over the column-wise variant, because the lookup is executed less frequently in the first fragment than in the

Matrix	Row	Column	Reshaped
gre_1107	0.4	1.5	$2.1 \cdot 10^{-3}$
jagmesh1	0.3	1.1	$1.7 \cdot 10^{-3}$
orani678	2.2	8.8	$6.4 \cdot 10^{-3}$
steam2	0.1	0.5	$1.4 \cdot 10^{-3}$

Table 1. Execution Time in seconds

second, namely $\frac{1}{4} \cdot M \cdot N$ and $M \cdot N$ times respectively. However, the reshaped version is clearly superior, due to the elimination of all lookups. Although this experiment is rather simple, it illustrates the most important objective in the generation of sparse codes, namely that the number of operations performed must be kept proportional to the number of entries in the sparse matrix [14, 16, 23]. Skipping operations on zeros by means of conditionals is useless. Scanning sparse data structure to obtain an entry must be avoided as much as possible. For the automatic data structure selection and sparse code generation method this implies that it is very important to achieve consistency between all the access patterns through an implicitly sparse matrix. In this case the generation of constructs that limit the number of operations performed, become feasible.

3   Unimodular Matrices

In this section we give an outline of the general approach to loop transformations in terms of unimodular matrices. For an extensive overview of the theory, consult [4, 5, 15, 25, 26]. Every iteration-level loop transformation on n perfectly nested loops with stride 1 and regular loop bounds, consisting of a combination of loop interchanging, loop skewing, or loop reversal [1, 22, 24, 27, 28, 29] can be modeled by a mapping between the **original** and **target iteration space**, namely a linear transformation that is represented by a unimodular matrix U.

A **unimodular matrix** is an $n \times n$ integer matrix, i.e. all elements are integers, for which $|\det(U)| = 1$ holds. Each iteration $\bar{\imath}$ in the original iteration space is mapped to an iteration $\bar{\imath}' = U \cdot \bar{\imath}$ in the target iteration space. Because iterations in the target iteration space are also traversed in lexicographic order, application of a transformation effectively results in a new execution order on the instances. Each unimodular matrix can be decomposed into a number of such elementary loop transformations. Conversely, any combination of iteration level loop transformations is represented by a unimodular matrix. Therefore, this approach offers more flexibility than the traditional step-wise application, where the usefulness and validity of each transformation is considered separately.

Application of U is valid, if each data dependence in the original nesting is satisfied in the resulting nesting. Dependence distance vectors provide a convenient representation of data dependences. If iteration $\bar{\imath}'$ depends on iteration $\bar{\imath}$, then $\bar{\imath} + \bar{d} = \bar{\imath}'$ for some distance vector $\bar{d}$. Induced by the sequential semantics of DO-loops, iterations are executed in lexicographic order. Consequently, each distance vector of a loop-carried data dependence is **lexicographically positive**, denoted by $\bar{d} \succ \bar{0}$, i.e. its leading component (first nonzero component) is positive. Since U is a linear transformation, $U \cdot \bar{\imath}' - U \cdot \bar{\imath} = U \cdot (\bar{\imath}' - \bar{\imath})$. Consequently, application of a unimodular transformation U is valid if and only if $U \cdot \bar{d} \succ \bar{0}$ for each dependence distance $\bar{d} \neq \bar{0}$ in the original nest. In [25, 26], a more abstract representation of data dependences, referred to as dependence directions, is incorporated in the validity test. Each component of a general dependence vector $\bar{d}$ can represent a possibly infinite range of integers. Directions '<', '>', '=', and '*' correspond to the ranges $[1, \infty]$, $[-\infty, -1]$, $[0, 0]$, and $[-\infty, \infty]$ respectively. A distance component d is denoted by the degenerate range $[d, d]$.

If all dependences are represented by lexico-graphically positive dependence vectors, i.e., each component is an interval $[l, r]$ with $l > 0$, dependence directions can also be handled by defining an arithmetic on these vectors. Addition of ranges and multiplication of a range by a scalar are defined as respectively $[l, r] + [l', r'] = [l + l', r + r']$ and $s \cdot [l, r] = [s \cdot l, s \cdot r]$, if $s \geq 0$, or range $[s \cdot r, s \cdot l]$ otherwise. Operations on ∞ are as expected (e.g. $0 \cdot \infty = 0$ and $-1 \cdot -\infty = \infty$). Using this new arithmetic, application of U is valid, if $U \cdot \overline{d} \succ \overline{0}$ for all dependence vectors $\overline{d}$. The converse implication does not hold. If loop skewings are used in U, dependence information may be lost.

The application of a unimodular matrix to a loop nest is implemented by rewriting the loop-body and generating appropriate loop bounds. Since $\overline{I} = U^{-1} \cdot \overline{I'}$ holds, the new body is obtained by replacing each I_j in the original body accordingly. The new loop bounds are determined by application of Fourier-Motzkin elimination [2, 13, 19] to the system of in-equalities that is obtained by substituting $U^{-1} \cdot \overline{I'}$ for $\overline{I}$ in the system defined by the original loop bounds. In [12], we present an implementation of Fourier-Motzkin elimination in which only integer arithmetic is involved and also present simplification methods to eliminate all redundant constraints from such a system, thereby improving the efficiency of the generated code.

Consider, for example, application of the unimodular matrix U to the following loop:

```
DO I₁ = 0, 50
  DO I₂ = 0, 50 - I₁
    DO I₃ = 0, 50
      L(I₁,I₂,I₃)
    ENDDO
  ENDDO
ENDDO
```

$$U = \begin{pmatrix} 1 & 1 & 1 \\ 1 & 0 & 0 \\ 0 & 1 & 0 \end{pmatrix}$$

$$U^{-1} = \begin{pmatrix} 0 & 1 & 0 \\ 0 & 0 & 1 \\ 1 & -1 & -1 \end{pmatrix}$$

We assume that application is valid. The resulting loop-body is obtained by replacing $\overline{I}$ according to equation $\overline{I} = U^{-1} \cdot \overline{I'}$. Application of Fourier-Motzkin elimination to the

following system of inequalities, obtained by substituting $U^{-1} \cdot \overline{I'}$ for $\overline{I}$ in the original system, is used to rewrite the system into a format that can be used to generate the resulting bounds:

$$\begin{array}{ccc} 0 \leq & I'_2 & \leq 50 \\ 0 \leq & I'_3 & \leq 50 - I'_2 \\ 0 \leq I'_1 - I'_2 - I'_3 \leq 50 \end{array}$$

After redundant inequalities have been eliminated, the following code is generated:

```
DO I'₁ = 0, 100
  DO I'₂ = 0, MIN(50,I'₁)
    DO I'₃ = MAX(0,I'₁-I'₂-50),MIN(50-I'₂,I'₁-I'₂)
      L(I'₂,I'₃,I'₁-I'₂-I'₃)
    ENDDO
  ENDDO
ENDDO
```

The conversion of the original iteration space into the target iteration space is illustrated in figure 1. It can be easily determined which iterations in the original iteration space are executed in one iteration of the resulting loops. For example, since $(1, 1, 1)$ is the first row of U, all iterations in the original iteration space that lie in the plane $I_1 + I_2 + I_3 = c_1$, for $c_1 \in \mathbf{Z}$, are executed in iteration $I'_1 = c_1$. Moreover, these planes are traversed in the direction $(1, 1, 1)$ in successive iterations of the outermost resulting loop, as illustrated in the first picture of figure 2. Because $(1, 0, 0)$ is the second row of U, all iterations in the intersection of the plane defined by the outermost loop and the plane $I_1 = c_2$, for $c_2 \in \mathbf{Z}$, are executed in iteration $I'_2 = c_2$. This line has direction $(0, 1, -1)$, as shown in the second picture of figure 2. An iteration along this line that also lies in a plane of which the normal vector is defined by the last row of U, i.e. $I_2 = c_3$, for $c_3 \in \mathbf{Z}$, is executed in the iteration $I'_3 = c_3$.

In general, the rows of an $n \times n$ unimodular matrix U, for $n \geq 2$, define the normal vectors of so-called hyperplanes in the n-dimensional iteration space.

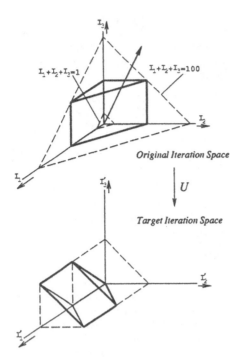

Original Iteration Space

U

Target Iteration Space

Fig. 1. Application of U

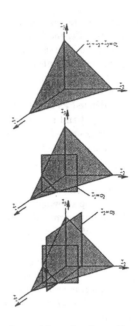

Fig. 2. Original Iteration Space Traversal

4 Reshaping Access Patterns

In this section, we present the construction of a unimodular matrix which will be used for changing the direction of access patterns.

4.1 Simple Method for Reshaping

The intersection of such hyperplanes determine which original iteration is executed in a particular iteration $\overline{I}' = \overline{c}$ of the resulting loop, according to equation $U \cdot \overline{I} = \overline{c}$. Consequently, all iterations that are executed in a complete execution of the innermost resulting loop are along a line through the original iteration, formed by the intersection of hyperplanes defined by the first $n-1$ rows of U. Moreover, since $\overline{I} = U^{-1} \cdot \overline{I}'$, the last column of U^{-1} defines the direction of this line. Along this line, original iterations are executed in successive iterations of the innermost resulting loop. For the previous transformation, this direction is $(0, 1, -1)$, i.e. the last column of U.

Consider the following general framework, in which an occurrence of an implicitly sparse matrix A appears in a perfectly nested loop at nesting depth $n \geq 2$, and where the subscripts functions are represented by a mapping $F_A(\overline{I}) = \overline{m} + M \cdot \overline{I}$ as defined in section 2.1:

```
DO I₁ ∈ V₁
    ...
    DO Iₙ ∈ Vₙ
S₁:    ... A( F_A(Ī) ) ...
    ENDDO
    ...
ENDDO
```

In order to achieve that the access patterns of this occurrence lie along lines with a particular desired direction $\overline{v} = (v_1, v_2)$, i.e. the directions become linearly dependent, we require that all index pairs (x, y) in one access pattern are on a line of the form $(x, y) = (c_1, c_2) + t \cdot (v_1, v_2)$. An important observation is that for any point $(x, y) = (c_1 + t \cdot v_1, c_2 + t \cdot v_2)$ on this line, the equation $v_2 \cdot x - v_1 \cdot y = v_2 \cdot c_1 - v_1 \cdot c_2$ holds. Therefore, the expression $v_2 \cdot x - v_1 \cdot y$ remains constant along a line of the previous form. Consequently, one way to enforce a desired direction $\overline{v}$ is to require that the expression $v_2 \cdot x - v_1 \cdot y$ for $(x, y)^T = F_A(\overline{I})$ is constant in one iteration of the *outermost* loop. Using the definition of section 2.1, x and y are defined as follows:

$$\begin{pmatrix} x \\ y \end{pmatrix} = \begin{pmatrix} m_{10} \\ m_{20} \end{pmatrix} + \begin{pmatrix} m_{11} \dots m_{1n} \\ m_{21} \dots m_{2n} \end{pmatrix} \cdot \overline{I}$$

The constraint that is induced by this approach can be written in the following form, where $k_i = v_2 \cdot m_{1i} - v_1 \cdot m_{2i}$ for $1 \le i \le n$:

$$(v_2 \cdot m_1 - v_1 \cdot m_2) + k_1 \cdot I_1 + \dots + k_n \cdot I_n = c'$$

Because only the variant part of this constraint is relevant, we simplify it as follows. In this expression, we define $\alpha_i = k_i/g$ for $g = \gcd(k_1, \dots, k_n)$, assuming that that $g \ne 0$:[2]

$$\alpha_1 \cdot I_1 + \dots + \alpha_n \cdot I_n = c \qquad (1)$$

A traversal of the original iteration space where in iteration $I_1' = c$, all iterations in the hyperplane $\alpha_1 \cdot I_1 + \dots + \alpha_n \cdot I_n = c$ are visited, is obtained by application of a linear transformation $\overline{I'} = U \cdot \overline{I}$, where the first row of U consists of $(\alpha_1, \dots, \alpha_n)$. In [21, 25], a completion method is presented that yields an $n \times n$ unimodular matrix of this form. In [11], we have extended this method to construct the inverse of this matrix efficiently by a simultaneous construction. This eliminates the need

---

[2] For most conversion, $g \ne 0$ holds. Only if no conversion is required, $g = 0$ can arise.

to explicitly compute the inverse afterwards. If no data dependences have to be accounted for, this completion method can be used to construct a loop transformation changing the direction of particular access patterns.

4.2 Double Loop Example

Suppose that regular diagonal-wise access patterns are desired in the following perfectly nested loop, in which access patterns with direction $(2, 4)$ occur:

```
DO I1 = 1, 6
  DO I2 = 1, 3
    ACC += A(I1+2*I2-2,4*I2-3)
  ENDDO
ENDDO
```

$$F_A(\overline{I}) = \begin{pmatrix} -2 \\ -3 \end{pmatrix} + \begin{pmatrix} 1 & 2 \\ 0 & 4 \end{pmatrix} \cdot \overline{I}$$

To achieve that the access patterns lie along lines with the desired direction $(1, 1)$, we require that expression $I_1 - 2 \cdot I_2$ is constant in one iteration of the outermost loop. If the dependence caused by the accumulation can be ignored, direct use of an automatically constructed matrix is possible:

$$U = \begin{pmatrix} 1 & -2 \\ 0 & 1 \end{pmatrix} \qquad U^{-1} = \begin{pmatrix} 1 & 2 \\ 0 & 1 \end{pmatrix}$$

This reshaping, illustrated in figure 3, results in the following fragment in which access patterns with direction $(4, 4)$ occur:

```
DO I1' = -5, 4
  DO I2'=MAX(1,⌈(1-I1')/2⌉),MIN(3,⌊(6-I1')/2⌋)
    ACC += A(I1'+4*I2'-2,4*I2'-3)
  ENDDO
ENDDO
```

4.3 Validity of Reshaping

Application of a unimodular transformation U is valid if $\overline{d'} = U \cdot \overline{d} \succ \overline{0}$ holds for all dependence distances $\overline{d} \ne \overline{0}$ in the original loop [3, 5, 25].

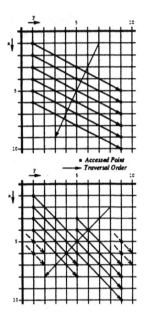

Fig. 3. Conversion of $(2, 4)$ into $(1, 1)$

This constraint is not always satisfied for a constructed transformation U. Fortunately, we can exploit the fact that several unimodular matrices can enforce traversal of hyperplanes that have the form (1), given in section 4.1. For double loops, the following proposition can be used:

Proposition 1 If there exists an $z_1 \in \{-1, +1\}$ such that $z_1 \cdot (\alpha_1, \alpha_2) \cdot \overline{d} \geq 0$ for all dependence distance vectors $\overline{d}$ in a double loop, then there exists an integer $z_2 \in \{-1, +1\}$ such that application of the following transformation V, where U is a unimodular matrix with first row (α_1, α_2), is valid.

$$V = \begin{pmatrix} z_1 & 0 \\ 0 & z_2 \end{pmatrix} \cdot U \quad V^{-1} = U^{-1} \cdot \begin{pmatrix} z_1 & 0 \\ 0 & z_2 \end{pmatrix}$$

PROOF Suppose there exists an $z_1 \in \{-1, +1\}$ such that $z_1 \cdot (\alpha_1, \alpha_2) \cdot \overline{d} \geq 0$ for all dependences distance vectors $\overline{d}$ in the original

nest. Let $\overline{d}$ be an arbitrary dependence distance vector in the original nest. We distinguish two cases. If $z_1 \cdot (\alpha_1, \alpha_2) \cdot \overline{d} > 0$, then $V \cdot \overline{d} \succ \overline{0}$ and application of V is valid. If $z_1 \cdot (\alpha_1, \alpha_2) \cdot \overline{d} = 0$, then $(\alpha_1, \alpha_2) \cdot \overline{d} = 0$, and, hence, $U \cdot \overline{d} = (0, t)^T$ for some $t \in \mathbf{Z}$. Therefore, we have $\overline{d} = U^{-1} \cdot (0, t)^T = t \cdot (-\alpha_2, \alpha_1)^T$. Since all dependences in the original nest are lexicographically positive we have, depending on the values of α_1 and α_2, *either* for all dependences $\overline{d}$ such that $(\alpha_1, \alpha_2) \cdot \overline{d} = 0$, $\overline{d}$ is of the form $t \cdot (-\alpha_2, \alpha_1)^T$ for some $t \geq 0$, *or* for all dependences $\overline{d}$ such that $(\alpha_1, \alpha_2) \cdot \overline{d} = 0$, $\overline{d}$ is of the form $t \cdot (-\alpha_2, \alpha_1)^T$ for some $t \leq 0$. Consequently, we can choose $z_2 \in \{+1, -1\}$ such that for any $\overline{d}$ with $(\alpha_1, \alpha_2) \cdot \overline{d} = 0$, we have $V \cdot \overline{d} = V \cdot U^{-1}(0, t)^T = (0, z_2 \cdot t)^T \succ \overline{0}$.

For example, making the direction through a matrix A and a desired direction $\overline{v} = (-1, 1)$ linearly dependent by application of the following constructed transformation U would violate the original dependences with distance $\overline{d} = (1, -1)^T$ in the following fragment:

```
DO I₁ = 2, 5
  DO I₂ = 1, 5
    B(I₁,I₂) = A(I₁,I₂) * B(I₁-1,I₂+1)
  ENDDO
ENDDO
```

$$\begin{pmatrix} 0 \\ -1 \end{pmatrix} = \begin{pmatrix} 1 & 1 \\ -1 & 0 \end{pmatrix} \cdot \begin{pmatrix} 1 \\ -1 \end{pmatrix}$$

Negation of the second row in U ($z_2 = -1$), eliminates this violation. Effectively, the direction within each access pattern is reversed:

```
DO I₁ = 3, 10
  DO I₂ = MAX(2,I₁'-5), MIN(5,I₁'-1)
    B(I₂',I₁'-I₂')=A(I₂',I₁'-I₂')*B(I₂'-1,I₁'-I₂'+1)
  ENDDO
ENDDO
```

The dependences within each access pattern are illustrated in figure 4.[3]

---

[3] Dependences are usually depicted in the iteration space. However, in this case accessed points correspond directly to iterations.

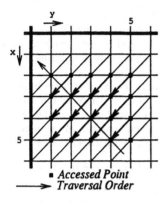

. *Accessed Point*
⟶ *Traversal Order*

Fig. 4. Dependences within one Access Pattern

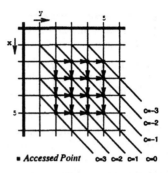

. *Accessed Point*   c=3 c=2 c=1 c=0

Fig. 5. Cyclic Ordering on Access Patterns

The method fails if the first component of $U \cdot \vec{d}$ is positive for some dependences, but negative for others. This occurs, for example, in the conversion that makes the direction of the access patterns through A and $(1,1)$ linearly dependent for the following fragment with dependence distances $(0,1)^T$ and $(1,0)^T$:

```
DO I₁ = 2, 5
  DO I₂ = 2, 5
  B(I₁,I₂)=A(I₁,I₂)*B(I₁,I₂-1)*B(I₁-1,I₂)
  ENDDO
ENDDO
```

In this case, for the two dependence distances, we get the following equations:

$$\begin{pmatrix} 1 & -1 \\ 1 & 0 \end{pmatrix} \cdot \begin{pmatrix} 0 \\ 1 \end{pmatrix} = \begin{pmatrix} -1 \\ 0 \end{pmatrix}$$
$$\begin{pmatrix} 1 & -1 \\ 1 & 0 \end{pmatrix} \cdot \begin{pmatrix} 1 \\ 0 \end{pmatrix} = \begin{pmatrix} +1 \\ 1 \end{pmatrix}$$

The reason for this problem is illustrated in figure 5. In diagonal-wise access patterns, all indices with $I_1 - I_2 = c$ are accessed before a next value of c is considered. However, the dependences imposes a cyclic traversal ordering on these access patterns.

4.4 Refinement of the Method

For double loops this simple method of reshaping is successful, because keeping expression (1) constant in one iteration of the *outermost* loop enforces a direction for the access patterns in the innermost loop, such that this direction and a desired direction $\overline{v}$ are linearly dependent. However, for general loops the method is too restrictive as illustrated below. Enforcing row-wise access patterns requires that expression $I_1 + 2 \cdot I_3$ is constant in one iteration of the outermost loop, and results in the next conversion:

```
DO I₁ = 1, 10
  DO I₂ = 1, 10
    DO I₃ = 1, 10
    ... A(I₁+2*I₃,I₂) ...
    ENDDO
  ENDDO
ENDDO
```

$$\downarrow \quad U = \begin{pmatrix} 1 & 0 & 2 \\ 0 & 1 & 0 \\ 0 & 0 & 1 \end{pmatrix} \quad \downarrow$$

```
DO I₁' = 3, 30
  DO I₂' = 1, 10
    DO I₃' = MAX(1,⌈(I₁'-10)/2⌉),
+               MIN(10,⌊(I₁'-1)/2⌋)
    ... A(I₁',I₂') ...
    ENDDO
  ENDDO
ENDDO
```

In the resulting fragment, *all* iterations that reference elements in the same row are executed in one iteration of the outermost loop. Each set of iterations is within a plane with normal vector $(1, 0, 2)$, as illustrated in figure 6. Although this kind of transformations can be useful for sparse code generation, because it tends to move the overhead for accessing sparse rows to a higher level in the loop nest, it provides little flexibility. Especially, if we want to change the directions of the access pattern of *several* occurrences of implicitly sparse matrices in a particular loop, it is unlikely that identical hyperplanes must be traversed in the outermost loop.

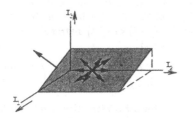

Fig. 6. Plane $I_1 + 2 \cdot I_3 = c$

More flexibility is obtained if we observe that iterations along *any* line within the previous plane reference (possibly identical) elements in the same row. Consequently, any transformation that induces a loop in which all iterations along a line in this plane are performed in one iterations of the resulting innermost loop can be used to enforce row-wise (or possibly scalar-wise) access patterns. In general, the direction of an access patterns and a desired direction $\overline{v}$ are linearly dependent, if the iterations that are executed in one iteration of the resulting *innermost* loop are on a line within a hyperplane that is given by equation (1). Since a line can only be within such a hyperplane if the direction $\overline{u}$ of that line is perpendicular to the normal vector $(\alpha_1, \ldots, \alpha_n)$

of that plane, i.e. $(u_1, \ldots, u_n) \perp (\alpha_1, \ldots, \alpha_n)$, the following constraint is imposed on $\overline{u}$:

$$u_1 \cdot \alpha_1 + \ldots + u_n \cdot \alpha_n = 0 \qquad (2)$$

The general solution of diophantine equation (2) has the form $\overline{u} = T^{-1} \cdot (0, t_2, \ldots, t_n)^T$ for arbitrary $t_i \in \mathbf{Z}$ for a matrix T with $\alpha_1, \ldots, \alpha_n$ as first row [3]. Matrix T^{-1} can be obtained during the construction of T as described in [11]. For instance, the direction $\overline{u}$ of a line through the plane $I_1 + 2 \cdot I_3 = c$ has the following general form:

$$\overline{u} = \begin{pmatrix} 1 & 0 & -2 \\ 0 & 1 & 0 \\ 0 & 0 & 1 \end{pmatrix} \cdot \begin{pmatrix} 0 \\ t_2 \\ t_3 \end{pmatrix} = \begin{pmatrix} -2 \cdot t_3 \\ t_2 \\ t_3 \end{pmatrix} \qquad (3)$$

Consequently, as observed at the end of section 3, any unimodular transformation U, for which the intersection of the hyperplanes defined by the first $n - 1$ rows form a line with a direction satisfying constraint (2), can be used to enforce a particular direction on the access patterns. For instance, since direction $(0, 1, 0)^T$ is an instance of (3), and the intersection of planes $I_1 = c_1$ and $I_3 = c_2$ is precisely a line in this direction, a unimodular matrix where the first and second row correspond to these planes can also be used to enforce row-wise access patterns in the previous example. The following matrix, modeling a single loop interchange, satisfies that form. Note that the last column of U^{-1} is identical to this direction:

$$U = \begin{pmatrix} 1 & 0 & 0 \\ 0 & 0 & 1 \\ \hline 0 & 1 & 0 \end{pmatrix} \qquad U^{-1} = \begin{pmatrix} 1 & 0 & 0 \\ 0 & 0 & 1 \\ 0 & 1 & 0 \end{pmatrix}$$

Indeed, interchanging the I_2- and I_3-loop in the previous example is another, more obvious, way to obtain row-wise access patterns through matrix A. In some cases, a penalty must be paid for this increased flexibility.

For example, because $(-2, 0, 1)^T$ is also an instance of (3), application of the following

matrix is also allowed, because the intersection of planes $I_2 = c_1$ and $I_1 + 2 \cdot I_3 = c_2$ is a line in this direction:

$$U = \begin{pmatrix} 0 & 1 & 0 \\ 1 & 0 & 2 \\ 0 & 0 & 1 \end{pmatrix} \quad U^{-1} = \begin{pmatrix} 0 & 1 & -2 \\ 1 & 0 & 0 \\ 0 & 0 & 1 \end{pmatrix}$$

This effectively reverses the I'_1- and I'_2-loop in the code that results after application of the first transformation discussed in this section, and scalar-wise access patterns result. An illustration of the kind of sparse sparse code that can be generated automatically if row-wise storage is selected by the compiler is shown below (for non-entries an address $\perp$ for which VAL($\perp$)=0.0 results [9]):

```
DO I = 1, 10
  DO J = 3, 30
    A = LKP(IND,LW(J),HGH(J),I)
    DO K = MAX(1,CEIL(J-10,2)),
+              MAX(10,FLOOR(J-1,2))
      ... VAL(A) ...
    ENDDO
  ENDDO
ENDDO
```

Because the same element is referenced in a complete execution of the innermost non-controlling loop, lookup overhead in this row is amortized over several iterations. Therefore, scalar-wise access patterns are considered acceptable, which is reflected in the fact that the scalar-wise direction $(0,0)$ and any other direction are linearly dependent. However, solutions in which row-wise access patterns occur are preferred.

4.5 General Method for Reshaping

In this section, we present a five-step method for obtaining the solution of the following problem: given p subscript functions $F^i(\overline{I})$ of several occurrences of implicitly sparse matrices in a perfectly nested loop of depth n, and desired directions $\overline{v}^i$, for $1 \leq i \leq p$, construct an $n \times n$ unimodular matrix U such

that application of U to this loop nest is valid and achieves that the direction of the access patterns induced by each resulting subscript function and the desired direction $\overline{v}^i$ become linearly dependent.

1. Construction of Hyperplanes In the first step, p hyperplanes of the form (1) in which expression $v_2^i \cdot x - v_1^i \cdot y$ where $(x, y)^T = F^i(\overline{I})$, remains constant, are constructed for each subscript function and desired direction:

$$\begin{cases} \alpha_1^1 \cdot I_1 + \cdots + \alpha_n^1 \cdot I_n = c_1 \\ \qquad \vdots \\ \alpha_1^p \cdot I_1 + \cdots + \alpha_n^p \cdot I_n = c_p \end{cases}$$

Occurrences for which this description of the hyperplane cannot be constructed because all coefficients are zero are ignored because any transformation will obtain an appropriate direction for the access patterns of such occurrences.

2. Construction of the Intersection In this step, the general form for the direction $\overline{u}$ of a line that lies within the intersection of these hyperplanes is determined. Since the direction of this line must be perpendicular to all vectors $(\alpha_1^i, \ldots, \alpha_n^i)$, the solution of the following homogeneous system of linear diophantine equations must be obtained:

$$\begin{cases} \alpha_1^1 \cdot u_1 + \ldots + \alpha_n^1 \cdot u_n = 0 \\ \qquad \vdots \\ \alpha_1^p \cdot u_1 + \ldots + \alpha_n^p \cdot u_n = 0 \end{cases} \qquad (4)$$

Fortunately, finding a solution of this system has been well-studied in the context of data dependence analysis. In [3, 5] it is shown, that if system (4) is represented by $(u_1, \ldots, u_n) \cdot A = \overline{0}$, where the $\alpha_1^i, \ldots, \alpha_n^i$ constitutes the ith column of A, and a unimodular $n \times n$ matrix R represents the operations to reduce the $n \times p$ matrix A to echelon form, i.e. $R \cdot A = S$ for an $n \times p$ echelon matrix S, then all solutions are given by $\overline{u} = (t_1, \ldots, t_n) \cdot R$ for arbitrary $t_i \in \mathbf{Z}$ such that $(t_1, \ldots, t_n) \cdot S = \overline{0}$. An algorithm to reduce a matrix to echelon

form, which means that nonzeros rows are ordered first and the nonzeros appear in staircase fashion, is given in [5]. If $r = \text{rank}(A)$, the first r rows of S are nonzero. Because a homogeneous system is considered, this implies that the general solution has the following form, for some $t_i \in \mathbf{Z}$:

$$\overline{u} = (\underbrace{0, \ldots, 0}_{r}, t_{n-r+1}, \ldots, t_n) \cdot R \qquad (5)$$

Since the intersection of the p hyperplanes given in (4) is constructed, $\overline{u} = \overline{0}$ is the only solution if $\text{rank}(A) = n$. In that case, a compromise must be found. Possible solutions are to ignore certain occurrences or to adapt a number of desired directions so that a nonzero solution exists. Ideally, such decisions are made automatically, but user interaction can be used to simplify this process.

3. Selection of a Suitable Line The result of the previous step is a general description of the direction $\overline{u}$ of lines lie within the hyperplanes constructed in the first step. In principle, an arbitrary nonzero instance of (5) can be taken. However, it is preferable to select an instance in which nonzero components appear at the position of controlling loops in the first, second, or any dimension of subscript functions for which column-, row- or diagonalwise access patterns are desired, in order to avoid the situation discussed at the end of section 4.4. Moreover, $\overline{u}$ is chosen such that $\gcd(u_1, \ldots, u_n) = 1$.

4. Construction of a Transformation In this step, a unimodular matrix must be constructed such that iterations in the original iteration space are executed along lines with direction $\overline{u}$. In earlier examples, it was shown that any unimodular transformation for which $\overline{u}$ constitutes the last column of its inverse can be used for this purpose. Either a new completion method can be used to obtain such a matrix, or the completion method of [11] can be adapted. First, a unimodular matrix T is

constructed with $\overline{u}$ as first row. This is possible because the components of $\overline{u}$ are relatively prime. Subsequently, we may define matrices U^{-1} and U as:

$$U^{-1} = (P \cdot T)^T \text{ and } U = (T^{-1} \cdot P^T)^T$$

$$\text{where } P = \begin{pmatrix} 0 & 1 & & \\ \vdots & & \ddots & \\ 0 & & & 1 \\ 1 & 0 \ldots 0 & \end{pmatrix}$$

5. Making the Transformation Valid The unimodular transformation constructed in the previous step is used directly if there are no dependences in the loop nest. Otherwise, we can use the fact that the following matrix V is also unimodular and that the last column of V^{-1} is either $\overline{u}$ or $-\overline{u}$, for any unimodular $(n-1) \times (n-1)$ matrix Z and integer $z \in \{-1, +1\}$:

$$V = \begin{pmatrix} Z & \overline{0} \\ \overline{0} & z \end{pmatrix} U \quad V^{-1} = U^{-1} \begin{pmatrix} Z^{-1} & \overline{0} \\ \overline{0} & z \end{pmatrix}$$

The following construction method will be used to enforce that for all dependence vectors $\overline{d}$ that represent loop-carried data dependences in the original loop nest, $\overline{d}' = V \cdot \overline{d} \succ \overline{0}$ holds. Starting with $Z = I$ and $z = 1$, the following steps are applied for $k = 1, \ldots, d-1$. At each step k, we select an index i with $k \leq i < n$, such that for all dependence vectors either all components $d_i' \leq 0$ or all components $d_i' \geq 0$. Subsequently, rows i and k in Z are interchanged followed by a reversal of row i if the components were non-positive. Dependence vectors for which the ith component become strictly positive do not have to be considered in following steps. Finally, z is chosen such that the nth component of all remaining dependence vectors is non-negative. Because Z is constructed by a permutation and reversals, Z^{-1} is equal to Z^T. If this construction breaks down, the reshaping method fails. This will occur, for instance, in situations that are similar to the one depicted in figure 5.

However, in general, we have more flexibility in selection of iteration space traversal than with the simple method of section 4.1.

4.6 An Example of Reshaping

Consider the following fragment with occurrences of three implicitly sparse matrices:

```
DO I₁ = 10, 15
  DO I₂ = 1, 3
    DO I₃ = 1, 50
      ... A(I₁+3*I₂+I₃,I₁+I₃) ...
      ... B(2*I₁+I₃,2*I₂)      ...
      ... C(I₁-3*I₂,I₃)        ...
    ENDDO
  ENDDO
ENDDO
```

Suppose that row-wise storage is desired for all matrices, and that there are data dependences with distances $(0,0,1)^T$, $(0,1,0)^T$ and $(1,0,0)^T$. Reshaping the access patterns accordingly seems to be a non-trivial task at first sight. Because the desired direction for the access patterns of the three occurrences is $(0,1)$, the following planes result in the first step:

$$\begin{cases} I_1 + 3 \cdot I_2 + I_3 = c_1 \\ 2 \cdot I_1 + I_3 = c_2 \\ I_1 - 3 \cdot I_2 = c_3 \end{cases}$$

In step 2, the general form for the direction $\overline{u}$ of line within these planes is determined. Echelon reduction yields the following form for $R \cdot A = S$, where $\text{rank}(S) = 2$:

$$\begin{pmatrix} 0 & 0 & 1 \\ 1 & 0 & -1 \\ 3 & 1 & -6 \end{pmatrix} \cdot \begin{pmatrix} 1 & 2 & 1 \\ 3 & 0 & -3 \\ 1 & 1 & 0 \end{pmatrix} = S$$

Direction $\overline{u}$ is described for arbitrary $t_3 \in \mathbf{Z}$ as $(0,0,t_3) \cdot R = (3 \cdot t_3, t_3, -6 \cdot t_3)$, indicating the direction of the line that is formed by the intersection of the previous planes. Vector $(3,1,-6)$ is an instance of this description for which the components are relatively prime,

and can be selected at step 3. Moreover, because all components are nonzero, the associated transformation will induce real row-wise access patterns. In the fourth step, matrices U^{-1} and U are constructed:

$$U = \begin{pmatrix} -1 & 3 & 0 \\ 0 & 6 & 1 \\ 0 & 1 & 0 \end{pmatrix} \quad U^{-1} = \begin{pmatrix} -1 & 0 & 3 \\ 0 & 0 & 1 \\ 0 & 1 & -6 \end{pmatrix}$$

Computation of $U \cdot \overline{d}$ yields $(0,1,0)^T$, $(3,6,1)^T$ and $(-1,0,0)^T$ respectively. Since all second components are non-negative, rows 1 and 2 in U are interchanged. Since only the resulting distance $(0,-1,0)^T$ must be considered, reversal of the the second row suffices to make the transformation valid:

$$V = \begin{pmatrix} 0 & 6 & 1 \\ 1 & -3 & 0 \\ 0 & 1 & 0 \end{pmatrix} \quad V^{-1} = \begin{pmatrix} 0 & 1 & 3 \\ 0 & 0 & 1 \\ 1 & 0 & -6 \end{pmatrix}$$

Indeed, row-wise access patterns result after application of this transformation:

```
DO I₁' = 7, 68
  DO I₂' = MAX(1,⌈(21-I₁')/2⌉),
  +        MIN(12,⌊80-I₁')/2⌋)
    DO I₃'= MAX(1,⌈(10-I₂')/3⌉,⌈(I₁'-50)/6⌉),
    +       MIN(3,⌊(15-I₂')/3⌋,⌊(I₁'-1)/6⌋)
      ... A(I₁'+I₂',I₁'+I₂'-3*I₃') ...
      ... B(I₁'+2*I₂',2*I₃')       ...
      ... C(I₂',I₁'-6*I₃')         ...
    ENDDO
  ENDDO
ENDDO
```

5 Data Structure Selection

The reshaping method presented in the previous section enables us to take a systematic approach to data structure selection. Consider, for example, the following formulation of the operation $C \leftarrow C + A \cdot B$, where A, B and C are implicitly sparse matrices [9, 18, 20, 23]:

```
DO I₁ = 1, 10
  DO I₂ = 1, 10
    DO I₃ = 1, 10
      C(I₁,I₂) += A(I₁,I₃) * B(I₃,I₂)
    ENDDO
  ENDDO
ENDDO
```

$$\begin{pmatrix} 1 & 0 & 0 \\ 0 & 0 & 1 \\ 0 & 1 & 1 \end{pmatrix} \cdot \begin{pmatrix} 1 & 0 & 1 \\ 0 & -1 & -1 \\ 0 & 1 & 0 \end{pmatrix} = \begin{pmatrix} 1 & 0 & 1 \\ 0 & 1 & 0 \\ 0 & 0 & -1 \end{pmatrix}$$

The reshaping method of section 4.5 enables us to explore all possible data structures. For any combination of e.g. row-, column- and the regular diagonal-wise storage of the three implicitly sparse matrices, the unimodular transformation that changes the direction of the access patterns accordingly can be determined, as illustrated in figure 7.

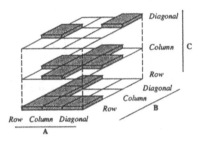

Fig. 7. Matrix Multiplication

For example, in case row-, column- and row-wise access patterns are desired for matrices A, B and C respectively, $\overline{u} = (0,0,1)$ results which, not surprisingly, gives rise to the unimodular transformation $U = I$. Consequently, a tile is placed on the row-column-row combination. All combination with row- and column-wise access patterns for A and B respectively are possible for $\overline{u} = (0,0,1)$ because the resulting scalar-wise access patterns for C matches all three directions. Reshaping for diagonal-wise access pattern for B and C and row-wise access patterns for A results in the following echelon reduction $R \cdot A = S$ with rank$(S) = 3$, so that no tile appears at the corresponding position:

6 Summary

In this paper we have presented a reshaping method which has been incorporated in a prototype restructuring compiler MT1 [8]. Given different occurrences in a perfectly nested loop, this method constructs a unimodular transformation that changes a direction of the access patterns of these occurrences into a desired direction. This reshaping method is necessary for the selection of compact data structures for implicitly sparse matrices that enables the generation of efficient sparse codes. For a simple fragment, the method can be used for an exhaustive search of the possible data structures for the different occurrences. However, since such an approach would induce an unacceptable increase of compile-time for real programs, a strategy to control the reshaping in combination with data structure selection must be developed.

References

1. Randy Allen and Ken Kennedy. Automatic translation of fortran programs to vector form. *ACM Transactions on Programming Languages and Systems*, Volume 9:491–542, 1987.
2. Corinne Ancourt and Francois Irigoin. Scanning polyhedra with do loops. In *Proceedings of Third ACM SIGPLAN Symposium on Principles and Practice of Parallel Programming*, pages 39–50, 1989.
3. U. Banerjee. *Dependence Analysis for Supercomputing*. Kluwer Academic Publishers, Boston, 1988.
4. U. Banerjee. Unimodular transformations of double loops. In *Proceedings of Third Workshop on Languages and Compilers for Parallel Computing*, 1990.

5. U. Banerjee. *Loop Transformations for Restructuring Compilers: The Foundations.* Kluwer Academic Publishers, Boston, 1993.

6. Aart J.C. Bik and Harry A.G. Wijshoff. Advanced compiler optimizations for sparse computations. In *Proceedings of Supercomputing 93*, pages 430–439, 1993.

7. Aart J.C. Bik and Harry A.G. Wijshoff. Compilation techniques for sparse matrix computations. In *Proceedings of the International Conference on Supercomputing*, pages 416–424, 1993.

8. Aart J.C. Bik and Harry A.G. Wijshoff. MT1: A prototype restructuring compiler. Technical Report no. 93-32, Dept. of Computer Science, Leiden University, 1993.

9. Aart J.C. Bik and Harry A.G. Wijshoff. On automatic data structure selection and code generation for sparse computations. In *Proceedings of the Sixth International Workshop on Languages and Compilers for Parallel Computing*, pages 57–75, 1993. Lecture Notes in Computer Science, No. 768.

10. Aart J.C. Bik and Harry A.G. Wijshoff. Nonzero structure analysis. In *Proceedings of the International Conference on Supercomputing*, 1994. To appear.

11. Aart J.C. Bik and Harry A.G. Wijshoff. On a completion method for unimodular matrices. Technical Report no. 94-14, Dept. of Computer Science, Leiden University, 1994.

12. Aart J.C. Bik and Harry A.G. Wijshoff. On strategies for generating sparse codes. Technical Report In Progress, Dept. of Computer Science, Leiden University, 1994.

13. George B. Dantzig and B. Curtis Eaves. Fourier-Motzkin elimination and its dual. *Journal of Combinatorial Theory*, Volume 14:288–297, 1973.

14. David S. Dodson, Roger G. Grimes, and John G. Lewis. Algorithm 692: Model implementation and test package for the sparse linear algebra subprograms. *ACM Transactions on Mathematical Software*, Volume 17:264–272, 1991.

15. Michael L. Dowling. Optimal code parallelization using unimodular transformations. *Parallel Computing*, Volume 16:157–171, 1990.

16. I.S. Duff, A.M. Erisman, and J.K. Reid. *Direct Methods for Sparse Matrices.* Oxford Science Publications, 1990.

17. I.S. Duff, Roger G. Grimes, and John G. Lewis. Sparse matrix test problems. *ACM Transactions on Mathematical Software*, Volume 15:1–14, 1989.

18. Fred G. Gustavson. Two fast algorithms for sparse matrices: Multiplication and permuted transposition. *ACM Transactions on Mathematical Software*, Volume 4:250–269, 1978.

19. Wei Li and Keshav Pingali. A singular loop transformation framework based on nonsingular matrices. In *Proceedings of the Fifth Workshop on Languages and Compilers for Parallel Computing*, 1992.

20. John Michael McNamee. Algorithm 408: A sparse matrix package. *Communications of the ACM*, pages 265–273, 1971.

21. Morris Newman. *Integral Matrices.* Academic Press, New York, 1972. Pure and Applied Mathematics, Volume 45.

22. David A. Padua and Michael J. Wolfe. Advanced compiler optimizations for supercomputers. *Communications of the ACM*, pages 1184–1201, 1986.

23. Sergio Pissanetsky. *Sparse Matrix Technology.* Academic Press, London, 1984.

24. C.D. Polychronoupolos. *Parallel Programming and Compilers.* Kluwer Academic Publishers, Boston, 1988.

25. Michael E. Wolf and Monica S. Lam. A data locality optimizing algorithm. In *Proceedings ACM SIGPLAN 91 Conference on Programming Languages Design and Implementation*, pages 30–44, 1991.

26. Michael E. Wolf and Monica S. Lam. A loop transformation theory and an algorithm to maximize parallelism. *IEEE Transactions on Parallel and Distributed Algorithms*, pages 452–471, 1991.

27. Michael J. Wolfe. Loop skewing: The wavefront method revisited. *International Journal of Parallel Programming*, Volume 15:279–293, 1986.

28. Michael J. Wolfe. *Optimizing Supercompilers for Supercomputers.* Pitman, London, 1989.

29. H. Zima. *Supercompilers for Parallel and Vector Computers.* ACM Press, New York, 1990.

Evaluating Two Loop Transformations for Reducing Multiple-Writer False Sharing

François Bodin*   Elana D. Granston†   Thierry Montaut*
bodin@irisa.fr   granston@cs.rice.edu   montaut@irisa.fr

* IRISA, Campus de Beaulieu, 35042 Rennes, Cedex, France

† Rice University, Center for Research on Parallel Computation
6100 S. Main Street, Houston, Texas 77005, USA

Abstract. Shared virtual memory (SVM) simplifies the programming of parallel systems with memory hierarchies and physically distributed address spaces, by providing the illusion of a flat global address space where coherency is maintained at the page level. The success of the SVM abstraction depends on efficient page management, which in turn depends on the efficient handling of *false sharing* and the resulting *ping-pong* effects that it can cause. We evaluate two loop transformations for attacking this problem. The first is a simple, new technique for reducing the ping-pong effects that result from multiple-writer false sharing. The second is our previously-proposed technique for eliminating multiple-writer false sharing itself. Both have been implemented in the Fortran-S compiler, which generates code that runs on the iPSC/2 under the KOAN SVM. Preliminary performance results are presented.

1 Introduction

Shared virtual memory (SVM) [1] simplifies the programming of parallel systems with memory hierarchies and physically distributed address spaces, by providing a virtual address space consisting of pages. A *page* is defined as the unit of data to which coherency is applied. In practice, this coherency unit may be a physical page, a cache line, or a multiple or portion thereof. Pages are physically distributed across the system according to some mapping function.

The success of this SVM abstraction depends heavily on page caching and on the existence of page-level locality. Unfortunately, *false sharing* can prevent the exploitation of this locality. Especially problematic is *multiple-writer* false sharing, which arises when two or more processors are writing distinct data on the same page in an unsynchronized fashion. Assume that the system supports an invalidate-based coherence protocol whereby, before a processor can write to a page, all other copies must be invalidated. Then multiple-writer false sharing causes writes to be serialized. Furthermore, it causes a minimum of n_P-1 page faults for a given page, where n_P is the number of processors simultaneously accessing that page. To reach this minimum, each processor must be able to complete all of its accesses to that page before the next processor begins. When

Loop Nest 1

```
DO I₁ = 0 TO N₁-1
   DOALL I₂ = 0 TO N₂-1
      A[2 * I₁ + 10 * I₂ + 1] = h(I₁, I₂)
   END DOALL
END DO
```

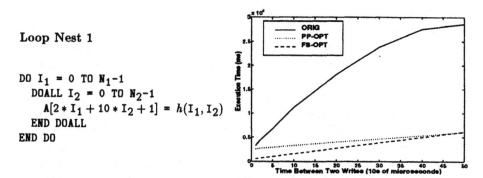

Fig. 1. *Execution times for three versions of Loop Nest 1.*

this is not the case, the page can bounce back and forth repeatedly between processors, causing the number of page faults to rise much higher. These additional page faults are referred to as *ping-pong* effects. The term *ping-pong* is used because the affected page bounces back and forth between processors.

For example, consider Loop Nest 1. Execution times are shown in Fig. 1 for three versions of this loop nest:

- the original loop (ORIG),
- a version optimized to reduce ping-pong effects only (PP-OPT), and
- a version optimized to eliminate multiple-writer false sharing (FS-OPT).

All three versions were executed on 16 processors of a 32-processor iPSC/2 under the KOAN SVM system [2], which supports the aforementioned invalidate-based coherence protocol and employs a page size of 4 KB (512 double-precision numbers). The problem size was $N_1 = N_2 = 10^3$. The performance difference between the two optimized versions and ORIG provides a conservative approximation of the degradation attributable to multiple-writer false sharing alone, and to multiple-writer false sharing compounded by ping-pong effects.

In this paper, we briefly describe the two transformations used in the aforementioned experiment. We also present preliminary performance results for these transformations. The remainder of this paper is organized as follows. Sect. 2 and Sect. 3 discuss the application of PP-OPT and FS-OPT to loops containing a single static write reference. Sect. 4 extends these techniques to loops containing multiple static write references. Sect. 5 presents performance results. Sect. 6 compares our approach to related work in the area of false sharing. Sect. 7 summarizes this work and discusses future research directions.

2 Reducing Ping-pong Effects (PP-OPT)

Ping-pong effects occur only when at least one processor is writing to a page multiple times *and* there is sufficient time between successive writes by this processor for a second processor to acquire the page, thus causing this first processor to fault on a successive write. This phenomenon can be seen in Fig. 1, where the time between successive writes is varied along the x-axis. As the time increases, so do the ping-pong effects. The phenomenon is due to a combination of the page-transfer protocol and the relative magnitude of the network latency in comparison to the time between writes. Although the values are characteristic of KOAN, these trends should generalize to other SVM systems.

Therefore, ping-pong effects can be reduced by minimizing the time between successive writes by the same processor to the same page. This can be effected by stripmining the parallel loop and then delaying the non-local writes within each strip until the strip's end, causing these writes to be performed in quick succession. The advantages of this simple, new technique are its wide applicability and its simplicity of implementation at the compiler level. The result of applying this optimization to Loop Nest 1 can be seen in Loop Nest 2. The local array **buff** serves as a software write buffer which stores results locally between the time that they are computed and the time that they are written out. As one might expect, there is a space–performance tradeoff: the larger the buffer, the better PP-OPT performs. For more details on this transformation and on the cost–benefit tradeoffs involved in selecting buffer sizes, see [3, 4].

Loop Nest 2

```
LOCAL ARRAY: buff[0:buffsz-1]          /* Copy-out loop: A ← buff */
                                        J = 0
DO I₁ = 0 TO N₁-1                       DO I₂ = II₂
   DOALL II₂ = 0 TO N₂-1 BY buffsz            TO MIN(II₂+buffsz, N₂)-1
                                              A[2 * I₁ + 10 * I₂ + 1] = buff[J]
   /* Main loop */                            J = J + 1
   J = 0                                END DO
   DO I₂ = II₂                        END DOALL
         TO MIN(II₂+buffsz, N₂)-1   END DO
      buff[J]=h(I₁,I₂)
      J = J + 1
   END DO
```

3 Eliminating False Sharing (FS-OPT)

For cases where reducing ping-pong effects is insufficient, we review our previously proposed transformation for eliminating multiple-writer false sharing itself. In this section, we present examples of applying this optimization to loop nests containing a single static write reference. In the interest of brevity, we restrict our discussion to cases that occur in the benchmarks discussed later in this paper.

Handling One-Dimensional Loop Nests: Consider Loop Nest 3. Multiple-writer false sharing can be eliminated by partitioning pages into blocks of k pages, known as *k-blocks*. Then the computation can be partitioned such that, during any given DOALL loop iteration, the I-loop iterations that are executed are exactly those that map to some distinct k-block.

Loop Nest 3

Loop Nest 4

```
                              DOALL II = 0 TO ⌈(N + φ)/β⌉-1
                                 /* I-loop iterates over exactly one k-block */
                                 DO I = MAX(⌈II * β - φ⌉, 0)
   DOALL I = 0 TO N-1                  TO MIN(⌈(II + 1) * β - φ⌉, N)-1
R:     A[3*I] = h(I)          R:      A[3*I] = h(I)
   END DOALL                      END DO
                              END DOALL
```

where

$$\beta \in \left\{ \beta^{A}(k) = k * \frac{m}{3} \mid k \in \mathbb{P} \right\}$$

$$\phi \in \left\{ \phi^{A}(n) = \frac{(o(A[0]) + n*m) \bmod (k*m)}{3} \mid n \in [0 : k)_{\mathbb{N}} \right\}.$$

Assume that a page can hold precisely m elements of A and that $o(A[expr])$ is the offset of A[expr] on some page, where $0 \le o(A[expr]) < m$. The code to accomplish this partitioning is shown in Loop Nest 4.[1] Depending on the choice of k, applying this transformation may lead to the use of a non-integer *block size* β. The *alignment factor* ϕ compensates for the fact that the array element accessed during iteration I=0 falls in the middle of a k-block. A comprehensive discussion of this optimization can be found in [5].

As an example, let $m = 4$ and $o(A[0]) = 3$.[2] We arbitrarily choose $k = 2$ and $n = 0$, so that the block size is $\beta = 8/3$ and the alignment factor is $\phi = 1$. Below is the partitioning of iterations/pages into k-blocks that results.

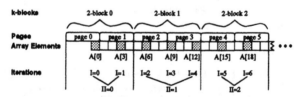

Because $k = 2$, the I-loop iterations that are executed during any given iteration of the II-loop (the outer loop after stripmining the original DOALL loop) are exactly those that map to some 2-block.

In particular, consider elements A[9] and A[12], which both lie on page 3 and are accessed during iterations I=3 and I=4, respectively. To prevent false sharing of this page, both of these iterations must be executed by the same processor.[3] This is ensured in two steps. First, the iteration partitioning strategy

---

[1] We use the following set notation: $\mathbb{N} = \{0, 1, \ldots\}$, $\mathbb{P} = \{1, 2, \ldots\}$, and $\mathbb{R}$ is the set of real numbers. $[mn : mx) = \{r \in \mathbb{R} \mid mn \le r < mx\}$. $[mn : mx)_S = [mn : mx) \cap S$, where $S \in \{\mathbb{N}, \mathbb{P}\}$.

[2] For illustrative purposes, an unrealistically small page size has been chosen.

[3] Had we chosen a larger, more realistic page size, there would have been more cases similar to this.

maps both of these iterations to the same 2-block. Then, it guarantees that all iterations that map to this 2-block are executed by the same processor.

Because the blocking factor is not an integer, the number of iterations that map to a k-block can vary by one from block to block. There are $k = 2$ possible pairings of pages into 2-blocks. By choosing $n = 0$, page 0 has become the first page in some 2-block. Had we chosen $n = 1$, page 0 would have been the second page in some 2-block.

Handling Two-Dimensional Loop Nests: Consider Loop Nest 5. In this section, we show how to eliminate multiple-writer false sharing and other sources of page migration from this example loop nest. A more general discussion of two-dimensional loop nests can be found in [4, 5].

Loop Nest 5   **Loop Nest 6**

```
                               DO I₁ = 0 TO N₁-1
                                 DOALL II'₂ = 0 TO P-1
                                   pid = GetPid()
                                   DO II₂ = firstIter^A(pid,I₁)
                                             TO ⌈(N₂ + φ/β)⌉ - 1 BY P
                                   /* I₂-loop iterates over exactly one k-block */
      DO I₁ = 0 TO N₁-1              DO I₂ = MAX(⌈II₂ * β - φ⌉, 0)
        DOALL I₂ = 0 TO N₂-1                   TO MIN(⌈(II₂ + 1) * β - φ⌉, N₂)-1
R:        A[4 * I₁ + 3 * I₂]    R:        A[4 * I₁ + 3 * I₂] = h(I₁,I₂)
            = h(I₁,I₂)                END DO
      END DOALL                   END DO
      END DO                    END DOALL
                               END DO
```

where

$$\beta \in \left\{ \beta^A(k) = k * \frac{m}{3} \mid k \in \mathbb{P} \right\}$$

$$\phi \in \left\{ \phi^A_{I_1}(n) = \frac{(o(A[0]) + 4*I_1 + n*m) \bmod (k*m)}{3} \mid n \in [0:k)_{\mathbb{N}} \right\}$$

$$\mathit{firstIter}^A(\mathrm{pid}, I_1) = \left(\mathrm{pid} - \left\lfloor \frac{o(A[0]) + 4*I_1 + n*m}{k*m} \right\rfloor \right) \bmod P .$$

In the above loop nest, page faults due to write references could arise from one or more of the following sources:

- **Source 1:** cold start misses,
- **Source 2:** multiple-writer false sharing within a single execution of a DOALL loop, and
- **Source 3:** overlap between the sets of pages written during two distinct executions of a DOALL loop.

In our experience, cold start misses are generally insignificant compared to those arising from the remaining two sources; therefore, we ignore these. To eliminate page migrations of the second and third sources, we apply the same technique as in the case of one-dimensional loop nests, but impose the additional restrictions that (1) the same partitioning of pages into k-page blocks must be used during every iteration of the I_1 loop and (2) a surjective mapping must be established between k-blocks and processors that is enforced at run time, so that each processor executes exactly those iterations associated with "its" k-blocks. The mapping that we choose maps every P^{th} k-block to the same processor, where P is the number of processors. This effects a block-cyclic schedule.

The transformed code is shown in Loop Nest 6. It is assumed that if a DOALL loop with P iterations is executed, then each distinct DOALL loop iteration is mapped to a distinct processor.

As an example, assume that $m = 4$ and that $o(A[0]) = 3$. We arbitrarily choose $k = 2$ and $n = 0$, so that the blocking factor is $\beta = 8/3$ and the alignment factor is $\phi = ((3 + 4 * I_1) \bmod 8)/3$. Below is the mapping between k-blocks and processors that results.

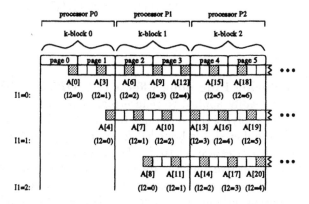

As a second example, recall Loop Nest 1. The performance benefit of applying this technique (FS-OPT) to that loop nest can be seen graphically in Fig. 1.

To maximize parallelism and reduce synchronization overhead, it is generally preferable, when legal, to interchange loops so that the DOALL loop is outermost.

Note that FS-OPT eliminates page migrations across multiple executions of the same doall loop by employing the same mapping between pages and processors during each execution. This same sort of affinity can be provided across distinct loop nests that each contain write references to the same array variable by choosing the same values of k and n in each case.

4 Optimizing Loop Nests with Multiple Write References:

In practice, programs often contain DOALL loops with more than one static write reference. This section briefly introduces three methods for extending the aforementioned loop transformations to handle multiple write references. The three differ in their aggressiveness and generality. As a running example throughout this section, we will use Loop Nest 7, a key loop nest from a two-dimensional explicit hydrodynamics code fragment known as Lawrence Livermore Kernel 18.

Loop Nest 7

```
/* Key loop nest from Lawrence Livermore Kernel 18 */
DOALL II₂ = 0 TO ⌈(N − 2)/β⌉ − 1
  DO I₁ = 2 TO 6
    DO I₂ = MAX(⌈II₂ * β⌉+2, 2) TO MIN(⌈(II₂ + 1) * β⌉+2, N)-1
```

R^{ZU}: $ZU[I_2,I_1] = ZU[I_2,I_1] + S * (ZA[I_2,I_1] * (ZZ[I_2,I_1] - ZZ[I_2+1,I_1]))$
            $- ZA[I_2-1,I_1] * (ZZ[I_2,I_1] - ZZ[I_2-1,I_1])$
            $- ZB[I_2,I_1] * (ZZ[I_2,I_1] - ZZ[I_2,I_1-1])$
            $+ ZB[I_2,I_1+1] * (ZZ[I_2,I_1) - ZZ[I_2,I_1+1)))$

R^{ZV}: $ZV[I_2,I_1] = ZV[I_2,I_1] + S * (ZA[I_2,I_1] * (ZR[I_2,I_1] - ZR[I_2+1,I_1]))$
            $- ZA[I_2-1,I_1] * (ZR[I_2,I_1] - ZR[I_2-1,I_1])$
            $- ZB[I_2,I_1+1] * (ZR[I_2,I_1] - ZR[I_2,I_1-1])$
            $+ ZB[I_2,I_1+1] * (ZR[I_2,I_1] - ZR[I_2,I_1+1)))$

```
      END DO
    END DO
  END DOALL
```

Technique 1: Reducing Ping-pong Effects (PP-OPT): The technique from Sect. 2 can be readily applied to reduce ping-pong effects for both references. An example of applying this technique to Loop Nest 7 is depicted in Loop Nest 8. The effective buffer size is bounded from above by the block size β. In Loop Nest 8, the buffer sizes are set to β. The copy-in loops, where ZU and ZV are read into their respective buffers, are not strictly necessary for this loop nest. However, we include them here because they may be needed to handle the general case and consequently are generated by default by the compiler in which these optimizations are currently implemented.

Technique 2: Eliminating False Sharing for One Reference Group and Reducing Ping-pong Effects for the Remainder (FS-PP-OPT): A *reference group* is a set of one or more write references with the same page offsets, the same array dimensions (excluding the outermost dimension), the same size elements, and the same subscript expressions (these need not be references to the same variable). A reference group has the property that the footprint of each reference in the group moves through memory at the same speed and crosses page boundaries at the same time. For example, in Loop Nest 7, ZU and ZV have the same size elements and the same subscript expressions. If they also have the same innermost dimension and the same offset, then they belong to the same reference group. Otherwise, they belong to distinct reference groups. In general, there are at most a few reference groups within a given loop nest. This is especially true if arrays are aligned with page boundaries when possible.

A reference group has the additional property that the set of block sizes and alignment factors that can be used to eliminate false sharing is the same for each reference in the group. Therefore, we can eliminate multiple-writer false sharing and Source 3 page migrations (Sect. 3) *within* a given reference group G, by applying our false sharing elimination techniques from Sect. 3, when applicable.

Loop Nest 8

```
/* Technique 1: Reducing ping-pong           /* Main loop */
   effects for both write references         J = 0
   from Loop Nest 7 (PP-OPT). */             DO I2 = I2MIN TO I2MAX
LOCAL ARRAY: buffZU[0:β-1]                       buffZU[J] = buffZU[J] + ···
LOCAL ARRAY: buffZV[0:β-1]                       buffZV[J] = buffZV[J] + ···
                                                 J = J + 1
DOALL II2 = 0 TO ⌈(N-2)/β⌉ - 1               END DO
  DO I1 = 2 TO 6
    I2MIN = MAX(⌈II2 * β⌉+2, 2)              /* Copy-out loops:
    I2MAX = MIN(⌈(II2 + 1) * β⌉+2, N)-1         ZU ← buffZU, ZV ← buffZV */
                                                 J = 0
    /* Copy-in loops:                            DO I2 = I2MIN TO I2MAX
       buffZU ← ZU, buffZV ← ZV */    R^ZU:         ZU[I2,I1] = buffZU[J]
    J = 0                                            J = J + 1
    DO I2 = I2MIN TO I2MAX                        END DO
      buffZU[J] = ZU[I2,I1]                       J = 0
      J = J + 1                                    DO I2 = I2MIN TO I2MAX
    END DO                                  R^ZV:     ZV[I2,I1] = buffZV[J]
    J = 0                                            J = J + 1
    DO I2 = I2MIN TO I2MAX                        END DO
      buffZV[J] = ZV[I2,I1]
      J = J + 1                                END DO
    END DO                               END DOALL
```

If there is only one reference group, then both these sources of page migrations are eliminated altogether. If there is more than one reference group, we can also apply our ping-pong reduction techniques to reduce ping-pong effects elsewhere.

For example, assume that ZU and ZV belong to distinct reference groups. Loop Nest 9 shows the result of optimizing to eliminate false sharing for the reference to ZU and optimizing to reduce ping-pong effects for the one to ZV.

Technique 3: Eliminating Multiple-Writer False Sharing for All References (FS-OPT): Under certain circumstances, multiple-writer false sharing and Source 3 page migrations can be eliminated simultaneously for multiple reference groups by applying the following compound transformation:
- **Step 1:** Distribute the DOALL loop to encapsulate the references from each group in distinct DOALL loops.
- **Step 2:** Independently select block sizes and alignment factors for each reference group (equivalently, each loop nest).
- **Step 3:** Fuse the DOALL loops back together so that no additional synchronization is necessary.

The circumstances under which this optimization can be performed are described in [4]. An example of applying this optimization to Loop Nest 7 is depicted in Loop Nest 10. For this example, it is again assumed that the references to ZU and ZV belong to different reference groups.

Loop Nest 9

/* *Technique 2: Eliminating false*
  sharing for R^{ZU} *and reducing*
  ping-pong effects for R^{ZV} *from*
  Loop Nest 7 (FS-PP-OPT). */
LOCAL ARRAY: buffZV[0:$\beta^{ZU}(k)$-1]

```
DOALL II'_2 = 0 TO P-1
  pid = GetPid()
  β = β^ZU(k)
  DO II_2 = 0 TO ⌈(N-2)/β⌉-1 BY P
    DO I_1 = 2 TO 6
      φ = φ_{I_1}^{ZU}(n)
```

/* *All elements of ZU written*
   during iterations
   (I_1, I_2MIN : I_2MAX) *lie*
   within some k-block that is
   mapped to processor pid */

```
      I_2MIN = MAX(⌈(II_2+
              FirstIter^ZU(pid,I_1))
              *β - φ⌉+2,  2)
      I_2MAX = MIN(⌈(II_2+
              FirstIter^ZU(pid,I_1)
              +1) * β - φ⌉+2, N)-1
```

/* *Copy-in loop:* buffZV ← ZV */
```
J = 0
DO I_2 = I_2MIN TO I_2MAX
  buffZV[J] = ZV[I_2,I_1]
  J = J + 1
END DO
```

/* *Main loop* */
```
J = 0
DO I_2 = I_2MIN TO I_2MAX
  ZU[I_2,I_1] = ZU[I_2,I_1] + ···
  buffZV[J] = buffZV[J] + ···
  J = J + 1
END DO
```

R^{ZU}:

R^{ZV}:

/* *Copy-out loop:* ZV ← buffZV */
```
J = 0
DO I_2 = I_2MIN TO I_2MAX
  ZV[I_2,I_1] = buffZV[J]
  J = J + 1
END DO

    END DO
  END DO
END DOALL
```

5 Preliminary Experimental Results

The optimizations to reduce ping-pong effects (Sect. 2) and eliminate false sharing (Sect. 3) have been implemented in the Fortran-S compiler [6], which generates code that runs on the iPSC/2 under the KOAN SVM [2]. The KOAN SVM system is embedded in the operating system of the iPSC/2. Pages of size 4 KB are physically distributed across processors' local memories. KOAN uses a distributed-manager algorithm based on [1], with an invalidation protocol that ensures that the shared memory is coherent at all times [7]. Under this protocol, pages can have one of three access modes: *read-only*, *write-exclusive* and *invalid*. Multiple copies of a page are permitted only when all copies are in read-only mode. When a processor needs to write to a page and either has a read-only copy or no copy at all, the processor must send a message to the page's manager requesting write-exclusive access. Once all other copies of that page are invalidated, a write-exclusive copy is sent to the requesting processor, which can then proceed with its write.

The Fortran-S compiler generates code using static scheduling. When P processors are allocated to the resulting code there is an initial fork onto all P processors and a join at the end. The starts and ends of DOALL loops are re-

Loop Nest 10

```
/* Technique 3: Eliminating false
   sharing for both write references
   from Loop Nest 7 (FS-OPT). */
DOALL II'_2 = 0 TO P-1
   pid = GetPid()


   /* Loop nest containing ZU after
      splitting main loop */
   β = β^ZU(k)
   DO II_2 = 0 TO ⌈(N-2)/β⌉-1 BY P
      DO I_1 = 2 TO 6
         φ = φ^ZU_{I_1}(n)


         /* All elements of ZU written
            during iterations
            (I_1, I_2MIN : I_2MAX) lie
            within some k-block that is
            mapped to processor pid */
         I_2MIN = MAX(⌈(II_2+
                     FirstIter^ZU(pid,I_1))
                     *β - φ⌉+2, 2)
         I_2MAX = MIN(⌈(II_2+
                     FirstIter^ZU(pid,I_1)
                     +1) * β - φ⌉+2, N)-1
         DO I_2 = I_2MIN TO I_2MAX
R^ZU:        ZU[I_2,I_1]
                = ZU[I_2,I_1] + ···
         END DO
      END DO
   END DO
```

```
/* Loop nest containing ZV after
   splitting main loop */
β = β^ZV(k)
DO II''_2 = 0 TO ⌈(N-2)/β⌉-1 BY P
   DO I_1 = 2 TO 6
      φ = φ^ZV_{I_1}(n)


      /* All elements of ZV written
         during iterations
         (I_1, I_2MIN : I_2MAX)  lie
         within some k-block that is
         mapped to processor pid */
      I_2MIN = MAX(⌈(II_2+
                  FirstIter^ZV(pid,I_1))
                  *β - φ⌉+2, 2)
      I_2MAX = MIN(⌈(II_2+
                  FirstIter^ZV(pid,I_1)
                  +1) * β - φ⌉+2, N)-1
      DO I_2 = I_2MIN TO I_2MAX
R^ZV:    ZV[I_2,I_1]
            = ZV[I_2,I_1] + ···
      END DO
   END DO
END DO
END DOALL
```

placed by P-processor barrier operations as needed. Whenever a DOALL loop is executed, iteration $I = j$ of that DOALL loop is executed on processor P_j, where $0 \le P_j < P$, which provides some affinity across DOALL loops.

The remainder of this section includes case studies of several Fortran 77 benchmarks. For each benchmark, the Fortran-S compiler was used to generate several versions: ORIG, PP-OPT and FS-OPT. For the ORIG and PP-OPT versions, each processor was assigned a consecutive chunk of $\beta = N/P$ iterations, where N is the problem size. For the PP-OPT version, a buffer size of β was chosen. For the FS-OPT version, each processor was assigned a consecutive chunk of $\beta = \beta(k)$ (equivalently, k "pages" of) iterations, where k that was chosen to yield the block size $\beta(k)$ that was closest to N/P. For all three versions, the innermost DOALL loop was parallelized. To maximize the grain of parallelism, loop interchanging was then applied when legal.

DMXPY: Loop Nest 11 depicts the Fortran kernel DMXPY from LIN-PACKD [8] which performs matrix–vector multiplication. Fig. 2 depicts the performance of the ORIG, PP-OPT and FS-OPT versions of DMXPY for two different problem sizes. As can be seen in Fig. 2(a), the overhead for applying either PP-OPT or FS-OPT is less than 10% of the sequential execution time. Therefore, as the number of processors increases and the degree of false sharing with it, the optimized versions quickly outperform ORIG. The curves that correspond to the optimized versions are smoother as well. This makes the performance of the optimized versions easier to predict, which facilitates program tuning.

For this benchmark and the range of processors studied, the performance of PP-OPT and FS-OPT is similar. The only exception occurs when the number of processors is very small in comparison to the problem size. In this case, the degree of false sharing is too small to offset the load unbalancing caused by FS-OPT. However, this trend quickly reverses as the number of processors is increased. This effect can be seen in Fig. 2(b).

Triangularized DMXPY: Because there is processor affinity across executions of the I_1 loop in DMXPY, the reference pattern is the same on every execution of this loop, so the degree of false sharing is not very high. To study false sharing effects when the reference pattern changes across I_1-loop executions, we created the triangularized version of DMXPY shown in Loop Nest 12.

The performance of the triangularized version of DMXPY can be seen in Fig. 3. Again, the optimized versions outperform the unoptimized versions. This time, however, the FS-OPT version significantly outperforms the PP-OPT version. There are several reasons for this. First, because of the triangulation, the PP-OPT version no longer has the advantage of affinity across DOALL loop executions, but the FS-OPT version still does. Second, the number of iterations per processor and, hence, the buffer size decrease as I_1 increases. Because the benefits of PP-OPT are proportional to the buffer size, PP-OPT becomes less effective as execution of the triangularized kernel progresses.

LLK18: Fig. 4 presents execution times for unoptimized and optimized versions of LLK18, a two-dimensional explicit hydrodynamics code, known as Lawrence Livermore Kernel 18. This code contains three loop nests similar to the one depicted in Loop Nest 7. Although each loop nest contains multiple write references, the references within each loop nest belong to the same reference group. This is because they have the same dimensions and subscript expressions, and the Fortran-S compiler aligns arrays with page beginnings, when possible. Consequently, if false sharing is eliminated with respect to one write reference in each loop nest, it is automatically eliminated with respect to both.

As can be seen in Fig. 4, both PP-OPT and FS-OPT again significantly outperform ORIG. As the number of processors increases, FS-OPT increasingly outperforms PP-OPT. Note that this is true for both graphs in Fig. 3 as well. This trend is due largely to the constraints that FS-OPT imposes on the scheduling policy. In general, with any program, increasing parallelism past some threshold will cause performance to worsen. Finding this point, however, is non-trivial.

Loop Nest 11

```
/* DMXPY */
DO I₁ = 0 TO N₁
   DO I₂ = 0 TO N₂
R:      Y[I₂] = Y[I₂] + X[I₁]
             * M[I₂,I₁]
   END DO
END DO
```

Loop Nest 12

```
/* Triangularized version of DMXPY */
DO I₁ = 0 TO N₁
   DO I₂ = I₁+1 TO N₂
R:      Y[I₂] = Y[I₂] + X[I₁]
             * M[I₂,I₁]
   END DO
END DO
```

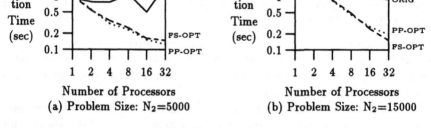

Fig. 2. *Execution times for original and optimized versions of* DMXPY *(Loop Nest 11) with the inner loop parallelized and interchanged.* $N_1 = 10$.

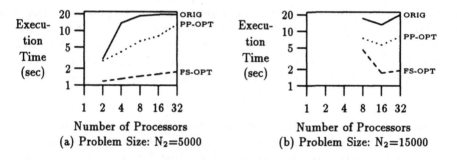

Fig. 3. *Execution times for unoptimized and optimized triangularized versions of* DMXPY *(Loop Nest 12) with inner loop parallelized (no interchanging).* $N_1 = 100$.

Because FS-OPT treats pages as indivisible units (i.e., all writes to a given page must be performed by the same processor), the maximum amount of parallelism is bounded from above by the number of pages. Therefore, FS-OPT has the side effect of bounding the amount of parallelism that can be exploited.

In contrast, PP-OPT does not make any such requirement. Therefore, as the number of processors increases, the number of iterations per processor decreases. Because the maximum effective buffer size is bounded from above by the number of iterations per processor, the maximum effective buffer size decreases as well. Because the benefits of PP-OPT are proportional to the buffer size, PP-OPT

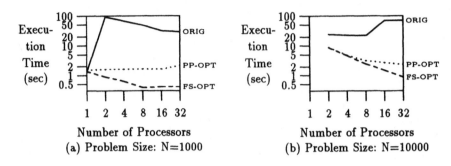

Fig. 4. *Execution times for original and optimized versions of* LLK18, *with inner loops parallelized and interchanged. All arrays are aligned with page boundaries, so there is only one reference group per loop nest.*

becomes less effective as the number of processors is increased. Note that, for these experiments, we set the actual buffer size equal to the maximum possible buffer size. Regardless of the buffer size chosen, however, the same trend would be observed beyond some threshold.

The best example of this effect can be seen in Fig. 4(a), where performance more or less flattens out after 8 processors, increasing only slightly beyond this point. The flattening out occurs because no more processors will be used even if they are available. The slight but steady increase after this point occurs for two reasons. First, in the current version of the compiler, no attempt has been made to prevent the execution of empty loop iterations. Second, the program is forked across all available processors, regardless of whether they are used. Both of these could be overcome at least partially in a more mature compiler, in which case performance would be expected to level out even more. Had we been able to run experiments on larger systems, we would have expected to see this same trend in Fig. 4(b) as well.

Key Loop Nest from LLK18 with Multiple Reference Groups: To test our extensions for handling loop nests containing multiple reference groups, we changed the bounds of array ZV from Loop Nest 7 so that they no longer match ZU. In Fig. 5, we compare the original version of this loop nest (ORIG) to the three optimized versions PP-OPT, FS-PP-OPT, and FS-OPT, depicted as Loop Nests 8, 9 and 10. For ORIG, PP-OPT and FS-OPT, block and buffer sizes are chosen as described earlier. For FS-PP-OPT, the block size is the same as in FS-OPT, and the buffer size equals the block size.

In general, for 2 to 32 processors, all three optimized versions greatly outperform ORIG. Note that, in the case of both PP-OPT and FS-PP-OPT, the maximum possible buffer size shrinks as the number of processors increase. In PP-OPT, the shrinkage is effectively unbounded for the reasons mentioned earlier. Therefore, the performance benefits of PP-OPT will eventually diminish as the number of processors is increased (this can already be seen for the smaller problem size as the number of processors approaches 32). In both the FS-OPT and FS-PP-OPT versions, the amount of parallelism is bounded from above,

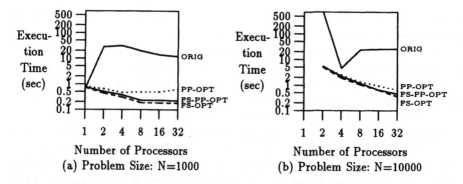

Fig. 5. *Execution times for original and optimized versions of Loop Nest 7 from LLK18, with inner loops parallelized and interchanged. ZU and ZV are declared with different dimensions, so that Loop Nest 7 contains two reference groups.*

because of the indivisibility of pages. Consequently, in FS-PP-OPT, the buffer size cannot grow smaller than $\beta(1)$, the smallest possible block size. Therefore, the performance curves for both these versions will more or less flatten out for the reasons mentioned earlier. FS-OPT slightly outperforms FS-PP-OPT, but the differences for this benchmark are negligible.

One advantageous side effect of the optimizations under study is that page-level locality is increased and the working set size is decreased. Occasionally the effects are dramatic. For example, in Fig. 5(b), ORIG performs very poorly on two processors because of thrashing. Because of the smaller working sets of the optimized versions, all three perform much better.

6 Related Research

The potential performance degradation that can be caused by false sharing has been studied by several researchers. Based on this research, data layout optimizations to reduce false sharing, such as array padding [2, 9, 10] and array reindexing [11], have been proposed. Others have studied data layout optimizations to reduce false sharing in languages with structures and pointers [12].

In many cases, when coherency units are small, compiler-directed program transformations that increase temporal and spatial locality without directly considering the size of the coherency unit alleviate much of the problem. These include transformations such as loop interchanging that increase locality within an individual loop nest [13, 14, 15] as well as optimizations that increase locality across loop nests, for example [16, 17, 18]. Unfortunately, when the coherency unit becomes larger, such techniques no longer suffice.

One run-time solution to the false sharing problem is to relax the consistency model. Systems such as Treadmarks [19] (by default) and KOAN [2] (as an option) allow multiple copies of writable pages to exist and merge modifications only at synchronization points. While these run-time techniques are more general than the compile-time techniques that we study here, they entail a significant space cost to keep track of modifications as well as a time cost associated with both the bookkeeping and the merging.

For this study, we targeted the elimination of false sharing to improve performance. Because of our assumptions of a page-coherent system (supported in either hardware or by the run-time system), the resulting program would execute correctly regardless of whether false sharing was eliminated. Therefore, we did not consider any transformations that would require the insertion of additional synchronization. In contrast, on systems where no hardware or run-time support for coherence is provided, false sharing *must* be eliminated to ensure correctness. Breternitz et al. [20] study this problem. They insert additional synchronization as needed so that the compiler can maintain coherence. Consequently, their techniques are more general than ours. However, on page-coherent systems, the overhead for the additional synchronization may outweigh the performance gain from eliminating false sharing.

Eliminating false sharing is only one optimization that a good SVM compiler should perform. Several researchers have begun exploring techniques to reduce synchronization overhead and hide latencies on SVM systems [11, 17, 21].

7 Conclusions

In this paper, we have distinguished between false sharing and its chief symptom, the ping-pong effect. We have evaluated two compile-time techniques for attacking multiple-writer false sharing for the purpose of improving performance (as opposed to ensuring program correctness). The first is PP-OPT, a new loop transformation that reduces the ping-pong effect by encouraging processors to perform multiple writes to a page before relinquishing the page. It is simple to implement and has wide applicability. We have shown that using this technique to reduce ping-pong effects can eliminate much of the performance degradation attributed to false sharing. For cases where a more aggressive approach is merited, we evaluated a second technique FS-OPT that targets false sharing directly. This loop transformation partitions iterations into blocks of "pages" and assigns these blocks to processors as indivisible units, thus ensuring that no page is written by more than one processor.

For both techniques, computation can be done symbolically at compile time if necessary. Triangular loops and loops with non-unit strides can be handled. Many commonly occurring cases of loops containing multiple references can also be handled. We are currently working on techniques to generalize these optimizations even further.

Overall, both techniques increase locality and, hence, reduce thrashing. Our experimental results have shown that run-time overhead is generally low and quickly offset as the number of processors is increased to even a moderate number. A secondary benefit to both optimizations is that performance becomes more predictable, which facilitates both manual and automatic program tuning.

In general, for any fixed problem size, increasing the amount of parallelism beyond some threshold will cause an application's performance to deteriorate.

One of the benefits of FS-OPT is that, as a side effect of treating pages as indivisible units, the amount of parallelism that will be utilized is bounded from above by the number of pages. This helps prevent performance from deteriorating when the number of processors available becomes too large. In contrast, PP-OPT does not impose any limits on parallelism or even provide any hints as to what the bound should be.

Consequently, in general, when the number of processors is increased beyond this threshold, FS-OPT should increasingly outperform PP-OPT. Below this threshold, however, the performance of the two optimizations is expected to be comparable in many cases. These trends can be seen in the preliminary experimental data presented in this paper. Because this threshold is often difficult to determine, the profitability margin of FS-OPT is likely to be higher. Moreover, FS-OPT has the advantage of naturally providing affinity across doall loops. However, PP-OPT has the advantage over FS-OPT of being simpler to implement and more generally applicable. Therefore, an aggressive compiler should probably support both FS-OPT and PP-OPT; FS-OPT should be applied where possible and PP-OPT used for the remaining cases. In a less aggressive compiler, it would probably suffice to support PP-OPT only.

Because the performance degradation due to page migrations is proportional to page size, so is the benefit of applying our techniques. Although we targeted systems with page-sized coherency units, it should also be possible to realize (albeit smaller) performance gains on SVM systems with cache-line-sized coherency units.

Clearly, eliminating false sharing is only one of several optimizations that a good SVM compiler should perform. In the future, we hope to study and incorporate optimizations to reduce synchronization, to hide latencies where communication is unavoidable, and to handle irregular accesses.

Acknowledgements

The authors would like to thank Thierry Priol and Zakaria Lahjomri for providing access to and assistance with KOAN, Preston Briggs, Ervan Darnell, William Jalby, Ken Kennedy, Ajay Sethi and the anonymous referees for their helpful comments and suggestions, and Debbie Campbell for proofreading this paper.

François Bodin and Thierry Montaut are supported by the Esprit Agency DG XIII under Grant No. APPARC 6634 BRA III and Intel SSD under Grant No. 1 92 C 250 00 31318 01 2. Elana D. Granston is supported by the Center for Research on Parallel Computation under Grant No. CCR-9120008, a grant from the International Business Machines Corporation, and a Postdoctoral Research Associateship in Computational Science and Engineering under National Science Foundation Grant No. CDA-9310307.

References

1. K. Li, *Shared Virtual Memory on Loosely Coupled Multiprocessors*. PhD thesis, Yale University, Sept. 1986.

2. Z. Lajormi and T. Priol, "KOAN: A Shared-Memory for the iPSC/2 Hypercube," in *CONPAR/VAPP92*, LNCS 634, Springer-Verlag, Sept. 1992.

3. T. Montaut and F. Bodin, "False Sharing in Shared Virtual Memory: Analysis and Optimization," tech. rep., IRISA, 1993.

4. F. Bodin, E. D. Granston, and T. Montaut, "Experiences Reducing False Sharing in Shared Virtual Memory Systems." Submitted for publication.

5. E. D. Granston, "Toward a Compile-Time Methodology for Reducing False Sharing and Communication Traffic in Shared Virtual Memory Systems," in the *Sixth Annual Workshop on Languages and Compilers for Parallel Computing*, Aug. 1993.

6. F. Bodin, L. Kervella, and T. Priol, "Fortran-S: A Fortran Interface for Shared Virtual Memory Architectures," in *Supercomputing '93*, pp. 274–283, Nov. 1993.

7. L. Censier and P. Feautrier, "A New Solution to Coherence Problems in Multicache Systems," *IEEE Trans. on Computers*, pp. 1112–1118, Dec. 1978.

8. J. Dongarra, J. Bunch, C. Moler, and G. Stewart, *LINPACK User's Guide*, 1979.

9. W. J. Bolosky, R. P. Fitzgerald, and M. L. Scott, "Simple But Effective Techniques for NUMA Memory Management," in *ACM Symp. on Operating Systems Principles*, pp. 19–31, Dec. 1989.

10. J. Torrellas, M. S. Lam, and J. L. Hennessy, "False Sharing and Spatial Locality in Multiprocessor Caches," Aug. 1992. Submitted to *IEEE Trans. on Computers*.

11. S. P. Ammarsinghe, J. M. Anderson, M. S. Lam, and C.-W. Tseng, "Design and Evaluation of Compiler Optimizations for Scalable Address Space Machines," 1994. To be published.

12. S. J. Eggers and T. E. Jeremiassen, "Eliminating false sharing," in *Int. Conf. on Parallel Processing*, pp. 377–381, Aug. 1991.

13. F. Bodin, C. Eisenbeis, W. Jalby, and D. Windheiser, "A Quantitative Algorithm for Data Locality Optimization," in *Code Generation-Concepts, Tools, Techniques*, Springer-Verlag, 1992.

14. K. Kennedy and K. S. McKinley, "Optimizing for Parallelism and Data Locality," in *Int. Conf. on Supercomputing*, pp. 323–334, July 1992.

15. M. E. Wolf and M. S. Lam, "A Data Locality Optimizing Algorithm," in *SIGPLAN '91 Conf. on Programming Languages Design and Implementation*, pp. 30–44, June 1991.

16. J. Fang and M. Lu, "A Solution to the Cache Ping-Pong Problem in RISC Based Parallel Processing Systems," in *Int. Conf. on Parallel Processing*, Aug. 1991.

17. B. Appelbe, C. Hardnett, and S. Doddapaneni, "Program Transformation for Locality Using Affinity Regions," in the *Sixth Annual Workshop on Languages and Compilers for Parallel Computing*, Aug. 1993.

18. J. Anderson and M. Lam, "Global Optimizations for Parallelism and Locality on Scalable Parallel Machines," in *SIGPLAN '93 Conf. on Programming Languages Design and Implementation*, June 1993.

19. P. Keleher, S. Dwarkadas, A. Cox, and W. Zwaenepoel, "Treadmarks: Distributed Shared Memory On Standard Workstations and and Operating Systems," in *Winter Usenix Conf.*, 1994.

20. M. Breternitz, Jr., M. Lai, V. Sarkar, and B. Simons, "Compiler Solutions for the Stale-Data and False-Sharing Problems," Tech. Rep. 03.466, IBM Santa Teresa Laboratory, Apr. 1993.

21. R. Michandaney, S. Hiranandani, and A. Sethi, "Improving the Performance of DSM Systems via Compiler Involvement," in *Supercomputing '94*, 1994.

Parallelizing Tree Algorithms: Overhead vs. Parallelism

Jon A. Solworth and Bryan B. Reagan

University of Illinois at Chicago

Abstract. We consider techniques to efficiently exploit large scale parallel execution of tree operations. Both arbitrary and fixed order operations on trees are considered. An arbitrary order execution must be equivalent to a sequential execution of these operations in *some* order, while a fixed order execution specifies a *specific* order.
Arbitrary order versions are significantly more parallel than fixed order; the parallelism and overheads of all of tree and graph interference, both arbitrary and fixed order are characterized, and the tradeoffs explored.

1 Introduction

It has been previously shown that sets of operations on trees, including inserts, finds, and deletes, can be highly parallel when parallelism is exploited at the leaves. Since most of the updates, even on balanced tree structures, take place near the leaves and since the number of leaves is linear in the size of the tree, there is close to linear parallelism to exploit. For example, we have demonstrated an algorithm called *tree interference* which achieves an average of 1000-fold parallelism while inserting 32K values into a 4K node tree [SR93].

The stereotypical paradigm for a tree operation occurs in two phases: In the first phase, a traversal begins at the root and follows a path down towards a leaf, performing only reads. In the second phase, the traversal is reversed performing writes up to some level. This *read-down, write-up paradigm* applies both to simple binary trees as well as self adjusting trees such as AVL, B-trees, and Red-Black trees.

Since every operation accesses the root, serializing root accesses results in at most logarithmic parallelism vs. the linear parallelism of leaf-based approaches. Hence, it is necessary to replicate the root and to ensure exclusive access to the root only if it is to be written.

Since tree operations are notoriously short lived, the overhead of parallelization must be reduced to achieve acceptable speedup.

The tree interference algorithm previously presented performs its set of operations by greedy scheduling. While its semantics are sequential, the operations in the set may be logically performed in any order — enabling the system to have

---

[0] This research was supported in part by ONR, grant number ONR 93-1-0655 and NSF, grant number CCR-9208631.

op_0	op_1	op_2	op_3
$x \Leftarrow 1$	$y \Leftarrow z$	$w \Leftarrow p+q$	$q \Leftarrow r^*s$
$y \Leftarrow v - z$	$m \Leftarrow w-x$	$q \Leftarrow r\&p$	$p \Leftarrow v$

Fig. 1. Arbitrary order operations

wide latitude in achieving effective parallelizations. However sometimes fixed order semantics are needed. Clearly, this loss of freedom of determining sequential order results in lower parallelism and higher overheads, but at what costs?

This paper presents the performance and overhead of two algorithms, *tree interference* and *graph coloring*, in both arbitrary and fixed order variants. We shall see that these overheads are quite modest, and moreover can be effectively tuned by reducing aggressiveness of parallelism exploitation. A simple adaptive algorithm is given which performs this tuning.

The rest of the paper is organized as follows. Section 2 describes in more detail the semantics of our iterations. Section 3 describes the various approaches to tree-based algorithms, while section 4 describes how the various algorithms can be implemented. Performance results are presented in Section 5, followed by the Conclusions.

2 Arbitrary order

In this paper, arbitrary order as well as fixed order operations on tree data structures are considered. The execution of a collection of *arbitrary ordered* operations must be equivalent to the execution of those operations *in some sequential order*. For example, an arbitrary order loop with five iterations labeled $i_0...i_4$ could be executed in the order i_0, i_1, i_2, i_3, i_4 or i_1, i_4, i_3, i_2, i_0 or any other permutation of those elements. Arbitrary ordered operations are *not* explicitly parallel — they are sequential operations whose order is unspecified.

Arbitrary order operations were first introduced in SETL [SDDS86], a purely sequential programming language. They are often used in algorithm books as a natural way of specifying computations using such notation as $\forall x \in set$ or $\exists x \in set | P(x)$ [AHU75]. Arbitrary order iterations reduce over-specification while enabling independent choice of data structures and algorithm.

They have also been proposed for specifying implicitly parallel algorithms, both pointer-based [Sol90] and numeric [Wol92]. When the order is not important, arbitrary order allows the compiler and the runtime system to often produce more parallel and lower overhead executions. They are the sequential analog of parallel techniques such as Linda's tuple space [ACG86].

In Figure 1, a set of 4 operations are to be performed, each operation consists of two assignments. We shall say that two operations **conflict** iff one operation writes a location that the other operations accesses (either reads or writes). Note that op_0 conflicts with op_1 on x and y; op_1 conflicts with op_2 on w; op_2 conflicts with op_3 on p and q. The conflicts relation is symmetric so if op_i conflicts with op_j then op_j also conflicts with op_i. The conflicts can be represented with an undirected *conflict graph* whose nodes are operations and edges correspond to conflict relations.

To perform these operations in parallel, it is sufficient that each of these operations be performed atomically. Atomicity can be implemented by scheduling concurrently only subsets of operations which do not conflict; for such subsets, no synchronization is needed among the operations in the subset. Since op_1 and op_3 do not conflict, they can be executed in parallel. Similarly, op_0 and op_2 do not conflict, and can be run in parallel. Hence, the four operations could be performed in two phases, with odd numbered operations in one phase and even numbered operations in the other. We shall call a set of operations whose elements pairwise do not conflict to be a *conflict free set (cfs)*. The concurrent execution of a *cfs* is semantically equivalent to executing the *cfs* in any sequential order. Note that without arbitrary order semantics, the above example requires sequential execution, since op_i conflicts with op_{i+1}.

The conflict graph in the above example could be computed statically, since the only locations specified were simple variables. However, in the more general case of arrays, pointers, and other memory aliasing techniques the conflict sets cannot in general be statically determined. Furthermore, if the locations written include indices for arrays or pointers, the conflict set changes after each phase and needs to be recomputed. Compile time analysis of conflict graphs has been studied by Larus and Hillfinger [LH88].

Run-time conflict algorithms using rollback include [Kat86] as well as Salz et. al's work [SMC91] on inspector-executor.

Arbitrary order operations lead to interesting compile-time and run-time optimizations to enable efficient executions. In previous papers we have considered the effect of these operations over list [Sol88, Sol91] and graph based data structures [Sol92] and trees [SR93]; in this paper we consider the the parallelism vs. overhead for operations on tree-based data structures, and in particular the cost of performing arbitrary and fixed order operations on trees, and the parallelism attainable with fixed order operations.

3 Tree-based Algorithms

There has been wide interest in detecting and optimizing tree based algorithms for both sequential and parallel executions [HHN92, CWZ90, Har92]. Most of the optimization have been in the area of pointer disambiguation; by refining alias information it becomes possible to map nodal data to registers, improving locality. There has been relatively little work in the area of parallelizing tree operations, although [CRRH93, SR93] are exceptions. In this paper, we consider the parallelization of sets of operations on trees.

Consider a set of tree operations which include inserts, searches, and deletes. With homogeneous sets of operations, where each operation is of the same type, arbitrary ordered sets of operations (or equivalently, any fixed order set of operations) will always return the same results. Consider a set of elements to be inserted into a tree. Independent of the order inserted into the tree, subsequent

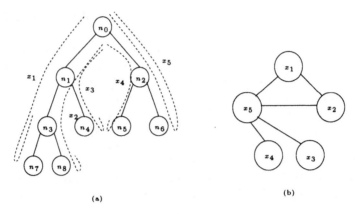

Fig. 2. (a) Tree inserts of arbitrary order operations and (b) the resulting conflict graph

searches will still find the same set of elements; subsequent deletes will still remove the same set of elements. Hence, three arbitrary order iterations — one each for inserts, searches, deletes — will insert, find, and remove the same set of elements as fixed order iterations. However, the shape of the resulting tree depends on the order in which operations are performed [SR93].

The techniques discussed here exploit not only the tree structure, but of the typical way in which the tree is traversed and updated. Consider the AVL tree insertions. All operations start at the root and traverse down to the bottom fringe of the tree, at which the update is performed. Then a rebalancing step is performed as the path down to the insert path is traced in reverse. This read-down, write-up paradigm is characteristic of AVL trees, B-trees, Binary Search trees, [AHU75] Red-Black trees, and many other tree structures. In fact, Splay trees [ST85] are the only tree-structure which the authors are aware which does not fit into this paradigm; however, the large, tree-global data structure changes of splay trees makes it unlikely to perform well in parallel.

This paradigm is illustrated with the tree interference diagram shown in Figure 2a. Five operations, labeled $x_1...x_5$, are to be performed in arbitrary order. These operations are shown in the figure as dotted lines. An operation reads the nodes from the root to the fringe on the way down, and then modify nodes coming up to some level. For example, x_1 read nodes n_0, n_1, n_3, n_7 on the way down, and then modifies nodes n_7, n_3 on the way up. We shall use Figure 2a as a running example to show how the various strategies for implementing arbitrary and determined order operations on trees work[1].

When pointers are present, the problem of finding conflict-free sets (*cfs*) of operations becomes more expensive since the set of locations accessed depend on the order in which the iterations are performed. For example, after an insertion

---

[1] We assume in the example that the conflict set is invariant with respect to the order of execution. This is not the case in general but serves as an adequate first order approximation

is performed the tree is changed, and so is the path (and conflicts) for future operations. Hence, the size of the *cfs* has two impacts on performance: with larger *cfss*, there is both more parallelism and less overhead for determining the other *cfs*. The tree-based interference produces a partitioning which is not a *cfs* but which is guaranteed to be equivalent to some sequential execution.

4 Implementing Arbitrary Order Operations

In this section we consider two methods for implementing arbitrary order operations on trees. Both methods perform a trial execution, find a subset of iterations which can be executed in parallel, and commit the subset of operations (changing the global store). The process is repeated with the remaining operations. These methods fall into two categories, differing by the method in which they find the parallel set. For arbitrary order, the following suffices:

Graph coloring interference (GI) The parallel set is any conflict free subset (ie, no read-write, write-read or write-write conflicts).

Tree-based interference (TI) The parallel set is any subset which has no write-write conflicts.

For fixed ordering, the subset is restricted to an initial prefix of the iterations remaining to be executed.

We shall need some terminology to describe both the ordering which is selected, as well as its execution. For the ordering we shall use semicolons (*"$x; y$"*) to indicate that x is semantically ordered before y and braces (*"$\{x, y\}$"*) to indicate that the order of x and y is immaterial, that is

$$\{x, y\} \text{ means that } (x; y) = (y; x).$$

In the fixed order semantics we shall assume from here on that the order is $x_1; x_2; x_3; x_4; x_5$. For execution we shall use double bars (*"$x||y$"*) to indicate x can be executed concurrently with y, and semicolons (*"$x; y$"*) to indicate that x completes before y begins execution.

4.1 Graph Coloring Interference

Arbitrary order We review the graph interference introduced in [Sol92].

Arbitrary order loops have different dependencies than fixed order loops. One way of creating a parallel execution at runtime is with an optimistic scheme which first executes each iteration in isolation. An isolated execution of an iteration performs a read of a location by first looking for that location in a local cache. If the value is in the cache, it is retrieved from there, otherwise a read is performed to the global store. A write is always performed only to the cache. Then, any subset of iterations, I, whose only shared locations (if any) are read only can be executed in parallel by committing its written cache location to the global store[2]. The process of optimistic execution is then repeated on the remaining unexecuted iterations. The sequential semantics are preserved since a concurrent execution of I is equivalent to a sequential execution of any permutation of I.

Graph coloring explicitly builds an interference graph which can then be colored, each color corresponding to a phase in the parallel execution — nodes which have the same color can be executed in parallel. This has been shown to be efficiently implementable in the case of a graph [Sol92].

For example, in the tree updates shown in Figure 2a, have a conflict graph as shown in Figure 2b. This conflict has a clique of size 3 (x_1, x_2, x_5), and requires three colors. Hence, these updates could be performed in three phases:

$$x_5; (x_2 || x_3 || x_4); x_1$$

yielding a semantic order of

$$x_5; \{x_2, x_3, x_4\}; x_1$$

Fixed order In fixed order, x_1 must be executed first, and since x_2 conflicts with it, only x_1 can be executed in the first phase. In the second phase, x_2, x_3, x_4 can all be executed, followed by x_5. Hence, the execution is as follows

$$x_1; (x_2 || x_3 || x_4); x_5$$

4.2 Tree interference

Arbitrary order Tree interference algorithm which works as follows:

1. Perform a preliminary execution of the operations on a tree.
2. Let $Lev(op)$ be the distance from the root, at which the write closest to the root occurs for operation op.
3. Operations without write-write conflicts can be scheduled to the same partition. Priority is given to the operations with the maximum Lev.
4. Repeat recursively on the remaining unexecuted operations.

Using tree interference, all of the operations shown in Figure 2a can be performed in a single phase. Note that there is a conflict between the reads performed in part 1 and the writes performed in part 3; hence the read down phase must occur before the write up phase. This occurs naturally within the tree interference algorithm since scheduling (and hence reading) must be performed before any writes.

We have previously shown what that sequential order of operations in a parallel partition P is (partially) ordered by Lev.

---

[2] The execution of any two iterations (in an arbitrary order loop) is pairwise *raceless* if no location which is used in both iterations can be written by either one. Two raceless iterations i_0, i_1 can be executed concurrently or in either $i_0; i_1$ or $i_1; i_0$ order with exactly the same result.

Hence, given the tree in Figure 2a, we have the sequential order

$$x_2; \{x_1, x_3, x_4\}; x_5$$

Note that this is the semantically equivalent sequential execution order; in fact, the execution of these operation is completely in parallel.

Fixed order The fixed order tree interference has one advantage over the fixed order graph coloring. The fixed order tree interference can execute past read write conflicts if the write belongs to a semantically later iteration than the read. Hence, x_5 can be executed concurrently with x_4 (however, x_1 cannot be executed concurrently with x_2). The resulting execution is therefore:

$$x_1; (x_2 \| x_3 \| x_4 \| x_5)$$

5   Performance

Having described the various algorithms, this section shows experimental results of the parallelism achieved and the overhead for achieving that parallelism. Each experimental data point is the average from 10 different executions.

5.1   Experiments of AVL tree inserts

We wish to at least show the amount of parallelism that such an algorithm would have for example on an AVL tree. We consider a tree of size S, having either $8S$, S, or $S/8$ inserts. For example consider an AVL tree with $S = 2048$ nodes, we consider the cases of inserting $16K, 2K,$ and 256 additional nodes. Both the AVL tree and the additional nodes are randomly generated.

Obviously, the more nodes that are inserted, the more the potential for parallelism since there are more inserts which can be done in parallel. However, the more nodes to be inserted, the greater the conflict, as multiple inserts occur at the same nodes in the tree.

First, the parallelism available is shown. This parallelism is measured by the number of phases; the fewer the number of phases, the more operations which are performed on average per phase and hence the more parallelism exploited. In Figure 3a–c, the number of phases required (y-axis) is shown for each of the algorithms as a function of increasing tree size (x-axis).

Clearly, any arbitrary order algorithm is better than any fixed order algorithm for sufficiently large S, and for a given ordering semantics, tree interference is better than graph coloring. Moreover, the difference is increasingly important as the size of the tree (and the number of inserts) increases.

Several other observations may be made:

- The algorithms are much closer together for a relatively sparse number of inserts ($S/8$) than for a dense number of inserts ($8S$).

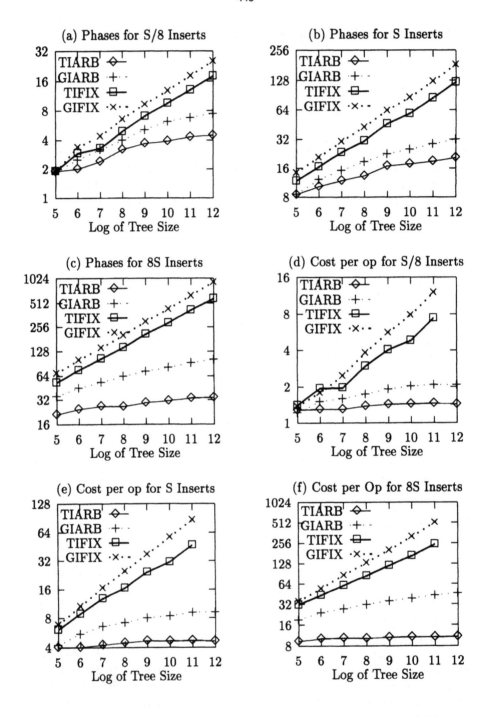

Fig. 3. Number of phases (first 3 graphs) and cost per operation are shown for various tree sizes and number of inserts

- The fixed ordered algorithms, TIfix and GIfix, do not improve performance by attempting to perform larger sets of inserts. Each time we increase the number of nodes to be inserted by 8, we get almost an 8 fold increase in the number of phases. (It is somewhat less than this, because the tree is growing hence later inserts are more parallel since they are performed on larger trees).
- The arbitrary ordered algorithms, TIarb and GIarb, have substantially slower growth in number of phases as the number of inserts grows. Increasing tree size is a major factor which is moderated by intensified congestion as the inserts become less uniform.
- The best arbitrary order vs. the best fixed order for a tree of size 2K has over 8 times fewer phases at $8S$. Clearly, arbitrary order algorithms result in much more parallelism than fixed order.

Parallelism, of course, is not the whole story. Next, the cost of performing these operations is measured by the number of times each operation must be tried before it can actually be performed. Ideally, each operation would need to be tried only one time and would with very high probability succeed. However, the more aggressively parallelism is exploited, the higher the overhead.

Figure 3d–f show the number of times each operation is tried assuming that each operation is tried every phase until completed. The following observations can be made:

- For $S/8$, GIarb has an average number of trials of somewhat over 2, while TIarb has an average number of trials of 1. For both of these algorithms, and TIarb in particular, almost all the inserts are done in the first try. Congestion is the reason multiple trials are required further out, but the congestion has a large impact on the number of phases, not on the overhead.
- For S, the number of trials roughly quadruple for each of TIarb and GIarb. Congestion dominates in both of these cases, as clusters of inserts result in cliques in the interference graph.
- For $8S$, the number of trials increase by a factor of 2–3. Clearly, the effect of larger trees is starting to take hold, as the earlier inserts increase the parallelism of later inserts.

It is worth looking at the number of operations completed during each phase. These are shown in Figure 4. Clearly, much more work is accomplished in the earlier phases than in the later phases — for example in TIarb over 96 percentage of operations are completed in half the phases. Not only does graph coloring based interference require significantly more phases, but the number of operations per phase decreases much more slowly. This is important since the number of trials per operation is equal to the sum of the fraction not done at the beginning of each phase. The result is that trial operations need to be performed many more times in GI than TIarb.

The numbers converge even faster when considering $S/8$. For $S/8 = 512$, it can clearly be seen that GI and TIfix are almost linear in their completion rate,

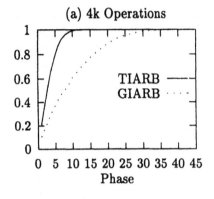
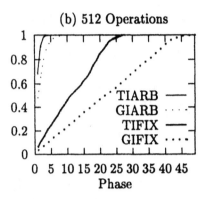

Fig. 4. Fraction of operations completed per phase for 4K inserts on a tree of size 4K and 512 inserts on a tree of size 512

whereas GIarb and TIarb converge very rapidly. The tail of these graphs approaches 100% slowly; this indicates that in a parallel implementation it might be best to use parallelism for the first 99% of operations, and then to use a sequential algorithm for the remaining and thus remove the overhead of parallelism for the last few phases.

5.2 Analytic Results

In this section, we estimate analytically the amount of parallelism for graph and tree interference in both fixed and arbitrary order variants.

The analysis begins with the number of elements inserted per phase in a complete binary tree in which each insert writes only a leaf. Let

- l be the number of leaves, and
- n is the number of elements to be inserted.

(The size of a complete binary tree with l leaves is $2l - 1$.) Given these assumptions we now describe the number of expected writes.

Arbitrary order Arbitrary order is modeled as an urn problem, in which each of the l leaves is an urn. The problem is then given n inserts on l leaves, what is the expected number of non-empty urns? The probability of inserting an element at a leaf is $1/l$ and the expected number of inserts is:

$$Ex\{\# \text{ inserts}\} = l \left(1 - \left(1 - \frac{1}{l}\right)^n\right) \qquad (1)$$

Note that as $n \to \infty$, the expected number of inserts is l. Hence, arbitrary order in the limit can achieve parallelism proportional to the number of leaves, and that a 4K node tree has an expected number of inserts of 2K in the limit.

Fixed order The fixed order case can be modeled by the length of a sequence chosen with replacement from a set of size l, such that no element repeats (to a maximum of n). This problem is also known as the "birthday problem" and as we shall see the expected value is significantly smaller than l. The probability that the number of inserts is greater than or equal to j is:

$$Pr\{\# \text{ inserts} \geq j\} < \prod_{i=0}^{j-1} \frac{l-i}{l} \qquad (2)$$

(This inequality is exact if none of the inserts go above a leaf). Hence, the expected number of inserts is:

$$Ex\{\# \text{ inserts}\} = \sum_{j=0}^{n} Pr\{\# \text{ inserts} \geq j\} \qquad (3)$$

Using the above formula, the expected number of inserts on a 4K node tree is 59, a factor of 71 times smaller than the arbitrary order case!

Shadow The above equations apply to a complete binary tree in which writes occur no higher than the leaves. The assumption of a complete binary tree is reasonable since the trees are balanced.

However, the assumption that writes take place only at a leaf, and hence that two operations conflict only at a leaf, is not sufficient. In this section we compute the average number of leaves which a single update obscures, which we call the *shadow*, for both graph and tree interference.

The number of nodes obscured depends on the height of the highest write. If the highest write is at the leaf, than it obscures only that single leaf node. However, a higher write also (partially) obscures adjacent leaf nodes.

Graph Interference When performing balanced tree inserts, the number of leaves is decreased by the fact that some inserts must write at levels of the tree higher than the leaf. This throws a "shadow" on other leaf nodes, eliminating them from the pool of possible inserts. Hence, we next compute the average size of this shadow for Tree and Graph Interference.

For graph interference, the size of the shadow depends on how many levels above the leaf the insert occurs. If the insert occurs k levels above the leaf, than the shadow falls on 2^k leaves, preventing any leaf within that subtree from being updated. When weighted by the probability, we get:

$$Ex\{\# \text{ of leaves shadowed by an op}\} = \sum_{i=0}^{\log P} P_i \cdot 2^i \qquad (4)$$

Where P_i is the probability that an operation's highest write occurs i levels above a leaf.

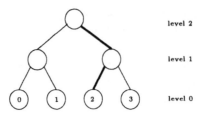

Fig. 5. The effect of a write occurring at level 2

Tree Interference For tree interference, an insert at level k creates a path of writes containing k nodes. The tree interference shadow is only for those writes whose path intersects the operation's path.

Consider a write which occurs at level $k > 0$. The write obscures the leaf touched by the write path. Unlike graph interference, it only partially obscures the adjacent nodes in the 2^k neighborhood. In Figure 5, the result of a write at level 2 is shown. In the case of graph interference, this would shadow leaves 0 through 3; however, in tree interference it:

- shadows node 2
- shadows node 3 only for writes to node 3 which have a height ≥ 1,
- shadows nodes 0 and 1 only for writes to those nodes whose height ≥ 2.

Hence, the expected number of leaves shadowed by a write of height k is:

$$Ex\{\# \text{ leaves shadowed by a } k \text{ level write}\} = \sum_{i=0}^{l} \sum_{j=i}^{\infty} P_j 2^{max(i-1,0)} \qquad (5)$$

and the expected value of being shadowed by any update is:

$$Ex\{\# \text{ leaves shadowed by an insert}\} = \sum_{i=0}^{l} P\{i = k\} Ex\{i\} \qquad (6)$$

5.3 Analytic vs. Experimental results

The AVL tree, as in other balanced trees, has a probability P_i that its highest update is i levels above the leaf. For $i > 1$, $P_{i+1} = \frac{1}{2} P_i$.

The size of the shadow for a 4K tree can now be computed. Under tree interference (eq. 6) we obtain 2.506 nodes and under graph interference (eq. 4) we obtain 7.43. Hence the shadow of tree interference is roughly $\frac{1}{3}$ that of graph interference for a 4K node tree. (This factor grows with the tree size).

The shadow is used to effectively reduce the number of leaves, computing the number of "synthetic leaves" by dividing the number of leaves by the shadow size. Hence on a 4K tree there are 2K leaves, and 817 synthetic leaves for tree interference and 276 synthetic leaves for graph interference.

	TIfix		GIfix		TIarb		GIarb	
	exp	anl	exp	anl	exp	anl	exp	anl
16	15.7	15.2	14.8	15.8	15.8	15.9	15.5	15.6
64	29.9	34.7	20.1	20.5	60.8	61.6	55.1	57.2
256	29.9	35.5	20.1	20.5	205.6	219.9	160.0	166.9
1024	29.9	35.5	20.1	20.5	531.2	583.9	339.4	275.4
4096	29.9	35.5	20.1	20.5	865.6	811.7	449.3	275.5

Table 1. Experimental and analytical values for the number of writes

Attempted	Achieved	Fract of Opt	Overhead
8	7.966	0.010	1.004
64	61.594	0.075	1.039
512	380.609	0.466	1.345
4096	811.694	0.993	5.046
8192	817.077	1.000	10.026

Table 2. Overhead vs. Parallelism achieved on a 4K nodes

The experimentally achieved (exp) and analytically calculated (anl) number of writes are shown in Table 1.

The correlations is very high (within 10%) for the fixed order algorithms as well as for TIarb. However, they diverge above 512 inserts for GIarb. The average shadow size is inaccurate, since as more leaves are obscured the arbitrary order will begin to select only those nodes which small shadows (but this just postpones the large nodes to the next cycle, it does not eliminate them). This effect is evident in GIarb but not TIarb because TIarb has a much smaller shadow size and hence smaller variability in selection.

We now look at overhead versus parallelism obtained, as shown in Table 2. From 2 to 512 attempted inserts in a tree of size 4K, we achieve 46.6% percent of maximum parallelism, while considering each node just 1.345 times on average – or 34.5% overhead. If each node is examined twice (thrice), 75% (93%) of peak parallelism is achieved. Beyond that, more aggressive parallelism reaches diminishing returns.

All of the experimental results obtained here were for insertions on AVL trees. In this section, we argue that these results are generally applicable to other operations (such as delete) as well as to other trees, such as B-trees and Red-Black trees. In each of these cases, $P_{i+1} = pP_i$ where p is typically $\frac{1}{2}$, hence each exhibits an exponential backoff of writing higher in the tree. Hence in all of these algorithms, there is an exponentially decreasing probability of writing higher levels in the tree.

Weight	Avg. Parallelism	Overhead
0.75	263.27	1.44
1.00	272.74	1.74
1.50	281.86	2.22
2.00	282.40	2.55

Table 3. An adaptive algorithm performance as a function of weight (average parallelism when inserting 4K nodes into a tree of size 4K)

5.4 A practical adaptive algorithm

The previous section showed that to achieve 75% of peak parallelism, a sufficiently large window (number of elements) should be schedule each phase. Unfortunately window size depends on the shadow size, and changes as inserts or deletes are performed on the tree. Since it is not evident a priori how to choose this window size, we have chosen an adaptive strategy:

- The initial window size equal to some fraction of the input size.
- successive window sizes are chosen as the sum of the number of elements scheduled in the last two phases times some weighting factor.

In Table 3, the results of the adaptive is shown; note that effectively all of the parallelism can be achieved with low overhead (less than 3).

6 Conclusions

We have shown a promising technique for parallelizing a set of arbitrary ordered tree updates, under the very general condition that those tree updates are of a generic and widely applicable form. In particular:

- Arbitrary order operations on trees provide substantial parallelism increase over fixed order operations.
- By reducing parallelism it is possible to achieve executions which require close to one trial operation per node.
- A simple adaptive window-based algorithms achieves high parallelism with small overhead.

Acknowledgements The authors gratefully acknowledge the comments of the referees and Jerry Stamatopoulos.

References

[ACG86]   S. Ahuja, N. Carriero, and David Gelertner. Linda and friends. *Computer*, 19(8):26–34, August, 1986.

[AHU75]   A. V. Aho, J. E. Hopcroft, and J. D. Ullman. *The design and analysis of computer algorithms*. Addison-Wesley, Reading, Mass., 1975.

[CRRH93]   Martin C. Carlisle, Ann Rogers, John H. Reppy, and Laurie J. Hendren. Early experiences with olden. In Uptal Banerjee, David Gelernter, Alex Nicolau, and David Padua, editors, *Languages and Compilers for Parallel Computing*, pages 1–20. Spring-Verlag, 1993.

[CWZ90]   David R. Chase, Mark Wegman, and F. K. Zadek. Analysis of pointers and structures. In *Programming Language Design and Implementation*, pages 296–310. ACM, June 1990.

[Har92]   W. Ludwell Harrison. Generalized iteration space and the parallelization of symbolic languages. In Ian Foster and Evan Tick, editors, *Workshop on Computation of Symbolic Languages for Parallel Computers*. Argonne National Labs, October 1992.

[HHN92]   Laurie J. Hendren, Joseph Hummel, and Alexandru Nicolau. Abstraction for recursive pointer data structures: Improving the analysis and transformation of imperative languages. In *Programming Language Design and Implementation*, pages 249–260. ACM, June 1992.

[Kat86]   Morris J. Katz. Paratran: A transparent, transaction based runtime mechanism for the parallel execution of scheme. Master's thesis, MIT, June 1986. Masters Thesis.

[LH88]   James R. Larus and Paul N. Hilfinger. Detecting conflicts between structure accesses. In *SIGPLAN'88 Conference on Programming Language Design and Implementation*, pages 21–34, June 1988.

[SDDS86]   Jacob T. Schwartz, R. B. K. Dewar, E. Dubinsky, and E. Schonberg. *Programming with sets: an introduction to SETL*. Springer-Verlag, New York, New York, 1986. setl book.

[SMC91]   Joel H. Saltz, Ravi Mirchandaney, and Kay Crowley. Run-time parallelization and scheduling of loops. *IEEE Trans. on Computer*, 40(5):603–612, May 1991.

[Sol88]   Jon A. Solworth. Programming language constructs for highly parallel operations on lists. *The Journal of Supercomputing*, 2:331–347, 1988.

[Sol90]   Jon A. Solworth. The PARSEQ project: An interim report. In *Languages and Compilers for Parallel Computing*, pages 490—510. Pittman/MIT, 1990.

[Sol91]   Jon A. Solworth. On the performance of parallel lists. In *Advances in Languages and Compilers for Parallel Computing*, pages 152—171. Pittman/MIT, 1991.

[Sol92]   Jon A. Solworth. On the feasibility of dynamic partitioning of pointer based data structures. In *5th Workshop on Programming Languages and Compilers*, pages 82–96, August 1992.

[SR93]   Jon A. Solworth and Bryan Reagan. Arbitrary order operations on trees. In Uptal Banerjee, David Gelernter, Alex Nicolau, and David Padua, editors, *Workshop on Programming Languages and Compilers for Parallel Processing*, pages 21–36. Springer-Verlag, 1993.

[ST85]   Daniel Dominic Sleator and Robert Endre Tarjan. Self-adjusting binary search trees. *JACM*, pages 652–686, July 1985.

[Wol92]   Michael Wolfe. Doany: Not just another parallel loop. In *5th Workshop on Programming Languages and Compilers*, pages 421–433, August 1992.

Autoscheduling in a Distributed Shared-Memory Environment *

José E. Moreira   Constantine D. Polychronopoulos

{moreira,cdp}@csrd.uiuc.edu
Center for Supercomputing Research and Development
and Coordinated Science Laboratory
University of Illinois at Urbana-Champaign
1308 W. Main St.
Urbana, IL 61801-2307 – USA

Abstract. The ease of programming and compiling for the shared memory multiprocessor model, coupled with the scalability and cost advantages of distributed memory computers, give an obvious appeal to distributed shared memory architectures. In this paper we discuss the design and implementation issues of a dynamic data management and scheduling environment for distributed shared memory architectures. In contrast to the predominantly static approaches used on distributed and message passing machines, we advocate the advantages of dynamic resource allocation, especially in the case of multi-user environments. We propose hybrid data and work distribution techniques that adjust to variations in the physical partition and achieve better load balance than purely static schemes. We present the architecture of our execution environment and discuss implementation details of some of the critical components. Preliminary results using benchmarks of representative execution profiles support our main thesis: With minimal control, the load balancing and resource utilization advantages offered by dynamic methods often outweigh the disadvantage of increased memory latency stemming from slightly compromised data locality, and perhaps additional run-time overhead.

1 Introduction

The distributed shared memory model has been the architecture of choice of the majority of the latest high-performance computers, such as the Cray T3D and the Convex Exemplar. The distributed shared memory architecture offers the programming and compiling advantages of shared memory, and at the same time, the scalability and cost advantages of distributed memory architectures. By virtue of being the successors to shared memory and distributed memory (or more precisely message-passing) architectures, distributed shared memory (or DSM) machines have also inherited some of the programming methodologies and architectural features of their predecessors. The indisputable importance of data locality has favored static approaches to data placement and scheduling on DSM machines, just like it did on earlier generation message-passing

---

* This work was supported by the Office of Naval Research under grant N00014-94-1-0234.

machines. Thus far, this has also been the underlying guide in the design of HPF[10], Fortran D[5], and to a lesser degree of the Cray MPP Fortran[19].

In this paper we give preliminary evidence of the importance of dynamic solutions to the data management and scheduling problems. We present the architecture of distributed autoscheduling, a dynamic environment for DSM adopted from our previous work on uniform access shared memory environments. We argue that dynamic methods can achieve better load balance, and improve resource utilization (especially in multi-user environments), while they can still exploit data locality. In addition to the performance advantages, dynamic environments can deal more effectively with hardware failures; they can also take advantage of unexpected changes in the availability of resources (processors) which is common in multiprogramming environments.

The distributed autoscheduling model borrows many of the characteristics of autoscheduling, which has been the subject of some of our recent work [6, 7, 15]. We assume that like autoscheduling a user application is decomposed² into a collection of well-defined subcomputations (tasks). During execution, the firing of tasks is performed dynamically by means of compiler generated code, which enforces data and control dependences. A ready-task queue is used to enqueue executable tasks; idle processors allocated to an address space repeatedly dispatch and execute tasks from the queue.

The major aspect of our new model is incorporation of capabilities for exploiting data locality while preserving dynamic scheduling and load balancing. This paper is organized as follows: Section 2 describes our target machine architecture and our program model. Section 3 describes the architecture of the run-time system that implements autoscheduling in a shared-memory multiprocessor. Data and load distribution issues are addressed in Section 4. The storage of data structures in distributed autoscheduling is described in Section 5 and the task queue in Section 6. Parallel loops are discussed in Section 7. Experimental results are presented in Section 8, related work is discussed in Section 9, and concluding remarks are given in Section 10.

2 Machine and Program Model

We consider specifically as target architecture a multiprocessor machine with a shared virtual and physical address space, built with commercial microprocessors. The global physical memory is divided into *modules*, and each module is connected to one particular processor. A processor can access its memory module faster than that of another processor, thus creating a nonuniform memory. All the processors assigned to a process use the same virtual to physical mapping, so a virtual address always corresponds to the same physical address.

The program model for autoscheduling is the *hierarchical task graph* (HTG), an intermediate program representation that encapsulates data and control dependences at various granularity levels, and from which autoscheduling code is generated. It represents a program in a hierarchical structure, thus facilitating task-granularity control. Information on control and data dependences allows the exploitation of functional (task

---

² Partitioning into tasks can be done by a parallelizing compiler or supported by programming language features.

level) parallelism in addition to data (loop level) parallelism. A brief summary of the properties of the HTG is given here, and details can be found in [2, 6, 14, 21].

The hierarchical task graph is a directed acyclic graph $HTG = (HV, HE)$ with unique nodes START and STOP $\in HV$, the set of vertices. Its edges, HE, are a union of control (HC) and data dependence (HD) arcs: $HE = HC \cup HD$. The nodes represent tasks of a program and can be of three types: *simple, compound,* and *loop.* A simple node represents the smallest schedulable unit of computation. A compound node is recursively defined as an HTG and is therefore composed by smaller nodes. A loop node represents a task that is either a serial loop (all iterations must be executed in order) or a parallel loop (the iterations can be executed simultaneously in any order). The body of a loop can be an HTG. An HTG may have local variables, which can be accessed by any task in the HTG, and in the general model each task can have task-local variables, which are internal to the task.

Each HTG is associated with a set of boolean flags (local variables) that mark the execution of nodes and arcs in the HTG. Also, each node is associated with an *execution tag*: an expression on the boolean flags that is derived from the data and control dependences and represents the execution condition for that node. Let $\varepsilon(x)$ denote the execution tag of node x. Whenever the values of the boolean flags cause $\varepsilon(x)$ to evaluate to TRUE, node x has been *enabled* and is ready to execute. The execution of an HTG starts with its START node, and therefore $\varepsilon(\text{START}) = \text{TRUE}$. The execution terminates when the STOP node is executed.

3 General Architecture of the Run-Time System

The execution environment of an autoscheduling program consists of the code and data area, defining an address space, a (time-variant) set of $n(t)$ physical processors assigned to that address space, a *task ready queue*, and a *cactus-stack* [20]. Using conventional terminology, an executing program is a *process*.

The set of processors $n(t)$ assigned to a process at time t is called a *partition* and is controlled by the operating system, which distributes the available processors in a machine to the processes. Scheduling policies at the OS level are beyond the scope of this paper and will not be discussed further.

The *task ready queue* is a (user space) data structure that holds *task identifiers* of the ready tasks. A task identifier contains task-specific information, including the starting address of the task and a pointer to context information, such as the *activation frame* of the task. Each processor allocated to a process executes a loop of the following type:

```
do
        get task from task queue
        execute task
forever
```

When a task completes execution, its *drive code* injected by the compiler evaluates the execution tags $\varepsilon(x)$ of the affected tasks and the new ready tasks are inserted in the queue; this is the basic scheduling operation. The execution of a program begins with its START task in the ready queue and terminates when its STOP task finishes.

The *activation frames* of a parallel program cannot be implemented with the simple stack structure normally used in sequential programs, since several instances of subroutines and loop iterations can be active at the same time. Instead, a *cactus-stack*, equivalent to a (dynamic) tree of activation frames, is used. All data structures reside in shared memory, and all activation frames are organized in the cactus-stack. Stacks are not associated with processors. The only information processors need in order to execute a task is the beginning address of the code and the base address of the activation frame. Therefore, any processor can execute any task, and switching between tasks involves only loading the code pointer and frame pointer in the appropriate registers.

The drive code injected by the compiler before and after each task node in the HTG take the form of *entry* and *exit* blocks respectively. The major functions of the entry and exit blocks are as follows:

ENTRY Blocks
- Allocate private activation frame
- Link to parent activation frame
- Execute initialization code
- Loop scheduling policy
- Granularity control

EXIT Blocks
- Barrier synchronization
- Update control & data dependences
- Testing of execution tags
- Queue ready tasks
- Granularity control

Granularity control, listed in both the entry and exit blocks, is a key feature of autoscheduling. It works by dynamically deciding which compound tasks are to be split into smaller tasks for parallel execution, and which are to be executed as serial code, in order to achieve a good balance between the number and size of parallel tasks. A parallel program must generate enough tasks to keep all the processors in its partition busy. However, as the number of tasks increases, so does the overhead for managing these tasks. By controlling the granularity of tasks, autoscheduling avoids the generation of unnecessary parallelism that cannot exploit any more processing power, but may add to the overhead.

Autoscheduling is a dynamic scheduling environment, adjusting the number and size of tasks generated by a process at run-time in order to better exploit the resources available to a process at any given time. When operating in multiprogrammed mode the resources of a multiprocessor must be divided among computing processes executing simultaneously. Ideally, the amount of resources that an individual process receives should be a function of the total workload on the machine. Programs written for fixed configurations of processors are not appropriate for execution in such dynamic environments. Autoscheduling uses the partition allocated to a process effectively and efficiently, and adjusts to variations in the partition, making multiprogramming in multiprocessors very efficient.

4 Data and Load Distribution

In a distributed shared memory machine with nonuniform memory access, the access to remote memory can be orders of magnitude slower than access to local memory. Therefore, it is important to distribute data and computations in such a manner that the computations performed by a processor involve mostly local memory accesses. In general, the higher the locality of access, the greater the performance. However, enforcing locality can degrade load balance, since the predefined distribution of work leaves less room for dynamic adjustments of load.

In order to preserve the main properties of autoscheduling that facilitate the efficient execution of simultaneous concurrent processes, we consider data distribution under the following constraints: (1) we assume that the partition assigned to a process is not known until run-time and is time-variant, and (2) load balance must be preserved. These goals are achieved through the following mechanism:

- Data are partitioned at compile time across sets of virtual processors defined by the user (or by a smart compiler), in a manner similar to HPF [10].
- Virtual processors are assigned on demand to physical processors during run-time. Virtual processors can migrate between physical processors during the execution of a process and may even, at times, not be assigned to any physical processor. The precise mechanism is discussed in Section 5.
- Data mapped to a virtual processor are allocated on demand in the local memory of the physical processor to which the virtual processor is assigned at the time of allocation. Data can also migrate from one processor to another on demand. The precise mechanism for data allocation and migration is also discussed in Section 5.
- Iterations of parallel loops and tasks can be mapped to virtual processors. This assignment is similar to a *hint* that these iterations and tasks should be executed in a particular virtual processor (most likely because they use mostly data local to the processor). These tasks and iterations can still be executed by any processor because the shared address space in autoscheduling allows any task to be executed in any processor.

Our approach to data distribution uses features from Fortran D [5], HPF [10], and Cray MPP Fortran [19]. In the description below, let the notation $X(Y_1, Y_2, \ldots, Y_n)$ denote an n-dimensional array with size Y_i in the i-th dimension. The valid indices along the i-th dimension are the integers $1, \ldots, Y_i$. The notation $X(y_1, y_2, \ldots, y_n)$ represents that particular element of X with index y_i along the i-th dimension, for $i = 1, \ldots, n$. Also, let H denote the set of physical processors in the machine. The data and load distribution is accomplished as follows:

1. The user defines one or more *virtual processor* arrays $V(P_1, P_2, \ldots, P_m)$. There is no implied relationship between a processor in array V_1 and a processor in another array V_2, even if both arrays have the same number of dimensions and the same sizes along each dimension. During execution, each virtual processor of a virtual processor array V is assigned to at most one physical processor at any given time t; but the physical processor can vary during execution. A physical processor may be assigned multiple virtual processors. The mapping $M : V \times t \rightarrow H$ represents this assignment of virtual to physical processors.

2. The user defines one or more *decompositions* $D(N_1, N_2, \ldots, N_n)$. A decomposition is an abstract problem domain that corresponds roughly to a *grid* where the data are placed and computations are performed (points in the grid correspond to points in the iteration space). For each decomposition D, the user defines a *distribution*

$T : D \rightarrow V$, which maps each element $D(j_1, j_2, \ldots, j_n)$ of a decomposition D to exactly one element $V(k_1, k_2, \ldots, k_m)$ of a virtual processor array V. Each decomposition can be associated with only one distribution at any given time; n and m are not necessarily equal.

Example (1): Consider the decompositions $D(100, 100, 10)$, with a total of 100,000 problem points. This decomposition can be mapped to a processor array $V(100, 100)$ in such a way that point $D(i, j, k)$ is mapped to processor $V(i, j)$; that is, all the elements with the same i and j are mapped to the same processor.

Example (2): Let $V(4, 4)$ be a two-dimensional virtual processor array (16 processors), and $D(100, 100)$ be a two-dimensional decomposition. A distribution

$$T : D(i, j) \rightarrow V(((i - 1)/15 \bmod 4) + 1, ((j - 1)/15 \bmod 4) + 1)$$

causes the mapping shown in Figure 1.

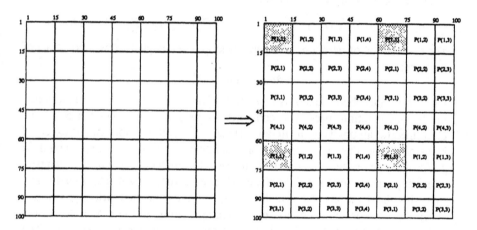

Fig. 1. Distribution of a decomposition $D(100, 100)$ across a processor array $P(4, 4)$ through the mapping $T : D(i, j) \rightarrow V(((i - 1)/15 \bmod 4) + 1, ((j - 1)/15 \bmod 4) + 1)$.

3. The user *aligns* array data structures of the form $R(S_1, S_2, \ldots, S_p)$ to a decomposition D using an *alignment* $L : R \rightarrow D$ which maps each data element $R(i_1, i_2, \ldots, i_p)$ of R to one or more points $D(j_1, j_2, \ldots, j_n)$ of D; p and n are not necessarily equal. An alignment maps a data point to a problem point in a decomposition, which in turn is mapped to a virtual processor. Each data element will be placed in the memory of the mapped virtual processor, but notice that the final mapping from virtual processor to physical processor is delayed until execution time. When an element $R(i_1, i_2, \ldots, i_p)$ is assigned to more than one point of D, this element is *replicated* in all the points to which it is assigned. All the copies of a data element are kept coherent.

Example (1): Let $R(100, 100)$ be an array of data elements, and $D(10, 10, 10)$ be a decomposition. Then defining the alignment L such that $R(i, j)$ is mapped to

$D((i-1)/10+1, (j-1)/10+1, 1 : 10)$ (the operator $/$ represents the quotient of integer division) has the effect of partitioning R into 10×10 blocks of size 10×10, and then replicating the entire block of data in 10 different sets of problem points. Each of the problem points $D(i, j, 1 : 10)$ gets the whole block of data $R((i-1)*10+1 : i*10, (j-1)*10+1 : j*10)$, and a change of R in one problem point is reflected in the other nine points in which the data are replicated.

Example (2): Let $X(100, 100)$, $Y(100, 100)$, and $Z(100, 100)$ be data array, and the computation

$$Z_\Delta = X_\Delta + Y_\Delta^T$$

is to be performed, where Z_Δ represents the lower triangular half of matrix Z (and correspondingly for matrices X and Y; Y is first transposed, and then the lower triangular left is selected). The iteration space is then a subset of decomposition $D(100, 100)$, and to avoid remote accesses it is desirable that elements $X(i, j)$, $Y(j, i)$, and $Z(i, j)$ be all mapped to the same decomposition point $D(i, j)$. This can be accomplished by the alignments

$$L_1 : X(i, j) \rightarrow D(i, j), \quad L_2 : Y(i, j) \rightarrow D(j, i), \quad L_3 : Z(i, j) \rightarrow D(i, j).$$

4. The distribution of iterations of a parallel loop is accomplished by a construct of the form:

doall E on D $\{\mathcal{B}\}$

where D is a distribution and E is a *space descriptor* that selects a subset of the points in D as the iteration space. This construct asserts that the computation $\mathcal{B}$ is to be performed for all points of the iteration space E, that all iterations can be executed in parallel, and that the iteration corresponding to $D(j_1, j_2, \ldots, j_n)$ should be *preferentially* executed by the virtual processor to which this point of D is mapped. In our implementation each of the physical processors cooperating in a loop starts by executing the iterations of E which are mapped to its assigned virtual processors. When a processor completes its set of iterations (from all the virtual processors mapped to it), it starts helping other active processors by *stealing* iterations. The execution of the **doall** terminates when all iterations in E are executed. This **doall** construct is similar to the Cray MPP Fortran construct, in which a perfect nest of DO loops is used to identify the iteration space, and the DOSHARED directive asserts that all iterations are independent and can be executed in parallel. In Cray MPP Fortran, however, the mapping is done directly through a distributed array (there are no decompositions), and the mapping is *binding*, in that an iteration assigned to processor i must execute on processor i.

Example : We represent space descriptors through *regular section descriptors* (RSDs) [12], which are sequences of triples $l_i : u_i : s_i$, where l_i, u_i, and s_i indicate the lower bound, upper bound, and step, respectively, along the i-th dimension of the RSD. We also allow the descriptor of index i to depend on the values of indices $1, \ldots, i-1$. The computation of $Z_\Delta = X_\Delta + Y_\Delta^T$ can thus be expressed by:

doall $(i, j) = (1 : 100, 1 : i)$ **on** D {
    $Z(i, j) = X(i, j) + Y(j, i)$
}

which specifies that the preferred location for the computation of $Z(i, j)$ is the physical processor assigned to the virtual processor to which $D(i, j)$ is mapped. If D is distributed as in Figure 1, then the iterations assigned to $P(1, 1)$ are the those in the shaded region in the lower triangular half of the decomposition.

5. Preferred locations for the execution of individual tasks can also be asserted, either through compiler analysis or directly by the user. The construct:

$$\textbf{task } x \textbf{ on } v \; \{T\}$$

asserts that task x, with body T, is to be preferentially executed on virtual processor v. This does not say anything about the subtasks of x, if it has any. Each task can have its own assertion, or none at all.

```
PARAMETER (N = 100)
PROCESSOR P(4,4)
DECOMPOSITION D(N,N)
DISTRIBUTE D(15,15) ONTO P
REAL X(N,N), Y(N,N), Z(N,N)
ALIGN X(I,J) WITH D(I,J)
ALIGN Z(I,J) WITH D(I,J)
ALIGN Y(I,J) WITH D(J,I)
DOALL (I,J) = (1:N,1:I) ON D
  Z(I,J) = X(I,J) + Y(J,I)
ENDDOALL
```

Fig. 2. Program to compute $Z_\Delta = X_\Delta + Y_\Delta^T$.

To illustrate some programming language issues we present the code to compute $Z_\Delta = X_\Delta + Y_\Delta^T$ in Figure 2. Two types of statements require more explanation:

1. The DISTRIBUTE statement: To simplify the code generation process and to avoid constructs that can cause a large run-time overhead, only block-cyclic distributions are allowed. The statement

$$\text{DISTRIBUTE } D(s_1, s_2, \ldots, s_n) \text{ ONTO } P$$

where D is a decomposition of dimension n, and P is a virtual processor array of dimension less than or equal to n tiles decomposition D with blocks of size $(s_1, s_2, \ldots, s_n)$ and then assigns the blocks cyclically along each dimension. An s_i equal to a "*" specifies that distribution is not to be performed along dimension i, effectively making the block size along dimension i equal to the decomposition size along this dimension. The statement

DISTRIBUTE D(15,15) ONTO P

implements the distribution shown in Figure 1.

2. The `ALIGN` statement: The alignment of data arrays to decompositions is accomplished through the construct:

$$\texttt{ALIGN } R(i_1, \ldots, i_p) \texttt{ WITH } D(f_1(i_1, \ldots, i_p), \ldots, f_n(i_1, \ldots, i_p))$$

where R is a p-dimensional data array, D is a n-dimensional decomposition, and the functions $f_1, f_2, \ldots, f_n$ specify the mapping between elements of R and points of D. There are restrictions on the form of these functions, in order to allow efficient implementation (basically, $f_j = \alpha + \beta i_k$, i.e., f_j is a linear expression on at most one of the indices, and α and β are coefficients independent of the indices).

5   Distribution of Activation Frames

Activation frames are created dynamically in virtual memory by three types of events:

1. *At program start:* The global data activation frame is created at this point. It often holds the largest data structures. This activation frame is shared by all the processors that join the execution of the program. It is deallocated when the program terminates.
2. *At function start:* When a function begins execution it is necessary, in general, to create an activation frame for its local variables. This activation frame is shared by all the processors that cooperate on the execution of that function. A function activation frame is deallocated when the function terminates.
3. *At parallel loop start:* Activation frames are also created for parallel loops with local variables. One activation frame is created for each physical processor participating in the execution of the loop[3]. When a processor terminates executing its share of the loop, it deallocates its own loop activation frame.

The basic requirement for the layout of an activation frame in virtual memory is that data mapped to different virtual processors must reside in separate virtual memory pages. This way, each virtual memory page is uniquely associated with a virtual processor. The physical layout of an activation frame is built during run time, together with the mappings M from virtual processor arrays to the physical processors.

The scheme works as follows: When a processor array V is defined, the mapping $M : V \times t \rightarrow H$ is empty, and when an activation frame is created, all its virtual pages are initially unmapped. Whenever a virtual page is accessed for the first time, a page fault occurs in the physical processor y that performed such access, which generates a *user space trap*, handled by a routine inserted by the compiler. The trap checks to which virtual processor $v \in V$ this page is mapped. If the page is not mapped to any virtual processor, because it contains non-distributed data, then a call to the operating system is made to allocate a physical frame for the virtual page in the local memory of processor y. If the page is mapped to virtual processor v, but v is not currently assigned to any physical processor, then an addition is made to M to assign v to physical processor

---

[3] One activation frame per processor is sufficient because in our execution model there can only be a maximum of P (number of physical processors) iterations of any given instance of a parallel loop under simultaneous execution.

y^4, and a call to the operating system is made to allocate a physical frame in the local memory of processor y. If the page is mapped to virtual processor v, and v is already assigned to a physical processor x, then a call to the operating system is made to allocate a physical frame in the local memory of processor x. Figure 3(a) is a flowchart of this mechanism.

If a page has to be swapped out of memory, then the (virtual $\rightarrow$ physical) memory mapping is updated to reflect that, and the next access to that page will cause a page fault; the same criteria as above will be used to determine where to load the page. If a physical processor has to leave a partition, then all the mappings between virtual processors and this physical processor have to be deleted. The virtual processors that lost this mapping will remain unassigned to any physical processor until an unmapped page associated with them is referenced.

The following illustrates a situation where there is data migration. Assume virtual processor v was mapped to physical processor x, which had n pages of v in its local memory. When processor x leaves the partition, v becomes unassigned, but the n pages of v remain in the local memory of x (Figure 3(b_1)). While the other processors in the partition reference only those n pages of v, and none of those pages are purged from the local memory of x, processor v remains unmapped. When a physical processor y references a page of v that was not part of those n pages, or that was purged out of x's local memory, then v is mapped to this processor y. From that point on, all pages of v that need to be allocated will be so in the local memory of processor y (Figure 3(b_2)). As the old pages in the local memory of p have to be purged to free space for the current computations in x, they will be reloaded in y, and the data will gradually migrate from x to y (Figure 3(b_3)). Alternatively, a wholesale migration of the data can be accomplished by simply purging all n pages out of x's local memory when this processor leaves the partition; this will cause v to be reassigned on the first access to some v data, and the data set will be reloaded on the new physical processor y according to demand.

6 The Distributed Task Queue

For a distributed shared memory MPP, a single task queue causes unacceptable contention, especially when task sizes are small, the number of processors is large, or both. A single queue also makes it difficult to select specific processors for the execution of each task, which is desirable when the code exhibits a high degree of data locality. The distributed queue scheme proposed here uses a two-level queue organization: one task queue per processor (*local* queue), and one additional task queue for the entire partition (the *central* queue). All queues reside in the shared address space, and any queue can be accessed by any processor in the partition. The enqueueing/dequeueing policies work as follows:

 – *Dequeueing:* A processor always tries to dequeue tasks first from its local queue. If its local queue is empty, then it tries to dequeue from the central queue. Only if

---

[4] The central issue of this scheme is that assignments of virtual processors to physical processors are done on demand. Instead of assigning the virtual processor to the physical processor where the fault occurred, alternative policies such as round robin and least loaded processor can also be used.

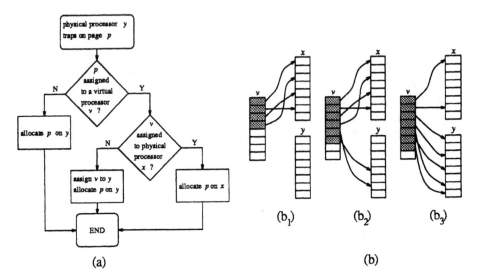

Fig. 3. (a) Flowchart for the mechanism that assigns virtual to physical processors. (b) Migration of data assigned to virtual processor v from physical processor x to physical processor y. (b₁) Originally, v is mapped to x and all the data assigned to v are stored in x. (b₂) v is reassigned to y, old data remain in x but new data are allocated in y. (b₃) As time passes, old data are purged from x and reassigned to y.

---

the central queue is empty will a processor then start searching for tasks from other processor queues.

- *Enqueueing:* When a task is enabled by an exit block executing in a given processor, it can be queued in the local queue of the corresponding processor, in the central queue, or in any other processor local queue. The criteria used to decide where to queue the tasks are the following, applied in the order enumerated:

  1. If the compiler has identified a preferential virtual processor for the execution of this task, either by analysis or through language constructs, and this virtual processor is assigned to a physical processor, then the task is enqueued in the local queue of the physical processor. If the virtual processor in unassigned, then the task is placed in the central queue.

  2. If the task is *large*[5] and has no preferential virtual processor to execute, then it is placed in the central queue. The extra overhead of enqueueing and dequeueing from the central queue is less significant in this case.

  3. If the task has no preferential virtual processor to execute and it is *small*, it is enqueued in the processor local queue, unless this queue is full, in which case it is enqueued in the central queue.

---

[5] A threshold size that differentiates between large and small tasks can be computed using machine-specific parameters and other criteria, such as overhead for remote task enqueueing and dequeueing.

When a physical processor is forced to leave a partition, it must transfer the tasks in its queue to the central queue, including the continuation of the task that was suspended, (if the processor was interrupted in the middle of a task). All virtual processors assigned to this physical processor become unassigned, and the virtual processors may be assigned to new physical processor(s). The data that were already mapped to the processor local memory remain there, but new data are allocated on the new processors, as are tasks directed to the virtual processors.

When a new processor joins a partition, its queue is empty, and it starts fetching tasks from the central queue. It will eventually build its own queue of tasks and can start fetching from there. Also, it may be assigned one or more virtual processors, in which case it will receive tasks associated with these virtual processors.

7 Execution of DOALLs

Consider the parallel loop:

doall $(E = (e_1, e_2, \ldots, e_n))$ **on** D $\{\ \mathcal{B}\ \}$

where D is a decomposition mapped to processor array $V(P_1, P_2, \ldots, P_m)$, and E is the iteration space. This loop can be rewritten as:

$$
\begin{aligned}
&\textbf{doall } (p_1, p_2, \ldots, p_m) = (1 : P_1, 1 : P_2, \ldots, 1 : P_m)\ \{ \\
&\qquad \textbf{doall } (E' = (e_1', e_2', \ldots, e_n'))\ \{\ \mathcal{B}'\ \} \\
&\}
\end{aligned}
$$

where E' and $\mathcal{B}'$ are modified versions (semantically equivalent) of the iteration space and loop body, and $(1 : P_1, 1 : P_2, \ldots, 1 : P_m) \times E' = E$. The array references in $\mathcal{B}'$ must be modified to be functions of the new iteration indices $p_1, \ldots, p_m, e_1', \ldots, e_n'$.

The outer loop iterates over the space of virtual processors in array V, and iteration $(p_1, p_2, \ldots, p_m)$ is assigned to virtual processor $V(p_1, p_2, \ldots, p_m)$. The inner loop is local to each virtual processor. Each iteration of the outer loop is queued in the local task queue of the physical processor to which the corresponding virtual processor is assigned. If the virtual processor is not assigned at all, then the iteration is queued in the central queue, so that some physical processor can eventually dispatch it (thus also inheriting its corresponding virtual processor). Each iteration of the outer loop creates an inner loop. The task for the inner loop is queued in the local queue of the processor that was executing the corresponding iteration of the outer loop. This processor will then start fetching iterations from the inner loop, but other physical processors can also participate in its execution by fetching iterations from this inner loop[6]. A variety of loop scheduling policies can be used for the inner loop.

---

[6] This may happen when both the local queue of a physical processor and the central queue are empty.

8 Results

The experimental results presented here were obtained through simulation of the execution of high-level code in the autoscheduling environment described in the paper. The benchmark suite consists of five simple programs that illustrate the main advantages of dynamic scheduling over static, and a sixth program that demonstrates the benefits of exploiting functional parallelism in this environment. Each of the first five programs has some properties that allow the comparison between static and dynamic scheduling for different types of computation:

1. *Block matrix add:* regular and balanced computation, poor temporal cache locality (only benefit is from prefetching a cache line).
2. *Block matrix multiply:* regular and balanced computation, with good cache locality (both temporal and space).
3. *Block triangular matrix add:* regular but unbalanced computation, poor temporal cache locality.
4. *Block triangular matrix multiply:* regular but unbalanced computation, good cache locality.
5. *Life:* irregular and unbalanced, good cache locality.

Each of these programs uses three matrices: A, B, and C. Each matrix is of size $N \times N$ and blocked as a $p \times p$ matrix of blocks of size $m \times m$, where $N = mp$. The computations are performed on a linear array V of p virtual processors. A decomposition D of size $N \times N$ is used to control the assignment of array elements and iterations to the virtual processors. All the computations are performed by a two-dimensional **doall** loop, each iteration operating on one block. Elements $A(i, j)$, $B(i, j)$, and $C(i, j)$, and iteration (i, j) are all mapped to decomposition element $D(i, j)$. Decomposition D is distributed across the processor array in a block row manner; that is, $D(i, j)$ is mapped to virtual processor $V((i - 1)/m + 1)$, or correspondingly, $V(1)$ gets the first row of blocks, $V(2)$ the second, ..., $V(p)$ the last.

The *life* benchmark requires some explanation. This program uses *life* on a $p \times p$ grid to determine which computations are performed in each time step. For each time step, one iteration of life is performed, computing the value of a new grid, then for this time step, for all cells (x, y) of the grid that are alive, block $A(x, y)$ and $B(x, y)$ are multiplied to generate block $C(x, y)$. This is a very irregular and unbalanced computation, with great variation in the pattern of computations between time steps. The program is sequential in the time steps, but parallel within a time step. The number of time steps used is p.

The sixth program is a complex matrix multiply. Let X and Y be two square matrices with complex elements, and consider the computation $Z = XY$. Let $X = A + jB$ and $Y = C + jD$, then $Z = XY = (AC - BD) + j(BC + AD)$. The complex matrix multiply can be implemented as four independent real matrix multiplies followed by two real matrix adds. By using functional parallelism and performing all four multiplications concurrently, a four-fold improvement in exploitable parallelism is obtained as compared to the case where only the loop parallelism in each multiplication is exploited. The matrices are of size $N \times N$, blocked as before with blocks of size $m \times m$, and a linear array V of p virtual processors is used ($N = mp$). The matrix multiplication is parallelized along only one dimension, so the maximum loop parallelism available is p. The static scheme exploits only loop parallelism.

The results presented here are speedup curves with respect to the physical number of processors used in the execution of the programs. This number is kept constant during the entire execution. In both the static and the dynamic scheduling the virtual processors are first assigned cyclically to the physical processors, and time starts to count after this assignment. The difference in the dynamic scheduling is that a processor is allowed to *steal* iterations from virtual processors not assigned to it, whereas in static scheduling it will only execute those iterations mapped to virtual processors assigned to it.

In the simulations, execution time is computed by counting the work in arithmetic operations (1 time unit), memory reads (1 time unit for cache, 10 for local, 100 for remote), memory writes (1 time unit), and iteration fetches (in the case of dynamic scheduling only, 10 time units for local, 100 or 1000 for remote). Cache line size is 8 words, and a whole line is prefetched when a word is accessed. The cache in each processor is large enough to hold the entire problem set, so there are only cold misses.

In the following plots (Figures 4 to 9), the dashed line represents linear speedup. The bullets (•) represent static scheduling, the diamonds (◇) represent dynamic scheduling with a cost of 100 units for remote iteration fetch, and the stars (⋆) represent dynamic scheduling with a cost of 1000 units for remote iteration fetch. $N = 256$, $p = 32$, and $m = 8$, except for Figure 9, where $N = 64$, $p = 8$, and $m = 8$.

From Figure 4 it can be seen that for matrix addition, static scheduling performs mildly better than dynamic, except for some cases in which the load balancing is particularly bad because some physical processors get one virtual processor while others get two. It is also seen that dynamic scheduling with a remote iteration fetch cost of 100 time units is very competitive.

In Figure 5, for matrix multiplication, both cases of dynamic scheduling perform very similarly and are either almost equal to or better than static; this happens because of the large size of iterations.

For triangular matrix add (Figure 6), in which the cost of each iteration is small (approximately 400 time units), dynamic scheduling performs better than static when the cost of remote fetches is low (100 time units), but worse when this cost is high (1000 time units).

For triangular matrix multiply (Figure 7), which has larger iterations, the dynamic scheme is consistently better, and essentially insensitive to variations from 100 to 1000 time units in the cost of remote fetches.

Life (Figure 8) represents the case in which dynamic has the largest advantage over static scheduling. However, since the iteration size is not as large as in matrix multiply (here it is only a block multiply, instead of a block-row × block-column), there is a noticeable difference in performance between the two cases of dynamic scheduling, and between them and static.

For the complex matrix multiply (Figure 9), the static scheme can only exploit loop parallelism, so speedup saturates after 8 processors. But the dynamic schemes can also exploit functional parallelism, resulting in a maximum speedup 3.3 times greater.

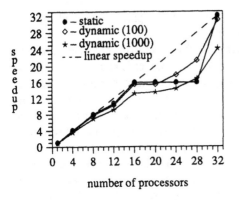

Fig. 4. Block matrix add.

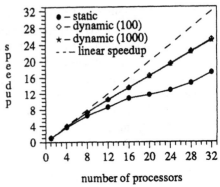

Fig. 7. Block triangular matrix multiply.

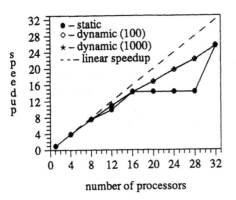

Fig. 5. Block matrix multiply.

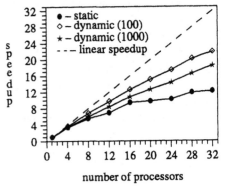

Fig. 8. Life.

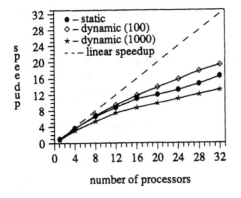

Fig. 6. Block triangular matrix add.

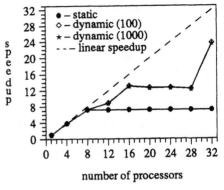

Fig. 9. Complex matrix multiply.

9 Related Work

For a survey of distributed shared memory architectures, see [17]. Detailed information on the architecture and programming model of the Cray T3D can be found in [4, 18, 19].

Examples of languages that support the specification of data distribution include Fortran D [5], Vienna Fortran 90 [1], High Performance Fortran [10, 13], and Cray MPP Fortran [19]. Compilation issues for these languages, including the actual implementation of the data distributions, code generation, and communication of distributed data across procedure boundaries, are discussed in [3, 9, 11, 12, 23].

Research is also being conducted on the field of automatic data partitioning techniques [8, 16]. In particular, [16] extends the HTG with information on data accesses, and from there derives data partitioning and processor assignment.

10 Conclusions

We have addressed many of the issues involved in the implementation of autoscheduling in a distributed shared-memory environment: data distribution, load distribution, task queue implementation, enqueueing and dequeueing policies, activation frame allocation, virtual to physical processor mapping, loop scheduling, and loop distribution. Our results demonstrate that a dynamic scheduling mechanism such as autoscheduling is very competitive with static scheduling for distributed shared-memory architectures. Autoscheduling supports multiprogramming in a multiprocessor very efficiently because processes can be executed on partitions of time-variant size, allowing a dynamic space partitioning of the resources across the simultaneously executing processes.

Acknowledgements

José E. Moreira has an appointment with the University of São Paulo, Brazil, and would like to thank the Fundação de Amparo à Pesquisa do Estado de São Paulo (FAPESP - São Paulo State Research Support Foundation).

References

1. Siegfried Benkner, Barbara M. Chapman, and Hans P. Zima. Vienna Fortran 90. In *Proceedings of the Scalable High Performance Computing Conference SHPCC-92*, pages 51–59, 1992.
2. Carl J. Beckmann. *Hardware and Software for Functional and Fine Grain Parallelism*. PhD thesis, Department of Electrical and Computer Engineering, University of Illinois at Urbana-Champaign, 1993.
3. Alok Choudhary, Geoffrey Fox, Sanjay Ranka, Seema Hiranandani, Ken Kennedy, Charles Koelbel, and Chau-Wen Tseng. Compiling Fortran 77D and 90D for MIMD distributed-memory machines. In *Proceedings of the Fourth Symposium on the Frontiers of Massively Parallel Computation*, pages 4–11, 1992.
4. Cray Research Inc. *CRAY T3D System Architecture Overview Manual*, 1994.
5. Geoffrey Fox, Seema Hiranandani, Ken Kennedy, Charles Koebel, Uli Kremer, Chau-Wen Tseng, and Min-You Wu. Fortran D language specification. Technical Report COMP TR90-141, Department of Computer Science, Rice University, December 1990.

6. M. Girkar and C. D. Polychronopoulos. The HTG: An intermediate representation for programs based on control and data dependences. Technical Report 1046, Center for Supercomputing Research and Development, University of Illinois at Urbana-Champaign, May 1991.

7. Milind Girkar and Constantine Polychronopoulos. Automatic detection and generation of unstructured parallelism in ordinary programs. *IEEE Transactions on Parallel and Distributed Systems*, 3(2), April 1992.

8. Manish Gupta and Prithviraj Banerjee. Demonstration of automatic data partitioning techniques for parallelizing compilers on multicomputers. *IEEE Transactions on Parallel and Distributed Systems*, 3(2):179–193, March 1992.

9. Mary W. Hall, Seema Hiranandani, Ken Kennedy, and Chau-Wen Tseng. Interprocedural compilation of Fortran D for MIMD distributed memory machines. In *Proceedings of Supercomputing'92*, pages 522–534, 1992.

10. High Performance Fortran Forum. *High Performance Fortran Language Specification, Version 1.0*, May 1993.

11. Seema Hiranandani, Ken Kennedy, and Chau-Wen Tseng. Compiler support for machine-independent parallel programming in Fortran D. Technical Report COMP TR91-149, Department of Computer Science, Rice University, January 1991.

12. Seema Hiranandani, Ken Kennedy, and Chau-Wen Tseng. Compiling Fortran D for MIMD distributed-memory machines. *Communications of the ACM*, 35(8):66–80, August 1992.

13. David B. Loveman. High Performance Fortran. *IEEE Parallel & Distributed Technology*, 1(1):24–42, February 1993.

14. Milind Girkar. *Functional Parallelism: Theoretical Foundations and Implementation*. PhD thesis, Department of Computer Science, University of Illinois at Urbana-Champaign, 1992.

15. José E. Moreira and Constantine D. Polychronopoulos. On the implementation and effectiveness of autoscheduling. Technical Report 1372, Center for Supercomputing Research and Development, University of Illinois, 1994.

16. Tsuneo Nakanishi, Kazuki Joe, Hideki Saito, Constantine Polychronopoulos, Akira Fukuda, and Keijiro Araki. The data partitioning graph: Extending data and control dependencies for data partitioning. In *Proceedings of the Seventh Annual Workshop on Languages and Compilers for Parallel Computing. Ithaca, NY*, 1994.

17. Bill Nitzberg and Virginia Lo. Distributed shared memory: A survey of issues and algorithms. *IEEE Computer*, 24(9), August 1991.

18. Wilfried Oed. The Cray Research Massively Parallel Processor System – CRAY T3D. Technical report, Cray Research GmbH, November 1993.

19. Douglas M. Pase, Tom MacDonald, and Andrew Meltzer. MPP Fortran programming model. Technical report, Cray Research, Inc., March 1994.

20. Per Stenström. VLSI Support for Cactus Stack Oriented Memory Organization. In *Proceedings of the 21st Annual Hawaii International Conference on System Sciences, vol I.*, pages 211–220, 1988.

21. Constantine D. Polychronopoulos. Autoscheduling: Control flow and data flow come together. Technical Report 1058, Center for Supercomputing Research and Development, University of Illinois at Urbana-Champaign, 1990.

22. Ravi Ponnusamy, Joel Saltz, Raja Das, Charles Koebel, and Alok Choudhary. A runtime data mapping scheme for irregular problems. In *Proceedings of the Scalable High Performance Computing Conference SHPCC-92*, pages 216–219, 1992.

23. Hans P. Zima and Barbara Mary Chapman. Compiling for distributed-memory systems. *Proceedings of the IEEE*, 81(2):264–287, February 1993.

Optimizing Array Distributions in Data-Parallel Programs

Krishna Kunchiṭhapadam   *Barton P. Miller*
krishna@cs.wisc.edu   bart@cs.wisc.edu

Computer Sciences Department
University of Wisconsin–Madison
1210 W. Dayton Street
Madison, WI 53706

Abstract

Data parallel programs are sensitive to the distribution of data across processor nodes. We formulate the reduction of inter-node communication as an optimization on a colored graph. We present a technique that records the run time inter-node communication caused by the movement of array data between nodes during execution and builds the colored graph, and provide a simple algorithm that optimizes the coloring of this graph to describe new data distributions that would result in less inter-node communication. From the distribution information, we write compiler pragmas to be used in the application program.

Using these techniques, we traced the execution of a real data-parallel application (written in CM Fortran) and collected the array access information. We computed new distributions that should provide an overall reduction in program execution time. However, compiler optimizations and poor interfaces between the compiler and runtime systems counteracted any potential benefit from the new data layouts. In this context, we provide a set of recommendations for compiler writers that we think are needed to both write efficient programs and to build the next generation of tools for parallel systems.

The techniques that we have developed form the basis for future work in monitoring array access patterns and generate on-the-fly redistributions of arrays.

This work is supported in part by Wright Laboratory Avionics Directorate, Air Force Material Command, USAF, under grant F33615-94-1-1525 (ARPA order no. B550), NSF Grants CCR-9100968 and CDA-9024618, Department of Energy Grant DE-FG02-93ER25176, and Office of Naval Research Grant N00014-89-J-1222. The U.S. Government is authorized to reproduce and distribute reprints for Governmental purposes notwithstanding any copyright notation thereon. The views and conclusions contained herein are those of the authors and should not be interpreted as necessarily representing the official policies or endorsements, either expressed or implied, of the Wright Laboratory Avionics Directorate or the U.S. Government.

1. INTRODUCTION

Parallel programming languages provide a programmer with abstractions tha ease the development of code. Data parallel programming languages [1] allow the programmer to reason about a single thread of control that executes in parallel on a large collection of data. The mechanisms of parallel execution, communication and synchronization are all handled automatically by the compiler; the details are hidden from the programmer. While the abstraction of these details can simplify the programmer's life, they can also obscure the cause of performance problems. Careless or naive array declarations or loop structures can cause poor performance, with no obvious explanation.

The performance of parallel programs is usually sensitive to the distribution of data amongst the processing nodes. For good performance, the programmer must choose an appropriate algorithm and a matching data distribution that minimizes communication. Figuring out optimal (or even acceptable) data distributions can be a non-trivial problem–except in the simplest cases.

Current data parallel languages [2-4] require the programmer to specify data distributions. Our goal is to help the programmer improve their data distributions so that their programs run faster. In this work, we monitor the execution of a parallel program and use this information to improve the array distributions. We present an approach based on the execution-time tracing and post-mortem analysis of a data-parallel CM Fortran program. We formulate the optimality criterion in terms of a novel graph-coloring problem and provide some simple techniques for approximating an optimal solution.

We experiment with these techniques on a real mechanical engineering application program running on our TMC CM-5. Starting with an unfamiliar application program and using only the information provided by our analyses, we were provided clear information for modifying the array distribution directives in the program. These modifications resulted in a 30% reduction in predicted communications (based on our weighted graph representation).

Actual performance improvements were prevented in part because the CM Fortran compiler generated code that counter-acted our distribution directives (we describe this in more detail in Section 5). We provide a set of recommendations for compiler writers that we think are important in allowing both programmers and tool builders to make the best use of parallel programming environments.

Our current analysis of array accesses is post-morten, but our goal is to be able to monitor and evaluate access patterns on-the-fly (while the program is running). In systems that support execution time data redistributions (such as described in the HPF specification [5]), programmers would be able to improve their array distributions automatically.

1.1. Data Distribution in Parallel programs

Almost all parallel programming environments require programmers to specify the distribution of their data structures across the target hardware. In message passing programs, the data distribution and access is explicit and under the control of the programmer. In a data parallel language, the compiler and runtime system provide a set of data distribution pragmas that describe the layout of parallel data structures. We develop our initial work in the context of parallel arrays.

Data distribution pragmas specify the details of the layout of a parallel array onto the nodes of a parallel machine. For example, CM Fortran (which we used in our study) provides block-structured layout pragmas. A language like Fortran-D [4] supports both block and cyclic layouts while the HPF language definition mentions arbitrary and dynamically changeable permutations of arrays.

Usually, a programmer chooses a simple data layout scheme or lets the compiler choose a default layout. However, it is easy to come up with examples where a default layout can result in poor performance.

Much of the current work on this problem has focused on static compiler analysis [6]. The compiler either tries to figure out a good distribution from the control and data flow graphs of a program or explores a small number of canonical distributions for suitable ones. Static analysis is not always able to determine good data distributions, especially for access patterns that are dependent on the input data. An execution-time approach like the one we suggest would be useful in such cases.

Ultimately, we envision a combination of both static and runtime analysis; with compiler analysis determining static access patterns and runtime analysis tracking those parts of the program that are not amenable to static analysis. In addition, static analysis may also provide a good starting point for the runtime analysis tools.

2. OPTIMIZING DATA DISTRIBUTION AS A GRAPH COLORING PROBLEM

We model the access patterns of a program execution as a colored graph. Each vertex of the graph represents a part of an array and the color of a vertex represents the current processing node to which this array part is assigned. Edges of the graph represent assignments of values arising from part of one or more arrays to part of another array (assuming an owner-computes [7] model). This notion is made more precise below. Our approach to finding good data distributions is based on graph coloring with a specific conservation property on the graph. Our approach also weights communication costs over computation costs.

Proximity Graph Definition:

We define a *proximity graph* $G = (V, E, W)$ as follows:

V is the set of vertices of the graph. Each vertex $v \in V$ has a name $n_v \in N$ and a color c_v. Each element of each unique parallel array in a program forms a vertex in the proximity graph. The name n_v of a vertex is the name of the array containing the data element v. N is the set of all variable names used by the application. The initial color of a vertex is the node to which the data element was assigned by the compiler. The number of colors used in the graph G corresponds to the number of nodes of the parallel machine executing the application.

E is the set of directed edges of the graph. Each edge $e = (u, v)$ has a source vertex u, a destination vertex v, and a weight w_e. An edge e between vertices u and v

in the graph corresponds to the fact that the data elements corresponding to u and v were used together in a computation in the parallel program. More precisely, all assignment statements in a program can be written as *lvalue=expression (rvaluelist)*. If we eliminate all temporary variables in the *rvalue* list, then the proximity graph for this statement will have an edge from each *rvalue* to the *lvalue*. An edge from u to v therefore indicates that the element corresponding to u was read and the element corresponding to v was written. The weight w_e of an edge from u to v represents the number of times u and v were used together (in the manner defined above) in the program.

W is the weight of the graph G and is defined as the sum of the weights of all edges e from u to v, such that $c_u \neq c_v$; only edges (or computation) between vertices of different colors (data elements located on different nodes of the parallel machine) contribute to the weight (communication cost). Computation involving data elements located on the same node does not contribute to the weight of the graph. ∎

Balance Conservation Property:

The colors of the vertices V satisfy the conservation property that, for each name $n \in N$, with $n_i = n_j$, the number of vertices with colors c_i and c_j are equal for all vertex pairs (i,j), i.e. there is a balanced distribution of array elements across the nodes of a parallel machine. This property is also important in stating the minimization criterion on the proximity graph. ∎

To perform optimizations on the data distributions, we define *balance preserving functions* that operate on G.

Balance Preserving Function:

We define a function F on graph G as follows:
$F(G) = (G')$, such that
1. $G = (V,E,W)$ and $G' = (V',E,W')$,
2. For all $u,v \in V$, $u',v' \in V'$, $c_u = c_{v'}$ and $c_v = c_{u'}$,
3. $n_u = n_{u'} = n_v = n_{v'}$. ∎

In other words, the function F exchanges the colors of two vertices u and v (condition 2) iff they correspond to data elements of the same array (condition 3). Note that F preserves the balance conservation property of the graph. G' corresponds to a data distribution that is exactly like that of the original graph G, except that data elements corresponding to u and v have exchanged home nodes.

Given the above, the graph optimization problem would reach an ideal result when a sequence of applications of the function F to G produces $W(F^*(G)) = 0$; i.e., a sequence of color exchanges (data redistributions) that reduces the weight of the graph (communication costs) to zero. If such a sequence can be found, then the data distribution resulting from this sequence of applications of F to G will not lead to any communication during program execution and will therefore be optimal (assuming that computation costs are always negligible). In practice, we can hope only to find a sequence of color exchanges that minimizes the weight of the graph (since some communication may always be required).

We can now also motivate the need for a balance conservation property. If there were no restrictions on the number of vertices of a given color, then a trivial solution would assign the same color to all vertices; i.e. all parallel arrays are stored on one node, effectively reducing the application to a sequential one). Such a trivial coloring certainly has a zero communication cost, but is not interesting to parallel programmers. The balance conservation property is one way of ensuring a balanced data distribution onto the nodes of a parallel machine.

The proximity graph does not model any spatial or temporal locality in communication. If the compiler optimizes communication via block-transfers or caching, the optimization must be factored in when constructing the proximity graph.

3. THE STEPS IN OPTIMIZING ARRAY DISTRIBUTIONS

The problem of optimizing array distributions can be divided into three steps: (1) collecting dynamic array reference data to build the proximity graph, (2) computing a new (and better) array distribution by re-coloring the graph, and (3) converting the new distribution back to pragmas specifiable in the source language. We first describe some of the variations in each step, and then describe the variations that we have explored in our experiments.

Data Collection: Trace Granularity and Storage

Our model in Section 2 is based on counting the data movements between each pair of array elements referenced in a program statement. The basic trade-off is between post-mortem versus on-the-fly evaluation. The reference data could be collected by generating a trace record for each execution of a program statement; this collection of traces would be processed to construct the proximity graph. Alternatively, the data could be summarized as the program was executing; this would require a state space proportional to the number of pairs of array locations referenced during execution (potentially as large as the square of the program's total array space). The amount of primary memory needed for post-mortem tracing is simply the size of memory used to buffer the traces before they are written to secondary storage (or sent to another process for on-line reduction). If the traces are written directly to secondary storage, then secondary storage space requirements are proportional to the length of the program execution.

One technique for reducing the amount of data space needed by on-the-fly data collection is *data blocking*. Each array is divided into blocks and reference data is recorded in terms of the block in which an array location resides. Blocks could be formed by dividing an array into equal size rectangles. Data blocking also can reduce the size of secondary storage space needed for the post-mortem tracing. Regular patterns of access to an array will benefit from this technique. Irregular patterns, such as occur using index arrays (A(B(i))), could perform poorly using such a technique.

The granularity of trace data also has an impact on the size of the proximity graph. As the blocking factor is increased, the maximum number of possible edges (and vertices) in the graph decreases (as does the complexity of computing colorings). Data can be blocked at any time up to the moment of constructing a proximity graph, though if data is combined during instrumentation, the lost details cannot be recovered in the later stages.

Computing an Improved Distribution: Graph Coloring Algorithms

Once the array access data is collected, we use it to build a proximity graph and then use this graph to optimize array distributions. The initial coloring of vertices is based on the current assignment of array locations to processor nodes. Given an initial coloring, we evaluate the amount of inter-node communication caused by the coloring (array distribution) and compute a new coloring that attempts to reduce the amount of inter-node communication. The assumption is that reduced communication should result in improved program performance.

While computing the optimal coloring of the graph is NP-complete [8] there are many possible heuristics that we can use. Simple greedy algorithms are preferable because they are fast. Other possibilities include genetic algorithms [9], simulated annealing [10] and algorithms based on optimization problems [11]. The basic tradeoff is between the complexity of the algorithm and the quality of the solution. A simple, fast algorithm is more appropriate in the context of application steering.

Realizing a Distribution: Mapping a Coloring to Language Pragmas

The colorings produced by an optimization algorithm need to be expressed in terms of the data-distribution pragmas provided by the source language. It is possible that the pragmas of the source language are not powerful enough to express the data distribution patterns produced by the coloring.

Extracting a data distribution from a proximity graph is a form of pattern-matching; a formal description of the array distribution directives in the language would be matched against the proximity distribution.

A simpler approach would be to investigate a small number of array distribution specifications that we know are expressible in the source language. It is easy to compute the weight of a proximity graph based on a given distribution and compare it with the weight of the computed coloring. The enumerations that result in weights closest to the computed coloring are candidates for further investigation.

A third approach is to simply animate or visualize the data distributions produced by the graph coloring algorithm [12]. The programmer may be able to identify global patterns in a picture and map them to a array distribution pragma; block and cyclic distribution patterns may be especially easy to recognize in this manner. We expect that a practical tool would use some combination of the above techniques.

If the data access patterns of an application do not depend either on the problem size or on the degree of parallelism, we can construct a detailed proximity graph for a small problem running on a small number of nodes and use powerful optimization techniques to come up with good solutions to both the graph coloring and the distribution-to-pragma mapping problems. The cost of a detailed analysis can then be amortized over a large number of runs of the application on large data sets.

Carefully chosen training data-sets will also help in finding distributions that work well for most large-scale executions of the application.

4. RESULTS

4.1. The Experimental Testbed

To experiment with some of the ideas that we described in the previous section, we chose a mechanical engineering application written in CM Fortran. The application, DRBEM (Dual Reciprocity Boundary Element Method), was written by members of our Mechanical Engineering Department; therefore, we did not use any knowledge of the semantics of the program in any of our studies. The application was 2,200 lines long, distributed among 18 source files.

DRBEM is a non-linear solution technique used for heat-transfer and vibration analysis applications. The technique allows non-linearities to be solved as boundary integral problems. Like other boundary element methods, it relies on Green's theorem to reduce a two-dimensional area problem into a one-dimensional line integral. The line-integral is then solved by discretizing and solvings sets of linear equations.

The application program reads in initial conditions from a file, sets up a system of linear equations, solves the equations for a series of time steps and finally writes the results to a file.

The sequence of viscous dissipation and convection computation, transient effect *curing* and linear-systems solution is repeated a large number of times (200 in our case) to obtain convergence. Therefore, even small array sizes have a significant impact on the execution time of the program. For example, array sizes of 100×100 result in an execution time of over a minute, while a full-scale run with arrays of sizes 1000×1000 take over an hour to complete.

To trace access to individual array elements, we hand-instrumented the program to write out array geometry and data access information to files. Hand-instrumentation is tedious, but was used only for this initial study. With the availability of def/use information from the compiler, the instrumentation step is straight-forward to automate. Ultimately, we expect to use binary rewriting [13] or dynamic instrumentation [14].

All program versions were run on a 32-node partition of a CM-5 computer (without using the vector units). The applications were compiled with CM Fortran (version 2.1.1-2) with optimization enabled. The trace data collected from the instrumented runs was used to build our proximity graph.

4.2. Our Investigations

In this section, we describe our algorithms and experiments, which cover a small subset of the different possibilities enumerated in Section 3.

Data Collection: Trace Granularity and Storage

In our experiments, we studied a single problem size–one involving arrays of size 32×32. This was done to keep the volume of trace data small. The application program was instrumented to trace all data accesses and a post-mortem filter used to vary trace granularity. The advantage of this approach was that we could use data collected from a single run of the application many times.

For this problem size, we constructed proximity graphs based on the following trace granularities: (1) full tracing (2) tracing assuming a blocking factor of 2×2, 1×4, and 4×1 (3) tracing assuming a blocking factor of 4×4, 1×16, and 16×1.

Computing an Improved Distribution: Graph Coloring Algorithms

To compute a better coloring of the proximity graphs constructed in the previous step, we used a simple greedy algorithm. Our coloring algorithm was written to be as fast as possible. Its heuristic is very similar to a restricted version of the Kernighan-Lin [15] optimization algorithm; we examine only 2-neighbors while the Kernighan-Lin algorithm examines arbitrary n-neighbors.

Realizing a Distribution: Mapping a Coloring to Language Pragmas

To map the distribution given by the optimized proximity graphs, we used a simple visualization approach to assist the programmer in identifying regular patterns in the distributions.

In our experiments, a set of scripts extract the coloring information for arrays that were redistributed by the coloring algorithm and plot a picture of the original and modified distributions. We were able to immediately identify both the nature of the redistributions and the pragmas that could be used to specify the new distributions from looking at these pictures.

4.3. Evaluating the Tracing, Coloring and Remapping Steps

Our experiments report the difference in the weights of the proximity graphs for the default distribution and the distribution produced by the coloring algorithm. The reduction in the weights of the graphs is an upper bound on the reduction in execution times of the application–for a given coloring algorithm.

The first set of results shows the behavior of our graph coloring algorithm with variation in the tracing granularity. The metric used for evaluating the coloring algorithm is the reduction in the weight of the graph. In an ideal scenario, a reduction in graph weight should manifest as a reduction in execution time for the new distribution. The second set of results present the nature of the new distributions that were obtained from the coloring algorithm. For this step, we used a collection of scripts that would draw pictures of an array before and after the coloring (using different screen colors for different graph colors); here we were looking for simple and easy-to-identify patterns.

4.4. Evaluating the Coloring Algorithm

Table 1 summarizes the performance of our greedy graph coloring algorithm. The first column represents the trace granularity; a trace block size of $m \times n$ means that all array elements within rectangular blocks of dimensions $m \times n$ are represented by a single vertex in the proximity graph. A larger value for m and n results in the corresponding proximity graph having a smaller number of vertices and edges. The second column indicates the size of the proximity graph (as $|V|$, and $|E|$, where V and E are the vertex and edge sets of the proximity graph. The third, fourth and last columns show the initial weight of the graph, the weight after using our greedy coloring algorithm, and the percentage change in graph weights.

Block Size	Graph Size		Initial Weight	Final Weight	Change
	$|V|$	$|E|$			
1×1	32,032	293,930	502,941	354,773	-29.5%
2×2	14,496	43,031	485,850	342,820	-29.4%
1×4	23,392	63,770	496,442	351,292	-29.2%
4×1	10,208	54,468	490,219	456,897	-6.8%
4×4	7,904	8,105	454,257	320,611	-29.4%
1×16	20,512	22,421	454,458	319,896	-29.6%
16×1	4,256	13,617	424,195	419,428	-1.1%

Table 1: Proximity Graph Data for DRBEM.

The results in Table 1 are grouped into three sets of rows. Each set represents a different number of array locations represented by a vertex in the proximity graph; the first row (1×1) has one element per vertex, the second set of rows has four elements per vertex, and the last set has 16 elements per vertex.

The execution time of the algorithm is (obviously) sensitive to the number of edges in the proximity graph. There is about an order of magnitude reduction in the running times from one granularity group to the next, as the blocking factor is increased.

It is interesting to note that except for the case of the $m \times 1$ blocking, all the other granularities for blocking trace data do not seem to perturb the coloring algorithm; the reduction in the weight of the proximity graph is the same. The differences between the original and new distributions also did not show any qualitative variation with the different blocking factors.

The default distribution that was chosen by the compiler was a column-major ordering of the arrays. Since the $m \times 1$ blocking treats elements of different columns (and hence different initial colors) as being identical, it loses some essential information and produces a poor proximity graph. The $m \times n$ and $1 \times n$ blocking heuristics both reduce trace sizes and preserve the initial distribution patterns and thus lead to more accurate proximity graphs.

Based on mapping information collected during the tracing of the application, we were able to tell which of the arrays of the application were redistributed[†], namely: drm_temp:s, drm_temp:scopy, drm_temp:dfx, and drm_temp:dfy. We discuss only changes made to two-dimensional arrays; the redistributions of vectors were not significant.

4.5. Visualizing the Array Redistributions

To get an intuitive feel for how the coloring algorithm redistributed the above mentioned arrays, we extracted the geometry information of the arrays from the original traces and from the new distributions. We then displayed this information as a picture of the two distributions using different screen colors for different graph colors.

For the 1×1 blocking, the redistribution of the arrays `drm_temp:s` and `drm_temp:scopy` was immediately apparent. The CM Fortran compiler had allocated these two arrays by co-locating elements along the column while our coloring algorithm had co-located elements along the rows. Figure 1 shows the redistribution suggested by the coloring algorithm. The *rotation* of the original picture into the new one was unmistakable.

Original distribution   *Optimized distribution*
of array drm_temp:s   *of array drm_temp:s*

Figure 1. Redistribution of array drm_temp:s

For granularities of 2×2 and 4×4, this *rotation* of the axis was equally apparent. However, for the $1 \times n$ and $m \times 1$ blocks, the pictures did not provide any insight into the new distribution or the way in which it differed from the original. It is possible that the arrays at which we were looking were too small for such blocking geometries to be useful. It is also interesting that the $1 \times n$ blockings not only provided no visual insight into the redistribution of the arrays but performed no better than the $n \times n$ blockings with respect to the graph colorings.

The pictures for the remaining two arrays `drm_temp:dfx` and `drm_temp:dfy` were similar to each other but not as striking as those for the previous two arrays. Once again, the compiler had originally allocated these arrays

---

† The names are of the form `function_name:array_name`.

by co-locating elements along the column. In the new distribution, each of these arrays showed a wavefront pattern of distribution in the bottom right of the arrays (higher values of the row and column indices). The original and optimized distributions are shown in Figure 2.

Original distribution
of array drm_temp:dfx

Optimized distribution
of array drm_temp:dfx

Figure 2. Redistribution of array drm_temp:dfx

When we examined the code that used the arrays `drm_temp:dfx` and `drm_temp:dfy` in detail, we found that the arrays were involved in only two kinds of operations: transposition and vector-matrix multiplication. The transposition causes a wavefront to appear in the optimized distribution. The interaction between the vector-matrix multiplication and the transposition pushes the origin of the wavefront to the observed position. Finally, the balance conservation property of our coloring algorithm causes the breakup of the wavefronts as they get larger. Since matrix transposition is a common operation in scientific code, we feel that compilers will need to be able to support data distributions that allow efficient transpose operations to be performed on arrays.

4.6. Evaluating the effect of Redistributions

Based on the observations we made in the previous section, We modified the distribution of arrays `drm_temp:s` and `drm_temp:scopy` using the pragmas provided by CM Fortran. It was impossible to redistribute the other two arrays as indicated by the coloring without a language that supported arbitrary distribution primitives (like HPF). We rebuilt the application program with the geometries of the two arrays modified to favor co-location of elements along rows. Even though the geometry modifications we specified were close to optimal (within 1%), they had no discernible effect on the execution times of the application. The next section discusses reasons for the absence of performance improvements.

5. THE USER VS. THE COMPILER

5.1. Initial Results

We were initially encouraged to see a significant reduction in the weight of the proximity graph for the application. We expected to see the same (or comparable) reduction in execution time. However, the redistributions we specified did not change the runtime at all..

The CM Fortran compiler provides an interface to a few inquiry functions in the CM runtime system †. We used an array geometry description function to see if the arrays were being redistributed according to our new specifications. It turned out that the compiler was ignoring our distributions and using the default layout.

We tried a number of different distribution directives to get the compiler to generate the exact distribution we wanted but the CM Fortran compiler seemed to show a propensity for column-major distributions (while we wanted row-major distributions for our arrays). In the end we were only able to get the compiler to layout the arrays in N-row x M-column blocks, where N < M (but N is never equal to 1, which is what we wanted).

When we ran the applications with these somewhat sub-optimal distributions, we still expected a decrease in runtime. However, there was either no change or a very slight increase in runtimes.

Using a compiler option, we then examined the names of communication functions and points in the code where they were called. It turned out that in each case where the specified distribution was in any way different from the default distribution, the compiler had inserted runtime system functions to redistribute these arrays into the canonical form before performing a parallel operation (and functions to redistribute any results back to the distribution specified by us). In essence, the compiler was undoing any possible optimizations that we specified.

5.2. Testing Simple Kernels: Matrix Multiplication

Since our application program was fairly complex with many interactions between different arrays, we started to work with small kernels to better understand the compiler.

Matrix multiplication is a simple kernel for which we knew the optimal data distribution. We wrote parallel versions of the kernel (using the intrinsic `matmul` and `dotproduct` functions). In each case, we varied the distribution of the source and destination arrays involved in the computation.

Once again, we noted that in each case where our distributions were different from the default ones, the compiler had generated code to redistribute the arrays into a canonical form.

---

† For example, a CM Fortran application can use these functions to determine/print the size and geometry of an array.

CM Fortran does not generate parallel code unless the programmer uses parallel constructs or intrinsic functions. However, using these constructs or intrinsic functions constrains the programmer to use the canonical distribution, even though this distribution may be sub-optimal for the operation involved.

Moreover, for operations like matrix multiplication even the canonical distribution requires individual node-to-node communication. However, this communication is hidden within the runtime system. Even when the programmer specifies an optimal distribution, the compiler undoes the optimization to conform to the runtime system interface, and runtime system then re-redistributes the operands back into a more optimal configuration. Needless to say, it is better not to have redundant data moves in the first place.

5.3. Recommendations for Compiler support

Our experience is based on one compiler and runtime system on a small collection of programs. However, we would like to make the following general recommendations to parallel-compiler writers.

- The compiler should trust the programmer's data distributions, even if they are different from canonical ones. We found it very difficult to get the compiler to accept our data layout, let alone generate efficient code for it.

- A corollary to the previous recommendation is that in every case of automated analysis that a compiler makes on an application, it must provide manual interfaces of comparable quality so that knowledgeable programmers can perform the optimizations most appropriate to their code.

- The interface between the compiler and runtime system should be made either broader (e.g., the runtime system should provide different matrix multiplication clones, each best suited for certain combinations of operand layout) or narrower (e.g., the runtime system provides a single matrix multiplication function that is guaranteed to work with operands of all distributions, without the need for the compiler to specify data movements). With the current interface, neither the compiler nor the runtime system can make optimizations with the guarantee that they will not be undone by the other.

The above recommendations are of paramount importance if programmers are to get any benefit from using different kinds of data distribution pragmas. Strategies such as the one used in CM Fortran make data distribution pragmas redundant.

In addition, we would like compiler writers to provide tool builders with detailed information on compile-time analysis. Many of the problems we faced were specific to CM Fortran, but unless all compilers provide a reasonable amount of information, tool builders will not be able to write their tools.

- The compiler must use a consistent internal namespace to identify parallel data objects. For example, the CM Fortran compiler uses descriptors to identify arrays, but the meaning of a descriptor is different depending on whether the associated array is a parameter to a subroutine or is a local. There should be a one-to-one mapping between descriptors and array data.

- The compiler should also provide a mapping of descriptor names to source level names. Currently tools use ad hoc techniques to present results to the programmer in a usable form.

- We used source-level instrumentation in our study since no other way to get information on array references. If compilers provided a summary of the dependence analysis (in the form of def-use points in the code), tool builders would be able to use either binary rewriting or runtime instrumentation on the programs. Not only is this approach simpler than source instrumentation (or compiler modification), it allows tool writers to experiment with more programs–it is easier to obtain binaries than it is to get source code.

- The compiler should also provide information on the kind of optimizations it performs. Otherwise, there may be little correlation between the specifications made by the user, the optimizations done by the compiler and the analysis done by external tools.

6. CONCLUSION

In this work, we presented a graph-coloring based model for analyzing the data access patterns of an application and a simple algorithm that produces reorderings of the distributions that would result in reduced communication.

Our experiments with a real-world application and with test kernels show that compiler and runtime system interfaces need to be improved so that programmers and tools can make use of optimized data layout pragmas. We have provided a set of features that we, as tool builders, would like to see in compilers for parallel systems.

This work complements other approaches. We can use distributions from static analyses as an initial guess and tune it with data from a program execution. From typical data parallel compilers that treat array distributions as a given and then optimize code organization and data movement, we provide the additional dimension of choosing more effective data distributions. In this context, our work also forms the basis for generating on-the-fly data redistributions of arrays.

7. REFERENCES

1. W. D. Hillis and G. L. Steele, Data Parallel Algorithms, *Communications of the ACM*, December 1986, 1170-1183.

2. CMFortran Reference Manual (Online document), *Thinking Machines Corp.* Version 2.2.1-2 .

3. C*: C-star Reference Manual (Online document), *Thinking Machines Corp.* Version 7.1 .

4. G. Fox, S. Hiranandani, K. Kennedy, C. Koelbel, U. Kramer and C. Tseng, Fortran-D Language Specification, *Technical Report, Computer TR90-141, Rice University*, 1990.

5. High Performance Fortran Language Specification, *High Performance Fortran Forum Version 1.0* (May 1993).

6. U. Kremer, J. Mellor-Crummey, K. Kennedy and A. Carle, Automatic Data Layout for Distributed-Memory Machines in the D Programming Environment, *Technical Report CRPC-TR93-298-S, Rice University*, .

7. A. Rogers and K. Pingali, Process Decomposition Through Locality of Reference, *Proc. of the 1989 Conf. on Programming Language Design and Implementation*, Portland, Oregon, June 1989, 69-80.

8. U. Kremer, NP-Completeness of Dynamic Remapping, *Proceedings of the Fourth International Workshop on Compilers for Parallel Computers*, December 1993, 135-141.

9. L. D. Whitley, Foundations of Genetic Algorithms, *M. Kaufmann Publishers*, San Mateo, California, 1993.

10. D. S. Johnson, C. R. Aragon, L. A. McGeoch and C. Schevon, Optimization by Simulated Annealing: An Experimental Evaluation, *Operations Research 39*, 3 (May-June 1991), 378-406.

11. J. R. Evans and E. Minieka, Optimization Algorithms for Networks and Graphs, *M. Dekker*, New York, 1992.

12. B. H. McCormick, T. A. DeFanti and M. D. Brown, Visualization in Scientific Computing, *Computer Graphics 21*, 6 (November 1987).

13. J. R. Larus and T. Ball, Rewriting Executable Files to Measure Program Behavior, *Software—Practice & Experience 24*, 2 (Feb, 1994), 197-218.

14. J. K. Hollingsworth, B. P. Miller and J. Cargille, Dynamic Program Instrumentation for Scalable Performance Tools, *1994 Scalable High-Performance Computing Conf.*, Knoxville, Tenn., 1994.

15. B. Kernighan and S. Lin, An efficient heuristic procedure for partitioning graphs, *Bell Systems Technical Journal 49* (1970), 291-307.

Automatic Reduction Tree Generation for Fine-Grain Parallel Architectures when Iteration Count is Unknown

Satoshi SEKIGUCHI[†], *and*   Kei HIRAKI[‡]

[†]Electrotechnical Laboratory, MITI
[‡]University of Tokyo
Email: *sekiguchi@etl.go.jp, hiraki@is.s.u-tokyo.ac.jp*

Abstract. Over the last few years, the research trend in future generation high-performance computing systems has been moving toward a multi-threaded parallel architectures. Thus the importance to exploit and control parallelism has growing parallel activities must be both synchronized and reduced. In fine-grain parallel computation, designing efficient micro synchronization, at the same level of granularity as the grain size, is essential for implementation. This article discusses methods of synchronizing parallel activities, focusing on the case when the number of activities to be gathered is determined at run time. A new reduction graph, without loss of parallelism, is proposed. It is especially useful if the number of parallel activities is determined dynamically. This method is basically developed for instruction-level dataflow computers. Its full potential should be realized when trends in parallel processing return to finer grain sizes.

1   Introduction

Over the last few years, research in future generation high-performance computing systems has been moving from two different approaches toward a multi-threaded parallel architecture world. One approach uses an optimizing compiler to exploit as much parallelism as possible from conventional language, in other words, it reduces the grain size of parallel activity. In the other approach, the compiler reassembles threads with small portions of the program, so that they can be executed in parallel. To reduce overheads, the structure is based on a fine-grain, *i.e.* instruction level, dataflow architecture. An appropriate implementation might use registers in pipeline bubble structure.

The general issues that must be addressed for optimizing compiler development are how to create threads and how to break them down into parallel segments. It becomes important to both exploit parallelism and control it; parallel activities must be both synchronized and reduced. In fine-grain parallel computing, the key to fast computations is designing efficient micro synchronization at a level of granularity which is the same as the given grain size.

[†] Electrotechnical Laboratory, MITI
1-1-4 Umezono, Tsukuba, Ibaraki, JAPAN 305

This article discusses methods of synchronizing parallel activities, focusing especially on the case when the number of activities to be gathered is determined at run time. Since dataflow operators don not have state, the implementation of barrier synchronization in pure dataflow is quite challenging. We solve this problem with a small dataflow scheme consisting of a cyclic interconnection of dataflow operators, which does not compromise parallelism. It is particularly useful when the number of parallel activities is determined dynamically. We expect that this method's full potential will be realized, when the trends in parallel processing return to finer grain sizes.

2 Reduction code when iteration count is known

We have performed a number of experiments using the first real-scale dataflow parallel supercomputer, the SIGMA-1[1] [3], which has been operational at the Electrotechnical Laboratory of Japan since 1987. It consists of 32 clusters connected via a global network, where each cluster consists of 4 processing elements and 4 structure elements connected by a crossbar switch. Each processing element has an instruction-level dataflow architecture with peak performance values of 3.3 MFLOPS and 5 MIPS. Total performance peaks at 427 MFLOPS and 640 MIPS. We now use the SIGMA-1, a representative of technology for fine-grain dataflow, to clarify existing problems and present their solutions.

Consider the following simple program:

```
while(P){
        create_thread();
};
signal  =  sync();
/* wait for completion of every thread */
```

While the predicate P is true, this example creates threads. The $sync()$ function is invoked after creating each thread to dispose of its completion signal. In the following, it is assumed that: (1) there are no data dependencies between any two of the threads created, and (2) every thread sends out a completion signal as soon as it finishes. The question arises, "What kind of code should be generated for $sync()$?" This is especially difficult to answer for an instruction-level dataflow machine.

2.1 A simple solution

We begin with a simple case. That is, the count of the **while** iteration can be determined at compile time. Without losing generality, in the following discussions,we assume a number of iterations, N, equal to 6.

1 shows a simple reduction tree to collect all the completion signals, $(sig0, sig1, \ldots, sig5)$, producing a single signal indicates the completion of all the threads created in the loop.

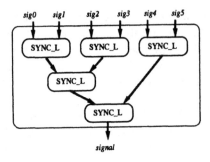

Fig. 1. Simple reduction tree for collecting a fixed number of completion signals

A **SYNC_L** node is a dataflow instruction where incoming operands and outgoing results are represented as tokens containing particular values. It synchronizes two incoming tokens and produces a token according to the operand on the left. This tree may be partially executed in parallel, but an algorithm forming a tree with an arbitrary number of nodes, except the number is two's power, is somewhat complicated.

Another simple reduction tree block is shown in 2. Although there is no parallelism in this tree, it is simple and easily produced by a compiler.

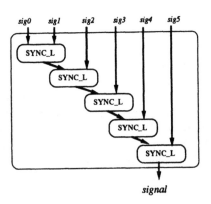

Fig. 2. Another simple reduction tree

In the two cases above, both blocks have N inputs and produce a single output, namely, the functional blocks have no internal state. Thus, they seem to be suitable for implementation in dataflow machines, even if the compiler must generate code to connect each completion signal with a different input port.

2.2 Solution using counter

Another possible solution uses a counter to monitor the number of signals remaining. Counter operations should include:

SET: Set an integer in the counter variable,
INC: Increment the counter value by one,
DEC: Decrement the counter value by one, if it has been reduced to zero, DEC produces a token.

The following code could be used for our example:

1. Before executing the loop, **SET** $N(= 6)$ to the counter when the control is passed to the **while** statement.
2. Send a **DEC** instead of a completion signal,
3. After e counter has been reduced to zero, DEC sends out a token to indicate completion.

The above method is impossible in the pure dataflow model, because it assumes that state can be held in the counter. Furthermore, **DEC** operation is usually produces no tokens. This violates the functionality of the dataflow model. According to the dataflow model, every node should generate at least one token to acknowledge proper execution. Of course, a counter implementation is possible in an extended dataflow model. For example, the SIGMA-1 has this feature included in its Structure Element [2] as a high level von Neumann memory. This method is rather simple because the threads created are exactly identical. As in the previous method, the input ports for each completion signals to be sent should really be different for each thread. We should notice that the solution with counters is like 2 in that it has no parallelism, since the decrements operate sequentially.

3 Reduction code when iteration count is unknown

The methods we have already discussed, forming a reduction tree or using a counter, are restricted to the case where the compiler can determine the number of iterations. Having examined this special case, we may now turn to the general case, where the number of iterations can neither be determined at compile time statically, nor can be known just before executing the loop, *i.e.*, before executing any iterations of the loop. In the latter case, even if the iteration count is not known to the compiler, it is still possible for the compiler to generate code that will dynamically produce a reduction tree or that will use a counter discussed in 2.2. In the following discussions, we would like to focus attention on the case where the iteration count is not known until the iterations are actually forked.

In addition to the assumptions considered in the previous section, it is reasonable to assume the followings:

- The stream of boolean values originated from the predicate P is available for use. According to boolean values, it consists of N signals with a value of true and one signal with false. Thus, $N + 1$ signals result for N threads.
- Both the completion and boolean signals have loop index identifiers. This identifiers could also be considered as colors in terms of a tagged token dataflow architecture. A token produced during the first iteration has a color of 0, which is the same as that outer loop. That is, 1 stands for the second iteration, 2 stands for the third, and so on.

3.1 A conceptual solution with counters

Clearly, a reduction tree solution is impossible because, by definition, the compiler is unable to determine the number of input ports for the block.

Considering the block with counters operation, it is reasonable to assume that both the boolean and completion signals arrive asynchronously at the counter. If not, all signals with the same identifier would have to be synchronized step-by-step. 3 shows signal behavior. It is similar to the ideas found in [5]. It is overly simplified, though. All of the parallelism between threads is lost, however, we should clarify an important distinction: if 2, the iterations may run in parallel, but just the signal gathering is sequential, whereas in 3, even the iterations run sequentially. Further, our final solution in 3.2 is as sequential in its signal gathering as is 2.

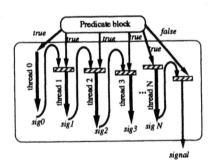

Fig. 3. Behavior of signals synchronized at each step

Let us return to the case, where signals arrive asynchronously. Although too simple for our purposes, another solution exists which corresponds to **INC** signal and a **DEC** signal. With this correspondence, an error would result if a DEC happened to reduce the counter into zero due to an incorrect signal. Such an error is very likely because the signals arrive asynchronously.

In conceptual block model with two counters (4), counter **A** is used to determine executed iteration number, which is increased by one with each of signal

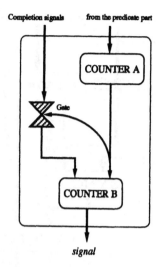

signal

Fig. 4. A conceptual block with two counters

true. With the false signal, the number is removed and placed in counter **B**. In all other respects, except that the gate must be closed before a false signal leaves an iteration count in counter **B**, it is quite similar to the case when the number of iterations is known. At present, this model is merely conceptual because several implementation issues remain to be solved. For example, the order of boolean signals must be guaranteed, otherwise the false signal would arrive at counter **A** before any of the true signals, causing an incorrect count to be reported. There also must be some way to confirm the order in which number is placed in counter **B** and the gate is opened.

3.2 A dataflow implementation

The conceptual model discussed above has the preferable feature that is it never interferes with the parallel execution of main threads. In this section we propose an implementation of the model with an instruction set for a fine-grain dataflow machine.

5 shows a dataflow implementation template to dispose of an unknown number of signals. Before explaining how it works, several dataflow instructions must be described.

SYNC_L: The function of node is as described. Note that this node is executed only if both the left and right operands, are available and their color is identical (6a).

COPY: This node copies the input value and forwards it to the output ports (6b).

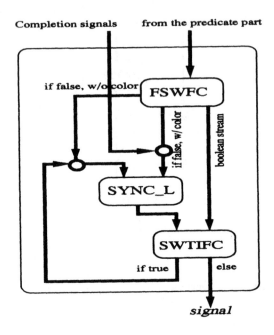

Fig. 5. A smart template with a dataflow instruction set to dispose of an unknown number of signals produced in a while-type loop.

I_INC: Increment the color. That is, change the color of an input token to be used in the following loop index (6c). For example, a token with an index of 2 (which means the token was generated in the third iteration), has its color changed to as 3 throughout the I_INC node. Once done, it can be matched with tokens produced during the fourth iteration.

I_CLR: Clear the color. That is, reset any color of an input token to zero so it can be used outside the loop (6d).

SW: Switch the destination of an input token at the data port according to the boolean value received at the control port (6e). For instance, if the control is true, output should be placed at port **T**, otherwise, at port **F**.

FSWFC: A compound node with a single input port and three output ports: a boolean stream output, a false token output port with the last iteration index, and false token output port with the cleared color. This function is composed as shown in 7a. It is the realization of the first counter discussed in 3.1. The optional outgoing branch, "if false, w/ color," means the other two branches "boolean stream" and "if false, w/o color" should be connected to other nodes.

SWTIFC: A compound node which acts like a SW (6e) with I_INC and I_CLR commands (7b).

○: A merge operation that simply forwards either input to the output.

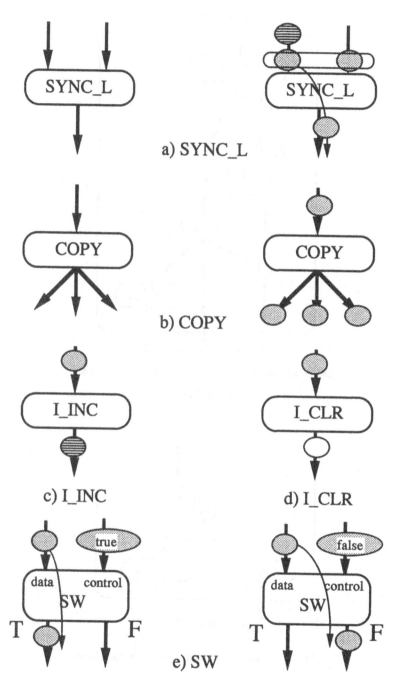

Fig. 6. Specification of simple dataflow nodes.

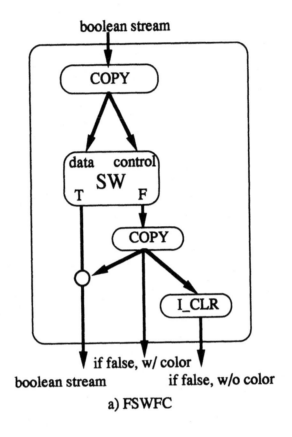

a) FSWFC

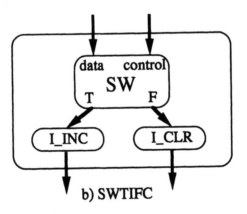

b) SWTIFC

Fig. 7. Compound nodes for the reduction block

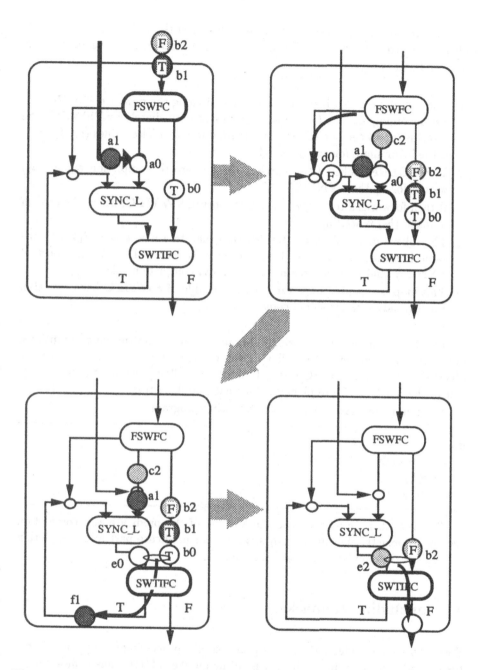

Fig. 8. A smart template with a dataflow instruction set to dispose of an unknown number of signals produced by a while-type loop.

Now we can explain how the smart template 5 works. 8 shows the transition, where N is three (*i.e.* two threads are created and three boolean values two true and one false, come out).

1. The completion signals (a_0, a_1) are buffered along the right arc of **SYNC_L**. The incoming boolean (b_0, b_1, b_2) is processed immediately by **FSWFC**. The result is fed to the boolean stream. It produces two false values (c_2, d_0) only if the incoming boolean (b_2) is false.
2. The **I_CLR**ed token (d_0) matches to the zero-th completion signal (a_0) waited for by the **SYNC_L**.
3. It then forwards a token (e_0) to the left port of **SWTIFC**, where the zero-th T-token (b_0) is waiting.
4. The tokens matched by the **SWTIFC** generate a new token (f_1) with the same identifier as the next loop index. It is returned to the left port of **SYNC_L** and matched again with the next completion token (a_1).
5. This loop is repeated until the control variable of **SWTIFC** becomes false. Finally, only a single signal comes out.

This block can be be used widely, because there are no special assumptions, except for those in general dataflow. Even though we have designed it for the SIGMA-1, which has a CISC instruction set that allows new instructions to be added, the block can be implemented on RISC architectures.

To examine one last, consider the following program:

```
do{
        create_thread();
} while(P);
signal = sync();
```

This is rather simplistic since the number of the predicate and completion signals are exactly the same. both signals from predicate part and completion are exactly the same. 9 shows the template.

4 Concluding Remarks

We proposed new code block for fine-grain parallel processing to dispose of signal tokens without loss of parallelism, where the number of iterations is determined at run time. We used the method in the DFCII [4] compiler targeting for the SIGMA-1. It has a fine-grain dataflow architecture because reduction tree execution can be done in sub processors without interfering with the main execution. The method should show its greatest utility in threading approaches where parallel activities are controlled dynamically for efficient execution. It would be interesting to benchmark the proposed method on a variety of architectures.

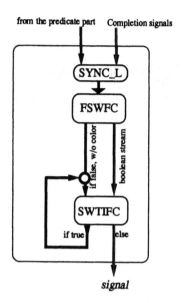

from the predicate part　　Completion signals

Fig. 9. A smart template with a dataflow instruction set which disposes of an unknown number of signals produced in a do-while-type loop.

Acknowledgments

We would like to thank Professor Toshio Shimada, Nagoya University, for his fruitful discussions, and Dr. Kimihiro Ohta, Director of Computer Science Division, Electrotechnical Laboratory, for his supporting our research work. Finally, we wish to express our gratitude to the anonymous referees for their helpful suggestions.

References

1. Hiraki, K., Sekiguchi, S., and Shimada, T., "System architecture of a dataflow supercomputer", *Proc. TENCON 87*, IEEE, Seul, August 1987, IEEE.
2. Hiraki, K., Sekiguchi, S., and Shimada, T., "Efficient vector processing on a dataflow supercomputer SIGMA-1", *Proc. Supercomputing'88*, IEEE, Orlando, November 1988, IEEE.
3. Hiraki, K., Sekiguchi, S., and Shimada, T., "Status report of SIGMA-1: a data-flow supercomputer", Gaudiot, J.-L., and Bic, L. (eds.), *Advanced Topics in Data-Flow Computing*, chapter 7, Prentice Hall, 1991, chapter 7.
4. Sekiguchi, S., Shimada, T., and Hiraki, K., "Sequential description and parallel execution language DFC II for dataflow supercomputers", *1991 Intl. Conf. on Supercomputing*, ACM, Cologne, June 1991, ACM.
5. Traub, T. R., "A compiler for the MIT tagged token dataflow architecture", Master's thesis, MIT, 1986.

Springer-Verlag
and the Environment

We at Springer-Verlag firmly believe that an international science publisher has a special obligation to the environment, and our corporate policies consistently reflect this conviction.

We also expect our business partners – paper mills, printers, packaging manufacturers, etc. – to commit themselves to using environmentally friendly materials and production processes.

The paper in this book is made from low- or no-chlorine pulp and is acid free, in conformance with international standards for paper permanency.

Lecture Notes in Computer Science

For information about Vols. 1–814
please contact your bookseller or Springer-Verlag

Vol. 815: R. Valette (Ed.), Application and Theory of Petri Nets 1994. Proceedings. IX, 587 pages. 1994.

Vol. 816: J. Heering, K. Meinke, B. Möller, T. Nipkow (Eds.), Higher-Order Algebra, Logic, and Term Rewriting. Proceedings, 1993. VII, 344 pages. 1994.

Vol. 817: C. Halatsis, D. Maritsas, G. Philokyprou, S. Theodoridis (Eds.), PARLE '94. Parallel Architectures and Languages Europe. Proceedings, 1994. XV, 837 pages. 1994.

Vol. 818: D. L. Dill (Ed.), Computer Aided Verification. Proceedings, 1994. IX, 480 pages. 1994.

Vol. 819: W. Litwin, T. Risch (Eds.), Applications of Databases. Proceedings, 1994. XII, 471 pages. 1994.

Vol. 820: S. Abiteboul, E. Shamir (Eds.), Automata, Languages and Programming. Proceedings, 1994. XIII, 644 pages. 1994.

Vol. 821: M. Tokoro, R. Pareschi (Eds.), Object-Oriented Programming. Proceedings, 1994. XI, 535 pages. 1994.

Vol. 822: F. Pfenning (Ed.), Logic Programming and Automated Reasoning. Proceedings, 1994. X, 345 pages. 1994. (Subseries LNAI).

Vol. 823: R. A. Elmasri, V. Kouramajian, B. Thalheim (Eds.), Entity-Relationship Approach — ER '93. Proceedings, 1993. X, 531 pages. 1994.

Vol. 824: E. M. Schmidt, S. Skyum (Eds.), Algorithm Theory – SWAT '94. Proceedings. IX, 383 pages. 1994.

Vol. 825: J. L. Mundy, A. Zisserman, D. Forsyth (Eds.), Applications of Invariance in Computer Vision. Proceedings, 1993. IX, 510 pages. 1994.

Vol. 826: D. S. Bowers (Ed.), Directions in Databases. Proceedings, 1994. X, 234 pages. 1994.

Vol. 827: D. M. Gabbay, H. J. Ohlbach (Eds.), Temporal Logic. Proceedings, 1994. XI, 546 pages. 1994. (Subseries LNAI).

Vol. 828: L. C. Paulson, Isabelle. XVII, 321 pages. 1994.

Vol. 829: A. Chmora, S. B. Wicker (Eds.), Error Control, Cryptology, and Speech Compression. Proceedings, 1993. VIII, 121 pages. 1994.

Vol. 830: C. Castelfranchi, E. Werner (Eds.), Artificial Social Systems. Proceedings, 1992. XVIII, 337 pages. 1994. (Subseries LNAI).

Vol. 831: V. Bouchitté, M. Morvan (Eds.), Orders, Algorithms, and Applications. Proceedings, 1994. IX, 204 pages. 1994.

Vol. 832: E. Börger, Y. Gurevich, K. Meinke (Eds.), Computer Science Logic. Proceedings, 1993. VIII, 336 pages. 1994.

Vol. 833: D. Driankov, P. W. Eklund, A. Ralescu (Eds.), Fuzzy Logic and Fuzzy Control. Proceedings, 1991. XII, 157 pages. 1994. (Subseries LNAI).

Vol. 834: D.-Z. Du, X.-S. Zhang (Eds.), Algorithms and Computation. Proceedings, 1994. XIII, 687 pages. 1994.

Vol. 835: W. M. Tepfenhart, J. P. Dick, J. F. Sowa (Eds.), Conceptual Structures: Current Practices. Proceedings, 1994. VIII, 331 pages. 1994. (Subseries LNAI).

Vol. 836: B. Jonsson, J. Parrow (Eds.), CONCUR '94: Concurrency Theory. Proceedings, 1994. IX, 529 pages. 1994.

Vol. 837: S. Wess, K.-D. Althoff, M. M. Richter (Eds.), Topics in Case-Based Reasoning. Proceedings, 1993. IX, 471 pages. 1994. (Subseries LNAI).

Vol. 838: C. MacNish, D. Pearce, L. Moniz Pereira (Eds.), Logics in Artificial Intelligence. Proceedings, 1994. IX, 413 pages. 1994. (Subseries LNAI).

Vol. 839: Y. G. Desmedt (Ed.), Advances in Cryptology - CRYPTO '94. Proceedings, 1994. XII, 439 pages. 1994.

Vol. 840: G. Reinelt, The Traveling Salesman. VIII, 223 pages. 1994.

Vol. 841: I. Prívara, B. Rovan, P. Ružička (Eds.), Mathematical Foundations of Computer Science 1994. Proceedings, 1994. X, 628 pages. 1994.

Vol. 842: T. Kloks, Treewidth. IX, 209 pages. 1994.

Vol. 843: A. Szepietowski, Turing Machines with Sublogarithmic Space. VIII, 115 pages. 1994.

Vol. 844: M. Hermenegildo, J. Penjam (Eds.), Programming Language Implementation and Logic Programming. Proceedings, 1994. XII, 469 pages. 1994.

Vol. 845: J.-P. Jouannaud (Ed.), Constraints in Computational Logics. Proceedings, 1994. VIII, 367 pages. 1994.

Vol. 846: D. Shepherd, G. Blair, G. Coulson, N. Davies, F. Garcia (Eds.), Network and Operating System Support for Digital Audio and Video. Proceedings, 1993. VIII, 269 pages. 1994.

Vol. 847: A. L. Ralescu (Ed.) Fuzzy Logic in Artificial Intelligence. Proceedings, 1993. VII, 128 pages. 1994. (Subseries LNAI).

Vol. 848: A. R. Krommer, C. W. Ueberhuber, Numerical Integration on Advanced Computer Systems. XIII, 341 pages. 1994.

Vol. 849: R. W. Hartenstein, M. Z. Servít (Eds.), Field-Programmable Logic. Proceedings, 1994. XI, 434 pages. 1994.

Vol. 850: G. Levi, M. Rodríguez-Artalejo (Eds.), Algebraic and Logic Programming. Proceedings, 1994. VIII, 304 pages. 1994.

Vol. 851: H.-J. Kugler, A. Mullery, N. Niebert (Eds.), Towards a Pan-European Telecommunication Service Infrastructure. Proceedings, 1994. XIII, 582 pages. 1994.

Vol. 852: K. Echtle, D. Hammer, D. Powell (Eds.), Dependable Computing – EDCC-1. Proceedings, 1994. XVII, 618 pages. 1994.

Vol. 853: K. Bolding, L. Snyder (Eds.), Parallel Computer Routing and Communication. Proceedings, 1994. IX, 317 pages. 1994.

Vol. 854: B. Buchberger, J. Volkert (Eds.), Parallel Processing: CONPAR 94 – VAPP VI. Proceedings, 1994. XVI, 893 pages. 1994.

Vol. 855: J. van Leeuwen (Ed.), Algorithms – ESA '94. Proceedings, 1994. X, 510 pages.1994.

Vol. 856: D. Karagiannis (Ed.), Database and Expert Systems Applications. Proceedings, 1994. XVII, 807 pages. 1994.

Vol. 857: G. Tel, P. Vitányi (Eds.), Distributed Algorithms. Proceedings, 1994. X, 370 pages. 1994.

Vol. 858: E. Bertino, S. Urban (Eds.), Object-Oriented Methodologies and Systems. Proceedings, 1994. X, 386 pages. 1994.

Vol. 859: T. F. Melham, J. Camilleri (Eds.), Higher Order Logic Theorem Proving and Its Applications. Proceedings, 1994. IX, 470 pages. 1994.

Vol. 860: W. L. Zagler, G. Busby, R. R. Wagner (Eds.), Computers for Handicapped Persons. Proceedings, 1994. XX, 625 pages. 1994.

Vol: 861: B. Nebel, L. Dreschler-Fischer (Eds.), KI-94: Advances in Artificial Intelligence. Proceedings, 1994. IX, 401 pages. 1994. (Subseries LNAI).

Vol. 862: R. C. Carrasco, J. Oncina (Eds.), Grammatical Inference and Applications. Proceedings, 1994. VIII, 290 pages. 1994. (Subseries LNAI).

Vol. 863: H. Langmaack, W.-P. de Roever, J. Vytopil (Eds.), Formal Techniques in Real-Time and Fault-Tolerant Systems. Proceedings, 1994. XIV, 787 pages. 1994.

Vol. 864: B. Le Charlier (Ed.), Static Analysis. Proceedings, 1994. XII, 465 pages. 1994.

Vol. 865: T. C. Fogarty (Ed.), Evolutionary Computing. Proceedings, 1994. XII, 332 pages. 1994.

Vol. 866: Y. Davidor, H.-P. Schwefel, R. Männer (Eds.), Parallel Problem Solving from Nature - PPSN III. Proceedings, 1994. XV, 642 pages. 1994.

Vol 867: L. Steels, G. Schreiber, W. Van de Velde (Eds.), A Future for Knowledge Acquisition. Proceedings, 1994. XII, 414 pages. 1994. (Subseries LNAI).

Vol. 868: R. Steinmetz (Ed.), Multimedia: Advanced Teleservices and High-Speed Communication Architectures. Proceedings, 1994. IX, 451 pages. 1994.

Vol. 869: Z. W. Raś, Zemankova (Eds.), Methodologies for Intelligent Systems. Proceedings, 1994. X, 613 pages. 1994. (Subseries LNAI).

Vol. 870: J. S. Greenfield, Distributed Programming Paradigms with Cryptography Applications. XI, 182 pages. 1994.

Vol. 871: J. P. Lee, G. G. Grinstein (Eds.), Database Issues for Data Visualization. Proceedings, 1993. XIV, 229 pages. 1994.

Vol. 872: S Arikawa, K. P. Jantke (Eds.), Algorithmic Learning Theory. Proceedings, 1994. XIV, 575 pages. 1994.

Vol. 873: M. Naftalin, T. Denvir, M. Bertran (Eds.), FME '94: Industrial Benefit of Formal Methods. Proceedings, 1994. XI, 723 pages. 1994.

Vol. 874: A. Borning (Ed.), Principles and Practice of Constraint Programming. Proceedings, 1994. IX, 361 pages. 1994.

Vol. 875: D. Gollmann (Ed.), Computer Security – ESORICS 94. Proceedings, 1994. XI, 469 pages. 1994.

Vol. 876: B. Blumenthal, J. Gornostaev, C. Unger (Eds.), Human-Computer Interaction. Proceedings, 1994. IX, 239 pages. 1994.

Vol. 877: L. M. Adleman, M.-D. Huang (Eds.), Algorithmic Number Theory. Proceedings, 1994. IX, 323 pages. 1994.

Vol. 878: T. Ishida; Parallel, Distributed and Multiagent Production Systems. XVII, 166 pages. 1994. (Subseries LNAI).

Vol. 879: J. Dongarra, J. Waśniewski (Eds.), Parallel Scientific Computing. Proceedings, 1994. XI, 566 pages. 1994.

Vol. 880: P. S. Thiagarajan (Ed.), Foundations of Software Technology and Theoretical Computer Science. Proceedings, 1994. XI, 451 pages. 1994.

Vol. 881: P. Loucopoulos (Ed.), Entity-Relationship Approach – ER'94. Proceedings, 1994. XIII, 579 pages. 1994.

Vol. 882: D. Hutchison, A. Danthine, H. Leopold, G. Coulson (Eds.), Multimedia Transport and Teleservices. Proceedings, 1994. XI, 380 pages. 1994.

Vol. 883: L. Fribourg, F. Turini (Eds.), Logic Program Synthesis and Transformation – Meta-Programming in Logic. Proceedings, 1994. IX, 451 pages. 1994.

Vol. 884: J. Nievergelt, T. Roos, H.-J. Schek, P. Widmayer (Eds.), IGIS '94: Geographic Information Systems. Proceedings, 1994. VIII, 292 pages. 19944.

Vol. 885: R. C. Veltkamp, Closed Objects Boundaries from Scattered Points. VIII, 144 pages. 1994.

Vol. 886: M. M. Veloso, Planning and Learning by Analogical Reasoning. XIII, 181 pages. 1994. (Subseries LNAI).

Vol. 887: M. Toussaint (Ed.), Ada in Europe. Proceedings, 1994. XII, 521 pages. 1994.

Vol. 888: S. A. Andersson (Ed.), Analysis of Dynamical and Cognitive Systems. Proceedings, 1993. VII, 260 pages. 1995.

Vol. 889: H. P. Lubich, Towards a CSCW Framework for Scientific Cooperation in Europe. X, 268 pages. 1995.

Vol. 890: M. J. Wooldridge, N. R. Jennings (Eds.), Intelligent Agents. Proceedings, 1994. VIII, 407 pages. 1995. (Subseries LNAI).

Vol. 891: C. Lewerentz, T. Lindner (Eds.), Formal Development of Reactive Systems. XI, 394 pages. 1995.

Vol. 892: K. Pingali, U. Banerjee, D. Gelernter, A. Nicolau, D. Padua (Eds.), Languages and Compilers for Parallel Computing. Proceedings, 1994. XI, 496 pages. 1995.

Vol. 893: G. Gottlob, M. Y. Vardi (EDS.), Database Theory – ICDT '95. Proceedings, 1995. XI, 454 pages. 1995.